THE BIBLE IN THEORY

SBL

Society of Biblical Literature

Resources for Biblical Study

Tom Thatcher
Editor (New Testament)

Number 57

THE BIBLE IN THEORY
Critical and Postcritical Essays

THE BIBLE IN THEORY

CRITICAL AND POSTCRITICAL ESSAYS

By
Stephen D. Moore

Society of Biblical Literature
Atlanta

THE BIBLE IN THEORY
Critical and Postcritical Essays

Copyright © 2010 by the Society of Biblical Literature

All rights reserved. No part of this work may be reproduced or transmitted in any form or by any means, electronic or mechanical, including photocopying and recording, or by means of any information storage or retrieval system, except as may be expressly permitted by the 1976 Copyright Act or in writing from the publisher. Requests for permission should be addressed in writing to the Rights and Permissions Office, Society of Biblical Literature, 825 Houston Mill Road, Atlanta, GA 30329 USA.

Library of Congress Cataloging-in-Publication Data

Moore, Stephen D., 1954–
    The Bible in theory : critical and postcritical essays / Stephen D. Moore.
        p. cm. — (Society of Biblical Literature resources for biblical study ; no. 57)
    Includes bibliographical references and index.
    ISBN 978-1-58983-506-1 (paper binding : alk. paper) — ISBN 978-1-58983-507-8 (electronic library copy : alk. paper)
    1. Bible--Criticism, interpretation, etc. 2. Poststructuralism. I. Title
    BS511.3.M665 2010
    220.6'—dc22   2010020799

18 17 16 15 14 13 12 11 10   5 4 3 2 1
Printed on acid-free, recycled paper conforming to
ANSI/NISO Z39.48-1992 (R1997) and ISO 9706:1994
standards for paper permanence.

Contents

Abbreviations vii
Acknowledgments ix
Foreword/Preface/Introduction/Preamble/Exordium
    Amy-Jill Levine xi

Introduction: On the Inside Looking Out While on the Outside
Looking In 1

Postmodernity

1. The "Post-" Age Stamp: Does It Stick? Biblical Studies and the
   Postmodernism Debate 9
   Further Reading on Postmodernity 23

Textuality

2. Illuminating the Gospels without the Benefit of Color: A Plea for
   Concrete Criticism 27
3. The Gospel of the Look 53
4. Are There Impurities in the Living Water That the Johannine Jesus
   Dispenses? Deconstruction, Feminism, and the Samaritan Woman 81
5. The Quest of the New Historicist Jesus (co-authored with Susan
   Lochrie Graham) 99
   Further Reading on Poststructuralism and New Historicism 122

Autobiography

6. True Confessions and Weird Obsessions: Autobiographical
   Interventions in Literary and Biblical Studies 127
7. The Divine Butcher 147
   Further Reading on Autobiographical Criticism 171

Masculinity

8. Taking It Like a Man: Masculinity in 4 Maccabees (co-authored with Janice Capel Anderson) 175
9. Gigantic God: Yahweh's Body 201
   Further Reading on Masculinity Studies 221

Sexuality

10. The Song of Songs in the History of Sexuality 225
11. Unsafe Sex: Feminism, Pornography, and the Song of Songs (co-authored with Virginia Burrus) 247
12. Sex and the Single Apostle 273
    Further Reading on Queer Studies 304

Postcoloniality

13. Questions of Biblical Ambivalence and Authority under a Tree outside Delhi; or, the Postcolonial and the Postmodern 309
14. "The Romans Will Come and Destroy Our Holy Place and Our Nation": Representing Empire in John 327
    Further Reading on Postcolonial Studies 350

Posttheory

15. A Modest Manifesto for New Testament Literary Criticism: How to Interface with a Literary Studies Field That Is Postliterary, Posttheoretical, and Postmethodological 355
16. After "After Theory" and Other Apocalyptic Conceits in Literary and Biblical Studies (co-authored with Yvonne Sherwood) 373
    Further Reading on the "After Theory" Debate 404

Works Cited 407
Index of Modern Authors 455

Abbreviations

AB	Anchor Bible
ABD	*Anchor Bible Dictionary*. Edited by David Noel Freedman. 6 vols. New York: Doubleday, 1992.
ABRL	Anchor Bible Reference Library
AGJU	Arbeiten zur Geschichte des antiken Judentums und des Urchristentums
ALGHJ	Arbeiten zur Literatur und Geschichte des hellenistischen Judentums
AnBib	Analecta Biblica
Bib	*Biblica*
BibInt	*Biblical Interpretation*
BibInt	Biblical Interpretation Series
BJS	Brown Judaic Studies
CBC	Cambridge Bible Commentary
CBQ	*Catholic Biblical Quarterly*
ConBNT	Coniectanea Biblica: New Testament Series
EKKNT	Evangelisch-Katholischer Kommentar zum Neuen Testament
FCB	Feminist Companion to the Bible
FCNTECW	Feminist Companion to the New Testament and Early Christian Writings
FRLANT	Forschungen zur Religion und Literatur des Alten und Neuen Testaments
GBS	Guides to Biblical Scholarship
GPBS	Global Perspectives on Biblical Scholarship
HAR	*Hebrew Annual Review*
HNT	Handbuch zum Neuen Testament
HR	*History of Religions*
HSM	Harvard Semitic Monographs
HTR	*Harvard Theological Review*
HTS	Harvard Theological Studies
ICC	International Critical Commentary
JAAR	*Journal of the American Academy of Religion*

JBL	*Journal of Biblical Literature*
JECS	*Journal of Early Christian Studies*
JSNT	*Journal for the Study of the New Testament*
JSNTSup	Journal for the Study of the New Testament Supplement Series
JSOTSup	Journal for the Study of the Old Testament Supplement Series
JSP	*Journal for the Study of the Pseudepigrapha*
JSPSup	Journal for the Study of the Pseudepigrapha Supplement Series
NCBC	New Century Bible Commentary
NIGTC	New International Greek Testament Commentary
NovT	*Novum Testamentum*
NovTSup	Supplements to Novum Testamentum
NTS	New Testament Studies
OBT	Overtures to Biblical Theology
OTL	Old Testament Library
PMLA	*Publications of the Modern Language Association*
RSR	*Religious Studies Review*
SBLDS	Society of Biblical Literature Dissertation Series
SBLEJL	Society of Biblical Literature Early Judaism and Its Literature
SBLMS	Society of Biblical Literature Monograph Series
SBLRBS	Society of Biblical Literature Resources for Biblical Study
SemeiaSt	Semeia Studies
TBei	*Theologische Beiträge*
THKNT	Theologischer Handkommentar zum Neuen Testament
VT	*Vetus Testamentum*
WBC	Word Biblical Commentary
WUNT	Wissenschaftliche Untersuchungen zum Neuen Testament
ZAW	*Zeitschrift für die alttestamentliche Wissenschaft*

Acknowledgments

1. "The 'Post-' Age Stamp: Does It Stick? Biblical Studies and the Postmodernism Debate" was first published in *JAAR* 57 (1989): 543–59. Reprinted by permission.

2. "Illuminating the Gospels without the Benefit of Color: A Plea for Concrete Criticism" was first published in *JAAR* 60 (1992): 257–79. Reprinted by permission.

3. "The Gospel of the Look" was first published in *Semeia* 54 (1991): 159–96. Reprinted by permission.

4. "Are There Impurities in the Living Water That the Johannine Jesus Dispenses? Deconstruction, Feminism, and the Samaritan Woman" was first published in *BibInt* 1 (1993): 207–27. Reprinted by permission.

5. "The Quest of the New Historicist Jesus" (co-authored with Susan Lochrie Graham) was first published in *BibInt* 5 (1997): 437–63. Reprinted by permission.

6. "True Confessions and Weird Obsessions: Autobiographical Interventions in Literary and Biblical Studies" was first published in *Semeia* 72 (1995): 19–51. Reprinted by permission.

7. "The Divine Butcher" was first published as "God's Own (Pri)son: The Disciplinary Technology of the Cross" in Francis Watson, ed., *The Open Text: New Directions for Biblical Studies?* (London: SCM, 1993), 121–39. Reprinted by permission.

8. "Taking It Like a Man: Masculinity in 4 Maccabees" (co-authored with Janice Capel Anderson) was first published in *JBL* 117 (1998): 249–73. Reprinted by permission.

9. "Gigantic God: Yahweh's Body" was first published in *JSOT* 70 (1996): 87–115. Reprinted by permission.

10. "The Song of Songs in the History of Sexuality" was first published in *Church History* 69 (2000): 328–50. Reprinted by permission.

11. "Unsafe Sex: Feminism, Pornography, and the Song of Songs" (co-authored with Virginia Burrus) was first published in *BibInt* 11 (2003): 24–52. Reprinted by permission.

12. "Sex and the Single Apostle" was first published as "Que(e)rying Paul" in David J. A. Clines and Stephen D. Moore, eds., *Auguries: The Jubilee Volume of the Sheffield Department of Biblical Studies* (JSOTSup 269; Sheffield: Sheffield Academic Press, 1998), 250–74. Reprinted by permission.

13. "Questions of Biblical Ambivalence and Authority under a Tree outside Delhi; or, the Postcolonial and the Postmodern" was first published in Stephen D. Moore and Fernando F. Segovia, eds., *Postcolonial Biblical Criticism: Interdisciplinary Intersections* (The Bible and Postcolonialism 8; New York: T&T Clark, 2005), 79–96. Reprinted by permission.

14. "'The Romans Will Come and Destroy Our Holy Place and Our Nation': Representing Empire in John" was first published in Stephen D. Moore, *Empire and Apocalypse: Postcolonialism and the New Testament* (The Bible in the Modern World 12; Sheffield,: Sheffield Phoenix, 2006), 45–74. Reprinted by permission.

15. "A Modest Manifesto for New Testament Literary Criticism: How to Interface with a Literary Studies Field That Is Postliterary, Posttheoretical, and Postmethodological" was first published in *BibInt* 15 (2007): 1–25. Reprinted by permission.

Foreword/Preface/Introduction/Preamble/ Exordium

Amy-Jill Levine

The task enjoined on me by Tom Thatcher, New Testament editor for the SBLRBS series, is to epitomize and eulogize this collection. Specifically, he asked me to write a "foreword"[1] of 1,500–2,000 words that "would simply provide some context for Stephen's work"[2] and announce the "significance of his contribution."[3] Thatcher concluded his request with his appreciation of my "endorsement."

My task is thus to comment on this collection, its broader literary corpus, and its author—and not the ideal or implied or narrativized author, but the real Stephen D. Moore. The standard procedure in addressing this type of task is to draw together fragmentary remarks, support them by citations and paraphrases lifted out of context, and retreat behind an all-powerful, omniscient, tantalizingly brief self-revelatory prose enhanced by the guise of humility. But Stephen's work is anything but standard fare, and a preface to his volume of collected essays thus should be more than summary *cum* complement/compliment. On the other hand, a bit of mimesis is not inappropriate. Therefore, the following comments are also marked by what is not said (John 20:30),

---

1. A later email from Thatcher spoke about a "preface." There is space here for genre study: "preface," "foreword," "note" (not lyrical enough), "prologue" (too Johannine), "salutation" (too historical-critical), "introduction" (too academic); who writes them?; what are the conventions?; how does the "foreword" function intertextually with the content?; what is *not* stated in the foreword?; how might this foreword reread given other forewords—the song by Linkin Park (enter cultural criticism), for example?; the relation of "pre" to "face" (enter linguistics and philology); and so forth. Each word draws its association, sets up its boundaries, anticipates its deconstruction, and fights to escape the page.

2. "Context?" I'd have to spend more than my allotted space talking about the text, the con, the con/text, and then mull around in the intertextual muck.

3. "Significance" … and signifiers, and signs, and sign posts, and post-cards, and post-every-thing-else.… Who the hell needs all this?

influenced by the styles in which Stephen has conveyed his thoughts, and, appropriately, composed while I am sitting under a tree outside a deli and eating a tongue sandwich.[4]

The polite response to Thatcher's invitation would have been, "Stephen D. Moore needs no foreword," but, given that he still, to some New Testament scholars, represents the THREAT OF _____ [fill in the term: literary studies, poststructuralism, postmodernism, deconstruction], perhaps he does. I'm not sure that my introduction could render his work kosher (not likely the metaphor the nay-sayers would use), let alone appetizing, for them, but perhaps it might help.

The better term for these introductory comments might be "forward" (or, if we must, "for[e]ward"), for Stephen's writing moves in this direction, even when he is looking back at the history of (the) discipline. His work has always been, to use the cliché and in honor of his father, "cutting edge": it opens the bodies of texts, reveals the subcutaneous strands overlooked by more ham-fisted (the right metaphor) readers, and leaves many a secure interpretation decentered, eviscerated, or at the very least exposed. From his "external, defamiliarizing vantage point"—he defines this point as his immersion in theory, gender/sexuality studies, cultural studies, etc.; he also, having his cake and eating it, too, gets to be both the "white male with tenure" and the Other, the Irish Catholic colonized subject living in Diaspora—he cocks his eye[5] at biblical studies, and under his typing fingers the text and the discipline prove themselves malleable, penetrable, unstable, and ultimately yielding. Stephen helps readers to smell the texts, to taste and touch what they offer, to dwell on the single word before moving on for the grand scheme or the main point, itself now subject to mo[o]re critique.

Sometimes seen as obscure (even as intentionally so?), indeed to some as a scandal and a folly (which may prove that he really does have gospel to preach), Stephen is, to the contrary, a clear and jolly guide to both text and reading strategies. His language is precise; each word does what it needs to do, and more; the pun and the playfulness advance the argument while also making the experience enjoyable. Hardly dry, his prose oozes with seepage, leakage, and seminal conceptions.

Sometimes seen as the go-to guy for providing a predigested meal of the latest servings of literary, cultural, gender/sexuality, and postcolonial studies and now, adequately seasoned, a few posttheoretical dishes, Moore is much more than this. He not only describes approaches toward reading; he also

---

4. The setting does make sense, dear reader; if it does not yet, read on into the volume.

5. A fraught mixed metaphor, and a potentially painful one.

shows how they work.⁶ Thus, at the end of his meal, there is not the dreaded "see how I've come up with something we already knew by using a new reading strategy that I've just spent 400 pages summarizing [and resummarizing and re-resummarizing…]" but a new way of celebrating the feast, of experiencing both the text and the reading of it.

Sometimes seen as holding the mantle (the fort, the door) only of literary approaches to Scripture, Stephen is also a careful historian—of the Roman court, of philology, of ancient Mediterranean society, of the study of the Bible from the patristic period through the scholastic era to the Reformers and beyond to the latest major commentaries both liberal and evangelical. Despite his penchant for "strategic anachronism," his works offer culturally specific insights ranging from first-century Roman society to the twenty-first-century Society of Biblical Literature (another empire of sorts). To critique approaches, such as the historical-critical, one needs to know them; to critique is not necessarily to dismiss, but to employ with awareness, to know both benefits and limitations.

I do not know if Stephen would accept the label "theologian," but that label also fits him. Comments on the divine—as Caesar, torturer, executioner, sufferer, estrogenized weight lifter, lover, absent, all-too-present—infuse his work. His revelatory analyses include an appreciation of the mysterious, the overflowing, the aesthetic, and the apophatic; they also foreground attention to the political, for his is a practical theology that impacts real people, real bodies. Stephen's readings lead not to final solutions/creedal pronouncements but to new questions. This is not to say that he has no conclusions, no "take away" and "write that down" insights—numerous apercus are sprinkled throughout his writings. It *is* to say that the encounter with his studies at the least changes received perceptions of the text. For the sympathetic reader, the encounter can also change the way of reading: from intellectual endeavor to sensory reception; from single meaning to multiple possibilities.

As for the "real" Stephen D. Moore, he begins this collection by locating himself "late in [his] career"—nonsense. He is hardly ready for retirement (John 8:57 is not far off the mark). He has done some work in autobiographical criticism (as this collection attests), but he's fairly coy about what he reveals, especially about his personal as opposed to professional present. A look at the Drew University website states that he is a native of Ireland,

---

6. Granted, I'm complicit in appreciating his attention to theory; my husband, erstwhile chair of the American Academy of Religion's Critical Theory Group, courted me by whispering in my ear, "Derrida, Foucault, Lacan, Cixous." Good thing he did not try "Heidegger, Habermas, and Adorno"; theory does sound better in French. "Žižek" might have worked.

received his Ph.D. in New Testament from the University of Dublin (Trinity College) in 1986, and taught at Trinity, Yale Divinity School, Wichita State University, and the University of Sheffield before coming to Drew in 1999. He has written/is in the process of writing twelve volumes, has edited ten more, and has published more articles than I care to count. Notable, throughout his publishing career and demonstrated in this collection, are his co-authored works (all four in this collection with women; a point on which he does not directly comment). These works, together with the numerous edited volumes, signal a remarkable unselfishness as well as attendant courage: a willingness to collaborate (rare within the humanities), to promote the work of others, and to challenge one's own reading and writing.

I know Stephen personally, and I like him very much. We've had several fabulous conversations; we've both been dead (a nice little autobiographical lagniappe); he was a monk, I wanted to be pope; we're both married to Jews. He looks more like Jesus than I do (his removing his pony tail helped), but, as I have learned from being in his Beauty Parlor and Gym, I probably look more like the full-frontal view of the Divine than he does. More than liking him and admiring him, I've learned from him. He has shown me things in texts that I would never have seen on my own; he has commended to me writers whose names do not typically appear in the footnotes of the *Journal of Biblical Literature* or *Catholic Biblical Quarterly*; he has changed my pedagogical moves, and he has inspired me toward more creative work while requiring that it be no less rigorous. These essays, only a sampling of Stephen D. Moore's contributions to biblical studies broadly defined, challenge, delight, inspire, and inform. Let them be, for all readers, appetizers to his larger banquets already prepared as well as anticipatory foretastes of new meals with unexpected ingredients yet unimagined.

Amy-Jill Levine
E. Rhodes and Leona B. Carpenter Professor of New Testament Studies
Vanderbilt University

Introduction: On the Inside Looking Out While on the Outside Looking In

To be invited late in one's career to cull one's best articles and essays for collection between the covers of a single volume is cause for gratitude. To set about making the selections, however, sifting through one's past arguments and analyses, pronouncements and presumptions, meanderings and imaginings, is a somewhat unsettling task that confronts one with assorted earlier selves, some considerably brasher than one's less flamboyant present self, some now, indeed, strangers to oneself. And yet my work of the past twenty years is not entirely devoid of continuity, it seems to me, despite the proliferation of authorial personae. Two themes in particular appear to unite it.

One theme, although not the main one, is *gender*—gender in biblical texts, gender and biblical texts; feminine gender, masculine gender, indeterminate gender, asymmetrical gender; gender continually traversed by the constitutive yet complicating factors of sex and sexuality; gender constantly constructed and deconstructed. It appears that eight of the sixteen essays gathered here (beginning with the earliest and including two of those that are co-authored) deal centrally with gender, while several of the remaining essays treat it in an ancillary way.

The principal unifying theme, however (to continue in this unpoststructurist vein—ironically, as we'll see in a moment), is reflected in the book's main title. Since before the beginning of my publishing career I have been centrally interested in *theory* and with reading biblical texts with, through, and in spite of it. The theory in question is principally poststructuralist theory—a formulation that, however, borders on the redundant, for the term *theory* has, for the past three decades or more (see Culler 1982, 8; 2007, 4), in literary-leaning regions of the humanities at any rate, been a codeword or synecdoche for poststructuralism—or, better, assorted poststructuralisms, such as deconstruction, New Historicism, postcolonial theory, queer theory, and major academic variants of "third-wave" feminism.[1] Hence the "post" in

---

1. Poststructuralism is notoriously difficult to define, but a definition would seem to

the book's subtitle. If "critical" refers to biblical criticism as customarily practiced—as more than two centuries of incremental institutional conditioning has predisposed us to practice it—then "postcritical" refers to the efforts certain of the essays make to burst out of that enclosure, ample though it is. Other essays, meanwhile, are content to pace back and forth behind the bars, lean comfortably against them, or pretend they don't exist.

---

be in order nonetheless, given the prominence of poststructuralism in this volume. The term evokes a congeries of interrelated topoi:

(1) The systematic dismantling of "metaphysical" concepts (origin, being, essence, transcendence, etc.) and hierarchical oppositions (presence/absence, speech/writing, primary/secondary, central/marginal, white/nonwhite, colonizer/colonized masculine/feminine, heterosexual/homosexual, human/animal, etc.). This is a wholly heterogeneous project with its roots in early Derridean deconstruction (e.g., Derrida 1976; 1978b; 1981a) but extending into deconstructive racial/ethnic studies (e.g., Gates 1986), postcolonial studies (e.g., Bhabha 1994d), third-wave feminism and queer theory (e.g., Butler 1990), and, most recently, animal studies (or, better, posthuman animality studies), a burgeoning subfield of ecocriticism that draws much of its energy from Derrida 2002b; 2008.

(2) The meticulous analysis of the ways in which literary, critical and philosophical arguments are inevitably destabilized by the figures and tropes they necessarily employ—a project especially associated with Paul de Man (e.g., 1971; 1979) and "early" American deconstructive literary criticism.

(3) The exposure of the exclusions, omissions, and systemic blind spots that enable texts, and entire societies, to function—a strategy of reading also closely associated with Jacques Derrida but adapted and extended once again by politically minded critics of various stripes (e.g., Spivak 1988a).

(4) The unearthing of the constructedness (i.e., nonnaturalness) of certain of the most solid-seeming features of our cultural landscapes—"man," the body, insanity, sexuality, etc.—as in Michel Foucault's successive "archeological" and "genealogical" projects, the most influential of which was his *History of Sexuality* (1978; 1985; 1986), a crucial resource for queer theory and masculinity studies.

(5) The investigation of the ineluctable role of power in the fabrication of truth and knowledge, another Foucauldian obsession (see esp. 1977a; 1978) and also a central preoccupation of New Historicism and certain versions of cultural studies.

(6) The exploration of the internal heteronomy fissuring every human subject—which is to say, Jacques Lacan's "return to Freud" (see esp. Lacan 1977a, 146–78), specifically, Freud's unsettling early vision of the human subject as irremediably split or disunified, Lacan further radicalizing that vision by filtering it through a (post)structuralist philosophy of language.

(7) The examination of the ways in which every text, independently of the conscious intentionality of any author, invokes innumerable other texts, ceaselessly recycling and rewriting them—that is, radical intertextuality in the mode of Julia Kristeva (e.g., 1980d) and the later work of Roland Barthes (e.g., 1977b).

And so on.

My own most memorable early encounter with theory occurred at my first, awe-struck pilgrimage in 1986 to that colossal cerebral festival that was the Joint Annual Meeting of the American Academy of Religion and the Society of Biblical Literature. I had been prowling around the edges of certain program units where narrative criticism and reader-response criticism had begun to bloom. Near the end of the conference I strayed into a session of a rather different sort. David Fisher was delivering a difficult paper entitled "The Texts and Their Owners," and George Aichele, David Jobling, and Gary Phillips were responding in kind. All four papers were sodden with theory. This dense discourse did not, of course, spring fully formed from the foreheads of the four presenters. It had been incubating for several years in certain AAR program units and the SBL's Structuralism and Exegesis Seminar, which was in fact hosting the session. Listening in 1986, nevertheless, to presentations officially billed as SBL papers, yet redolent with references to Derrida, Foucault, Barthes, and their exotic ilk, was, for me at least, an exhilaratingly disorienting experience, like stepping through a gray door into a Technicolor dreamscape. I had spent the previous year anxiously unemployed in Topeka, Kansas, where I had moved from Ireland for romantic reasons, following the completion of my doctoral degree. But now I wasn't in Kansas any more, whether literally or metaphorically. Although I did not realize it then, the discursive performances I was witnessing were simultaneously situated inside and outside biblical studies. Fisher's primary training was in philosophical theology, as was Aichele's, while Jobling and Phillips were both transitioning from biblical structuralism (the "high" kind associated with deep structures, semiotic squares, and actantial models), which had been their disciplinary habitat. In other words, these heady theoretical performances were taking place on the outermost rim of the biblical studies discipline and were tethered to the core values of the discipline only by the feeblest and most unstable of orbits.

Even today, of course, theory of the poststructuralist stripe is thoroughly external to the humdrum daily business of biblical scholarship, while it has been the bread and butter of literary studies for approximately three decades (although many literary critics have begun to gag on it of late, a reflex discussed in the last two essays of this collection). Throughout my career as a biblical scholar I have read intensively in literary studies (and hence also in critical theory, gender and sexuality studies, cultural studies, postcolonial studies, etc.), primarily because I found it afforded me an external, defamiliarizing vantage point from which to view what we do as biblical critics. I have always desired to write as simultaneously an insider and an outsider to the field of biblical studies, on the inside looking out while on the outside looking in. The essays assembled in this volume (at any rate those for which I am the sole author) all reflect that Janus-faced ambition to a greater or lesser degree, although I doubt that any actually come close to achieving it.

Apart from the final essay, "After 'After Theory,' and Other Apocalyptic Conceits in Literary and Biblical Studies," which Yvonne Sherwood and I co-authored, all of the others have been published previously. The invitation to assemble this collection came with the suggestion that some of the selections be unpublished conference papers. That sounded like a splendid idea, but when I began to exhume and examine these unpublished conference papers, I had a rather dispiriting epiphany: they sit moldering in drawers rather than yellowing in journals because they weren't very good to begin with. I have also spared the reader my juvenilia—my articles and essays from the period 1986–1989. Admittedly, the opening essay, "The 'Post-' Age Stamp: Does It Stick? Biblical Studies and the Postmodernism Debate," is juvenile enough in places to make me cringe, but it seemed to provide a scene-setting lead-in, nonetheless, to the second and third essays in the volume. Specifically, the first essay provides a theoretical exposition of the particular brand of poststructuralism that finds exegetical expression in the second and third essays. The sequence of the essays throughout the collection is broadly chronological, but not strictly so. All told, I was more interested in continuity than chronology and, where possible, in having a particular essay seem to take up where the previous one left off. Each essay is prefaced with a specially composed headnote that attempts to contextualize it in hindsight. Cumulatively if obliquely, these headnotes attempt to turn the volume's table of contents into an unfolding tale—that of a professional life lived in the interstices of Bible and theory, which simultaneously, although incompletely, is a tale of two disciplines.

To a greater or lesser extent, all of the essays have been revised—greater with regard to the earlier essays, lesser with regard to the later, and barely at all with regard to the four that have been co-authored. Those that received significant revision did so according to the following ground rules. I did not attempt to take on board scholarship that appeared subsequent to the essay's original date of publication. That prospect proved too daunting, given that ten to twenty years had elapsed since more than half of the pieces originally appeared and the stack of relevant scholarly literature had grown ship-sinkingly high. I did, however, streamline certain of the essays, or, alternatively, flesh out certain of their arguments. Most of all, I tinkered with their style. Repeatedly, the elder me has impatiently snatched the pen from the younger me and "improved" a paragraph, a sentence, or a turn of phrase. Age has its prerogatives, after all.

In terms of primary literature, the essays range through the Song of Songs (chs. 10 and 11), the Gospel of Mark (ch. 2 and part of ch. 5), the

Gospel of Luke and the Acts of the Apostles (ch. 3), the Gospel of John (chs. 4 and 14), the Letter to the Romans (ch. 12 and part of ch. 7), Josephus's *Jewish War* (more precisely, small portions thereof; ch. 5), 4 Maccabees (ch. 9), and the ancient Jewish mystical text known as the *Shi'ur Qomah* (ch. 8), to name only the principal stops on the itinerary. None of the half-dozen or so articles and essays on the book of Revelation that I have published over the years is included in this volume, as I am planning to gather those pieces in a separate collection.

Theoretically and methodologically, the essays assembled in the present volume span postmodernism in relation to poststructuralism and feminism (ch. 1); Derridean deconstruction (chs. 1, 2, and 4) and other poststructuralisms—Lacanian (ch. 3), Foucauldian (chs. 3, 7, and 11), and Kristevan (ch. 1); deconstruction in relation to feminist biblical criticism (ch. 4); New Historicism in relation to biblical historical criticism, epitomized by the quest for the historical Jesus (ch. 5); autobiographical criticism in relation to feminism, poststructuralism, and contextual biblical hermeneutics (ch. 6); cultural studies (chs. 8 and 15), masculinity studies (chs. 8, 9, and 12), and queer theory (chs. 10, 11, and 12); queer theory in relation to feminist biblical criticism (ch. 11); postcolonialism in relation to poststructuralism and postmodernism (ch. 13); postcolonial biblical criticism (ch. 14); postmethodological developments in literary studies and their implications for biblical studies (ch. 15); and the "after theory" debate in literary studies and its ramifications for biblical studies (ch. 16).

Thematically, the essays are grouped in seven sections: "Postmodernity," "Textuality,"[2] "Autobiography," "Masculinity," "Sexuality," "Postcoloniality," and "Posttheory." One of these sections has only one essay in it, as the reader will notice, while others have only two. Like all such containers, moreover, the sections have numerous leaks: "postmodernity" drips into the "postcoloniality" section, "textuality" trickles into the "autobiography" section, "masculinity" seeps into the "sexuality" section, and so on. Still, these divisions seemed to me, nonetheless, on consideration to be the "logical" ones—the main themes

---

2. This term also merits definition. A term redolent with poststructuralist associations (Derridean, Barthesian, Kristevan…), "textuality" connotes the capacity of texts (and not only literary texts) to mean and mean again, incessantly and uncontrollably, beyond the intentions of their original authors, and generally to exceed and even to eclipse their original circumstances of production. Textuality evokes plural contexts of reception (and hence multiple politics of interpretation) as distinct from a singular context of production. Yet the concept is not necessarily inimical to historiography, as the example of New Historicism demonstrates (see ch. 5 below). For New Historicism, however, history is knowable only through its vestigial textual traces—which is to say, only in, through, and in spite of textuality.

that the essays, collectively, seemed to treat, the principal parts into which the volume, overall, seemed to fall.

At the end of each section, I have slotted in an annotated bibliography of suggestions for further reading on the specific section topic or topics. (That, too, has been determinative of the divisions into which I have carved the collection. Earlier I was tempted by the sage suggestion of an anonymous reviewer of the book proposal that I combine my "Masculinity" and "Sexuality" sections into a less exclusionary sounding "Gender and Sexuality" section, until the challenge of compiling a single short bibliography that would adequately orient the reader to that vast combined field proved too overwhelming.) The volume is hardly well suited to serve as a basic introduction to critical theory and literary studies in relation to biblical studies, but I hope that it might at least serve as an "advanced" introduction to this biblical interdiscipline and that readers with some prior familiarity with biblical literary criticism might find the volume relatively comprehensible and reasonably useful.

It was in Tom Thatcher's brain, not my own, that this volume was first conceived. I am immensely grateful to Tom for taking the notion that such a collection would be a worthwhile addition to the Resources for Biblical Study series that he edits, and I am also deeply grateful to Bob Buller, SBL Editorial Director, for agreeing to the idea. I feel honored and humbled that Amy-Jill Levine, whose scholarship I have always greatly admired, accepted Tom's invitation to write a foreword for the volume. The volume is also enhanced by the fecund intellect and unique erudition of each of the four co-authors who contributed to it: Janice Capel Anderson, Virginia Burrus, Susan Lochrie Graham, and Yvonne Sherwood. Collaborative authorship has always been extremely important to me. Frequently I have known what I mean only when I have seen what the other person has to say. "One must be several in order to write," Derrida once remarked (1987c, 152). But several must be one in order to write collaboratively—an altogether trickier exercise, but exhilarating when it succeeds. Finally, I wish to thank my supportive dean and generous colleagues at Drew Theological School, whose provision of a research semester enabled me to rouse these slumbering essays from their resting places, dress them up as best I could, and send them out once more into the world.

Postmodernity

1

The "Post-" Age Stamp: Does It Stick? Biblical Studies and the Postmodernism Debate*

Postmodernism was a shiny new concept in biblical studies in the mid- to late 1980s. Indeed, it still bore the sheen of the new even in academia at large. In my *Literary Criticism and the Gospels* I could declare with youthful confidence that the "important statements" (by which I meant notable books) in postmodernism numbered five (Moore 1989, 130 n. 21)—and I didn't mean in biblical studies but in general. It was only in the succeeding decade that the literature on postmodernism began to flood the academic landscape.

In my own mind (if nowhere else), postmodernism in biblical studies begins in earnest with certain papers that Gary Phillips presented at the SBL in the mid-1980s (papers that used the emergent literature on postmodernism to frame poststructuralism and, ultimately, biblical criticism) and extends from there in a (singularly unpostmodern) straight line to *The Postmodern Bible* (The Bible and Culture Collective 1995).[1] Within that trajectory, poststructuralism folded neatly into postmodernism—poststructuralism was, indeed, quintessential academic postmodernism—and this was also the tack I myself took in *Literary Criticism and the Gospels*.

But here I was less confident, it seems, because in the essay that follows (which dates from the same year as the book) I call the postmodernism/poststructuralism conflation into question and argue that poststructuralism should instead be regarded as a late inflection of (aesthetic) modernism, which I distinguish from

---

* First published in the *Journal of the American Academy of Religion* 57 (1989): 543–59.

1. Other points on that line include Fowler 1989, Burnett 1990, and Phillips 1990a, as well as my own early work (esp. 1989, 108–78). I associate a related, more recent trajectory with the industry of A. K. M. Adam (1995, 2000, 2001, 2006).

(Enlightened) modernity. I would still hold by these arguments and distinctions (which were not original to me, in any case). What strikes me now, however, on rereading the piece is how eager I still was to identify postmodernism with all that was politically progressive and, most of all, with feminism. Within a few years that was no longer possible, Fredric Jameson's landmark book on postmodernism (Jameson 1991) having convinced me that it is better understood as "the cultural logic of late capitalism" (to cite the book's appositional title).

Feminism looms large in this essay, as I have already implied, and it was my first sustained attempt to engage with it in my writing. The attempt is hardly successful. I draw a sharp line between French feminism and North American feminism without yet realizing that there are other important lines to be drawn as well—racial/ethnic lines, class lines, global North/global South lines. The essay's feminism is insufficiently politicized, in other words, while its postmodernism is excessively politicized.

[T]his might be the postmodernism whose coming has been foretold.... Beneath the glimmering boreal light, mirrored polar ice groans and heaves. (Tyler 1987, 59)

"Postmodernism"—a multidisciplinary throng of book and article titles today sport this secularized mark of the Beast. The mark has just started to appear in biblical-scholarly titles. What do biblical scholars mean by it? The instinct of the biblical scholar who takes on the sorter's task of separating what is postmodern in critical thought from what is modern would seem to be one of affixing the postmark to any critical practice issuing from any region far removed from positivist biblical scholarship. This is Edgar V. McKnight's instinct, for instance, in his *Postmodern Use of the Bible* (1988). McKnight's postmark, "which allows readers to use the Bible today is that of a radical reader-oriented literary criticism, a criticism which views literature in terms of readers and their values, attitudes, and responses" (1988, 14–15). Robert M. Fowler (1989) surrenders to the same instinct, confidently affixing the postmark to reader-response criticism, the philosophies of Gadamer, Wittgenstein, and J. L. Austin, the media criticism of Walter Ong, Derridean deconstruction, and various forms of political criticism. But the instinct is not unique to biblical scholars. Among literary critics (e.g., Hassan 1987) the label "postmodernist" is most often reserved for literary experiments that thoroughly debunk standard literary conventions, such as American surfiction or the French New and New New Novel. Other critics argue, however, that such experimental fictions are best seen not as postmodernist artifacts but as extreme instances "of modernist autotelic self-reflection" (Hutcheon 1998, 40). What of experimental *critical* texts, those of Jacques Derrida, for example, whom Fowler suspects is "the exemplar of the post-modern intellectual" (1989, 17)? Gary A. Phillips, too, sees "postmodern currents of thought ... exemplified in the deconstructive criticism of Derrida" (1989, 11). Should we conclude that deconstructive biblical criticism exemplifies postmodernism in biblical studies?

Is Poststructuralism Really Postmodern?

It is certainly tempting to read the celebrated "two interpretations of interpretation" passage in Derrida's "Structure, Sign, and Play" as a classic formulation of the modern/postmodern dichotomy. The first interpretation of interpretation (the Rousseauistic one) "seeks to decipher, dreams of deciphering a truth or an origin which escapes play and the order of the sign, and ... lives the necessity of interpretation as an exile," while the second interpretation of interpretation (the Nietzschean one) "is no longer turned toward the origin, affirms play," and "tries to pass beyond man and humanism" (1978b, 292).[2] A modern/postmodern construal of the passage seems further encouraged by Derrida's veiled closing reference to "the as yet unnamable which is proclaiming itself and which can do so ... only under the species of the nonspecies, in the formless, mute, infant, and terrifying form of monstrosity" (1978b, 293). French poststructuralism, however, Derrida's version of it included, seems better read as a reinscription of modernism. Derrida's procedure in *Dissemination* (1981a; French original 1972), a stylistic watershed between his more propositional early work and subsequent paraliterary experiments, is telling. *Dissemination*'s first and second essays, "Outwork" and "Plato's Pharmacy," deconstruct Hegel and Plato respectively. The third essay, however, "The Double Session," and the concluding title essay, which treat literary experiments by *fin de siècle* symbolist poet Stéphane Mallarmé and New Novelist Philippe Sollers, respectively, are *not* exercises in deconstruction, at least as we know it. Derrida's strategy in the pivotal Mallarmé essay, for instance, presaged by earlier readings of avant-garde playwright Antonin Artaud (Derrida

---

2. These two interpretations of interpretation are not, however, chronologically successive: "we live them simultaneously and reconcile them in an obscure economy" (Derrida 1978b, 293). The essay dates from 1966 and as such predates the postmodernism debate per se.

1978b, 169–95, 232–50), is to apprentice himself to *Mimique,* a short Mallarméan text (Mallarmé, of course, being a seminal *modernist):* "we are … in the process of determining in what way there *is* no 'philosophy' in [Mallarmé's] text, or rather that that text is calculated in such a way as no longer to be situated *in* philosophy" (Derrida 1981b, 207 n. 24, his emphasis)—which is where Derrida wants to be as well. Subsequent paraliterary experiments (e.g., *Glas* [1986b], *The Truth in Painting* [1987c]) have Derrida riding in the slipstream of other modernist writers and visual artists. Derridean discourse is, to this extent, an extension of the discourse of modernism.

The case is similar for Roland Barthes, who already in "Introduction to the Structural Analysis of Narratives" declares: "Narrative does not show, does not imitate.… '[W]hat happens' in narrative is, from the referential (real) point of view, literally, *nothing,* what 'takes place' is language alone, the adventure of language, whose coming never ceases to be celebrated" (1988 [French original 1966], 134–35). Appended to Barthes's hyper-(post)structuralist pronouncement, however, is a snippet from Mallarmé's *Crayonne au théâtre:* "A dramatic work shows the succession of the externals of action without any moment's keeping its reality and without there happening, ultimately, anything at all" (Barthes 1988, 135 n. 72). He might equally have quoted Flaubert, who wished to write "a book about nothing, a book without external attachments which would hold together by itself through the internal force of its style."[3] Center stage in French critical theory is, as Andreas Huyssen observes, held by the classical modernists: "Flaubert, Proust and Bataille in Barthes; Nietzsche and Heidegger, Mallarmé and Artaud in Derrida; Nietzsche, Magritte and Bataille in Foucault; Mallarmé and Lautréamont, Joyce and Artaud in Kristeva; Freud in Lacan; Brecht in Althusser and Macheray, and so on" (1986, 208–9). French (post)structuralism does, of course, have a *political* face that high modernist statements such as Barthes's tend to obscure; but the modernist avant-garde too was capable of intense political fervor, as Dada and surrealism amply attest. As some critics have recently come to see, then (e.g., Krauss 1980; Ulmer 1983; Huyssen 1986, 206–16), the modernist revolution in the arts, exhausted and at an impasse by the 1960s, has, through the agency of French poststructuralism, been renewed in *critical* discourse, which has finally been affected by the crisis of representation that marked the birth of modernist art and literature more than a century ago.

---

3. Quoted in Huyssen (1986, 54) from an undocumented source.

1. THE "POST-" AGE STAMP 13

"Post-" What, Precisely?

Modernism itself is hardly a clear term. (Newman 1985, 21)

If affixing the "post-" age stamp to Derrida, Barthes, and other French thinkers is problematic, what of the more moderate figures listed by Fowler and McKnight as witnesses of the postmodern: Gadamer, Wittgenstein, J. L. Austin, Stanley Fish, Wolfgang Iser et al.? McKnight does recognize that "postmodernism assumes different forms because of different expressions of modernism" (1988, 25 n. 1). This is, indeed, a crucial if neglected factor for any discussion of postmodernism.

Just as there are two interpretations of interpretation, there are at least two interpretations of modernism. The first is an *aesthetic* interpretation centered on literature since Flaubert, plastic art since Manet, and their deconstruction of verbal and visual language respectively. As it happens, this usage of the term modernism is by far the most common one in the postmodernism debate (at any rate, outside of biblical studies). The second interpretation of modernism, or better in this case of *modernity*, is an *epistemic* interpretation, which locates the birth of modernity in the scientific revolution and/or the Enlightenment. As defined by Jürgen Habermas, for example, the project of modernity, which "comes only into focus when we dispense with the usual concentration upon art," was formulated in the eighteenth century by the philosophers of the Enlightenment and "consisted in their efforts to develop objective science, universal morality and law, and autonomous art according to their inner logic" (1983, 8–9). Timothy Reiss associates the birth of modernity more with the scientific revolution. Modernity's signal characteristic, for Reiss, is its *analytico-referential discourse*, which "assumes that the world, as it can be and is to be known, represents a fixed object of analysis quite separate from the forms of discourse by which men speak of it and by which they represent their thoughts" (1982, 44). Aesthetic modernism—the crisis of representation that erupted in nineteenth century art and literature—can thus be seen as a crisis of philosophical and scientific modernity's analytico-referential paradigm. The iconoclastic aesthetic of nascent modernism amounted to a rejection of the early modern *épistème* and the canons of representation that it legitimized (in the visual arts, for example, the iconoclastic trajectory extends from impressionism, expressionism, and cubism through Dada and surrealism and on down to abstract expressionism, to name only the principal movements). Later the analytico-referential paradigm would be assailed within its own traditional strongholds: in physics by Einstein, for instance, and in mathematics by Gödel.

Historical criticism of the Bible, an offshoot of the scientific revolution and the Enlightenment (modernity in the expanded sense), is currently in the grip of an epistemic crisis. On this there is widespread agreement. But how severe is this crisis? In my view, it cannot yet be regarded as severe. The challenge to historical criticism posed by reader-oriented literary theory and criticism, for example (of which McKnight and Fowler both have much to say), amounts to a much-delayed replay within biblical studies of Kant's epochal deflection of critical attention from the object of knowledge considered in itself to the partially constitutive activity of the knower, thought to give that object its appearance and intelligibility. But does this quiet Kantian revolution gathering force in biblical studies (anticipated by Bultmann and others who announced the impossibility of presupposition-free exegesis decades ago) require the postmodern stamp? McKnight believes it does (although he does not style the revolution a Kantian one):

> A *radical* reader-oriented criticism is postmodern in that it challenges the critical assumption that a disinterested reader can approach a text objectively and obtain verifiable knowledge by applying certain scientific strategies. A radical reader-oriented approach sees the strategies, the criteria for criticism and verification, the "information" obtained by the process, and the use made of such "information" in light of the reader. The reader is no more autonomous than the text in postmodernism; the reader and the text are interdependent. (1988, 15, his emphasis)

What McKnight has described seems to me better viewed as a case of positivistic biblical scholarship awakening from its "dogmatic slumber" (as Kant might phrase it) to a still more enlightened modernity. Biblical studies has yet to experience its own analogue of the modernist revolution that erupted in the arts in the century following Kant. The major premises of the modernist artwork can be characterized as "the rejection of all classical systems of representation, the effacement of 'content,' the erasure of subjectivity and authorial voice, the repudiation of likeness and verisimilitude, the exorcism of any demand for realism of whatever kind" (Huyssen 1986, 54). And French and North American poststructruralists have partially reenacted that revolution in an academic register, as we have seen.

What would be the effects of such a revolution in the biblical arena? Certain stretches of Mark C. Taylor's *Erring: A Postmodern A/theology* (1984, 103–20, 170–82) offer suggestive sketches of that spectacle, although Taylor's project is an a/theological rather than a biblical one. Taylor's principal accomplice is Derrida, not surprisingly, specifically the Derrida who radicalized the structuralist dictum that linguistic systems are irreducibly relational. The linguistic signifier (sound pattern) is able to signify solely by its relationship to other signifiers; it has no *innate* significance. The sound *tree*, for instance, is intelligible to a speaker of English not because of what it *is*, strictly speaking, since there is no resemblance whatsoever between that sound (or its appearance when written) and either the concept of a tree or the physical object that flourishes under that name. Instead, the sound is intelligible precisely because of what it *is not*, which is to say *three*, *the*, *tea*, and every other word in the English language or any language. All of that Derrida gleaned from the structural linguist Ferdinand de Saussure, as did every other Parisian intellectual of the 1960s. But Derrida boldly picks up where Saussure nervously left off. If the signifier has no innate significance, Derrida continues, then neither is it possessed of *presence*:

> [T]he movement of signification is possible only if each so-called "present" element is related to something other than itself, thereby ... constituting ... the present by means of this very relation to what it is not.... [B]ut this interval that constitutes it as present must, by the same token, divide the present in and of itself, thereby also dividing, along with the present, everything that is thought on the basis of the present. (1982, 13)

And what has been thought on the basis of the present in the West is not inconsiderable, as it turns out. "[A]ll the names related to fundamentals ... have always designated an invariable presence—*eidos*, *arche*, *telos*, *energeia*, *ousia* (essence, existence, substance, subject), *aletheia*, transcendentality, consciousness, God, man..." (Derrida 1978b, 279–80). To that which deconstructs presence even as it constructs it, Derrida gives the name *writing* (*l'écriture*), understood as "a fabric of traces marking the disappearance of an exceeded God or of an erased man" (1978b, 294), and which includes among its effects: (1) writing as ordinarily conceived, that is, as an instrumental substitute for speech; (2) speech as ordinarily conceived, that is, as the privileged locus of presence and hence of truth; (3) presence itself in all its variations, and, as such, extending to every hierarchical binary opposition based on the presence/absence dichotomy (affirmation/negation, being/nonbeing, identity/difference, speech/writing, etc.).

Following Derrida's own thread (e.g., 1978b, 64–78), Taylor stitches Derridean *Écriture* to *Scripture*. "In the liminal time-space of scripture, hard-and-fast oppositions are shattered and every seemingly stable either-or is perpetually dislocated." Scripture "is" the divine milieu that "is neither fully present nor absent.... It neither is nor is not.... The paradoxical divine milieu presupposes a 'logic of contamination and the contamination of logic'" and "is not thinkable within the terms of classical logic" (Taylor 1984, 117, quoting Derrida 1981a, 149, 153). Nor is it thinkable in terms of transcendence. Linguistic signs are commonly thought to designate concepts or actual objects in the world. But insofar as signs are altogether unintelligible apart from other signs, the sign can only ever be "a sign of a sign" (Taylor 1984, 105). Words, writing, scripture are not so much *about* something as they *are* that something itself. "To interpret God as word is to understand the divine as scripture or writing" (1984, 104). And scripture thus reinscribed cannot affirm the transcendent but only subvert it, giving birth to an irreducibly incarnational christology: "the divine is *forever* embodied" (1984, 104, his emphasis). Incarnation thus reconceived "is not a once-and-for-all event, restricted to a specific time and place" (1984, 104). Writing is bodily or incarnate. In scriptural a/theology, materiality precludes transcendence: "word is made flesh and flesh is made word" (1984, 106).

Taylor's a/theology, a chilling "plunge into the horizontality of a pure surface" (Derrida 1978b, 298), sends rip(ple)s through the traditions of theological and biblical reflection inherited from the Enlightenment. "[T]he tailor is profoundly interested in surfaces and completely preoccupied with appearances," puns Taylor (1984, 180). But "the tailor does not weave the material he cuts and sews. He stitches together textiles that have been woven by others" (1984, 180). Taylor's text(ile)s, notwithstanding the postmark of his book's subtitle (*A Postmodern A/theology*),[4] are those of aesthetic modernism. The (poststructuralist) texts Taylor stitches together are recycled literary and painterly texts; they bespeak the insistent flatness of the modernist canvas, coupled with the defiant cry of Artaud that resounds through modernist literature: "When I write there is nothing other than what I write" (quoted in Derrida 1978b, 169). These texts enter *Erring* via the French poststructuralist rewriting that first transformed them into critical texts. Deconstructive a/theology does not mark a funeral, then—"the attempt to keep the wake after the death of God going on forever" (Stout 1987, 22)—so much as a rebirth: that of aesthetic modernism as a/theological discourse.

This is not to conclude, however, that post-modernism, whether in theology or in general, is nothing more than "a dash surrounded by a contradiction" (Newman 1985, 17), or that there can be nothing truly new under the waning Western sun after a century of modernist experiments. In his article "Postmodern Biblical Criticism," Robert Fowler identifies as

> one grand index of the postmodern ... an increasing recognition that reading and interpretation is always interested, never disinterested; always significantly subjective, never completely objective; always committed and

---

4. Although the term *postmodern* in theology has commonly denoted the Barthian project, it now not infrequently denotes the (not entirely unrelated) Heideggerian and Derridean projects of certain radical theologians in addition (Taylor, Raschke, Scharlemann, Winquist, Caputo et al.).

therefore always political, never uncommitted and apolitical; always historically-bound, never ahistorical. The modernist dream of disinterested, objective, distanced, abstract truth is fading rapidly. (1989, 22)

That dream was already fading in the nineteenth century. But the crisis of representation today has a face that it could not have had for Nietzsche, Flaubert, Manet, or their successors. The concern with what can be represented and what cannot has become to an unprecedented degree a *political* concern to expose the systems of power that authorize certain representations while prohibiting or invalidating others. And "[a]mong those prohibited from Western representation, whose representations are denied ... legitimacy, are women" (Owens 1983, 59)—a situation the historical avant-garde, the political vanguard of aesthetic modernism, did exceedingly little to change, as it happens: it "was, by and large, ... patriarchal, misogynist, and masculinist" (Huyssen 1986, 60). To the extent that it exceeds enlightened modernity *and* aesthetic modernism, then, exposing their master narratives as narratives of male mastery, feminism can be said to represent an authentic *post*modern swerve in Western culture.

Related to the emergence of feminism in Western culture is an awareness that other cultures must be met by means other than conquest, domination or assimilation (cf. Huyssen 1986, 220). That awareness, too, must be translated into types of intellectual work different from those of the typical modernist artist or intellectual who tended to speak with the confidence of standing at the cutting edge of history and culture, and from that imaginary position blithely spoke for geographical and cultural others (cf. Huyssen 1986, 220). Latin American, African and Asian exegetes are beginning to force that awareness on North American and European biblical scholars, arguably a further index of a nascent postmodern biblical criticism.

To label feminist and "Third World" exegetes postmodern(ist), however, is to continue to speak for others. The postmodernism debate is largely a North American concern that has been little exported to date. Even in fields where the debate has flourished (cultural studies, art history, literary studies, etc.), feminist critics have paid tellingly little heed to it (cf. Huyssen 1986, 198). Totalization's announced death rattle has all too often turned out to have been a clearing of the throat. "I cannot speak of feminism in general," Gayatri Chakravorty Spivak remarks in a different context; "I speak of what I do as a woman within literary criticism" (1988b, 77). Critics such as Spivak seem to have internalized a commendable "incredulity toward metanarratives," Jean-François Lyotard's grand index of the postmodern (Lyotard 1984, xxiv). Others (myself included, no doubt) allow various metanarratives to slip in unheeded as they swap modern tales of the postmodern.

Postmodernisms and Feminisms

"And yes," says Molly, carrying *Ulysses* off beyond any book and toward the new writing: "I said yes, I will Yes." (Cixous 1980a, 255),

We have distinguished a high modernism in the arts, extending into certain sectors of academic culture, that is antithetical to Enlightened modernity, and to its realist canons of representation in particular. We have also distinguished a postmodernism of resistance, opposed to the andocentric and Eurocentric canons of Enlightened modernity and high modernism alike. But hypermodernist criticism and postmodernist criticism need not be mutually exclusive. Derrida's periodic grappling with the issue of phallocentrism is an illuminating case in point (e.g., 1979b, 1985b, 1987e). Still more instructive is the case of *l'écriture féminine,* the utopian writing of Hélène Cixous and the writings of Julia Kristeva and Luce Irigaray associated with it.[5] "Woman must write herself," announces Cixous in her manifesto, "The Laugh of the Medusa" (1980a, 245). Woman has been without a voice of her own, and has thus been obliged to speak "the language of men and their grammar" (1980a, 257). Madeleine Gagnon, another writer of the feminine, puts it yet more forcefully: "The phallus, for me, ... represents repressive capitalist ownership, the exploiting bourgeois, the higher knowledge ... that watches, analyzes, sanctions, ... everything that wants regimentation and representation.... I am a foreigner to myself in my own language and I translate myself by quoting all the others" (1980, 180). Kristeva, for her part, distinguishes two kinds of women's writing. The first kind speaks the propositional language of the patriarchal regimen, although only in order to subvert it. (Feminist biblical criticism invites description of this sort, as we shall see.) The second kind, meanwhile, "flee[s] everything considered 'phallic' to find refuge in the valorization of a silent underwater body" (1980a, 166).

This submerged aqueous body is that of the Mother, which (in Lacanian parlance) is sealed off by the Law of the Father (cf. Lacan 1977a, 67; 198–249 passim). Lacan's poststructuralist rereading of Freud is critically reread in turn by the French writers of the feminine. The Law of the Father is that which cuts the child off from symbiotic union with the mother. This severing is partially effected by the child's acquisition of language—or, rather, by language's acquisition of the child. For Cixous, Irigaray and Kristeva, the "reasonable" language of the Father is the crucial site of woman's struggle. Irigaray writes of "the dry desolation of reason" (1985a, 191). Woman

---

5. Irigaray, less obviously indebted than Cixous or Kristeva to aesthetic modernism, will not feature significantly, however, in the ensuing discussion.

must "flee the logic that has framed her," sidestepping "obvious 'truths' that actually hide what she is seeking" (1985a, 93). Cixous similarly urges destruction of the syntax of philosophical-theoretical discourse, a severing of "that famous thread ... which acts for men as a surrogate umbilical cord" (1980a, 256).

Although the history of writing has been confounded with the history of reason, there have, however, been certain exceptions, concedes Cixous, failures "in that enormous machine that has been operating and turning out its 'truth'" for centuries (1980a, 249). For *l'écriture feminine*, the gender of writing is what counts, while the biological gender of the writer is secondary. Cixous singles out Jean Genet—iconoclastic author, queer icon, petty criminal, prison inmate ... —as an exemplary failure in the machine, a prototypical writer of the feminine: "under the name of Jean Genet, what is inscribed in the movement of a text which divides itself, breaks itself into bits, regroups itself, is an abundant, maternal, pederastic femininity" (1980c, 98). Kristeva elaborates more fully what is at stake in such texts: "in a culture where the speaking subjects are conceived of masters of their speech, they have ... a 'phallic' position. The fragmentation of language in a text calls into question the very posture of this mastery" (1980a, 165).

Like Derrida, Barthes, and other male poststructuralists, Kristeva and Cixous take their cue from the classic modernists: "For at least a century, the literary avant-garde (from Mallarmé and Lautréamont to Joyce and Artaud) has been introducing ruptures, blank spaces, and holes into language.... All of these modifications in the linguistic fabric are the sign of a force that has not been grasped by the linguistic or ideological system" (Kristeva 1980a, 165; cf. Kristeva 1974; Cixous 1972). To this unassimilable force, the unsayable of phallic Western discourse, Kristeva gives the name *woman:* "In 'woman' I see something that cannot be represented" (1980c, 137). "Woman," the excluded object of primal repression, marks "the fragile limits of the speaking being, closest to its dawn" (Kristeva 1982, 18), before language and identity supervene. But the purpose of writing—specifically, the libidinal writing of feminine *jouissance*—is to expedite the return of the repressed. In the prototypical literary utterance (Kristeva's example is Molly Bloom's soliloquy in Joyce's *Ulysses*), "the writer approaches the hysterical body [*hystera*: womb] so that it might speak ... of what eludes speech and turns out to be the hand to hand struggle of one woman with another, her mother, of course, the absolute because primeval seat of the ... excluded, the outside-of-meaning.... Atopia" (Kristeva 1982, 22).

The projects of Kristeva, Cixous, and certain other French female intellectuals, like those of certain of their male counterparts (notably Barthes and Derrida), are thus, in no small part, extensions or transpositions of the projects of aesthetic modernism. Their radical feminism[6] distances Kristeva and Cixous from the fathers of modernism, however, and locates them in a postmodernist space. But although their politics are (to that extent) postmodernist, their writings are modernist through and through.[7] Their iconoclastic desire to rock the Western edifice of representational language on its foundations (the quintessential modernist desire) distinguishes them from North American feminist critics, including feminist critics of the Bible. While all these feminists might be termed postmodernist in their deep suspicion of modernity's masculinist universalism, the French writers of the feminine emerge from the traditions of aesthetic modernism, as we have seen, whereas the North American feminist critics (and the feminist biblical critics in particular) tend to emerge from less iconoclastic, more reformist regions of modernity. Socio-historical studies of women in the biblical world, coupled with literary-critical studies of women in the biblical narratives, have been among the fastest growing areas of biblical studies in the 1980s. The following description of North American feminist criticism (Marks and de Courtivron 1980, xi) applies especially to such biblical criticism: "American feminists are interested in going back, in resurrecting lost women, ... in reconstructing a past—'herstory.' They are engaged in filling in cultural silences and holes in discourse." (Contrast Kristeva's affirmation of "ruptures, blank spaces, and holes in language" [1980a, 165].) "The assumption is that women have been present but invisible and that if they look they will find themselves." (Schüssler Fiorenza's *In Memory of Her* [1983] would be the classic biblical-scholarly instance of such a quest.) "American feminists tend also to be focused ... on describing the material, social, psychological condition of women.... Their style of reasoning, with few exceptions, follows the Anglo-American empirical, inductive, anti-speculative tradition. They are often suspicious of theories and theorizing."

A second style of feminist biblical criticism centers more on the patriarchal language of the Bible. Motivated by the recognition "that biblical texts are not the words of God but the words of *men*" (Schüssler Fiorenza 1984, x–xi, her emphasis), it is somewhat nearer to *l'écriture féminine*. For both projects, a transformation in language is imperative. There is, however, an important

---

6. Note, however, that both Cixous and Kristeva have, at different times, rejected the label "feminist" for their work.

7. Symptomatically, Kristeva's statement on postmodernist writing (Kristeva 1980b) is populated by modernist heroes—Mallarmé, Joyce, Artaud et al. In this she resembles Lyotard (the foremost French expositor on the postmodern), who outlines "an aesthetic that is far more closely related to the traditional ideologies of high modernism proper than to current postmodernisms, " as Fredric Jameson astutely notes in his foreword to Lyotard's *The Postmodern Condition* (Lyotard 1984, xvi).

difference of degree. For the French writers of the feminine, the language of patriarchy does not need reforming, it needs destroying. In Cixous's quasi-apocalyptic idiom, the return of the repressed feminine will be "an explosive, *utterly* destructive, staggering return, with a force never yet unleashed" (1980a, 256, her emphasis).

This difference of degree is even better measured by Kristeva's *Powers of Horror* (1982), which contains the first extended reading of Jewish and Christian scripture by a French writer of the feminine (see also Kristeva 1987c, 83–100, 139–50, 234–64; Irigaray 1989). Lacan's speaking subject is constituted in part, as we noted earlier, by a catastrophic loss of unity with the maternal body and a concomitant repression of forbidden desire. Kristeva terms this primal repression *abjection,* and the object of repression *the abject.* The abject object of prohibited desire is also an object of dread; its encroachment menaces the fragile identity of the subject. Constituted initially by "a violent, clumsy breaking away" from the maternal entity, the subject runs the "constant risk of falling back" (1982, 13)

Powers of Horror is no *Texts of Terror* (Trible 1984). In contrast to North American feminist readings of the Bible, the repressed "woman" exhumed in *Powers of Horror* resists simple identification with any oppressed female, biblical or otherwise. Kristeva's hypothesis is that different religious systems (pagan, Jewish, Christian) correspond to different structurations of the subject against the danger and fascination of the abject. In various pagan cultures the danger seems to come from outside. Rites of purification spring up, as do prohibitions of nutritive and other substances, "the exclusion of which coincides with the sacred since it sets it up" (1982, 17). Kristeva reads nascent Judaism as a "tremendous forcing that consists in subordinating maternal power (whether historical or phantasmatic, natural or reproductive) to symbolic order"—that is, to the Law of the Father here embodied in an intricate legal system (1982, 91). The sacred, an external force for the pagan, penetrates deep into the life of the Jew through the Law. Each subject must now wage a struggle "in order to become separate" (from the maternal abject/from contaminated objects) so as "to become a speaking subject and/or subject to the Law" (1982, 94). But it is only with Christianity, contends Kristeva, that the contaminating danger is perceived no longer as external to the subject but as fully internal. Although classically expressed in the Pauline concept of flesh (*sarx*), Kristeva finds the interiorization if impurity in progress everywhere in the New Testament. "[E]vil, thus displaced *into* the subject, will not cease tormenting him from within, no longer as a polluting or defiling substance, but as the ineradicable repulsion of his henceforth divided and contradictory being" (1982, 116, her emphasis). Implicitly, for Kristeva, Pauline "man" prefigures Lacan's "split subject" driven by desire of the (M)Other, the nonfulfillment of which is the precarious condition of his ever unstable identity.

Kristeva's analysis of biblical religion leads inexorably to its declared supersession. Whereas organized religions resist the abject, literature uncovers it. Literature (modernist literature, naturally; here she names Baudelaire, Lautréamont, Kafka, Bataille, the Sartre of *Nausea,* and Céline) poises itself "on the fragile border ... where identities ... do not exist or only barely so" (1982, 207). Aesthetic productivity, for Kristeva, is "rooted in the abject it utters" and is "the essential component of religiosity." As such, "it is destined to survive the collapse of the historical forms of religions" (1982, 17). What collapses above all in Kristeva's analysis is transcendence. *Powers of Horror* pushes relentlessly to "the ultimate point that can be reached by what a moralist would call nihilism" (1982, 208), but what Kristeva would prefer to call a "[b]lack mysticism of transcendental collapse" (1982, 206). Such countertranscendentalism is entirely consonant with the French feminist project of utterly decentering the phallus—understood as that which rises up to oversee and control and thereby transcend—in all its cultural manifestations. In and through *Powers of Horror*, Nietzsche's "strangest of guests" (nihilism) knocks on the back door of the biblical-scholarly institution, demanding admission.

Which strategy is likely to prove more effective politically—the uncompromising iconoclasm of a Kristeva or the more moderate approach of most North American feminist critics, biblical feminists included? Many feminists, American and French alike, are skeptical of the claims Kristeva and Cixous make for the political efficacy of avant-garde writing. "True, conventional narrative techniques, as well as grammar and syntax, imply the unified viewpoint and mastery of outer reality that men have claimed for themselves," concedes Ann Rosalind Jones. "But literary modes and language itself cannot be the only targets for transformation" (1985, 373). Jones and others urge attention to the political, economic, and other material factors that prop up the masculinist establishments (Jones 1985, 367–75; cf. Moi 1985, 121–26, 147–48, 170–72; Spivak 1988b, 134–53). What is being urged in effect by such critics is a politicized postmodernism of resistance—critical and complicitous at once, simultaneously outside and inside the dominant social discourses (cf. Hutcheon 1988, 222)—beyond a modernist practice of experimental writing. Hermetic writing, it is implied, is self-marginalizing and hence self-defusing. North American feminist readers of the Bible, thus far at least, draw no such criticisms. For better or worse, and unlike Gayatri Spivak, Barbara Johnson, Jane Gallop, Shoshana Felman and numerous other secular feminists immersed in poststructuralism, they can be said to be postmodernist critics who have never known a modernist revolution.

But I have spoken too much for others. "Men must learn to be silent," writes Marguerite Duras. "This is probably very painful for them" (1980, 111). Very painful, indeed, at least for some, because the "post" of postmodernism must be driven deep into the privilege of the white, Western male. That, arguably, is the real stake in the postmodernism debate.

Further Reading on Postmodernity

Adam, A. K. M. 1995. *What Is Postmodern Biblical Criticism?* GBS. Minneapolis: Fortress. Considers deconstruction, ideological criticism and certain styles of feminist criticism under the umbrella of postmodernism.

———. 2006. *Faithful Interpretation: Reading the Bible in a Postmodern World*. Minneapolis: Fortress. Considers postmodernism's implications for such interrelated topics as biblical theology, hermeneutics and ethics.

———, ed. 2000. *Handbook of Postmodern Biblical Interpretation*. St. Louis: Chalice. A mini-encyclopedia of theories (e.g., deconstruction, queer theory), theorists (e.g., Foucault, Irigaray) and topics (e.g., historiography, postcolonialism).

———. 2001. *Postmodern Interpretations of the Bible—A Reader*. St. Louis: Chalice. A collection of exegetical essays designed as a companion to the *Handbook*.

Aichele, George, Peter Miscall and Richard Walsh. 2009. An Elephant in the Room: Historical-Critical and Postmodern Interpretations of the Bible. *JBL* 128:383–404. Attempts to catalyze an authentic dialogue between historical-critical and postmodern practitioners of biblical studies.

The Bible and Culture Collective. 1995. *The Postmodern Bible*. New Haven: Yale University Press. A manifesto for a politicized postmodernism in biblical studies, each chapter of which is the collaborative work of the ten scholars who make up the collective.

Cahoone, Lawrence E., ed. 2003. *From Modernism to Postmodernism: An Anthology*. 2nd ed. Oxford: Blackwell. Anthologies in postmodernism abound, but this one is panoramic in scope, its fifty-five selections beginning with Descartes and extending down to Jameson (and beyond).

Clines, David J. A. 1998. *On the Way to the Postmodern: Old Testament Essays, 1967–1998*. 2 vols. JSOTSup 293. Sheffield: Sheffield Academic Press. Of particular interest is "The Pyramid and the Net: The Postmodern Adventure in Biblical Studies" in vol. 1.

Collins, John J. 2005. *The Bible after Babel: Historical Criticism in a Postmodern Age*. Grand Rapids: Eerdmans. Considers the impact of postmodernism on biblical studies (especially Hebrew Bible/Old Testament studies), with special attention to the crisis in historiography and the challenges from postcolonial and feminist critics.

Jameson, Fredric. 1991. *Postmodernism, or, The Cultural Logic of Late Capitalism*. Durham, N.C.: Duke University Press. Dense, dystopian, magisterial. Argues that postmodernism is (among other related things) "the consumption of sheer commodification as a process."

Jobling, David, Tina Pippin, and Ronald Schleifer, eds. 2001. *The Postmodern Bible Reader*. Oxford: Blackwell. The authors anthologized in this companion to *The Postmodern Bible* include critical theorists, literary critics and liberation theologians, most well-known figures and all writing on or around the Bible.

Lyotard, Jean-François. 1984. *The Postmodern Condition: A Report on Knowledge*. (French orig. 1979.) Translated by Geoff Bennington and Brian Massumi. Minneapolis: University of Minnesota Press. Best known for its endlessly cited definition of the postmodern as "incredulity toward metanarratives."

Textuality

2

Illuminating the Gospels without the Benefit of Color: A Plea for Concrete Criticism*

"Derrida? Ach, he's a madman!" exclaimed the charismatic German theologian whose opinion on the controversial French philosopher I had solicited during my first year of doctoral work (hence, in 1982). Since this professor, whom I remember with considerable affection, happened to be on my dissertation committee (to employ American argot, although the place was Ireland), Derrida was not cast in the lead role in my dissertation, to put it mildly. Not only did my professor's brusque dismissal, however, predictably increase my curiosity about Derrida; it also constituted an uncannily accurate encapsulation of Derrida, as I eventually came to realize.

It was not, of course, that Derrida was certifiable. But his cumulative oeuvre constituted such an unrelenting assault on the normal, the natural, the commonsensical, the goes-absolutely-without-saying as frequently to amount to something altogether akin to madness. The Derrida who is best known is the "early" Derrida who single-mindedly deconstructs the hierarchical binary oppositions of Western metaphysics and hence of ordinary thought and everyday speech (this is also the Derrida of ch. 4 below). The present essay and the next one, however, emerge out of a fascination I had developed by the late 1980s with a slightly later Derrida, the progenitor of paraliterary experiments such as *Glas* (1986b) and *The Post Card* (1987a). I had become convinced by then that the intensely graphic way of writing and the intensely concrete way of thinking (actually one and the same activity) characteristic of these paraliterary texts

---

*First published in the *Journal of the American Academy of Religion* 60 (1992): 257–79.

better equipped me to come to grips with the visceral, parabolic language of the Gospels than the bloodless, propositional language of standard Gospel scholarship. And I find that I still think that today, even if I'm no longer mad enough still to be writing quite that way.

In this essay and the next one, then, I'm in resolute rule-breaking mode. If critical biblical scholarship was built upon the scrupulous avoidance of historical anachronism, I wanted to embrace anachronism with open arms like a long-lost friend (as indeed it was: I was a born-again Bible reader well before I became a biblical critic). I even dubbed my method "strategic anachronism." If precritical exegesis was the constitutive other of critical exegesis, then I wanted to exegete postcritically in a register redolent of precritical exegesis. And so on. Small wonder that the "plea" of the essay's subtitle went unheard (eventually even by me).

What do you get if you mix the illuminated Gospel manuscript with the modernist literary experiment (notably Joyce's *Finnegans Wake*, itself much preoccupied with a certain Gospel manuscript, as we shall see), and add in the paraliterary experiment in academic discourse, exemplified by certain texts of Derrida (e.g., 1986b; 1984a; 1987a, 1–256; 1987b, 237–70; 1987c, 149–253; 1981a, 287–366; 1982, ix–xxix; 1979a)? The answer is a cementation of styles that I propose to call *concrete criticism*. Why these particular ingredients should be mixed, and why the end product should be termed "concrete," will be explained in due course. First, I propose to take some concrete criticism, ready-mixed, and apply it to the Gospel of Mark

Jesus' Post Cards

> When I enter the post office of a great city I tremble as if in a sacred place. (Derrida 1987a, 69)

> I never dramped of prebeing a postman.... (Joyce 1939, 488.19)

Shall we ever be finished with the reading and rereading of Mark, a Gospel of absent apocalypse in which the living letter never quite reaches its destination, or is dead on arrival, which amounts to the same thing? "Are you the Messiah, the Son of the Blessed One?" the high priest demands of Jesus at his trial. "I am," replies Jesus, "and 'you will see the Son of Man sitting at the right hand of the Power,' and 'coming with the clouds of heaven'" (Mark 14:61–62; cf. Dan 7:13). Apocalypse, unveiling, tearing aside to uncover or reveal. On hearing Jesus' blasphemy, the high priest ritually tears his own garment, inadvertently miming the apocalypse his adversary has just predicted. He pronounces its name while refusing to hear it.

The sound of cloth being sundered is also heard at Jesus' death: "And the veil the temple was torn in two [*echisthē eis duo*], from top to bottom" (15:38).[1] Which veil? The temple had two veils, or curtains, it seems: an outer one, which covered the main entrance, and an inner one, which covered the entrance to the holy of holies. The Greek term used by Mark, *to katapetasma*, suggests the second veil to most scholars (cf. Exod 27:16 LXX), the inner one that separated the awesome presence of the God of Israel from those cringing outside. But when at Jesus' death the veil of the temple is torn in two, it reveals the presence of God as ... absence.

According to Josephus, whose description of the Herodian temple is the most detailed that has come down to us, the holy of holies contained ... nothing whatsoever (*ouden holōs en autō*; *Jewish War* 5.5.4.219; cf. 2 Bar 6:7–8; 2 Macc 2:4–8). Derrida comments:

> The structure encloses its void within itself, shelters only its own proper interiorized desert, opens onto nothing, confines nothing, contains as its treasure only nothingness: a hole, an empty spacing, a death.... Nothing behind the curtains. Hence the ingenuous surprise of a non-Jew when he opens ... or violates the tabernacle ... and after so many ritual detours to gain access to the secret center, he discovers nothing—only nothingness....
>
> One undoes the bands, displaces the tissues, pulls off the veils, parts the curtains: nothing but a black hole.... It is the experience of the powerful Pompey at the end of his greedy exploration....
>
> The tent of the tabernacle, the stone of the temple, the robe that clothes the text of the covenant—is finally discovered as an empty room, is not uncovered, never ends being uncovered, as it has nothing to show. (1986b, 49–50)

You undo the bands, unfurl the cloth or shroud, tear back the veil—endlessly. You wait endlessly for apocalypse.

On Golgotha, too, God's presence, in his son, is disclosed precisely as the sun is eclipsed (15:33), as the son absents himself. It is not that Jesus' absence as such precipitates comprehension in Mark. The subsequent announcement

---

1. His career ends as it began, then; cf. 1:10: "As he was coming up out of the water, he saw the heavens torn asunder [*schizomenous tous ouranous*]." On the connection between the two tearings, see Ulansey 1991.

of the young man at the empty tomb, a jubilant proclamation of absence—"He has been raised; he is not here" (16:6)—merely elicits confusion: "they went out and fled from the tomb, for terror and amazement had seized them…" (16:8). Jesus' living presence among his disciples precipitated confusion; the absence of his dead body at the tomb precipitates confusion. The climactic scene of comprehension in Mark, the centurion's "confession" at the foot of the cross—"Truly this man was a son of God" (15:39)—follows Jesus' desolate cry of abandonment at the apparent absence of God: "why have you forsaken me?" (15:34). At the precise moment in which Jesus departs his body, becoming absent, the centurion realizes in whose presence he has been, recognizes the son as an absent presence.

The centurion must be content, then, with a bare, tantalizing glimpse of Jesus as he slips away. The rupturing of the temple veil, Yahweh's hymen, coupled with the centurion's penetrating glance ("the curtain of the temple was torn in two…. And when the centurion … saw that in this way he breathed his last…"), does not bring immediate consummation. The consummation of presence must await Jesus' *parousia* (9:1; 13:26; 14:62). Full presence is subject to postponement, deferral, detour in Mark. And detour—the mandatory detour through Galilee, for instance ("he is going ahead of you to Galilee; there you will see him"—16:7)—is always subject to the risk of accident, of nonarrival, in this Gospel: "they went out and fled from the tomb … *and they said nothing to anyone, for they were afraid*" (16:8).

In short, Jesus' message in Mark is subject to the *postal principle*—"postal maneuvering, relays, delay, anticipation, destination, telecommunicating network, the possibility … of going astray" (Derrida 1987a, 66). Indeed, Jesus' message *as* mark is already subject to that principle. If, as Saussure assures us, language is a differential system that depends for its intelligibility on the differences that distinguish each of its elements from every other element in the system, then "within every sign already, every mark, … there is distancing, the post, what there has to be so that it is legible for another" (Derrida 1987a, 29). Nothing, therefore, "neither among the elements nor within the system, is anywhere ever simply present or absent. There are only, everywhere, differences and traces of traces" (Derrida 1981c, 26). *Trace:* reshuffle its letters and you are dealt a *carte*, perhaps even a *carte postale*.

A depthless object, the postcard is a hopeless container. It cannot retain meaning. Meaning plays over its surface and splashes off. Hardly object-ive, barely meaning-full, it gives little satisfaction to the scholar. The disinterested posture is foreign to the postcard; it is the most personal (and personable) of communications. It can also be the most cryptic.

Ever the nonbook, the postcard begs to be judged by its cover. Evaluating the collection *Writing and Sexual Difference* (Abel 1982), Jane Gallop is as intrigued by its cover as by its contents. In other words, she reads it like a postcard. The cover has

> pictures of people writing: on the front is a woman, on the back a man. Together they compose a particularly well-articulated illustration of "writing and sexual difference." The woman is writing a letter; the man a book. Women write letters—personal, intimate, in relation; men write books—universal, public, in general circulation. The man in the picture is in fact Erasmus, father of our humanistic tradition; the woman, without a name. In the man's background: books. The woman sits against floral wallpaper, echoed in reverse by her patterned dress. (Gallop 1988, 163)

The woman could just as easily be writing a postcard, of course, that most decorative and indecorous of texts. The same, however, cannot be said of Erasmus. We do not know what Erasmus is writing, but we suspect that it is no longer addressed to us. The postcard is the stamp of our post-age system in a way that Erasmus's book no longer can be, a system of mass communication in which informal, anecdotal address is everywhere juxtaposed with graphic imagery—look no further than the network news and the advertisements around which it is structured.[2] And thanks to feminism and poststructuralism, the personal, the anecdotal and the graphic are now to be heard and seen with unprecedented frequency in academic discourse as well.

The postcard is a postmodern text, then. But that is not to say that there are no ancient postcards. If the postcard can be said to contain the recipe for the texts that some of us are now eager to produce, it also contains the recipe for the texts that some of us are still eager to devour—the biblical texts, for example. This is the case whether we choose to read the Bible as a love letter sent from God to God's people, a cryptic missive, admittedly, but one strategically left open for all the world to see (a postcard, in other words); or whether we choose to read it instead as a miscellaneous collection of human, all-too-human communications, all too closely tied to local particulars of time and place, accident and circumstance ("when you come, bring the cloak that I left with Carpus at Troas"—2 Tim 4:13). They are, moreover, communications exposed to the pious, prurient gaze of a readership populous beyond the wildest nightmares of the senders, communications nearly always unsigned, addresses to persons almost never named, and long since dead anyway, "[l]etters open, but like crypts" (Derrida 1987a, 53)—in short, a bundle of yellowed and tattered postcards.

---

2. Advertisements that themselves tend to be structured around puns. The pun is the trope of our age. It bombards us from every billboard, every newspaper stand, every television screen.

"The guardians of tradition, the professors, academics, and librarians, the doctors and authors of theses are terribly curious about correspondences," as Derrida notes, "private or public correspondences (a distinction without pertinence in this case, whence the post card, ... half-private, half-public, neither the one nor the other...)" (1987a, 62). We biblical scholars earn our living by peeking into other people's mail. Working long shifts in the Dead Letter Office we examine the writings of the dead for clues of their identity and whereabouts. We perform postmortems on dead letters. The blades of our letter-openers run red.

(The scholar's defense: "Everything is opened and read in order to divine, with the best intentions in the world, the name of a sender or of an addressee. When I came ... into possession of these letters ... they had in effect been opened. Once more become the post cards that at bottom they already were." [1987a, 50])

In Mark the message, the letter, that Jesus mails and remails to his disciples (although marked urgent, it is repeatedly returned unopened—8:31–33; 9:31–32; etc.) is eventually read at the foot of the cross, although by a third party (the centurion) to whom it had not been addressed. "We are ... dealing with a letter which has been diverted from its path," as Lacan remarks of another purloined letter, "or [in] the language of the post office, a *letter in sufferance*" (1988b, 43, his emphasis). No sooner does Jesus absent himself than the centurion reads his letter in sufferance, his letter of suffering. Here, however, the intrusion may be desired.

(Jesus' love for the centurion: "They will have only post cards from me, never the true letter, which is reserved uniquely for you." [Derrida 1987a, 81]).[3]

But the centurion is allowed to read the letter only when Jesus has left the room. Could the letter have been mailed, opened and read when Jesus was still present, still living, not yet a corpse? After all, letters normally presuppose the physical dissociation of addresser and addressee(s). Jesus' message in Mark functions like a letter: it makes sense only when Jesus is away.

(Jesus to his disciples: "Do I write to you in order to bring you near or in order to distance you...? The question is posed when you are in the next room, or even when in the same room, barely turning my back to you, I write to you again, when I leave a note under your pillow or in the letter box upon

---

3. Jesus is not the speaker in Derrida's text. But is the reading of Mark that Derrida performs in *The Post Card* any less insightful for being unwitting? The better Derrida unknowingly reads Mark, moreover, the more evidence he amasses for his assertion that the possibility of being read in ways unintended and unimaginable is the ineradicable birthmark of the written (1988d, 5ff.).

2. ILLUMINATING THE GOSPELS

leaving, the essential not being that you are absent or present at the moment when I write to you but that I am not there myself, when you are reading."

The disciples' desire for Jesus: "To have the other within oneself, right up close but stronger than oneself, and his tongue in your ear before being able to say a word while looking at yourself in the depths of the rearview mirror."

Jesus: "I want you to look at the envelope for a long time before you open me" [Derrida 1987a, 79, 60, 110].

But will the envelope, when opened, contain anything but a post card, or open crypt?)

Rejected, Jesus' emitted sense, his seed, falls along the path, on rocky ground, among thorns: "postmark, stamp, and return to sender" (1987a, 24). His post cards are returned unread—except by strangers, of course; such is the perpetually exposed condition of the post card. Athough he wants to keep them private, he cannot: "[Jesus] said to him, 'See that you say nothing....' But he went out and began to proclaim it freely" (Mark 1:44–45; cf. 7:36). (Derrida too exclaims in agony: "The secret of the post card burns—the hands and the tongues—it cannot be kept" [1987a, 188].) Moreover, everything that passes between Jesus and his disciples is surreptitiously rerouted to us. Indeed, even while he is in the very act of writing them, Jesus' post cards are already being intercepted, already being readdressed. "Let the reader understand," urges Mark *sotto voce* (13:14), interrupting Jesus even in mid-sentence.

(Jesus to himself: "I am suffering ... from a real pathology of destination: I am always addressing myself to someone else [no, to someone else still!], but to whom? I absolve myself by remarking that this is due, before me, to the power of ... the 'first' mark, to be remarked, precisely, to be repeated, and therefore divided, turned away from whatever singular destination."

The reader to herself: "I receive as a present the chance to which this card delivers me. It falls to me. And I choose that it should choose my by chance, I wish to cross its path."

Mark to itself: "I am somewhat hung up on post cards: so modest, anonymous, ... stereotyped ...—and absolutely indecipherable, the interior safe itself that the mailmen, the readers, the collectors, the professors finally pass from hand to hand with their eyes, yes, bound."

Jesus to Mark: "There is nothing I fear more than this exposition without envelope" [1987a, 112, 47, 68].)

Mark's epistemology is an epistle-ology, then. And his hermeneutic is a postal hermeneutic, which is to say a hermetic hermeneutic, Hermes the messenger being the patron not only of interpreters but also of postmen. But to be (a) post-man is to be past the age of man. Is Mark really (a) postman or simply another male man?

It all depends on where you stand—at the foot of the cross or at the empty tomb. Mark 15:40–41 states: "There were also women looking on [at the crucifixion] from a distance.... These used to follow him and provided for him when he was in Galilee; and there were many other women who came up with him to Jerusalem." Mary Ann Tolbert writes: "They have not betrayed, denied, and fled, as did the male disciples, but have remained with Jesus through tribulation and persecution. Although some scholars treat the women basically as surrogates or stand-ins for the disciples, ... *how* they are described, and their identity *as women* all depict a group similar to but *much better than* the Twelve. They are not surrogates but superiors" (1989, 291–92, her emphasis).

Tolbert is surely right. But is excellence rewarded in the Markan workplace? Mark is hardly a manifesto for equal-opportunity employment. "And entering the tomb, they saw a young man..." (16:5; cf. 14:51). Jesus' final message addressed to the eleven, collected by the mysterious young (mail)man and carried to the tomb or office where everything *should* be sorted (out), threatens to become yet another card adrift in a bag, yet another victim of a strike or sorting accident. And thanks to whom? Mark's female postal workers? Has Mark used his author-ity over these women to place them in a compromising position? His(s)tory recounts that they resigned without notice just when they were most needed (16:8). Even Tolbert admits as much: "The seed has fallen on rocky ground once again, as fear, not faith, motivates their actions. Like the Twelve before them, the women too flee in silence" (1989, 295).[4]

(The women on their failure to become the readers Mark will not let them be: "What does a post card want to say to you? On what conditions is it possible? Its destination traverses you, you no longer know who you are. At the very instant when from its address it interpellates you, uniquely you, instead of reaching you it divides you or sets you aside.")[5]

Letters are always at risk, as Derrida (himself a postphilosopher) reminds us: "a letter does *not always* arrive at its destination, and from the moment that this possibility belongs to its structure one can say that it never truly arrives, that when it does arrive its capacity not to arrive torments it with an internal drifting" (1987a, 489, his emphasis). This risk, this internal capacity for going astray, is what Mark will not erase from his own letter. The disciples *may* eventually get Jesus' note to meet him in Galilee ("he is going ahead of you to Galilee..."—16:7). Indeed, they *must* get it, even if he has to deliver it in person. But will they eventually get it even if he does deliver it by hand?

---

4. Other feminist scholars (e.g., Schüssler Fiorenza 1983, 320ff.; Malbon 1983) give Mark the benefit of the doubt, interpreting the role accorded to the women in 16:8 more benignly.

5. From Derrida's statement on the dust jacket of *The Post Card* (1987a).

Person-to-person delivery has proved astonishingly ineffective throughout this Gospel. Possibly they may never get it at all. Mark keeps this possibility open, holds its legs apart, not caring who it frustrates or offends.

(Mark to itself: "I love the delicate levers which pass between the legs of a word, between a word and itself, to the point of making entire civilizations tremble" [1987a, 78].)

The possibility, although open, is nevertheless closed to investigation. And the way that Mark has signed off, the way he has sealed his legacy, crossed his own legs, suggests that it will ever remain so.

(Mark to the executors of his estate: "I have enclosed everything in a virgin envelope. I [have] signed on the border, on the V, you know, where the two parts stick to each other, the lips, the one on the other, such that the letter [cannot] be opened without deforming my signature" [1987a, 137].)

The disciples' fate is sealed, then, forever tucked away out of sight. But this does not mean that Mark lacks a resurrection appearance. Is not Mark itself Jesus' resurrected body, the reappearance that its ending predicts but does not depict? Jesus' corpse, soon to become a literary corpus, and a colossal one at that—"the world itself could not contain the books that would be written" (John 21:25)—is raised up in the very act of being read. And so the body of Christ can now indeed be eaten, but only as one would devour a book. And the tomb is indeed empty ("Look, there is the place they laid him"—Mark 16:6), but only as a bookshelf might be empty, empty of the very book whose flesh the reader is in the act of ingesting.

(Mark to Jesus: "Your absence is reality for me, I don't know any other."

Jesus to Mark: "You mark for me both reality and death.... You mark me" [Derrida 1987a, 181].)

But what of Jesus' remains? Mark tells us that the tomb was vacant. And yet there must have been a remains, a residue. If Jesus had been *totally* translatable he would have vanished into Mark, utterly become Mark. He would have been completely devoured and digested, nothing remaining. Tradition does insist that Mark was a skilled *hermēneutēs* ("interpreter," "translator").[6] But that Mark could not totally translate Jesus is attested by the fact of subsequent Gospels. Mark must have left something to be desired, to be devoured, to be digested—some uneaten scraps on the mortuary slab. But if Jesus had been totally *un*translatable he would simply have remained, untouched, in the tomb, a cryptic and unappetizing remains. As writing, as text, Jesus *is* translated, not completely, yet triumphantly. "Triumphant translation is neither the

---

6. So Papias, as quoted by Eusebius: "Mark, having become the *hermēneutēs* of Peter, wrote down accurately all that he remembered of the things said and done by the Lord..." (*Hist. eccl.* 3.39.15).

life nor the death of the text," writes Derrida, "only or already its living *on*, its life after life, its life after death" (1979a, 102–3, his emphasis). "It lives and lives on in mutation" (1986e,183). This, in so many words, is what the angel tells the women at the mortuary, now become a library. Jesus is no longer stored in the tomb; instead he is storied in the tome. He has risen to an eternal (shelf) life. But he can no longer be read in the original. Like Enoch of old, a type (script) of the book he has become, Jesus can only be found in translation: "By faith Enoch was translated [*metetethē*] that he should not see death; and he was not found because God had translated him" (Heb 11:5, KJV; cf. Gen 5:24). Unable to read the translation, the women run from the library.

Or is it rather that they have been unable to locate the volume? "He is not here," declares the librarian (16:6). The book "is *missing from its place*," declares Lacan,[7] "as the call slip puts it when speaking of a volume lost in the library" (1988b, 40, his emphasis). Even if the volume were "on an adjacent shelf or in the next slot" it would be no less hidden, "however visibly it [might] appear" (1988b, 40). Confronted with it, the women might not recognize it—John and Luke tell us as much: "She ... saw Jesus standing there, but she did not know that it was Jesus" (John 20:14; cf. 21:4); "Jesus himself came near ... but their eyes were kept from recognizing him" (Luke 24:15–16).

Jesus' death initiates his transformation into a book.[8] Writ(h)ing in pain upon his cross, Jesus can at last be read: "Truly this man was a son of God!" (Mark 15:39). Nailed, grafted onto the tree, Jesus' body is becoming one with the wood. His flesh, shredded and beaten to a pulp, joined by violence to the wood, is being transformed into processed wood pulp, into paper, as the centurion looks on. As tree and budding book, Jesus is putting forth leaves, the leaves of a Gospel book, whose opening sentence the centurion has just read: "The beginning of the good news of Jesus Christ, son of God" (1:1).

Doubled over in pain, folded like a stack of leaves, Jesus is bound to a hard wooden spine. Graphted onto the tree, he is leafing his body, in order to readturn as a book. He will spend tree days in the tome. But in death his voice will acquire the volume that it lacked in life.

(Jesus to himself: "My foos won't moos. I feel as old as yonder elm.... My ho head halls. I feel as heavy as yonder stone.... Lsp! I am leafy speaking. Lpf!.... Not a sound falling. Lispn! No wind no word. Only a leaf, just a leaf and then leaves" [Joyce 1939, 215.34–36, 216.1, 619.20–23]).[9]

---

7. Who, however, is not speaking of Jesus.

8. The event is announced in the *Gospel of Truth*: "Jesus appeared; he put on that book.... He published the edict of the Father on the cross" (20:24–25; cf. Col 2:14).

9. *Finnegans Wake* does not lack a Christ (albeit an idiot Christ), although he, too, is not the speaker here.

"From the fig tree learn its lesson: as soon as its branch becomes tender and puts forth its leaves, you know that summer is near. So also, when you see these things taking place, you know that he is near, at the very gates" (Mark 13:28–29). What is the lesson of that other, newly sprung tree (the cross) in whose bark Mark has carved his Gospel (for this is a book that bleeds)? Is it that Jesus' body, grafted onto the cross, become one with it, and thus become branch, tree, book and leaf, inscribed with letters of blood, can now at last be read, no longer an indecipherable code but an open codex? And that in its (now) re(a)d(able) ink, lately invisible, the message that was scratched into the fig tree is indelibly transcribed: outside the gates, but only just, the summer Son is shining in full strength?

But what if the Son were really a black hole, a gigantic vacuum cleaner, a S(p)on(ge)?

The Sponge of God

He who will drink from my mouth will become like me. (Gospel of Thomas, saying 108)

I sink I'd die down over his feet, humbly dumbly, only to washup. (Joyce 1939, 628.10–11)

Mark 15:36 reports: "And someone ran, filling a sponge [*spoggos*] with sour wine, put it on a reed, and gave it to him to drink...." What did the crucified Son of God read in this sponge swollen with *oxos* (cheap, sour wine, or wine vinegar), poised to assault his palate? Himself God's own Sponge, destined to wipe away sin (14:24; cf. 10:45) and soak up readings insatiably, did he see a simulacrum of himself in the body of this prodigy: a zoophyte with wine for blood?

The sponge is supported on a reed, or reading. Being overheavy with liquids (vinegar, wine, blood) it is fated to bend and break every reading, every reed. Grotesquely swollen, nonsaturable, the sponge drips continually, incurably, incontinently. It finds "its irreducible force in a passivity without limit, absorbing everything": clean or filthy water, fine wine or rotgut, strong or insipid readings. "It is a remarkable figure for a receptacle," as Derrida remarks (1984a, 66).

What must be wiped clean in order that Derrida's Sponge (the antihero of his nonbook *Signsponge*)[10] be resurrected as Mark's Son? The p-ge, seemingly, or page. But if we erase Derrida's p(a)ge, it is only in order to clear a space for

---

10. The subject of this small, strange book is the prominent French poet Francis

Mark within its margins, and thereby read a christography where none was intended.

Jesus as S(p)on(ge) of God, then, the apocalyptic pun-chline held in reserve by God to bring his(s)tory to a shattering climax. As God's parabler, and as such his wordsmith, Jesus is himself a punster; to pun "is to pound words, to beat them into new senses, to hammer at forced similes" (Culler 1988a, 1–2),

The Father means to mop up with the S(p)on(ge), and the unclean spirits are understandably nervous: "What do you want with us, Jesus of Nazareth? Have you come to wipe us out [*ēlthes apolesai hēmas*]?" (Mark 1:24). But for those who long to be clean, the Sponge overflows with compassion: "A leper came to him begging him, and kneeling he said to him, 'If you choose, you can make me clean [*dunasai me katharisai*].' Moved with pity, Jesus stretched out his hand and touched him, and said to him, 'I do choose. Be made clean.' Immediately the leprosy left him, and he was made clean" (1:40–42). "Receptive, open, welcoming, ... ready, in its guile, to receive all impressions, the sponge" (Derrida 1984a, 80)—God's own beloved S(p)on(ge). This medical sponge absorbs bodily spillages, drying them up with a touch: "Now there was a woman who had had a flow of blood for twelve years.... She ... came up behind him in the crowd and touched his cloak, for she said, 'If I but touch his clothes, I will be made well.' Immediately the flow of blood dried up [*exēranthē hē pēgē tou haimatos*]" (5:25–29).

The Sponge is intimately associated with water, as we might expect. God's initial acclamation of Jesus as S(p)on(ge) occurs only after he has been doused in water: "And just as he was coming up out of the water, he saw the heavens torn apart.... And a voice came from heaven, 'You are my Son, the Beloved'" (1:10–11). The sponge is "able to hold gases or liquid alternatively, 'to fill itself with wind or water'" (Derrida 1984a, 70). Not unexpectedly, therefore, Jesus has authority over these elements. "Who then is this, that even the wind and the sea obey him?" exclaim the disciples as the turbulent waters grow calm (4:41; cf. 6:48b). Moreover, the destiny of those who engage with the Sponge is reward by reason of water, or punishment by means of it: "Whoever gives you a cup of water to drink because you bear the name of Christ will by no means lose his reward. If any of you put a stumbling block before one of these little ones who believe in me, it would he better for you if a great millstone were hung around your neck and you were thrown into the sea" (9:41–42).

The Sponge cleans deep to remove dirt and stains. As a result, it can itself appear filthy, together with those who are absorbed by it:

Ponge, upon whose surname (French for "sponge") Derrida puns relentlessly. But why? The epistemology of the homonym will be elaborated in the final section of this essay.

> They noticed that some of his disciples were eating with defiled hands [*koinais chersin*], that is, without washing them [*tout estin aniptois*]. (For the Pharisees, and all the Jews, do not eat unless they thoroughly wash [*ean mē ... nipsōntai*] their hands ... and they do not eat anything from the market unless they wash it; and there are also many other traditions that they observe, the washing [*baptismous*] of cups, pots, and bronze kettles.) So [they] asked him, "Why do your disciples not live according to the tradition of the elders, but eat with soiled hands?" (7:2–5)

They fail to see that this is no ordinary sponge. It does not simply clean hands and eating utensils (of food stains and other blemishes); it cleans the food itself. Any further washing is therefore unnecessary: "'Do you not see that whatever goes into a person from outside cannot soil, since it enters, not the heart, but the stomach, and goes out into the sewer?' (Thus he cleansed all foods [*katharizōn panta ta brōmata*])" (7:18–19). This Sponge attacks stains at their source. Appropriately enough, therefore, when the p(a)ge is finally pulled back and the transfigured Sponge is revealed for what it has been all along—a Son—its "clothes bec[o]me dazzling white, such as no detergent on earth could bleach them [*stilbonta leuka lian hoia gnapheus epi tēs gēs ou dunatai houtōs leukanai*]" (9:3).

Disciples of the Sponge are challenged to match him drink for drink, even if it kills them: "Are you able to drink the cup that I drink, or be washed with the washing with which I am washed [*ē to baptisma ho egō baptizomai baptisthēnai*]?' They replied, 'We are able.' Then Jesus said to them, 'The cup that I drink you will drink; and with the washing with which I am washed you will be washed'" (10:38–39). But later, having soaked up the entire contents of "an alabaster flask of ointment of pure nard, very costly," which has been poured over him (14:3–9), and having secured a room in which to celebrate Passover by the novel (but not unspongely) device of having his disciples tail a man "carrying a jar of water" (14:12–16), and having had his half-oblivious followers finally drink him under the table ("This is my blood ... which is poured out for many.... I will never again drink ... until ... I drink ... in the kingdom of God"—14:23–22), even the Sponge has had one drink too many and can barely keep the last one down ("Abba, Father, ... remove this cup from me"—14:36).

In short, and to return to where we began, far more can be squeezed out of the sponge of Mark 15:36—Jesus erected on a stake, his lips parted to merge with a sponge, itself erected on a reed—than Mark has seen fit to give us. Yet that excess can easily be wrung out of what has been hung out to dry on Mark's other lines, as we have begun to see, lines dripping with water and wine, with pus and blood.

"Insofar as it ingests, absorbs, and interiorizes everything, proper or not, the sponge is certainly 'ignoble,'" admits Derrida (1984a, 72)—but its ignobility is precisely what makes it serviceable. Indeed, the Sponge is designed to serve and not to be served (Mark 10:45). "It can also, when applied to a surface, expunge, wipe, and efface." Moreover, "it is also the chance for purification, something which sponges away the stain, and even … expunges the debt" (1984a, 72).

Unquestionably, our insatiable Sponge has begun to overflow Mark's margins by now (even though this is a Gospel written on blotting paper:[11] it soaks up readings faster than we can write them) to mop up other texts round about. It wipes off their dusty surfaces to uncover fresh inscriptions: "Behold the Sponge of God who wipes away the sin of the world," for instance (John 1:29, 36). The Johannine Jesus, endlessly read and reread, is also bread—the bread of life (6:35ff.). But note that "crumb has a texture akin to that of sponges" (Derrida 1984a, 84). We should not be at all surprised, therefore, to discover that the bread of life satisfies thirst as well as hunger: "I am the bread of life. Whoever comes to me will never hunger, and whoever believes in me will never thirst [*ou mē dipsēsei*]" (6:35).

Am I wringing this Sponge metaphor dry? Sea creatures dread dryness, as do I. Or, situated as it is on the sea-bed of language, does the Sponge not refill faster than I can compress it?

Still (s)pun(ge)-diving in these texts, then (in the depths of their ink, superficial yet abyssal), we find that the Sponge partakes of more than one substance. A taxonomic anomaly, it is "neither simply a thing, nor simply vegetal, nor simply animal" (Derrida 1984a, 72). Neither simply divine nor simply human, the S(p)on(ge) is an animal plant, a divine human being. It has emptied itself, humbled itself, to take on a form that is serviceable: only read Philippians 2:7–8. John, too, recounts how the S(p)on(ge), on the night before he suffered, "knowing that the Father had given all things into his hands, and that he had come from God and was going to God, got up from the table, took off his outer robe, and tied a towel [*lention*] around himself. Then he poured water into a basin and began to wash [*niptein*] the disciples' feet and to wipe [*ekmassein*] them with the towel that was tied around him" (13:3–5). But the towel no less than the sponge is a figure for the incarnate Son. And can we confidently say where the Sponge ends and the Towel begins? From the preexistent sponge, or raw material, "will have been cut, to give it form, a *serviette-éponge* [sponge-towel]," says *Signsponge* (Derrida 1984a, 84). "Because it is less natural—it comes from a factory, a process of production can be read in it—it also comes closer to us" (1984a, 82).

---

11. Or "drinking paper," as in French (*papier buvard*).

The eminently serviceable sponge-towel—as a towel, the sponge can clean still deeper to remove stubborn stains—can be said, although not without injustice, to be "the very example of the worthless, of the no-thing or the such-a-little-thing, the no-matter-what of low price, the nameless or nearly so in the mob of small things" (1984a, 88). The *serviette-éponge* is the quintessential thing of low extraction: "He was despised, and we esteemed him not" (Isa 53:3). And what of the *bloody* S(p)on(ge-towel), said by some to have emerged from between the immaculate thighs of a virgin? Virtually without value, it is practically priceless. The exaltation of this *serviette-éponge* (on a reed, or reading, for example, to assuage the thirst, perhaps to mop the brow, of the suffering Son of God, now wrung out so that his perforated body streams cleansing blood and water) is therefore a scandal of particularity. Why the S(p)on(ge-towel) in particular? Why *this* S(p)on(ge-towel) on his particular (towel-)rack of pain?

Thus perforated, dark squiggles of blood covering his stretched skin, the S(p)on(ge) is once again Writing. Although only a muscle filled with wind *(pneuma)*, the Sponge can absorb anything and everything that is poured into it. So too the text (a prosthetic organ designed to reproduce vocal sounds, and hence itself also an artificial wind-muscle or sponge) can soak up readings endlessly. However grotesquely bloated they become, neither the S(p)on(ge) nor the text—least of all the Gospel text—ever appear in any real danger of bursting.

(The Sponge confesses its gluttony: "Bursting with emotion, I wanted to swallow myself by opening my mouth very wide and turning it over my head so that it would take in my whole body, and then the Universe, until there would be nothing more than a ball of eaten thing which little by little would be annihilated; that is how I see the end of the world" [Derrida 1986b, 198].)

And so as S(p)on(ge), Jesus is once again writ(h)ing, this time with a wooden pen too massive for him to maneuver (and to which he is in any case pinned, fingers clenched around other pens whose nibs have been hammered through his palms), his own nib dipped in perspiration, in vinegar, in blood.

"And someone ran, filled a sponge with sour wine, put it on a reed, and gave it to him to drink..." (Mark 15:36). As the unweaned sponge rears up on its reed, impatient to drink from Jesus even as he drinks from it, and then to suck down the entire Gospel in long, greedy gulps, Mark's fabric parts to reveal a cleavage, or abyss. "In order to be abyssal, the smallest circle must inscribe in itself the figure of the largest" (Derrida 1987c, 27). The sponge is just such an abyssal inscription, as I have been attempting to show.

The Gospel in Hieroglyphics

> ...that strange exotic serpentine, since so properly banished from our scripture. (Joyce 1939, 121.20–21)

I have been trying to write graphically, in the manner of a Gospel. The pictorial language of a Gospel is not the abstract propositional language of a theological treatise; Gospels are more like dreams than dissertations. "Abstract expressions offer the same kind of difficulties to representation in dreams as a political leading article in a newspaper would offer to an illustrator," notes Freud (1900, 5:340). Like the illustrator, the dream must render in concrete terms a subject matter that is commonly "colorless and abstract" (1900, 5:339). But biblical scholars and theologians are neither dreamers nor cartoonists, for the most part, preferring to take a pneumatic drill to the concrete language of the Gospels, to replace graphic images with abstract categories. Generally vivid, sometimes startling, a Gospel is a postcard, a pictogram, a picture puzzle. But a dream too is a picture puzzle (*Bilderrätsel*), according to Freud (1900, 4:278). As such it can be compared to hieroglyphic writing: "The interpretation of a dream is completely analogous to the decipherment of an ancient pictographic script such as Egyptian hieroglyphics" (1913, 177). To invent a "pictographic" script fitted to the wor(l)d of print, therefore, would be to compose in the manner of a dream—or a Gospel. It would be to reinvent a script precisely as primitive as was Freud's ascription of meaning to the dream in the first place: "Freud appeared ... to revert to the most archaic thinking—reading something in dreams" (Lacan 1988a, 1).

This is where Derrida comes into the picture. In texts such as *Glas* (1986b), *The Post Card* (1987a) and *Signsponge* (1984a), he has "adopt[ed] hieroglyphic writing as a model, translating it into a discourse, producing thus in philosophy distortions similar to those achieved by those movements, labeled 'cubist' and 'primitivist,' which drew on the visual arts of non-Western cultures in order to deconstruct the look of logocentrism" (Ulmer 1985, 18)—more on which below. The challenge is to mime, in an alphabetized, printed script, idiographic writing, thereby reinventing academic discourse.

Regressive? Not at all, as it happens. The pictographic intersection of the visual and the verbal is everywhere in evidence in contemporary popular culture—in advertisements and video games, newspapers and magazines, book and album jackets, cartoons and comic strips. What is most recent, then, is also most ancient. And most biblical.

Speaking on behalf of every stylist worried about his figure(s), Somerset Maugham protests: "The Bible is an oriental book. Its alien imagery has nothing to do with us. Those hyperboles, those luscious metaphors, are foreign to our genius.... To write good prose is an affair of good manners, ... good prose should resemble the conversation of a well-bred man"[12]—or a well-read scholar. For me, however, the task would rather be that of replying to the Gospels in kind, speaking in a related dialect, responding to a pictographic text pictographically, to a narrative text narratively, writing a critical text that is no less visceral than the text it purports to read.

It is not that there have not been graphic readings of, say, Mark before now; there have been many, beginning with Matthew and Luke. Some of them have been considerably more graphic even than Mark itself. Take the *Book of Kells*, for instance, an illuminated copy of the four Gospels and the most spectacular of a family of manuscripts created in Ireland and northern Britain between the seventh and tenth centuries. Umberto Eco has described it as a work of "erudite and whimsical composition, crazy and lucid, civilized and barbaric, ... a continuous exercise in the decomposition and rearrangement of spoken language and figurative forms" (1989, 78). Erudite but not "earudite," it is a biblical commentary that enters through the eye:

> In a total refusal of realism, there was a flowering of *entrelacs*, of highly stylized and elegant animal forms in which small, monkey-like figures appear among an incredible geometrical foliage capable of enveloping whole pages. These are not repetitions like the themes of an ornamental carpet, for every line, each corymb represents an invention, a complexity of abstract, wandering spiral forms which deliberately ignore geometrical regularity. Delicate colors fan outward from red to yellow orange, from lemon to mauve. We find quadrupeds and birds, lions with bodies of other beasts, greyhounds with swans' beaks, unthinkable humanoid figures, contorted like the circus athlete who puts his head between his knees, thereby composing the initial of a letter. Beings as malleable and foldable as colored elastic are introduced into the maze of lacing; they peek out from behind abstract decorations, twist around the capital letters, and insinuate themselves between the lines. The page no longer stops before the gaze but assumes its own life. The reader no longer succeeds in choosing a reference point. There are no boundaries between animals, spirals, and *entrelacs*; everything mixes with everything. Nonetheless, figures or hints of figures emerge from the background, and the page tells a story, an inconceivable, unreal, abstract, and above all, fable-like story composed of protean characters whose identities are continuously disappearing. (1989, 78–79)

Hieroglyphic writing (in the strict sense), therefore, is not the only model for a concrete criticism. The version of Mark that I have begun to sketch in

---

12. Undocumented quotation in Hartman 1989, 94–95.

this essay bears the imprint of the Kells scriptorium. Like those of the Kells illuminators, my own arabesques are designed to "conceal, embellish, and reveal a page of gospel" (Tindall 1959, 239). I aspire to be an inventive copyist, able to illuminate the Gospels without the benefit of color, to inscribe elaborate and extravagant designs in their margins, to write a critical page that "no longer stops before the gaze but assumes its own life," to heap story upon surrealistic story—"inconceivable, unreal, abstract, and above all, fable-like ... composed of protean characters whose identities are continuously disappearing." Hence a Jesus who is a bloodstained scrap of paper one moment, and a common bathroom item the next. I am willing, at least for a time, to deal only marginally (in the manner of a marginal illustrator) with what the Gospels have been thought to be about.

The *chi* page from the *Book of Kells* exemplifies the technique that interests me. A Greek letter *chi*, huge and swollen, is sprawled across the page:

> Surrounding the curved flowing lines of this initial of Christ are all sons of living things. Apart from tiny human figures on the left-hand side, we can see an otter bending down with a fish [symbol of Jesus] in its mouth at the bottom of the page. Near the otter, to the left, two cats sit facing each other, with their kittens. Two have climbed on to the backs of the mother-cats. Two are sharing the little round white disc which they nibble [according others, these last two are not kittens but rats]. This disc, marked with a cross, suggests the sacred communion bread of the eucharist. A butterfly with spreading wings is tucked away near the top right-hand corner of the page. (Simms 1988, 50)

How do we get from there to here? Joyce slips into the breach, showing us how to paint in print. A facsimile of selected plates from the *Book of Kells* followed him into exile. He would "[pore] over its workmanship for hours," searching for new ways to write (Ellmann 1982, 545). And he picked his subject matter from whatever lay ready to hand, particularly as he composed *Finnegans Wake*, "the last word in stolentelling" (Joyce 1939, 424.35). Not surprisingly, then, the *Wake* contains a lengthy pastiche of Sir Edward Sullivan's scholarly introduction to the *Book of Kells* facsimile (Joyce 1939, 107–24; cf. Sullivan 1920, 1–48). Here, for example, is Sullivan-Joyce on the manuscript's *Sitz im Leben*:

> Every person, place and thing in the chaosmos of Alle anyway connected with the gobblydumped turkery was moving and changing every part of the time: the travelling inkhorn (possibly pot), the hare and turtle pen and paper, the continually more or less intermisunderstanding minds of the anti-collaborators, the as time went on as it will variously inflected, differently

pronounced, otherwise spelled, changeably meaning vocable scriptsigns. No, so holp me Petault, it is not a miseffectual whyacinthinous riot of blots and blurs and bars and balls and hoops and wriggles and juxtaposed jottings linked by spurts of speed: it only looks as like it as damn it; and, sure, we ought really to rest thankful that at this deleteful hour of dungflies dawning we have even a written on with dried ink scrap of paper at all to show for ourselves, tare it or leaf it ... after all that we lost and plundered of it, ... cling to it as with drowning hands, hoping against hope all the while that, by the light of philophosy, ... things will begin to clear up a bit one way or another within the next quarrel of an hour.... (Joyce 1939, 118.21–119.6)

In particular "Joyce seems to have regarded the 'TUNC' page of [the *Book of Kells*], the incredibly involved illumination of Matthew xxvii. 38 (TUNC CRU—CIFIXERANT—XPI CUM EO DU—OS LATRONES ['Then they crucified Christ and with him two robbers']), as having special affinity with his own art" (Litz 1961, 98; cf. Joyce 1939, 122.22–23). In the Kells illuminators' interpretation of Matthew's interpretation of Mark's interpretation of Jesus' demise, "[t]he description of the Crucifixion is set out in the form of a cross. The scribe seems to feel that he should not write in straight lines as he thinks about Jesus hanging on a cross between two thieves. The words 'Christ [XPI] and with him two robbers' are shaped like a diagonal or St. Andrew's Cross.... This way of writing with criss-cross words makes a great impression on the reader" (Simms 1988, 53). Criss-cross words for the reinscription of a crucifixion: like concrete poetry, the *Book of Kells* shows us how to write with decorative designs instead of in straight lines. It shows us the contours of an alternative mimesis bound to the shapes of words. *In our own black-and-white wor(l)d of print, the closest analogue would be the pun,* a technique no less bound to the look (and the luck) of the word, to the material specificity of the letter.

Here, again, we draw near to the dream, that royal road to the unconscious. "[I]f you open a book of Freud," notes Lacan,

> and particularly those books which are properly about the unconscious, you can be absolutely sure ... to fall on a page where it is not just a question of words ... but words which are the object through which one seeks for a way to handle the unconscious. Not even the meaning of the words, but words in their flesh, in their material aspect. A great part of the speculations of Freud is about punning in a dream.... (1970, 187; cf. Freud 1900, 1901, 1905a)

To put it another way, the unconscious is irreducibly "literary" in its workings. It is a realm of metaphoric condensations, metonymic displacements, graphic word-images, startling associations, surrealistic spectacles, bad jokes, and Joycean multilingual puns. It is a tasteless assemblage of "alphybettyformed verbage," "messes of mottage," "quashed quotatoes," and "once current puns" (Joyce 1939, 183.13, 22–23). Elsewhere, speaking in the name of that "goddess" (the unconscious) whose mystique drew Freud into a lifelong pursuit, Lacan declares: "I wander about in what you regard as being least true in essence: in the dream, in the way the most-far fetched witticism, the most grotesque nonsense of the pun [*calembour*] defies sense, in chance, not in its law, but in its contingency..." (1977a, 122, translation modified).

What *are* puns, anyway, and why do we belittle them so? Could we put the question to the Puntiff, the Puntriarch himself (Joyce, of course), how might he reply? "The pun is letter-day apocalyptic," he might begin, "a quivering tic of the pen or lip, a pen-or-lip-trick, apocalipstick." But why should it induce such apoplectic reactions? "Because its babelings illicit an epiphony of chaosmic upevil."

Imagine that you have encountered a word "in a severely impoverished context," and let that word be *God*. "[I]t appears on a scrap of paper pushed under the door, for instance, or is spoken in a dream" (Attridge 1988, 142).[13] The word's normal range of meanings, ample but orderly, thereby broadens uncomfortably:

> No longer is language's potential for semantic expansion hinted at but simultaneously kept at bay; it has become threatening and confusing. Remove even more of the context and the expansion accelerates rapidly: imagine the word being encountered by someone who knows no English, or no Indo-European language, or no human language. Eventually its meaning becomes infinite and, at exactly the same moment, disappears. (1988, 142)

"God" would become everything and nothing at once.

On the brink of this I-splitting silence (cataracts of sense falling away into nonsense) the pun is s(l)i(p)tuated. Puns are slits in the great body of discourse that we erect to protect ourselves from the unconscious. They babel obscenely of what they have seen: an ecstasy of meaning so immense that one could forever lose one's self in it.

To the extent that homophonic writing is writing with a point, a point that ought not to be missed, a point intended for the reader (to impale himself or herself on), it is a patriphallocentric writing. But to the extent that it is an unweaned writing, it is a writing that threatens the paternal regimen: it seeks to (re)inscribe the (M)other. It is at once tormented with phallacious fantasies

---

13. Attridge's own example, however (untheological fellow that he is), is not the word "God" but the word "port."

and (b)re(a)stless longings. Both aspects surface in Derrida's description of his dredging operation in *Glas*:

> I am seeking the good metaphor for the operation I pursue here. I would like to describe my gesture, the posture of my body behind this machine.... I see ... a sort of dredging machine. From the dissimulated, small, closed, glassed-in cabin of a crane, I manipulate some levers and, from afar, I saw that done at Saintes-Maries-de-la-mer at Eastertime, I plunge a mouth of steel in the water. And I scrape the bottom, hook onto stones and algae there that I lift up in order to set them down on the ground while the water quickly falls back from the mouth.
>
> And I begin again to scrape, to scratch, to dredge the bottom of the sea [*mer*], the mother [*mère*]....
>
> The toothed matrix only withdraws what it can, some algae, some stones. Some bits [*morceaux*], since it bites [*mord*]. Detached. But the remains [*reste*] passes between its teeth, between its lips. You do not catch the sea. She always reforms herself.
>
> She remains. There, equal, calm. Intact, impassive, always virgin. (1986b, 204–5)

In Derrida's more audacious texts (paraliterary or paraphilosophical, as you prefer—*Glas* [1986b] and *Signsponge* [1984a]; "Envois" from *The Post Card* [1987a] and its postscript, "Telepathy" [1988e]; "+R" and "Cartouches" from *The Truth in Painting* [1987c]; *Dissemination*'s [1981a] title piece; "Hear Say Yes in Joyce" [1988a]; and much more besides), we find him exploiting chance associations between words across several languages—associations traditional scholarship would disregard as inconsequential—performing interpretations that engage in textual congress with the *letter* of the text being read—its accidents of expression, the minutiae of its style, the look of its words as well as their sound—as opposed to the ideality of its content. The distinction of letter and idea is, however, the first casualty of these experiments.

Derrida's project in such writings can be understood in part as an attempt to extend to the domains of philosophical and critical analysis Freud's pioneering explorations of dreams, slips of the tongue and pen, purposeful forgetting, and all the other "accidents" of conscious life that we ordinarily shunt into the margins (cf. Derrida 1978b, 230). "[T]he whole domain of verbal wit is put at the disposal of the dreamwork," as Freud noted (1900, 5:340). Why should it not also be put at the disposal of academic work? "We must decide to scandalize those illiterate scientisms ... shocked by what can be done with a dictionary" (Derrida 1984a, 120; cf. Derrida 1986c). Gregory Ulmer prefaces his intriguing study of Derrida with the observation:

> His detractors accuse him of superficial wordplay, and sometimes even the deconstructors consider the images and puns as nonfunctional subversion of academic conventions. What I had not expected, what in fact astonished me, is the fully developed homonymic program at work in Derrida's style, a program as different from traditional academic discourse and assumptions as it is productive in its own terms of knowledge and insight. I say I was astonished because it is one thing to engage in wordplay, but another thing to sustain it and extend it into an epistemology. (1985, xi–xii; cf. Ulmer 1988)

Ulmer later goes so far as to claim: "the extent of [Derrida's] reliance on … puns for the generation of his strategies can never be overestimated" (1985, 19). Derrida's wordwork plays on the assumption "that language itself is 'intelligent,' hence that homophones 'know' something" (1985, 46). Ulmer also says of Lacan (an even more impudent punster than Derrida) that "he adopts a manner of speaking … which allows language to say what it knows" (1985, 201). "Let that be our first assignment," urges Ulmer, "to let language do some thinking for us" (1985, 315).

Such a project would entail the disorganization of a cluster of hierarchical oppositions that happen—not by chance—to form the foundations of academic discourse, the discourse of biblical scholarship included: rational/irrational, intended/unintended, essential/accidental, necessary/contingent, serious/trivial, central/marginal, content/form, idea/ornament, critical writing/creative writing.… These hierarchies tend to be accepted as natural and self-evident, as though they had not been established at certain junctures, as though they had no history. Frozen, reified, they paralyze thought even as they enable it. But take, for example, the exclusion of noninferential associations from the Western intellectual tradition—the homonym, homophone or garden-variety pun. This exclusion can be traced back to such contingencies as Aristotle's strictures against homonyms (cf. Derrida 1982, 240–41, 247ff., 271), and Plato's exclusion of poets from his ideal state.

For the serious scholar, puns and anagrams are jest a joke. Language should be heard and not seen. Texts such as *Glas*, however, give us a glimpse (and even a whiff, a taste and a touch) of an academic writing no longer fixated solely on the voice. (Smell, taste and touch also figure in this new writing together with sight, but that is a tale for another time.) Homophonic and other associative clusters, moreover, disrupt binary thinking. A thinking that lives in vertical, two-tiered, oppositional, hierarchical structures is necessarily unsettled by a nomad thinking that picks its steps through horizontal, single-tiered, associative, open-ended word clusters. Outside the city, with Plato's poets, on ground that academe has long deemed a swamp, there is ample room for a different academy that would house alternative approaches to reading and writing. What might the city council say to a Babelian edifice in its own back

2. ILLUMINATING THE GOSPELS

yard? "Shun the Punman!" advises Shem the Penman, author of *Finnegans Wake* (Joyce 1939, 93.13). "What [an] institution cannot bear is for anyone to tamper with language," adds Derrida in an essay that does just that. "It can bear more readily the most apparently revolutionary ideological sorts of 'content,' if only that content does not touch the borders of language and all of the juridico-political contracts that it guarantees" (1979a, 94–95).

Derrida will not pull his pun-ches, then, as long as language has something left to say. But the more pun-ishing his style becomes, the nearer he draws to *Finnegans Wake*. As the *Book of Kells* was for Joyce, so is *Finnegans Wake* for Derrida: a model to be emulated. "[Y]ou stay on the edge of reading Joyce—for me this has been going on for twenty-five or thirty years—and the endless plunge throws you back onto the river-bank, on the brink of another possible immersion, *ad infinitum*" (Derrida 1984b, 148).[14] All through Derrida's edifice, the ghost of Joyce rattles his homonymic chains: "every time I write, and even in the most academic pieces of work, Joyce's ghost is always coming on board" (1984b, 149).[15] Derrida recalls how in his very first book, "at the very centre of [that] book," he "compared the strategies of Husserl and of Joyce: two great models, two paradigms with respect to thought, but also with respect to a certain 'operation' of the relationship between language and history.... Husserl proposes to render language as transparent as possible, univocal, limited to that which, by being transmittable or able to be placed in tradition, thereby constitutes the only condition of possible historicity" (1984b, 149; cf. Derrida 1978a, 102–3). Parallels with the project of traditional biblical scholarship hardly need spelling out. The other great paradigm, for Derrida, would be the Joyce of *Finnegans Wake*, the Joyce who declared "I'm at the end of English" (Ellmann 1982, 546):

> He repeats and mobilizes and babelizes the (asymptotic) totality of the equivocal, he makes this his theme and his operation, he tries to make outcrop, with the greatest possible synchrony, at great speed, the greatest power of the meanings buried in each syllabic fragment, subjecting each atom of writing to fission in order to overload the unconscious with the whole memory of man: mythologies, religion, philosophies, sciences, psychoanalysis, literatures. This generalized equivocality of writing does not translate

---

14. *Finnegans Wake* "ends," goes underground, in mid-sentence—"A way a lone a last a love a long the"—resurfacing in the book's opening words: "riverrun, past Eve and Adam's...." *Glas* also begins and ends in mid-sentence, not coincidentally.

15. Although Derrida has never before "dared to write *on* Joyce" (1984b, 148, his emphasis). Encouraged by his first attempt, seemingly, he has since published *Ulysse gramophone: Deux mots pour Joyce* (1987d). Lacan, Cixous, Kristeva and Sollers, along with other masters and mistresses of French thought, have also been intrigued by the *Wake*.

one language into another on the basis of common nuclei of meaning...; it talks several languages at once. (Derrida 1984b, 149)

In the multiverse of *Finnegans Wake* the printed pages silently explode like distant stars, although with laughter. Its lines *appear* to march in standard, parallel formation, i's fixed straight ahead, but in reality each line of soldiers is not marching but doing a tap dance, is not in uniform but in drag. More than a wave of sound, each line is a weave of superimposed vocables,[16] an elaborate arabesque or grotesquerie, thanks to the intricacy of the *Wake*'s punning texture, its undecorous, but highly decorative, D(o)ublin' talk, a speech that demands to be seen.[17]

The pictography of the Gospels is not of this sort, needless to say. Here, by and large, it is not the look of the word that counts, but the concreteness of the concept (seed, water, bread, wine, blood, cross...). Yet the Gospel of the Lion is eminently capable of springing in either of two directions, as are its three companions, the ox, the eagle and the man. It can immerse itself in standard academese, a vat of paint-stripper that swiftly relieves it of its residual hieroglyphic brilliance. But what of the other possibility?

One option for a concrete criticism (the one I have pursued here) would be to plant Mark's pictographic seed in the furrow of one's own text and watch its shoots push up through one's page; to push the principle of pictorial writing through to its logical or graphical conclusion; to write a Markan criticism that is yet more Markan, more attentive the graphic mark, than the Gospel of the Mark itself.

Joyce's technique of "stratification," evocative of the ancient or medieval palimpsest, and analogous to certain techniques adopted by Derrida in several of his paraliterary writings, offers one model for such criticism: multiple layers of meaning are superimposed, thereby producing an effect of simultaneity or many-sidedness, analogous to the cubist canvas.[18] Obligingly, language would think for one. Reasoning would be the meticulous unpacking of a metaphor, argumentation the delicate unfolding of an image. The word would lead the

---

16. Compare the *Book of Kells:* "The most distinguishing feature of the colouring or the decoration ... is the use of several colours painted one on top of another" (Brown 1980, 91). Joyce: "Yes. Some of the means I use are trivial—and some are quadrivial" (quoted in Ellmann 1982, 546).

17. Joyce was tormented with eye problems as he wrote the *Wake*. Yet "there was no possibility of dictating; he must write and see what he was writing, he said" (Ellmann 1982, 573).

18. Cubism, and modernist painting generally, deconstructed the illusion of perspective. Homophonic writing deconstructs a parallel illusion, that in which writing is conceived as stored speech and nothing more (what Derrida terms "logocentrism").

idea (cf. Barthes 1977c, 152), take it gently yet firmly by the hand. And such a method would have no inherent boundaries, other than the skill of the scribe or illustrator.

The task as I see it, finally, is not to *immerse* the GospeL in hieroGLyphics (to watch it cleave the surface of the paint at the place reserved for it, the space between the G and the L). Should the Lion and the other Gospels only choose to shake themselves, drops of technicolored hieroglyphic would fly off in every direction. Taking my (curli)cue from the anagram yet again, I would say that the task is rather one of re(in)statement: to *rel(oc)ate* the GOSPEL in hiErOGLyPhicS.

3
The Gospel of the Look*

If the previous essay originated as a series of doodles in the margins of certain of Derrida's texts, the present essay originated as a series of scribbles between the lines of certain of Lacan's and Foucault's texts. I was drawn to the French thinkers not only because of what they thought but also because of how they wrote (abstractly and abstrusely, to be sure, but also aphoristically and lyrically). More proximate models were provided by the three American poststructuralists whose styles of writing and modes of analysis I most admired: Barbara Johnson, Jane Gallop, and Shoshana Felman (see esp. Johnson 1980; Gallop 1982, 1985; Felman 1982). Except for Foucault, as it happened, all of these writers punned compulsively, Derrida and Lacan even erecting elaborate epistemologies upon the homonym (I touch on this in the previous essay; see further Moore 1992, 61–84, 105–8, 154–58). Small wonder that I punned as well and at will and attempted to lace my text more generally with surreal and visceral imagery, flashes of lyricism, strategic anachronism, and all the other mannerisms that so captivated me at the time. (The entry on "Jesus" in the index to my *Mark and Luke in Poststructuralist Perspectives: Jesus Begins to Write* [1992, 190–91], the book into which the present essay and the previous one grew, suggests the extent of that infatuation: "Jesus: as amoeba...; as castrated subject...; as corpse...; as fish...; as *je suis*...; as phallus...; as photographic model...; as psychoanalyst...; as smell...; as sound...; as sponge...; as Sun of God...; as theorist...; as towel...; as umbrella...; as writer...; as writing....") The 1989 conference paper out of which the present essay emerged was the

---

* First published in *Semeia* 54 (1991): 159–96.

first in which I gave free rein to this new way of writing, which, for me at least, was also a new way of reading.

What I failed to articulate adequately in the essay, but what most strikes me now on revisiting it, is that its latter, Foucauldian half is attempting to perform narrative criticism in a poststructuralist register (a project with which I have again become preoccupied, impelled by the intriguing work of a former student; see Elliott 2009; Moore 2008). New Testament narrative criticism morphed out of structural narratology, as is well known. Here I am attempting to use Foucauldian poststructuralism to interrogate certain commonplaces of narrative criticism, not least its quasi-theological concepts of authorial omniscience and omnipresence. That Foucault himself had little or no apparent interest in narratology only added to the interest of the project (such was my mindset in those years). Foucault being Foucault, however, the reading of Luke-Acts that results is predictably dark and sinister, even though the subject of that reading is light and sight.

…thousands of eyes posted everywhere. (Foucault 1977a, 214)

On Lukan theology, Christology, soteriology, pneumatology and ecclesiology much ink been been spilled. Lukan epistemology, by comparison, is a virginal sheet. Is this an "-ology" of which Luke is innocent? Or does Luke-Acts also contain a discourse on knowledge about knowledge, an epistemology or theory of knowledge?

Knowledge *is* a theoretical matter in Luke-Acts. Theory stems from the verb *theōreō*, as Heidegger reminds us, in which *thea* and *horaō* have fused. "*Thea* (cf. Theatre) is the outward look, the aspect, in which something shows itself.… To have seen this aspect, *eidenai*, is to know." *Horaō*, the second root, means "to look at something attentively, to look it over, to view it closely" (Heidegger 1977, 164). Theory is looking (so as) to know, then. Let theory denote a certain look that is also (a) certain knowledge, and we are ready to look at Luke-Acts.

God's Word-Thing

Do you hear what I'm seeing…? (Joyce 1939, 193.10–11)

Caught in the act of looking: knowing glances are exchanged in Luke-Acts as the shutter slides back and the critic's eye fills the aperture. What the critic has seen, everywhere, is characters in the act of observing.[1] In Look-Acts, moreover, seeing is believing. Let us glance at some of these scenes.

Following an angelic epiphany, the shepherds urge each other to "go over to Bethlehem and see [*horaō*] this thing that has happened" (Luke 2:15). What they see when they arrive seems unspectacular at first glance, a "child lying in a manger" (2:16); but it is a sight that has already been read for them ("This will be a sign [*sēmeion*] for you: you will find a child…"), and with spectacular brilliance at that ("the glory of the Lord shone around them"—2:12, 9).

"Meaning is only ever erected," observes Jacqueline Rose (1982, 43). What makes meaning erect is an act of authority, here a decree by Authority itself: the divine Author in the person of his reliable spokesperson. And what the angel decrees is that the signifier in the crib be read for what it manifestly is not (cf. 2:18: "and all who heard it were amazed [*ethaumasan*] at what the shepherds told them").

How does the seminar gathered around the *sēmeion* read it following the shepherds' presentation? Is Luke's sign theory, his semiology, similar to that of Plato? Recall that *thea* "is the outward look, the aspect, in which something shows itself" (Heidegger 1977, 164). Now, "Plato names this aspect in which what presences shows what it is, *eidos*. To have seen this aspect, *eidenai*, is to know" (1977, 164). Earlier Heidegger notes:

> We, late born, are no longer in a position to appreciate the significance of Plato's daring.… For *eidos*, in the common speech, meant the outward aspect that a visible thing offers to the physical eye. Plato exacts of this word, however, something utterly extraordinary: that it name what precisely is not and never will be perceivable with physical eyes. For *idea* names … the nonsensuous aspect of what is physically visible. (1977, 20)

Can Luke's *sēmeion* then be read as an allegory of Plato's boldest gesture—*eidos* as outward appearance transparent on *eidos* as idea (whatever it is the shepherds have seen that those who are amazed have not); God's messianic power (cf. 1:32–33, 35, 43; 2:11) present in the powerless infant; the senses displaced by the sense? The *sēmeion* would then be a metaphysical ideogram, *eidos* as outward aspect *(physikos)* pointing beyond *(meta)* to *eidos* as idea.

---

1. See, e.g., Luke 2:15, 17, 26, 29–30; 3:6; 4:18 (a chiasmus, apparently, that puts sight at the center); 5:8; 7:22, 44a; 8:10; 10:18, 23–24, 31–33; 11:34–36; 15:20; 18:34, 42–43 (restored sight contrasts with the renewed blindness of the Twelve); 19:3, 37, 42; 22:61; 23:7–8 (cf. 9:9), 35, 47–49; 24:31; Acts 2:33; 3:4, 9; 4:13–14, 20; 7:55–56; 8:13; 9:8–9, 17–18; 13:11–12; 14:11; 22:14–15; 26:16–18; 28:26–27. See further Hamm 1986, who perceptively discusses many of these scenes, and Nuttall 1978, who argues that Luke is fascinated by the "dialectic of … ignorance and knowledge, of … blindness and the moment of insight" (13).

Luke's Semitic *sēmeion*, however (cf. Exod 3:12; 1 Sam 2:34; 14:10; 2 Kgs 19:29; 20:9; Isa 37:30; 38:7), would hardly be content with this Platonic relationship to meaning. In the Septuagint, whose style Luke's birth stories mimic, *sēmeion* usually translates *'ôth*, the Hebrew word for "sign." K. H. Rengstorf notes: "From a whole series of sayings which contain *'ôth*, it may be gathered with certainty that what is denoted thereby can be perceived with the senses and is often meant to be so. As a rule the reference is to visual perception" (1971, 211). Should Luke's *sēmeion* be seen as an *'ôth*, then?

To see is indeed to know in the nativity scene—but only if one has first heard a word that doubles as a *thing*, a word one sees as well as hears: "Let us go over to Bethlehem and see this *rhēma* that has happened, which the Lord has made known to us" (Luke 2:15). *Rhēma* normally means "word" (cf. 1:38; 2:17). But in the Septuagint (where it often translates *dābār*), *rhēma* can also mean "thing," "matter," or "deed."[2] Like the word (*logos*) of logocentric metaphysics, the *rhēma* to be heard at Bethlehem is a word that lives and breathes.[3] It is a "child lying in a manger" (2:16). But unlike that aerated *logos*, this *rhēma* is something to see: "Let us go and see this word-thing."

Luke's ideology finds its natural support in this *logos* capable of being seen (*idein*). "What we call ideology is precisely the confusion of linguistic and natural reality," writes Paul de Man (1986, 11). The effect of the *rhēma* is rhetorical, then: to (con)fuse "the materiality of the signifier with the materiality of what it signifies" (1986, 11).

The confusing logic of this uncommonly sensible *logos* is further glossed by Jean-Joseph Goux: "If the signifier *stands for* the thing, in simple equivalence, it is because it *is* the thing itself. Here the signifier appears to refer neither to an ideal signified nor even, beyond the signified, to the absent thing: it is a *double* of the thing, with the same properties, powers, faculties" (1990, 173, his emphasis).[4] Goux is here speaking of a primitive mode of signifying that shades over into magic. And the fusion characteristic of this mode of signifying is also characteristic of the unconscious.

Israel's Messiah is indeed a dream child. "Words are often treated as things in dreams," observes Freud (1900, 5:603).[5] Into the hole that gapes between words and things, a word-thing, by divine fiat, is inserted. The shepherds see it

---

2. "This is a deed that speaks," says Brown (1977, 405). According to Plummer (1922, 59), *logos* in classical Greek can also denote "deed" or "thing," although he lists but one example, Herodotus 1.21.2.

3. "To think being as life in the mouth, that is the *logos*," writes Derrida (1986b, 72).

4. Not that Goux is commenting on Luke.

5. Cf. Abraham and Torok 1986, 46: "It is a word that operates only from the Unconscious, that is, as a *word-thing*" (their emphasis).

clearly. Can they also hear, touch, and smell it? Later others will taste it: "This is my body" (Luke 22:19). Possibly it dreams of what it already is: "even the ... simplest dreams of the child ... show miraculous or forbidden objects" (Lacan 1977a, 263).

This *rhēma*, if it is still mute, will not be mute for long. It is ripe with the promise of truth-bearing speech. The flesh of the signifier undulates to the breath of the signified. Contrast this ripening word with the husk of the empty tomb: "when they went in, they did not find the body" (Luke 24:3). Alien to a metaphysics of the voice (sense present to sound in speech), the empty tomb signifies absence as the condition of life. It is a hieroglyph etched in stone. Goux's remarks are again apposite:

> The *glyph* is sacred, the signifier of a mystery that it manifests but does not elucidate or articulate; it is the indecipherable, *enigmatic* sign of a hierarchically superior, overwhelming meaning; like an intercessor, it bears eternal witness to the impenetrability of a transcendent generative mystery, which it signifies in a cryptophoric rather than a metaphoric way, since it cannot reflect this mystery. (1990, 171, his emphasis)

The tomb is such a cryptophor.

The crib, however, is the reliquary of a phantasmic word-thing. It is attended by interpreters who are custodians of the authoritative reading: "they made known what had been told them about this child" (2:17). The crypt, in contrast, contains no-thing: the absent object of desire ("He is not here"—24:5). It is attended by garden-variety interpreters who have no choice but to read: the women and Peter, presented with a text more cryptic than swaddling cloths (cf. 2:12), namely, the grave cloths empty of their expected contents: "looking in, he saw the linen cloths by themselves" (24:12). One *sēmeion* has been displaced by another (cf. 11:30). Each is material, each maternal. The first was phantasmic, barely conceivable: "'you will conceive in your womb and bear a son....' Mary said, '...How can this be, since I do not know man?' The angel said to her, '... nothing will be impossible with God.' Then Mary said, '...let it be done unto me according to your *rhēma*'" (1:30–38). The second is the sign of an open crypt that keeps the necessity of reading alive, precisely because it resists penetration and possession. Not surprisingly, this unmasterable sign of a tomb (womb), borne by women ("returning from the tomb, they told all this to the eleven and to all the rest"—24:9), is greeted as so much *lēros* (nonsense, idle talk, women's chatter) by the eleven apostles—although the disputed v.12 does have Peter rising and rushing at the tomb in an effort to uncover and penetrate its mysteries. But all that is offered him is cloth, weave, text—the grave cloths of an already absent signified: "stooping and looking in, he saw the grave cloths [*ta othonia*] by themselves; and he went home wondering at what had happened." What he finds is not a living word, but writing. Sarah Kofman observes: "Writing, that form of disruption of presence, is, like the woman, always put down and reduced to the lowest rung ['these (women's) words seemed to them an idle tale, and they did not believe them'—24:11]. Like the feminine genitalia, it is troubling, petrifying—it has a Medusa effect" (1973, 125–26). An open script, itself made of stone, the crypt petrifies all the apostles except Peter: "But Peter rose and ran to the tomb...." He comes to violate a sepulcher, but is brought up short by an inscription in stone. Even he will turn back frustrated, his tail (limp) between his legs: "he went home wondering at what had happened."

Peter goes away hungry, then. He has come to feast with his eyes, but his teeth have shattered on the stone. He can be compared to the lost explorer who wanders into Derrida's "Fors":

> I am thinking (detached illustration) of the paleontologist standing motionless, suddenly, in the sun, bewitched by the delicate stay of a word-thing, an abandoned stone instrument, like a tombstone burning in the grass, the double-edged stare of a two-faced Medusa. And then I can feel, on the tip of my tongue, the angular cut of a shattered word. (1986a, xlviii)

Luke, Look, Lack, Lacan

> ...the gaping chasm of castration. (Lacan 1990, 85)

Let us turn to another of the infancy stories, the presentation of Jesus in the temple. It has been revealed to Simeon "by the Holy Spirit that he should not see [*horaō*] death before he [hasl seen [*horaō*] the Lord's Christ" (Luke 2:26). Immediately upon seeing and handling the Christ, however ("he took him in his arms"), Simeon is ready to see death: "Now you may release [*apolyō*] your slave, Master ...; for my eyes have seen [*horaō*] your salvation" (2:28–30).[6]

(Simeon's desire for Jesus: "[A]ll of a sudden ... the small volume was there, on the table, I didn't dare touch it.... [F]or a long time I believed that I would not be given the thing, that I would be forever separated from it. I wound up spreading the pages while holding the bound cover in both hands. I didn't know where to start reading, looking, opening.... It would be good if I died tonight ... after having seen the thing at the end of the race.")[7]

But what exactly has Simeon seen that so spectacularly effects his release?

---

6. In the Septuagint, *apolyō* is a euphemism for the release of death, e.g., Gen 15:2; Num 20:29; Tob 3:6, 13 (cf. Brown 1977, 439; Fitzmyer 1981, 428). Salvation is also "seen" in Ps 97[98]:3; Isa 40:5; 52:10; Bar 4:24.

7. From Derrida 1987a, 208–10 (who, however, is not speaking for, or about, Simeon).

Let Lacan take Simeon aside for a moment. Meanwhile, a partial recital of the Lacanian myth of origins will be in order, although Lacan himself shied away from such distillations. "My discourse proceeds in the following way," he said; "each term is sustained only in its topological relation with the others" (1978, 89). Each circles the others like the elements of a mobile. Attempts at a Lacanian *summa* nonetheless abound.[8] "Their interest will be that they transmit what I have said literally," he declared, "like the amber which holds the fly so as to know nothing of its flight" (1977b, xv).[9] Discarding our flyswatter if not our amber, let us hazard a few remarks on this firefly.

For Lacan, cutting into the Freudian corpus with instruments forged in a bewildering variety of workshops—philosophy and anthropology, linguistics and semiotics, psychiatry and psychology, mathematics and theology, literature and the visual arts...—the human subject is irremediably split, barred from symbiotic union with the mother through being inserted into a *symbolic order* (sociocultural, linguistic), whose first "thou shalt not" is the prohibition of such (con)fusion. To refuse to tie this symbolic k/not is to risk psychosis. Henceforth the subject's primordial desire (to be the sole desire of the M/Other) will be deflected through an interminable chain of substitutions, none of which can ever stop up that hole in being, that lack, or want-to-be (*manque-à-être*). Lacan terms this lack *castration*, after Freud—not in the sense of a threatening sword of Damocles hovering over the (male) subject, however, but the constitutive condition of *every* subject, male or female, who accedes to the symbolic order. And Lacan terms the agent of castration the *Name-of-the-Father*, the symbolic locus of the Law's emphatic No (*non/nom du père*).[10]

How does Lacan's myth of human origins relate to the Lukan myth of Jesus' origins? Jesus' subjection to his Father (cf. Luke 2:49) is inaugurated by a symbolic castration ("at the end of eight days ... he was circumcised"—2:21) and completed by his consecration in the temple. Moreover, it is to the *Law* of the Father that Jesus is made subject; note the insistent repetition of the term *nomos* ("law") in the passage—an insistence all the more striking for the fact

---

8. Lemaire 1977 was the first, although Ragland-Sullivan 1986 is the most exhaustive at the time of writing.

9. Attempts to capture Lacan in flight have included Felman 1987, Gallop 1985, and MacCannell 1986. The most readable (i.e., anecdotal) books on Lacan are Clément 1983 and Schneiderman 1983, but for the official court history, see Roudinesco 1990. On Lacan and narrative, see Davis 1983; and on Lacan and religion, see Wyschogrod et al. 1989; Taylor 1987, 83–113; Hogan and Pandit 1990, 185–204.

10. "It is in the *name of the father* that we must recognize the support of the symbolic function which, from the dawn of history, has identified his person with the figure of the law" (Lacan 1977a, 67, his emphasis; cf. 1977a, 199, 310–11).

that "there was ... no Mosaic or customary requirement that parents present their first-born in the Temple" (Esler 1987,112).

> When the time came for their purification according to the law [*kata ton nomon*] of Moses, they brought him up to Jerusalem to present him to the Lord (as it is written in the law of the Lord [*kathōs gegraptai en nomō kyriou*], "Every firstborn male shall be designated as holy to the Lord"), and they offered a sacrifice according to what is stated in the law of the Lord [*kata to eirēmenon en tō nomō kyriou*], "a pair of turtledoves or two young pigeons."
> ... [A]nd when the parents brought in the child Jesus, to do for him what was customary under the law [*kata to eithismenon tou nomou*], Simeon took him in his arms.... When they had finished everything required by the law of the Lord [*kata ton nomon kyriou*], they returned into Galilee.... (2:22–24, 27–28, 39)

It is to the "so shall you do" that the social is due. Jesus is a subject, then, but is he more? His accession to the Law of the Father coincides with Simeon's release: "Now you may release your slave [*doulos*], Master" (2:29). How is this release to be read? As a release from *desire*, Simeon's desire regaining in a glance ("my eyes have seen your salvation"—2:30) the lost object for which it has always looked?[11] Can the look in Luke repair the lack, Lac(k)an notwithstanding? What if the object of the look were himself to lack being (*manque-à-être*, the Lacanian lacuna), were himself a Son of Man(que), requiring regular injections of meaning from some outside supplier (God, the Holy Spirit, angelic interpreters, scripture...), being himself subject to the desire of the Other, a desire that displaces his own ("Father, if you are willing [*ei boulei*] ...; yet, not my will [*to thelēma mou*] but yours be done"—22:42; cf. 23:46)?[12]

Jesus' hole in being, however, does not prevent him from filling a phallic position in Luke-Acts, from being erected by acts of authority (cf. Luke 4:32,36; 5:24; 6:5,19; 7:7–8; 8:25; 10:17–19; 19:37; 20:2ff.; 21:27; 22:69) and by order of the Father (cf. 3:22; 4:43; 9:35; 10:22; 11:20; 20:13; 22:29) to the position of master of the house and overseer of the Father's business ("Did you not know that I must be in my Fathers house/about my Father's business

---

11. Cf. Nolland 1989, 119: "This patient slave ... is now being released by his Master ... from his duty as watchman..., because the goal of his watching is now accomplished."

12. Here the desire of the Other bespeaks a corresponding lack in the Other. Lacan seems to have seen both the Jewish and Christian traditions as pivoting on the contradictory concept of a desiring deity (cf. 1990, 89–90; 1981, 323ff.).

[*en tois tou patrou mou*]?"—2:49).[13] Significantly, it is Luke's leading female character, Jesus' mother, who is the main beneficiary of this lesson in home management (2:48, 51). The Father has handed Jesus a blade on the assumption that he knows what to do with it (" 'Your mother and your brothers are standing outside, desiring [*thēlontes*] to see you.' But he said..., 'My mother and my brothers are those who hear the word [*logos*] of God and do it' "— 8:20–21; cf. 2:35).

Simeon's "cure" contrasts interestingly with that of Simon. Lacan remarks: "When I speak to you of the unconscious ... you may picture it to yourselves as a *hoop net* ... at the bottom of which the catch of fish will be found" (1978, 143–44, his emphasis). The scene of (self-)recognition centered on the marvelous catch of fish (Luke 5:1–11) is the scene of analysis. On Jesus' advice, Simon "put[s] out into the deep [*epanagō eis to bathos*] and let[s] down [his] nets for a catch." The result is traumatic, dreamlike: "When they had done this, they caught so many fish that their nets were beginning to break. So they signaled their partners in the other boat to come and help them. And they came and filled both boats, so that they began to sink." Ordinarily the unconscious announces itself in the *lapsus*, the slip. So this slithering morass must have been all but screaming at Simon. But it is a silent scream, a written communiqué: it presents itself as something to be read ("when Simon Peter saw [*horaō*] it..."). Faced with the subaqueous representatives of his own unconscious writ(h)ing grotesquely in the analytic net (cf. 2:35: "the inner thoughts of many will be revealed"), Simon yields his own soft underbelly to the analyst's knife, lets himself be cleaned like a fish, spills his guts at the analyst's feet: "he fell down at Jesus' knees, saying, 'Go away from me, Lord, for I am a sinful man!' " Filleted, Simon is forced to acknowledge that he too is a split subject. But only that he might better serve as bait. "Henceforth you will be catching live human beings [*anthropous esē zōgrōn*]," Jesus reassures him.

In Acts the therapy continues. Simon Peter must decipher yet another manifestation of his own unconscious writ(h)ing: "he fell into a trance [*ekstasis*]. He saw the heaven opened and something like a large sheet coming down.... In it were all kinds of four-footed creatures and reptiles and birds of the air" (10:11–12). His cure is effected only as he accepts the "unclean thing" ("I heard a voice saying to me, 'Get up, Peter; kill and eat.' But I replied, 'By no means, Lord; for nothing profane [*koinon*] or unclean [*akatharton*] has ever entered my mouth' "—11:7–8), that is, uncircumcision (cf. 11:3), the obverse of that arbitrary cut that forms the precarious basis of his own self-identity. This is the "bloody scrap" that Lacan speaks of become, impossibly, "the signi-

---

13. Or "I must be among those who belong to my Father," a less frequent translation of this difficult expression (cf. Brown 1977, 475–77; Nolland 1989, 131–32).

fier of signifiers" (1977a, 265).[14] For Peter to accept that the other is *not* cut, or rather, that he or she is cut differently, is to accept the contingent character of his own cut. Only then can he be in a position to take the other alive (cf. Luke 2:10), to let him or her be in his or her difference.

The Sun of God

> I could not see because of the brightness of that light.... (Acts 22:11)

> [T]he greatest light is also, is it not, the source of all obscurity? (Lacan 1988a, 238)

What makes seeing possible in Luke-Acts? On the mount of transfiguration Peter, John and James are permitted a glimpse behind the veil: "they saw [*horaō*] his glory [*doxa*]" (Luke 9:32). It is a dazzling sight: "the appearance of his face changed, and his clothes became dazzling white/white as lightning" [*leukos exastraptōn*—9:29; cf. 17:24]. Jesus as Sun of God (cf. Acts 9:3; 22:6, 9, 11; 26:13)?[15] Certainly, without light there can be neither sight nor reading. "[T]he metaphor of darkness and light (of ... revelation and concealment) [is] the founding metaphor of Western philosophy as metaphysics," as Derrida notes. "[I]n this respect the entire history of our philosophy is a photology, a name given to a history of, or treatise on, light" (1978b, 27).[16] And elsewhere: "Everything ... that passes through ... *eidos* ... is articulated with the analogy between ... the intelligible ... and the visible sun" (Derrida 1982, 253–54; cf. Heidegger 1977, 106–7).

Now, whereas the transfiguration is implicitly articulated with the analogy between the intelligible and the visible *sun,* it is explicitly articulated with the analogy between the intelligible and the visible *Son:* "This is my Son..., listen to him!" (Luke 9:35). But the light is too bright for Peter to see or read by (cf. 9:33); he might as well be reading in the dark. "Christ and the saints in glory," exclaims Plummer in his commentary on the passage; "the chosen three blinded by the light; the remaining nine baffled by the powers of darkness [9:40]" (1922, 254). A phosphorescent Jesus makes a poor reading lamp.

Elisabeth Roudinesco's *Jacques Lacan & Co.* records a similar epiphany:

---

14. Furthermore, what Peter's *ekstasis* has exposed him to is that dangerously pleasurable threat to selfhood that Lacan terms *jouissance*—a hard-to-translate term whose nearest English equivalent is "ecstasy" (cf. Lacan 1982b, 137–48).

15. "Ra, the Rabbi cut in two, is perhaps the Egyptian God as well, the sun or light" (Derrida 1986d, 343; cf. Derrida 1981a, 82ff.).

16. For the roles of light in early Christianity, see Malmede 1986, esp. 61–75.

What was striking was the kind of *radiant influence* emanating from both [his] physical person and from his diction, his gestures. I have seen quite a few shamans functioning in exotic societies, and I rediscovered there a kind of equivalent of the shaman's power. I confess that, as far as what I heard went, I didn't understand. And I found myself in the middle of an audience that seemed to understand.... (1990, 362, emphasis added)

The speaker is not Peter, however, but Claude Lévi-Strauss. And the venue is not the mount of transfiguration, but the seminar of Jacques Lacan. Perhaps Lacan can shed some light, then, on Luke's irradiated Jesus—or at least provide some Songlasses through which to read him.

Teetering on the edge of sleep in a dreamscape ("[they] were drowsy with sleep"), Peter and his daz(zl)ed companions are able to gaze at the master signifier ("Master, it is good for us to be here..."), now unveiled in all its naked glory, only by diffusing its brightness through a misreading: "'let us make three dwellings, one for you, one for Moses, and one for Elijah'—not knowing what he said," adds the Beloved Physician, also an adept Analyst (Luke 9:32-33). Lacan may well be right: "[the phallusl can play its role only when veiled" (1977a, 288).[17] But our text already knows that. It says: "this word-thing [*rhēma*] was veiled [*ēn parakekalummenon*] from them" (9:45; cf. 18:34; 24:16)—veiled, that is, by the Father (cf. Ernst 1977, 310; Marshall 1978, 394; Schűrmann 1969, 1.573).

The *rhēma* stipulated that "the Son of Man must [*dei*] suffer many things, and be rejected ... and be killed, and ... be raised" (9:22; cf. 22:37; 24:26, 44). Now, *dei* ("it ought," "it must") is used seven times in Luke to designate the Law of the Father that binds and obligates his Son (9:22; 13:33; 17:25; 22:37; 24:7, 26, 44).[18] But the Law that binds also blinds; demanding that the Son suffer, it also demands that the disciples not see why until the Sun should have risen ("at early dawn, they went to the tomb..."—24:1; cf. 24:45-46, 26-27).

---

17. The Lacanian phallus is not the penis; rather; it is the signifier of that (unconscious) lack in every subject that feeds desire while keeping it insatiable. It is "'the signifier which has no signified" (Lacan 1982b, 152). More controversially, it is "the privileged signifier" (Lacan 1977a, 287). Debate still rages among feminists as to whether the Lacanian phallus connotes complicity with, or critique of, the phallocratic social order (e.g., Irigaray 1985b, 86-105; Gallop 1985, 133-56; Ragland-Sullivan 1986, 267-308; Grosz 1990,147-87). Whatever about the Lacanian corpus, the patriarchal phallus appears to be prominent in the Lukan corpus, Jesus' authority ("who ... gave you this authority?"—Luke 20:2) proceeding directly from the Father ("This is my Son, my Chosen, listen to him!"—9:35; cf. 3:22).

18. Elsewhere in Luke-Acts, *dei* is used more innocuously (see Cosgrove 1984 for details).

Luke, look, lack, Lacan.... In the Lukan text, as in Lacan's, the paternal *dei* bars the desiring subject from ever completely possessing the phallus. The *dei* in Luke-Acts is inerasably inscribed in its *deity*, and so the LACK in LuKe-ACts is literally irremovable.

Thus "the phallus ... always slips through your fingers" (Lacan 1982a, 52) whenever you try to seize it ("passing through the midst of them he went away"—Luke 4:30). It may erupt "in sudden manifestations..., in a flash" (Lacan 1982a, 48), as here on the mount of transfiguration, also a mount of phallophany. But it permits these titillating glimpses of itself only to disappear again, thereby luring you on ("they recognized him; and he vanished from their sight"—Luke 4:31; cf. Acts 1:9). It always slips away, and sometimes you can't even be sure that it has *come* ("Are you he who is to come, or shall we look for another?"—Luke 7:18). And although it attempts to persuade you of its solidity ("Touch me, and see..."—24:39), "the phallus, even the real phallus, is a ghost" (Lacan 1982a, 50; "they were startled and frightened, and supposed that they saw a ghost [*pneuma*]"—Luke 24:37).

By a stroke of luck—or is it Luke?—the term commonly translated "appearance" in the phrase "the appearance of his countenance was altered" (Luke 9:29) is *eidos*, whose tracks we detected earlier in the nativity scene but which we now come upon in broad daylight—the enhanced daylight of the transfiguration.[19] More than any other term, *eidos* connotes the subsumption of visibility in intelligibility, signifier in signified, body in mind, and mat(t)er in the paternal Law. Everything in Look-Acts that is refracted through *eidos-idein-eidenai* is articulated with the analogy between Son and sun, enlightenment and light, insight and sight, and never more brilliantly than here.

That Obseen Object of Desire

> ... the spirit of seeing, with which comes desire. (Testament of Reuben 2:4)

The longer we stare at the Son, however, the less we are likely to see. There is a dark side to seeing that we are liable to overlook. "Sight registers surfaces," observes Walter Ong, "which means that of itself it encourages one to consider even persons not as interiors but from the outside. Thus persons, too, tend to be thought of somehow as objects" (1981, 228). Freud associated the act of seeing with anal activity, with control and the desire for mastery (cf.

---

19. Or Sonlight, at any rate. The detail "drowsy with sleep" (Luke 9:32) "may be Luke's way of indicating that it was night" (Fitzmyer 1981, 801–2; cf. Luke 9:37).

1905, 157; 1915, 129). Lacan, as always, goes further: "in this matter of the visible, everything is a trap" (1978, 93),[20] a verdict that is echoed by Foucault.[21]

It is women, however, who have expressed the strongest discomfort with (under) the (male) gaze. "[T]he *gaze* enacts the voyeur's desire for sadistic power," writes Toril Moi, "in which the object of the gaze is cast as its passive, masochistic, feminine victim" (1985, 180 n. 8, her emphasis; cf. Mulvey 1975; Owens 1983, 70–77; Rose 1986, 165ff.). And Luce Irigaray states: "*Seeing remains the special prerogative of the Father*. It is in his gaze that everything comes into being" (1985a, 323, her emphasis). "As for the mother," she later adds, "let there be no mistake about it, *she has no eyes,* or so they say, no gaze.... And if one were to turn back toward her in order to re-enter, one would not have to be concerned about her point of view. The danger would rather be of losing one's bearings (or perhaps finding them?). Of falling into a dark hole where lucidity may founder" (1985a, 340, her emphasis).

Within the optical economy of Luke's epistemology the primary focus of the look, Jesus, is not an object of the gaze in Ong's sense. The look commended in Luke is the one that does *not* glance off the surface (the look of the shepherds, Simeon, or Anna, for instance, or that of the centurion at the foot of the cross). Moreover, even when the gaze directed at Jesus is superficial, he can hardly be said to be its victim. Rather, those who do the gazing (the *atenizontes* in Luke 4:20, for example) are themselves cast as victims of blindness.[22] Luke's scopic economy has one fundamental law of exchange: sight's shallow superficiality must ever be capable of being converted into deep insight.

But this is not to say that Luke is innocent of the imperial eye.

---

20. Part 2 of this volume (Lacan 1978) is entitled "Of the Gaze." Lacan's famous "Seminar on 'The Purloined Letter'" is also structured around the glance—or three glances, to be precise (see 1988b, 32).

21. "Visibility is a trap," declares Foucault in the "Panopticism" chapter of *Discipline and Punish* (1977a, 200). Cf. "The Eye of Power" (Foucault 1980a), in effect an addendum to this chapter; also "Seeing and Knowing" in *The Birth of the Clinic* (Foucault 1973, 107–23). Increasingly commentators have stressed the importance of vision for Foucault's work as a whole (e.g., Deleuze 1988, 32–69 passim; Jay 1986; Rajchman 1988). Notable perspectives on vision have also been provided by Heidegger, Sartre, Merleau-Ponty, Levinas, Bataille, Derrida, and Irigaray.

22. Similar reversals occur in Luke 6:7–11, 14:1–6 and 20:20–26. In each case, Jesus is the object of the verb *paratēreō* ("watch," "scrutinize"; cf. Acts 9:24). According to Hamm, *paratēreō* connotes "a special kind of non-seeing," "a manipulative scrutiny of surfaces which cannot perceive ... his true identity" (1986, 467, 476).

Look-Ax: Luke's Cutting Glance

> ...knowledge ... is made for cutting. (Foucault 1977b, 154)

> ...the master of that slave will ... cut him in pieces. (Luke 12:46)

In the elegant antechamber that forms the entrance to this Gospel, the narrator, *Look,* introduces himself: "Inasmuch as many have undertaken to compile a narrative of the things which have been accomplished among us, just as they were delivered to us by those who from the beginning were eyewitnesses [*autoptai*] and ministers of the word"—with a gracious bow, he invites you to accompany him—"it seemed good to me also, having followed all things closely for some time past, to write an orderly account for you, most excellent Theophilus"—this is not your name, but you let it pass—"that you may know the truth concerning the things of which you have been informed" (Luke 1:1–4).

He leads and you follow. Together you ascend the tower that looms above this written wor(l)d. Gradually you realize that you have entered a pen-itentiary.

Foucault might put it thus: "an uninterrupted work of writing links the center and the periphery.... [P]ower is exercised ... according to a ... hierarchical figure, in which each individual is constantly located, examined and distributed" (1977a, 197). In this stretch of *Discipline and Punish: The Birth of the Prison*, Foucault is describing the Panopticon, Jeremy Bentham's late eighteenth-century design for the perfect disciplinary institution. "[A]t the periphery, an annular building; at the center, a tower; this tower is pierced with wide windows that open onto the inner side of the ring; the peripheric building is divided into cells.... All that is needed, then, is to place a supervisor in a central tower and to shut up in each cell a madman, a patient, a condemned man, a worker or a schoolboy" (1977a, 200). However, "the arrangement of this machine is such that its enclosed nature does not preclude a permanent presence from the outside: ... anyone may come and exercise in the central tower the functions of surveillance" (1977a, 207). Enter the reader.

As we are about to see, Look's written wor(l)d is a panoptic disciplinary mechanism designed not only to monitor the discipline of its inmates—its madmen ("demons came out of many"—Luke 4:41), its patients ("all those ...who were sick"—4:40), its condemned men ("Two others, who were criminals [*kakourgoi*], were led away to be put to death with him"—23:32), its workers ("Master, we toiled all night and took nothing! But at your word I will let down the net"—5:5), its schoolboys ("Good Teacher, what shall I do...?"—18:18)—but to transform readers into disciples in addition. The reader is enlisted to assist the author in disciplining and punishing the inmates of the work(house). Strict order is maintained by means of a sharp, cutting glance passed back and forth between Look and the reader and used unsparingly on the inmates. But the reader too is subjected to a regimen of model discipleship even as she exercises her functions of surveillance in this prison, asylum, workhouse and hospital whose director is "the beloved physician" (cf. Col 4:14).

Of course, there are twists and turns in this labyrinthine mechanism that my own Punopticon, undisciplined and punnish as it is, will be unable to monitor. The trickiest twist of all concerns my own place in the design. It arises from the fact that while I am attempting to read against the restraints, the straitjacket, of an institution(alized discipline), I am also reading by means of them.

Look—we are in the "transparent, circular cage, with its high tower, powerful and knowing" (Foucault 1977a, 208). This multistoried watchtower is what makes Look's story possible. One ascends it by means of stares. The tower's design is such that the character-inmates are always visible from within it, but are themselves unable to see into it: "in the peripheric ring, one is totally seen, without ever seeing; in the central tower, one sees everything without ever being seen" (1977a, 202). The characters have a name for this invisible overseer, who sometimes speaks to them through a megaphone ("This is my Son, my Chosen; listen to him!"—Luke 9:35; cf. 3:22). They call him God.

The secret of Look's power is his tower: it enables him to be *omnipresent* in his wor(l)d (cf. Chatman 1978, 212). That is how Look, who admits that he himself was not an eyewitness of the events he recounts (Luke 1:2), can nevertheless conjure up in his reader the illusion of unmediated reference. The out-of-body experience that gets the Gospel of Look off the ground is not the least of its many miracles. Look's spatial relationship to his written wor(l)d is a special one: it is that of a disembodied observer.

Look has a press card that permits him to move freely in his wor(l)d, bringing live coverage to the reader. Legend has it that Luke was a painter;[23]

---

23. It seems that Luke painted a portrait of the Virgin, which later fell into the hands of the Empress Eudoxia of Constantinople, who passed it on to her daughter, from whom it eventually made its way to Venice, where it can still be seen (Plummer 1922, xxi–xxii). If so, Luke might also have painted himself into Luke-Acts, in the manner of Velázquez in *Las Meninas*. Foucault's comments on Velzáquez's technique would then apply to Luke. "The painter is turning his eyes towards us only in so far as we happen to occupy the same position as his subject"—the inscribed reader whose role he is sketching. His "gaze, addressed to the void confronting him outside the picture, accepts as many models as there are spectators"—or readers. "As soon as they place the spectator in the field of their gaze, the painter's eyes seize hold of him, force him to enter the picture, assign him a place at

more likely he was a photographer. In Luke-Acts the narrating "I" (cf. Luke 1:3; Acts 1:1) turns out to be an Eye: that of a roving-eye or at-the-scene reporter. It is also the eye of a detective fitted out with the latest surveillance equipment. "Taking photographs sets up a chronic voyeuristic relation to the world," as Susan Sontag notes (1973, 11). Look is a private eye for whom no scene is too private, whether it be Zechariah's or Mary's troubled encounters with the angel (Luke 1:8–23, 26–38), or Jesus' struggles with temptation (4:1–13; 22:41–45). These and other such scenes are narrated, not as having been told to a narrator-researcher (1:2–3 notwithstanding), but as directly witnessed by an on-the-spot narrator-observer.

Luke-Acts is replete with what narrative theorist Käte Hamburger would call *situation verbs* (1973, 96), verbs that designate the experiential "here and now" of a character. Take Luke's nativity account (2:1–7), for example. Up to and including the description of Jesus' birth ("And she gave birth to her firstborn son..."), the narrative is general and summary in accordance with the temporal perspective, which is one of distance: "And it came to pass in those days [*egeneto de en tais hēmerais ekeinais*]...." Luke 2:7b, however ("and she wrapped him in bands of cloth, and laid him in a manger"), marks a significant shift in presentational mode. Abruptly we are no longer in the past of a narrator but in the "present" of a character, invisible spectators of the minutiae of her daily existence, courtesy of the omnipresent narrator.

Today, live coverage is no longer the province of the historian. Situation verbs ("wrapped him in bands of cloth..., laid him in a manger") are not normally used "to make statements about points of time that are either indefinite or that lie far back within the distant past. We can say: yesterday, or a week ago, Peter cycled to the city, but we do not usually say something like: ten years ago, or at the start of this century, Peter cycled to the city, or got up from a chair" (Hamburger 1973, 96).[24] Luke, however, while purporting to present events long past relative to the time of writing, has Peter, Jesus, and every other major character cycling to the city or getting up from chairs at every turn—"he rolled up the scroll, and gave it back to the attendant, and sat down" (Luke 4:20); "they beckoned to their partners in the other boat to come and help them" (5:7); "his disciples plucked some heads of grain, rubbed them in

---

once privileged and inescapable"—a predetermined role of reading (1970, 4–5). Touch the canvas or the page and the work snaps shut behind you.

24. Bennison Gray terms this presentational mode *moment-by-moment narration*: "an event can be stated in two different ways. It can be presented moment-by-moment, with or without transitional summaries, and thus constitute a statement *of* an event. Or it can be narrated in summary, with little or no moment-by-moment presentation, and thus constitute a statement *referring* to an event. The first way is characteristic of literature. The second way is characteristic of history" (1975, 100, his emphasis).

their hands, and ate them" (6:1); "he lifted up his eyes on his disciples" (6:20); and so on.

Here we touch on what Foucault has called "the infinitely small of political power." Complete supervision seeks "ideally to reach the most elementary particle, the most passing phenomenon." Such supervision, to be successful requires an "instrument of permanent, exhaustive, omnipresent surveillance, capable of making all visible," while itself remaining invisible. It has "to be like a faceless gaze that transform[s] the whole social body into a field of perception: thousands of eyes posted everywhere" (1977a, 214).

Seeing all is not sufficient, however; Luke must also hear all, as we are about to learn. Luke's Panopticon (he sees without being seen) is also a confessional (he hears without being seen)—his is a Gospel of repentance, after all (cf. Fitzmyer 1981, 237–39). Luke is "the one who listens and says nothing" (Foucault, 1978, 62).[25] Of course, Luke's many penitents are deaf to the fact that he is listening. And blind to the fact that the confessional encaging them is also a television set.

Arguably, Luke-Acts concerns a conflict between light and darkness (cf. Garrett 1991, 95–96, 100–105). Luke turns it into a living-room war. He transmits live audio as well as video; direct speech proliferates in Luke-Acts.[26] Now, if the situation verb permits moment-by-moment presentation, the direct speech report epitomizes it, "the temporal sequence of words occurring one after another as they are uttered" (Gray 1975, 114; cf. Hamburger 1973, 83–84). There is a corresponding dearth of indirect speech report in Luke-Acts.[27] In short, Luke puts Jesus and his interlocutors on television.

Contemporary historiography cannot compete with television, needless to say, or even with televangelists such as Luke. In a modern history or biography, direct speech implies "that the words recorded between quotation marks have a documented source, and that they are reproduced word for word, [whereas] represented [or indirect] speech does not.... 'He would be going to Saint Moritz again in August—could Marcel come too?' implies only that Robert de Montesquiou said something *like that* to Marcel Proust, that this sentence captures the 'gist' of the conversation" (Banfield 1982, 260, her emphasis). Contrast the speech of Lukan characters, which is seldom trans-

---

25. Foucault is commenting here on the penitential rite.
26. *Legō* ("say") is far and away the most common verb of speech in Luke-Acts, occurring either alone (Luke 1:13, 18, 24; etc.) or in participial phrases (1:19, 67; 3:10; etc.). Other verbs used to introduce direct speech (of which there are few) include *anakrazō* ("cry out"—4:33), *apaggelō* ("report"—8:20) and *blasphēmeō* ("blaspheme"—23:39).
27. The principal examples in Luke are 6:11; 7:18; 9:10, 31; 11:53; 22:4–5; 23:9. These are all of a rudimentary kind; the topic of the speech event is indicated, but no attempt is made to paraphrase its content.

mitted indirectly as something that was said "way back then," the gist of which is now reported. The actors in Luke's docudrama are instead foregrounded as figures that can be "directly" experienced in the act of speech.

Look-Acts brings audiovisual technology, then, to Jeremy Bentham's eighteenth-century Panopticon. The Panopticon was dreamed up by Bentham as a more "enlightened" penal institution: "no more bars, no more chains, no more heavy locks" (Foucault 1977a, 202). Acts 12:7 speaks of this reform: "an angel of the Lord appeared and a *light* shone in the cell.... And the chains fell off his [Peter's] wrists." But a panoptic mechanism *is* light, dispensing with the "heaviness of the old 'houses of security,' with their fortress-like architecture" (1977a, 202). Peter does not know that it is Look, his enlightened supervisor, who has arranged his "escape." "Full lighting and the eye of a supervisor capture better than darkness, which ultimately protected" (1977a, 200). Thanks to panopticism, power "throw[s] off its physical weight; it tends to the noncorporal." In the case of written narrative, it becomes light as paper. But "the more it approaches this limit, the more constant, profound and permanent are its effects" (1977a, 203). Panopticism thus "makes it possible to perfect the exercise of power. It does this in several ways: because it can reduce the number of those who exercise it"—in the case of narrative, it reduces it to one—"while increasing the number of those on whom it is exercised" (1977a, 206)—in the case of a Gospel, it increases it incalculably

In Look-Acts, supervision is pen-al: it derives from a certain style of writing. Text, weave, fabric, fabrication, fiction. "A real subjection is born mechanically from a fictitious relation" (1977a, 202). Look-Acts is a penoptic mechanism, then, a prison house of language. Its theology is a technology of power. "Inspection functions ceaselessly. The gaze is alert everywhere" (1977a, 195).

To a remarkable extent, then, Foucault's reflections on the panoptic mechanism apply *mutatis mutandis* to the omnipresence device in fictional narrative.[28] "We are much less Greeks than we believe," claimed Foucault. "We are neither in the amphitheatre, nor on the stage, but in the panoptic machine" (1977a, 217). But the omnipresence technique in fiction prefigures Foucault's "disciplinary society," one whose emblem is the Panopticon, one less of spectacle than of surveillance. (Today the Lukan Jesus' claims would

---

28. Certain observations in Spanos 1987 (156ff.), together with Foucault's own "Behind the Fable" (1988a), got me started on this line of thinking. In the latter article, Foucault at one point states: "Right next to the principal characters, speaks a shadow that shares their privacy, knows their faces, their habits, their vital statistics, and also their thoughts and the secret folds of their character; it listens to their dialogues, but it also registers their feelings as if from within" (1988a, 2).

lead him, not to the cross, but to the psychiatric ward. Having been examined by Dr. Pilate, he would be led away for further observation.)

Luke's historiographic assumptions allow him the use of an omnipresent narrator. This enables his own assumption, or ascension, his translation to a sphere free of spatial limitation: his apotheosis. The author of Luke-Acts is long dead. Enter his tome, however, and you will not find his body ("He is not here…"—Luke 24:5). Reborn as an omnipresent narrator, he has exited the tomb (womb) of mat(t)er, like the hero of his tale (for neither is the risen Jesus bound by material constraints: "he vanished out of their sight…. As they were saying this, Jesus himself stood among them"—Luke 24:31, 36; cf. 24:51; Acts 1:9; 9:3ff.). But unlike Jesus, who, still in a body, is subject to touch ("handle me"—Luke 24:39), Look is wholly spirit. Aptly, therefore, this Gospel of the Look is also known as the Gospel of the Holy Spirit.

But even if Look *is* God in his wor(l)d, First Person of the Blessed Trinity of Implied Author, Protagonist and Narrator, he nevertheless works a nine-to-five job. Thanks to the omnipresence device, the Implied Author can assume a secret identity in his written wor(l)d, can be transformed from a mere ear-witness ("I have heard from some who were told by others who said they were there…"—cf. Luke 1:2) into an eyewitness, can present the Good News as the Network News. And the reader is made an eye-and-earwitness by extension, thanks to the roving camcorder and floating mike that is the Lukan narrator.

But to be an eyewitness in Look-Acts is to qualify not only for the rank of reporter but for a seat on the board of directors of the Good News Network itself. It is to qualify for the position of apostle. Acts 1:21–22 states the hiring policy—"one of the men [*andrōn*] who have accompanied us during all the time that the Lord Jesus went in and out among us, beginning from the baptism of John until the day when he was taken up from us—one of these must become a witness with us to his resurrection" (cf. 10:39–41; Luke 24:48)—after which the job is offered to the successful candidate: "the lot fell on Matthias; and he was added to the eleven apostles" (Acts 1:26). And although the particular reader whose career we are about to follow has been so well trained by Luke that she succeeds in outperforming the entire managerial corps of Jesus' corporation (his reanimated corpse being its main investment), she is passed over for the position advertised in Acts 1.[29]

Her training course has, in fact, been exceptionally rigorous. To read this Panoptic Gospel is to be submitted to a battery of exacting tests. "[T]he Panopticon was also a laboratory," explains Foucault; "it could be used as a

---

29. As are the women who have followed Jesus from Galilee (Luke 8:2–3), who have also outperformed the apostles (23:49, 55), and have been the first witnesses of the resurrection (24:1–11, 22–24).

machine to … alter behavior, to train or correct individuals" (1977a, 203). The model reader is (s)trapped in(to) the text, made to swallow the role of reading pre-scribed for her by the Beloved Physician. Luke, then, is guilty of mal(e)practice.

But what if our author was actually a woman,[30] and the reader actually a man, like the Theophilus to whom "Luke" ostensibly addresses herself (Luke 1:3; Acts 1:1)? Would the implied author of Luke-Acts be any less phallic on that account? Would her implied reader be any less pliable? "[T]he phallic personality needs a receptive audience or womb," writes Norman O. Brown (1966, 125). But the owner of the phallus might well be a woman, just as the owner of the womb might well be a man.

Luke's superpowers are not limited to omnipresence. This panoptic overseer is but one of a pantheon of narrators who seem to "have complete control [over their narrative worlds] owing to [their] godlike privileges of unhampered vision, penetration to the innermost recesses of [their] agents' minds, free movement in time and space, and knowledge of past and future" (Sternberg 1978, 257). This divine stance is, to put it mildly, hardly "amenable to the usual canons of probability" (1978, 295). Traditionally it has been termed the narrator's *privilege*, and its telepathic trajectory (the ability to read characters' minds) has been termed the narrator's *omniscience*.

"Come, let us build ourselves … a tower with its top in the heavens" (Gen 11:4). God might be permitted a moment of anxiety as the elevator doors open and the omniscient and omnipresent narrator steps forth. Luce Irigaray writes of

> the gaze of God which, ever on high, sees everything at one and the same time, looming over the whole universe.… From that perspective one cannot glimpse, calculate, or even imagine what the vanishing point might be.… Supreme erection that exceeds every horizon; even the sharpest, the most piercing gaze will be incapable of calculating its angles of incidence, for the eye remains captive in the world of the visible.… Light that nothing resists.… [A]lien to all shadow, outshining the Sun itself.… Gaze that no bodily organ … can limit. Without any blind spot, even one that might represent something forgotten. (1985a, 328–29)

But is Luke really in this league?

Luke's narrator can "know" any of his characters at will (in the biblical sense, needless to say). His (g)lance is able to penetrate every body in his writ-

---

30. As Jane Via, for example, has suggested (1987, 49–50 nn. 37–40), undeterred by Luke 1:3, which applies the masculine form of the participle (*parēkolouthēkoti*) to the narrator.

3. THE GOSPEL OF THE LOOK 73

ten wor(l)d. Wayne Booth writes of a narrator's "most important privilege" being "that of obtaining an inside view of [a] character" (1983, 160), and of narrators who provide inside views differing "in the depth and the axis of their plunge" (1983, 177).

Again, we are back in the dark recess of the confessional, a place designed for (self-)disclosure. The power of the Father Confessor, like that of the omniscient narrator, "cannot be exercised without knowing the inside of people's minds, without exploring their souls, without making them reveal their innermost secrets" (Foucault 1983, 214).[31] "Nothing is covered up that will not be uncovered," says Look, "and nothing is secret that will not become known" (12:2; cf. 8:17).

However, "Knowing All need not mean Telling All," as Seymour Chatman sagely observes (1978, 212). Luke is a photographer, and the confessional is his darkroom. Too much light would spoil the plot he is developing (although a modicum of light is essential). Does Luke respect the confidentiality of the confessional, then? Not entirely. He confides his characters' inner states to Theophilus, forgetting that others too are listening. From this gossiping Gospel we learn that Mary "was much perplexed" (*dietarachthē*) by the angel's words "and considered in her mind [*dielogizeto*] what sort of greeting this might be" (Luke 1:29), that the congregation "wondered" (*ethaumazon*) at Jesus' words (4:22), that Jesus "was moved with pity" (*esplagchnisthē*) for the bereaved mother (7:13), that the Pharisee "said to himself [*eipen en heautō*] 'If this man were a prophet...'" (7:39), that Herod "was perplexed" (*diēporei*) by reports of Jesus (9:7), that Peter "remembered" (*hypemnēsthē*) Jesus' prediction (22:61), and so on.[32]

Most of these plunges are relatively shallow. This is particularly true of the emotional states (astonishment, fear, joy, anger, anxiety, sorrow), which barely qualify as data that could not be inferred by strictly "natural" means—the

---

31. Foucault's topic here is "pastoral power."
32. Limiting ourselves to the Gospel, we find that Luke uses inner-action verbs to disclose his characters' *astonishment* (1:63; 2:18, 33, 17, 48; 4:22, 32, 36; 5:9, 26; 8:25, 56; 9:43; 11:14, 38; 20:26; 24:41), *fear* (1:65; 2:9; 7:16; 8:25, 35, 37; 9:34, 45; 20:19; 22:2; 24:5, 37), *joy* (1:58; 10:17; 13:17; 19:6; 22:5; 23:8; 24:52), *anger* (4:28; 6:11; 13:14), *anxiety* (1:12, 29), *sorrow* (18:23; 22:45), *inner reflection* (1:66; 2:19, 51; 3:15), *suppositions* (2:44; 19:11; 24:37), *knowledge or ignorance* (1:22; 2:50; 8:53; 9:33; 9:45; 18:34), *disbelief* (24:11, 41), *perplexity* (9:7), *recognition* (24:31), *recollection* (22:61), *thoughts* (7:39), and *hopes* (23:51; cf. 2:26). Sometimes a phrase is used instead of a single verb; e.g., "they were filled with fear" (*ephobēthēsan phobon megan*—2:9). At other times, two or three inner-action verbs or phrases are used in a single sentence; e.g., "they were afraid and they marveled...." (*phobēthentes de ethaumasan*—8:25); "he was very glad [*echarē lian*], for he had long desired to see him [*thelōn idein auton*] ... and he was hoping [*ēpizen*] to see some sign..." (23:8).

ordinary glance of an observer as distinct from the extraordinary glance of a narrator. The border between external and internal observation is, in any case, an ambiguous one. "[P]urely 'external' vision," notes Tzvetan Todorov, "the one that confines itself to describing perceptible actions without accompanying them with any interpretation, any incursion into the protagonist's mind, never exists in the pure state: it would lead into the unintelligible" (1981, 34). What Dorrit Cohn says of the earliest modern novelists can also be said of Luke, namely, that he dwells mainly on "manifest behaviour, with the characters' inner selves revealed only indirectly through spoken language and telling gesture" (1978, 21).[33] Once again, Luke takes photographs.

(Jesus to the reader: "What determines me ... is the gaze that is outside. It is through the gaze that I enter light.... Hence it comes about that the gaze is the instrument through which ... if you will allow me to use a word, as I often do, in a fragmented form—I am *photo-graphed*.")[34]

Photography too can be phallic, as Susan Sontag has noted (1973, 13–14),[35] but its penetration is relatively shallow. Shallow penetration is all that Look needs, however, in order to impregnate his text with meaning—meaning that the reader will be expected to adopt. To put it another way, it is not necessary that (the) Look probe deeply, for it is cosmetic surgery that is

---

33. This is not without significance for historiography. Culpepper suggests that the inside views in John (which are similar to those in Luke-Acts) preserve a measure of verisimilitude by reason of their limited depth. Such knowledge "may be credibly, if not entirely, accounted for as insights gained after the fact" (1983, 22–23). Hamburger anticipated a similar objection, namely, that verbs such as "to believe," "to intend" or "to think" can be used in a modern history. It can be stated, for instance, that Napoleon believed he would conquer Russia. However, "the use of 'believe' here is only a derived one," argues Hamburger. "From those documents transmitted to us it is derived, or concluded, that Napoleon was of the belief that he would conquer Russia. In a historical ... account, however, Napoleon cannot be portrayed as someone in the act of believing 'here and now.' That is, he cannot be portrayed in the subjectivity ... of his inner, mental processes.... Should this occur, we would find ourselves in a novel about Napoleon, in a work of fiction" (1973, 82–83). Cohn adds: "Narrative fiction is the only literary genre, as well as the only kind of narrative, in which the unspoken thoughts, feelings, perceptions of a person other than the speaker can be portrayed" (1978, 7). Such pronouncements beg questions of another sort, needless to say. But to test the various "cans" and "cannots" in these citations, to see whether and under what circumstances they would bend, or to ask when and why they became necessary (cf. Foucault 1979) is beyond the scope of this essay.

34. From Lacan 1978, 106, his emphasis. Etymologically, photography is a writing (*graphē*) with light (*phōs*).

35. Cf. Barthes 1980, 48: "A word exists in Latin to designate that wound, that prick, that mark made by a pointed instrument.... I will thus call it *punctum*.... The *punctum* of a photo, it's that accident which, in it, stings me."

being performed, and not on the characters but on the reader. Henceforth the reader will *look* better: he or she will see more clearly.

Eyes Only: A Classified Gospel

> This speaking eye would be ... the master of truth. (Foucault 1973, 115)

"To photograph ... means putting oneself into a certain relation to the world that feels like knowledge—and, therefore, like power," writes Sontag (1973, 4). The knowledge-power equation is, however, especially associated with Foucault. In the introduction to his *History of Sexuality*, Foucault famously insists that power should not be thought of as emanating from some central, sovereign or exterior site. Neither is it to be thought of as a group of institutions or a system of regulations; "these are only the terminal forms power takes" (1978, 92). Instead, power is a "moving substrate" of relations that are ubiquitous, unequal, and unstable—economic relations, sexual relations, knowledge relations (1978, 93–94; cf. Foucault 1977a, 26ff.). But if power cannot be sited, can it at least be sighted? Yes and no, Foucault would seem to say. Certainly, there is no uncompromised high ground from which to observe the workings of power, to take an "instant photograph of multiple struggles continuously in transformation" (1989a, 188). Luke is a keen photographer, as we have seen. What would he say to Foucault?

Like Foucault, Luke has a thing about power. His Gospel "uses the term 'power' (*dynamis*) more frequently than either Matthew or Mark," as Susan Garrett observes, "introducing it into several accounts where it was not present in his source (Luke 4:36; 5:17; 6:19; 9:1; see also 10:19; 24:49). On occasion the evangelist's narration indicates that he conceived of 'power' in material terms: it is like a substance that flows forth from someone (Luke 6:19; 8:46; cf. Acts 5:15; 19:12)"—or through someone—although Garrett rejects John Hull's suggestion that power in Luke-Acts is "impersonal and free-floating" (Garrett 1989, 65–66; cf. Hull 1974, 105–14).[36] For Garrett, all power in Luke-Acts is centered in God, Satan, and their respective agents. But what of the power of that other Lukan deity, its omniscient and omnipresent narrator?

In Luke-Acts, the textual technique of the inside view works less to foster the reader's intimate identification with the characters, Jesus included,[37] than

---

36. Foucault's decentered notion of power, nonetheless, is in some respects a very ancient one (cf. Castelli 1991a, 45ff.).

37. Exposure of Jesus' inner life is sporadic and depthless: "he was hungry" (Luke 4:2), "he was amazed" (7:9), "he was moved with pity" (7:13), "he rejoiced" (10:21). The most exposive inside view of Jesus (or of any Lukan character) is Luke 22:44: "being in an agony

to effect a certain distribution of knowledge, and hence of power, between narrator, characters and audience. This distribution involves a cumulative apportioning to the reader of certain classified (eyes only) information, which, in its entirety, is unavailable to anyone in the story world except Jesus and his Father. Wedded to Jesus at penpoint, the reader is inducted into the family business ("I must be about my Father's business"—Luke 2:49). Yet is not as if the reader is privately taken aside and directly coerced by the God/Father of this immeasurably powerful family. Power here "has its principle not so much in a person as in a certain concerted distribution of bodies, surfaces, lights, gazes; in an arrangement whose internal mechanisms produce the relation in which individuals are caught up" (Foucault 1977a, 202). How exactly does this work?

First, the reader is given access to classified information that is withheld from most of the story participants. Here are some examples from the Gospel:

- 1:59–61: The reader knows why Elizabeth and Zechariah must name their son John (cf. 1:13), whereas their neighbors and kinsfolk are utterly in the dark.
- 1:66, 4:36, 8:25, 9:9: Groomed by the narrator, the smug reader knows the answers to all these unanswered questions.
- 2:48–50: The reader is better equipped than Jesus' own parents to make sense of their son's explanation.
- 3:15: The reader knows better (cf. 2:11, 26) than to subscribe to the popular opinion of John.
- 4:22: The congregation's question, "Is not this Joseph's son?" has the reader positively smirking once again (cf. 5:21).
- 11:14–54: The performance of the characters (crowds, religious authorities) is especially inept in this sequence, giving the reader a further opportunity to shine.
- 16:30–31: The reader knows that the Pharisees are altogether unaware that Jesus is referring to himself.

Second, without having to sign for it, every Lukan reader is extended a dossier of highly classified information ("tell this to no one"—Luke 9:21; cf.

[*en agōnia*] he prayed more earnestly [*ektenesteron proseucheto*]...." (The verse is omitted from many manuscripts, however; see Ehrman and Plunkett 1983 for the arguments for and against its inclusion.) But even here disclosure depends primarily on external data—the words of Jesus' prayer and the detail of his sweat "like great drops of blood." The appearance of the strengthening angel would also seem to be an externally observable event, like Satan's temptations earlier (4:1–13). Similarly, the revelation at Jesus' baptism, although intended primarily for him ("you are [*su ei*] my beloved Son"—3:22; cf. Matt 3:17: "this is [*houtos estin*] my beloved Son"), is presented as an observable occurrence ("the Holy Spirit descended ... in bodily form [*sōmatikō eidei*]"; cf. Mark 1:10; Matt 3:16).

4:41; 5:14; 8:56). Among the human characters, the disciples alone have access to this file. Reader response becomes reader responsibility. Luke's wor(l)d is carefully drafted so as to underscore the solemn character of the disciples' contract with its Central Intelligence, mediated through the agency of his Son. The contract begins: "To you it has been given to know the secrets [*ta mystēria*] of the kingdom of God; but for others [*tois de loipois*] they are in parables, so that 'looking they may not perceive and listening they may not understand'" (Luke 8:10; cf. Isa 6:9–10). But the reader, under the narrator's adept supervision, will soon out-perform Jesus' inept trainees.

The reader's infiltration of Jesus' core group is made possible not so much by Look's omniscience (which he shares with Jesus)[38] as his omnipresence (which he withholds even from Jesus until the latter has accomplished his mission). From the moment the adult Jesus makes his entrance in Luke-Acts as God's special agent (Luke 3:21), the narrator, Look, who, as we have seen, is the author's private investigator in the story world (cf. 1:3: "after investigating [*parēkolouthēkoti*] everything carefully…"), is expected to tail Jesus throughout Galilee and Judea—although as omnipresent, Look can also bilocate so as to photograph Satan's mole Judas, for example, on his errand of betrayal (22:3–6), or Peter in the act of breaking his contract (22:54b-62). Look will only look, however; being a voyeur he will never intervene. "Photographing is essentially an act of non-intervention" (Sontag 1973, 11).

Where Look leads, the reader must follow. Unable to escape except by suicide (that is, by ceasing to read), the reader is stuck in a gumshoe role. But it is a role in which she is made to excel. For instance, on reaching Jairus's house, Jesus will allow no one to enter the sleeping chamber with him "except Peter, John, and James, and the child's father and mother" (Luke 8:51). But the reader-in-the-text is already between the covers; she is already an undercover disciple. And so she slips in unnoticed to witness a spectacle that Jesus wants covered up: "he ordered them to tell no one" (8:56). Jesus' position is swiftly becoming impossible.

(Jesus to Look: "What you will never know, what I have hidden from you and will hide from you, barring collapse and madness, until my death, you already know it, instantly and almost before me. I know that you know it.")[39]

By the time of Jesus' second passion prediction (Luke 9:44), the disciples are struggling to survive his brutal training regime (cf. 8:25a; 9:33, 40), and things will only get tougher (cf. 9:46, 49–50, 54–55, etc.). Their painful pre-

---

38. Jesus displays his omniscience in Luke 5:22, 6:8, 9:47, 11:17, 20:23, and 24:38, although it fails him mysteriously in 8:45–46 (and possibly also in 9:18, depending on whether we take his question to be rhetorical or not).

39. From Derrida 1988e, 15.

dicament is triply highlighted in 9:45—"they did not understand ... and it was concealed from them ... and they were afraid to ask"—and in a form that suggests that their ignorance is due to a decision at the top: the passive verbal construction "it was concealed" (*ēn parakekalummenon*) implies the agency of a Central Intelligence (cf. 18:34; 24:16), as we noted earlier. Jesus' secret instructions constantly vanish into the shredder before the disciples have had a chance to decipher them. But first they must cross the desk of the reader, who is being trained to crack their code.

Reading Luke-Acts, however, is no desk job. The reader is constantly in the trenches with Jesus, clad in the trenchcoat of a fictional follower. And to be assigned the role of a tail in this way is to make one's way through this tale as a model disciple. In the confusion attending Jesus' arrest, for instance, the disciples are finally shaken off his tail. Peter does try to follow "at a distance" (Luke 22:54), but he breaks under interrogation (22:53—62). The reader follows Jesus with ease, however, never letting him out of her sight—until he gives even her the slip by descending into the tomb (23:53). Here at last is a lead-lined vault that even Look's super vision cannot penetrate.[40] The reader is obliged to turn and walk away with Look, as he follows some women home (23:56).

Poststriptum

Our author's traditional name, Luke, alerts us to his scopophilia by sounding so like *Look*: such is the luck of the homonym. Complicity of the look and the book: Luke's narrator is omniscient and omnipresent, his Gospel panoptic as well as synoptic. Luke's sharp glance, his pointed look, is able to penetrate every body in his written wor(l)d.

If Luke acts superior to Jesus, however, presuming to penetrate even him, it is not because he is in fact superior. The Son is at the center of Luke's photological fantasy, his Sunoptic Gospel. In the light of the Son there is only (in)sight or blindness, brightness or deep shadow. Luke too is subject to the Son, for he writes by the Son's light. Luke-Acts is not light reading, but it *is* light writing, as we have seen: photo-graphy. Jesus is a model in Luke-Acts—a model for Paul, Peter and Stephen, as has often been observed, but a photographic model as well. Luke the photographer circles endlessly around

---

40. The tomb would remain secure until 1522, when Hans Holbein the Younger painted *The Body of the Dead Christ in the Tomb*. The crypt, as Holbein represents it, is claustrophobically constricted and coffin-like. Julia Kristeva describes the effect: "Holbein's Christ is alone. Who sees him? [...] There is, of course, the painter. And ourselves.... The viewer's gaze penetrates this closed-in coffin from below..." (1989, 242, 265).

his photogenic Jesus. So does everybody and everything else in the Lukan cosmos. Luke's system of knowledge is a solar system. The centrality of the Son is its first law of (meta)physics.

Luke's probing look is fashioned from a voice, that of the Lukan narrator. And that voice is pitched so as to penetrate the reader. "[S]ound ... *penetrates* us*,*" writ(h)es Derrida. "[I]ts reception is obligatory.... I can close my eyes, I can avoid being touched by that which I see.... [But v]oice penetrates into me violently, it is the privileged route for forced entry" (1976, 240, his emphasis; cf. Derrida 1985a, 33). Even the reader does not escape the Beloved Physician, then, without a rubber-glove examination ("The doctor will see you now..."). Of course, even if we cannot close our ears, we can always close the book. We can cease reading, commit readerly suicide. Or we can counterread, as here.

4
ARE THERE IMPURITIES IN THE LIVING WATER THAT THE JOHANNINE JESUS DISPENSES? DECONSTRUCTION, FEMINISM, AND THE SAMARITAN WOMAN*

This essay (which began life as a 1988 conference paper) finds me still replaying, in time-lapse mode, the history of deconstruction in America. If the first phase of that history was characterized by a euphoric embrace of deconstruction's revolutionary epistemology, the second phase entailed a determined rolling up of sleeves in order to translate that theoretical revelation into models for social revolution. In consequence, the thoroughgoing poststructuralization of U.S. literary studies that marked the 1980s was simultaneously a thoroughgoing politicization of U.S. literary studies. (The potential for self-deception in this enterprise was, of course, colossal in a national culture in which the political and the intellectual are virtual antonyms; more on this problem in ch. 13 below.)

To put it another way, whereas the first wave of American deconstruction was primarily preoccupied with the intricate internal workings of literary texts, the second wave, rushing toward the shore by the mid-1980s, was primarily preoccupied with the intricate relations of literary texts to (other) social and cultural realia, not least gender and sexuality, race and ethnicity, and colonialism and postcolonialism. This second wave, like the first, was centrally preoccupied with hierarchical binary oppositions and was discovering Derrida's deconstructive strategies for dismantling such oppositions to be a crucial resource. But whereas the first wave, taking its lead from "early" Der-

---
* First published in *Biblical Interpretation* 1 (1993): 207–27.

rida, tended to obsess about such hierarchies as presence over absence and speech over writing, the second wave was beginning to obsess about such hierarchies as male over female, white over black, colonizer over colonized, and heterosexual over homosexual.

It is with the first of the latter set of hierarchical oppositions—male over female—that the present essay is centrally concerned, and with one male and one female in particular: the Johannine Jesus and the Samaritan woman. And to deconstruct that hierarchy I find that I do not need to have recourse to any of the demanding Derridean theory that informed, say, my earlier "Illuminating the Gospels without the Benefit of Color." All that is necessary, ultimately, for my reading is the relatively simple two-step tactic articulated by Derrida, as will be seen, in a 1971 interview. This was deconstruction by numbers, if the truth be told, which is why I only attempted it once. I leave it to the reader to decide whether or not the numbers add up.

Jesus' Desire

Jesus, weary from his journey, is sitting on the lip of the well. The Samaritan woman arrives to draw water. The crowd parts to let her through. Some have brought binoculars, other are already taking notes.

For many who have written on the scene at the Samaritan well, the woman's oblivion to her own need, so much greater than that of Jesus, is the pivot on which the irony turns. Paul D. Duke, for example, remarks: "Jesus greets the woman with a request for water (cf. Gen 24:17), an irony in itself in view of who will eventually give water to whom" (1985, 101). Gail R. O'Day elaborates: "She assumes that she is in conversation with a thirsty Jew; this Jew informs her that if she knew both the gift of God and the identity of the person with whom she was speaking, she would recognize that she herself was the thirsty one" (1986, 60). Teresa Okure concurs:

> In Jesus' case, his exercise of humility is outstanding by the fact that though he is the one with "the gift of God" to offer (v 10), he nonetheless approaches the woman as a beggar [...] Ironically ... the woman is the one who needs to drink. Jesus' thirst and her as yet unrecognized thirst are thus inseparably linked [...] The whole point of v 10, therefore, is that if only the woman knew it, she, not Jesus, is the beggar who needs to ask and receive from him the gift of eternal life, given freely for the asking. (1988, 86–87, 95, 98)

4. ARE THERE IMPURITIES IN THE LIVING WATER? 83

Raymond E. Brown distills the dialogue thus: "*Jesus* asks the Samaritan for water, violating the social customs of the time.... *Woman* mocks Jesus for being so in need that he does not observe the proprieties.... *Jesus* shows that the real reason for his action is not his inferiority or need, but his superior status" (1966, 177, his emphasis). Rudolf Schnackenburg is yet more blunt: "It is not Jesus who is in need of anything, but the woman; and she is confronted with the one person who can satisfy the deepest needs of man" (1968, 426). But are Jesus' own needs in this scene really any less than those of the woman?

"Give me a drink," asks Jesus. The demand would appear to be double. Seated wearily at a well whose water is beyond his reach, Jesus desires a drink. But he has another desire that well water cannot satisfy, as 4:10 suggests: "If you knew the gift of God, and who it is that is saying to you, 'Give me a drink,' you would have asked him, and he would have given you living water." What Jesus longs for from this woman, even more than refreshing spring water, is that *she* long for the living water that *he* longs to give *her*. Jesus thirsts to arouse *her* thirst. His desire is to arouse her desire, to be himself desired. His desire is to be the desire of this woman, to have her recognize in him that which she lacks in herself. His desire is to fill up *her* lack. Only thus can his own deeper thirst be assuaged, his own lack be filled. To this lack, one of several holes around which my reading is organized, I shall later return.[1]

Sizing Up the Oppositions

The Samaritan woman appears to be incapable of distinguishing the literal and material from the figurative and spiritual. "Sir," she finally says, "give me this water, so that I may never be thirsty or have to keep coming here to draw water" (4:15). A two-storey ironic structure is thereby erected.[2] "Below," at ground level, is the apparent meaning, in which the woman, as unwitting victim, is trapped. It would seem that the only door in this ironic structure leads upstairs, although the woman has yet to discover it. "Above" is a higher level of meaning, a second floor of which the woman is unaware, unlike the reading or listening audience, who have just now taken up residence there along with Jesus and the Johannine narrator, who share a double bed.

---

1. This language of lack and desire is adapted from the French poststructuralist Freudian, Jacques Lacan. Further on Lacan, lack, and the Gospel Jesus(es), see "The Gospel of the Look" above.

2. To use a metaphor beloved of the literary commentators; see esp. Culpepper 1983, 167–68; Duke 1985, 13–14. The metaphor seems to have originated with D. C. Muecke (1969, 19).

This two-storey structure is a hierarchical opposition. The Fourth Gospel contains row upon row of such structures. The road to the well, for example, is lined with them: knowledge/ignorance (1:10, 26, 31; 3:10–11; cf. 1:18), spiritual/literal (2:19–21; 3:3–4), spirit/flesh (3:6; cf. 1:13), heavenly things (*ta epourania*)/earthly things (*ta epigeia*) (3:12; cf. 3:31), light/darkness (3:19–21; cf. 1:7–9), baptism in the Holy Spirit/water baptism (1:31–33; cf. 3:5), miraculous wine/water for ritual cleansing (2:6ff.), heavenly ascent/descent (1:51; 3:13; cf. 3:31), and so on.

As much as anything, deconstruction is a dismantling of "the binary oppositions of metaphysics" (Derrida 1981c, 41). Of course, all oppositions are not created equal. "Each pair operates with very different stakes in the world," as Barbara Johnson has observed (1987, 2). The exchange between Jesus and the woman of Samaria, an ironic two-tiered structure according to the majority reading, is itself housed within a much larger enclosure, that of the opposition between male and female, a gigantic pavilion whose stakes extend very deep into the world indeed.

Deconstruction and Feminism

The Samaritan woman contrasts sharply with Jesus' previous conversation partner. "When Jesus speaks with Nicodemus in John 3, he speaks with a male member of the Jewish religious establishment. In John 4 he speaks with a female member of an enemy people," Gail O'Day notes. "Nicodemus has a name, but the woman is unnamed; she is known only by what she is—a foreign woman" (1992, 295). The conversation between Jesus and the woman is, apparently, a scandalous one, as O'Day goes on to remark; Jewish men were not supposed to speak with Samaritan women (4:9, 27), seemingly,[3] and Jewish rabbis (4:31) were not supposed to speak in public with any kind of woman.[4] Jesus breaches this double boundary by engaging the Samaritan woman in dialogue.

In addition to O'Day, at least two other feminist biblical scholars, Regina St. G. Plunkett and Sandra M. Schneiders, have recently advanced readings of this scene (Plunkett 1988; Schneiders 1991, 180–99). Despite substantial differences of approach, the common burden of all three readings has been to redress the ill-treatment that the Samaritan woman has endured at the hands of male interpreters. The issue centers on Jesus' "prophetic" declaration to the

---

3. C. K. Barrett cites the talmudic tractate *Niddah* in support of this view: "The daughters of the Samaritans are menstruants from their cradle [i.e., perpetually unclean]" (*Niddah* 4.1, quoted in Barrett 1978, 232).

4. For the relevant rabbinic sources, see Barrett 1978, 240.

woman, "You have had five husbands, and the one you have now is not your husband" (4:18; cf. 4:19). Should this declaration be taken *literally,* that is, as a statement about an irregular marital and sexual career (which is how the implications of the literal reading have almost invariably been construed)?[5] This reading has resulted in an exceedingly long litany of disapproving or dismissive comments on the woman, ranging, in modern times, from Theodor Zahn's reference to her "immoral life, which has exhibited profligacy and unbridled passions for a long time" (1921, 244), to Paul Duke's description of her as "a five-time loser … currently committed to an illicit affair" (1985, 102).[6] Or should the verse be read *figuratively* instead, that is, as a statement about the religious infidelity of Samaria itself, represented here by the woman? Samaria had worshiped the gods of five foreign tribes (cf. 2 Kgs 17:13–34) and apparently its current Yahwism was also adulterated ("the one you have now is not your husband"). This has been the dominant form of the figurative or symbolic reading.

What might deconstruction contribute to this debate? At least two insights. First, deconstruction tends to work with the heuristic assumption that the literary text is capable of deftly turning the tables on the critic who sets out to master it. The critic, while appearing to grasp the meaning of the text from a position safely outside or above it, has unknowingly been grasped by the text and pulled into it. He or she is unwittingly acting out an interpretive role that the text has scripted in advance. As Shoshana Felman puts it, introducing a highly effective demonstration of such conscription: "The scene of the critical debate is thus a repetition of the scene dramatized in the text. The critical interpretation, in other words, not only elucidates the text but also reproduces it dramatically, unwittingly *participates in it*. Through its very reading, the text, so to speak, acts itself out" (1982, 101, her emphasis).[7]

---

5. O'Day, however, questions this common construal: "The text does not say … that the woman has been divorced five times but that she has had five husbands. There are many possible reasons for the woman's marital history.… Perhaps the woman, like Tamar in Genesis 38, is trapped in the custom of levirate marriage and the last male in the family line has refused to marry her" (1992, 296).

6. Others assume more generally that Jesus is "lay[ing] bare the woman's sin" (Hoskyns 1947, 242), that he has "exposed her bawdy past" (Staley 1988, 101) or her "immoral life" (Beasley-Murray 1987, 61), that she is "wayward" (Schnackenburg 1968, 433), "of low morals" (Olsson 1974, 120), "markedly immoral" and a doer of "evil deeds" (Brown 1966, 171, 177), or guilty of "loose living" (Dodd 1968, 313). Lyle Eslinger goes even further, arguing that the woman, whom he calls "coquettish," "coy," "lascivious," "brazen," and "carnal," makes "sexual advances" to Jesus (1987, 171, 177–78).

7. Felman's text is Henry James's *The Turn of the Screw.* For similar quotations from

How might this apply to our scene? The majority of Johannine commentators have preferred the literal reading of 4:18 to the figurative one. They have included such authorities as C. K. Barrett (1978, 235), G. R. Beasley-Murray (1987, 61), Raymond Brown (1966, 171), Rudolf Bultmann (1971, 187), Ernst Haenchen (1984, 221), Barnabas Lindars (1972, 185), and Rudolf Schnackenburg (1968, 433). At the same time, these commentators have scrupulously noted the repeated failure of the woman to grasp the nonliteral nature of Jesus' discourse. In opting to take Jesus' statement in 4:18 at face value, then, they effectively trade places with the woman. They reenact what they purport to be describing. They mimic the literal-mindedness that marks her as inferior in their eyes. The standard reading of 4:18 conceals a double standard, then. To interpret Jesus literally is a failing when the woman does it, but not when the commentators follow suit. This double standard is, however, also a double bind. They can condemn her only if they participate in her error, can ascribe a history of immorality to her only by reading as "carnally" as she does—at which point the literal reading of 4:18 threatens to become a displaced reenactment of yet another Johannine episode, one in which another unnamed woman is similarly charged with sexual immorality by accusers who themselves stand accused (8:1–11).

Let us move on to a second, more substantial contribution that deconstruction can make to the nascent feminist debate on John 4. Traditionally, commentators have tended to view the Samaritan woman's literal-minded responses to Jesus' pronouncements as a rich example of Johannine irony. Tellingly, Sandra Schneiders makes no mention whatsoever of irony in her feminist reading of John 4:1–42 (1991, 180–99), nor does Gail O'Day in her own reading of it in her *Women's Bible Commentary* essay on John (O'Day 1992), even though her earlier study of the episode in her book, *Revelation in the Fourth Gospel*, was precisely a study of its irony (1986, 49–92). And Regina Plunkett (1988) has argued that, contrary to appearances, the Samaritan woman is not in fact a victim of irony. The term "victim" is significant here. Recent feminist readers of John 4:1–42 have been countering a traditional tendency on the part of male commentators to victimize the Samaritan woman—to reduce her to a sexual stereotype, to patronize her for her intellectual "inferiority"[8]—thereby providing yet another biblical warrant for the unequal treatment of

---

Jacques Derrida, Paul de Man, J. Hillis Miller, and Barbara Johnson, and for a discussion of Mark and its interpreters from this perspective, see Moore 1992, 28–38.

8. Examples of the latter tendency also abound; two will suffice to give the general idea. Dodd remarks on 4:15 that the woman, "as usual, fails to understand," indicating "a crass inability to penetrate below the surface meaning" (1968, 313). For Beasley-Murray, too, at this point, "the woman's misunderstanding becomes crass" (1987, 61).

contemporary women in the church, the academy, and society at large (cf. Schneiders 1991, 188; O'Day 1992, 296). The challenge would seem to be that of showing that the Samaritan woman is indeed a worthy conversation partner for Jesus, and this O'Day, Plunkett, and Schneiders undertake to do, each in her own way.[9] "The woman is the first character in the Gospel to engage in serious theological conversation with Jesus," concludes O'Day (1992, 296).

What remains unquestioned, however, in these readings is Jesus' own superiority to the Samaritan woman. He retains his privileged role as the dispenser of knowledge—"the subject presumed to know," as Jacques Lacan would say (1977a, 232–33)—while the woman retains her traditional role as the compliant recipient of knowledge, a container as empty as her water jar, waiting to be filled. The hierarchical opposition of male and female—the male in the missionary position, the female beneath—remains essentially undisturbed. And as long as that hierarchy remains intact, Jesus' boundary-breaching activity and challenge to the status quo in this episode, while not inconsequential, remains a minor tremor rather than a major upheaval. But what if the Samaritan woman were found to be the more enlightened partner in the dialogue from the outset? What if her insight were found to exceed that of Jesus all along? Impossible? Not at all, as I hope to show.

The Hydraulics of a Liquid Metaphor

> We will not, as do positive historians, account for all that could have flowed into this text *from the outside*. (Derrida 1982, 275, his emphasis)

The issue in John 4:7–15 can be refocused as follows. Two kinds of water, literal and figurative, slosh around in the Samaritan woman's head, it would seem, mingling where they should not (vv. 11–12, 15). For me, however, the real question is whether Jesus himself can keep the living water pure and clear, uncontaminated by the profane drinking water. To discover the answer we shall have to track the course of this water downstream. It flows underground through the Gospel, for the most part, surfacing again only in chapters 7 and 19. To these water-stained pages we now turn.

On the last day of the Feast of Tabernacles, "the great day," Jesus again speaks of thirst, drinking, and the supramundane living water: "As the scripture has said, 'Out of his heart [lit. belly] shall flow rivers of living water

---

9. This is also the task that Teresa Okure takes on, as we shall see. She accepts the majority reading of 4:18, however, as a disclosure by Jesus of the woman's sinfulness, although she argues that his purpose is simply "to let her know that [he] possesses supernatural knowledge," not to confront her with her guilt (1988, 110–11).

[*potamoi ek tēs koilias autou rheusousin hydatos zōntos*]'" (7:38). Out of whose heart? Jesus' heart or that of the believer? The earlier exchange at the well would seem to authorize either reading. In 4:10 Jesus gestured to himself as the source of the living water. Rivers of living water might therefore be said to flow out of him. But he added that once the believer has drunk of this water, it becomes a spring in him or her "gushing up to eternal life" (4:14). Rivers of living water can also be said to flow out of the believer, then—but only if the believer has first been filled with the water that issues forth from Jesus. The believer is more than a mere receptacle for surplus water, therefore, an overflow; rather, he or she is a channel, or conduit, in his or her own right.[10]

Let us return to the Feast of the Tabernacles. We may still be in time to see the procession enter through the Water Gate and the priest pour out the daily water libation. Surrounded by so much water we cannot refrain from asking, Is Jesus really the origin of the living water in the Fourth Gospel? Is he the spring, the source, from which it flows? As we have seen, Jesus attempts to authorize himself as the source by appealing to scripture ("As the scripture has said [*kathōs eipen hē graphē*]..."). In so doing, however, he inadvertently creates a rival. Might this scriptural verse not itself be the real source of the living water imagery in the Fourth Gospel, the water that first springs up in the course of Jesus' discourse at the Samaritan well (4:10)? In that case, Jesus would himself be a mere conduit for a stream that originated elsewhere, that flowed into this Gospel from outside it. But if this verse *is* the source of the living water in the Fourth Gospel, it is a hidden source. The words "quoted" by Jesus have no exact parallel either in the Masoretic Text or the Septuagint. Equipped with divining rods, Johannine scholars have combed all the relevant fields, ranging from the Jewish scriptures and the rabbinic commentaries to the parched desert region of the Dead Sea Scrolls, but their findings have been inconclusive at best (for details, see Beasley-Murray 1987, 116–17).

This particular source-hunt can be considered paradigmatic of the many source-hunts of historical criticism. The elusive source-text in this instance is itself *about* a source, a water-source ("Out of his belly shall flow rivers of living water"), and a highly elusive source at that, if the owner of the belly is Jesus.[11] In the preceding scene, the text has Jesus say to those who would seize him,

---

10. Deconstruction is "very interested in reading the logic of metaphors, absolutely literally," as Gayatri Chakravorty Spivak explains (1990a, 164). In the present context this will take the form of swimming with the current of the Johannine water imagery and seeing where it takes us. And it will involve writing a critical text that is itself saturated with water images.

11. The belly may also belong to the believer, as we saw, in which case Jesus and the believer would be conjoined twins.

"You will search for me, but you will not find me" (7:34, 36; cf. 8:21; 13:33). Once again, the text has thematized and dramatized its own reception, the commentators *on* the text inadvertently taking up positions *within* the text. Those who search for the source find neither him nor it.

To the reintroduction of the figure of living water in 7:38 the Johannine narrator adds an important gloss: he interprets the figure as being "about the Spirit, which believers in him [Jesus] were to receive" (7:39). The narrative depiction of that reception is deferred, however: "As yet there was no Spirit [*oupō gar ēn pneuma*], because Jesus was not yet glorified" (7:39).[12] And Jesus' glorification will be interpreted in turn as the hour of his exaltation on the cross, an exaltation that will prefigure his resurrection (12:23–24, 28; 13:31–32; 17:1, 5; cf. 3:14; 12:32).

Capsizing the Oppositions

The motifs of thirst and drinking well up once again as Jesus hangs dying on the cross. More precisely, it is *desire* that wells up, ostensibly desire for a drink. "I thirst," cries the source of the living water (19:28), and we are back once again at the well ("Give me a drink"—4:7).[13] Again it is about the sixth hour (4:6; 19:14; Lightfoot 1956, 122), and again Jesus needs more than just a drink. Recall that in the scene at the Samaritan well, Jesus' real desire was to complete the desire of the woman, to fill up that which she lacked. In the crucifixion scene, we can safely assume that Jesus is physically thirsty, as in 4:7, but the context likewise suggests a more consuming thirst. According to the narrator, Jesus announces his thirst "in order to fulfill the scripture [*hina teleiōthē hē graphē*]." Here, as at Cana (2:6–10), well water has been replaced with wine (19:29). And it has sometimes been asked whether this sour wine or vinegar (*oxos*) offered to Jesus would not have aggravated his thirst rather than quenched it.[14] But his deeper thirst *is* assuaged, nonetheless. What is essential is that the drink be drawn from scripture ("He said in order to fulfill the scripture, 'I am thirsty'"), and assuredly this one is (see Ps 69[68]:22, LXX: "for my thirst they gave me *oxos*"). Having accepted the drink Jesus announces "It is finished" and promptly expires (19:30). He has

---

12. On which see Kelber 1990, 88. It was Kelber who initially prompted me to track the course of the living water through John 4, 7, and 19.

13. R. H. Lightfoot appears to have been one of the first critical commentators to note this connection. John 4:7 and 19:28 beg comparison, "these being the only two passages in John which allude to thirst on [Jesus'] part" (1956, 122).

14. "If this was so one wonders why the soldiers drank it," Barrett sensibly responds (1978, 553).

fulfilled the scripture, completed it, made up what was lacking in it.[15] The following homology emerges: as the wine is to the well water, so is scripture to the Samaritan woman, Jesus' desire drifting between all four terms. But in bringing his desire to completion, has Jesus allowed common *oxos*, "the inferior popular drink" (Schnackenburg 1968, 283), to mingle with the living water, thereby compromising its purity? It is time we tested a sample of this living water.

Announcing "It is finished," Jesus yields up—what? His spirit? The Spirit? (The Greek simply has *to pneuma*, which could mean either.) The Spirit is not *formally* handed over until 20:22: "He breathed on them and said to them, 'Receive the Holy Spirit.'" We need not drop "Spirit" from our reading of 19:30 on that account, however; both meanings can be kept in the air simultaneously. This in fact is what Raymond Brown does, taking *to pneuma* in 19:30 to be yet another Johannine double entendre: "In vii 39 John affirmed that those who believed in Jesus were to receive the Spirit once Jesus had been glorified, and so it would not be inappropriate that at this climactic moment in the hour of glorification there would be a symbolic reference to the giving of the Spirit.... This symbolic reference is evocative and *proleptic*, reminding the reader of the *ultimate* purpose for which Jesus has been lifted up on the cross" (1970, 931, his emphasis).

We are now in a position to capsize the hierarchical opposition that earlier established the parameters of the dialogue between Jesus and the Samaritan woman, that between literal and living water, an opposition closely linked to several others, as we saw, such as spiritual/material, heavenly/earthly, and even male/female, given the context. As Jesus hangs dying on the cross, these hierarchies are teetering, about to topple over, needing only the slightest push. Having requested a last drink, as prescribed by scripture, Jesus announces "It is completed," after which he expires and surrenders the *pneuma* (his spirit/ the Spirit). The satiation of Jesus' *physical* thirst, therefore, is the necessary precondition for the proleptic yielding up of that which is intended to satiate the *spiritual* thirst of the believer, namely, the Holy Spirit (see 7:37–39; cf. 4:10, 13–14). But it is an arrestingly strange precondition (cf. Kelber 1990, 88). In the dialogue at the Samaritan well, the earthly, material, literal level, represented by the thirst for spring water, was declared superseded by a heavenly,

---

15. In place of the more usual *plēroō* (e.g., 19:24, 36), John uses *teleioō* here for "fulfill (scripture)." Since John also uses *teleioō* for the completion of Jesus' work (e.g., 17:4, 23; cf. 19:30), several commentators have suggested that its use in 19:28 means that scripture is brought to complete fulfillment as Jesus dies (e.g., Brown 1970, 908–9). Interestingly, *teleioō* is also used of the completion of Jesus' work in the discourse at the well (4:34). Lightfoot connects 4:34 with 19:30 (1956, 122), as does Schnackenburg (1982, 283).

spiritual reality, represented by the living water, and summarily thrust into the background. But this material, literal domain is curiously reinstated at the hour of Jesus' glorification, again in the form of physical thirst, now decreed by scripture, and coupled with physical death. The repressed has made a forceful return. The material order has reasserted itself as the necessary precondition that enables the Spirit, emblem and emissary of the spiritual order (cf. 14:16–17, 26; 15:26; 16:13–15), to come into being for believers (cf. 7:39: "For as yet there was no Spirit, because Jesus was not yet glorified").[16] The hierarchical opposition established at the well is inverted at the cross, the ostensibly superior, pleromatic term (living water, Spirit) being shown to depend for its effective existence on the ostensibly inferior, insufficient term (literal well water), contrary to everything that the narrative has led us to expect up to this point. "What is born of the flesh is flesh," as Jesus confidently summarizes the issue for Nicodemus, "and what is born of the Spirit is spirit" (3:6).[17]

DROWNING THE OPPOSITIONS

To content oneself simply with *overturning* a hierarchical opposition, however, "is still to operate on the terrain of and from within the deconstructed system," according to Derrida (1981c, 42). It is still to think in dualistic, hierarchical categories, even if what was once face up is now face down, even if the opposition is now floating on its belly instead of its back. It is to continue to reside "within the closed field of these oppositions," thereby confirming its tenacity and reifying its authority (1981c, 42). A second phase is therefore necessary in the deconstructive operation, one that would entail "the irruptive emergence of a new 'concept,' a concept that can no longer be, and never could be, included in the previous regime," that would inhabit the hierarchical opposition only to resist, paralyze and incapacitate it (1981c, 42–43).[18]

---

16. As has often been remarked, no distinction is made between ontology and soteriology in 7:39b, the Spirit being presented as though it had no effective existence prior to Jesus' glorification (notwithstanding 1:32, "I saw the Spirit descend ... and it remained on him"). See further Hooke 1962–63.

17. See also 1:13; 3:31; 4:13–14, 24, 33–34; 6:26–27, 31–33, 49–50, 58, 63; 8:23; 12:25; and 17:2.

18. Derrida's term for these subversive concepts is "undecidables" (1981c, 42–43), as each of them has "a double, contradictory, undecidable value" (1981a, 221). He makes extensive use of them to read against the grain of the Western philosophical tradition, and Western culture in general, which has invested so heavily in hierarchical binary oppositions: transcendent/immanent, intelligible/sensible, spirit-mind-soul/body, presence/absence, necessary/contingent, primary/secondary, nature/culture, human/animal, male/female, masculine/feminine, heterosexual/homosexual, normal/abnormal, sane/insane,

Sure enough, as if on cue, such a concept makes its appearance immediately after the scene we have been discussing. The proleptic yielding up of the Spirit ("he gave up the *pneuma*"), which is to say the living water (cf. 7:39), is followed by the reemergence of material water, long gone underground, as Jesus' side is pierced and blood and water issue forth (19:34). "Here the paradoxical thing is not the blood but the water" (Bultmann 1971, 678 n. 1), and the latter has provoked a stream of supraliteral interpretations down through the ages, the modern rationalizations of pathologists and surgeons (e.g., Edwards, Gabel, and Hosmer 1986) doing nothing to staunch the flow. Some connection between the water discourse of 7:37–39 and the stream of water in 19:34 has often been suggested (e.g., Hoskyns 1947, 532; Dodd 1968, 428; Bultmann 1971, 678 n. 1; Barrett 1978, 556; and esp. Brown 1970, 949–50). Intermingled with the former passage, as we have seen, are the water libations that formed part of the ritual of Tabernacles. Given the association of earthly water with living water and the Spirit, therefore, not only in the Tabernacles discourse and the dialogue at the Samaritan well but also in the dialogue with Nicodemus (3:5), the flow of water from Jesus' side can be read as, among other things, a further token of the promised living water or Spirit, which has now become available through Jesus' glorification. That leaves us with a symbol (the flow of water) of a metaphor (living water) for the Spirit.[19]

When water reappears in this Gospel from an unexpected quarter, therefore—Jesus' side—following an extended drought, it is as an "undecidable" term that fills the literal and figurative categories or containers simultaneously, along with the material and spiritual containers and the earthly and heavenly containers, in such a way as to flood these hierarchical structures and put them temporarily out of commission. Let me attempt to clarify this statement by retracing the stream yet again. At the Samaritan well, literal earthly water was declared superseded by figurative living water (4:13–14), which was later interpreted as the Holy Spirit (7:39), which has now become

---

conscious/unconscious, religion/superstition, white/black-brown-red-yellow, inside/outside, central/marginal, object/representation, objective/subjective, history/fiction, serious/trivial, literal/metaphorical, content/form, original/copy, text/interpretation, speech/writing, etc. For extended practical examples of his strategy, see Derrida 1976, 141–64; 1981a, 61–171. It entails demonstrating that the border separating the two terms in a hierarchical opposition is an arbitrary, artificial one rather than a natural, inevitable one, and as such can always be redrawn.

19. Taking "symbol" in its simplest sense as "a visible token of something other than itself" (Barrett 1982c, 66). Equally simply, I am taking "metaphor" to denote "a transfer of meaning from the word that properly possesses it to another word which belongs to some shared category of meaning" (McLaughlin 1990, 83).

available through Jesus' death as symbolized both by his giving up the *pneuma* as he expires (19:30) and by the fresh flow of water from his side (19:34). But this water is neither simply material and literal, since it is symbolic, nor fully spiritual and figurative, since it is physical. It is a spiritual material and a literal figure. Literality and figurality intermingle in the flow from Jesus' side, each contaminating the other, which is to say that we cannot keep the literal clearly separate from the figurative in the end.

Significantly, the water that dissolves this distinction is part of Jesus' own body, as much a part of his body as his blood ("at once blood and water came out"), and Jesus' body is a site of paradox throughout the Fourth Gospel. As C. K. Barrett rightly remarks in an intriguing essay on the latter topic, "The paradox of the [Johannine] Son of Man is that even when on earth he is in heaven; … effectively the Son of Man is in both places at once" (1982b, 110–11). Indeed, it is because he inhabits both realms simultaneously, manifesting the unknowable otherness of God in finite flesh (cf. 1:18), that he makes communication between the two realms possible (cf. 1:51; Barrett 1982b, 110, 113). He dissolves the partition between heaven and earth, spirit and matter, figure and letter. He is not "a physical mixture, of which the elements may be separated out," so much as "a chemical compound, where the compounding elements have combined to form a new substance" (1982b, 105).[20] But he himself fails to see that he is a chemical compound. Mistaking his place on the table of elements, he speaks to the Samaritan woman and all his other interlocutors as though he *were* a mixture composed of separable elements, as though the living water *could* be cleanly distinguished from spring water, the bread of life from common bread, the figurative from the literal, the spiritual from the material, and the heavenly from the earthly. What Jesus *says* is contradicted by what he *is*.

The Erosion of Johannine Irony

But what Jesus *is* is affirmed by what the Samaritan woman *says*. The distinction between the material and the spiritual is no sooner made by Jesus than it is muddied by the woman. Jesus carefully distinguishes the spring water from the living water, to which she replies: "Sir, give me this water, that I may never be thirsty"—it would seem the denarius has finally dropped—"*or have to keep coming here to draw water* [*mēde dierchōmai enthade antlein*]" (4:15). "The woman has not moved with Jesus!" exclaims O'Day, echoing the response of countless other commentators. "She has understood his words in part, that his water is better than the water in Jacob's well, but she does not understand why.

---

20. "Christ is the absolute hybrid," claims Jean Soler (quoted in Crossan 1982, 34).

She interprets Jesus' words about the quenching of thirst as referring solely to physical thirst, and requests the gift of water from Jesus so that she will no longer be obliged to come to the well to draw water" (1986, 64). But can we really be so sure that the water on which the woman's mind is set is material and literal only?

The exchange between Jesus and the woman is conducted under the eyes of the police. "Give me a drink," says Jesus, and the Law responds, "How is it that you, a Jew…?" (4:7, 9). "From the dawn of history," notes Lacan, patriarchal culture has identified the person of the Father "with the figure of the law" (1977a, 67). But there is more than one Father in this scene.

Jesus' own Father is nearby, needless to say. Jesus gestures to him in 4:23, giving expression to the Father's desire ("such the Father seeks to worship him"). But the woman points to a different father, or rather, to different fathers. First there is "our father Jacob, who gave us the well, and with his sons and his flocks drank from it" (4:12). Then there are "our fathers" who "worshiped on this mountain" (4:20). The woman's own identity would seem to be closely bound up with the legacy and customs of these fathers. Teresa Okure is unusually sensitive to this fact. Here is a catena of the passages in which she mentions it:

> For the woman, the well is a living testimony to her people's descent from Jacob…. She compares [Jesus] to Jacob, the giver of the well whose water, in her view, Jesus seems to slight. Her reply in vv 11–12 is, in effect, a defense of the ancestral water. Not only does Jesus' offer of living water appear ridiculous to the woman, but as far as she is concerned, no water can be better than that of Jacob's well…. This is not just any well, but one that is renowned for its antiquity and whose usage goes back to the founding father himself: he, his family and all his livestock drank from it; so did generations after him. Yet despite the centuries of use, the well has neither dried up nor become exhausted. Thus, in addition to its revered ancestry, the well has a character which is almost eternal. Can Jesus, then, possibly produce anything better? (1988, 89, 99, 100)

The woman's well water now has begun to sound a good deal less like a crude dilution of Jesus' living water. "The well is deep," as she says (4:11). Blend Okure's remarks with those of Schnackenburg: "Water provides almost endless symbolism for the Oriental, to whom it appears as the most indispensable factor in life—purifying, stilling thirst, giving and renewing life and fruitfulness—which could easily be applied to the higher needs and blessings of man" (1968, 427). It begins to sound as though the water bubbling up from Jacob's well is, for the woman, more than something with which to satisfy a physical need. Indeed, it has begun to sound more and more like the water

4. ARE THERE IMPURITIES IN THE LIVING WATER?

that will later flow from Jesus' side. It is not simply literal nor is it purely figurative. Another literal figure, it overflows both containers.

The reader arrives at the cross, then, only to be returned, in effect, to the well, carried by the current of a stream that flows equally between literality and figurality. As such, the narrative has forced a "sublime simplicity" on us that it led us earlier to transcend[21]—that of the woman of Samaria who desired the living water so that she might no longer have to come to the well to draw, but also that of Nicodemus perplexed that he should have to reenter his mother's womb in order to be born anew (3:4), that of the crowd who would fill their bellies with the imperishable bread (6:26-27, 34), and that of the puzzled disciples unable to distinguish plain speech from figurative (cf. 16:25, 29). In each case, two levels of meaning are collapsed that should have been kept apart. The ironic structure that positioned us on a level above these characters depended on our being able to keep the literal and figurative levels clearly separate. But the events of the death scene have collapsed the levels, disallowing their separation. Irony—which depended on the clean separation of flesh and glory, earthly and heavenly, material and spiritual, literal and figurative, water and "water"—now collapses in paradox (cf. Kelber 1990, 89).[22]

In the process, that other hierarchical structure within which Jesus and the Samaritan woman conversed has also suffered some water damage. I refer, of course, to the hierarchy of male over female. If what Jesus has *said* to the Samaritan woman is indeed contradicted by what he *is*, and if what Jesus *is* has indeed been affirmed by what she has *said*, then the female student has outstripped her male teacher, even though he himself was the subject of their seminar. She has insisted, in effect, that earthly and heavenly, flesh and Spirit, and figurative and literal are symbiotically related categories: each drinks endlessly of the other, and so each is endlessly contaminated by the other. To draw a clear line between them, as Jesus attempts to do, is about as effective as drawing a line on water.[23]

---

21. The term "sublime simplicity," used in this way, is borrowed from Paul de Man (1979, 9). De Man's deconstructive analyses of the intricate operations of figural language in literary texts form a further model for my reading of the Johannine living water motif in this essay.

22. This is similar to Jeffrey Staley's claim that the implied reader of the Fourth Gospel is occasionally the victim of its irony (1988, 95-118), except that in my reading it is the implied author, the narrator and the protagonist (i.e., the Johannine Jesus) who are the main ironic casualties.

23. This is to say that our deconstruction of the hierarchical opposition spiritual/material has resulted in an inversion of the hierarchical opposition male/female. This inverted

God's Desire

Earlier I argued that the flow of water from Jesus' side can be read as, among other things, a further token of the promised living water or Spirit that has now become available through Jesus' death, leaving us with a symbol (the flow of water) of a metaphor (living water) for the Spirit. But does this figurative waterslide come to a halt with the Spirit? What if the Spirit were itself a substitute for something else? Sounding uncannily Derridean, Raymond Brown defines the Johannine Paraclete as "another Jesus," "the presence of Jesus when Jesus is absent" with the Father (1970, 1141).

Tracing the water imagery upstream, therefore, we arrive at its apparent source. Contrary to what one might expect, Jesus himself is not that source. The stream does not issue from Jesus' presence; rather, it is from Jesus' *absence* that it flows. The time in which the Fourth Evangelist is writing is the time of the Paraclete (cf. 14:26; 15:26; 16:7–15; 20:22–23), a time when Jesus is away with the Father (cf. Porsch 1974, esp. 242). And absence is the source of desire. The water imagery in John is a river of desire, then; it issues from the Fourth Evangelist, although it cannot be said to have originated with him.

But neither can this river of desire be said to empty into Jesus. For Jesus too is driven by desire, carried along in its current, until he reunites with his Father in death, as a river reunites with the sea from which it sprang. The Father is the ultimate object of Jesus' desire in the Fourth Gospel. But even the Father is not free of desire. It was to accomplish the Father's *thelēma* (will, wish, desire) that the Son was sent into the world (4:34; 5:30; 6:38; 7:16; 8:28, 42; 12:49; 14:10, 24; 15:10; 17:4). And so the sea into which the river finally empties itself is a chasm hollowed out by desire—the Father's desire to be the desire of the Son and those whom he draws to himself through the Son (6:44, 65; cf. 12:32; 17:20–26). As Lacan has insightfully remarked, what distinguishes both the Jewish and Christian traditions from most Asian religious traditions is that the former turn not on God's "bliss" (*jouissance*) but on God's desire (1990, 89–90; cf. 1981, 323ff.). God's desire is a black hole that slowly draws the Johannine cosmos into it.[24]

For many who have written on the scene at the Samaritan well, the woman's oblivion to her own need, assumed to be so much greater than that

---

opposition could, of course, be deconstructed in its turn, should space permit it or strategy require it.

24. This would be my reply to Hendrikus Boers, apropos of the Fourth Gospel, when he writes: "It has always been my interest to discover a kind of metaphysics of New Testament texts. I want to know what holds the text together from its inside" (1988, xv).

of Jesus, is the pivot on which the irony of their dialogue turns. Deeper by far, however, is the irony that Jesus' own need—not to mention that of his Father—is just as great as the woman's. "The well is deep," as the woman says (4:11). Desire, however, is bottomless.

5
THE QUEST OF THE NEW HISTORICIST JESUS*

Co-authored with Susan Lochrie Graham

This essay—a collaborative venture with Susan Lochrie Graham, and, among other things, an experiment in authorial voice—was written for a thematic issue of the journal *Biblical Interpretation* on New Historicism (see Moore 1997). The headnote to the previous essay spoke of the simultaneous poststructuralization and politicization of U.S. literary studies in the 1980s. Arguably, New Historicism was one of the two most visible products of that synthesis (the other being colonial discourse analysis, later renamed postcolonial theory, and the subject of ch. 13 below). At base, New Historicism was an attempt to press positivist historiography through a poststructuralist wringer. Officially, the brand name on the wringer was Foucault's, and certainly Foucault's dystopian conception of power as ubiquitous and nontranscendable permeates the New Historicist mindset, obsessed as it also is with power, as the essay explains. But whereas Foucauldian New Historicism was regularly pitted against Derridean deconstruction in the halcyon days of American high theory, in hindsight New Historicism itself seems singularly deconstructive in its dual preoccupation with textuality and historicity—"the historicity of texts and the textuality of history," as one of its most frequently intoned formulae phrases it (Montrose 1989, 20). As such, New Historicism was a very different enterprise than biblical historical criticism, as this essay sets out to show. What the essay also reveals is the extent to which New Historicism was preoccupied with early modern European colonialism, even before the emergence into prominence of postcolonial studies. In my view, New

---

First published in *Biblical Interpretation* 5 (1997): 437–63.

Historicism is a significant potential resource, largely untapped as yet, for postcolonial biblical criticism.

Essentially in this essay, Susan and I are attempting to read the putative charter document of New Historicism, Stephen Greenblatt's *Renaissance Self-Fashioning* (1980), as an inadvertent but incisive commentary on the seminal text of the Third Quest, John Dominic Crossan's *The Historical Jesus* (1991). The abstract we composed for the piece was nothing if not brash. We announced:

> Our ambition in this article is to use the New Historicism as a spade with which to open up the grave where John Dominic Crossan's historical Jesus was unceremoniously dumped, exhuming certain assumptions buried there in the process. As we dig and sieve the contents of this burial site ("Why do you seek the living among the dead? He is not here"), we uncover a rock-hewn tomb from which to summon a shadowy protean figure shrouded in contingency—a New Historicist Jesus.

Certainly we summoned him; but did he actually come?

He comes to us as One unknown, without a name, as of old.... (Schweitzer 1968 [1906], 403)

He comes as yet unknown into a hamlet of Lower Galilee. (Crossan 1991, xi)

¶1. I[a] propose to frame certain texts, ancient and modern, of which Jesus of Nazareth is now composed, with a certain set of questions ripped from a second set of texts, those of the New Historicists.[b] Yet another paper incarnation of the Nazarene, more crumpled and torn than most, will float across your field of vision. But that will not lessen my longing to behold him, or even to

---

a. The "I" is always something of a fiction, don't you find? Especially the academic "I." And doubly so in this instance.

b. Will the questions violently torn from these texts resent their transportation into the scorching Judean landscape (which is where they will mainly find themselves)? Will they repay the discomfort by torturing the texts they interrogate, forcing them to confess to indecent acts they would rather have denied? And will these reprobate texts be redeemed through the agony of being stretched on my reading frame? The danger is that having completed their task, the questions will then turn on me in the same fashion and with the same results.

5. THE QUEST OF THE NEW HISTORICIST JESUS

hold him; for this paper—this paper Jesus—began with a desire to speak with the dead (cf. Greenblatt 1988,1). The flimsy handful of questions used for my framework does not exhaust the questions New Historicism might raise about the current quest for the Nazarene, I need hardly add, any more than **John Dominic Crossan's *The Historical Jesus*** (upon whose broad peasant shoulders my own Jesus will be content to ride until he is able to stand on his own two feet) exhausts the results of that quest. But you may find, unless you play differently, that the answers are always the same.^c

¶2. "Marlowe and the Will to Absolute Play," the penultimate chapter of Stephen Greenblatt's seminal New Historicist study, *Renaissance Self-Fashioning* (1980, 193–221), "moves through five moments," as H. Aram Veeser observes in his provocative introduction to *The New Historicism Reader* (1994, 5). Each of these moments, each of these moves, can arguably be said to be exemplary of New Historicist strategy. They are: **anecdote, outrage, resistance, containment,** and **autobiography**.¹

¶3. Greenblatt typically leads off a chapter or essay with a historical anecdote. So do other New Historicists, but **the inaugural anecdote** is something of a Greenblattian trademark nonetheless, employed with faint restraint in his earlier work, but with abject abandon in his later work. Three of the six chapters of *Renaissance Self-Fashioning* open with an anecdote, as do five of the eight essays of *Learning to Curse* (a collection spanning the years 1976 to 1990), but all four chapters of *Shakespearean Negotiations* (1988)² are launched with an anecdote, while the introduction to *Marvelous Possessions* contains the following admission: "It will not escape anyone who reads this book that my chapters are constructed largely around anecdotes, what the French call *petites histoires*, as distinct from the *grands récits* of totalizing, integrated, progressive history, a history that knows where it is going" (1991, 2). An endnote appended to this statement refers us, significantly, to Joel Fineman's "The History of the Anecdote" (Fineman 1989).³ For if Greenblatt was the first New Historicist to deploy the anecdote determinedly, Fineman was the first New Historicist to theorize its deployment thoroughly. The exemplary anecdote, for Fineman, would be a spanner in the works of the "old" historicists. It would introduce an opening into the teleological (and frequently theological), epic-addicted traditions of historiography. It would mark **an irruption of**

---

c. Some explanation of the rules of the game is, perhaps, in order. You play by reading, but it is a writing game. You must resist as you read, but resist differently. Refuse to follow my order(s). Read associatively, in fragments. I have been so **bold** as to suggest some paths for you to follow, some fingers pointing the way. Mine is an electronic Jesus, freed by the logic of hypertext, and you may find your lost freedom there, too. There are other rules also, of course, but we will make them up as we go along.

the contingent, the inexplicable, the unassimilable into these tightly plotted histories.

¶4. Greenblatt supplies a searing example of such anecdotal subversion in his introduction to *Learning to Curse* (1990, 11–12). This grisly anecdote exhumed from the archives is credited to a certain Edmund Scott, principal agent for the East India Company in Bantam, Java, from 1603 through 1605. It tells of his treatment of an unnamed Chinese goldsmith whom he suspected of theft. With chilling matter-of-factness, Scott relates how he had the man "burned under the nails of his thumbs, fingers, and toes with sharp, hot iron," after which the nails themselves were torn out; how he had the man's sinews ripped out "with rasps of iron"; had all his fingers and toes mangled with pincers; and so on.[4]

¶5. What is one to do with such an account? wonders Greenblatt.[d] What is "history" to make of it? Like a severed body part wrapped up as **a ghastly gift, this anecdote** arrived on Greenblatt's desk prepackaged. The outermost layer of wrapping was supplied by the Haklyut Society, which in 1943 reprinted *The Voyage of Sir Henry Middleton to the Moluccas, 1604–1606*, which in turn quotes the above anecdote from Edmund Scott's 1606 tome, *Exact Discourse of the Subtilities, Fashions, Pollicies, Religion, and Ceremonies of the East Indians* (see Foster 1943, 121–22). Greenblatt notes how the Haklyut Society editor, Sir William Foster, passes over this festering fragment, this bit that will not fit, in silence.[e] Sir William styles Scott's *Exact Discourse* "an epic story of a grim struggle against disease and dangers of many descriptions, sustained by a dogged determination to keep the flag flying at all costs" (the year, remember, is 1943). Scott's "proudest boast," continues Sir William, "is that, small as were the resources of the English, they yet won and kept the good opinion of the Asiatics by whom they were surrounded, at the same time maintaining the honour of their sovereign and the good name of their country" (1943, xxxix–xl).

¶6. Are there first-century analogues to this anecdotal undermining of a rousing historical *grand récit*? At least one immediately leaps to mind, the anecdote of the cannibal mother from **Josephus's *Jewish War***. Let us turn, then, from the clumsy patriotic pirouettes of a twentieth-century aristocratic

---

d. Not much **outrage** here.

e. Greenblatt seems to find the silence of the editor of the modern reprint more reprehensible than the physical torture: "The moral stupidity of this drivel obviously reflects the blind patriotism of a nation besieged"(1990, 12). I, in turn, wonder what one is to do with *that*. But on with the tales of maimed and mangled bodies! Their nastiness appeals to my lewdness (and yours?), and, after all, no one actually gets hurt. But does anything actually get done?

5. THE QUEST OF THE NEW HISTORICIST JESUS   103

historian to the more intricate ideological footwork of a first-century aristocratic historian.

¶7. In the sixth book of the *Jewish War*, while describing (yet again) the frightful famine that gripped Jerusalem during the Roman siege, Josephus makes a startling announcement: he is "about to describe an act unparalleled in the history whether of Greeks or barbarians, and as horrible to relate as it is to hear" (6.199).[5] (It may also be pure invention, of course, designed by Josephus himself as a fulfillment of scriptural prophecy; cf. Deut 28:53, 56–57; 2 Kgs 6:24–29.) The anecdote (for such it turns out to be) concerns a certain Mary, once "eminent for her family and wealth" (6.201) but now reduced to starvation and desperation along with all the other denizens of the doomed city. "Pierced through her very bowels and marrow" by the famine, she "proceeded to an act of outrage upon nature [*epi tēn physin echōrei*]" (6.204). Snatching up her infant son, she exclaimed:

> "Poor babe, amidst war, famine, and sedition, why should I preserve you? With the Romans slavery awaits us, should we live till they come; but famine is forestalling slavery, and crueller than either are the rebels. Come, be my food, to the rebels an avenging fury, and to the world a tale such as alone is wanting to the calamities of the Jews." With these words she slew her son, and then, having roasted the body and devoured half of it, she covered up and stored the remainder. At once the rebels were upon her and, scenting the unholy odour, threatened her with instant death unless she produced what she had prepared. Replying that she had reserved a fine portion for them also, she disclosed the remnants of her child. Seized with instant horror and stupefaction, they stood paralysed by the sight. She, however, said, "This is my own child, and this is my handiwork. Eat, for I have had my share [*phagete, kai gar egō bebrōka*]." (6.205–210)

Declining the horrid invitation, the rebels slink away "trembling, in this one instance cowards, though scarcely yielding even this food to the mother" (6.212). In fact, continues Josephus, the "whole city," upon learning of the crime, "shuddered" as if they themselves had been the perpetrators of such horror (6.212).

¶8. The sorry tale is soon told to the besiegers; "of them some were incredulous, others were moved to pity, but the effect on the majority was to intensity their hatred of the nation" (6.214). But what of Titus, commander of the besieging army now and destined to be emperor within a decade, under whose patronage and upon whose pension Josephus is penning the *Jewish War*? What is Titus's reaction to the desperation of the starving mother? Josephus's motivation for including the anecdote in his history (beyond a desire to provide lurid entertainment for his audience) becomes apparent in the response that he crafts, or recrafts, for his hero. "As for Caesar," he begins—a title of destiny repeatedly bestowed on Titus in the *Jewish War*, causing the glory of emperorship to radiate proleptically from the brow of the general—

> he excused himself before God in this matter [*apelogeito kai peri tou tō theō*] protesting that *he* had offered the Jews peace, independence, and an amnesty for all past offences, while *they*, preferring sedition to concord, war to peace, famine to plenty and prosperity, and having been the first to set fire with their own hands to that temple which he and his army were preserving for them, were indeed deserving even of such food as this. He, however, would bury this abomination of infant-cannibalism [*to tēs teknophagias mysos*] beneath the ruins of their country, and would not leave upon the face of the earth, for the sun to behold, a city in which mothers were thus fed. (6.215–17)

¶9. The *Jewish War* is built upon the theological foundations of biblical historiography, as has often been noted (e.g., Lindner 1972, 21–48; Rajak 1983, 78–79, 94–103; Bilde 1988, 75, 184–91). God, who goes "the round of nations," entrusting "to each in turn the rod of empire," and who formerly rested over Assyria, Babylonia, Persia, and Greece, "now rest[s] over Italy" (*War* 5.367)—so much so, indeed, that the Jewish rebels "are warring not against the Romans only, but also against God" (5.378), who had determined to punish them by permitting the Romans to sack Jerusalem, slaughter its citizens, and level its temple. Josephus trots out the anecdote of the cannibal mother to lend support to his theological metanarrative: the Jewish God along with his elect agent, the Gentile general and emperor-to-be, acted justly in destroying Jerusalem. The existence of a monstrously "unnatural" mother within the walls of the city is presented as the ultimate warrant for its annihilation.[f]

---

f. I have **one of these little stories** to tell you myself, as it happens. It took place just recently. I thought it was important to tell you, although why I should think so is a subject for still further footnotes. It also has to do with an abusive parent, like so much else that I find myself writing about. The Children's Services people brought charges against a pregnant woman who is addicted to sniffing glue. She has had three other children, the last two born with brain damage because of her addiction. The agency asked the court to rule that she should be held in custody and required to undergo treatment for her addiction. Finding the woman mentally incapable of caring for herself, the judge ruled, on the basis of a seldom-used legal principle, *parens patriae*, that the court may force protection upon adults who are mentally unfit. The woman has been photographed coming out of the courtroom, shielding her face with her hands, which clutch a lighted cigarette. Advocates for the government have loudly proclaimed the need to force her to undergo treatment, both for herself and her unborn child. She herself remains mute. The lower court has demanded

¶10. But the anecdote turns renegade in its turn and blows a hole in the high-walled enclosure of the metanarrative. The hole is created by the awkward fact that the woman is not herself a rebel; on the contrary, she is a sorry victim of the rebels, who have already stripped her of her wealth, and now rob her even of the pitiful scraps of food that she manages to scrape together for herself and her emaciated infant. In the end she pronounces these "seditious rogues" a more insufferable source of torment than the prospect of either slaughter or enslavement at the hands of the Romans, or than the terrible famine itself (*War* 6.202–7). It may have registered belatedly with Josephus that the outrage he ascribes to Titus is logically unstable. After having Titus indignantly announce that "he would bury this abomination of infant-cannibalism beneath the ruins of their country, and would not leave upon the face of the earth, for the sun to behold, a city in which mothers were thus fed," Josephus has him concede (Caesar's serene brow momentarily creasing with uncharacteristic uncertainty?) that "such food is fitter for the fathers than for the mothers to eat of, since it is they that continue still in arms, even after such horrors" (6.217–18). The woman has become the scapegoat for the siege of which she is the victim, and Titus comes perilously close to admitting as much. The anecdote unravels the (theo)logical thread of Josephus's historical design. Theodicy is the theme of this design, as we have seen; Josephus is at pains to explain why the Jewish God allowed the destruction of his city and house. By tugging on the design's loose threads, however, the anecdote calls into question not only the justice of **Titus** but also the justice of the deity who has used the general as his instrument.g

---

that she be incarcerated in an approved drug treatment facility, and she has been detained in a local hospital. Her lawyer has argued successfully on appeal that the courts have no jurisdiction to take people into custody if they have not broken the law, and the higher court has ordered her release. In a statement issued to the press, however, she has broken her silence to say that she will comply with the original decision and remain institutionalized until the birth of her child.

g. Does my **anecdote** of the pregnant glue sniffer not tear a similar hole in the rousing *grand récit* of liberty and justice for all? Within this benign dispensation we "freely" choose those actions best calculated to guarantee life, liberty, and the pursuit of happiness. I do not, of course, have the right to break into your house, murder you, and steal your possessions. Fortunately for you, having sufficient possessions of my own, I have no desire to take yours or do you harm. But what if it were not so? How might I resist a social order in which I found myself seriously disadvantaged? This woman tried to escape, however ineptly. But her resistance only resulted in her further oppression, as the courts moved in to contain and defuse her defiance. In her ultimate acceptance of incarceration, does she become complicitous in her own oppression?

¶11. The impulse to whip out **a shocking anecdote** in the course of, or as a prelude to, a sober historical recital is a trait that the ancient historian and the New Historicist share in common.[6] The incident with which Greenblatt's "Marlowe and the Will to Absolute Play" opens, however, is considerably less gruesome either than the anecdote of the cannibal mother or the anecdote of the Chinese goldsmith, although a grim read nonetheless, like so many New Historicist anecdotes. It tells how a small fleet set out from Gravesend, at the mouth of the Thames, in June 1586, bound for the South Seas. "It sailed down the West African coast, sighting Sierra Leone in October..." (Greenblatt 1980, 193). On board was a merchant, **John Sarracoll**, who now picks up the tale: "The fourth of November we went on shore to a town of the Negroes ... which we found to be but lately built: it was of about two hundred houses...." The crew entered the town "with such fierceness" that all its inhabitants fled. A tour of inspection followed. The crew found the town "to be finely built ... and the streets of it so intricate that it was difficult for us to find the way out that we came in at. We found their houses and streets so finely and cleanly kept that it was an admiration to us all, for that neither in the houses nor streets was so much dust to be found as would fill an egg shell." Yet the account ends with the following admission: "Our men at their departure set the town on fire, and it was burnt (for the most part of it) in a quarter of an hour, the houses being covered with reed and straw" (Sarracoll 1903–1905, 206–7, quoted in Greenblatt 1980, 193).

¶12. What is most striking about Sarracoll's anecdote, as Greenblatt notes, "is the casual, unexplained violence. Does the merchant feel that the firing of the town needs no explanation? If asked would he have had one to give?" (1980, 194). All such questions, however, are "met by the moral blankness that rests like thick snow"—or fine ash?—"on Sarracoll's sentences" (1980, 194). Veeser glosses Greenblatt's point: "Sarracoll's bland moral vacancy, so like that of Arfie in *Catch-22* and Pyle in Graham Greene's *The Quiet American*, seems endemic to imperialism" (Veeser 1994, 5).[h] "But so is its negation, **resistance** and rebellion," Veeser goes on. "Greenblatt now introduces just such a nay-sayer, Christopher Marlowe, who rebels against every secular and divine orthodoxy..." (Veeser 1994, 5–6). Greenblatt writes, "If, on returning to England in 1587, the merchant and his associates had gone to see the Lord Admiral's Men perform a new play, *Tamburlaine the Great*, they would have

---

h. The moral blankness of imperialism has a corollary in the ethical bankruptcy of institutions, even, or especially, when what is at stake is life, liberty, and the pursuit of happiness. So how might I resist? I do not lack for models. Greenblatt's Marlowe, for one. And, as you'll see, Crossan's Jesus. My own Jesus, too, for that matter. And this poor, addicted woman.

5. THE QUEST OF THE NEW HISTORICIST JESUS 107

seen an extraordinary meditation on the roots of their own behavior" (1980, 194). "[I]conoclast, foe of hypocrisy, intransigent outsider"—such was Chris Marlowe (Veeser 1994, 6). But increasingly of late the same is being said of another Chris, or rather Christ. I especially have in mind John Dominic Crossan's "historical" Jesus (1991; 1994a; 1994b; 1995)—not quite and yet more than a Christ: iconoclast supreme, enemy of hypocrisy, unassimilable outsider, countercultural rebel.

¶13. The casual connection that I have just effected between the sixteenth-century dramatist and the first-century sage (which will be crucial for the remainder of this article) is both typical and atypical of New Historicist method. It is typical in that New Historicists tend to combine seemingly disparate materials so as to create meticulously staged "coincidences," "impossible" linkages, startling juxtapositions, and other contingent connections that bypass the causal models of explanation that undergird traditional historical narratives. But it is atypical in that the texts thereby linked (and I have merely forged the first link in a long chain) are more disparate, temporally, than in the average New Historicist essay—a series of Elizabethan texts, on the one hand, refracted through a late twentieth-century literary-critical text; and a series of early Christian texts, on the other hand, refracted through a late twentieth-century biblical-critical text. Can the chain stand the strain? That remains to be seen as I proceed to read **"Marlowe and the Will to Absolute Play"** as a ☞ ¶19
commentary on Crossan's *The Historical Jesus*.

¶14. Political power (religio-political power included), most of all when it purports to be absolute power, coupled with the resistance that such power invariably elicits, is a recurrent New Historicist preoccupation. Here New Historicism is at its most Foucauldian (see Lentricchia 1989; Newton 1990; Hamilton 1996, 133–44). But Crossan's *The Historical Jesus* turns on these same themes, as we are about to discover. Consider in particular Crossan's construal of Jesus' enigmatic action in the Jerusalem temple (Mark 11:15–19 and pars.; John 2:13–22).

¶15. Crossan is "quite convinced" the temple incident actually occurred (1991, 359). And not only Crossan, of course; E.P. Sanders, especially, is equally certain of its historicity, making it the cornerstone of his reconstruction of the historical Jesus' career (1985, 11, 61–76; 1993, 252–69). I myself, while capable of admiration for an argumentative tour de force by a Jesus scholar (such as Sanders's case for the historicity of the temple incident), tend toward agnosticism in the matter of the true sayings and authentic deeds of the elusive Galilean. I admire, indeed I emulate, the arguments of such scholars nonetheless because I myself have plunged through the same black holes in post-Enlightenment faith and passed into the same discursive universe. And I readily affirm the relative untranscendability of this shared discursive space, but also its relative relativity. Which is to say that a historical fact, for me, is a discursively determined interpretation, impressively solid-seeming for now, but only for now, since critical and even commonsense discourse is itself subject to unceasing historical change and hence to continual erosion.[i]

¶16. But enough vanitas; let us return to the task at hand. Jesus' "attack" on the Jerusalem temple, if it indeed occurred, would have been an attack on authority, it seems safe to say—but which authority, which authorities? The "religious" authorities, epitomized by the august figure of the Jewish high priest, Joseph Caiaphas? Or the "secular" authorities, epitomized by the less august but arguably more powerful figure of the Roman prefect of Judea, Pontius Pilate? Or is it even possible to disentangle these two authorities, beyond a certain point? It is probably safe to surmise that the long relationship of Caiaphas and Pilate was not free of conflict. Yet that it was essentially a symbiotic relationship, a mutually advantageous partnership, is strongly suggested by the fact that Caiaphas managed to remain in office for eighteen years (longer than any other high priest under Roman rule), the last ten of which coincided with Pilate's prefecture over Judea. It appears that a hand-in-glove arrangement prevailed, then, the thickly padded glove, ceremonial yet practical, composed of the high priest, his council, and his temple guards; and the hand composed of the prefect and his lightly manned garrisons—a surprisingly small hand, perhaps, but able to bunch up into a formidable fist in a brawl because it could call on the muscle of the Syrian legate and his legions. Given this arrangement, could it not plausibly be argued that Jesus' attack on the Jewish temple was ultimately directed at the Roman state?

¶17. This is Crossan's position, implicitly, although he arrives at it by a different route. In common with the majority of critical scholars, Crossan construes Jesus' action in the temple as "not at all a purification but rather a symbolic destruction" (1991, 349). "Here then is my historical reconstruction of what happened," he states.

> I am not sure that poor Galilean peasants went up and down regularly to temple feasts. I think it quite possible that Jesus went to Jerusalem only once and that the spiritual and economic egalitarianism he preached in Galilee exploded in indignation at the Temple as the seat of all that was nonegalitarian, patronal, and even oppressive on both the religious and political level.

---

i. "Facts" only become historical when an historian elects to enflesh them in narrative. But what selective and combinative criteria are employed by the collector of anecdotes and other historical detritus? Why should it seem important to me, for instance, to invest **the anecdote of the pregnant glue-sniffer** with significance, while ignoring innumerable other "human interest" stories in the daily news?

[☞ note f]

5. THE QUEST OF THE NEW HISTORICIST JESUS 109

Jesus' symbolic destruction simply actualized what he had already said in his teachings, effected in his healings, and realized in his mission of open commensality.[7]

Crossan sees Jesus' symbolic action in the temple, therefore, as a natural, even necessary, extension of Jesus' social program ("the historical Jesus had both an ideal vision and a social program" [1991, 349]), but he sees that social program in turn as an expression of peasant resistance to imperial oppression, a notion he seems to have borrowed from Richard Horsley (see Horsley and Hanson 1985; Horsley 1987). Crossan contends "that the most proximate background for Jesus must be the full trajectory of peasant social unrest, which can be mapped across a hundred years before it comes to a first and awful consummation in the revolt against Rome" (1991, 100; cf. 124–36, 313–18). And so he is prone, especially in *Jesus: A Revolutionary Biography* (which also turns out to be the biography of a revolutionary), to make claims such as the following:

> [Jesus] not only discussed the kingdom of God; he enacted it, and said others could do so as well. If all he had done was talk about the Kingdom, Lower Galilee would probably have greeted him with a great big peasant yawn. But you cannot ignore the healings and the exorcisms, especially in their socially subversive function. You cannot ignore the pointedly political overtones of the very term *Kingdom of God* itself. It is, unfortunately, one of the abiding temptations of pastors and scholars to reduce Jesus to words alone, to replace a lived life with a preached sermon or an interesting idea. To remove, however, that which is radically subversive, socially revolutionary, and politically dangerous from Jesus' *actions* is to leave his life meaningless and his death inexplicable (1994b, 93, his emphasis; cf. 76; 1991, 95).

¶18. Crossan's story of Jesus, therefore, is a story of religio-political power (absolute in principle) and a singular instance of creative resistance mounted in response to that power. Greenblatt's story of Marlowe is likewise a story of religio-political power (absolute in principle) and a singular instance of creative resistance mounted in response to that power.[j] But Greenblatt's tale also has **a tragic last act**, one in which power is depicted as effortlessly absorb-   ☞ ¶21

---

j. What of my own resistance? I resist the only way I can (or dare): I write. I have models for this too: Greenblatt, even Crossan. But what of the practical effects of their resistance (or of mine)? The force they exert is poetic. Marlowe must have supposed that the pen was mightier than the sword, and naturally I am tempted to agree. Do I want to change the world if it means risking my livelihood? The question remains academic, of course.

ing the very resistance it elicted, one that many would see as typical of New Historicism.

¶19. Midway through **"Marlowe and the Will to Absolute Play,"** Greenblatt performs "the strong **containment** move," as Veeser aptly styles it. Authority "flicks … Marlowe aside. In Marlowe's supposedly destabilizing drama, attacks on social norms … are 'exposed as unwitting tributes to that social construction of identity against which they struggle'" (Veeser 1994, 6, quoting Greenblatt 1980, 209). Despite their best, or worst, efforts, Marlowe's heroes remain enveloped in the standard scripts of their culture, contends Greenblatt. True, they eagerly embrace what respectable society deems taboo, and in so doing imagine that they have burst the bars of their cage. But all they have really managed to do is define, and thereby reify, society's "crucial structural elements" (Greenblatt 1980, 209). "[T]heir acts of negation not only conjure up the order they would destroy but seem at times to be themselves conjured up by that very order" (1980, 209). Although ostensibly engaged in subversive self-fashioning, they are nevertheless compelled to employ tools and models manufactured by the dominant culture (1980, 210).

¶20. Consider the case of Marlowe's Faustus, for instance, who concludes the signing of his infamous bargain with the words "*Consummatum est*." To unfurl the significance of this citation of the Johannine Jesus' dying words, Greenblatt attempts to reinsert them into their original literary context. The words come in the wake of Jesus' acceptance of a draught of vinegar "in order to fulfill the scripture" (John 19:28–29), namely Psalm 69:21, "for my thirst they gave me vinegar to drink." "Christ's thirst is not identical to the body's normal longing for drink," claims Greenblatt,

> but an *enactment* of that longing so that he may fully accomplish the role darkly prefigured in the Old Testament. The drink of vinegar is the final structural element in the realization of his identity. Faustus's use of Christ's words then evokes the archetypal act of role-taking.… But whatever status Faustus can thereby achieve is limited to the status of a brilliant parody. His blasphemy is the uncanny expression of a perverse, despairing faith, an appropriation to himself of the most solemn and momentous words available in his culture to mark the decisive boundary in his life.… (1980, 213–14, his emphasis)

Faustus is "tragically bounded by the dominant ideology" against which he struggles, therefore, like all of Marlowe's iconoclastic protagonists. Far from destroying, or even destabilizing, this dominant ideology, they pay it unwitting tribute instead, argues Greenblatt. At such moments, argues Veeser— "archetypal, inevitable moments" for New Historicism—"leftist, feminist,

5. THE QUEST OF THE NEW HISTORICIST JESUS

oppositional, liberationist critics have traditionally walked out:[k] who wants to hear that the good fight is **doomed to fail?**" (1994, 6; cf. Veeser 1991, 3–4, 7–8).   ☞ ¶31

¶21. I shall return to this problem later. First let me reflect further on the good fight of Jesus the peasant resister. Can Crossan's Jesus succeed where **Greenblatt's Marlowe failed**? The Roman state, the ultimate, ubiquitous object of Jesus' peasant resistance movement, casually crushes Jesus for his symbolic destruction of the Jerusalem temple. "[I]t is now impossible for us to imagine the offhand brutality, anonymity, and indifference with which a peasant nobody like Jesus would have been disposed of," claims Crossan (1991, xii; cf. 1994b, 152). Yet that is but the first step. The second step is infinitely more terrifying. The same colossal sandal (Jesus' minute mashed corpse still adhering unnoticed to its sole) is later raised as high as it will go and brought down with frightful force upon the entire anthill. The city of Jerusalem and its temple are flattened, along with many, or most, of the city's inhabitants. Josephus (admittedly given to exaggeration in such matters) tells us that 1,100,000 perished, and that a further 97,000 were taken captive (*War* 6.420).

¶22. But this second step has the incidental effect of draining Jesus' death of any meager drops of meaning that might still have clung to it, if, as Crossan suspects, that death was the direct result of Jesus' symbolic destruction of the temple (1991, xii, 360; 1994b, 133). For it is the imperial oppressor, not the peasant resister, who, as it turns out, literally annihilates the temple—but not before the oppressor has reflexively squashed the resister for presuming to enact, even through symbol, that which should be the oppressor's prerogative alone: the obliteration of the central structure of the subject people's symbolic universe.[l] The upshot is that Titus, conqueror of Jerusalem, ironically switches places with Jesus. The soon-to-be emperor brings to completion the symbolic action performed by **the soon-to-be crucified peasant**, thereby emptying it   ☞ ¶29
of its subversive import.

¶23. Another intertext now beckons. In order to press my analysis further I shall have to set Crossan's Jesus aside temporarily and turn to an infinitely more influential Jesus. Does Mark's Jesus fare any better than Crossan's in his

---

k. To reassemble in the mountains? Are guerrilla tactics, rather than direct assaults on the ramparts, less likely to be contained? The trick would be to stay out of the loop. And to expose the degree to which institutions, too readily imagined as being self-consistent and immutable, are rift with internal contradictions and hence unstable. Can we thereby create conditions that make social change possible? Staging a guerrilla war requires faith in the power of the few against the many, certainly, and in the possibility of moral agency. Does New Historicism's plan of attack preemptively eviscerate such faith?

l. It's convenient for the oppressor, is it not, that the symbolic structure in question is architectural first and foremost, and hence that much easier to raze, or erase? It will be replaced with a more resilient structure, the oral and written Torah.

contest with the Roman state? Listen closely as Mark's Jesus and **Josephus's Titus** whisper conspiratorially amid the ruins of Jerusalem and its temple—unbeknown to either author, needless to say (New Historicism wouldn't have it any other way).

¶24. Even a casual cross-reading of the Gospel of Mark and the *Jewish War* turns up a panoply of intriguing, and altogether contingent, connections.[m] Mark's suffering sovereign, Jesus (15:17–19, 26, 32), is God's elect agent, his chosen instrument (1:11; 8:29; 9:7; 14:61–62), whose career was foretold from of old in the Jewish scriptures (1:2–3; 4:11–12; 11:7–10; 12:10–11,35–37; 13:24–26; 14:27, 49, 62; 15:24, 34). Josephus's sovereign, Titus, meanwhile, is likewise God's elect agent and instrument, as was Titus's father, Vespasian, before him. The *Jewish War* is styled theologically on biblical historiography, as noted earlier, God "now resting over Italy" (5.367), just as he had formerly rested over Assyria, Babylonia, Persia, and Greece, so that the Jewish rebels are "warring not against the Romans only, but also against God" (6.378). Josephus's brazen claim, indeed, is that Vespasian's glorious career, and by extension that of his son, was foretold from of old in the Jewish scriptures. The Jewish revolt was fueled by "an ambiguous oracle [*chrēsmos amphibos*] ... found in their sacred scriptures, to the effect that at that time one from their own country would become ruler of the world. This they understood to mean someone of their own race, and many of their wise men went astray in their interpretation of it. The oracle, however, in reality signified the sovereignty of Vespasian who was proclaimed emperor on Jewish soil" (6.312–13).[8]

☞ ¶9

¶25. The connections between Mark's Jesus and Josephus's Titus are far more intricate than this, however, and converge on the Jerusalem temple. At least one of Jesus' followers is full of admiration for the temple, according to Mark: "As he came out of the temple, one of his disciples said to him, 'Look, Teacher, what large stones and what large buildings'" (13:1). Arguably this unnamed disciple is to be regarded as speaking also for his fellow followers; this, at any rate, is Matthew's and Luke's understanding of the scene

---

m. The Latin *contingere* connotes, etymologically and antithetically, causal connection, on the one hand, and **chance connection**, on the other (cf. Veeser 1994, 4–5; Ross 1990, 490–93). New Historicists regularly produce readings that oscillate between these two contradictory senses of contingency, reacting to an historiographic tradition that has tended to absolutize the first sense while sternly setting aside the second. In the New Historicist cosmos, as in the medieval cosmos, everything can be connected with everything else.

But to what end? To that of demonstrating repeatedly that resistance is ever predestined to be contained? Why should *this* be the necessary upshot of privileging chance over cause? Couldn't one deploy associative and anecdotal strategies to arrive at an altogether different destination? To read resistantly, yet elude capture?

(Matt 24:1; Luke 21:5). Jesus himself, however, sternly refuses to show respect for the temple (Mark 11:15–17; 13:2; cf. 14:56–59; 15:29–30, 37–38). Titus, in a chiastic inversion of the Markan scenario, is full of admiration for the temple; it is his followers who fail to show it respect. First, Titus's admiration: he "went into the building with his generals," claims Josephus, "and beheld the holy place of the sanctuary and all that it contained—things far exceeding the reports current among foreigners and not inferior to their proud reputation among ourselves" (6.260).[n] Now, his subordinates' lack of respect: one of the soldiers, "awaiting no orders and with no horror of so terrible a deed, but moved by some supernatural impulse, snatched a brand from the burning timber and, hoisted up by one of his comrades, flung the fiery missile through a low golden door" (6.252). Before long the entire army is engaged in looting and burning the sacred building.[o]

¶26. Jesus himself does not destroy the temple, then—how could he? But that only thickens his complicity with Titus. For neither does Titus destroy the temple, at least on Josephus's account: "Titus was resting in his tent after the engagement, when a messenger rushed in with the tidings. Starting up just as he was, he ran to the temple to arrest the conflagration" (6.254). Titus is unsuccessful, however, in his near-frantic efforts to have the blaze quenched. Josephus concludes: "Thus the sanctuary was set on fire in defiance of Caesar's wishes [*ho men oun naos houtōs akontos Kaisaros empiatai*]" (6.266)—a claim that undoubtedly must be taken with a grain of salt, or several.[p]

¶27. Let us now consider some final conjunctions and disjunctions. In Mark's narrative, the virtuous action of a destitute woman (12:41–44) introduces Jesus' prediction of unprecedented (13:19), but thoroughly deserved, suffering for the Jewish people. According to Mark, the Jerusalem temple was destroyed as a punishment on those who had rejected the kingdom of God centered on his son, Jesus.[q] In Josephus's narrative, the *wicked* action

---

n. It has sometimes been suggested that the bold entry of the pagan conqueror into the holy of holies is the event cryptically referred to in Mark 13:14: "And when you see the abomination of desolation standing where *he* should not be [*hotan de idēte to bdelygma tēs erēmōseōs hestēkota hopou ou dei*]." See, e.g., Branderburger 1984, 82; Lührmann 1987, 22; Hooker 1991, 314.

o. Note how we are returned to **Greenblatt's Sarracoll** and the casual burning of beautiful buildings by the plundering arm of empire. ☞ ¶11

p. The fourth-century Christian chronicler Sulpicius Severus, although clearly aware of Josephus's claim, contradicts it, contending more plausibly (even if unprovably) that Titus himself decreed the temple's destruction (*Chronica* 2.30.6–7). Josephus even appears to contradict himself on this point (*Ant.* 20.250; *War* 7.1).

q. As is well known, Mark has cleverly cut in half the story of Jesus cursing the fig tree and stuffed his account of Jesus "cleansing" the temple between the two slices (11:12–21),

of a destitute woman (the cannibal mother) introduces *Titus's* prediction of unprecedented,[r] but thoroughly deserved, suffering for the Jewish people, as we saw earlier.[s] According to Josephus, the Jerusalem temple was destroyed as a punishment on those who had rejected the divinely ordained rule of Rome, centered on Titus at the time in which Josephus is writing.

¶28. The upshot of this curious complex of contingencies is that Titus is to the *Jewish War* as Jesus is to the Gospel of Mark. Moreover, Titus takes up where Jesus leaves off. Jesus mimes the temple's destruction, but only Rome can effect it. Authority flicks Jesus aside precisely by *taking* his side, having first taken his life. Whether one looks at Crossan's pre-messianic peasant resister, therefore, or at Mark's resistant peasant messiah in their respective relations to the Jewish temple, on the one hand, and the Roman state, on the other, the same configuration springs into view (at least when focused through **a New Historicist lens**), that of power, resistance, and containment.

☞ ¶40

¶29. Of course, I have barely begun to plumb the astonishing extent of the containment that the resistance movement initiated by **the Galilean peasant** elicits (to return to Crossan's Jesus). For in time this resistance movement will *become* that which it was designed, ultimately, to resist: the Roman state itself. History will turn Jesus into a new Romulus, the founder of a new Rome. The Roman state will not only contain, then, but actively manipulate the threat represented by Christianity, by turning Christianity into a version of itself, or, rather, by turning itself into a version of Christianity. The strong containment move will assume surreal proportions. Crossan himself is not unaware of this

---

a prime example of his so-called "sandwich technique," one of several that you and I are asked to swallow.

r. Mark 13:19, referring to the tragic outcome of the Jewish revolt, reads, "For in those days there will be suffering, such as has not been from the beginning of the creation that God created until now, no, and never will be" (cf. Dan 12:1), while *War* 6.429 reads, "The victims thus outnumbered those of any previous slaughter, human or divine."

s. Josephus's anecdote of the cannibal mother undermines his theological construal of the temple's destruction, as we also saw. Does Mark's anecdote of the selfless widow similarly undermine his own construal of the same event, similarly cause that construal to come crashing down with the temple? Ultimately it does—although in a less electrifying fashion than Josephus's eye-popping anecdote, admittedly. More like the (news) story of the pregnant glue sniffer, then; the shocks it sends through the foundations of the meta-narrative are relatively subtle. Anyway, the tired theological problem the widow anecdote poses is one with deep roots in the sapiential tradition: why must the righteous suffer along with the wicked? Why must the virtuous widow, or her numerous faceless and equally nameless counterparts, be subjected to the frightful punishment soon destined to descend upon the population of Jerusalem and the Jewish people generally? Like Josephus, Mark manages, altogether inadvertently and through the agency of an anecdote, to raise disturbing questions about divine power that he is utterly unable to answer.

5. THE QUEST OF THE NEW HISTORICIST JESUS 115

conundrum. In the epilogue to *The Historical Jesus* we find him meditating gloomily on the irony:

> It is hard, indeed, not to get very, very nervous in reading [Eusebius's] description of the imperial banquet celebrating the Council of Nicaea's conclusion:
>> Detachments of the bodyguards and troops surrounded the entrance of the palace with drawn swords, and through the midst of them the men of God proceeded without fear into the innermost of the imperial apartments, in which some of the Emperor's companions were at table, while others reclined on couches arranged on either side. One might have thought that a picture of Christ's kingdom was thus shadowed forth, a dream rather than a reality.
>
> The meal and the kingdom still come together, but now the participants are the male bishops, and they recline, with the Emperor himself, to be served by others. Maybe Christianity is an inevitable and absolutely necessary "betrayal" of Jesus, else it might all have died among the hills of Lower Galilee. But did that "betrayal" have to happen so swiftly, succeed so fully, and be enjoyed so thoroughly? (1991, 424, quoting Eusebius, *Vita Constantini* 3.15)

Crossan later recycles these reflections in *Jesus: A Revolutionary Biography*, where they actually form the concluding lines of the book (1994b, 201). Yet again Crossan's Jesus is strikingly New Historicist in his lineaments, although this is probably a **chance contingency**: Crossan nowhere indicates that he has read the New Historicists. The difference between them and him, however, is that what he holds sadly over for a cautionary epilogue—the spectacle of state power further inflating by absorbing the very resistance that arose in reaction to it—a New Historicist like Greenblatt would tend to make the mainspring of the plot.[t]

☞ note m

¶30. But why? Why this fascination with the enervating notion that state power, at its most efficient, is able effortlessly to anticipate and co-opt the

---

[t]. No wonder Crossan is nervous. I too glance over my shoulder, wondering how thoroughly I am being contained. When the political institutions whose ideology I contest absorb my opposition; when the academic institutions whose ideology I resist reward me for that resistance; when my thoughts collude with those they confront, I too am a collaborator, complicitous in my own oppression and that of others.

But the temple *did* come down nonetheless: a crack here, a breach there, a spark that exploded into flame. And our own institutions, with their monolithic metanarratives, are no less vulnerable. They are buttressed with contingencies; they are not irresistible, neither are they invincible.

most determined resistance it triggers? Because the notion is true? But true for whom? Certainly it would seem to be true for left-leaning academics in the topmost turrets of the ivory tower, such as Stephen J. Greenblatt himself, the 1932 Professor of English at the University of California at Berkeley, who is not only permitted by the state (local and federal) to write denunciatory statements about state power but is handsomely rewarded for it. Admittedly the state that is the target of Greenblatt's barbs is not the one headed by the Governor of California, nor even the one headed by the President of the United States, so much as the one headed by Elizabeth I; but other New Historicists who specialize in American rather than Renaissance studies have been rewarded no less lavishly for their subversive scribblings. The United States is able to defang its intellectual class with a facility that would have left Henry VIII—or Constantine the Great—gasping in admiration, all the while granting this class unfettered "freedom of expression." To this extent, New Historicism in the Greenblattian mode, with its frank fascination with the dreary dialectic of resistance and containment in its early modern manifestations, could be read as a Foucauldian "history of the present," an etiological exploration of how what is came to be—including the political marginality of New Historicism itself, which thereby becomes an exercise in displaced autobiography.

¶31. So how might **a New Historicist Jesus, doomed to ultimate impotence**, comport himself? How would he measure up to Marlowe's Promethean protagonists? Would Greenblatt's claims concerning the latter apply *mutatis mutandis* to the former? Would such a Jesus also feel compelled to live his life as a project, even in the midst of intimations that the project is an illusion? If so, his strength would not be sapped by these intimations; he would not withdraw into stoical resignation or contemplative solitude, nor would he endure for the sake of isolated moments of grace in which he would be in touch with a wholeness otherwise absent in his life. Instead he would take courage from the absurdity of his enterprise, a self-destructive, supremely eloquent, playful courage. This playfulness would manifest itself as subversive humor, a penchant for the outlandish and absurd, delight in role-playing, entire absorption in the game at hand and consequent indifference to what lies outside the boundaries of the game, and extreme but disciplined aggression. In his life, as in his teaching, the categories by which we normally organize experience would be insistently called into question. Is this a man whose recklessness suggests that he is out of control, we would ask, or rather that he is supremely *in* control—control so coolly mocking that he can calculate his own excesses? His will to play would flaunt his society's cherished orthodoxies, embrace what his culture found loathsome or frightening, transform the serious into the joke and then unsettle the category of the joke by taking it seriously, court

5. THE QUEST OF THE NEW HISTORICIST JESUS 117

self-destruction for the anarchic discharge of its energy. This would be play on the brink of an abyss, then—*absolute* play.[u]

¶32. Interestingly, it would also be play in the mode of John Dominic Crossan's Jesus—not the Jesus of *The Historical Jesus*, however, so much as Crossan's earlier, postmodernist Jesus, the protagonist of *The Dark Interval* (1975), *Raid on the Articulate* (1976), and *Cliffs of Fall* (1980).[v] After *Cliffs of Fall* Crossan adjusted his tie, smoothed down his hair, and began the more respectable line of research that would eventually result in *The Historical Jesus*,[w] with its correspondingly serious protagonist. This deeply politicized Jesus I have found to be strikingly well-suited for a role in a New Historicist drama of power, resistance, and containment. But now it begins to appear that the more this political Jesus embraces this tragic role, the more he begins to resemble the playful Jesus of *Cliffs of Fall* and its precursors. If so, Crossan's poststructuralist Jesus, the product of Crossan's now largely forgotten poststructuralist period, lies buried within the pages of *The Historical Jesus* ready to resurrect, or at least to spring out like a Jack-in-the-box upon the unsuspecting reader. Or rather like a Dom-in-the-box; for can one seriously doubt by now that Crossan's own intellectual biography is inextricably bound up with the mercurial biography of his perfectly protean subject?[x]

¶33. And so we come up against a familiar brick wall. On this wall hangs a mirror. In the uncertain light the historian peers anxiously into that mirror. Surely a sliver of glass is missing from its center? Delicately he extends a digit to test his hypothesis. No question about it, there appears to be a chink in the reflection. His pulse quickens. He stares yet more intently into the tiny aperture. Time passes and the gloom deepens. In the darkness, new hypotheses are hatched. First, that the brick that should be behind the chink is itself missing. Second, that the resulting peephole reveals a first-century Palestinian peasant home on the other side of the wall. Third, that a second mirror, an extremely crude one, has been cunningly hung by some unknown hand on the mud wall opposite the peephole. Fourth, that all previous historians

---

u. Apart from some minor adjustments and omissions, this entire sketch is lifted verbatim from Greenblatt 1980, 219–20, where it refers to Marlowe's heroes at first and then to the dramatist himself. "Marlowe is deeply implicated in his heroes," argues Greenblatt (1980, 220). And Greenblatt himself appears to identify deeply with Marlowe (1980, 113, 218–19).

v. Crossan's *Finding Is the First Act* (1979) is closely affiliated with this trilogy, as is his programmatic early book, *In Parables* (1973). A rough trajectory can be traced from the relatively restrained *In Parables* through to the exuberant excesses of *Cliffs of Fall*.

w. By way of *In Fragments* (1983), *Four Other Gospels* (1985), and *The Cross That Spoke* (1988).

x. Crossan's own protests notwithstanding (1995, 211–15).

privileged to discover the peephole became mesmerized by their own reflection in this second mirror, mistaking it for the house's most reclusive resident. And fifth, that a glimpse can be caught, in this same rudimentary mirror, of a window in an otherwise invisible wall, through which **the real Jesus** can be seen departing the hamlet on whose fringes the house is located.[y]

¶34. Crossan invents an anecdote to explain the circumstances of that departure. Indeed he opens *The Historical Jesus* with it:

> He comes as yet unknown into a hamlet of Lower Galilee. He is watched by the cold, hard eyes of peasants living long enough at subsistence level to know exactly where the line is drawn between poverty and destitution. He looks like a beggar, yet his eyes lack the proper cringe, his voice the proper whine, his walk the proper shuffle. He speaks about the rule of God, and they listen as much from curiosity as anything else. They know all about rule and power, about kingdom and empire, but they know it in terms of tax and debt, malnutrition and sickness, agrarian oppression and demonic possession. What, they really want to know, can this kingdom of God do for a lame child, a blind parent, a demented soul screaming its tortured isolation among the graves that mark the edges of the village? Jesus walks with them to the tombs, and, in the silence after the exorcism, the villagers listen once more, but now with curiosity giving way to cupidity, fear, and embarrassment. He is invited, as honor demands, to the home of the village leader. He goes, instead, to stay in the home of the dispossessed woman. Not quite proper, to be sure, but it would be unwise to censure an exorcist, to criticize a magician. The village could yet broker this power to its surroundings, could give this kingdom of God a localization, a place to which others would come for healing, a center with honor and patronage enough for all, even, maybe, for that dispossessed woman herself. But the next day he leaves them, and now they wonder aloud about a divine kingdom with no respect for proper protocols, a kingdom, as he had said, not just for the poor like themselves, but for the destitute. Others say that the worst and most powerful demons are found not in small villages but in certain cities. Maybe, they say, that was where the exorcised demon went, to Sepphoris or Tiberias, or even Jerusalem, or maybe to Rome itself, where its arrival would hardly be noticed amidst so many others already in residence. But some say nothing at all and ponder the possibility of catching up with Jesus before he gets too far. (1991, xi; cf. 1994b, 194–5)

---

y. He'll be incapacitated whether he stays put or makes a break for it, in this New Historicist cosmos: a victim predestined to fail in his resistance, whose act of revolt is ironically completed, as we saw, by those against whom it is directed. The freedom to think and act oppositionally is always illusory in such a constricted context.

5. THE QUEST OF THE NEW HISTORICIST JESUS

¶35. We end where we began, then, with **the opening anecdote**, the anecdote in its capacity to open up a reading. Recourse to an inaugural anecdote is yet another (**contingent?**) point of connection between Crossan and the New Historicists. Historians normally adduce anecdotes for purposes of explication. Crossan reverses the procedure. As *The Historical Jesus* unfolds, more and more of the corpus of early Christian literature, along with a much larger corpus of secondary literature, is pulled in to explicate the anecdote, until the book becomes a five-hundred page gloss upon the one page scene with which it began, a scholarly footnote blown up to nightmarish proportions (and ready to burst at the touch of a pin?). This reversal is also characteristic of Greenblatt's practice, as it happens. "The historical anecdote functions less as explanatory illustration than as disturbance, that which requires explanation, contextualization, interpretation," he explains (1990, 5)—although he has yet to gloss an anecdote with a footnote longer than an essay.

☞ ¶3

☞ note m

¶36. But Crossan goes beyond Greenblatt in other ways as well. Unable to find the anecdote that he needs in the archives, Crossan brazenly invents it instead. Not surprisingly, therefore, Crossan's opening anecdote, unlike one of Greenblatt's opening anecdotes, is not a disturbance that the remainder of the work will take pains to interpret, so much as an interpretation that the remainder of the work will take pains not to disturb.

¶37. And yet the interpretation announces itself implicitly at the outset as a work of invention. Such is the effect of Crossan's fictional anecdote. It deftly undercuts his subsequent insistence that a uniquely rigorous attention to methodology will enable him to steer safely between the Scylla of "do[ing] theology and call[ing] it history," on the one hand, and the Charybdis of "do[ing] **autobiography** and call[ing] it biography," on the other, in his Odyssean quest for the historical Jesus (1991, xxviii).[9] One senses a seamless ideological fit between Crossan's Jesus and Crossan himself throughout the book that tempts one to conclude what its first page in fact suggests—that Crossan's Jesus is ultimately Crossan's own invention, exquisitely crafted to give sublime expression to the author's most profound convictions. And the fit becomes a fusion in *Jesus: A Revolutionary Biography*. There the statements made by Crossan's passionately political Jesus prompt some of Crossan's own most passionate political pronouncements (e.g., 1994b, 58–62, 66–74), at which point the circularity driving his method has his wheels spinning in place and autobiography takes the form of vicarious biography.

¶38. Greenblatt grants autobiography a more forthright role in his work. The autobiographical move is one of the five characteristic moves that Veeser ascribes to Greenblatt, as we saw at the outset of this essay. But this move, or "moment," seems to arise more from personal proclivity than methodological conviction; other prominent New Historicists (Louis Montrose would be a case in point) do not evince the same passion for it. "Marlowe and the Will to Absolute Play" contains but a sliver of autobiography (1980, 216). The epilogue to *Renaissance Self-Fashioning* itself is unabashedly autobiographical, however (1980, 255–57), and repeatedly over the years Greenblatt has yielded himself up to the autobiographical impulse, most notably in "Laos is Open" (1996), a recent essay that, from start to finish, is explicitly personal and "confessional."[10] And it is certainly no accident that many of the major themes of Greenblatt's more formal work (especially *Marvelous Possessions* [1991]) are also prominent in this experiment in autobiographical criticism, a riveting account of a visit to Cambodia: exploration and exploitation, colonialism and capitalism, race and representation.

¶39. Crossan, no less than Greenblatt, is a gifted writer, a *creative* writer; but he seems less comfortable with his creativity than Greenblatt, perhaps because he is the denizen of a discipline that still draws a stern distinction between creativity and discovery. Crossan himself pays homage to that distinction in the prologue to *The Historical Jesus,* as we have seen, but the invented episode with which the book opens tells another story. Indeed, it is tempting to regard that episode as a limit example of **that lethal *petit genre*,** the New Historicist anecdote. It tweaks many of the cherished convictions of the average unschooled Christian, along with certain of the cherished convictions of the average Christian scholar. But the anecdote also tweaks its own tail, the tale of the Mediterranean Jewish peasant appended to its posterior. It does so by virtue of its own fictionality, suggesting that although the tail may bristle with historical-sounding data, the muscle that wags it is essentially novelistic. What do we conclude? That the historical is an outgrowth of the textual, the factual an outgrowth of the fictional? But what if the tail were wagging the dog at the same time that the dog was wagging the tail?[z] What if the textual were *also* an outgrowth of the historical, the fictional *also* an outgrowth of the factual?

¶40. Louis Montrose's oft-cited phrase, "the historicity of texts and the textuality of history" (see esp. 1996, 5–6), neatly encapsulates this double perspective. New Historicists refuse to choose **the bottle-bottomed distance glasses** of the historian over **the taped-up reading glasses** of the literary critic. Instead they thrust a bifocal both/and into our blindly outstretched hand. Small wonder if we squirm in the optometrist's chair. For New Historicism would make the search for **the hard-to-see Nazarene** harder, rather than easier, by bringing postpositivist sensibilities to bear upon a task that,

---

z. The canine in question would be one of those scavenger dogs into whose belly Crossan believes the historical Jesus eventually vanished (1994b,127, 154)—which rather limits the possibilities for a glorious emerging on Easter morning.

5. THE QUEST OF THE NEW HISTORICIST JESUS   121

up to now, has tended to be informed by positivist assumptions—hardly a resounding recommendation for New Historicism, I realize, given that the task in question already seems so difficult. But the dictum that has long held true for textual criticism should equally hold true for historical Jesus research: prefer the *lectio difficilior*.

Epilogue

But what's the point of it all? you may well ask. It all depends. What was your text, what was your route, what did you write? Even more, what game were you playing? The New Historicist fascination with contingent connections suggests, to me at least, another way to read. And in this enterprise, we have a new tool, the unexpected product of a new toy. That electronic toy was expected to enable us to do more work, faster, more efficiently, but not differently: business as usual here in the scriptorium. But the toy turned out to be a Trojan horse. The texts that spill out of its belly are fragmented and ephemeral. And free? But can the historical Jesus ever be reassembled out of electronic fragments that continually combine in ever-new associational configurations? Must the quest for the elusive Galilean always take the form of a paper chase? Is the fact that the origins of the quest lie close to the invention of print to be explained in terms of cause or chance? (The quest itself takes no chances. What, or who, is the ultimate cause of this perpetually proliferating pile of paper? it asks. Peel back the pages one by one until he is revealed, naked and shivering under our triumphant gaze.) Can the quest itself survive in hypertextual space?—a space into which New Historicism, although still print-bound, has sent exploratory probes, as we have seen: hence its interest for us. But if the quest cannot survive, then the historical Jesus himself cannot survive. He expires and is entombed once more, and in his place a New Historicist Jesus—or a still more unfamiliar, as-yet-to-be-conceived Jesus—emerges. He comes to us as one unknown, without a name, as of old.… ☞ ¶1

Endnotes

1. These strategies are not the whole campaign, as Veeser himself concedes.
2. Not counting the introductory chapter.
3. Greenblatt also muses on the function of the anecdote in his introduction to *Learning to Curse* (1990, 5–6). Here, too, he takes his lead from Fineman.
4. Compare the still more horrific anecdote with which Michel Foucault opens *Discipline and Punish* (1977a, 3–5, quoted on p. 153 below).
5. Here and in what follows, Thackeray's LCL translation is used, although subject to occasional modification.
6. Fineman, tongue-in-cheek, dubs Thucydides "the first New Historicist" on the basis of that similarity (1989, 51).

7. Crossan 1994b, 133, recycling Crossan 1991, 360 (cf. xii). The first sentence ("Here then is my historical reconstruction…") is not found in the earlier book; there the hypothesis is introduced less boldly as a "tentative and possibly unmethodological proposal" (1991, 360). Crossan seems to have become convinced by his own conjecture in the interval between the two books.

8. Tacitus, too, alludes to this oracle (*Hist.* 5.13), as does Suetonius (*Vesp.* 4). But which oracle is it supposed to be? For a sample of opinions, see Hengel 1989, 237–40, who himself favors Num 24:17.

9. Crossan's six-page introduction to his method begins: "I knew, therefore, before starting this book that it could not be another set of conclusions jostling for place among the numerous scholarly images of the historical Jesus currently available. Such could, no matter how good it was, but add to the impression of acute scholarly subjectivity in historical Jesus research. This book had to raise most seriously the problem of methodology and then follow most stringently whatever theoretical method was chosen" (1991, xxviii). He is also careful to add, however: "It is clear, I hope, that my methodology does not claim a spurious objectivity, because almost every step demands a scholarly judgment and an informed decision. I am concerned, not with an unattainable objectivity, but with an attainable honesty" (1991, xxxiv).

10. And as such partakes of a much larger phenomenon; see pp. 125–72 below.

Further Reading on Poststructuralism and New Historicism

Aichele, George. 1996. *Jesus Framed*. Biblical Limits. London: Routledge. Draws on poststructuralist theory, especially that of Roland Barthes, for a fresh approach to the narrative enigmas of the Gospel of Mark.

Beal, Timothy K. 1997. *The Book of Hiding: Gender, Ethnicity, Annihilation, and Esther*. Biblical Limits. London: Routledge. An eclectic array of French critical theorists—notably, Cixous, Irigaray, Levinas, Lacan, Kristeva, Derrida and Foucault—inform this incisive reading of the book of Esther

Belsey, Catherine. 2002. *Poststructuralism: A Very Short Introduction*. Oxford: Oxford University Press. An expert overview of poststructuralism in 128 pages. Theorists treated include Derrida, Barthes, Lacan, and Foucault.

Conway, Colleen M. 2009. Supplying the Missing Body of Onesimus: Readings of Paul's Letter to Philemon. Pages 475–84 in *Sacred Tropes: Tanakh, New Testament, and Qur'an as Literature and Culture*. Edited by Roberta Sterman Sabbath. BibInt 98. Leiden: Brill. A New Historicist reframing of Philemon and its reception history in relation to the issue of slavery.

Derrida, Jacques. 1996. *Deconstruction in a Nutshell: A Conversation with Jacques Derrida*. Edited by John D. Caputo. New York: Fordham University Press. The extended conversation with Derrida that forms the book's centerpiece is an excellent and accessible introduction to many of the major themes of his later thought, including democracy, justice and the messianic.

———. 2002. *Acts of Religion*. Edited by Gil Anidjar. London: Routledge. Eight essays on such topics as faith, the Babel narrative, hospitality, and Derrida's prayer shawl. An important (if disappointingly truncated) collection of Derrida's major writings on religion.

Gallagher, Catherine, and Stephen Greenblatt. 2000. *Practicing New Historicism*. Chicago: University of Chicago Press. An advanced introduction to New Historicism by two of its leading practitioners. Includes virtuoso analysis of assorted early modern cultural artifacts, ranging from paintings to potatoes.

Hens-Piazza, Gina. 2002. *The New Historicism*. GBS. Minneapolis: Fortress. Situates New Historicism, outlines its recurring characteristics, and discusses its implications for biblical criticism.

Jennings, Theodore W., Jr. 2005. *Reading Derrida/Thinking Paul: On Justice*. Cultural Memory in the Present. Stanford, Calif.: Stanford University Press. Employs the concept of justice beyond the law and other late Derridean themes (such as the gift, hospitality, cosmopolitanism, and forgiveness) to analyze Paul's concept of justice in the Letter to the Romans.

Jobling, David, and Stephen D. Moore, eds. 1991. *Poststructuralism as Exegesis. Semeia* 54. Atlanta: Scholars Press. Contains Derrida's "Des Tours de Babel" (in English, despite the title), one of the most interesting of his biblical forays, along with nine other essays by scholars of the Hebrew Bible and New Testament that engage with a variety of poststructuralist theorists.

Keller, Catherine, and Stephen D. Moore. 2005. Derridapocalypse. Pages 189–207 in *Derrida and Religion: Other Testaments*. Edited by Yvonne Sherwood and Kevin Hart. Chicago: University of Chicago Press. An introduction to some the major themes of Derrida's later thought and a reflection on the book of Revelation in light of them.

Moore, Stephen D. 1992. *Mark and Luke in Poststructuralist Perspectives: Jesus Begins to Write*. New Haven: Yale University Press. Attempts to perform biblical criticism in a register that deconstructs many of the distinctions between it and biblical literature.

———. 1994. *Poststructuralism and the New Testament: Derrida and Foucault at the Foot of the Cross*. Minneapolis: Fortress. An introduction to Derrida, Foucault, and poststructuralism in general, issuing in a Derridean reading of John and a Foucauldian reading of Paul.

———, ed. 1997. *The New Historicism*. BibInt 5:4 (thematic issue). Robert Carroll, Harold Washington, and Yvonne Sherwood on Hebrew Bible texts and themes, and Clive Marsh, Susan Graham, and Stephen Moore on the quest for the historical Jesus, all focused through New Historicism. Aram Veeser responds.

Polaski, Sandra Hack. 1999. *Paul and the Discourse of Power*. The Biblical Seminar 62; Gender, Culture, Theory 8. Sheffield: Sheffield Academic Press. A rare book-length appropriation of Foucauldian thought for biblical interpretation. Employs categories of analysis drawn from Foucault to investigate how Paul negotiates relationships of power with his assemblies and other Christian leaders.

Rutledge, David. 1996. *Reading Marginally: Feminism, Deconstruction and the Bible*. BibInt 21. Argues the relevance of Derridean deconstruction for feminist criticism in general and feminist biblical criticism in particular. The final chapter offers a reading of Gen 2:4b–3:24.

Seeley, David. 1994. *Deconstructing the New Testament*. BibInt 5. Leiden: Brill. Includes chapters on Matthew, Mark, Luke-Acts, John, and the letters of Paul. Argues the close relationship of deconstruction to source criticism and other traditional modes of biblical criticism.

Sherwood, Yvonne, ed. 2004. *Derrida's Bible (Reading a Page of Scripture with a Little Help from Derrida)*. New York: Palgrave Macmillan. Sixteen exegetical essays with an introduction and two response essays. The most significant feature of the collection is that most of the essays engage with "later" Derrida, as opposed to the "early" Derrida who has informed most deconstructive work in biblical studies.

Smith, James A. 2005. *Marks of an Apostle: Deconstruction, Philippians, and Problematizing Pauline Theology*. SemeiaSt 53. Atlanta: Society of Biblical Literature. Although Phil 1:18 is the primary focus of this work, the project of (re)constructing Pauline theology as such is the ultimate object of its deconstructive analysis.

Twomey, Jay. 2005. Reading Derrida's New Testament: A Critical Appraisal. *BibInt* 13:374–403. Incisive assessment by a literary critic of Derrida's various (and rather uneven) forays into the New Testament.

Veeser, H. Aram., ed. 1994. *The New Historicism Reader*. New York: Routledge. An anthology of fifteen selections divided into two parts, "The Beginnings" ("classic" New Historicist selections) and "Some Fractures and Futures of the New Historicism."

Wilson, Andrew P. 2007. *Transfigured: A Derridean Reading of the Markan Transfiguration*. New York: T&T Clark. Argues that the theological sensibilities traditionally brought to bear on the Markan transfiguration have failed to take its measure and performs an alternative reading.

Autobiography

6
True Confessions and Weird Obsessions: Autobiographical Interventions in Literary and Biblical Studies*

If the previous essay ends with the theme of autobiography, the present essay begins and ends with it. The essay was written as a de facto second introduction to the first collection on biblical autobiographical criticism (see Anderson and Staley 1995). Autobiographical criticism's moment has passed in literary studies, and even, it would seem, in biblical studies (see "Further Reading" on pp. 171–72 for its most notable achievements). It has, however, meant rather different things in the two fields. In literary studies, it represented the first significant upsurge of "posttheory" (a phenomenon that is the central topic of the final section of the present collection). As one of the critics quoted in the essay remarked at the time, "We've been living with poststructuralism since the 1970s, and a great weariness has set in, especially in the more rarified theoretical precincts of the profession" (Begley 1994, 57). Autobiographical criticism, a.k.a. personal criticism, was in no small part a reaction to the impersonal, abstruse, highly abstract modes of discourse associated with "high theory," and poststructuralist theory most of all. (And yet not all of it; see the headnote to "Illuminating the Gospels without the Benefit of Color" above).

Autobiographical criticism could not, of course, mean precisely the same thing in biblical studies, which was (and, for the most part, still is) in a pretheory rather than posttheory phase. Yet biblical academese (the lingua franca of traditional biblical studies) is, arguably at least, every bit as impersonal and depersonalizing, abstract and alienating, turgid and tedious as

---

* First published in *Semeia* 72 (1995): 19–51.

literary academese (the lingua franca of theory-infused literary studies). And there is at least one further reason why autobiographical biblical criticism should not simply be dismissed as a fluffy fad whose fifteen minutes has expired. The relationship of autobiographical or personal criticism to what I term in this essay "positional" criticism—and by which I mean contextual hermeneutics, minority criticism (cf. Bailey, Liew, and Segovia 2009), and every other variety of biblical-scholarly writing that emerges *explicitly* out of a specific community or more diffuse sociocultural location—is a complex and important one, as the essay attempts to show. Contextual biblical hermeneutics is not going away any time soon, it would seem. It is a transcontinental biblical-critical phenomenon that, even after several decades of proliferation, is still in ascent (albeit from the margins; cf. Sugirtharajah 2008). How one writes *contextually* will always also be a question of whether, how, or to what extent one writes *personally*, and so the issues raised by autobiographical criticism will, I believe, continue to be relevant for biblical criticism.

"What if everyone started doing it?" wonders Nancy K. Miller (1991, 3). Everyone *is* doing it, insists H. Aram Veeser (1996a, ix–x)—everyone, that is, in the humid hothouses of high theory or putative posttheory. "It" has been called many names in its short life, most conspicuously personal criticism, autobiographical criticism and confessional criticism.[1] For now, an autobiographical flourish in a critical essay is a fashion statement, a gold hoop dangling from the navel of one's argument, a garish tattoo unexpectedly leaping into view, startling the reader out of slumber. (Even if it occupies no more than forty seconds of a forty-minute talk, claims Veeser [1996a, x], the audience will ask questions only about those forty seconds.) But is it more?

Let us begin again. Reacting strongly and sharply to decades of forced immersion in malestream critical language ("I baptize you in the name of the Father…"), many female critics, followed by a few male critics, have begun to contest that abstruse idiom's spurious separation of theory and biography, reflection and emotion, public and private, political and personal (see esp. Tompkins 1993; Freedman, Frey and Murphy Zauhar 1993a). Renouncing, or at least revaluing, the austere, abstract, alienating language of high theory,

---

1. I shall use these terms interchangeably, not having been convinced by attempts to disentangle them (e.g., N. Miller 1991, 1; cf. Freedman 1996, 3–4).

6. TRUE CONFESSIONS AND WEIRD OBSESSIONS 129

these courageous discontents have begun to speak personally, confessionally, autobiographically. Nancy K. Miller even wonders whether personal criticism might not be for women only. "Or do women seem better at it because they've been awash in the personal for so long?" (1991, 19).

"There is no theory that is not a fragment, carefully preserved, of some autobiography," claimed Paul Valéry.[2] If so, the recent irruption of autobiographical criticism in literary studies would simply represent—once again, in yet another guise—the return of the repressed. But because similar autobiographical interventions have recently been recorded in biblical studies, as we shall see, autobiographical literary criticism may provide a yardstick with which to measure the (slighter) autobiographical swerve in biblical studies, and to assess the collision of the personal and the professional that has resulted from that swerve, along with its consequences or lack thereof.

I see a confessional flanked by a pew. The pew contains a queue of literary and cultural critics, mostly women. A few still sport the latest Parisian fashions, although most affect a more indigenous look. As I look on, a gaggle of biblical scholars, mainly men, several draped in the fashions of yesteryear (wide collared disco shirts open to the navel, exposing hirsute chests adorned with faux gold chains) slink in and shyly take their places at the end of the row. One by one, the critics enter the confessional.

Me and My Bladder

What, precisely, *is* personal (autobiographical, confessional) criticism? Let a minimalist definition suffice for now. "Personal criticism, as I mean the term in this book," explains Miller in *Getting Personal*, "entails an explicitly autobiographical performance within the act of criticism" (1991, 1; cf. Brownstein 1996, 31).

Miller's use of the term "performance" is interesting here. Veeser, wrestling with the question, "What does the confessional critic want?" (the very question that, "mutatis mutandis, stumped Freud"), hazards three answers, the first of which is, simply, that the confessional critic wants to perform *(1996a, xiii). Personally, I want them to perform, and to perform well. Perhaps I have contracted a deadly disease from my undergraduates, but increasingly I want to be entertained even as I am being informed. I want to be moved, amused, aroused, absorbed. Admittedly, these are the very things that* literature *is supposed to do to one, but the literary criticism I feel most drawn to is criticism that happens to be literary as well as critical.*

---

2. Undocumented epigraph to Olney 1980.

Personal criticism is a form of self-disclosure, but needless to say the degree of self-disclosure, of self-exposure, varies wildly. What is "personal," anyway? "Is it personal only if it's embarrassing?" muses Miller (1991, 19). At the "degree-zero" end of the scale of self-exposure, Miller places the "academic anecdote" (1991, 1), an autobiographical vignette set in the hallowed groves of academe, in which the professor plays, well, a professor: "As a young visiting instructor at DePauw University in 1954, I recall vividly the experience of standing before a blackboard with my back to a class of college students. I was lecturing on the synoptic problem..." (Farmer 1994, ix). What might we expect to encounter at the other end of the scale? Miller herself provides an arresting, if uncomfortable, example. Her concluding chapter, "My Father's Penis," is a well-wrought rumination on patriarchy, the phallus, and, yes, her father's penis ("I have seen his penis. I have even touched it.... [I]t felt soft and a little clammy" [1991, 144]). And Miller's central example in her opening chapter concerns Jane P. Tompkins's bladder.

Tompkins is perhaps better known to biblical scholars as the enterprising editor and agile theorist of *Reader-Response Criticism: From Formalism to Post-Structuralism* (Tompkins 1980). In 1987, however, she published a daringly unorthodox article entitled "Me and My Shadow," which, in hindsight, readily assumes the appearance of a pioneering work of personal criticism. A certain scene from "Me and My Shadow" has imprinted itself in my mind. And not just in mine, apparently. Miller (1991, 5–7) reports that hostile readers of the article (most of her own students included) have been unable to get past this scene, in which Tompkins, seated in her study, protests that she does not know how to enter the sterile academic debate that she is called upon to enter (she has a response article to write) "without leaving everything else behind—the birds outside my window, my grief over Janice [a friend who has recently committed suicide], just myself as a person sitting here in stockinged feet, a little bit chilly because the windows are open, and thinking about going to the bathroom. But not going yet" (Tompkins 1993, 28).[3]

In our residually prudish culture, explicit toilet-talk is the last bastion of intimacy (when it is not the first recourse of crudity), one that many lifelong couples never care to conquer. And in "polite society," whether in a formal or

---

3. The scene is replayed two pages later: "This is what I want you to see. A person sitting in stockinged feet looking out of her window—a floor to ceiling rectangle filled with green, with one red leaf. The season is poised, sunny and chill, ready to rush down the incline into autumn. But perfect and still. Not going yet" (1993, 30). Compare law professor Patricia J. Williams's self-portrait in her autocritographical "diary": "[Y]ou should know that you are dealing with someone who is writing this in an old terry bathrobe with a little fringe of blue and white tassles dangling from the hem, trying to decide if she is stupid or crazy" (1991, 4).

6. TRUE CONFESSIONS AND WEIRD OBSESSIONS   131

semiformal setting, and above all in mixed company, any volunteering of information concerning the status of one's bladder or bowels, beyond the exquisite euphemism "I need to use the bathroom" (if one is American), is taboo. A statement such as "I need to go, but I think I can hold out for another few minutes" would invite the putdown, "Thanks, but that's more than I need to know right now," unless the sufferer is four or under, in which case the putdown could be substituted with the beaming rejoinder, "My, but you're getting to be *such* a big girl!" Do such considerations account entirely for the derision, discomfort, and downright disgust that Tompkins's realist self-portrait (legs tightly crossed) has elicited, or is there more? Miller thinks there is. She reports that her students, "especially the women…, felt confused and put off" by the author's abdication throughout the article of "the very positions of academic authority" that they themselves "were struggling hard to mime, if not acquire" (1991, 6), an abdication that achieves its perigee, or perhaps its apogee, in the potty passage. Miller concludes: "To the extent that as academics we worry about our own ability to produce the authority effect, we're not sure we want ourselves going to the bathroom in public—especially as women and feminists—our credibility is low enough as it is" (1991, 8). Distinguished literary critic Frank Lentricchia, in contrast, can go the bathroom in public with impunity in his autocritographical experiment, *The Edge of Night*: "Halfway there I have to take a leak.… I can't hold it in for another three hours and twenty-eight minutes.… Dick in hand, I worry about my writing" (1994, 70). The moral of the tale, it would seem, is that personal criticism is more risky for women than for men.

Tompkins herself is not unaware of the danger. "Me and My Shadow" originated as a response to another article in the same issue of *New Literary History*, one by Ellen Messer-Davidow that inquired what the position of feminists should be toward the dominant male intellectual traditions. Tompkins began:

> There are two voices inside me answering, answering to, Ellen's essay. One is the voice of a critic who wants to correct a mistake in the essay's view of epistemology. The other is the voice of a person who wants to write about her feelings (I have wanted to do this for a long time but have felt too embarrassed). This person feels it is wrong to criticize the essay philosophically and even beside the point: because a critique of the kind the critic has in mind only insulates academic discourse further from the issues that make feminism matter. That make *her* matter. The critic, meanwhile, believes such feelings, and the attitudes that inform them, are soft-minded, self-indulgent, and unprofessional.
>
> These beings exist separately but not apart. One writes for professional journals, the other in diaries, late at night. One uses words like "context" and "intelligibility," likes to win arguments, see her name in print, and give

graduate students hardheaded advice. The other has hardly ever been heard from. She had a short story published once in a university literary magazine, but her works exist chiefly in notebooks and manila folders labeled "Journal" and "Private." This person talks on the telephone a lot to her friends, has seen psychiatrists, likes cappuccino, worries about the state of her soul. Her father is ill right now, and one of her friends recently committed suicide. (1993, 24, her emphasis)

A lively argument then ensues between the journal writer and the writer for journals. Of course, the former is given the last word: "So for a while I can't talk about epistemology. I can't deal with the philosophical bases of feminist literary criticism. I can't strap myself psychically into an apparatus that will produce the right gestures when I begin to move. I have to deal with the trashing of emotion [by male academics] and with my anger against it. This one time I've taken off the straitjacket, and it feels so good" (1993, 40).

"I was electrified by this piece when it first appeared," writes Miller (1991, 4). Well, so was I (I had stumbled on it quite by accident in the library), all the more so since Tompkins the theorist, author of the audaciously clever introduction to Reader-Response Criticism, *had been something of a role model for me as a graduate student vainly attempting to track the "implied reader" through some of the thornier thickets of Luke-Acts (she helped me to see that the tracks were mainly my own). Riveted, I didn't want the piece to end, and I remember realizing that this was the first time in ages that I had had that reaction to an academic article, so many of which I begin enthusiastically and end hurriedly, if at all.* "Sometimes, when a writer introduces some bit of story into an essay, I can hardly contain my pleasure," admits Tompkins. "I love writers who write about their own experience. I feel I'm being nourished by them, that I'm being allowed to enter into a personal relationship with them" (1993, 25). *And that, of course, was exactly how I felt reading "Me and My Shadow," although according to the argument mounted therein, I shouldn't have felt that way at all, being a man.*

The soft underbelly of the piece, an irresistible target for the cruel barbs of the critics (cf. N. Miller 1991, 7; Brownstein 1996, 35; Lang 1996, 52), is its stereotyping of gender roles, its gender essentialism. At one point in the article, for instance, Tompkins is dipping into selection of academic books plucked at random from her bookshelf. She quickly decides that "what is gripping, significant, 'juicy'" for men "is different from what is felt to be that way by women." It is a question of "what is important, answers one's needs, strikes one as immediately *interesting*. For women, the personal is such a category" (1993, 36, her emphasis).[4]

---

4. Related to this argument is a second one about emotion. "The public-private

Essentialism aside, it is of course statistically the case that, to date (and notwithstanding the risk noted earlier), very many more women than men have felt compelled to write personal criticism, at any rate in literary studies. "Maybe personal criticism is for women only," Miller surmised in her 1991 book (prematurely, as it turned out, for the next few years would see, in her own field alone, the appearance of Henry Louis Gates's *Colored People* [1994]; Frank Lentricchia's *The Edge of Night* [1994]; *The Intimate Critique* [Freedman et al. 1993] with its three male contributors—only three out of twenty-five, admittedly; and *The Confessions of the Critics* [Veeser 1996b] with its twelve male contributors—although four of them refuse to confess). "Or do women seem better at it because they've been awash in the personal for so long?" continues Miller (1991, 19). Or is it simply that some men are so bad at it? This brings me back to biblical autobiographical criticism.

Impersonal Criticism

I begin with the recently released first volume of *Reading from This Place*, edited by Fernando F. Segovia and Mary Ann Tolbert (1995a). A projected three-volume collection, *Reading from This Place* is designed to explore the intricate interface between social location and biblical interpretation. How does the former impinge upon the latter? How does one's gender, race, ethnicity, nationality, class, sexual orientation or religious affiliation affect one's exegesis? I should emphasize that *Reading from This Place* does not purport to be personal criticism; *positional* criticism might be a better term for the offerings assembled between its covers. Several of the essays in the inaugural volume, however, also happen to be examples of personal criticism,[5] while several others manage to be autobiographical and impersonal at once, as we are about to see.

---

dichotomy, which is to say, the public-private *hierarchy*, is a founding condition of female oppression," she contends (1993, 25, her emphasis). Why? Because Western epistemology "is shaped by the belief that emotion should be excluded from the process of attaining knowledge," and because "women in our culture are not simply encouraged but *required* to be the bearers of emotion," so that "an epistemology which excludes emotions from the process of attaining knowledge radically undercuts women's epistemic authority" (1993, 25–26, her emphasis; cf. 39–40).

5. Just as several of the essays in *The Intimate Critique*, the first collection devoted to autobiographical criticism in literary studies, happen to be explorations of social location. "While not essentializing, the writers in this volume assume the categories of gender, race, class, and ability are among matrices that influence their reading, knowing, and writing" (Freedman et al. 1993, 10).

Daniel Patte's "Acknowledging the Contextual Character of Male, European-American Critical Exegeses: An Androcritical Perspective" (1995a) is a spin-off from his book *Ethics of Biblical Interpretation* (1995b). I am in fundamental agreement with Patte's basic thesis, which is that the work of male European and North American biblical scholars, notwithstanding traditional claims for objectivity, neutrality, and universality, is every bit as interested, ideological, and contextual as that of any other constituency of scholars; and I admire the earnest passion with which he argues it. (After "Me and My Shadow," it's a little harder to write such sentences, however sincere. "Very nice, Jane. You sound so reasonable and generous. But, as anyone can tell you, this is just the obligatory pat on the back before the stab in the entrails" [Tompkins 1993, 26].) Reading Patte's essay, however (yes, here it comes), I was struck by its strange avoidance of autobiographical detail. Three pages into the piece we read:

> Though dispersed throughout the world and thus very different from each other, androcritical biblical scholars[6] share a common twofold experience: that of having been fundamentally challenged in our interpretive and pedagogical practices by feminist, womanist, *mujerista*, African-American, Hispanic-American, Native-American, and/or Third World liberation theologians and biblical scholars, among others; and that of striving to respond constructively to this challenge by radically transforming our practices as critical exegetes and teachers. (Patte 1995a, 37)

I'm intrigued. I've encountered this challenge as well, although I sense that Patte's experience of it has been more devastating than mine. But I want to hear the particulars. A further three pages into the essay, buried in a footnote, I come upon a cryptic reference to a certain conference, a "watershed event" for Patte and his confrère Gary Phillips, at which their failure and that of other unnamed "male European Americans" "to acknowledge and affirm [their] otherness was confronted by feminist, womanist, *mujerista*, African-American, Hispanic-American, and Jewish scholars in biblical criticism and ethics" (1995a, 40 n. 17). But what precisely was said? What did Patte and his white male colleagues say or do to anger or alienate this formidable phalanx of women and minority scholars? And what did the latter say or do in return? We are never told. The scene in question is implicitly presented as the essay's raison d'être. As such, it is potentially the essay's most powerful rhetorical resource, and begs to be shown. What we have here is a failure, or

---

6. Patte's term for white male biblical scholars who are critical of androcentrism.

inability, to stage an autobiographical "performance," and the essay's efficacy is diminished as a result.

Patte's essay is followed by Fernando F. Segovia's "Toward a Hermeneutics of the Diaspora: A Hermeneutics of Otherness and Engagement," which begins: "As the title of the present essay indicates, I believe that the time has come to introduce the real reader, the flesh-and-blood reader, fully and explicitly, into the theory and practice of biblical criticism; to acknowledge that no reading, informed or uninformed, takes place in a social vacuum or desert; to allow fully for contextualization, for culture and experience..." (1995c, 57). This sounds promising. But on the next page, a caveat is introduced: "In this essay I should like to propose, therefore, the beginnings of a hermeneutical framework for taking the flesh-and-blood reader seriously in biblical criticism, not so much as a unique and independent individual but rather as a member of distinct and identifiable social configurations, as a reader from and within a social location" (1995c, 58). A footnote qualifies the caveat: "I certainly do not mean to deny the presence of independence and uniqueness to individuals within such social groupings, but rather to focus on those aspects that characterize individuals as members of special social groupings" (58 n. 3). Segovia then proceeds to outline his own position "as a Hispanic American, with an emphasis on the general characteristics and similarities of this reality rather than on its distinguishing features or characteristics" (61). What follows is instructive and illuminating, yet not as effective as it might have been, or so it seems to me. More even than Patte's self-portrait, Segovia's is a study in abstract minimalism; nothing approaching an autobiographical anecdote is allowed to mar its spare lines and muted tones.[7] But does this not defeat the hermeneutic that Segovia is advocating, one, which in flat opposition to the claimed neutrality and universality of much traditional biblical scholarship, opts "for humanization and diversity" and "resists...any divestiture of all those identity factors that constitute and characterize the reader as reader..." (72). Surely those identity factors cannot simply be reduced to the depersonalizing particulars of a passport, a census form, an affirmative action questionnaire or a police report ("Hispanic male...")? Do Segovia's "hermeneutics of the diaspora" not cry out for personal testimony, autobiographical instance, first-person disclosure?

---

7. Paradoxically, Segovia's general introduction to the volume contains a little more in the way of explicit autobiographical information (1995a, 1–3 passim). (A peculiar rule of the scholarly game dictates here and throughout that I write as though Segovia, Patte and Phillips were merely implied authors, paper personae to me and not cordial acquaintances or longtime friends—possibly the most depersonalizing rule of all.)

Or are there compelling reasons why politically minded critics tend to avoid explicit autobiographical gestures? "Social location," the positional, has connotations of seriousness, of substance. Does the personal, by comparison, have connotations of levity, of triviality? "In the face of the visible extremes of racism or misogyny," Nancy Miller concedes, "the autobiographical project might seem a frivolous response" (1991, xiv). But she continues: "[T]he risk of a limited personalism, I think, is a risk worth running ... in order to maintain an edge of surprise in the predictable margins of organized resistances" (1991, xiv).

Personalism, however, particularly in biblical studies, carries a risk of another sort, namely, the suspension of criticism. The seventh essay in *Reading from This Place* is the first that is truly autobiographical. Justo L. González opens his "Reading from My Bicultural Place: Acts 6:1–7" with a reminiscence:

> I must have been six or seven years old. In a large Methodist church in Cuba, in rather broken Spanish, our missionary pastor was speaking of Peter's denial. "How was it that people knew that Peter was one of Jesus' followers?" he asked. And his answer was quite simple: "When you have been with Jesus, it shows on your face." It was a rather inspiring sermon, calling us all to closer fellowship with Jesus. The problem came later. After the service ended, I sat on a wall by the door, carefully looking at each parishioner as they filed out of the church, and deciding that not one of them had been with Jesus! (1995, 139)

A page or two later I abruptly realize that what I am reading is itself a sermon. This is confessional criticism of a rather different kind.

"Why is it sexy when literary critics do it, but not when biblical critics do it?" a frivolous little voice inside me wants to know. More substantially, I experience the same problem reading González's essay that I've experienced with so much liberation exegesis: it's confessional exegesis, written from faith to faith, written about a "we" that doesn't include me. ("The problem is that as a church we ..." [González 1995, 146]). *Of course, there's absolutely no reason why it should include me. But it does tend to aggravate a persistent little problem of my own, an itch I can't seem to scratch: Why am I still in biblical studies?*

Is it possible for a biblical scholar, committed to writing self-consciously out of his or her social location, to navigate successfully between the Scylla of insufficient personalism, on the one hand, and the Charybdis of insufficient criticism, on the other? I believe it is. I see it happening in Amy-Jill Levine's "'Hemmed in on Every Side': Jews and Women in the Book of Susanna," for example, which begins so compellingly ("I am a Jew. My interest in the origins of Christianity began when a neighbor accused me of 'killing the Lord'..." [1995, 175]), and continues as critically as the subject matter demands; or in

6. TRUE CONFESSIONS AND WEIRD OBSESSIONS   137

Regina Schwartz's "Nations and Nationalism: Adultery in the House of David" (1992), in which the author's reflections on early Israelite monarchy are skillfully refracted through her first-hand impressions of modern Israeli militarism; or in Robert Allen Warrior's "Canaanites, Cowboys, and Indians: Deliverance Conquest, and Liberation Theology Today," an eye-opening reading of the biblical conquest narratives by a Native American ("I read ... with Canaanite eyes" [1989, 262]); or in Jeffrey Staley's *Reading with a Passion: Rhetoric, Autobiography, and the American West in the Gospel of John* (1995), about which I shall have much to say below.

Shortly after beginning this section, right after I had quoted Tompkins on the stab in the entrails, I myself was disemboweled. The heavens opened and a great sword descended, or at any rate the doorbell rang. It was the mail, including a mystery envelope from Fortress Press, which turned out to contain, not a check, to my disappointment, but a copy of a review of my last book by somebody whose own work I've read and whom I once ran into at a conference (where else?). Anyway, he has some very nice things to say about the book initially, but I won't bore you with those. The part of the book that least impressed him, however, is the part that most impressed me (is it ever otherwise?), my first foray into autobiographical criticism, which begins "My father was a butcher" (which he was), goes on in that (opened) vein for a paragraph or two, and then cuts to an extended meditation on Paul's fixation with Jesus' gruesome demise in light of Foucault's Discipline and Punish, *particularly its grisly opening scene, the public dismemberment of an eighteenth-century regicide. By way of inclusio, I wax autobiographical again at the end. Well, the reviewer was entirely unconvinced that "the story of a sensitive young Irish boy ... who witnessed the slaughter of animals by his butcher father, but who did not collapse until a priest preached of the dreadful slaying of Jesus at a Good Friday service," could have anything to do with Paul's contagious crucifixion. He concludes: "It appears to me that there are sounder ways of making sense of Pauline Christology (especially via the apocalyptic paradigm advocated by J. C. Beker)." Yes, but a dutiful display of sound sense could have been enacted in this case only at the cost of a certain repression, a strong, silent misrepresentation of what the crucifixion has really meant in my life, and at the time I wasn't willing to pay the price.*

Anyway, what I want to mull on here is my sense, undoubtedly exaggerated, that this reviewer and I hail from different dimensions. Because if Patte is correct, the reviewer and I should be shoulder to shoulder on the same team, covertly pursuing our group's common interests and concerns. I'm white, male, and of Irish Roman Catholic stock, and so is he. We should be golf buddies, surely. And perhaps to a casual observer, a third biblical scholar from the Third World, say, this individual and I might indeed appear as alike in our exegetical strategies as two peas in the proverbial pod, although I doubt it. You see, this person happens to be a Roman Catholic priest, whereas I, on a good day, am an agnostic. Yes, we do have a common set of professional interests to promote—the perpetuation of an expert discourse on the Bible, something that is essential to our material survival (mine more than his, perhaps)—but I assume that's true of everyone, anywhere, who makes, or ekes, a living from teaching and writing on this perennial best seller. I don't know for certain, of course, but I suspect that this person's scholarly research has the overall effect of validating his original decision to become, his daily decision to remain, a priest. I do know for certain that my own scholarly research has had the (no less convenient) effect of validating my own unbelief. And I further suspect that that is the real reason why he and I can have so much, and yet so little, in common.

Why am I still in biblical studies? Simple: because I'm stuck here. I do still love the Bible, but I'm no longer in love with it (much less with Him), and I haven't been for a very long time. There are many other things—literature, popular culture, art...—that I could imagine teaching or researching instead, and with a passion. Still, I plan to remain faithful to the Bible till retirement do us part. Of course, the temptation to squeeze all my other interests into my biblical work has long proved irresistible. ("What are you working on?" a colleague from English politely inquires. "The muscular male body," I reply. [Pause.] "And the Bible?" she prompts dubiously. With minor variations, this scene has replayed itself again and again over the years; only the inquirer and my reply vary.) I've just completed a manuscript (on the Bible—what else?) that begins: "This is an intensely personal book. Its three parts spring from a phobia and two fascinations, each of which has shadowed me since childhood...." Autobiography by any other name? Assuredly. Self-indulgent? Perhaps. But whom should I indulge instead? The stern fathers of our discipline (as it is so aptly named)?

INSUBSTANTIAL SELVES

If confessional criticism is currently "hot" in literary studies, that is due in no small part to the stages on which it is being performed, such as the English department at Duke University, that sizeable stable of expensive intellectual thoroughbreds no fewer than six of whose faculty have recently abandoned themselves to the autobiographical impulse (Davidson 1993; Kaplan 1993; Lentricchia 1994; Sedgwick 1993; Tompkins 1993, 1996a, 1996b; Torgovnick 1994). Why this sudden outbreak of autobiographical moonlighting among critics whose day job, after all, is the explication of literary texts (cf. Veeser 1996a, x)? "I'm not supposed to be writing this," Lentricchia guiltily confesses, "I'm supposed to be finishing my never-ending book on modernism, the last chapter, the others have been done for so long (I almost wrote 'dead for so long')" (1994, 123). "This swerve into the autobiographical mode," one commentator explains, "indicates the exhaustion of the dominant critical idiom. We've been living with poststructuralism since the 1970s, and a great weariness has set in, especially in the more rarified precincts of the profession" (Frederick Crews quoted in Begley 1994; cf. N. Miller 1991, 20).

Yet the very audible splash that personal criticism is making at certain elite institutions is but the froth on a wave that has been cresting for quite some time. Feminism, for instance, has long been predicated on the personal; one immediately thinks of the early feminist slogan "The personal is political" (cf. Brownstein 1996, 32; Freedman 1996, 8). Most academic feminists, however, did not write a personalized prose. Miller notes that although the writings of pioneering feminist literary critics "were clearly fueled by a profound understanding of the consequences of taking the personal as a category of thought," these critics nonetheless opted to express themselves in PhD-ese (1991, 14). The subsequent "triumph of theory," so-called, poststructuralist theory in particular, only served further to depersonalize academic feminism (cf. Tompkins 1993, 24, 36–37). Much confessional criticism, then, especially that issuing from feminist circles—which is to say, most of it to date—can be read as an attempted recovery of feminism's personal, experiential, autobiographical base.

What else might be impelling the autobiographical turn in literary studies? It cannot be unrelated to the upsurge of interest in the *study* of autobiography that the profession has witnessed in recent years (e.g., Olney 1972, 1980; Spengemann 1980; Gunn 1982; Eakin 1985; Lejeune 1989; Folkenflik 1993; Ashley et al. 1994; Marcus 1994). This interest is not itself unrelated to feminism, since much of it has focused on women's autobiographies (e.g., S. Smith 1987; Benstock 1988; Personal Narratives Group 1989; Smith and Watson 1992; Stanley 1992; Gilmore 1994; Kosta 1994; Perreault 1995). "During the past five hundred years," as Sidonie Smith argues, "autobiography has assumed a central position in the personal and literary life of the West precisely because it serves as one of those generic contracts that reproduces the patrilineage and its ideologies of gender" (1987, 44). For most of this period, women have been consigned to the margins of the dominant autobiographical tradition; with few exceptions, the letter, the diary, the journal and other "culturally muted" media of self-representation have been their assigned province (1987, 44). The issue assumes a particular intensity and importance in the colonial context. Traditionally, the quintessential subject of autobiography has been conceived of as male, or even as "Man," the universal human subject, alias the "straight white Christian man of property" (Watson and Smith 1992, xvii). Over against this representative Man, Western thought, at least since the "age of discovery," has tended to set the colonized, an anonymous, amorphous, "opaque collectivity of undifferentiated bodies"

(1992, xvii). It is the self-representation, oral or written, of the colonized subject, and above all the colonized female subject, that is the focus of much of the most provocative recent work on autobiography (see esp. Lionnet 1989; Smith and Watson 1992).

The postcolonial condition receives a rather different treatment in Jeffrey Staley's *Reading with a Passion* (1995), the first book-length experiment in biblical autobiographical criticism The book is divided into two parts. Part 1 is entitled "Reading the Text," the text in question being the Fourth Gospel, and part 2 is entitled "Reading the Reader," the reader being the author himself. "The arguments raised against formalist reader-response criticism have finally worked their way under my thick skin," the second part begins (1995, 113). Staley is now ready to come clean and confess that the "implied reader" of the Fourth Gospel, the protagonist of his published doctoral dissertation (1988), was really Staley himself all along. But Staley is going to need some time to don a new persona. "When you've been hiding behind implied and encoded readers as long as I have, it's not easy to slip into something more comfortable, curl up in a chair, and tell a stranger who you are" (1995, 114). And Staley insists that he doesn't know who he is in any case, as we shall see.

When Staley was seven years old, his white missionary parents moved the family to the Navajo Indian reservation in northeastern Arizona. Staley's sojourn on the Navajo reservation is the subject of "Not Yet Fifty: Postcolonial Confessions from an Outpost in the San Juan Basin," the autobiographical, and pivotal, chapter of *Reading with a Passion*. As literature, the chapter beggars summary, except of the most banal sort. For present purposes, I shall restrict myself to those passages in which Staley reflects on the roles that the Gospel of John has played in his life and the roles that *he* has played in *John's* life. "I have uncovered St. John every time that I have peered into my past," he writes. "In my childhood years on the Navajo reservation it flowed with the muddied waters of the San Juan River of northern New Mexico and southern Utah. It lay deep beneath the snowcapped San Juan Mountains of southern Colorado" (1995, 197). On the banks of the San Juan, Staley learned that

> the word *john* was pejorative reservation slang derisively used by Anglos and "town Navajos" for any Navajo who had not made the transition from traditional Indian culture to the dominant Caucasian culture and its values. Like a chapter from my childhood (like the red-letter text of John in my missionary parents' home or the two-dimensional topographical map on our schoolroom wall), John seems to me to be a Gospel that outwardly has a simple message, clearly stated and transparent. But underneath that message there is another which—like the john world outside my childhood front door, or the three-dimensional desert floor—often seems to subvert and controvert the previously established norm. As I approach the end of my fifth decade of

life, I am beginning to think that I have long been the unsuspecting victim of two johns, two geographies, and two existential ironies. (1995, 195)

The john world was a harsh one, in many ways, for the gestating Johannine scholar. "Outside our childhood home, white-skinned people were dirty, smelly, and stupid," he recalls. "To most of the Navajo children we played with, our heads were strangely shaped, protruding out from the backsides of our necks like grossly overgrown tumors; likewise our genitals were curiosity pieces, a topic of frequent speculative conversations. We transmitted ghost-sicknesses, and a strange cow-like odor followed us wherever we went" (1995, 170). He recalls how he and his brother once incurred the wrath of four Navajo men, one brandishing a shotgun, by swimming in a small irrigation reservoir near the mission. "As it turned out, the Navajos were afraid that our pallid skin would somehow wash off in the coffee-colored water, spreading deadly diseases to their sheep that drank from the reservoir" (171). Through this and other trials, the misplaced missionaries' son soon learned "that brown skin denoted intelligence, along with beauty, cleanliness, and everything that was good in the world" (172).

What conclusions does the elder Staley, explorer of St. John's Gospel, draw from the cultural misadventures of the younger Staley, explorer of the john world of the San Juan basin? In the preceding chapter he speculates that the theory of "Johannine reader victimization," which he first conceived in *The Print's First Kiss* (1988, 95–118) and is further fleshed out in *Reading with a Passion* (1995, 85–109)—the notion that the implied reader of the Fourth Gospel is the foremost victim of its ironies—"was rooted in [his] own childhood experience of being a victim of ethnic and racial discrimination as much as it was rooted in [his] professional reading of literary criticism" (1995, 115). If this is indeed the case, the critics of biblical reader-response criticism would be proved right ("What Staley's reader construct masks is the critic himself; Staley's reader reads the way Staley does," etc.), Staley's scholarship being shown to be unconscious, unacknowledged autobiography.

As will by now be apparent, Staley treads a fine line in his autobiographical reminiscences and reflections. The risk he ran was that of writing something that would be read as a resentful tale of reverse discrimination. It seems to me that he has successfully circumvented that danger. There is not a trace of bitterness in his tone. He shows himself to be well aware both of the horrific history of exploitation and oppression that made the reservations "necessary" in the first place, and of the fact that his Caucasian features and complexion sufficed to open up innumerable doors for him in the world outside the reservation that would forever be closed to his Navajo friends (see esp. 1995, 184–85).

Staley's book constitutes a double challenge to biblical scholars. First, he challenges us to come out from behind the assorted ceremonial masks that we don whenever we exegete the biblical texts, whether those masks bear the blurred features of a hypothetical "original" reader or hearer of the texts (what most historical critics like to hide behind), or the highly stylized, heavily made up features of an "implied" reader of the texts (what most literary critics like to hide behind), or, more generally, the cold, withdrawn, impassive features of a strenuously impersonal style of writing (what most of us like to hide behind most of the time). But this is a challenge that has already been voiced by others, including myself (1989, 71–107). What sets Staley's book apart is his determination to press beyond the now facile formula, "I am a white, male, middle-class, heterosexual, Protestant biblical scholar," and expend the same amount of energy exegeting his own investments, biases and neuroses as an interpreter as he expends in exegeting the biblical text.

This is commendable, but uncommonly difficult. For what Staley discovers, as we shall see, is that the self is no less slippery than the text, and never more so than when the interpreter is reaching out, hammer in hand, to grasp it and nail it down. Then it begins to thrash uncontrollably. And even should the interpreter succeed in gripping it, he or she might find that it is not a single self after all, but a fistful of selves, which slither surreptitiously between the fingers and slip away. This brings us finally to structuralism and poststructuralism; for although the self of which many postcolonial critics write is indeed a split self, a self constituted by two or more conflicting cultural identities, it is with French critical theory that the fragmented self has been supremely associated, and the relationship of this to personal criticism must now be considered.

Two things, arguably the only things, linking Lévi-Strauss, Lacan, Barthes and Foucault, the four thinkers routinely singled out in 1960s France as most representative of structuralism, were (1) a fixation with language as the supreme semiotic system and, as such, the fundamental element in socialization, coupled with (2) an implacable opposition to any system of thought that accorded a preeminent, or even a privileged, position to the individual human subject. (2) appeared to follow inexorably from (1). For if one's subjectivity is purely the result of one's insertion into the infinitely fecund matrix of language, then language, whether in its simpler or more complex manifestations (as system, structure, code, culture, etc.), must be accorded absolute primacy in any rigorous system of thought, and the subject must be regarded merely as language's most impressive "effect," admittedly intricate, but ultimately ephemeral. For structuralism in general, moreover, and for Lacan and Barthes in particular, the subject that emerges in and through language is necessarily a fractured, fragmented, decentered, disunified subject.

6. TRUE CONFESSIONS AND WEIRD OBSESSIONS   143

Structuralism's sleight-of-hand elision of the comfortable, solid-seeming self of traditional humanism appeared to have far-reaching consequences both for biography and autobiography; for if inside each of us there is not, after all, an essential, integral, inalienable self, predisposing us to act within certain more or less predictable parameters as the plot, or script, of our lives unfolds, then how can it be possible to capture on paper the discernible contours, the internal coherence, the underlying logic of a life? This is not to say that autobiography could be of no interest to structuralism or its mutant cousin poststructuralism. On the contrary, autobiography could provide the latter with a text through which to dismantle classic conceptions of the self. And *Roland Barthes by Roland Barthes* (1977c) would be the classic case in point.[8]

Biography was offensive to Barthes as a literary genre because it represented "a counterfeit integration of its subject" (Sturrock 1979, 53; cf. Calvet 1995, xi-xiv). Barthes's second book, *Michelet par lui-même*, opened with the following disclaimer: "In this little book the reader will not find either a history of Michelet's ideas, or a history of his life, still less an explanation of one by the other" (1954, 1). And his *Sade/Fourier/Loyola* ended with parodic biographies of Sade and Fourier (1976, 172–84). Fourier's "life," for instance, consists of a chaotic and altogether arbitrary list of "facts" numbered from 1 to 12 (e.g., "4. Fourier hated old cities: Rouen" [1976, 183]). Predictably, therefore, Barthes declared of himself, "I have no biography" (1981, 245).

What, then, are we to make of *Roland Barthes by Roland Barthes*? "It must all be considered as if spoken by a character in a novel," we are cautioned on the first page.[9] Needless to say, the novel in question is no *Bildungsroman*, no tightly integrated plot of inexorable progress toward harmonious selfhood. Indeed, when the preliminary caution is later reiterated, Barthes adds: "…or rather by several characters" (1977c, 119). As though to figure this irreducible plurality in the autobiographical subject, *Roland Barthes by Roland Barthes* is written for the most part in the third person—it begins: "In what he writes, there are two texts…" (1977c, 43)[10]—punctuated with passages in the first

---

8. Also worthy of note is Derrida's "Circumfession" (1993), which combines oblique philosophical reflection on such texts as Augustine's *Confessions* with autobiographical reminiscence. The latter too is oblique, as one might expect from a thinker who once blurted out, in response to an interviewer's probing: "Ah, you want me to tell you things like 'I-was-born-in-El-Biar-in-the-suburbs-of-Algiers-in-a-petit-bourgeois-Jewish-family-which-was-assimilated-but….' Is this really necessary? I just couldn't do it, you'll have to help me" (Derrida 1988b,74). Further on Derrida and autobiography, see R. Smith 1995, esp. 40–48.

9. Cf. Barthes 1971, 89: "[A]ny biography is a novel that dares not speak its name."

10. The first forty-two pages are taken up with photographs of the (mostly) younger Barthes, with ironic or lyrical captions by the elder Barthes.

and, less often, the second person. Soon after the book appeared, Barthes was invited to review it himself (see Calvet 1995, 206–7), an opportunity to stage a Barthes on Barthes by Barthes that he gleefully accepted: the author as amoeba.

Refusing a unified autobiographical subject, *Roland Barthes by Roland Barthes* also refuses a conventional autobiographical plot. Instead it is made up entirely of fragments (as is his *Michelet*). "To write by fragments: the fragments are then so many stones on the perimeter of a circle: I spread myself around: my whole little universe in crumbs; at the center, what?" (1977c, 92–92). The fragments themselves are small slabs of prose composed sometimes of a single sentence, sometimes of several paragraphs, each with its own title, each entirely self-contained. Their order of succession is largely alphabetical by title (*Actif/réactif, L'adjectif, L'aise…*), which is to say arbitrary or aleatory; the scraps of a life can always be assembled differently.[11] In short, *Roland Barthes by Roland Barthes* is less an autobiography than an *an/autobiography*, a relentless exploration, or rather a ruthless exposure, or, better still, an extraordinarily austere renunciation of identity as a fiction (cf. Barthes 1975, 62; Moriarty 1991, 173).

Awkward questions do arise, nonetheless, as one contemplates Barthes's project in this book. Isn't there something a little disingenuous about it? Isn't there a sense in which *Roland Barthes by Roland Barthes*, with its resolute refusal of a teleological plot, is given the lie by Roland Barthes's curriculum vitae? Indeed, the book ends with a two page "Biography," a conventional compilation of dates, events, and accomplishments. The final item is dated 1962 and reads, "Director of studies at the École pratique des Hautes Études…" (1977c, 184). Of course, Barthes's ascent up the academic ladder did not end there. In 1976 he was appointed to a chair at the Collège de France, the most prestigious academic appointment in the Francophone world. Barthes's biographer, Louis-Jean Calvet (1995), despite an impressive show of scruples in his preface at the very idea of writing a biography of this arch antibiographer, nevertheless lets Barthes's CV dictate much of the biographical plot: chapter 7, for example, is entitled "The École, At Last," while chapter 10 is simply entitled "The Collège de France."

Of course, Barthes is not the only structuralist or poststructuralist whose dismissive pronouncements on the self or subject have elicited awkward questions. In recent years it has become commonplace in certain circles to point out how, coincidentally, or perhaps conveniently, the dramatic "disappearance" of the subject staged by structuralist and poststructuralist theorists in the 1960s and 1970s—white male theorists, almost without exception—

---

11. Barthes would again employ the fragmentary technique and the alphabetical arrangement in *A Lover's Discourse* (1978).

6. TRUE CONFESSIONS AND WEIRD OBSESSIONS

occurred just as women and racial/ethnic minorities were themselves finally achieving unprecedented status as full subjects and free agents—and in precisely those parts of the world where structuralism and poststructuralism were flourishing (Western Europe and North America).

In still other circles, however, including those from which personal criticism has begun to emerge, the poststructuralist erasure of the subject is dismissed with a casual shrug. More precisely, it is read in hindsight as a rhetoric of hyperbole, useful, even necessary, in its day, but not any longer. Jane Tompkins, for instance, asked by an interviewer "how she reconciles her autobiographical voice with postmodernist notions of the self as a fractured entity," responds with a blank "Who needs to say that anymore?" (Begley 1994, 57); while Nancy Miller would posit a causal connection between the demise of the kind of theory that presumed to say such things in the first place and the rise of personal criticism (1991, 29).

Yet again, one can refuse to choose between theory and self, summoning up the specter of the insubstantial subject even while engaging in personal criticism. This Jeffrey Staley does deep into *Reading with a Passion*, summarily dismissing the solid-seeming self whose interpretive misadventures, first in St. John's Gospel and then in the San Juan Basin, he has been narrating:

> I have discovered nothing from reading myself as a reader. Nothing except that I can as easily hide and lie about myself as I can about the Gospel of John. And if the critics of reader-response criticism tell me my Johannine "reader" is a fiction, critics of autobiography tell me that the "self" I have read reading the Gospel of John is no less a fiction. The "I" of this chapter is nothing more than print and paper conceived from the unholy trinity of Tony Hillerman's popular, quasi-anthropological detective novels, my own piecemeal memory, and sacred Scripture. But then, the same can be said of Jesus' self-disclosing "I Am" in John's Gospel. It is not his own either. It is merely the text of Exodus 3:14 pinned precariously to his lips by some nameless author. All our reconstructed personae are intertextual and linguistic fictions, whether the referent (or "deferent") is "Jesus," "Jeffrey," or the "Johannine encoded reader." (1995, 198)[12]

Yes, but so what? The notion of an undivided self, an ontologically prior essence, an internal fountain of truth capable of expressing itself without

---

12. Cf. Simpson 1996, 86, who asserts that "[a]fter Foucault and many other critics and philosophers … the private voice of Jane Tompkins or anyone else" can no longer bear any necessary correlation to a self, such selves having once and for all been exposed "as nothing more than a string of attributes and contingent connections masquerading as an entity."

misrepresenting itself is certainly a fiction. But this fiction is by no means necessary in order for selves to communicate, imperfectly but adequately, with other selves, and thereby effect change in the material conditions of their existence. Yet even that is not the bottom line. Theory may indeed cause the unproblematized self to shimmer, flicker, and finally vanish. But the fictional, unfragmented self reappears, or had better reappear, the moment one begins to interact again with other selves, or else one risks confinement in one of those highly unpleasant holding places that our society reserves for ill-formed selves.[13]

Does such an uncontroversial assertion need substantiation? I speak from experience, in case it does, although it was not megadoses of Lacan, Foucault, and Derrida (LFD?) that caused it; rather, it was megadoses of LSD. I was through with hallucinogenics by 1972, but they weren't through with me. Two years later I experienced a religious conversion that took the form of a six-week LSD flashback, at the height of which I became convinced that I was God bringing Myself into existence (I'm nothing if not modest), and that resulted in an involuntary confinement (my second), complete with electric shock therapy. Yes, I had to be crazy to become a biblical scholar (for that's how it all began). Best leave the last word to Tompkins, then: "This one time I've taken off the straitjacket, and it feels so good" (1993, 40).

---

13. In fairness to Staley it should be noted that he too raises, and wrestles with, the "so what?" question, although from a different angle (see esp. 1995, 19–20, 199, 236ff.).

7
THE DIVINE BUTCHER*

In March 2004 I sat in a sold-out auditorium in my local multiplex watching gore splatter the silver screen. The movie was not the remade *Texas Chainsaw Massacre*, however, which had been released some months earlier, nor yet the *Friday the 13th/A Nightmare on Elm Street* crossover, *Freddy vs. Jason*, also from around this time. Instead it was a splatter flick of another kind, Mel Gibson's *The Passion of the Christ*, and its interminable flogging scene was fully underway. To my dismay I began to feel the onset of a queasiness that I associate with the gruesome Good Friday sermons of my Irish Catholic childhood ("Next, dear brethren, the hammering home of the nails. But 'nails' is too mild a term for the monstrous spikes, crusted over with the dried blood of earlier victims, that would undoubtedly have been used to inflict the utmost agony on our blessed Lord…"). "How are you doing?" I whispered to my wife, hoping she would reply "Not so good" so that I could offer to accompany her outside for a breath of fresh air. "I'm all right," she answered serenely. To prove it she had taken out her knitting. I glanced across at the friends with whom we had come, Jewish like my wife, and curious, like her, to see what all the fuss was about. They too seemed to be taking the flogging in stride; and all around the crowded auditorium, indeed, ordinary-looking people of all ages were calming munching their popcorn and sipping their sodas while the atrocious violence unfolded on the screen. I closed my eyes and sank into a cold half-faint, in which state I remained for most of the rest of the film.

---

* First published in Francis Watson, ed., *The Open Text: New Directions for Biblical Studies?* (London: SCM, 1993), 121–39, under the title "God's Own (Pri)son: The Disciplinary Technology of the Cross."

Afterwards I found it difficult to articulate why it was that I felt *The Passion of the Christ* was symptomatic of a pathology intrinsic to all crucifixated variants of Christianity. I mumbled that the film's spectacular violence is enacted under the aegis of the doctrine of atonement: the text of Isa 53:5 ("But he was pierced for our transgressions, he was crushed for our iniquities; the punishment that brought us peace was upon him, and by his wounds we are healed") is displayed in one of the film's opening frames. But in fact I had articulated the argument a decade earlier in the essay that follows. Clearly my take on the crucifixion and its thick theological encrustations is visceral as well as intellectual and phobic as well as personal (as the reviewer whom I quote in the previous essay rightly recognized). What I am attempting in this essay is the transformation of intense emotion into intellectual analysis, as well as the exorcism of certain of my personal demons, as the autobiographical fragments that frame the essay attest. Did it work? Not as therapy; the demons are still in residence. Whether or not it works as argument I leave the reader to judge.

"Father, save me from this hour...." (John 12:27)

"Father, ... remove this cup from me...." (Mark 14:36)

"Father, don't you see I'm burning?" (Freud 1900, 5:510)[1]

I begin with a confession, although it is not yet my own. "Now my soul is troubled [*nun he psychē mou tetaraktai*]," confesses the Johannine Jesus in an uncharacteristic moment of uncertainty as the hour of his flogging and crucifixion draws near. "And what shall I say? 'Father, save me from this hour?'" All too quickly he collects himself: "No, it is for this reason that I have come to this hour. Father, glorify your name" (John 12:27–28). As it happens, the Father has something quite exquisite up his sleeve. He will arrange for his Son to be condemned to death around noon on the day of preparation for the Passover (19:13–16)—the precise hour when the slaughter of the passover lambs

---

1. This question forms the climax of a dream that was reported third-hand to Freud, a dream that seems to have affected him deeply, as it does me (see Freud 1900, 5:509–11; cf. 533–34, 542, 550, 571).

will begin in the temple precincts nearby (cf. 19:29, 36; Exod 12:22, 46; Num 9:12; 1 Cor 5:7).[2] In truth, however, Jesus' throat was cut from the moment that he first strayed, bleating, into this Gospel: "Here is the Lamb of God who takes away the sin of the world!" exclaims John the Baptist upon first spotting him (1:29). The next day, Jesus staggers by again, still bleeding profusely (cf. Rev 5:6). "Look, here is the Lamb of God!" John again exclaims (1:36; cf. Acts 8:32ff.; 1 Pet 1:18–19; Rev 5:6–13). Two of the Baptist's disciples set off hungrily after Jesus (1:37), following a trail of blood. The trail leads straight to the cross, which is also a spit, for it is as *roast* lamb that Jesus must fulfill his destiny (cf. 6:52–57: "How can this man give us his flesh to eat?"). Justin Martyr saw this more clearly than most: "[T]hat [passover] lamb which was commanded to he wholly roasted [Exod 12:8–9] was a symbol of the suffering of the cross which Christ would undergo. For the lamb, which is roasted, is roasted and dressed up in the form of the cross. For one spit is transfixed right through the lower parts up to the head, and one across the back, to which are attached the legs of the lamb" (*Dialogue with Trypho* 40.3, ANF trans.).

My own father too was a butcher, and a lover of lamb with mint sauce. As a child, the inner geographical boundaries of my world extended from the massive granite bulk of the Redemptorist church squatting at one end of our street to the butcher shop guarding the other end. Redemption, expiation, sacrifice, slaughter.... There was no city abattoir in Limerick in those days; each butcher did his own slaughtering. I recall the hooks, the knives, the cleavers; the utter terror in the eyes of the victim; my own fear that I was afraid to show; the crude stun-gun slick with grease; the stunned victim collapsing to its knees; the slitting of the throat; the filling of the basins with blood; the skinning and evisceration of the carcass; the wooden barrels overflowing with entrails; the crimson floor littered with hooves.

I also recall a Good Friday sermon by a Redemptorist preacher that recounted at remarkable length the atrocious agony felt by our sensitive Savior as the spikes were driven through his wrists and feet. Crucifixion, crucifixation, crucasphyxiation.... Strange to say, it was this somber recital, and not the slaughter-yard spectacle, that finally caused me to faint. Helped outside by my father, I vomited gratefully on the steps of the church.

---

2. Colossal quantities of passover lambs, if Philo is to be believed (*On the Special Laws* 2.27.145). Most of the major commentators on the Fourth Gospel note in passing the connection between the commencement of the slaughter and Jesus' sentencing. Raymond Brown is more loquacious than most (1970, 883; 1994, 1:847–48).

MORS TURPISSIMA CRUCIS

> Then they will hand you over to be tortured.... (Matthew 24:9)

The central symbol of Christianity is the figure of a tortured man. Attending an exhibition of instruments of torture in Rome, classicist Page duBois reports: "I gazed uneasily at the others visiting this spot.... I tried to imagine what brought them there. Was it a historical curiosity about the Middle Ages, or the same desire that brings people to horror movies, or sexual desire invested in bondage and discipline? I was there too" (1991, 2). Such unease would be almost unimaginable in a Sunday service, and yet the central spectacle is not altogether dissimilar. The Gospels do nothing to disturb the bland equanimity with which the average Christian views this grisly spectacle. The Evangelists seem smitten with verbal constipation as they describe the scourging and crucifixion of Jesus. Tersely John tells us that "Pilate took Jesus and flogged him [*elabon ho Pilatos ton Iēsoun kai emastigōsen*]" (19:1). Mark and Matthew relegate the scourging to a subordinate clause: "and after flogging Jesus, he handed him over to be crucified [*kai paredōken ton Iēsoun phragellōsas hina staurōthē*]" (Mark 15:15; cf. Matt. 27:26). Luke has Jesus publicize his flogging well in advance (18:33), but passes over the event itself in silence (although see 23:16, 22). What none of the Evangelists find it necessary to say is that the scourging would almost certainly have been administered with a short *flagrum* composed of several single or braided leather thongs, each adorned with jagged fragments of bone, or weighted with metal balls, or both; or that the severity of the flogging, when it was a prelude to crucifixion, was commonly calculated to bring the condemned to the edge of the grave, thereby shortening his sojourn on the cross (cf. Mark 15:44; John 19:33; see further Leclercq, 1907–53; Blinzler 1959, 222–55 passim). Contrast Josephus, who telling of the flogging of a different Jesus before a different Roman procurator, cannot resist throwing in a graphic detail: "he was scourged till his bones were laid bare [*mastixi mechri osteōn xainomenos*]" (*Jewish War* 6.5.3, my trans.).[3] Earlier he claims that he himself had certain of his Galilean enemies scourged "until the entrails of all of them were exposed [*mechri pantōn ta splagchna gymnōsai*]" (*Jewish War* 2.21.5, my trans.; cf. Josephus, *Life* 30.147).

The restraint exercised by the Evangelists in their accounts of Jesus' flagellation is matched only by the restraint exercised in their accounts of his crucifixion. "They crucify him [*staurousin auton*]" is all that Mark will say (15:24). Luke is no less tight-lipped (23:33), while Matthew and John actually consign the event to a subordinate clause: "And when they had crucified

---

3. The Jesus in question is Jesus son of Ananias, and the procurator is Albinus.

him [*staurōsantes de auton*], they divided his clothes..." (Matt 27:35; cf. John 19:18). The Gospel of Peter drains the scene still further of its horror: "And they brought two criminals and crucified the Lord between them. But he himself remained silent, as if in no pain" (4:1, trans. from R. Miller 1995; cf. Apoc. Pet. 81:15–23).

It would not be difficult, however, to imagine the crucifixion of Jesus retold in the merciless manner of another contemporary work, 4 Maccabees,[4] which recounts in unsparing detail the execution by torture of an elderly Jew, Eleazar, under the baleful glare of the Syrian tyrant Antiochus IV Epiphanes—an execution, which, as it happens, also commences with a flogging:

> After they had tied his arms on each side they cut him with whips [*mastixin katēkizon*], while a herald who faced him cried out, "Obey the king's commands!" But the courageous and noble man ... was unmoved, as though being tortured [*basanizomenos*] in a dream; yet while the old man's eyes were raised to heaven, his flesh was being torn by scourges, his blood flowing, and his sides were being cut to pieces. Although he fell to the ground because his body could not endure the agonies, he kept his reason upright and unswerving. (6:3–7, NRSV)

After this, Eleazar is led away to be subjected to more elaborate agonies, although his entire ordeal is merely a warm-up for the slow butchering and broiling of seven brothers, witnessed by their mother, which follows (8:10–12:19; cf. 2 Macc 6:18–7:42).

Martin Hengel's classic study, *Crucifixion in the Ancient World and the Folly of the Message of the Cross*, amounts to a Maccabean elaboration of the stark statement, "they crucified him." When I tracked down Hengel's book in the college library I was intrigued to find that it was not shelved in the religion section, as I had expected, but in a dusty corner of the history section devoted to torture. Hengel's theological monograph was flanked by lavishly illustrated treatises on medieval torture, on the one hand, and Amnesty International reports, on the other—as effective a defamiliarization of "the message of the cross" as anything attempted in the present essay.

The burden of Hengel's study is to show, through extensive appeal to ancient sources, why crucifixion was regarded as the most horrific form of punishment in the ancient world. The original German edition of the work bore the Latin title *Mors turpissima crucis*, "the utterly vile death of the cross," a quotation from Origen (*Comm. on Matt.* 27.22). Josephus similarly deemed crucifixion "the most wretched of deaths" (*Jewish War* 7.6.4), while Cicero called it "that

---

4. Further on 4 Maccabees, see "Taking It Like a Man" below.

most cruel and disgusting penalty" and "the ultimate punishment" (*Verrine Orations* 2.5.165, 168).[5] According to Hengel, far from being a dispassionate execution of justice, "crucifixion satisfied the primitive lust for revenge and the sadistic cruelty of individual rulers and of the masses" (1977, 87).

> Even in the Roman empire, where there might be said to be some kind of "norm" for the course of the execution (it included a flogging beforehand, and the victim often carried the beam to the place of execution, where he was nailed to it with outstretched arms, raised up and seated on a small wooden peg), the form of execution could vary considerably: crucifixion was a punishment in which the caprice and sadism of the executioners were given full rein. All attempts to give a perfect description of *the* crucifixion in archaeological terms are therefore in vain; there were too many different possibilities for the executioner. (1977, 25, his emphasis)[6]

The implication, of course, is that the bald statement, "they crucified him," still retains certain of its secrets no matter how thoroughly the historians and archaeologists interrogate it.

Spectacle and Surveillance

…the crowds who had gathered there for the spectacle…. (Luke 23:48)

…they will be tortured with fire and sulfur in the presence of the holy angels and in the presence of the Lamb. And the smoke of their torture goes up for ever and ever. (Revelation 14:10–11)

Now I begin to be a disciple…. Let fire and the cross; let the crowds of wild beasts; let tearings, breakings, and dislocations of bones; let cutting off of members; let shatterings of the whole body; and let all the dreadful torments of the devil come upon me. (Ignatius of Antioch, *Epistle to the Romans* 5, ANF trans.)

---

5. See also Cicero, *On Behalf of Babirus* 5.16 (even the term "cross" should be far from the eyes, ears and thoughts of a Roman citizen), Seneca, *Epistle* 101.14 (the cross is an "accursed tree"), Justinian, *Digest* 48.19 (crucifixion is "the supreme punishment") and Augustine, *City of God* 19.23 (crucifixion is "the worst of deaths"), together with 1 Cor 1:18, 23; Gal 5:13; Heb 12:2.

6. The specimen texts here include Josephus, *Jewish War* 5.11.1, and Seneca, *To Marcia on Consolation* 20.3: "I see crosses there, not just of one kind but fashioned in many different ways: some have their victims with head down toward the ground; some impale their private parts; others stretch out their arms on the crossbeam" (trans. from Brown 1994, 2:948).

7. THE DIVINE BUTCHER

Seventeen-hundred years later we find the executioners exploring still other possibilities. Michel Foucault's *Discipline and Punish: The Birth of the Prison* opens with the following scene:

> On 2 March 1757 Damiens the regicide was condemned "to make the *amende honorable* before the main door of the Church of Paris," where he was to be "taken and conveyed in a cart, wearing nothing but a shirt, holding a torch of burning wax weighing two pounds"; then, "in the said cart, to the Place de Grève, where, on a scaffold that will be erected there, the flesh will be torn from his breasts, arms, thighs and calves with red-hot pincers, his right hand, holding the knife with which he committed the said parricide, burnt with sulphur, and, on those places where the flesh will be torn away, poured molten lead, boiling oil, burning resin, wax and sulphur melted together and then his body drawn and quartered by four horses and his limbs and body consumed by fire, reduced to ashes and his ashes thrown to the winds." (1977a, 3)[7]

According to witnesses, the execution was badly botched; the quartering went on interminably, two more horses had to be brought in, "and when that did not suffice, they were forced, in order to cut off the wretch's thighs, to sever the sinews and hack at the joints…" (1977a, 3). The victim, meanwhile, forgave his executioners, Jesus-like, and begged them not to swear as they struggled to dismember him.

In time, as Foucault reports, the ritual of public torture became intolerable. "Protests against the public executions proliferated in the second half of the eighteenth century: among the philosophers and theoreticians of the law; among lawyers and *parlementaires*; in popular petitions and among the legislators of the assemblies" (1977a, 73). The more spectacular forms of public execution gradually ceased, and judicial punishment was reestablished on a more "humane" foundation. "In the worst of murderers, there is one thing, at least, to be respected when one punishes: his 'humanity.' The day was to come, in the nineteenth century, when this 'man,' discovered in the criminal, would become the target of penal intervention, the object that it claimed to correct and transform, the domain of a whole series of 'criminological' sciences…" (1977a, 74; see further Foucault 1975). No longer could judicial punishment be justified as the rightful vengeance of a sovereign on a rebellious subject.

A giant step forward in the history of judicial practice? Foucault does not think so, which is what makes *Discipline and Punish* remarkable. For Foucault, the feudal "society of the spectacle" was succeeded in the modern period

---

7. Foucault is quoting from the *Pièces originales et procédures du procès fait à Robert-François Damiens* (1757).

by something altogether more sinister. The fearsome spectacle of brutal punishment being publicly exacted on the body of a condemned criminal had at least the advantage of being open and direct. The degree of *covert* control over the individual that modern "disciplinary societies" aspire to would have been unimaginable under the old regimes. In particular, for Foucault, the prison reforms of the nineteenth century concealed an iron fist of totalitarianism in a velvet glove of humanitarianism. Hayden White paraphrases Foucault's perspective: "In the totally ordered, hierocratized space of the nineteenth-century prison, the prisoner is put under constant surveillance, discipline, and education in order to transform him into what power as now organized in society demands that everyone become: docile, productive, hard-working, self-regulating, conscience-ridden; in a word, 'normal' in every way" (White 1979, 106).

In an interview Foucault remarked: "I'm delighted that historians found no major error in [*Discipline and Punish*] and that, at the same time, prisoners read it in their cells" (1988b, 101). Recently, however, Page duBois has questioned the story that *Discipline and Punish* tells. She notes that the tripartite structure of the book shows "Torture" (the subject matter of part 1) yielding first to "Punishment" (part 2) and then to "Discipline" (part 3), the implication being that state-sanctioned atrocities such as the execution by torture of transgressors have now receded into history, "that we are all so thoroughly disciplined now, have so deeply internalized our own policing, that we no longer need the spectacle of punishment" (duBois 1990, 153). Foucault states confidently: "We are now far away from the country of tortures, dotted with wheels, gibbets, gallows, pillories" (1977a, 307). "Tell it to the El Salvadorans," replies duBois (1990, 154). In other words, the narrative of *Discipline and Punish* "is resolutely Eurocentric"; Foucault's "description of the transition from spectacular torture and execution to internalized discipline remains a local analysis" (1990, 154).[8] His narrative is further undermined by the fact that whereas state-sanctioned torture does seem to be the exception rather than the rule today in Western Europe and North America, the substantial role that certain Western democracies have played in propping up regimes that routinely employ torture to enforce public order suggests a disturbing, symbiotic relationship between the "societies of the spectacle" and the "disciplinary societies," one that the serene, seductive chronology of *Discipline and Punish* obscures (cf. duBois 1990, 154–57; Sáez 1992, 128ff.). These are serious criticisms. At the very least, they caution us that if we are to use *Discipline and Punish* as an analogical tool for a reconsideration of the relationship between violent punishment and internalized self-policing in early Christian interpre-

---

8. Foucault himself was not unaware of this: "I could perfectly well call my subject [in *Discipline and Punish*] the history of penal policy in France—alone" (1980e, 67).

7. THE DIVINE BUTCHER 155

tations of the crucifixion and its "spiritual" effects—which is what we shall be doing, focusing principally on the letters of Paul—we must allow for the possibility that the relationship may be symbiotic or parasitic.

"His Mighty and Annihilating Reaction"

> For the wrath of God is revealed from heaven against all ungodliness and wickedness.... (Romans 1:18)

> I ... give up body and life ... to bring to an end the wrath of the Almighty. (2 Maccabees 7:37–38)

Let us begin with Hengel's conclusion, which is that "the earliest Christian message of the crucified messiah demonstrated the 'solidarity' of the love of God with the unspeakable suffering of those who were tortured and put to death by human cruelty" (1977, 88). This is a poignant interpretation of the crucifixion, and, as it happens, one also encountered frequently in the writings of liberation theologians. In Leonardo Boff's *Passion of Christ, Passion of the World*, for instance, we read of Carlos Alberto, a Roman Catholic priest who became convinced that his ministry to his peasant parishioners necessitated "the promotion of their socio-political liberation," and was arrested and interrogated as a result (1987, 118). "Father Carlos Alberto was barbarously tortured and taken back to his cell. With what strength he had left he read the passion of our Lord Jesus Christ according to Saint John, and realized that he was identified with Christ in a glorious suffering" (1987, 123). And yet a troubling question arises, one that Boff himself does not address. Hengel too can ill-afford to address it, having argued that crucifixion "is a manifestation of trans-subjective evil, a form of execution which manifests the demonic character of human cruelty and bestiality" (1977, 87). The question is a deceptively simple one: Who inflicted the punishment of crucifixion on Jesus? Was it the procurator of Judea, acting on behalf of the Roman Emperor? Or was it an even higher power, acting through the Roman authorities—which is how several of the New Testament authors understand it (see Acts 2:23; 4:27–28; 1 Cor 2:6–8; cf. John 19:11; Rom 13:1–4; 1 Pet 2:13–14)?[9]

Certain feminist theologians have taken this question with the utmost seriousness. "Is it any wonder that there is so much abuse in modern society," Joanne Carlson Brown and Rebecca Parker write, "when the predominant

---

9. Whether "the rulers of this age" in 1 Cor 2:8 are to be construed as human authorities, supernatural authorities (cf. Col 2:15) or a combination of both does not substantially affect the issue.

image or theology of the culture is of 'divine child abuse'—God the Father demanding and carrying out the suffering and death of his own son? If Christianity is to be liberating for the oppressed it must itself be liberated from this theology" (1989, 26). After centuries of exquisitely subtle pronouncements and propositions by theological courtiers and diplomats, designed to finesse the dubious divine desire that eventually issued in the crucifixion (cf. Mark 14:36 par.), such statements have a disarmingly direct ring. What if the divine Emperor were found to be in a flagrant state of undress despite the most assiduous efforts of his theological tailors?

To interpret the Son's torture and execution as a spectacle staged by the Father is to move within the ambit of the doctrine of atonement, a term which, as John McIntyre explains, "has so established itself as to have become the generic name for the doctrine of the death of Christ," enfolding all the other names within its embrace: "propitiation," "expiation," "substitution," "ransom," "redemption," "reconciliation," and so on (1992, 39). The doctrine continues to exercise enormous popular appeal, even, or especially, in its propitiatory form, that form most calculated to cause contemporary theologians to squirm uncomfortably or become hot under the collar, clerical or otherwise (although not all, as we shall see).

Although it had a rich patristic history, the doctrine of atonement came fully into its own only with Anselm of Canterbury's eleventh-century treatise *Cur Deus Homo* (Why God Became Man), where it was formulated as a "theory of satisfaction." What Anselm laid was a new foundation for the slaughterhouse of Christian soteriology:

> Sin is an offence against the majesty of God. In spite of his goodness, God cannot pardon sin without compounding with honor and justice. On the other hand, he cannot revenge himself on man for his offended honor; for sin is an offence of infinite degree, and therefore demands infinite satisfaction; which means that he must either destroy humanity or inflict upon it the eternal punishments of hell.... There is but one way for God to escape this dilemma without affecting his honor, and that is to arrange for some kind of *satisfaction*. He must have infinite satisfaction because the offense is immeasurable.... Hence, the necessity of the *incarnation*. God becomes man in Christ; Christ suffers and dies in our stead. (Anselm 1966, viii)[10]

It is, of course, no coincidence that Anselm's construal of the crucifixion bears a marked resemblance to the feudal conception of judicial punishment as outlined in the opening chapters of Foucault's *Discipline and Punish*. Under the

---

10. From Alfred Weber's introduction to *Cur Deus Homo* (his emphasis).

feudal regime, "the law ... represented the will of the sovereign; he who violated it must answer to the wrath of the king.... Thus, the power and integrity of the law were reasserted; the affront was righted. This excessive power found its form in the ritual of atrocity" (Dreyfus and Rabinow 1983, 145). The term "ritual" is highly appropriate here. "Under this type of regime the notion of crime is still not fully distinguished from that of sacrilege, so that punishment takes the form of a ritual intended not to 'reform' the offender but to express and restore the sanctity of the law which has been broken" (Sarup 1993, 67).[11]

In *The Doctrine of Reconciliation*, the fourth and final volume of his *Church Dogmatics*, Karl Barth reiterates Anselm's assertion that sin is an infinite affront to the divine majesty, requiring infinite restitution. "The way in which it is put by Anselm of Canterbury," asserts Barth, "is very accurate and complete" (1956–61, 4:1:485; cf. 4:1:407, 412; Barth 1960). The fact that God put forward his own Son as the means of atonement "makes it plain what human guilt is," how horrendous it is (1956–61, 4:1:491). Any other means "would be quite inadequate ... even the severest punishment which might come upon us.... Even if he were eternally cast into hell, would not man still be the sinner that he is? What help would this punishment be?" (1956–61, 4:1:491). Instead, the punitive judgment of God is "executed in the death of Jesus Christ." Negatively put, this judgment, this sentence, is "the burning, the consuming fire, the blinding light of [God's] wrath" on "corrupt and sinful man" (1956–61, 4:1:514). This judgment and sentence is "that I am the man of sin, and that this man of sin and therefore I myself am nailed to the cross and crucified..., that I am therefore destroyed and replaced, that as the one who has turned to nothingness I am done away in the death of Jesus Christ" (1956–61, 4:1:515; cf. Barth 1933, 193–94, 199). For it was Jesus himself who, in "lowly obedience," "undertook to withstand the wrath of God in our place on the cross" (1956–61, 4:1:559; cf. Barth 1933, 105–6).

The language of wrath and punishment applied to the crucifixion is by no means defunct even among contemporary New Testament scholars. In his massive commentary on Romans, for example, Douglas Moo has recently defended the traditional attribution to Paul of a doctrine of divine wrath and retribution (1991, 94–97). What distinguishes Moo from other critical commentators on Romans is his austere refusal to dilute the doctrine of divine wrath to make it more palatable to modern tastes. "God's wrath is necessary to the biblical conception of God," he insists. "The OT constantly pictures God as responding to sin with wrath"—his examples include Exod 4:14; 15:7;

---

11. Sarup is paraphrasing Foucault, as are Dreyfus and Rabinow. Foucault himself uses language such as the following: "[T]orture forms part of a ritual. It is an element in the liturgy of punishment" (1977a, 34).

32:10–12; Num 11:1; Jer 21:3–7—and "Paul clearly works with this same conception…" (1991, 94–95). Moo singles out C. H. Dodd as representative of the apologetic school of thought to which he is opposed (see Dodd 1932, esp. 20–24). "[W]e cannot," Dodd declared, commenting on the motif of divine wrath in Rom 1:18, "think with full consistency of God in terms of the highest ideals of personality and yet attribute to Him the irrational passion of anger" (1932, 24).[12] Dodd's God doesn't foam at the mouth, then, tear the telephone out of the wall, say things he will regret in the morning, or return to the office with an assault rifle and a case of ammunition.

Barth was sternly critical of the Pauline apologists of his own day. "The critics of the term 'wrath of God,'" he insisted, "were quite wrong when they said that 'wrath' is not a quality or activity or attitude which can be … brought into harmony with [God's] love and grace" (1956–61, 4:1:490). For Barth, the sinner is "intolerable before God." "[C]onfronted by the majestic right of God," the sinner "must perish," must be "repaid according to his works. This man has to die." Upon him punitive judgment must fall "in all its inescapable … strictness" (1956–61, 4:1:539–40). Barth would surely cathect, then, with Anders Nygren's paraphrase of Rom 1:18: "As long as God is God, He cannot behold with indifference that His creation is destroyed and His holy will trodden underfoot. Therefore He meets sin with His mighty and annihilating reaction" (1949, 98, quoted approvingly in Moo 1991, 94). Here we are not far from the feudal world of Anselm, nor from the Roman world of Paul. We can almost hear the bones cracking on the wheel, accompanied by shrieks of hellish torment, as the might of the offended sovereign bears down upon the body of the condemned.

"What a Primitive Mythology"

…Christ Jesus, whom God put forward as a sacrifice of atonement by his blood. (Romans 3:24–25)

What primitive notions of guilt and righteousness does this imply? (Bultmann 1961, 7)

---

12. Similar is Ernst Käsemann's claim that the wrath of God in Rom 1:18 "is not to be viewed as an emotion," nor is "psychologizing language about holy indignation" applicable to it (1980, 37). C. E. B. Cranfield, however, like Moo, objects to Dodd's mild-mannered God (1975–79, 1:108–9). James D. G. Dunn also wishes to retain the Pauline concept of divine wrath, although for Dunn it is an exquisitely nuanced state, transcending the commonplace notions of "divine indignation" and "judicial anger against evil," not to mention divine vengeance (1988, 54–55, 70–71).

7. THE DIVINE BUTCHER

If the twentieth century's most influential theologian, Karl Barth, was entirely comfortable with the doctrine of atonement, its most influential New Testament scholar, Rudolf Bultmann, was acutely embarrassed by it. Traditionally the doctrine has been laid at the feet of Paul, where it lies in a slow-spreading pool of blood. For Bultmann, however, it should never have been left there in the first place.

Paul's thought regarding sin contains two distinct strands, according to Bultmann, which "are not harmonized with each other" (1952–55, 1:249). Bultmann reluctantly concedes that there is in Paul a "juristic conception of death as the punishment for sin" (1952–55, 1:249), but this Paul inherited from "the Old Testament-Jewish tradition" (1952–55, 1:246). According to this conception, "*Death is the punishment for the sin a man has committed*; sinners are 'worthy of death' (Rom. 1:32 KJ), they have 'earned' death"—even the "final" death that will be effected "by the verdict condemning them to 'destruction' which God will pronounce over sinners on the judgment day (Rom. 2:6–11)" (1952–55, 1:246, his emphasis). Faced with this glum prospect, sinners are in urgent need of justification through the blood of Jesus Christ, "a propitiatory sacrifice by which forgiveness of sins is brought about; which is to say: by which the guilt contracted by sins is canceled" (1952–55, 1:295). Intimately bound up, moreover, with the idea of propitiatory sacrifice is the idea of vicarious sacrifice, "which likewise has its origin in the field of cultic-juristic thinking" (1952–55, 1:296). "The same phrase (*hyper hēmōn*) that is translated 'for us' can also express this idea, meaning now: 'instead of us,' 'in place of us'" (1952–55, 1:296). Bultmann attributes a vicarious theology to Gal 3:13 ("Christ redeemed us from the curse of the law by becoming a curse for us—for it is written 'Cursed is everyone who hangs on a tree'") and 2 Cor 5:21 ("For our sake, he made him to be sin who knew no sin"; cf. Rom 8:3), and argues that both ideas, vicarious and propitiatory sacrifice, merge in 2 Cor 5:14ff. ("we are convinced that one has died for all; therefore all have died…. [I]n Christ God was reconciling the world to himself, not counting their trespasses against them") (1952–55, 1:296).

Bultmann himself, however, bristles at such ideas. "How can the guilt of one man be expiated by the death of another who is sinless—if indeed one may speak of a sinless man at all?" he splutters in his demythologizing manifesto "New Testament and Mythology" (1961, 7). "What primitive notions of guilt and righteousness does this imply? And what primitive idea of God? … What a primitive mythology it is, that a divine Being should … atone for the sins of men through his own blood!" (1961, 7). The sacrificial hypothesis entails a *sacrificium intellectus* that Bultmann is determined to avoid. He has no desire to see his own brain laid upon the sacrificial altar, quivering under the upraised knife.

In his *Theology of the New Testament*, therefore, Bultmann is scrupulously careful to highlight those passages in which Paul appears to interpret Jesus' crucifixion as *potential deliverance from the power of sin* and to gloss over passages in which Paul appears to interpret the crucifixion as *sacrificial atonement for actual sins committed*. The latter passages do "not contain Paul's characteristic view," he insists (1952–55, 1:296; cf. 46–47, 287).[13] For Paul, "Christ's death is not merely a sacrifice which cancels the guilt of sin (i.e., the punishment contracted by sinning), but is also *the means of release from the powers of this age: Law, Sin, and Death*" (1952–55, 1:297–98, his emphasis; cf. 287). In line with the judicial reformers of eighteenth-century Europe, then, Bultmann finds the idea of a vengeful sovereign capable of inflicting atrocious physical punishment on rebellious or unruly subjects to be morally intolerable. Such primitive ideas "make the Christian faith unintelligible and unacceptable to the modern world" (1961, 5).

"Once you suppress the idea of vengeance," writes Madan Sarup, glossing Foucault, "punishment can only have a meaning within a technology of reform" (1993, 67–68)—or a theology of reform, as here. The doctrine of atonement, in its classic Anselmian form, amounts to an interpretation of Jesus' torture unto death as public satisfaction for transgression, the righting of an affront to the sovereign power—the injured party not being the Roman Emperor, however (as those who administer the punishment unwittingly suppose), but the Divine Majesty Himself. Uncomfortable with such "primitive" notions, Bultmann prefers to attribute to Paul an interpretation of Jesus' crucifixion as a potential *reform*, a unique opportunity for the transgressor to be utterly transformed from within. The event of the cross promises freedom from sin. "But this freedom is not a static quality: it is freedom *to obey*. The indicative implies an imperative" (1961, 32, his emphasis).[14] A horrific act of violence, then, execution by public torture, gives birth to an altogether different order in which obedient action springs spontaneously from within and no

---

13. Bultmann consistently attempts to excise the "Jewish sacrificial" element from Paul's theology. This gives rise to a troubling question. Is it possible to isolate Bultmann's treatment of Paul in "New Testament and Mythology" (1941, later elaborated in his *Theology of the New Testament*, 1948–53) from the Nazi solution to the Jewish question, which was being implemented even as Bultmann wrote? In response to this concern, is it enough simply to cite Bultmann's public criticism of Nazi policy in his 1933 Marburg lecture (Bultmann 1960, esp. 165), courageous and commendable though it was? Did the anti-Judaic elements endemic to German theology of the period, including Bultmann's own, not contribute to the very phenomenon he was attacking? These are issues that have often been debated (see esp. Schwan 1976; also Georgi 1985, 82ff.; G. Jones 1991, 200–208 passim).

14. This sentiment is a commonplace of Pauline studies, hence its interest. In effect, it will be the primary object of analysis in the remainder of the essay.

God's Own (Pri)son

> Are they servants of Christ? ... I am a better one: with far greater labors, far more imprisonments.... (2 Corinthians 11:23–25)

One would he hard-pressed to find a Protestant New Testament scholar more squeamish about the blood of Jesus than Bultmann. One would be equally hard-pressed to find a Roman Catholic New Testament scholar more squeamish about it than Xavier Léon-Dufour, whose *Life and Death in the New Testament* returns obsessively to the motifs of sacrifice, expiation and atonement. Léon-Dufour is especially pained by a common tendency among Christians, loosely based on a sacrificial reading of Paul, to speak "of sin's 'offense' against God and of God's intention to punish and to chastize," on the one hand, and "of 'reparation,' of 'satisfaction,' and of 'merit' by which the human Jesus 'satisfied' divine justice," on the other hand (1986, 192). This leads to a "distressing attribution" to God of "inadmissible dispositions" (1986, 192).

Although Léon-Dufour does not say so explicitly, the dispositions in question are those of a cruel despot who keeps his fearful subjects in check through the threat of frightful physical punishment—the sort of despot who features prominently in the early chapters of *Discipline and Punish*. Interestingly, the public executions by torture in eighteenth-century Europe led to the precise phenomenon that Léon-Dufour deplores, an attribution to the sovereign of "inadmissible dispositions." Foucault writes: "It was as if the punishment was thought to equal, if not to exceed, in savagery the crime itself, to accustom the spectators to a ferocity from which one wished to divert them, ... to make the executioner resemble a criminal, judges murderers" (1977a, 9). Léon-Dufour's God, however, is not given to theatrical displays of power. As for Bultmann, a "healthy understanding of Jesus' death" would emphasize instead its transformative potential, how it is "active" in the believer through baptism and the eucharist "so that it exercises its influence in ordinary life" (Léon-Dufour 1986, 192). Once again, as in the eighteenth-century rhetoric of judicial reform, the recommended shift of emphasis is from corporal punishment ("painful to a more or less horrible degree," as one contemporary glossed it [quoted in Foucault 1977a, 33]) to internal reform leading to a transformation of everyday behavior.

What the transformational interpretation of the crucifixion attempts to exclude, however, is the issue of *power*, an issue all too close to the surface in the punitive interpretation, the power of one person over the body of another, a power never more evident than in the relationship of the torturer to the victim (cf. Scarry 1985, 27–59; Greenblatt 1990, 11ff.)—and never more disturbing, perhaps, than when torturer and victim are metaphorically figured as parent and child. But what if the transformation of the believer were merely a more efficient exercise of power, still exercised on the body but now reaching into the psyche as well to fashion acceptable thoughts and attitudes yielding acceptable behavior, of power absolutized to a degree unimaginable even in a situation of extreme physical torture? This, above all, is the question that *Discipline and Punish* prompts us to ask.

Let us rephrase the question: What if the crucified Jesus, as interpreted by Paul, were actually God's own (pri)son? The prison would contain a courtyard, however, and a scaffold would dominate the courtyard. For Paul's gospel of reform cannot simply be conflated analogically with the judicial reforms of eighteenth-century Europe. For the latter, the punitive liturgy of public torture had to be consigned once and for all to history. But for Paul, discipline remains indissolubly bound up with atrocity. Each believer must be subjected to public execution by torture: "Do you not know that all of us who have been baptized into Christ Jesus were baptized into his death?" (Rom 6:3). Paul refuses to separate torture from reform (cf. 1 Cor 1:18ff.; Gal 2:19–21). Unless the believer is tortured to death in the (pri)son, he or she cannot be rehabilitated: "We know that our old self was crucified with him so that the sinful body might be destroyed [*hina katargēthē to sōma tēs hamartias*]" (Rom 6:6; cf. Gal 5:24).

Of course, Christian discipline is also bound up with power: "[T]he kingdom of God does not consist in talk but in power [*en dynamei*]" (1 Cor 4:20). How is this power exercised and who is entitled to exercise it? Foucault's views on power may be pertinent here. "In thinking of the mechanisms of power," he explains, "I am thinking ... of its capillary forms of existence, the point where power reaches into the very grain of individuals, touches their bodies" (1980d, 39). For Foucault, "nothing is more material, physical, corporal than the exercise of power" (1980a, 57–58)—and for Paul too, seemingly. As Elizabeth A. Castelli has remarked of 1 Corinthians, "the human body provides a central series of images and themes for this text.... Food practices and sexuality occupy fully half of the letter's content.... It is also the case that explicit language about authority and power is used most frequently in the discussion of bodily practices..." (1991b, 209).

Discipline has only one purpose, according to Foucault: the production of "docile bodies." "A body is docile that may be subjected, used, transformed and improved," says Foucault (1977a, 136). "I punish my body and enslave [*doulagōgō*] it," says Paul (1 Cor 9:27). Indeed, the docility engendered by discipline is precisely that of the slave. Crucifixion in the Roman world was, above all, "the slave's punishment" (Cicero, *Verrine Orations* 2.5.169; Valerius Maximus, *Deeds and Sayings* 2.7.12; Tacitus, *Histories* 2.72.2; 4.11.3). Through Jesus' crucifixion, then, the Christian slave is disciplined and kept in line (cf. Phil 2:5–8). "Whoever was free when called is a slave [*doulos*] of Christ," writes Paul (1 Cor 7:22; cf. Rom 6:1.6–19), he himself being no exception (Rom 1:1; cf. Phil 1:1). Of course, there are slaves and "slaves" (cf. 1 Cor 7:21–24; Phlm 15–16), and Paul is in the latter category (cf. Martin 1990, 86–135). Even among "slaves," moreover, a strict hierarchy is observed; the man is the "head" (*kephalē*) of the woman, for example, even as Christ is the "head" of the man (1 Cor 11:3; 14:34). Christ himself is also a subject: "When all things are subjected to him, then the Son himself will also be subjected to the one who put all things in subjection under him" (1 Cor 15:28; cf. 11:3).

Given this hierarchy of subjection and submission, it is no wonder that Paul can define his apostleship, his mission, as that of bringing about "the obedience of faith" (*hypakoē pisteōs*—Rom 1:5)—that is, the faith that manifests itself as obedience, or alternatively the obedience that stems from faith.[15] As James Dunn has argued (1988, 17–18), "the obedience of faith" is "a crucial and central theme" of Paul's preeminent surviving letter (i.e., Romans), "structurally important in understanding [its] thrust," as is indicated by its reappearance in the letter's concluding sentence (16:26), thereby framing it, and by the prominence of *hypakoē* ("obedience") and its cognate, *hypakouō* ("I obey"), in the letter as a whole (5:19; 6:12, 16–17; 10:16; 15:18; 16:19; cf. 10:30–31).

Indeed, throughout all of Paul's letters, the issue of obedience is crucial to his interpretation of Jesus' crucifixion, as David Seeley (1990) has recently contended. For Seeley, as for several other sleuths, the trail of blood sprinkled across Paul's letters leads not to the Old Testament altar of sacrifice, nor to Isaiah 53 (where the Servant of Yahweh suffers in silence), nor to Mount Moriah (where Abraham has raised his knife to slit his son's throat), nor to the secret chambers where Hellenistic mystery rites are practiced, but to the torture chamber of Antiochus IV Epiphanes. In other words, Paul's interpretation of Jesus' crucifixion is primarily, although not exclusively, a martyrological one, and a blood relative of the interpretations of the Maccabean martyrs' deaths lightly sketched out in 2 Maccabees and given detail and (lurid) color in 4 Maccabees (a free expansion, apparently, of 2 Macc 6:12–7:42)—which brings us back to one of the slaughterhouses in which this essay opened.[16]

---

15. The first if the genitive in *hypakoē pisteōs* is epexegetical or appositional, the second if it is a genitive of source (Fitzmyer 1993, 237).

16. Seeley's claim, however, is not that Paul consciously mined the Maccabean literature but rather that he, in common with the authors of 2 and 4 Maccabees themselves,

Now, the heroic example set by the Maccabean martyrs is precisely the example of *obedience*. They embrace God's will, embodied in his law, no matter how horrific the cost. The martyrs are models, moreover, for the audiences of these books, who are implicitly urged to imitate their obedience. The elderly Eleazar, for example, on his way to the rack "of his own accord" rather than eat "things that it is not right to taste" (2 Macc 6:19–20), but pausing repeatedly en route to express stirring sentiments, declaims: "Therefore, by bravely giving up my life now I will … leave to the young a noble example [*hypodeigma gennaion*] of how to die a good death willingly and nobly for the revered and holy laws" (6:27–28). Lest the reader somehow miss the point, the narrator adds at Eleazar's expiration: "So in this way he died, leaving in his death an example of nobility and a memorial of courage [*hypodeigma gennaiotētos kai mnēmosynon aretēs*], not only to the young but to the great body of his nation" (6:31).

The young in question are, first and foremost, the seven brothers who are patiently waiting their turn at the rack. In 4 Maccabees this is made explicit. The brothers, also refusing "the defiling food" (pork), berate the tyrant "with one voice together, as from one mind" (8:29), resolving to despise his "coercive tortures," which their "aged instructor [*paideutes gerōn*]" has so admirably endured (9:6). Subsequently, as Seeley observes, "the brothers serve as models for one another" (1990, 92). "Imitate me, brothers [*mimnēsasthe me, adelphoi*]," cries the first (9:23), the wheel on which he is being broken being "completely smeared with blood," and the coals over which he is simultaneously being roasted "being quenched by the drippings of gore, and pieces of flesh … falling off the axles of the machine" (9:20). "I do not desert the excellent example of my brothers [*ouk apautomolō tēs tōn adelphōn mou aristeias*]," cries the seventh when his turn finally comes (12:16; cf. 10:13, 16; 11:14–15; 13:8–18). This mimetic chain, slick with blood, snakes out of the text and seeks to coil itself around the audience. Through his lingering, almost loving descriptions of these unspeakable deaths, the author seeks to inspire heroic obedience in his audience just as each martyr's slaughter inspires renewed obedience in his fellow martyrs (cf. Seeley 1990, 94).

"Be imitators of me [*mimētai mou ginesthe*], as I am of Christ," Paul similarly urges his addressees (1 Cor 11:1; cf. 4:16; Phil 3:17; 1 Thess 1:6; also Gal 4:12).[17] Again, a mimetic chain reaches out of the text and seeks to wrap itself

---

internalized particular inflections of an idealized notion—that of the Noble Death—"available to anyone who breathed the intellectual atmosphere of the Hellenistic Kingdoms and the early Roman Empire" (1990, 150).

17. Oddly enough, Seeley fails to connect these Pauline injunctions to imitation with those in the Maccabean literature. I have benefited from Castelli's searching analysis of

7. THE DIVINE BUTCHER

around the audience. Jesus' death, as Paul interprets it, was an utterly obedient death (Rom 5:19; Phil 2:8). Absolutely obedient to the will of his Father, and hence sinless (cf. 2 Cor 5:21), Jesus alone has quashed the rebellion of the flesh, even under extreme torture, and resisted the savage coercion of the cruel tyrant, Sin (cf. Seeley 1990, 148–49; Robinson 1952, 40). In order to emerge triumphant from the tomb, Jesus had first to emerge triumphant from the torture chamber. What does this mean for the believer? "Do you not know that all of us who have been baptized into Christ Jesus were baptized into his death?" inquires Paul in Rom 6:3. When you imitate a martyr's death, going to the rack or cross with the same obedient abandon, you triumph over the tyrant who would compel you to sin. Similarly, when you "die with" Christ, you reap the objective benefits that accrue from the literal reenactment of a martyr's death, even though you have not literally died. You gain a victory over the wicked tyrant (Sin), and reap the rewards of absolute obedience, as though you really had remained faithful under terrible torture, as though you really had died horribly rather than renounce God's will. Seeley hits the nail on the head (so to speak): Paul has "coalesced the two categories of literal and imaginative re-enactment" (1990, 148). Each Christian emerges from the baptismal water a bloodless martyr, with the heroic obedience of Jesus attributed to him or her, but without his stripes or stigmata.

Of course, the Christian is then ready for *real* floggings, and even real crucifixion. "Are they servants [*diakonoi*] of Christ?" Paul asks contemptuously of his Corinthian opponents. "I am a better one," he boasts, baring his hideously scarred back, "with far greater labors, far more imprisonments, with countless floggings [*en plēgais hyperballontōs*], and often near death. Five times I have received from the Jews the forty lashes minus one. Three times I was beaten with rods. Once I received a stoning" (2 Cor 11:23–25; cf. 6:4–5). Concluding his missive to the Galatians he utters a grim, if cryptic, warning: "From now on, let no one make trouble for me, for I carry the marks of Jesus branded on my body [*egō gar ta stigmata tou Iēsou en tō sōmati mou bastazō*]" (6:17). Despite the reader's polite protests, Paul is stripping off his shirt once again as he says this, exposing the map of his missionary journeys that has been cut into his back. (Significantly, the term *stigmata* was also common in the ancient Mediterranean world for the brands of slaves or prisoners, for a slave of Christ is precisely what Paul claims to be, as we saw earlier.)

Pauline mimesis in her *Imitating Paul* (1991a; see esp. 89–117). She, however, does not adduce the Maccabean parallels, even though she deals extensively with "discourses of mimesis" in antiquity (1991a, 59–87).

But Paul also wants his converts to have their own war wounds to show off. To the Thessalonians he writes: "And you became imitators [*mimētai*] of us and of the Lord, for in spite of much affliction/persecution [*en thlipsei pollē*] you received the word with joy inspired by the Holy Spirit, so that you became an example [*typon*] to all the believers in Macedonia and Achaia" (1 Thess 1:6–7). In submitting obediently to the word of proclamation, even in the face of persecution (cf. 2:14; 3:3–4), the Thessalonians successfully imitated Paul's own obedient imitation of Jesus' exemplary obedience (cf. 2:2, 15–16), and themselves became examples of obedience to be imitated by all the believers in the region. Again, the mimetic chain wends its way toward an audience that Paul never envisioned (you and I), but first it must pass through the ankle cuffs of a chain gang whose principal overseer is Paul himself, namely, the Thessalonian "imitators [*mimētai*] of the churches of God in Christ Jesus that are in Judea" (2:14). They too are likewise "in Christ," likewise in(mates of) God's own (pri)son.

"You received the word with joy inspired by the Holy Spirit...." The crucial role played by the Holy Spirit in all of this should not be overlooked. The imaginative reenactment of Jesus' death-torture, especially through the ritual of baptism, has objective effects precisely because it results in the Holy Spirit setting up a command post within the believer: "the Spirit of God dwells [*oikei*] in you" (Rom 8:9; also 8:11; 1 Cor 3:16; 6:19; 12:13; 2 Cor 1:22; Gal 4:6; cf. 2 Tim 1:14). You are no longer regulated from without, as formerly, but from within (Rom 8:5, 14; 2 Cor 3:3; Gal 5:16–18, 25; cf. Eph 3:16). No longer must you police your own thoughts, passions and desires; they are now overseen by an inner sentinel (cf. 2 Cor 10:5b) whose relationship to you is one of permanent penetration and absolute possession (cf. Rom 8:9b; 1 Cor 6:19; 2 Cor 10:7), closer than the most intimate act of love, closer than the most exquisite act of torture (cf. 1 Cor 2:10b; 6:17). The Spirit is *in* you, filling your every orifice (cf. Rom 5:5; also Eph 5:18), insinuating itself between you and yourself. Its fingers uncoil within you and extend outward until everything you once thought yourself to be is but a skintight glove adorning its open hand, always about to become a clenched fist (cf. 1 Cor 5:3–5, 11; 16:22; 2 Cor 10:6; Gal 6:1).[18] But the Spirit is also God's phallus, a (rigid) extension of his power. It penetrates you, it invades you, it annihilates you, causing you to "groan inwardly," to expel "sighs too deep for words" (Rom 8:23, 26).

---

18. James T. South, concluding his *Disciplinary Practices in Pauline Texts*, notes that Paul's letters contain no formal disciplinary code, but attributes this to Paul's "gospel of freedom" (1992, 185–86), failing to recognize that the internal self-policing made possible by the Holy Spirit renders all such codes crude and redundant.

In Gal 5:19–23 Paul lists "the works of the flesh" ("fornication, impurity, licentiousness…"), contrasting them with "the fruit of the Spirit" ("love, joy, peace…"). The *work* of the Spirit, however, is discipline, for the Spirit is God's rod (cf. Prov 13:24; 23:13–14). ("Shall I come to you with a rod [*en rhabdō*]…?" Paul threatens his Corinthian "children," fondling the instrument lovingly as he speaks—1 Cor 4:21; cf. 4:14–15.)[19] Like Aaron's rod, moreover (Num 17:8; cf. Heb 9:4), God's rod puts forth blossoms and fruit. The blossom of discipline is obedience, and the fruit of obedience—Christ's obedience, and the consequent obedience of the believer—is righteousness (Rom 5:19; 6:16–19; cf. 2:15), the supreme Pauline fetish. Obedience to whom? Ostensibly obedience to God, for even when Jesus' crucifixion is interpreted as a means toward internalized discipline rather than as retributive punishment for sin (although Paul is not uncomfortable with the latter interpretation, as we have seen), absolute power continues to be attributed to a monarchical God. But the question that inevitably arises is this: Who really stands to benefit from this attribution? And the answer that immediately suggests itself is *Paul* (cf. Castelli 1991a, 112–13). To appeal to one's own exemplary subjection to a conveniently absent authority in order to legitimate the subjection of others (cf. Rom 1:5; 15:18; 16:26; 1 Cor 14:37–38; 2 Cor 13:3) is a strategy as ancient as it is suspect. "Be imitators of me, as I am of Christ," urges Paul. Above all, imitate my obedience by obeying me (cf. 1 Cor 11:16; 2 Cor 2:9;10:6; Phlm 21; also 2 Thess 3:14).

The Dark Twins

[I]f you confess … you will be saved. (Romans 10:9)

I deemed it … necessary to extract by torture a confession of the truth from two female slaves. (Pliny the Younger, *Letters* 10.96, my trans.)

"It has often been said that Christianity brought into being a code of ethics fundamentally different from that of the ancient world," writes Foucault, adding that what is less often noted is that Christianity "spread new power relations throughout the ancient world" (1983, 214). This new form of power Foucault

---

19. Throughout his magisterial tome on the Holy Spirit in the Pauline letters, Gordon D. Fee strives valiantly, but unsuccessfully, to dispel the impression that being "led" by the Spirit confers a passive role on the Christian. On Gal 5:22–25, for example, he remarks: "Paul's point, of course, is that when the Galatians properly use their freedom, by serving one another through love, they are empowered to do so by the Spirit, who produces such 'fruit' in/among them. But they are not passive; they must walk, live, conform to the Spirit" (1994, 444; cf. 881–82). In other words, they must strive actively to submit passively.

terms "pastoral power." It "is not merely a form of power which commands; it must also be prepared to sacrifice itself for the life and salvation of the flock. Therefore, it is different from royal power, which demands a sacrifice from its subjects to save the throne" (1983, 214). Ultimately, for Foucault, "this form of power cannot be exercised without knowing the inside of people's minds, without exploring their souls, without making them reveal their innermost secrets. It implies a knowledge of the conscience and an ability to direct it" (1983, 214; cf. 1988c, 60ff.). Foucault is thinking particularly of the sacrament of penance here (cf. 1988e, 40–41), which assumed the status of a Christian obligation only after the Fourth Lateran Council in 1215 c.e., but which is deeply rooted in the ancient conception, especially prominent in the Jewish scriptures, of an all-seeing God who "searches" and "tests" the human heart, exposing its innermost secrets (e.g., 1 Sam 16:7; 1 Kgs 8:39; 1 Chron 28:9; Job 34:21–22; Pss 17:3; 26:2; 44:21; 90:8; 139:1–2, 23; Prov 5:21; 15:11; Jer 11:20; 12:3; 17:10).

Although this tradition does not achieve anything like its full flowering in Paul—that will have to await the institution of private confession—Paul does allude to it frequently (e.g., Rom 2:16, 29; 8:27; 1 Cor 4:5; 14:25). And in due course Paul's ecclesiastical descendents will appropriate for themselves the divine privilege of laying bare the human soul. "Since the Middle Ages at least, Western societies have established the confession as one of the main rituals we rely on for the production of truth…" (Foucault 1978, 58). But this form of discipline, too, will be closely bound up with atrocity. First, it is the death-torture of Jesus, interpreted as atonement for sin, that makes the sacrament of penance efficacious. God's forgiveness is extended to the sinner over the skewered, flayed body of his Son (e.g., Rom 5:8–11; 2 Cor 5:18–21). Second, as Foucault notes, "[o]ne confesses—or is forced to confess. When it is not spontaneous or dictated by some internal imperative, the confession is wrung from a person by violence or threat; it is driven from its hiding place in the soul, or extracted from the body. Since the Middle Ages, torture has accompanied it like a shadow, and supported it when it could go no further: the dark twins" (1978, 59).

Eventually, Foucault argues in effect, this coercive obsession with the state of the soul becomes the soul of the modern state. His hypothesis is that "the modern Western state has integrated in a new political shape, an old power technique," namely, pastoral power, with its investment in the regulation of the individual's inner existence (1983, 213; cf. 1991, 87–88, 94–95, 104). This power technique, "which over centuries—for more than a millenium—had been linked to a defined religious institution, suddenly spread out into the whole social body; it found support in a multitude of institutions" (1983, 215).

As it happens, these are the same institutions of surveillance and control that Foucault repeatedly attacked in his writings. They are not necessarily the institutions, however, that ordinarily leap to mind in this connection— the CIA, the KGB, etc. Power is at its most insidious and efficient, for Foucault, precisely when its workings are effaced—when its brow is furrowed with humanitarian concern, when its voice is warm with Christian compassion, when its menace is masked even, or especially, from itself. The institutions, or practices, at which Foucault took aim in his writings, therefore, are particularly those in which power wears a white coat and a professional smile. They include psychiatry, the secular sacrament of penance, which is the subject of *Madness and Civilization* (1965; cf. 1962); modern medicine, which exposes the innermost secrets of the human body to the scientific gaze, and is the target of *The Birth of the Clinic* (1973); the social sciences, which likewise turn the human subject into an object of scientific scrutiny, and is the target of *The Order of Things* (1970); modern methods of dealing with delinquency and criminality, which is the subject of *Discipline and Punish* (1977a); and the modern policing of sexual "normality," which is the subject of the first volume of his *History of Sexuality* (1978). Foucault once confessed in an interview: "A nightmare has pursued me since childhood: I have under my eyes a text that I can't read, or of which only a tiny part can be deciphered; I pretend to read it, but I know that I'm inventing" (1989b, 25). Foucault tempts us to invent in our turn, to write preludes and sequels to his own surreal historical narrative, one in which the melancholy murmur of a medieval penitential liturgy is heard echoing through the contemporary halls of science, of medicine, of justice and of government—the public dismemberment of the body of the deviant having been displaced by strategies of social control that seem to grow ever lighter the deeper they extend into each of us.[20]

Closing Confession: "Bless Me, Father..."

Then Ura'el, one of the holy angels who was with me,...said to me, "Enoch, why are you afraid like this?" I answered and said, "I am frightened because of this terrible place and the spectacle of this painful thing." (1 Enoch 21:9–10, *OTP* trans.)

Let this be enough, then, about the ... extreme tortures. (2 Maccabees 7:42)

---

20. Its touch is lightest of all in the case of television, a "disciplinary technology" that Foucault never examined. The obverse of the Bible's panoptic God, television's single blind eye polices and controls, not by being all-seeing, but by being seen by all.

I recall that each ornate confessional in the Redemptorist church in Limerick displayed, deep in its somber interior, the effigy of a tortured man, and that the column of confessionals was itself flanked by the fourteen Stations of the Cross, each one ornate and imposing, the spectacle of atrocity being inseparable, as I now realize, from the spectacle of docility. "Bless me, Father, for I have sinned...."

My own father was a warm, compassionate man. But he was also a butcher. Foucault's father too was a butcher of sorts, as I learned upon perusing *The Passion of Michel Foucault*:

> *These*, then, are the images that Foucault apparently shared on his deathbed with [Hervé] Guibert: the sunken continent of childhood revealed; ... the philosopher's most singular truths confessed....
>
> The first of the "terrible dioramas," writes Guibert, "shows the philosopher-child, led by his father, who was a surgeon, into an operating room in the hospital at Poitiers, to witness the amputation of a man's leg—this was to steel the boy's virility...."
>
> [This] first story, of being forced by his father to witness an amputation, Foucault told to at least one other person before he died. This, of course, does not mean that the story is "true," in the sense of accurately representing an event that actually occurred. The recollection of primal scenes from childhood, as Freud has taught us, often produces elaborations, omissions, strange and telltale ellipses, and fabrications....
>
> The image, certainly, has all the ingredients of a recurrent nightmare: the sadistic father, the impotent child, the knife slicing into flesh, the body cut to the bone, the demand to acknowledge the sovereign power of the patriarch, and the inexpressible humiliation of the son, having his manliness put to the test. (J. Miller 1993, 365–66, his emphasis)[21]

All of which brings us back to where we began: "Father, spare me from this hour...."

I received a postcard from Paris the other day, sent to me by my sister, who had just read an earlier draft of this essay. She writes of being put off her food for an entire day (truly a disservice to a tourist in Paris) remembering "the blood, entrails, and passion dramas" of that street "flanked by the two places of sacrifice" in Limerick where we lived as children, then adding, "although I must admit I remember the slaughterhouse in Adare much more vividly."

We moved from Limerick to Adare, "the prettiest village in Ireland," when I was seven and my sister five. The Catholic children's Bible used in the Chris-

---

21. Miller continues: "Like debris from a shipwreck, fragments of this scene keep bobbing up throughout Foucault's life and work" (1993, 366).

tian Brothers' school that I attended there contained a slaughterhouse even more terrible than my father's. (The latter was a scant hundred yards from the school; on hot summer days its stench would waft faintly through the opened classroom windows.) It was the abattoir of Antiochus IV Epiphanes in 2 Macc 7, site of the scalping, dismemberment and barbecuing of the seven hapless brothers, watched by their helpless mother, a Pietà to the power of seven. ("Do not fear this butcher!" she cries [7:29], as her youngest son is about to be dismembered.) The story held a horrible fascination for me. It seemed the very soul of this Bible, a soul racked with an agony that the anemic Jesus on the jacket, suffering the little children to come unto him, could never quite conceal—a Jesus who himself would soon be summoned to the torture chamber to take the place of the seventh brother, under the wrathful glare of his Father and the anguished gaze of his mother: "The king fell into a rage, and handled him even worse than the others..." (7:39).

FURTHER READING ON AUTOBIOGRAPHICAL CRITICISM

Anderson, Janice Capel, and Jeffrey L. Staley, eds. 1995. *Taking It Personally: Autobiographical Biblical Criticism*. Semeia 72. Atlanta: Scholars Press. The inaugural collection that introduced autobiographical/personal criticism to biblical studies.

Black, Fiona C., ed. 2006. *The Recycled Bible: Autobiography, Culture, and the Space Between*. Semeia Studies 51. Atlanta: Society of Biblical Literature. Attempts to bring autobiographical criticism and cultural studies into dialogue around biblical texts and their cultural afterlives.

Davies, Philip R., ed. 2002. *First Person: Essays in Biblical Autobiography*. Biblical Seminar 81. Sheffield: Sheffield Academic Press. Each essayist assumes the identity of a familiar character in the Hebrew Bible (e.g., Delilah, Isaiah, Haman) and uses his or her scholarly expertise and readerly imagination to fill in the gaps of the biblical text and affirm or adjust its ideology.

Freedman, Diane P., Olivia Frey, and Francis Murphy Zauhar, eds. 1993. *The Intimate Critique: Autobiographical Literary Criticism*. Durham, N.C.: Duke University Press. The first comprehensive introduction to autobiographical literary criticism. Most of its twenty-five essays address issues of gender, and many address issues of race and/or class in addition.

Freedman, Diane P., and Olivia Frey, eds. 2003. *Autobiographical Writing across the Disciplines: A Reader*. Durham, N.C.: Duke University Press. The fifteen disciplines featured include religion—although James Cone is assigned to prop it up solo. Still, the volume is essential reading for anybody interested in what the editors now term "self-inclusive scholarship."

Hallett, Judith P., and Thomas van Nortwick, eds. 1997. *Compromising Traditions: The Personal Voice in Classical Scholarship*. London: Routledge. Ten classicists wax autobiographical, "Getting Personal about Euripides," for example (to cite one of the essay titles).

Kitzberger, Ingrid Rosa, ed. 1999. *The Personal Voice in Biblical Interpretation*. London: Routledge.

———. 2002. *Autobiographical Biblical Criticism: Between Text and Self*. Leiden: Deo. Essentially, these two collections might be two volumes of a single work. Between them they contain a rich array of essays by an international cast of contributors whose customary methodological affiliations run the gamut from traditional historical criticism through literary criticism to liberationist and postcolonial criticism.

Miller, Nancy K. 1991. *Getting Personal: Feminist Occasions and Other Autobiographical Acts*. London: Routledge. An engaging reflection on the risks and benefits of personal disclosure in academic discourse.

Moore, Stephen D. 2001. Revolting Revelations. Pages 173–99 in Moore, *God's Beauty Parlor: And Other Queer Spaces in and around the Bible*. Contraversions: Jews and Other Differences. Stanford, Calif.: Stanford University Press. Autobiographical reading in and around the book of Revelation.

Seesengood, Robert Paul. 2006. *Competing Identities: The Athlete and the Gladiator in Early Christianity*. Library of New Testament Studies 346. New York: T&T Clark. Autobiographical criticism is a major resource for Seesengood, particularly in his chapters on Hebrews and Revelation.

Staley, Jeffrey L. 1995. *Reading with a Passion: Rhetoric, Autobiography and the American West in the Gospel of John*. New York: Continuum. Staley's brand of personal criticism emerges out of reader-response criticism, and the volume is structured accordingly, moving from liminal experiments in reader-response criticism into full-blown autobiographical criticism.

Veeser, H. Aram, ed. 1996. *Confessions of the Critics: North American Critics' Autobiographical Moves*. London: Routledge, 1996. Differs from Freedman et al. in that it combines essays that throw themselves unrestrainedly into the autobiographical enterprise with others that are critical of it and still others that fall into neither category precisely.

MASCULINITY

8
Taking It Like a Man:
Masculinity in 4 Maccabees*

Co-authored with Janice Capel Anderson

A respondent to a conference paper I presented around the time this essay was written joked that he had been brushing up on his Derrida in preparation for his bout with Moore only to find that Moore had fled poststructuralism for the field of classics. It was true that I had by then become eager to develop an alternative way of writing that I could wheel out from time to time, one that would be less peripheral to the ordinary waking concerns of the average biblical scholar. My collaboration with Janice Capel Anderson in the present essay, and in a related essay on Matthew and masculinity that followed (Anderson and Moore 2003), enabled me to explore and internalize that alternative style of writing (also an alternative mode of analysis), and for that she will always have my gratitude.

My foray into the field of classics, however, did not really amount to a flight from poststructuralism, since what interested me most in that field was the distinctive body of work on Greek and Roman masculinities, and sex and gender more generally, that had sprung up around the second and third volumes of Foucault's *History of Sexuality* (1985; 1986), a "school of Foucault" in classics that built upon his work, extending it, refining it, and critiquing it. To a greater or lesser extent, Foucault's flawed but fundamental work on sexuality, whether in direct or mediated fashion, informs the present essay, the two essays on the Song

---

* First published in *JBL* 117 (1998): 249–73.

of Songs (chs. 10 and 11 below), and the essay on the Letter to the Romans (ch. 12).

Janice and I had independent interests in masculinity studies going into this project, but what drew us to 4 Maccabees in particular was the intriguing fact that so many of the cultural assumptions about masculinity that are embedded in New Testament texts and other early Christian and Hellenistic Jewish texts, needing to be dug out and brushed off for display, are strewn all across the surface of 4 Maccabees, ready for the picking. In other words, there is an unusual degree of explicitness to the language of masculinity in 4 Maccabees, and I have since found that text a useful yardstick against which to measure other ancient texts in which the language of masculinity is more oblique or opaque.

Of course, I had long had a personal fascination as well—a horrid fascination—with the gruesome Maccabean martyr saga (a torturous read, if ever there was one), as the ending of the previous essay makes plain. But that traumatic tale is manfully repressed in the present essay. The author of 4 Maccabees would expect no less.

Some of the most innovative work in classical studies in recent years has centered on the cultural construction of gender in Greek and Roman antiquity. Feminist classicists, together with (or including) classicists concerned primarily with conceptions of masculinity (two complexly overlapping groups), have raised key questions about how femininity and masculinity were construed during this period. Influenced by the second and third volumes of Michel Foucault's *History of Sexuality*, for example, scholars such as David M. Halperin and John J. Winkler have attempted to measure the gap, if not the gulf, that exists between the ancient Greek and Latin words *anthrōpos, anēr, arsēn, homo, vir, masculus*, and their cognates, on the one hand, and the English words "man," "male," "masculine," and their cognates, on the other.[2] On

---

2. See Foucault 1978; 1985; 1985; Halperin 1990; Winkler 1990; Halperin, Winkler and Zeitlin 1990. All of these books attend carefully, although not exclusively, to the cultural construction of masculinity in antiquity. On the relationship of this work to that of feminist classicists, see Skinner 1996. For related work on gender construction in rabbinic texts, see Satlow 1994; 1995, esp. 1ff., 185–222 passim; 1996; 1997; Boyarin 1995; and much of Boyarin 1993. Foucault's conclusions were anticipated in part by K. J. Dover (1989 [1978]), among others, and have been critiqued most recently by Simon Goldhill (1995), who, however, also builds on them. Biblical scholars are only beginning to har-

the basis of such work it is now possible to hazard a broad definition of the preeminent conception of masculinity in the ancient Mediterranean world. Mastery—of others and/or of oneself—is the definitive masculine trait in most of the Greek and Latin literary and philosophical texts that survive from antiquity. In certain of these texts, as we shall see, a (free) man's right to dominate others—women, children, slaves, and other social inferiors—is justified by his capacity to dominate himself. Moreover, as we shall also see, this hegemonic conception of masculinity was less a dichotomy between male and female than a hierarchical continuum where slippage from most fully masculine to least masculine could occur. The individual male's position on this precarious gender gradient was never entirely secure. Especially intriguing to us are texts in which control of others is radically devalued in favor of self-control, the latter being represented as the supreme index of masculinity. Such a text is 4 Maccabees, as we shall be arguing. Interest in 4 Maccabees is currently high among scholars of Hellenistic Judaism and early Christianity. Attention to its gender dynamics should be an important part of the ongoing discussion.[3] Drawing on recent classical scholarship on gender, we shall show how 4 Maccabees both subverts and supports the ancient hegemonic conception of masculinity.

Through the medium of a baroque rhetorical style (the florid Asianic style as distinct from the more restrained Attic style), 4 Maccabees tells the hortatory tale of how Eleazar, an aged Jewish philosopher (specifically, a Stoic sage), and seven unnamed Jewish boys (*meirakia*—11:24; cf. 11:13) defeat a Gentile tyrant.[4] Eleazar and the boys outman Antiochus Epiphanes, who has

---

ness this body of work (e.g., Stowers 1994, esp. 42–82 passim; Martin 1995b, esp. 339ff.; cf. Martin 1995a, esp. 3–37, 174–79). Studies centered more directly on masculinity in biblical texts, which owe little or nothing to parallel studies in classics, have also begun to appear (e.g., Eilberg-Schwartz 1994; Glancy 1994; Clines 1995a; 1998; Parsons 1995; Moore 1996; Washington 1997). Across the humanities and social sciences, the literature on masculinity is already vast; for further bibliography, see Cornwell and Lindisfarne 1994, 214–30.

3. Robin Darling Young has made an excellent start with her pathbreaking essay on the Maccabean mother (1991). Classicist Brent Shaw has also produced a provocative discussion of gender in 4 Maccabees (1996). His comments are part of a larger argument about the significance of endurance in Hellenistic Jewish texts such as the Testament of Joseph, the Testament of Job and 4 Maccabees, as well as a number of early Christian martyrological texts.

4. 4 Maccabees is probably best classified as an epideictic speech (see Klauck 1989, 659). A variety of dates have been suggested for it, ranging from the mid-first century B.C.E. to the mid-second century C.E., or even later. E. J. Bickerman's thesis that it was composed sometime between 18 and 54 C.E. has proved the most influential (1976 [1945]), convincing scholars such as Moses Hadas (1953, 95–96; he attempts to narrow Bickerman's dates to ca. 40–41 C.E.), Stanley Stowers (1988, 923), and Hugh Anderson (1985, 534; 1992, 453).

them tortured to death for their faithfulness to their ancestral religion. That a physically feeble old man (cf. 7:13) and a handful of boys should overcome an elite male in his prime challenges the hegemonic concept of masculinity, as we shall show. What is even more striking, however, is that the (similarly unnamed) mother of the seven boys also "takes it like a man." The exemplary self-mastery the boys demonstrate proves them worthy of the designation "men" (14:11), but so does the even greater self-mastery displayed by their elderly, widowed mother (15:23, 28–30; 16:14) who endures still greater agonies (14:11; cf. 16:2). Paradoxically, the prime exemplar of masculinity in 4 Maccabees is a woman.

"Put Us to the Test Then, Tyrant": Trials of Manhood

In the Greco-Roman world the four cardinal virtues were prudence (*phronēsis*), temperance (*sōphrosynē*), justice (*dikaiosynē*), and courage (*andreia*).[5] Aristotle and the Stoics inherited this four-part schema, as did Philo of Alexandria (see esp. *Leg. all.* 1.63–72), the author of the Wisdom of Solomon (8:7), and the author of 4 Maccabees.[6] The latter adduces all four virtues and construes them as manifestations of "devout reason" (*ho eusebēs logismos*), by which he means reason subservient to the Mosaic law (see Aune 1994, 135).[7] Or as he

---

Unconvinced by Bickerman, however, J. W. van Henten (1986) opts for a date in the early second century C.E., following André Dupont-Sommer (1939, 75–81) and Urs Breitenstein (1978, 173–75, 179). John Barclay, too, opts for a later date, although not quite second century (1996, 369–80), while Douglas Campbell suggests a date no earlier than 135 C.E. (1992, 221–28). Whatever fragile consensus Bickerman's essay created is now apparently crumbling. The identity of the author of 4 Maccabees is also unknown, as is the place of composition, although Antioch has most often been suggested (e.g., Dupont-Sommer 1939, 69–73; Hadas 1953, 111–13; Anderson 1985, 535; van Henten 1986, 146–49).

5. As classically formulated by Plato (see esp. *Phd.* 69C).

6. 4 Maccabees is colored throughout by an unmistakable, if eclectic, Stoicism. Gutman's and Hadas's arguments that the book is modeled on Plato's *Gorgias* are unconvincing (Gutman and Hadas 1949, 35–37; Hadas 1953, 116–18). More compelling are Renehan's and Stowers's arguments that it has strong affinities with the middle Stoicism of Posidonius (Renehan 1972; Stowers 1988, 924). Further on the philosophical underpinnings of the work, see Dupont-Sommer 1939, esp. 33–38; Breitenstein 1978, 131–75 passim. Scholars are sharply divided on the question of whether 5:19–21 espouses or opposes the Stoic doctrine of the equality of sins, but that need not concern us here.

7. Aune also notes: "As far as I have been able to determine, 4 Macc is the first (and only) occurrence of this phrase ['devout reason'] in the standard Greek literature previous to the second century CE" (1994, 135). Paul L. Redditt argues that *nomos* functions in five ways in 4 Maccabees: "to teach the way of Jewish culture, to enable rational living, to encourage the faithful to persevere even in the face of persecution, to condemn/not con-

himself puts it, "Now reason [*logismos*] is the mind that with unerring logic esteems the life of wisdom [*ton sophias bion*]" (1:15).[8] And wisdom is nothing other than "instruction in the law [*hē tou nomou paideia*]" (1:17). But the forms of wisdom, for this thoroughly Hellenized Jew, consist of the four cardinal virtues. Of the four, "prudence [*phronēsis*] is the most authoritative,[9] since reason controls the passions [*tōn pathōn*] by means of it. Of the passions, the two most comprehensive types are pleasure and pain [*hēdonē te kai ponos*]" (1:19-20). And of those two, it is pain that most concerns our author. Through prudence, devout reason is able to master "the passions that impede courage [*andreias*], namely, rage, fear, and pain [*thymou te kai phobou kai ponou*]" (1:4).

The principal virtue exhibited by the heroes of our tale, therefore—Eleazar, the seven brothers and their mother—will be *andreia*, hence the usefulness of 4 Maccabees for examining constructions of masculinity in the ancient Mediterranean world. For as every student of elementary Greek knows, *andreia* derives from *anēr* ("man"), so that its root meaning is "manliness" (cf. Goldstein 1983, 307). Indeed, given that *andreia* and its cognates (*andreios, andreiōs, andrizomai*, etc.) frequently mean just that—"manliness" and *its* cognates ("manly," "manfully," "to play the man," etc.)—in both classical and *koine* Greek, it is not too much to suggest that built into the language itself was the notion that to act courageously was to act as befits a man. Thus, courage was conceived as essentially a masculine virtue. "I could prove to you from many different examples that reason is sovereign master of the passions," claims the author of 4 Maccabees, "but I can demonstrate it best from the manly courage [*andragathias*] of those who died for the sake of virtue, Eleazar and the seven brothers and their mother" (1:7-8).

As much as anything else, then, 4 Maccabees is about what it means to be a "true man." In 4 Maccabees the two types of sovereignty associated with masculinity—sovereignty over others and sovereignty over oneself—are implicitly contrasted. The book deftly recycles the Cynic-Stoic commonplace that the kingdom that counts is the kingdom within. To the mind God gave the law, avers the author, "and he who is subject to it shall have domain over a dominion [*basileusei basileian*] that is temperate, just, good, and courageous/

---

demn persons for their behavior, and to issue commands and prohibitions for right living" (1983, 254).

8. Unless otherwise indicated, all translations of 2 and 4 Maccabees are ours, based on Rahlfs's text.

9. This is classic Stoic doctrine. According to Zeno of Citium, *sōphrosynē, dikaiosynē* and *andreia* are mere manifestations of *phronēsis* (*Stoic*. 1.200–201). Philo, whose middle Platonism contains a strong admixture of Stoicism, also regards *phronēsis* as the preeminent virtue (*Leg. all.* 1.71).

manly [*andreian*]" (2:23). Antiochus Epiphanes exemplifies the hegemonic male who possesses absolute power in the outward, material realm. Now, according to the philosophical tradition in which our author stands (the philosophic *koine* of the Greco-Roman world; cf. Renehan 1972, 227), in order to be deemed worthy of dominating others, one first had to be able to dominate oneself. Xenophon's *Oeconomicus*, for example, states that to rule over "willing subjects" is "a gift of the gods ... bestowed on those who have been initiated into self-discipline [*sōphrosynē*]" (21.12).[10] So how does Antiochus measure up?

At the conclusion of his encomium to the martyred Eleazar, the author of 4 Maccabees notes that "some men seem to be ruled by their passions [*pathokrateisthai*] because of the weakness of their reason.... Only the wise and manly individual [*ho sophos kai andreios*] is ruler [*kyrios*] of the passions" (7:20–23).[11] The author then subtly introduces the paradox of the absolute ruler who is slave to his own passions:

> For when the tyrant had been publicly defeated in his first attempt, being unable to compel an old man to eat defiling foods, then in violent rage [*sphodra peripathōs*] he commanded that others of the Hebrew captives be brought, and that any who ate defiling food would afterwards be released, but if any refused he would torture them even more viciously [*pikroteron basanizein*]. (8:2)

This sets the scene for all that ensues. The physical torture of the youths and the psychological torture of their mother will prove their remarkable self-control, and hence their "manliness." But the torture itself, characterized by excess, is occasioned by the inability of Antiochus to control his own passions, especially his rage. The point is driven home by the following revelation, which introduces the torture of the eldest brother: "When they [the seven brothers] had said these things, the tyrant was not only indignant [*echalepainen*], as at men who are disobedient, but also enraged [*ōrgisthē*], as at men who are ungrateful. Then at his command the guards brought forward the eldest"— and the torture commences (9:10–11). We have now been told twice that Antiochus abandoned himself to anger in initiating the torture of the brothers. Rage is also implied in 10:17, in which "the bloodthirsty, murderous, and utterly despicable Antiochus," unable any longer to endure the defiant taunts of the fourth brother, orders that his tongue be cut out (cf. 2 Macc 7:4, 10).

---

10. Translation from Pomeroy 1994. Foucault lists and discusses many similar examples (1985, 75–77, 82–83; 1986, 84–86, 94–95).

11. Cf. Philo, *Mig.* 197: "We call wisdom kingship for we call the sage a king" (also Wisd 6:20).

Already in 10:5 the tyrant's fury has infected his subordinates: "Thoroughly infuriated [*pikrōs enegkantes*] by the man's [the third brother's] boldness, they dislocated his hands and feet with their instruments...."[12]

What is the virtue that should have enabled Antiochus to curb his rage, to keep it under control? The author has already informed us. Reason (*logismos*) should rule over the passions "that impede *andreia*, namely, rage [*thymos*], fear, and pain" (1:4). But if the torture of the seven youths is an expression of rage on the part of the tyrant, and as such a failure of *andreia* ("manliness"), it is also the occasion for a stunning exhibition of *andreia* on the part of the youths themselves, and even their elderly mother. By yielding to rage Antiochus has compromised his masculinity; by overcoming fear (*phobos*) and pain (*ponos*) the martyrs have confirmed theirs.[13]

Indeed, as interpreted by Eleazar earlier, the ordeal represented by the torture is precisely a trial of manliness. Eleazar boldly informs the king that the Mosaic law "teaches us temperance [*sōphrosynē*] so that we are in control of all our pleasures and desires, and it also trains us in manliness [*andreia*], so that we endure all suffering willingly..." (5:23; cf. 10:9–10). Then he boasts: "I am neither so old nor so unmanly [*anandros*] as not to be young in reason on behalf of piety. So get the torture wheels ready and fan the fire more vigorously!" (5:31–32).[14] (The brothers later imitate Eleazar's example: "But if old men of the Hebrews lived piously because of their religion and endured torture, it is even more fitting that we who are young should die despising your coercive tortures, which our aged instructor [*ho paideutēs hēmōn gerōn*] also overcame.... Put us to the test [*peiraze*] then, tyrant..." [9:6–7; cf. 9:17–18;

---

12. Greek authors regularly represented "barbarians" as being incapable of controlling their passions (see Hall 1989, 80–84, 124–33). "So Gentiles ... suffer the same depiction at the hands of Jewish writers," adds Stowers (1994, 60). Cf. Satlow 1996, 35–36, which notes how certain rabbinic texts associate Gentiles with women as lacking masculine self-control.

13. Antiochus's rage resembles that of Nebuchadnezzar, and the faithfulness of the youths that of the three young men in Dan 3:13–30, a story repeatedly evoked in 4 Maccabees (13:9; 16:3, 21; 18:12). Shaw (1996, 271–73) notes a similar loss of control by those in authority in Achilles Tatius's *Leucippe and Clitophon* (6.18–22) and in Jerome's account of an innocent woman accused of adultery (*Ep.* 1 [CSEL 54.1–9]).

14. In 2 Macc 7:27 Eleazar declares, "by manfully [*andreiōs*] giving up my life now, I shall show myself worthy of my old age." Compare, too, *Mart. Pol.* 9.1, in which the hero, also elderly, hears a heavenly voice urging, "Be strong, Polycarp, act like a man," as he enters the arena for the final test. Discussing Phlm 9, Craig S. Wansink argues: "There is reason to believe that an appeal to age would have created pathos. Ancient writers often refer to the tension and anxiety created when the elderly are forced to undergo public humiliation, torture or martyrdom" (1996, 163). His prime example is 4 Maccabees, although he also cites Philo, *In Flacc.* 4; Tacitus, *Ann.* 4.28; *The Martyrs of Lyons* 28; Eusebius, *Hist. eccl.* 6.39.2.

10:16]).[15] When Eleazar has finally expired, the author exclaims in the course of his panegyric to him: "O aged man, mightier than tortures; O elder, fiercer than fire.... But most wonderful of all, though he was an old man, the tautness of his body having slackened, his muscles having become flabby and his sinews feeble [*lelymenōn men ēdē tōn tou sōmatos tonōn perikechalasmenōn de tōn sarkōn kekmēkotōn de kai tōn neurōn*], he became young again in spirit by means of reason, and by reason like Isaac's triumphed over the multiheaded rack" (7:10–14).[16] Compare the sixth brother, physically still a boy (*meirakiskos*—11:13), who proudly informs Antiochus: "I am younger in years than my brothers, but just as mature mentally [*tē de dianoia hēlikiōtēs*]" (11:14). This statement would also apply to the seventh brother, presumably, who is still younger in years.[17] Following their martyrdom both are accounted "men" along with their elder brothers: "Do not consider it amazing that reason retained control over those men [*tōn andrōn ekeinōn*] in their torture" (14:11; cf. 1:10). And prior to their martyrdom the author invited us to imagine the self-pity to which the brothers might have yielded if some of them had been cowardly and "unmanly" (*anandroi*—8:16; cf. 8:17–26; 16:5–11). All in all, the message is plain in the case of the younger brothers, as in the case of Eleazar: true masculinity inheres in rational self-mastery rather than in a manly physique.

The author's Jewish spin on this philosophical commonplace is that reason in turn must be ruled by the Torah. As such, faithful adherence to "the paternal law" (*ho patrios nomos*—5:32; cf. 8:7) is implicitly cast in 4 Maccabees as the quintessential expression of masculinity. Observant Jews are a superior race of "men" (even when they happen to be anatomically female), since they are ruled, not by reason alone, but by "devout reason" (*ho eusebēs*

---

15. Commenting on 2 Macc 6:18–7:42, Darling Young remarks: "The author has constructed the narrative to demonstrate how effective Eleazar's *hypodeigma* ['example'] was, because the very example of manliness which he provided is immediately followed by the startling accounts of the 'manliness' of children and of a woman" (1991, 70). The comment is even truer of 4 Maccabees.

16. Isaac's greatness, for our author, inheres in the fact that "seeing his father's hand wielding a knife and descending upon him did not flinch" (16:20). To the author's assertion that Eleazar "became young again in spirit [*aneneasen tō pneumati*]," compare the conception of manhood exhibited in the *Shepherd of Hermas*. As Steve Young has shown, being manly in the *Shepherd* means, in part, "overcoming the weariness associated with old age by recovering one's youthful vigor" (1994, 250).

17. Lam. Rab. 1:50, in a variant form of our tale (more on which below), whimsically gives the age of the youngest brother at his death as two years, six months and six-and-a-half hours. Following his debate with the tyrant on the finer points of the scriptural teaching on idolatry, he is allowed to nurse at his mother's breast.

logismos), reason subservient to the Torah. The Maccabean martyrologies, like the court tales of Daniel 1–6, can thus be said to exhibit a "ruled ethnic perspective" (Wills 1990, 68). What John J. Collins has to say of the court tales applies *mutatis mutandis* to the martyrologies: "They are affirmations of the enduring worth, even superiority, of people who have lost political power" (1993, 44). Note, for example, the elder brother's boast to his torturers: "Your wheel is not so strong, filthy lackeys, as to strangle my reason. Sever my limbs, burn my flesh, twist my joints, and through all these torments I will prove to you that the children of the Hebrews alone are invincible where virtue is concerned [*hyper aretēs eisin anikētoi*]" (9:18). As such, the Jewish martyrs in 4 Maccabees (like those of 2 Macc 7:12) are models of masculine virtue, even for the Gentiles:

> Who did not marvel at the athletes [*athlētas*] of the divine legislation? Who was not astounded? The tyrant himself and his whole council marveled at their endurance.... For the tyrant Antiochus, when he observed the manliness of their virtue [*tēn andreian autōn tēs aretēs*] and their endurance under the tortures, commended them to his soldiers as an example for their own endurance, and this made them brave and manly [*gennaious kai andreious*] for infantry battle and siege, and he ravaged and conquered all his enemies. (4 Macc 17:16–24; cf. 6:12–13; 17:17)[18]

---

18. Shaw argues that the endurance (*hypomonē*) we see in this passage and elsewhere in 4 Maccabees is the book's preeminent virtue and a "novel value" (1996, 278–79). He also argues that the martyrs' endurance would have been seen "as weak, womanish, slavish, and therefore morally bad" (1996, 279) in terms of the dominant gender ideology of the ancient Mediterranean world. In 4 Maccabees we find "the explicit cooptation of passivity in resistance as a fully legitimized male quality—a choice that could be made by thinking, reasoning and logical men" (1996, 280). We agree with Shaw that the theme of the mastery of the passions and the framework of the athletic (and, we would add, martial) contest involve the deployment of traditional social values (1996, 277–78). We also agree that the book focuses on resistance to illegitimate power and presents suffering and death in accord with devout reason as a legitimate male activity. But we disagree with his contention that endurance is the preeminent virtue or a (completely) novel value in 4 Maccabees. Our own reading suggests that endurance is not singled out as a discrete value more important than others, but is closely bound up with self-mastery and the virtue of manly courage. The martyrs' manly courage and endurance are proof that they have mastered their passions. We also find that the masculine quality of endurance is assumed rather than argued in the book, suggesting that Shaw has overstated the novelty of this view of endurance. In the passage quoted above, for example (4 Macc 17:16–24), Antiochus unapologetically commends the endurance of the martyrs to his soldiers "as an example for their own endurance," which example renders them "brave and manly"; while in 15:30 the mother is described as more manly than men in *hypomonē*. Furthermore, if endurance were not assumed to be a masculine value in 4 Maccabees, needing no apologia, the irony of a feeble old man, seven young

But if the Jewish law is the supreme ally of reason in 4 Maccabees, the Gentile tyrant is the supreme ally of the passions. Antiochus is temptation incarnate in a passage such as 5:5–13, for example, his seductive advice to Eleazar ("Why should you abhor eating the very excellent meat of this animal?"), or 8:5–11, his flattering address to the seven brothers ("Young men, I admire each and every one of you and wish to show you favor"), or 12:3–5, his "compassionate" plea with the single surviving brother ("If you yield to persuasion you shall be my friend and have charge of the affairs of my kingdom"). For the author of 4 Maccabees, the tyrant's seductive psychological manipulation along with his brutal physical coercion is but the graphic externalization of the internal temptation that every "true man" must resist. For the notion of masculinity that undergirds the book is that *external* control exercised over others does not a man make, but only *internal* control exercised over oneself. The malignant tyranny of the Gentile tyrant, therefore, is pointedly contrasted with the beneficial tyranny of reason tempered by the Jewish law: "O reason of the children [i.e., the sons], tyrant [*tyranne*] over the passions!" (15:1; cf. 1:13).

In a paroxysm of apostrophe, Eleazar at one point exclaims: "I shall not play you false, O Law my instructor, nor shall I renounce you, beloved self-control [*enkrateia*]!" (5:33–34). The agonistic aspect of self-mastery was commonly expressed by *enkrateia* in antiquity, a term closely related in meaning to *sōphosynē*, although not identical to it (see North 1966, 202–3). "*Enkrateia*, with its opposite, *akrasia*, is located on the axis of struggle, resistance, and combat," notes Foucault; "it is self-control, tension, 'continence,'" the repression of the passions. In general, it refers "to the dynamics of a domination of oneself by oneself and to the effort that this demands" (1985, 65). Although *enkrateia* occurs in 4 Maccabees only in 5:34,[19] the book is studded throughout with cognates of the term. In the first two chapters alone, for example, we read that the author's purpose is to inquire "whether reason is sovereign master [*autokratōr*] of the passions" (1:13); that "reason controls [*epikrateō*] the passions that hamper temperance" (1:3); that temperance "is control [*epikrateia*] over desires" (1:31); and that reason is also "able to control [*epikrateō*] the appetites" (1:33).[20] "The temperate Joseph" is praised "because

---

boys and an aged woman exhibiting it as a mark of their manliness—a central irony in the book, as we argue—would be lost.

19. It occurs elsewhere in the LXX only in Sir 18:29 as a textual variant. In the New Testament it is found in Acts 24:25; Gal 5:23; 2 Pet 1:6.

20. The author's example is reason's capacity to control the craving for forbidden foods (1:33–34)—especially apt since the tyrant will later do his utmost to compel or entice the martyrs to eat such foods (see esp. 5:1–3, 6–9; 8:2, 12; 13:2–3).

through his mental faculties he gained control [*perikrateō*] over sexual desire" (2:2). "And not only over the frenzied urge of sexual desire is reason seen to exercise control [*epikrateō*]," adds the author, "but over all desire" (2:4). It is through reason, moreover, that a man "is controlled [*krateō*] by the law" (2:9). The law can even "prevail over" (*epikrateō*) a man's natural affection for his wife (2:11). And so on.[21]

Enkrateia received a distinctly masculine inflection in classical Greek literature; it was a manly virtue, a virile virtue (see Foucault 1985, 63–77 passim). The durability of this inflection is evident from the Shepherd of Hermas (late first to mid-second century C.E.), in which *enkrateia* is allegorized as a woman; her behavior, however, is said to be masculine. Hermas has a vision of a tower surrounded by seven women, the first of whom is Faith. Faith's daughter, "who has her garments tucked up and conducts herself as a man [*andrizomenē*], is called Self-Control [*enkrateia*].... Whoever then follows her will become happy in his life, because he will restrain himself from all evil works, believing that, if he restrains himself from all evil desire, he will inherit eternal life" (*Herm. Vis.* 3.8).[22] In classical Greek literature, moreover, *enkrateia* was often cloaked in military or athletic metaphors (see Foucault 1985, 65–70, 72–74).[23] Grimly taking up arms and emulating the well-disciplined soldier, one valiantly resisted the pitiless assaults of the passions, drove them back, and utterly defeated them. Alternatively, one faced off with them in the gymnasium or the stadium and vigorously wrestled them to the ground, or raced neck-and-neck with them for the prize.

Enkrateia was also a key term for the Stoics. And it was the Stoics who, following the Cynics, fully unfurled the philosophical motif of the moral struggle of the sage, compulsively couching it in martial, and especially athletic, imagery. "The true Agon of the sage is one of the most frequently recurring pictures in the moral discourses of Epictetus, Seneca, Marcus Aurelius, and Plutarch," writes Victor C. Pfitzner. "The contest into which a man enters, if he wishes to follow the Stoic way of life with its struggle against the

---

21. See also 1:5, 6; 2:6, 15, 20 (*krateō*); 1:9 (*perikrateō*); 1:14; 2:14 (*epikrateō*).

22. ANF translation, modified. Steve Young remarks on this and similar passages: "From the start it is evident that 'manliness' in the *Shepherd* cannot be a mere biological category; indeed, male anatomy is neither a necessary nor a sufficent precondition for 'being a man'" (1994, 238). The Christian adaptation of *enkrateia* tied it closely to the concept of chastity. As Giulia Sfameni Gasparro notes, "numerous sectors within early Christianity gave strong emphasis to *enkrateia* both in the sense of 'virginity' and 'marital continence' as a central value of the Christian life" (1995, 134).

23. Foucault's examples include Plato, *Rep.* 8.560B; 9.572D–573B; *Leg.* 1.647D; 8.840C; Xenophon, *Oec.* 1.23; *Mem.* 1.2, 19.

desires and passions, and the whims of fortune which threaten to disrupt his peace of mind, is the Olympic contest of life itself" (1967, 29; cf. 28–35).

That 4 Maccabees is saturated with military and athletic metaphors should come as no surprise, therefore, given the Stoic affiliations of its author.[24] In 3:6–18, for example, a martial anecdote is adduced to illustrate the author's martial philosophy. David has been fighting the Philistines all day and is parched with thirst. Although he has an abundance of water ready to hand, he is consumed by an "irrational desire" (*alogistos epithymia*) for a drink of the enemy's water. "Two vigorous young soldiers" (*duo neaniskoi stratiōtai karteroi*) voluntarily risk their necks to fill a pitcher of water for the king from the enemy's spring. Inspired by their manly example, David finally manages to defeat his internal enemy, irrational desire: although still burning with thirst, he pours the dearly-bought drink out as a libation to God.[25] David's moral victory pales, however, beside that of the warrior-sage, Eleazar: "No city besieged with numerous and ingenious war machines has ever put up such resistance as did that most holy man! Although his sacred life was set ablaze with scourgings and rackings, he conquered [*enikēsen*] the besiegers with the shield of his devout reason [*dia ton hyperastizonta tēs eusebeias logismon*]" (7:4).[26] The mother, for her part, is saluted as a "soldier of God in piety's cause [*di' eusebeian theou stratiōti*]" (16:14).[27] Her eldest son boasts to his torturers that "the children of the Hebrews alone are invincible [*anikētoi*] where reason is concerned" (9:18), as we noted earlier, and then exhorts his fellows: "Imitate me, brothers; do not become deserters in my struggle [*agōna*] or renounce our valiant brotherhood. Fight a sacred and noble fight [*hieran kai eugenē strateian strateusasthe*] for religion…" (9:23–24). And Antiochus himself, observing "the manliness of their virtue" (*tēn andreian autōn tēs aretēs*) and their astonishing imperviousness to physical pain (their Stoic *apatheia* or *anaisthēsia*, actually, although the author never uses either term),[28] commends them to his soldiers as a stirring example of martial prowess, with spectacular results,

---

24. Pfitzner surveys the athletic imagery in 4 Maccabees (1967, 57–64; cf. Breitenstein 1978, 188). Philo, too, favored athletic and, to a lesser extent, military metaphors (Pfitzner 1967, 38–48).

25. The story differs significantly from the scriptural versions (2 Sam 23:13–17; 1 Chron 11:15–19; cf. Josephus, *Ant.* 7.12.3).

26. The metaphor of the sage as a besieged city was a stock Stoic theme, especially in the early Roman Empire (see Stowers 1988, 929–30).

27. She is also hailed as "elder" (*presbyti*) in the same verse, "perhaps signifying an official of the synagogue," as Darling Young surmises, yet another masculine title "to match the *andreia* of her soul" (1991, 78).

28. Samuel Sandmel contrasts the martyrs of 4 Maccabees with the ten martyrs of the Hadrianic persecution depicted in rabbinic literature. The latter undergo "the acute pain

the metaphoric military conquests of the martyrs inspiring real military conquests on the part of the troops (17:16–24).

As for athletic metaphors, we are told that Eleazar, like a "noble athlete" (*gennaios athlētēs*), was victorious over his tormenters (6:10). The mother, for her part, merits the following apostrophe: "O mother of the nation..., winner of the prize in the contest of the heart [*tou dia splagchnōn agōnos athlophore*]!" (15:29). And her sons declare in unison, "Through this grievous suffering and endurance we shall obtain the prize of virtue [*ta tēs aretēs athla echomen*]..." (9:8). The final metaphor reserved for the mother and the sons in the book is also that of prizewinner: "But the sons of Abraham together with their mother, who carried away the prize [*syn tē athlophorō mētri*], are gathered together into the chorus of the fathers..." (18:23). But the most elaborate athletic imagery is found in 17:11–16:

> Divine indeed was the contest [*agōn*] in which they were engaged. For on that day virtue was the umpire [*hēthlothetei*] and tested them for their endurance. The prize [*nikos*] was incorruptibility in an endless life. Now, Eleazar was the first contestant [*proēgōnizeto*], but the mother of the seven sons also competed [*enēthlei*], and the brothers, too, contended [*hēgōnizonto*]. The tyrant was the competition [*antēgōvizeto*] and the world and the human race were the spectators [*etheōrei*]. Piety was the victor [*enika*] and awarded the crown to its own athletes [*tous heautēs athlētas stephanousa*]. Who did not marvel at the athletes [*athlētas*] of the divine legislation? Who was not astounded?

At one point, martial and athletic metaphors intertwine. The sixth brother, the mere boy (*meirakiskos*—11:13), while being simultaneously broken on the wheel, roasted over a fire, and run through with red-hot skewers, blithely exclaims:

> O contest [*agōnos*] befitting holiness, in which so many of us brothers have been summoned to an exercise in suffering [*eis gymnasian ponōn*] for religion's sake, yet have not been conquered [*ouk enikēthēmen*]! For religious knowledge, O tyrant, is invincible [*anikētos*]! Fully armed [*kathōplismenos*] with nobility I, too, shall die with my brothers...." (11:20–22)[29]

---

which their fidelity enable[s] them to endure," whereas the former "are portrayed as completely immune to the pain" (1978, 279).

29. Cf. Plutarch, *Mor.* 40: "The boys in Sparta were lashed with whips during the entire day at the altar of Artemis Orthia, frequently to the point of death, and they bravely endured this, cheerful and proud, vying with one another for the supremacy as to which one of them could endure being beaten for the longer time and the greater number of blows. And the one who was victorious was held in especial repute" (LCL trans.). According to Hecataeus of Abdera, Moses similarly expected Israelite youths "to cultivate man-

And later we learn that the brothers had earlier resolved: "Let us fully arm ourselves [*kathoplisōmetha*], therefore, with the control of the passions [*pathokrateian*] that comes from divine reason" (13:16).

As will by now be readily apparent, the real battle in 4 Maccabees is between the martyrs and themselves (although it is less a battle than a rout). A standard feature of popular Hellenistic moral philosophy was the distinction between the man who is "stronger than himself" (*kreittōn heauou*), that is, able to rein in his passions and appetites, and the man who is "weaker than himself" (*hēttōn heatou*), that is, a slave to his passions and appetites (and as such not fully a "man").[30] Predictably, this stock antithesis also crops up in 4 Maccabees: "Since the seven brothers scorned sufferings even unto death, therefore, all must concede that devout reason is absolute sovereign [*autodespotos*] over the passions. For if they had been slaves to their passions [*tois pathesi doulōthentes*] and had eaten defiling food, we would have said that they had been conquered by them [*elegomen an toutois autous nenikēsthai*]" (13:1-2). In the ancient Mediterranean world, "slave" and "woman" were not merely two of the antonyms that served to define the concept "man" (the third being "child," which could be extended to encompass "youth"; cf. Walters 1991, 30–31). "Slave" and "woman" were also variant terms for the internal "other" that posed a perpetual threat to masculine identity. "The enemy was also within," John J. Winkler writes of this peculiarly brittle concept of masculinity (1990, 49; cf. Foucault 1985, 67). A statement such as the following from Plato's *Laws* thus becomes fully legible: "Being defeated by oneself is the most shameful and at the same time the worst of all defeats" (1.626D-E). Why? Because it is tantamount to a defeat at the hands of women or slaves.[31]

In 4 Maccabees it is the paradoxical fate of the absolute monarch, Antiochus Epiphanes, to suffer defeat at the hands of a woman (cf. Judg 4:9; 9:54; Jdt 9:10; 13:15, 17; 14:18; 16:5-6), an old man,[32] and a gaggle of boys ("We

---

liness [*andreian*] and steadfastness, and generally to endure every hardship" (Diodorus Siculus 40.3.6). (We are indebted to J. W. van Henten for the latter reference.)

30. The distinction received its classic formulation from Plato, who adduces it repeatedly (see esp. *Rep.* 4.430C-431A). On the Stoic formulations, see Erskine 1990, 43–63 passim.

31. Cf. Philo's warning that the mind, which he codes as masculine, can be deceived by the senses, which he codes as feminine. When this happens, "reason is forthwith ensnared and becomes a subject instead of a ruler, a slave instead of a master, an alien instead of a citizen, and a mortal instead of an immortal" (*Op.* 59.165, LCL trans.).

32. Specifically, a physically feeble old man (7:13). As Marilyn B. Skinner has noted (1993, 111), physical infirmity due to old age tended to be viewed as a "feminizing" disability in a male: "Male status, the prerogative of the citizen and head of household, is a function of age as well as of sex, hinging upon control—control over wife and children,

six boys [*meirakia*] have destroyed your tyranny"—11:24). As such, 4 Maccabees is partly about the (fictitious) public shaming of this traditional villain. But this is simply to say, once again, that 4 Maccabees is in some sense about hegemonic manhood, for manhood was supremely a matter of public perception in the ancient Mediterranean world, of honor versus shame.[33] Being forced to dishonor one's fathers and one's god by eating forbidden food would be shameful enough, Eleazar avers, without giving the oppressor opportunity to laugh derisively (*epigelaō*) at one as a result (5:27), thereby compounding the insult to one's manhood. "But you will not have this laugh at my expense [*all' ou gelaseis kat' emou touton ton gelōta*]," he resolves (5:28). He is neither so old nor so "unmanly" (*anandros*) as to allow that to happen (5:30). Although shamefully abused, he refuses to be shamed.[34] First he is stripped naked, but need not be ashamed, for he is still "adorned with the beauty of his piety [*enkosmoumenon tē peri tēn eusebeian euschēmosynē*]" (6:2). Then he is flogged until he loses control of his body; he falls to the ground but again incurs no loss of honor, for he keeps his reason "erect and unbent [*orthon eichen kai aklinē ton logismon*]" (6:7).[35]

In the ancient Mediterranean world, *malakos* ("soft"; Latin *mollis*) was the adjective supremely used to differentiate women, girls, boys, youths, effeminate males, catamites and eunuchs from "true men" (see Walters 1991,

---

over slaves, over extrinsic political and economic affairs and, above all, over self. To maintain that status, constant physiological and psychological vigilance is required. Any loss of physical vigor due to old age, infirmity, or overindulgence in carnal pleasures, any analogous lapse of moral resolve, or any diminution of social standing, can weaken the bulwarks of masculinity and cause reversion to a passive 'womanish' condition." Philo's pronouncement on the "tenth stage" of a man's life thus acquires added significance: "during the tenth comes the desirable end of life, while the bodily organs are still compact and firm; for prolonged old age is wont to abate and break down the force of each of them" (*Opif.* 103, LCL trans.). So, too, does Sir 3:12–13: "My son, assist your father in his old age, and do not grieve him as long as he lives. Even if his mind fails, be considerate of him; do not dishonor him [*mē atimasēs auton*] in the fullness of your strength" (our trans.).

33. See Gilmore 1990, 36–38; Malina and Neyrey 1991, 41–43; Plevnik 1993, 95–97; Moxnes 1996. For an attempt to apply these categories to 4 Maccabees, see deSilva 1995a, 127–42; 1995b. Important critiques of some of the pioneering work on honor and shame in the Mediterranean world should, however, be noted (e.g., Chance 1994; Kressel 1994; deSilva 1995b, 32–33).

34. DeSilva remarks: "The author does not consider for a moment that the tortures and physical outrages to the martyrs' bodies affect their honor in any way. While such treatment is thought to include the destruction of a person's honor and place in society, for the martyrs it is a sign of honor" (1995b, 54).

35. The phrase appears to be a play on *orthos logos* ("right reason"), an important Stoic concept (see Erskine 1990, 16–17, 45).

29; cf. Dover 1978, 79; Winkler 1990, 50–52; Gleason 1995, 65, 69). Given that Eleazar has already framed his ordeal as a trial of "manliness," it is not surprising that *malakos* now makes its appearance in his discourse, embedded in a compound verb. Urged by his friends to spare himself further abuse by feigning to eat the pork, Eleazar indignantly replies: "Never may we, the children of Abraham, think so ignobly that, being soft/effeminate in spirit [*malakopsychēsantes*], we feign a role unbecoming to us" (6:17). To act in so unmanly a fashion would be dishonorable in the extreme:

> For it would be irrational if having lived our life in accordance with truth right up to old age and having guarded its reputation [*doxan*] in accordance with law, we should now change course and ourselves become a model of impiety to the young by setting them an example in the eating of unclean food. It would be shameful [*aischron*] if we should survive for only a short time and during it become a laughingstock [*katagelōmenai*] to all for our cowardice and be despised by the tyrant as unmanly [*anandroi*] for not defending our divine law to the death. (6:18–21)

This sentiment is later echoed by the author in his encomium to Eleazar: *su pater tēn eunomian hēmōn dia tōn hypomonōn eis doxan ekyrōsas* (7:9)—which Hadas aptly, if awkwardly, renders as "You, father, by your perseverance in the public gaze, have made strong our adherence to the Law," taking his cue from the fact that *doxa* could mean "public repute" (1953, 185).[36] To add that it could also mean "honor" would be almost redundant; in the ancient Mediterranean world, male honor and sound reputation were synonymous, and both values were intimately bound up with the dominant concept of masculinity. Antiochus's reaction to the (too) honorable demise of this "wise and manly" (*sophos kai andreios*—7:23) sage is to yield to rage, as we already noted: "For when the tyrant had been publicly defeated [*enikēthē perithanōs*] in his first attempt, being unable to compel an old man to eat defiling foods, then in violent rage he commanded that others of the Hebrew captives be brought…" (8:2; cf. 9:8). That a gain in honor on the part of one male regularly entailed a loss of honor on the part of another male was a fundamental law of the honor-shame economy, and it appears that Antiochus is only too well aware of this.

But so are the "Hebrew captives" that are now led forth, namely, the seven brothers. Indeed, they seem to believe that any unmanly weakness shown on their part will bring shame not only on themselves but on all their honorable male forebears as well. No sooner has Antiochus finished advising them to eat the forbidden food than they all "with one voice and as with one mind"

---

36. Anderson (1985, 552) concurs that this connotation of *doxa* is in play here.

reject his seductive arguments: "Why do you delay, tyrant? We are ready to die rather than transgress our forefathers' commandments [*tas patrious hēmōn entolas*]; for we are obviously bringing shame upon our ancestors [*aischynometha gar tous progonous hēmōn*] unless we show obedience to the Law and to Moses our counselor" (9:1–2). When four of the brothers have already been butchered, the fifth indignantly asks the tyrant what they have done to be treated in this shameful fashion. "Is it because we revere the Creator of all and live in accord with his virtuous Law? But these things deserve honors, not tortures [*alla tauta timōn ou basanōn estin axia*]" (11:5–6). Of course, the frightful tortures do provide the brothers with an invaluable opportunity to prove their incomparable manhood ("You unwittingly bestow glorious favors on us, tyrant"—11:12) by demonstrating absolute self-mastery over physical pain (*ēsan autokratores tōn algēdonōn*—8:28; cf. 13:1), thereby heaping up unprecedented honor not only for themselves but for their nation (cf. 17:10). And the honor consists both in the unbounded admiration that they win from their fellow men ("For they were a source of wonder, not only to all men [*pantōn anthrōpōn*], but even to their torturers on account of their manly courage [*andreia*] and endurance"—1:11; cf. 17:17, 23–24; 18:3) and in the approval that they win from their (male) god. Now "they are gathered together in the chorus of their fathers [*eis paterōn choron synagelazontai*]"—together with their manly mother (18:23)—in a heaven become an eternal haven for true men.

A Woman "More Manly Than Men"

The exemplary self-mastery the boys demonstrate proves them worthy of admiration, emulation and the designation "men": "reason retained control over those men [*tōn andrōn ekeinōn*] in their torture" (14:11; cf. 1:10). But their mother is depicted as yet more manly. Why? Because "even a woman's mind [*kai gynaikos nous*] scorned still more diverse agonies" (14:11; cf. 16:2).

What "agonies" (*algēdones*) does the author have in mind? For we eventually learn that the mother cheated the torturers: "Some of the guards reported that when she, too, was about to be seized and put to death she cast herself into the fire so that no one might touch her body" (17:1). The answer, apparently, is that the mother vicariously suffered the slow butchering of each of her boys, thereby enduring the death-torture, not once, but seven times (14:12). "No mother ever loved her children more than the mother of the seven boys," the author insists (15:6).[37] His grisly account of her vicarious torture follows:

---

37. Stowers notes that the Stoics "showed more interest in children and 'natural' familial bonds than did the other Hellenistic schools" (1988, 931). In overcoming or transform-

"She beheld the flesh of her children melting in the fire and their toes and fingers scattered on the ground, and the flesh of their heads right down to the jaws exposed like masks" (15:15), and so on. The account concludes: "How numerous, then, and how great were the torments that the mother suffered while her sons were tortured on the wheel and with the searing irons" (15:22).

Of course, it is not only with these hideous external pressures that the mother must wrestle; she must also contend with her own internal female "nature." The author has already mentioned in passing what he assumes his audience already knows, namely, that "mothers are *asthenopsychoi*" (15:5)—"weak-spirited," or "weak-souled," or simply "the weaker sex," as NRSV aptly paraphrases it.[38] But it is precisely this "innate" disability that the mother is depicted as heroically overcoming, thereby proving herself worthy of one of the more curious compliments that a Hellenistic male author could bestow upon a female character: she shows herself to be a true man at heart. First the author states: "But devout reason, filling her heart with manly courage in the very midst of her emotions [*ta splagchna autēs ho eusebēs logismos en autois tois pathesin andreiōsas*], strengthened her to disregard, for the time being, her parental affection" (15:23).[39] A few verses later he is prepared to go farther: "O mother of the nation, champion of the law, defender of true religion, and winner of the prize in the contest of the heart! More noble than men in perseverance and more manly than men in endurance [*andrōn pros hypomonēn andreiotera*]!" (15:28–30). And again: "By your endurance you have conquered even a tyrant, and by your deeds and words you have been found stronger than a man [*kai ergois dynatōtera kai logois eurethēs andros*]" (16:14). Throughout, the author is embroidering 2 Macc 7:21, which tells how the mother succeeded in "rousing her female reasoning with male courage [*ton thēlyn logismon arseni thymō diegeirasa*]."[40]

---

ing familial affection, the mother resembles her offspring who mastered their brotherly love (13:19–14:1; cf. Klauck 1990), a love that might have caused them to sin. Instead they encourage each other to die for the sake of the law.

38. Cf. 16:5: "For this, too, you must consider: If the woman had been timid of soul/fainthearted [*deilopsychos*]—being, as she was, a mother [*kaiper mētēr ousa*]—she would have lamented over them [her sons] and perhaps spoken as follows...." This rendering of *kaiper mētēr ousa* is Hadas's. He argues: "It is hard to see the force of the concessive *kaiper* ('although') in this context; and none of the suggestions offered by commentators is wholly convincing" (1953, 227). 15:5 lends support to his translation.

39. *Andreioō*, "fill with (manly) courage," appears to be a neologism (see Lust, Eynikel and Hauspie 1992, s.v. *andreioō*).

40. 2 Macc 6:12–7:42 seems to have functioned as the primary source for 4 Maccabees, the latter being a free expansion of the former. So Dupont-Sommer (1939, 26–32), Hadas (1953, 92–95), and most subsequent commentators, *pace* Freudenthal (1869, 72–90), fol-

She is stronger than a man, then, and not just any man. For the author of 4 Maccabees dares to imply that the martyr-mother's manly self-control exceeded even that of Daniel and his companion Mishael (Dan 3; 6): "Not so savage were the lions surrounding Daniel, nor so blazing hot was the raging fiery furnace of Mishael, as was the natural mother's love that burned in her when she saw her seven sons tortured in such varied ways. But by means of devout reason the mother quenched these many intense emotions" (16:3–4). Indeed, the martyr-mother with the "mind of adamant" (*hōsper adamantinon echousa ton noun*—16:13) begs comparison with no less a figure than Abraham himself. Far from being "weak-souled" (*asthenopsychos*—15:5) or "timid-souled" (*deilopsychos*—16:5), she possesses a soul like the father of her people: "But sympathy for her children did not sway the mother of the youths, whose soul was like Abraham's [*tēn Abraam homopsychon tōn neaniskōn mētera*]" (14:20). For her spectacular sacrifice of her sons in obedience to the divine will calls to mind and rivals Abraham's own (near-)sacrifice of *his* son: "as the daughter of God-fearing Abraham, she remembered his fortitude" (15:28; cf. 13:12; 16:20; Darling Young 1991, esp. 77, 79–80; Sandmel 1971, 56–59). Lamentations Rabbah (fifth or sixth century C.E.), which features a rather different performance of this martyrological tale, will go farther than our author dares, having the mother say to her youngest boy as he is about to be slaughtered, "My son, go to the patriarch Abraham and tell him, 'Thus said my mother, "Do not preen yourself [on your righteousness], saying I built an altar and offered up my son, Isaac." Behold, our mother built seven altars and offered up seven sons in one day. Yours was only a test, but mine was in earnest'" (1.50).[41]

The martyr mother may exhibit a masculinity equal to or greater than that of any man, but in this she is not unique. The literary and philosophical topos of the subject who is anatomically female but morally masculine is an exceptionally far-flung one, found in early Christian texts, and early Buddhist texts, as well as in ancient Jewish texts and pagan Greek and Roman texts.[42] Xenophon's *Oeconomicus*, for example, depicts Socrates recounting his conversation with a wealthy landowner, Ischomachus, in which the latter boasts of the prodigious progress in virtue exhibited by his precocious young wife as a result of his having deigned to instruct her in the proper management of

---

lowed by Deissmann (1900, 156), who argued that the authors of 2 and 4 Maccabees each had independent recourse to the (lost) five-volume work of Jason of Cyrene upon which 2 Maccabees purports to be based (2:23).

41. Translation from Freedman and Simon 1939. The story is quoted in full by Hadas (1953, 129–33). More on the rabbinic versions below.

42. For the Buddhist texts, see Paul 1979, 171–74; Schuster 1981.

her household. "By Hera, Ischomachus," exclaims Socrates, "you show that your wife has a masculine intelligence [*andrikēn ge epideiknyeis tēn dianoian tēs gynaikos*]!" (10.1).[43] Philo of Alexandria, for his part, extols the soul that succeeds in bringing together masculine and feminine elements—"not that the masculine thoughts may be made womanish, and relaxed by softness," he hastily adds, "but that the female element, the senses, may be made manly by following masculine thoughts and by receiving from them seed for procreation, that it may perceive [things] with wisdom, prudence, justice, and courage, in sum, with virtue" (*Quaest. in Gen.* 2.49; cf. 2.12).[44] Then, too, there is the now notorious saying with which the Gospel of Thomas ends. In response to Simon Peter urging his fellow male disciples, "Let Mary leave us, for women are not worthy of life," Jesus defends her by declaring, "I myself shall lead her in order to make her male, that she too may become a living spirit resembling you males. For every woman who will make herself male will enter the kingdom of heaven" (114).[45] As a final example, consider the climactic vision vouchsafed to the Christian martyr Perpetua, according to the "prison diary" contained in the Martyrdom of Perpetua and Felicitas. In the vision, Perpetua is led into the arena to confront her opponent, an Egyptian "of vicious appearance." "My clothes were stripped off," she reports, "and suddenly I was a man [Greek *egenēthēn arrēn*; Latin *facta sum masculus*]" (10). Unencumbered by her femaleness she succeeds in overcoming her opponent, as a symbolic prelude to her overcoming of fear in the real arena and her stalwart acceptance of death.[46] What these different examples, embedded in different texts, genres and cultural contexts, seem to share in common is a separation of masculinity from anatomy, coupled with a conception of mas-

---

43. Translation from Pomeroy 1994. Earlier the wife had revealed: "My mother told me that my duty is to practice self-control [*einai sōphronein*]." "By Zeus, wife," replies Ischomachus, "my father said the same to me" (7.14–15; cf. 7.26). Building on the *Oeconomicus*, Sheila Murnaghan (1988) has shown how the cultural categories of masculinity and femininity could refer in classical Greek literature, not to conditions based ultimately upon anatomy, so much as to degrees of self-mastery (*sōphrosynē*) in persons of either sex.

44. LCL translation. Elsewhere Philo states: "For progress [toward virtue] is indeed nothing else than the giving up of the female gender by changing into the male, since the female gender is material, passive, corporeal, and sense-perceptible, while the male is active, rational, incorporeal, and more akin to mind and thought" (*Quaest. in Ex.* 1.8, LCL; cf. *Det.* 28; *Leg.* 319). See further Baer 1970, 45–49; Aspegren 1990, 93–95; Mattila 1996.

45. Translation from Robinson 1988. See further Meyer 1985; Castelli 1991c, esp. 29–33.

46. Castelli treats this metamorphosis in some detail (1991c, 33–43), as does Aspegren (1990, 133–39, 142–43); see also P. C. Miller 1992, 60–61; Tilley 1994, 844–45. Similar examples could be multiplied; see Aspegren 1990, 99–164 passim; Vogt 1991, 170–86 passim.

culinity as the ultimate measure of virtue. Notwithstanding the fact that one of our examples appears to have been authored by a woman (Perpetua's prison diary is generally accepted as authentic), the topos denigrates women's biology and constructs female gender negatively. Kerstin Aspegren puts it succinctly: "If a woman achieved something good or distinguished herself in ethical, religious or intellectual matters, she was not praised as being a woman of good qualities but as a woman who had become manly" (1990, 11). (A merciless double standard prevailed, moreover: a man who had become womanly was regarded as a moral degenerate, as someone who deserved to be mastered by a real man [see Winkler 1990, 45–70 passim; Gleason 1995, 60–76; Sly 1990, 211–12].)[47] Unable to measure up to men in the arena of virtue, the best a woman could hope for was to be declared an honorary man. This is the laurel wreath that Perpetua awards to herself in her prison diary, the same wreath that is awarded to the martyr-mother in 4 Maccabees (17:11–16; 18:23). But even this recuperative gesture could arouse anxiety in certain male spectators, as we are about to see.

The mother is given the last word, or rather the last speech, in 4 Maccabees. But what a strange speech it turns out to be:

> The mother of the seven children also addressed these precepts to her offspring: "I was a chaste virgin and did not venture outside my father's house; but I kept guard over the rib that was fashioned [into the female body]. No seducer in the desert or corruptor in the field defiled me, nor did the destroying and deceitful serpent sully the purity of my virginity. In the days of my prime I remained with my husband.... While he was still with you, he taught you the law and the prophets. He read to you of Abel, slain by Cain, of Isaac, offered as a burnt offering, and of Joseph, in prison. He told you of the zeal of Phineas, and taught you about Hananiah, Azariah, and Mishael in the fire. He also sang the praises of Daniel in the lions' den and called him blessed. He reminded you of the scripture of Isaiah which says, 'Even though you pass through fire the flame shall not burn you.' He sang to you the psalm of David which says, 'Many are the afflictions of the righteous.' ... He affirmed the question of Ezekiel, 'Shall these dry bones live?' For he did not forget to teach you the song that Moses taught, which says, 'I kill and I make alive....'" (18:6–19)

Critical commentators have long noted the tacked-on appearance of this speech—it reads like an addendum—and some have not hesitated to brand it an interpolation (Freudenthal [1869, 155], for example, followed most

---

47. The labeling of a male opponent as feminine, therefore, was a stock polemical slur (see Kraemer 1994).

196   THE BIBLE IN THEORY

notably by Dupont-Sommer [1939, 153]), or at least a displacement (Deissmann [1900, 175] suggesting that it was originally a continuation of 16:23).[48] Hadas, writing in the early 1950s, confessed himself to be enchanted by the cozy images that the speech summons up: "Whether or not the passage is genuine, it presents a charming picture of domestic piety: the strict chastity of the maiden, the devotion of the wife to her husband, the love of children, the father reading Scripture to the family and instructing them in religion" (1953, 239).

Of course, the scene is not nearly so innocent. Today it is hard to avoid the suspicion that we are witnessing not just a domestic scene but a scene of domestication, that the martyr-mother is being tamed and herded into the patriarchal fold. In some respects, she has not been allowed to stray too far from the fold to begin with. Robin Darling Young notes that in 2 Macc 7 the woman is never once permitted to speak publicly; her remarks are confined to private exhortations to her sons in "the paternal tongue [*tē patriō phōnē*]" (7:21, 27), of which Antiochus is ignorant (1991, 70).[49] Similarly in 4 Maccabees, the woman is allowed to encourage all seven of her sons privately (12:7; 16:15–25), yet of the nine main martyrs in the book (counting Eleazar), she is the only one who does not address Antiochus and his men directly.

Contrast Lamentations Rabbah 1.50, the fullest rabbinic parallel to 2 Macc 7 and 4 Macc 8–18 (the tale of the mother and her seven sons),[50] which unequivocally presents the woman as the central character from the outset ("It is related of Miriam, the daughter of Tanhum, that she was taken captive with her seven sons…"), and later has her not only address the tyrant directly, but shame him by insulting him to his face.[51] The youngest son has just had

---

48. Townshend is content to label it a "digression" (1913, 655). The debate hinges on the style of the passage as well as its content. Freudenthal deemed the style inferior to the rest of the book (1869, 155); Deissmann disagreed (1900, 175). More recently Stowers (1988, 933–34), and especially Breitenstein (1978, 155–56), have declared the speech genuine, the latter in the course of a detailed stylistic analysis of the book.

49. The language is probably best understood as Hebrew (rather than Aramaic), which is how the author of 4 Maccabees interprets it (12:7); cf. Goldstein 1983, 297–98.

50. The other parallels are Git. 57b; S. Eliyahu Rab. 30; Pesiq. R. 43.

51. Nameless in 4 Maccabees, the mother is dubbed Miriam bat Tanhum, or Hannah, in the rabbinic tradition, Solomone in the Greek Christian tradition, and Mart Simouni in the Syriac tradition (see further Darling Young 1991, 67). The tyrant in the rabbinic versions, however, is not Antiochus Epiphanes but Hadrian: "Hadrian came and seized upon a widow…" (*S. Eliyahu Rab.* 30); "In the days of the *shemad* [the Hadrianic persecutions]…" (*Pesiq. R.* 43). The disparate versions of the story found in the Maccabean literature, on the one hand, and in the rabbinic literature, on the other, are best viewed as variant performances of a popular martyrological tale. Various scholars have argued that the tale has a firm historical foundation (e.g., Dupont-Sommer 1939, 24; cf. 20–25; Hadas 1953, 128;

a lively debate with the tyrant, which has afforded him ample opportunity to parade his encyclopedic knowledge of scripture (notwithstanding the fact that he is only two-and-a-half years old). Unimpressed by his erudition, the tyrant orders him slain. At this point Miriam intervenes:

> "By the life of your head, O emperor, give me my son that I may embrace and kiss him." They gave him to her, and she bared her breasts and suckled him. She said to the king, "By the life of your head, O emperor, put me to death first and then slay him." He answered her, "I cannot agree to that, because it is written in your Torah, *And whether it be cow or ewe, ye shall not kill it and its young both in one day*" (Lev 22.28). She retorted, "You unutterable fool! Have you already fulfilled all the commandments save only this one?" He immediately ordered him to be slain.[52]

The mother in 2 Maccabees 7, although a far cry from Miriam bat Tanhum, does cause Antiochus to suspect that he is being treated with contempt. He is unable to understand her address to her sons, yet his suspicions are aroused by her reproachful tone (*ho de Antiochos oiomenos kataphroneisthai kai tēn oneidizousan hyphorōmenos phōnēn...*—7:24). The author of 4 Maccabees eliminates this detail; in his version, the woman is not said to offer any affront to the monarch. Like a respectable Greco-Roman matron, she is seen but not (over)heard.[53] One suspects, nevertheless, either that the author of 4 Maccabees has had second thoughts, fearing that he has painted too masculine a portrait of his heroine, one that risks alienating his elite male readership,[54]

Darling Young 1991, 68). This position, however, is probably insufficiently critical. Collins (1981, 310) contends that the "legendary character" of 2 Maccabees 7 (and, by extension, 4 Maccabees 8–18) is suggested not only by "the highly implausible presence of the king" (influenced, perhaps, by Dan 3 and 5), "but also by the stock number of seven sons. There are numerous stories about seven sons even within ancient Judaism [e.g., *T. Mos.* 9; Josephus, *Ant.* 14.15.5].... Seven is the number of perfection, and seven sons is the proverbially perfect family."

52. Translation from Freedman and Simon 1939.

53. Nor is she seen overmuch. 18:7 ("I was a chaste virgin and did not venture outside my father's house") is perhaps intended to suggest that she would virtuously have preferred to avoid the public gaze altogether. Pliny the Younger, a contemporary or near-contemporary of our author, praises his wife for sitting demurely behind a curtain when he gives a public reading of his work, so that she may hear without being seen (*Ep.* 4.19; cf. Plutarch, *Mor.* 139C; 1 Cor 14:34–35; 1 Tim 2:11–12). In general, however, the exclusion of model women from the public gaze may have represented a male desideratum more than actual practice.

54. Stowers suggests that the author of 4 Maccabees writes from the perspective of the male ruling elite of his ethnic subculture (1994, 60). If so, he would likely have seen himself

and that he is hurrying to tone it down in 18:6–19; or, alternatively, that a later editor has undertaken to soften the portrait for him.[55] Whoever the author of the speech may be, its effect is the same. The "manly" woman is effectively, if clumsily, "feminized"; a share of the credit for the manliness of the sons is transferred from her to their father, and she is depicted as always having been properly subservient to him. Although she has shown that she can take it like a man, she remains a "proper" woman in the end.

The Cost of Victory

Mastery is synonymous with masculinity in most of the Greek and Latin texts that survive from antiquity. Such mastery could be directed outwards as domination of others or inwards as domination of oneself. Mastery of others was frequently justified on the basis of the master's putatively superior masculine reason and self-control. In 4 Maccabees, absolute control of the physical circumstances of others, epitomized by the Gentile despot Antiochus, is radically devalued in favor of absolute self-control, epitomized by the Jewish martyrs. The book presents a female, an aged male, and a group of physically immature males—all representatives of a conquered people—as ironic exemplars of masculinity at the expense of an ostensibly powerful, ultra-elite male in the prime of life. The martyrs themselves become icons of power in the process—of masculine power redefined as an affair of the will, which need have no recourse to physical force, a definition clearly consonant with the political circumstances of the subcultural, colonized group to which the book is addressed. The "weak" defeat the "strong" and moral mastery of oneself displaces political mastery of others as a defining male trait. Fourth Maccabees thereby constructs a Hellenistic Jewish version of Greco-Roman masculinity thoroughly tailored to the experience of imperial oppression. But this customized construction does not come without a repressive cost of its own.

Victory is achieved in 4 Maccabees only by accepting and reaffirming the dominant hierarchical continuum along which ruler and ruled, master and slave, male and female were positioned in ancient Mediterranean culture. The physically feeble old man, the boys, and especially the woman gain all the

---

as primarily addressing male peers who shared his social location (cf. Klauck 1989, 665).

55. Here it may be instructive to note the objections that Musonius Rufus anticipates to his argument that women should be allowed to study philosophy: "Yes, but I assure you, some will say, that women who associate with philosophers are bound to be arrogant [*authadeis*] for the most part and presumptuous [*thraseias*], in that abandoning their own households and turning to the company of men they practice speeches, talk like sophists, and analyze syllogisms, when they ought be to sitting at home spinning [*deon oikoi kathēmenas talasiourgein*]" (translation from Lutz 1947).

more stature from the fact that their masculine reason and courage are exhibited by those who might be expected to be among the mastered. Antiochus is feminized, his apparent superiority called severely into question because of his inferior level of self-control. But although Eleazar, the boys and their mother emerge as the true men in the end, the connection between masculinity and domination is not overturned, subverted, or even seriously challenged in this book.

Fourth Maccabees does modify the elite, hegemonic concept of masculinity by elevating self-mastery over mastery of social inferiors. Yet the martyrs master Antiochus in effect, so that mastery of others is still a central value and still celebrated. The irony of 4 Maccabees is that a feeble, flabby old man, a gaggle of boys, and an elderly widow—all persons who should rate low on the hierarchical continuum of (masterful) masculinity and (mastered) femininity—triumph over someone who should be at the privileged end of the continuum. The continuum must continue to exist and to function, however, or the irony cannot function. And the continuum still has masculinity at its superior, elevated end and femininity at its inferior, denigrated end. That the continuum is employed rather than destroyed in this text is especially apparent in the treatment of the martyr-mother. The tacked-on speech of 18:6–19 returns the woman to her proper place on the continuum in relation to her absent husband. She may be hypermasculine in relation to a Gentile tyrant, but not unfeminine in relation to her Jewish husband. She may have mastered the tyrant (both the external tyrant that is the Gentile despot and the internal tyrant that is her "womanly" emotions), but her own master is her husband. Consequently, she rates higher on the continuum than Antiochus, but lower than her husband. Masculinity in 4 Maccabees is both a process and a product; it is a moral state achieved and maintained through a sheer act of will (subjugation of the passions), and as such is independent of anatomy. Yet women are also predestined (by anatomy?) in 4 Maccabees to be subservient to men. The victory over oppression that 4 Maccabees celebrates is therefore double-edged. On the one hand, the oppressed have triumphed; on the other, they have been implicated in a contest of manhood that is itself inherently oppressive.[56]

---

56. The authors would like to thank Loveday Alexander for a valuable critique of an earlier draft of this essay.

9
GIGANTIC GOD: YAHWEH'S BODY*

As is clear from its opening lines, this essay (which quickly ballooned into the latter part of my book *God's Gym: Divine Male Bodies of the Bible* [1996]) also emerges explicitly out of my biography. It is less an exercise in autobiographical criticism, however, than an experiment in three of the other critical developments that erupted into prominence in literary studies in the 1990s: cultural studies, masculinity studies, and queer theory. The critical study of masculinity is most interesting for me when it is the study of masculinity's contradictions, instabilities, and aporias (failed man that I am, no doubt; read no further than the headnote to "The Divine Butcher"). As such it is a version of masculinity studies that is already in bed with queer theory (the latter notable for its tireless demonstrations of the fluidity, malleability and mutability of sexual identities and hence of gender identities), and remains a major focus of my work to this day. Cultural studies—quintessentially, the academic analysis of contemporary popular culture—is an area that I have moved in and out of over the years, but this essay was my first sustained excursion in this mode (as well as my first publication in Hebrew Bible).

To slap a final label on this essay, I would also see it as an exercise in intertextuality, and of the kind that has always intrigued me the most: that is, where the texts to be brought into contact with each other are ostensibly unrelated, not least because they are temporally and culturally remote from each other (or to put it more bluntly, where there is least danger of intertextuality becoming merely another name—a somewhat sexier name—for, say, the study of Synoptic interrelationships or New Testament citations of Jewish scripture). My contention in this essay is

---

* First published in the *Journal for the Study of the Old Testament* 70 (1996): 87–115.

that certain texts of the Hebrew Bible that discourse (however obliquely) on the body of Yahweh, together with certain Jewish midrashic and mystical texts dependent on them, are illuminated by the phenomenon and literature of contemporary bodybuilding and vice versa. In short, various intertexts, both ancient and (post)modern, are here used to fashion a critical midrash on the (unstable) hypermasculinity of the biblical God. As in the second and third essays of this collection, it is a case of responding to graphic, concrete, and corporeal texts graphically, concretely, and corporeally, and of responding to midrashic texts midrashically—or, which is to say the same thing, of writing postcritically in a para-precritical mode. In short, while the topic of masculinity unites this essay with the previous one, the approach taken to the topic could not be more different.

Have you an arm like God…? (Job 40:9)

I quit bodybuilding at age thirty-two because it was cutting too deeply into my research time. I set about building up my bibliography instead. The flesh began to peel away from my bones. I cut it into squares, stacked it in piles, and traded it for an assistant professorship.[1]

To the untrained eye, the hypermuscular male physique looks like a mass, indeed a mess, of large lumps and bumps, and other prodigious protuberances. (I never achieved this advanced level of lumpiness myself, sad to say—yet another reason I was happy to hang up my lifting belt.) To the trained eye, in contrast, each knob, ridge, and protrusion is fully legible, enhancing a whole whose parts have been built up according to laws as unambiguous and inflexible as those that once governed the construction of sonnets.[2]

---

1. Since then, bodybuilding itself has drifted into academia. With the boom in cultural studies and gender studies and the irruption of queer theory, the iron-pumped physique has increasingly come under the critical gaze; see, e.g., Honer 1985; Warner 1992; Klein 1993; Lingis 1994, 29–44; Simpson 1994, 21–43; Tasker 1993, esp. 77–83, 118–23; cf. Paglia 1992; Fussell 1994; Dutton 1995.

2. For practical reasons, my remarks on the bodybuilding physique will be confined to the male of the species. At present, the criteria governing women's competitive bodybuilding are ambiguous in the extreme. For male competitors, the invariable formula for success is muscle mass, symmetry, and "definition" (more on this below). One cannot have too much mass provided it is symmetrical and defined. But for female competitors there is an intangible fourth ingredient—femininity—that sets strict limits on the amount of

9. GIGANTIC GOD: YAHWEH'S BODY

To begin with the neck, it should be a thick, fluted column of muscle ("'pencil neck' is a bodybuilding term for the weak and impure," as Alan Klein notes [1993, 264]). The neck should he framed by fully developed trapezius muscles (known more familiarly as "traps"), two ridges that rise high above the shoulders on either side. The shoulders themselves (deltoids or "delts") should be fully developed in all three heads of the muscle ("cannonball delts" is the cliché regularly invoked to describe the resulting effect). The pectorals ("pecs") should he especially massive, two striated slabs of muscle eternally separated from each other by a deep groove running all the way up to the collar bone. The latissimus dorsi ("lats"), the workhorse muscles of the back, should sweep upwards and outwards from a wasp-like waist, achieving an altogether unlikely width as they approach the deltoids, and branding the bodybuilder's torso with the classic V shape. Across its length and breadth, moreover, the back should be a study in fine detail, each muscle group, major or minor, writhing like copulating serpents beneath the skin. The biceps at rest should be larger than cantaloupes, and they should rise to a near-pinnacle when flexed. Each head of the triceps muscle should be fully developed, producing the coveted "horseshoe" shape when displayed. The forearms too should be formidable, narrowing to relatively small wrists. The abdominals ("abs") should be as free of subcutaneous fat as an oak frieze, and should be replete with exquisitely chiseled details. The upper legs should be particularly massive ("tree-trunk thighs" is the cliché of choice here), the quadriceps ("quads") billowing out from the hips like sails, and the hamstrings ("hams") bulging out from below the buttocks like balloons. The quadriceps should also display a high degree of muscle separation, the four heads of the muscle divided by deep rivulets, and the striations on each head showing clearly through the skin. The calves should be colossal, carefully cut diamonds. The overall impression, finally, should be one of absolute symmetry, no one muscle group overpowering any other, but all combining to overpower the spectator instead.

---

muscle that can be amassed. *Flex,* the premier hardcore "musclemag," now features centerfolds of female bodybuilders posing nude. The shots are prefaced in each issue by the following statement, which says it all: "Women bodybuilders are many things, among them symmetrical, strong, sensuous, and stunning. When photographed in competition shape, repping and grimacing or squeezing out shots, they appear shredded, vascular and hard, and they can be perceived as threatening. Offseason they carry more bodyfat, presenting themselves in a much more naturally attractive condition. To exhibit this real, natural side of women bodybuilders, *Flex* has been presenting pictorials of female competitors in softer condition. We hope this approach dispels the myth of female-bodybuilder masculinity and proves what role models they truly are." For incisive analysis of bodybuilding's double standard, see Bolin 1992, 87–95.

Muscle mass and symmetry alone, however, are not sufficient to win major bodybuilding titles. Muscle "definition" is the third indispensable ingredient. In contest condition, the champion bodybuilder is an ambulatory three-dimensional anatomy chart. Each muscle, however minor, is clearly visible through the skin, which, stripped of almost all subcutaneous fat through a dangerously stringent dieting regime, adheres to the muscles as closely as Saran Wrap.

Corporeal God

How does Yahweh's body measure up to these exacting standards? Does the God of Israel even *have* a body? Apparently he does. His is a slippery body, as we shall see, but also a sizeable one and, of course, a perfect one. Hence the bodybuilding gym is the most obvious contemporary context in which to situate and comprehend it.

First, the slipperiness. The *in*corporeality of Yahweh is (perhaps) implied by Deut 4:12, 15–18:[3] "Then Yahweh spoke to you out of the fire. You heard the sounds of words but saw no form [*ûtĕmûnāh 'ênĕkem rōîm*].… Since you saw no form when Yahweh spoke to you at Horeb out of the fire, take care…so that you do not act corruptly by making an idol for yourselves.…" This passage would seem to be alone in suggesting that Yahweh has no body—if indeed it does, for even here there is no outright denial that he has *tĕmûnāh* (cf. Deut 5:4). Elsewhere, anthropomorphisms abound: Yahweh strolls in the garden of Eden in the cool of the evening (Gen 3:8), helpfully shuts the door of the ark behind Noah (7:16), appreciatively inhales the fragrance of Noah's sacrifice (8:21), curiously descends from heaven to see what is going on at the tower of Babel (11:5), and so on. Even the most passionate assertion of Yahweh's unrepresentability in the Hebrew Bible—that of Second Isaiah (40:12–26)—is itself riddled with anthropomorphisms.

The most intriguing anthropomorphism in the Hebrew Bible, however—certainly the most debated—is Gen 1:26: "Let us make humankind in our image [*ṣelem*], according to our likeness [*dĕmût*]." What precisely does this mean? Among the many solutions that have been proposed to the riddle, two in particular stand out. First, the image makes the human being God's representative or vice-regent, exercising dominion on his behalf over the rest of creation (cf. Gen 1:28; Ps 8:3–8). This interpretation, which goes back at least to Chrysostom on the Christian side, is extremely popular with modern commentators, who appeal to parallel Egyptian and Mesopotamian texts that

---

3. This, at any rate, is how it has generally been interpreted; see, e.g., Weinfeld 1972, 198; 1991, 204; Christensen 1991, 87.

depict the king as being in the image of a god (e.g., von Rad 1972, 59–60; Davidson 1973, 25; Jacob 1974, 10; Vawter 1977, 57–59; Wenham 1987, 30–32; Sarna 1989, 12–13).[4] Alternatively, the image consists of a physical resemblance between creature and creator.

Of course, these two interpretations are not mutually exclusive. The first specifies the function, consequences or benefits of the divine image, but it leaves us guessing as to what the image is in itself, as Gordon J. Wenham points out (1987, 32). Might it not consist of a physical resemblance between God and humankind? In support of this disarmingly straightforward reading is the fact that, outside of the passages that concern us (Gen 1:26 and its "echoes": 1:27; 5:3; 9:6), "(physical) image" is far and away the most common meaning of ṣelem in the Hebrew Bible.[5] Furthermore, in Gen 5:3 Adam is said to have fathered "a son in his likeness [dĕmût], according to his image [ṣelem]," presumably a reference to physical resemblance. Like many a commentator before him, however, Wenham squirms at the idea that the ṣelem of Gen 1:26 is solely, or even partly, a reference to physical resemblance. "The OT's stress on the incorporeality and invisibility of God makes this view somewhat problematic (cf. Deut. 4:15–16)," he demurs (1987, 30). But Deut 4:15–16 is the exception that proves the rule, as we saw earlier; elsewhere in the Hebrew Bible anthropomorphism predominates.[6] "The difficulty is increased," continues Wenham, "if, as is usually the case, the material is assigned to the late P source, for this would he too gross an anthropomorphism for exilic literature" (1987, 30). But is it any more gross than Ezekiel's description of Yahweh as having "something that appeared like a human form [dĕmût kĕmarēh 'ādām]" (1:26; cf. 8:2)—Ezekiel who was himself a priest in exile? (cf. von Rad 1972, 58, 172). Even if Gen 1:26 does not mean only that God's body resembles a human body, therefore, a compelling case can nonetheless be made for regarding this as part of its "intended" meaning.[7]

---

4. The chief dissenter is Westermann (1984, 153–54).

5. Ṣelem means "(physical) image" in Num 33:52; 1 Sam 6:5, 11; 2 Kgs 11:18 (= 2 Chr 23:17); Ezek 7:20; 16:17; 23:14; and Amos 5:26. (Dĕmût also refers to physical likeness in 2 Kgs 16:10 and 2 Chr 4:3.) Ṣelem is used figuratively in the two remaining examples of its occurrence, Pss 39:7 and 73:20, where it means something like "(mere) semblance."

6. Even in Deuteronomy itself (1:30–31, 34, 37, etc.), although to a lesser extent than in other materials, as Weinfeld has shown (1972, 191–209). But that hardly supports a non-anthropomorphic reading of Gen 1:26–27.

7. Essentially, this is also how the rabbis saw it; see, e.g., Genesis Rabbah 8:10; Leviticus Rabbah 34:3; Mekhilta de Rabbi Ishmael: Baḥodesh 8; b. 'Aboda Zara 43b; Tosefta Yebamot 8:4; Midrash Tana'im (Hoffman ed.) 132. See further Gottstein 1994; also Urbach 1975, 1:226–27; Boyarin 1990; Stern 1991, 97–101.

Who is permitted glimpses of the divine physique? Those selected for the privilege include the following (although we are rarely told just what it is that they see): Abraham (Gen 18:1ff.; cf. 12:7; Exod 6:3), Jacob (Gen 32:24–30; cf. 35:1; 48:3; Exod 6:3), Moses (Exod 33:17–23; cf. 3:6; 4:24; 33:11; Num 12:6–8; Deut 34:10) and seventy-three of his fellow wanderers (Exod 24:9–11), David (2 Chr 3:1; cf. 2 Sam 24:17 [= 1 Chr 21:16]), Solomon (1 Kgs 3:5 [= 2 Chr 1:7]; 9:2 [= 2 Chr 7:12]; 11:9), Micaiah (1 Kgs 22:19), Job (42:5; cf. 19:26), Isaiah (6:1, 5), Ezekiel (1:26–28; 8:2–4; 43:2–5), Amos (7:7; 9:1; cf. 7:1, 4) and Daniel (7:9).[8]

Most are impressed by what they see, none more than Ezekiel, whose attempt to drape the divine form in words carries him to the brink of aphasia:

> seated above the likeness of a throne was something that appeared like a human form. Upward from what appeared like the loins I saw something like gleaming amber, something that looked like fire enclosed all around; and downward from what looked like the loins I saw something that looked like fire, and there was a splendor all around. Like the bow in a cloud on a rainy day, such was the appearance of the splendor all around. This was the appearance of the likeness of the glory of Yahweh [*marēh děmût kěbôd-YHWH*]. (1:26–28; cf. 8:2)

Howard Eilberg-Schwartz remarks on this passage: "But even this description does not indicate whether God has a full body. It is not clear, for example, whether God's 'nether' regions are human in form" (1990, 193). But Eilberg-Schwartz is being over-cautious here. Cognate visions in the Hebrew Bible do not hesitate to ascribe feet, at least, to Yahweh: "And they saw the God of Israel. And under his feet [*ûtaḥat raglāyw*] there was something like a pavement of sapphire stone" (Exod 24:10).[9] Eilberg-Schwartz is correct, nevertheless, in claiming that God's body is "incompletely represented" in the Hebrew Bible (1990, 193).[10] Extreme circumspection in the representation of the divine body is the norm, even when the medium is verbal rather than visual. References to certain synecdochically charged body parts do abound—Yahweh's face, eyes, mouth, ears, arm, hand and feet are frequently mentioned—but

---

8. See also Gen 16:13; Exod 16:10; Lev 9:23; Num 14:10, 14; 16:19; 20:6; 24:4; Judg 6:12, 22; 13:3, 22; Pss 11:7; 17:15; 27:4; 84:7; Zech 3.

9. Some scholars suggest that Exod 24:10 actually underlies Ezek 1:26 (e.g., Greenberg 1983, 50). Yahweh's feet also appear in 2 Sam 22:10; 1 Chr 28:2; Pss 18:9; 99:5; 132:7; Isa 60:13; 63:3, 6; 66:1; Ezek 43:7; Nah 1:3; Hab 3:12; Zech 14:4. See further Wolfson 1992.

10. He has since suggested that this reticence arose in part from a desire "to veil the divine sex" (1992a, 31–32), an intriguing notion subsequently elaborated at length in his *God's Phallus* (1994, esp. 59–133).

anything approaching a head-to-toe description of the divine physique would be all but unimaginable in the context of the Hebrew Bible.

Colossal God

It is not left entirely to us, however, impertinently to imagine the unimaginable, to complete the biblical authors' (necessarily) incomplete thoughts on the body of Yahweh, to press the logic of their divine body-talk through to its (possibly unnatural) conclusion. For the unthinkable was long ago thought in the *Shiʿur Qomah*, a Jewish mystical writing extant in five separate recensions, abandoned offspring of a single parent text, according to the late Gershom Scholem, still the towering authority on ancient Jewish mysticism, and Martin S. Cohen, currently the *Shiʿur Qomah*'s most dedicated investigator.[11]

Shiʿur Qomah means "Measure of the Body," the body in question being that of Yahweh. The anonymous authors of the *Shiʿur Qomah* bring to the contemplation of Yahweh's corporeality a sensibility that would not be out of place in the pages of *Flex, Muscle & Fitness* or other contemporary bodybuilding magazines. In these magazines the gods of the sport are regularly reduced to their anatomical measurements—"In his prime, Arnold's arms measured 22 inches, his chest 57 inches, his waist 31 inches, his thighs 28 inches, his calves 20 inches," and so on. The hero of the *Shiʿur Qomah* is also big—bigger even than Arnold, as it turns out:

> What is the measure of the body of the Holy One, blessed be He, who lives and exists for all eternity, may His name be blessed and His name exalted…? From His right shoulder to His left shoulder is 160,000,000 parasangs.[12] The name of the right shoulder is Tatmehininiah and the name of the left is Shalmehininiʾel.[13] From His right arm to His left arm is 120,000,000 para-

---

11. Scholem, however, dated the parent text to the late second century CE (1965, 36–42), while Cohen dates it to the seventh century (1983, 21–27, 51–76), and Peter Schäfer, another authority on ancient Jewish mysticism, casts doubt on its existence altogether, suggesting that the *Shiʿur Qomah* was never a single text to begin with (1988b, 75–83).

12. Ordinarily a parasang is a Persian mile, equivalent to about 1,320 yards. As the *Shiʿur Qomah* goes on to explain, however, a divine parasang "is four mils, and each mil is ten thousand cubits, and each cubit is three *zĕrātôt*. And His *zeret* fills the entire universe, as it is stated: 'Who measured the waters with the hollow of His hand, and the skies with His *zeret*?'" (lines 105–107). A mil is 5,000 feet, a cubit (in rabbinic literature) either five or six handspans, and a *zeret* either one handspan or the length of the little finger (Cohen 1983, 215–16 nn. 4–6).

13. The name of the right shoulder seems to be derived from *tāmāh*, "to wonder at, to be amazed," and probably means "God is my wonder." The name of the left shoulder is obscure (Cohen 1983, 212 nn. 56–57).

sangs.[14] His arms are folded. The name of His right arm is Gevar Hodiah and the name of the left is Va'ans. (*Shi'ur Qomah* lines 51–52, 91–95)[15]

This statuesque pose, arms folded to accentuate the thickness of the forearms, shoulders spread, chest flexed is also found in the mystical *Hekhalot* literature to which the *Shi'ur Qomah* is closely related (see *Hekhalot Rabbati* 11:2; 12:1). This is the pose that the deity favors when the celestial hosts are assembled before him to sing their songs of adulation (cf. Cohen 1983, 212 n. 58). "You are big [*gādôl*] and Your name is big," they cry. "You are strong and Your name is strong.… You are awesome and Your name is awesome…" (*Shi'ur Qomah* lines 5, 8, 10).

How did the *Shi'ur Qomah* come about?[16] Cohen is convinced that it was the product of a "school" of practical mysticism "developed around the set of Biblical descriptions of the godhead rooted in the notion of divine *gĕdûllāh*. The adjective *gādôl*, usually translated as 'great' or 'magnificent' was taken at its most literal, and understood to mean simply 'big'" (1983, 9; cf. 104–105; Idel 1988, 157–58). And so when the psalmist exclaims "Our Lord is *gādôl*" (147:5), for instance, he is simply taken at his word;[17] while v. 19 of the same Psalm, understood to he saying, "He reveals his dimensions to Jacob," is treated as evidence "that the God of Israel intended all along for His physical dimensions to be known to the elect of Israel" (Cohen 1983, 11). In addition, the detailed description of the body of the bridegroom in the Song of Songs (5:10–15), the bridegroom being identified as Yahweh, may also have provided the authors of the *Shi'ur Qomah* with a scriptural model and pretext for their speculations (Scholem 1965, 37, 39; 1971, 63–64; 1987, 20). The result,

---

14. An oddly meager measurement, given the width of the divine shoulders. Elsewhere in the text, the distance from the right arm to the left arm is given as 770,000,000 parasangs, which seems in better proportion (lines 17–18). The discrepancy is not a trivial one, since, for the *Shi'ur Qomah*, knowledge of God's precise measurements is the path to salvation (lines 120–23).

15. The name of the right arm means "man of thanksgiving," the name of the left is obscure (Cohen 1983, 212 nn. 59–60). The translation quoted here is Cohen's, who is using the *Sefer Haqqomah* recension of the text (Oxford ms. 1791). The five extant recensions are distributed over approximately thirty-four manuscripts, eight of the most important of which are reproduced in Cohen 1985, 183–212.

16. Leaving open the question of whether an *Urtext* of the *Shi'ur Qomah* ever existed. If not, the phrase *Shi'ur Qomah* would simply refer to a category of Jewish esoteric knowledge represented by a cluster of closely related texts (cf. Janowitz 1992, 186).

17. Divine *gĕdûllāh* is also celebrated in Deut 7:21; 10:17; 2 Chr 2:4; Neh 1:5; 8:6; 9:32; Pss 77:14; 86:10; 95:3; 99:2; 135:5; 147:5; Isa 12:6; Jer 10:6; 32:18; Dan 9:4.

in any case, is a text that, as Scholem aptly puts it, "reads like a deliberate and excessive indulgence in anthropomorphism" (1965, 36).[18]

Let us ponder some further excesses. The first man was made in the image and likeness of God, according to Genesis 1:26–27.[19] Independently of the *Shiʻur Qomah* but with impeccable logic (cf. 1 Kgs 8:27 [= 2 Chr 6:18]; 2 Chr 2:5–6; Isa 66:1), Adam too turns out to be gigantic in other ancient Jewish sources.[20] We learn that Adam's physical dimensions were truly Brobdingnagian, reaching from heaven to earth and from East to West—and not because he was prodigiously obese. For in addition to his impressive size, Adam also possessed the most perfectly formed physique the world has ever seen (cf. Ezek 28:12, 17).[21] (In these sources, as in modern muscle magazines, the male form is the yardstick of physical perfection. Eve was the most beautiful woman who ever lived, we are told, but "compared with Adam, Eve was like a monkey").[22] What we have in this oversized Adam is, as Louis Ginzberg long ago observed, a "special application of the idea that all primordial creations came out fully developed" (1909–59, 5:78 n. 21). Adam at his creation was twenty years old[23]—an extraordinarily precocious age at which to achieve full muscular development. Alas, Adam's brawn was not matched by his brain. According to numerous other sources, Adam was a brainless hunk at first, devoid of intellect, which the Creator only later installed.[24] In the beginning was the body.

---

18. Scholem adds: "Small wonder that it has deeply shocked later and more sober Jewish thought.... Jewish apologetics has always tried to explain it away" (1965, 36). Why not simply ignore it? Because "it was hailed by the Kabbalists of the Middle Ages as the profound symbolic expression of the mysteries of what could be called the Kabbalistic *plērōma*" (1965, 36; cf. 1971, 63).

19. As was the first woman, of course (*'ādām* is used generically here), but that's another story.

20. See, e.g., Genesis Rabbah 8:1; 21:3; 24:2; Leviticus Rabbah 14:1; 18:2; b. Ḥagigah 12a; b. Sanhedrin 38b; Pirqe Rabbi Eliezer 11. Here and in what follows, I am indebted to Ginzberg 1909–59 for directing me to many of the sources (see esp. vol. 5). Urbach 1975 (esp. 2:787ff.) also proved invaluable in this regard.

21. See b. Baba Batra 58a; cf. Genesis Rabbah 12:6; Leviticus Rabbah 20:2; Pesiqta de Rab Kahana 4, 12, 36b, 101a; Pesiqta Rabbati 14, 62a.

22. B. Baba Batra 58a; contrast Apocalypse of Sedrach 7:6–7, which seems to suggest that Eve was more beautiful than Adam. On the androcentrism of rabbinic Judaism, see Boyarin 1993, esp. 94–106 passim; and further on the fortunes of Eve in rabbinic tradition, see 1993, 77–106, along with Bronner 1994, 22–41, and Weissler 1992.

23. See, e.g., Genesis Rabbah 14:7; Numbers Rabbah 12:8.

24. See, e.g., Pesiqta Rabbati 23 (cf. 46, 115a, 187b); Yalqut Shimʻoni 34. In part, this tradition seems to have been an attempt to harmonize the two creation accounts: if Adam has already been created in Gen 1:27, then what is God about in 2:7?

Adam's splendid physique, then, mirrored Yahweh's own—so much so, indeed, that the angels initially mistook him for the deity: "When the Holy One, blessed be he, came to create the first man, the ministering angels mistook him [for God, since he was in God's image]."[25] But a puzzling question now arises. If Yahweh possesses a body, and a perfect body at that—"What blemish in any manner is heard of him? What defect is heard of him?"[26]—why is the vision of God in the Hebrew Bible so often confined to his face?

The answer biblical scholars generally give runs along the following lines. Semantically, *pānîm* far exceeds the standard usages of the English noun "face." *Pānîm* can be a synecdoche for the entire person, for example, as when Yahweh declares to Moses, "My face will go with you [*pānay yēlēkû*] and I will give you rest," to which Moses replies, "If your face will not go [*im-'ên pānêkā hōlĕkîm*], do not carry us up from here" (Exod 33:14–15; cf. 2 Sam 17:11; Isa 63:9; Lam 4:16; Pss 21:10; 139:7). More generally, *pānîm* is the most common term for "presence" in the Hebrew Bible. In particular, to "see the face" of a king is to be granted an audience with him or to be allowed to enter his presence (e.g., 2 Sam 3:13; 14:28, 32; 1 Kgs 12:6; 2 Kgs 25:19; Esth 1:10). To see the face of Yahweh, therefore, is to be granted the awesome privilege of a personal audience with him (which is only for the very few, as we have seen). More common is the circumlocutionary *niph'al* phrase, "to be seen (i.e., to appear) before the face of Yahweh [*nir'āh lipnê-YHWH*], which generally denotes a visit to his sanctuary (e.g. Exod 23:17; 34:23; Deut 16:16; 31:11; 1 Sam 1:22; Ps 42:2; Isa 1:12).[27]

To content ourselves with such a sensible explanation, however, would be to fall sadly short of the sublime exegetical standards set by the ancient Jewish sages. Surely there are other reasons for Yahweh's agonizing shyness in the Hebrew Bible? Why does he not want anyone to see his body?

The rabbis once again supply the clue, although they fail to follow it through. In our earlier appraisal of Adam's admirable physique, we omitted to note one small abnormality: initially he had two faces, a condition that persisted until the creation of Eve.[28] Indeed, Eve's creation was possible only because of Adam's two faces, say our sources, for one of the faces was female. In each of these sources another tradition is also cited—essentially, however, it is the same tradition—according to which Adam was created initially as an

---

25. Genesis Rabbah 8:10; cf. Ecclesiastes Rabbah 6:10; Life of Adam and Eve 13–15. The translation of Genesis Rabbah used here and in what follows is Jacob Neusner's (1985).

26. Genesis Rabbah 12:1. Abot de Rabbi Nathan 2A even suggests that Yahweh is circumcised.

27. For exhaustive treatments of Yahweh's face, see Nötscher 1969, esp. 3–9, 85–98, 147–70; Reindl 1970, esp. 7–52.

28. See, e.g., Genesis Rabbah 8:1; 17:6; Leviticus Rabbah 14:1; b. Berakot 61a; b. ʿErubin 18a; Tanḥuma Tazriaʿ 2.

9. GIGANTIC GOD: YAHWEH'S BODY

androgyne: "When the Holy One, blessed be he, came to create the first man, he made him androgynous, as it is said, 'Male and female created he them.'"[29] Subsequently, this androgyne was anesthetized by Yahweh (cf. Gen 2:21), who had decided to separate it into its male and female components. The surgery, although crude, was a success: "When the Holy One, blessed be he, came to create the first man, he created him with two faces, then sawed him in two and made a back on one side and a back on the other."[30]

"Let us make humankind in our image," declares God in Genesis 1:26. This "image" (*ṣelem*) includes the idea of bodily image, as we have seen. The resulting creation is a two-faced androgyne. The implications are interesting, to say the least; it follows that the God of Israel is also androgynous—*physically* androgynous, I hasten to add. The more familiar form of the argument runs something like this: Gen 1:26–27 is a "plain declaration of the existence of the feminine element in the Godhead, equal in power and glory with the masculine." So wrote Elizabeth Cady Stanton in *The Woman's Bible* (1895–98, 1:14). A century later, we find Susan Niditch in *The Women's Bible Commentary* echoing Stanton's comment: "Without establishing relative rank or worth of the genders, the spinner of this creation tale indicates that humankind is found in two varieties, the male and the female, and this humanity in its complementarity is a reflection of the deity" (1992, 12–13). This now popular interpretation has, I realize, an essential role to play in countering the exclusion of the feminine from Jewish and Christian conceptions of the divine and the subjugation of women that such exclusion has reinforced. But what this interpretation brackets, it seems to me, is the awkward yet intriguing fact that the biblical God is an embodied being, and the question of whether or not this body is a gendered one. The remainder of this essay will be staged inside these brackets (a space that is a posing dais as well as a stage, as we shall see).

---

29. Genesis Rabbah 8:1 (the Greek term *androgynos* is used in the original). It is not only in rabbinic texts that the androgynous Adam is found; see, e.g., Jubilees 2:14 (although some would say that Adam is not fully androgynous here); Apocalypse of Adam 1:4–5.

30. Genesis Rabbah 8:1. According to Boyarin, the two-face tradition is best understood as "a specification and interpretation" of the androgyne tradition. The first human, which had genitals of both sexes, "was like a pair of Siamese twins who were then separated by a surgical procedure" (1993, 43). The myth of a primal androgyne was widespread in the ancient world (1993, 36–44 passim; Ginzberg 1909–59, 5:88–89; Urbach 1975, 1:228–30). Independently of the rabbinic and other ancient sources (which she does not cite), Phyllis Trible has arrived at a similar position, arguing that *'ādām* is "sexually undifferentiated"; prior to the creation of the female it cannot be regarded as male (1978b, 80). Trible's *'ādām* is not androgynous, however, for androgyny "assumes sexuality" (1978b, 141 n. 17). Mieke Bal has developed Trible's argument further (Bal 1987, esp. 112–14). For a sympathetic critique of both versions of the argument, see Pardes 1992, 20–33.

Androgynous God

The God of Israel is an androgyne, a hermaphrodite, a she-male, as we have seen. But is s/he also two-faced, like the original Adam? The crucial prooftext here is Exod 33:18–20. "Show me your glory [*kābôd*] I pray," pleads Moses, to which Yahweh replies, "I will make all my goodness [*kol tôbî*] pass before you, and will proclaim before you the name, 'Yahweh.' ... But you cannot see my face [*l'ō tûkal lir'ōt et-pānāy*]; for no one shall see me and live" (cf. 19:21; Gen 16:13; Lev 16:2: Judg 13:22; Isa 6:5). He continues, however, in a more conciliatory tone: "See, there is a place by me where you shall stand on the rock; and while my glory passes by I will put you in a cleft of the rock, and I will cover you with my hand until I have passed by; then I will take away my hand, and you shall see my back [*wĕrā'îtā et-'aḥōrāy*]; but my face shall not be seen" (Gen 33:21–23).[31]

Now, Yahweh would have had a splendid back, fanning out from a near nonexistent waist to a truly awe-inspiring width, every square inch of it tattooed with exquisitely chiseled details. Brevard Childs remarks, "Even to be allowed a glimpse of [Yahweh's] passing from the rear is so awesome to the man Moses that God himself—note the strange paradox—must shield him with his own hand" (1974, 596). Should we conclude, therefore, that Yahweh is simply showing Moses one of his better body-parts? ("Fully, massively, powerfully and deeply developed from the base of the skull to the top of the pelvis and from armpit to armpit, the back is one of a bodybuilder's greatest assets," declares Joe Weider [1983, 129], bodybuilding's ultimate guru.) No, for then we too would be taken in by Yahweh's ruse. What is really significant in this scene is not what Yahweh is purporting to show but what he is attempting to hide. And it is not his face that he is attempting to cover up, for he does disclose it elsewhere, even to Moses himself (Exod 33:11; Deut 34:10; cf. Num 12:6–8). Yahweh does not have two faces, then. But s/he does have another condition that s/he wishes to conceal. Had Moses been afforded a full-frontal peek at the divine physique, he would have glimpsed a massively muscular chest (naturally), but one that was also unmistakably female.[32]

---

31. Although as R. W. L. Moberly observes, the term *'āhôr* "is not the usual term for 'back' in the physical or anatomical sense (*gaw, gēw*), but more vaguely means 'hinder part,' thus conveying the idea of a view from behind, while being less explicit about exactly what is seen" (1983, 82). This raises the delicate question of what Moses might have glimpsed in addition to Yahweh's back (cf. Eilberg-Schwartz 1994, 70).

32. Trible trembles on the threshold of this realization (1978a, 61). Biale boldly plunges through (1982). Neither of them is reflecting on Exod 33:18–33, however, but rather on a possible connection between the divine epithet *'ēl šadday* and the word for breasts, *šādayîm* (see esp. Gen 49:25). What does a massive muscular female chest look

9. GIGANTIC GOD: YAHWEH'S BODY

That we are still on the right track is confirmed by an intriguing tradition preserved in *Hekhalot Rabbati*, a compilation of Jewish esoteric lore from the late antique and early medieval periods. A vision of the divine glory forms the near-unattainable summit of the mysticism enshrined in this material. And one of the principal objects of this vision is the *ḥālûk*, a long shirt-like robe in which the deity is draped. This is no mere nightshirt, however. Incomparably radiant (cf. Ps 104:2; Dan 7:9b; 1 Enoch 14:29; 71:10), it is covered with repetitions of the Tetragrammaton (see esp. *Hekhalot Rabbati* 3:4). No doubt the *ḥālûk* displays the contours of the divine musculature to good effect. (In his bodybuilding memoir, *Muscle*, Sam Fussell recalls his own acquisition of a *ḥālûk*: "From the back of the bodybuilding magazines, I sent off for XXL T-shirts specially cut for bodybuilders.... Just eighteen months before, these shirts would have billowed over my bony frame. Now, they stretched over my mountains of muscle like a taut second skin" [1991, 68].) And yet, even in the moment of supreme bliss, the visionary is left in the oddly prurient position of having to imagine what God would look like without his clothes. We are now in a position to recognize, however, that the purpose of the *ḥālûk* is less to frustrate the visionary than to keep the divine breasts a secret.

Certain pieces of our puzzle are still missing, nonetheless. Let us see if we can track them down. Yahweh's physique is phenomenal, according to the *Shi'ur Qomah*. How did s/he get so big? The Hebrew Bible supplies several important clues.

First, there is Yahweh's diet, which is composed primarily of red meat; for the Hebrew Bible does speak repeatedly of sacrifices as Yahweh's food. Some scholars refuse to take this seriously. Walther Eichrodt, for instance, while conceding that there are indeed frequent references to sacrifices as Yahweh's food in the Hebrew scriptures, that "the meat is sometimes boiled before being offered," that salt is used to make it more "tasty," that "[t]he subsidiary offerings of food and wine ... recall the drink and side-dishes which go with the main meat course," and even that "the Israelite sacrifice *ultimately derives* from the conception of the feeding of the deity," nevertheless concludes that "it is extremely doubtful whether this conception was still a *living* reality in Israel" (1961, 1:142–43, his emphasis). Jacob Milgrom, too, while conceding that "the original aim of the sacred furniture of the Tabernacle-Temple—the table for the bread of presence, the candelabrum, and the incense altar—was

---

like? To find out, pick up any hardcore bodybuilding magazine. Former bodybuilder Sam Fussell fondly recalls his night of bliss with G-spot, a female iron-pumper: "There was barely room for our lips to meet above our swollen, pumped up chests. When, finally, I reached below her gold dumbbell pendant for her breast, I found it harder than my own" (1991, 158).

to provide food, light, and pleasant aroma for the divine residence," likewise concludes that "these words, objects, and mores are only fossilized vestiges from a dim past, which show no signs of life in the Bible" (1991, 440). Against this anorexic school of thought, Gary A. Anderson argues:

> [O]ne must account for the enormous amount of evidence that portrays Israelite sacrifice as food for YHWH.... The altar itself is called "the table of YHWH" [e.g., Ezek 41:22; 44:16; Mal 1:7, 12]. The sacrifices can be called "YHWH's food" [e.g., Lev 3:11, 16; 21:6, 8, 17, 21–22; 22:25; Num 28:2, 24; Ezek 16:19: 44:7; Mal 1:7, 12]. The aroma of the burnt offerings is said to be "a sweet savor to YHWH" [e.g., Gen 8:21; Exod 29:18, 25, 41; Lev 1:9; 6:21; 8:21; Num 15:3, 13, 14, 24; 18:17]. All of this is dismissed by some biblical scholars as ancient relics of Israel's pagan past. No account is made of the fact that these terms and phrases are *freely* introduced into *all genres* (cultic and epic narratives, psalms, and more) of Israel's literature in all periods.... While one can point to a few isolated poetic texts that speak of YHWH's freedom from human needs such as food [esp. Ps 50:13], one must dismiss dozens of other texts from a variety of genres as unrepresentative, or as relics from an archaic past. (1992, 872, his emphasis, my examples; see further 1987, esp. 14–19)

What are the implications of this colossal daily intake of animal protein? Clearly it suggests that Yahweh is a bodybuilder. In the off-season, competitive bodybuilders consume a minimum of 1.25 grams of protein daily for every pound of body weight. "To become a selfwilled grotesque is no mean feat," concedes Fussell, referring to the hugely drab and dreary diet of the heavyweight contender, who may inflate to 300 lbs. in the off-season (1994, 48). "With breakfast being the most important meal of the day, I don't hold back and will scarf down a dozen eggs," confesses champion bodybuilder Mike Matarazzo. "With my eggs, I'll have two cups of oatmeal and six or seven wholewheat pancakes" (1993, 21). The second of Mike's five square meals features a further dozen pancakes, along with three turkey patties; his third meal features more turkey patties together with a pound of macaroni; his fourth meal features a pound and three-quarters of flank steak; and his final meal features a second pound and three-quarters of steak, although for variety he will sometimes substitute two pounds of jumbo shrimp (not an option for Yahweh, of course—cf. Lev 11:10–12; Deut 14:10).[33]

---

33. Matarazzo 1993, 21–22. Compare Gaines and Butler's description of the young Arnold, out for a light lunch, cruising "across a patio of small people eating spinach salads" to his table, where he orders "a side dish of four scrambled eggs with his Stuffed Sirloin Spectacular" (1974, 52).

9. GIGANTIC GOD: YAHWEH'S BODY

Needless to say, however, Yahweh's daily consumption of red meat dwarfs even that of Mike Matarazzo: "Now this is what you shall offer on the altar: two lambs a year old regularly each day" (Exod 29:38; cf. Num 28:3; Ezek 46:13). (Thus it becomes possible to calculate Yahweh's minimal bodyweight. For example, if his or her protein intake is estimated conservatively at 100 lbs. per day, representing at least 1.25 grams of protein for each pound of bodyweight, then the latter must be at least 36,288 lbs.)[34] Far from being "fossilized vestiges from a dim past, which show no signs of life in the Bible," therefore, the repeated references to animal sacrifices as Yahweh's principal source of nutrition point to some of his or her most profound needs—physical but also psychological, as I explain below.

The second clue to the secret of Yahweh's stupendous size lies in his or her violent temper. For the biblical God is a God of wrath, as everyone knows. Yahweh's frequent outbursts of fury and accompanying acts of violence (e.g., Num 16:20–35, 44–49; Deut 29:19–28; Josh 7:25–26; 1 Sam 6:19; 2 Sam 6:6–7; 24:1,15; Isa 63:3–6), coupled with his or her gross physical bulk, suggest only one thing: anabolic steroids. The wrath of the biblical God is nothing other than "'roid rage." Alan Klein defines the latter as "aggressive behavioral outbursts" induced by excessive steroid use (1993, 151). The substances in question might include methyl-testosterone, thyroid, rhesus monkey hormones and human growth hormone drawn from the pituitary gland of cadavers (Fussell 1994, 49; cf. 1991,117–23). (Would Yahweh have flouted his own prohibition in order to partake of the latter? "Whoever touches anything made unclean by a corpse [$hannōgē'a\ běkol-těmē'-nepeš$] ... shall be unclean"—Lev 22:4–6; cf. Num 19:11ff.) Fussell writes of his own years on steroids: "I was fueled by my own anger, which I seemed to draw from an inexhaustible source.... I wasn't just aching for a fistfight, I was begging for it. I longed for the release. So I strutted through the city streets, a juggernaut in a do-rag, glaring at and menacing anyone who dared meet my eye" (1991, 130). Compare Yahweh's admission in Isaiah 63:5–6: "So my arm brought me victory, and my wrath [$waḥamātî$] sustained me. I trampled down peoples in my anger [$bĕ'appî$], I crushed them in my wrath [$baḥamātî$], and I poured out their lifeblood on the earth."

---

34. This does not take into account the additional quantities of meat that Yahweh regularly consumed beyond his or her basic ration (see esp. Lev 1–7; Num 28–29), nor the massive binges in which s/he sometimes indulged: 700 oxen and 7,000 sheep on one occasion (2 Chr 15:11), for example, and 22,000 oxen and 120,000 sheep on another (1 Kgs 8:63 [= 2 Chr 7:5]; cf. 1 Kgs 8:5). Cf. Matarazzo 1993, 24: "I adhere to this [disciplined] meal plan six days a week; the seventh is my cheat day. That's when all the rules are off."

216   THE BIBLE IN THEORY

The irascible Yahweh has not lacked apologists. Gary A. Herion's remarks are typical:

> At best, only a very few passages seem to suggest that, like other ANE deities, Yahweh could behave in an irrational manner unrelated to any moral will: Gen 32:23–33 [Eng. 32:22–32]; Exod 4:24–26; 19:21–25; Judg 13:21–23; and 2 Sam 6:6–11.... The objects of such anger tend to be those who, unfortunately, are simply in the wrong place at the wrong time. (1992, 993)[35]

But as Yahweh became more powerful, he also became more paranoid. Paul D. Hanson has argued convincingly that local rampages such as Isa 63:1–6 contain the seeds of a full-blown apocalyptic eschatology, one that "construes the enemy increasingly in terms of absolute evil. All the nations of the world would be portrayed as one monolithic force confronting the Divine Warrior Yahweh in the final cosmic battle" (1979, 207).

Of course, neither side will have to face the final posedown unaided. Fussell recalls his own final contest: "As soon as I opened the door [of the men's room] I saw him: a short, stocky competitor bending down, the syringe in his palm, his thumb working the plunger, the needle inserted deep into his calf muscle. It was Escline, the last minute inflammatory. 'Shit,' he groaned, feeling the rush as his calves swelled before my eyes" (1991, 229–30). But Fussell's own body was ballooning even as he beheld this chemical miracle. Earlier his accomplice, Nimrod, had handed him a vial of pills: "'They're niacin, friend. Pop four of them right now and watch your veins explode....' I threw five of the little white 250-milligram pills down my throat.... Within minutes the niacin kicked in and I was breathing fire" (1991, 228–29). "Oh yes! Oh yes! Judgment Day!" Fussell's other brother-in-iron, Vinnie, screams rapturously when Fussell finally takes the stage, now himself a Divine Warrior (1991, 231).[36]

Yahweh's use of steroids also explains his or her androgyny. Certain steroids can produce a condition known as gynecomastia ("bitch tits" in gym vernacular). To counteract the steroid-induced flood of testosterone, the male body boosts its manufacture of estrogen. "If the estrogen/testosterone ratio is changed in favor of estrogen, dormant mechanisms in the male are stimulated—among them, breast development" (Brainum 1994, 211). Ordinarily this breast development does not advance beyond a bulbous swelling under one or both nipples. In Yahweh's case, however, it would appear that the

---

35. Other scholars are yet more defensive of the rage-prone Yahweh; see esp. Heschel 1962, 279–98; cf. 299–306.

36. "You're the fucking King of Kings, man!" Vinnie had exclaimed earlier as Fussell awaited his turn (Fussell 1991, 228).

9. GIGANTIC GOD: YAHWEH'S BODY

immeasurable quantities of testosterone unleashed in the divine body produced a prodigious estrogen reaction, leading not just to tumor-like swellings below the nipples, but to bona fide mammary glands. The effect on Yahweh's genitals may have been just as drastic ("My testicles had shrunk to the size of cocktail peanuts," confesses former Mr. Universe Steve Michalik [in Klein 1993, 150]); on this the Hebrew Bible, and even the rabbis, are (ominously?) silent.

But an important question remains: Does Yahweh actually lift weights? On this the Bible is also silent,[37] but certain mystical and midrashic texts afford us valuable vignettes of the divine workout. Yahweh's arm routine in particular deserves mention ("Have you an arm like God...?" Yahweh asks Job, flexing his mountainous bicep under the awed mortal's nose—40:9; cf. Exod 6:6; 15:6; Deut 7:19; Ps 44:3). The *Shi'ur Qomah* reports: "He hangs *mĕ'ônāh* [the sixth heaven] on His arm." Midrash Konen states that the primeval Torah hangs from the divine arm, and in Seder Rabbah de Ber'eshit we learn that the entire world is suspended from the arm of God.[38] Throughout, the divine posterior never rises from the seat of the *merkābāh*; therefore the arm exercise in question would most likely have been seated dumbbell curls, the unimaginable weight being curled inexorably upwards in a semicircular arc toward the shoulder, first by one arm, then the other, while the hosts of heaven look on in awe. His training partner in several of these texts is the supernal archangel Metatron, himself of singular size. Metatron recalls: "[T]he Holy One, blessed be he, laid his hand on me and blessed me with 1,365,000 blessings. I was enlarged and increased in size till I matched the world in length and breadth" (3 Enoch 9:1–2, *OTP* trans.).[39]

Third Enoch testifies eloquently to the effectiveness of Yahweh's arm routine. The visionary in 3 Enoch (as so often in the *merkābāh* literature, not least the *Shi'ur Qomah*) is Rabbi Ishmael, and his celestial tour guide is Metatron. The seer is shown all the mysteries of the seventh heaven, but the most sublime secret of all, the supreme hidden reality, is "the right arm [*yāmîn*] of the Omniscient One.... From it all kinds of brilliant lights shine, and by it the 955

---

37. Although it frequently lauds his impressive strength (e.g., Exod 6:1; 13:3, 9, 14, 16; 15:6; 32:11; Josh 4:24; 1 Chr 29:12; Job 9:4; Pss 29:1; 62:11; 68:34; Jer 50:34).

38. See Cohen 1983, 253 n. 35 for exact references and further examples.

39. Metatron's story (3 Enoch 3–16) is the ultimate "before and after" testimonial. He began life as Enoch, who "walked with God; then he was no more, because God took him" (Gen 5:24; cf. 1 Enoch 70–71). Translated into heaven, Enoch acquired a new name—and a magnificent new body (cf. 2 Enoch 22:10). Other massively built angels also populate the pages of 3 Enoch (see 17–26 passim).

heavens were created" (48A:1).[40] Third Enoch climaxes with Rabbi Ishmael's vision of the Arm:

> I went with him, and, taking me by his hand, he bore me up on his wings and showed it to me, with all kinds of praise, jubilation, and psalm: No mouth can tell its praise, its honor, and its beauty. Moreover, all the souls of the righteous who are worthy to see the joy of Jerusalem stand beside it, praising and entreating it, saying three times every day, "Awake, awake! Clothe yourself in strength, arm of the Lord [Isa 51:9], as it is written, 'He made his glorious arm go at the right hand of Moses [Isa 63:12].'" (48A:2–3)

In general, therefore, whether from the biblical texts themselves or from midrashic unfurlings of their contents, it emerges that Yahweh is a God who, from all eternity, has been intent on amassing the defensive trappings of hegemonic hypermasculinity, preeminently an awe-inspiring physique. "Hypermasculinity is an exaggeration of male traits, be they psychological or physical," explains Klein. "Whether one looks at hypermasculinity through a psychological or sociological lens, there is embedded in it a view of radical opposition to all things feminine. Male self-identity is the issue here" (1993, 221).

Why would Yahweh have had any doubts about his masculinity (at any rate, in his preandrogynous state)? His diet again provides the clue. Although monstrous by human standards, Yahweh's daily intake of animal protein would have been positively anorexic relative to that of many of his divine cousins in the ancient Near Eastern pantheons. The Akkadian god Anu and his consort Antu, for example, along with certain other deities "dwelling in the city of Uruk," enjoyed a daily bill of fare (spread over four meals) of

> twenty-one first-class, fat, clean rams which have been fed barley for two years; two large bulls; one milk-fed bullock; eight lambs; thirty *marratu*-birds; thirty [...]-birds; three cranes which have been fed [...]-grain; five ducks which have been fed [...]-flour; two ducks of a lower quality than those just mentioned; four wild boars; three ostrich eggs; three duck eggs. (*ANET*, 344)

---

40. Philip S. Alexander, the *OTP* translator of 3 Enoch, renders *yāmîn* as "right hand" rather than "right arm." In adjusting his translation to favor the right arm, I am following Michael Fishbane (1994, 275–92 passim) who explicates 3 Enoch 48A by way of a parallel passage in Pesiqta de Rab Kahana 17:5, where *yāmîn* clearly means "right arm" rather than the more usual "right hand."

This was served with 243 loaves of bread, along with a corresponding quantity of beer, wine, milk, dates, figs and raisins, and rounded off with a daily supplement of ten additional "fat, clean rams" (343–44).[41] Yet A. Leo Oppenheim characterizes this particular diet as relatively "human" in scale as compared with "the gargantuan quantities of Egyptian sacrificial repasts" (1977, 188). (And it was not only the meals of the Egyptian gods that were gargantuan, according to Ezekiel 23:19–20. Feeling small and rejected, Yahweh bitterly accuses Jerusalem of "remembering the days of her youth, when she played the whore in the land of Egypt and lusted after her paramours there, whose members were like those of donkeys, and whose emission was like that of stallions [*'ašer běar hamôrîm běśārām wězirmat sûsîm zirmātām*]".) The implication is clear: these Egyptian and Mesopotamian deities would have dwarfed Yahweh physically, hence his determination to get bigger at any cost. Being a god, he was spectacularly successful in the attempt—too successful, in fact. So hypermasculine did he become that his body ceased to be merely male and began to sprout female parts. Far from being assuaged, his insecurities about his masculinity now had something new to feed on—a pair of female breasts.

Yahweh's mammiferous metamorphosis should not surprise us. "[E]very time men try to grasp something consolingly, sturdily, essentially masculine," notes Mark Simpson, "it all too easily transforms into its opposite. Bodybuilding gives an insight into the *flux* of masculinity right at the moment it is meant to solidify it in a display of exaggerated biological masculine attributes" (1994, 30, his emphasis). Towering on stage, engorged muscles ready to explode through his taut skin, the male bodybuilder seems a veritable caricature of the ultra-virile male. In all probability, however, as Sam Fussell discloses (and Ezek 23:19–20 notwithstanding), "he's pumped so full of steroids that he's literally impotent" (1994, 52). "But not only is he less of a man at his moment of majesty," continues Fussell, "he's actually more of a woman. Faced with a flood of surplus testosterone, the body reacts by temporarily shrinking the testicles (with a resultant sperm count drop) and releasing an estrogen counterbalance" (1994, 52), which can eventually engender a pair of pubescent breasts, as noted earlier. "Of course, the bodybuilder reacts with horror to this development, but that is just the horror of the caterpillar finding itself pupating," as Simpson sagely observes. "The bodybuilder does not understand that he was destined all along to be a transsexual butterfly (1994, 42). Suddenly everything about the bodybuilding lifestyle makes perfect sense: the meticulous

---

41. A colophon dates this unusually detailed text to "the reign of the kings Seleucus and Antiochus" (probably Seleucus I and his successor Antiochus I, whose combined reigns extended from 312 to 261 B.C.E.), but claims it is copied "from tablets which Nabuaplausur, king of the Sea Land, carried off as plunder from the City of Uruk" (*ANET*, 345).

removal of all body hair, whether by shaving, depilatory creams or electrolysis (not front-page material in the musclemags); the unrelenting obsession with diet and weight; the fact that musclemags, like old-style girly mags, come wrapped in plastic with fold-out centerfolds of near-naked physiques.[42] Pull the posing trunks off the entire enterprise and what is revealed? Simpson, who has looked, files the following report:

> The male bodybuilder dramatizes in his flesh the insecurity, the uncertainty, the enigma of masculinity. He is a living testament not so much to the capabilities of the male body, its phallic power, its massive irresistible virility ("I saw my chest swelling to such gargantuan proportions that no shirt on Earth could contain it"), but rather to…the fluidity of the categories male and female, masculine and feminine, hetero and homo, and the fabulous, perverse tricks they play. (1994, 42, quoting Fussell 1991, 49)[43]

Caught in this quandary, feeling the cool of the blade against his scrotum, Yahweh hit upon a brilliant strategy. He would create an androgynous being in his own image and likeness, and he would do to this being what he longed to do to himself—siphon off its female side and banish it altogether into another body, thereby eradicating it. (Note that the notion that it is not good for the androgyne to be alone comes not from the androgyne him/herself but from Yahweh—Gen 2:18.) Thus would Yahweh vicariously effect that which he had failed to accomplish through bodybuilding alone. To complete the therapy, he would later devise a sublimely perfect punishment for his objectified female self, making the woman's body a direct source of pain for her, and giving the man license to dominate her: "To the woman he said, 'I will greatly increase your pangs in childbearing [*harbāh arbeh 'issĕbônēk wĕhērōnēk*]; in pain [*bĕ'eseb*] you shall bring forth children; and your desire shall be for your husband, but he shall rule over you [*wĕhû' yimšāl-bāk*]'" (Gen 3:16).[44]

---

42. See further Simpson 1994, 42; Fussell 1994, 46–47; Dutton 1995, 293–307 passim; Lingis 1994, 37–38, 42; Walters 1978, 295. Simpson's chapter on male bodybuilding is tellingly titled "Big Tits!"

43. Certain gay bodybuilders, however, are deeply attuned to, and entirely comfortable with, this ambivalence. For example: "At the 1992 gay pride parade in New York City, there was a handsome, intensely muscular man in full leather regalia, sporting on his distended chest a T-shirt that read, KEEP YOUR LAWS OFF MY UTERUS" (Sedgwick 1993, xi). Further on queer muscularity, see Halperin 1995, 115–18; D. Miller 1992, 28–31.

44. Such, at any rate, is the traditional, Christian, infinitely influential way of translating this verse. For countertranslations/interpretations, see Meyers 1988, 95–121; Bledstein 1993.

The therapy, however, is only marginally successful. Afterwards Yahweh does note a slight increase in his ability to accept his own semi-female physique. In his stronger moments, he is even able to apply female metaphors to himself. In Isa 42:14 he styles himself "a woman in labor," for instance (cf. 45:10; 66:9),[45] and in Isa 66:13 a mother comforting her child (cf. 46:3–4; 49:15; Jer 31:20) (see further Bronner 1983–84; Gruber 1992). Similarly, in Pss 22:9 and 123:2 Yahweh is a midwife and a mistress respectively (although he himself is not the speaker in either instance).[46] Overwhelmingly, however, he still continues to refer to himself with male metaphors, including hegemonic male metaphors (designed to feed his fantasies of domination?), such as *king* (e.g., 1 Sam 8:78; Isa 33:17; Ezek 20:33), *military commander* (e.g., Isa 13:3; Josh 5:13–15; Joel 2:11), *warrior* (e.g., Exod 15:3; Isa 42:13; 63:1–6; Jer 20:11) and *judge* (e.g., Gen 15:14; Ps 75:2; Isa 3:13; Ezek 34:17, 20, 22). In addition, he ensures that masculine pronouns are consistently applied to him throughout the Hebrew scriptures. In the end, this unrelenting torrent of masculine pronouns powerfully reinforces "a male image of God, an image that obscures, even obliterates, female metaphors for deity," as even Phyllis Trible is obliged to concede (1978a, 23 n. 5). But that is exactly how Yahweh wants it.

Further Reading on Masculinity Studies

Adams, Rachel, and David Savran, eds. 2002. *The Masculinity Studies Reader*. Keyworks in Cultural Studies 5. Oxford: Blackwell. Twenty-two selections divided into five parts: "Eroticism"; "Social Sciences"; "Representations"; "Empire and Modernity"; and "Borders." Authors range from Freud and Fanon to Eve Sedgwick and Daniel Boyarin.

Clines, David J. A. 1995. David the Man: The Construction of Masculinity in the Hebrew Bible. Pages 212–43 in Clines, *Interested Parties: The Ideology of Writers and Readers of the Hebrew Bible*. JSOTSup 205; Gender, Culture, Theory 1. Sheffield: Sheffield Academic Press. This essay is programmatic for Clines's work on biblical masculinities in general.

———. 1998. Ecce Vir, or, Gendering the Son of Man. Pages 352–75 in *Biblical Studies/Cultural Studies: The Third Sheffield Colloquium*. Edited by J. Cheryl Exum and Stephen D. Moore. JSOTSup 266; Gender, Culture, Theory 7. Sheffield: Sheffield Academic Press.

---

45. Taken in context, however, this metaphor is less than tenderly maternal: see 42:13–15, which begins, "Yahweh goes forth like a soldier [*kaggibbôr*], like a warrior/man of war [*kĕ'îš milḥāmôt*] he stirs up his fury.…"

46. Through admirable sleight of hand, Trible manages to wrest various other female metaphors for God from the text of the Hebrew Bible (1978a, esp. 31–71; also 1976).

———. 2002. He-Prophets: Masculinity as a Problem for the Hebrew Prophets and their Interpreters. Pages 311–29 in *Sense and Sensitivity: Essays on Reading the Bible in Memory of Robert Carroll*. Edited by Alastair G. Hunter and Philip R. Davies. JSOTSup 348. Sheffield: Sheffield Academic Press.

———. 2003. Paul, the Invisible Man. Pages 181–92 in Moore and Anderson 2003.

Conway, Colleen M. 2008. *Behold the Man: Jesus and Greco-Roman Masculinity*. Oxford: Oxford University Press. Analyzes the construction of masculinity in the Pauline letters, Mark, Matthew, Luke-Acts, John, and Revelation, with special attention throughout to the potentially emasculating scandal of the cross.

Eilberg-Schwartz, Howard. 1994. *God's Phallus and Other Problems for Men and Masculinity*. Boston: Beacon. Argues that various Hebrew Bible texts and the Gospel infancy narratives are attempts to come to terms with the problem that the maleness of Yahweh posed for ancient Israelite and Jewish men.

Gardiner, Judith Kegan, ed. 2002. *Masculinity Studies and Feminist Theory: New Directions*. New York: Columbia University Press. Invaluable reading for anyone interested in the complex, sometimes strained relations between these two fields.

Krondorfer, Björn, ed. 2009. *Men and Masculinities in Christianity and Judaism: A Critical Reader*. London: SCM. The anthology's thirty-four selections include around a dozen that deal with masculinity in biblical texts, late ancient Christian texts, or rabbinic texts.

Kuefler, Mathew. 2001. *The Manly Eunuch: Masculinity, Gender Ambiguity, and Christian Ideology in Late Antiquity*. Chicago Series on Sexuality, History, and Society. Chicago: University of Chicago Press. Argues for a crisis of masculinity in Roman antiquity that Christian theologians attempted to resolve by drawing on early Christian teachings that privilege gender ambiguity.

Moore, Stephen D. 1996. *God's Gym: Divine Male Bodies of the Bible*. London: Routledge. The bodies in question are those of Yahweh and Jesus.

———. 2001. *God's Beauty Parlor: And Other Queer Spaces in and around the Bible*. Contraversions: Jews and Other Differences. Stanford, Calif.: Stanford University Press. Analyzes the masculinity of Paul's Jesus, Revelation's Jesus, and assorted popular-cultural Jesuses.

Moore, Stephen D., and Janice Capel Anderson, eds. 2003. *New Testament Masculinities*. SemeiaSt 45. Atlanta: Society of Biblical Literature. Includes ten essays that analyze masculine constructions in Matthew, Mark, Luke-Acts, John, the Pauline letters, Revelation, and the Shepherd of Hermas. Also includes three response essays and a twenty-page classified bibliography on masculinity studies.

Williams, Craig A. 2010. *Roman Homosexuality*. 2nd ed. Oxford: Oxford University Press. In effect, an encyclopedic synthesis of decades of work by classicists on the construction and performance of Roman masculinities.

Sexuality

10

THE SONG OF SONGS IN THE HISTORY OF SEXUALITY*

The previous essay veers into queer theory. The present essay, however, is a more single-minded plunge into that eclectic mode of theorizing and analyzing. Queer theory, which took literary studies by storm in the 1990s and remains immensely influential to this day, may tentatively be defined as a poststructuralist "take" on sex (homosex but also heterosex), sexuality, and sexual identity that argues (or assumes) their invariable instability, their de-essentializing fluidity, their contingent status as discursive constructions and/or products of performance.

This definition is tentative, however, or at least partial, because not everything that parades under the queer banner in academia drapes itself in the vestments of poststructuralism. Look no further than *The Queer Bible Commentary* (Guest, Goss, West, and Bohache 2006), little enough of whose 977 pages could be classified as poststructuralist in thrust. A literary studies volume of that size, however, with the word "queer" emblazoned in the title and scant reference to the work of Michel Foucault, Judith Butler, Eve Sedgwick, or their ilk inside would be all but unimaginable—yet another indication of how peripheral poststructuralism is even to the margins of biblical criticism. The reasons for this peripherality are complex, although Yvonne Sherwood and I begin to ponder them in "After 'After Theory'" below.

Just as one would be hard-pressed to name an ancient Jewish or Christian text that lends itself better than 4 Maccabees to the style of analysis associated with masculinity studies (see "Taking It Like a Man" above), so too would one be hard-pressed to name a biblical text that lends itself better to queer analysis than the Song of Songs. In no small part, of course, this is a simple

---

*First published in *Church History* 69 (2000): 328–50.

corollary of the fact that there is more "sex" (however loosely defined) in the Song of Songs than in any other biblical text. A second reason for homing in on the Song is that so much of its history of interpretation, Jewish but especially Christian, is queer in the extreme, as I attempt to demonstrate in this essay, and that history intersects in intriguing ways with "the history of sexuality" (a term made famous by Foucault), as the essay's title suggests: the demise of the allegorical tradition of Song of Songs interpretation coincides with the invention and dissemination of heterosexuality. A third reason is related to the second and, once again, is biographical. I first encountered Bernard of Clairvaux's astonishingly audacious commentary on the Song of Songs while I was a Cistercian novice monk long ago. Having a pretext to read Bernard again after all these years (even if no longer in the ankle-length man-dress of a monk) was not the least of the pleasures that writing this essay afforded me.

Solomon produced this book by divine inspiration in the language of a woman. (Rashi, *Commentary on the Song of Songs*, Prologue)

"So you actually read the Bible?" I asked in wonder. We had begun to converse two hours into the flight to San Diego and the MLA conference. She had interrupted her copious note taking on an issue of *GQ* (which magazine she had earlier claimed from a mildly bewildered flight attendant who had offered her *Vogue*) to whip out and consult an issue of *GLQ*[1]—at which point I could restrain my curiosity no longer. She turned out to be an English professor, not entirely unexpectedly, and when I admitted what I did for a living (usually a guaranteed conversation-killer) she casually revealed that she still read the Bible regularly. "But only the *beautiful* books," she added, hefting my Bible in one hand (she had caught it peeping out of my briefcase, shy as always about appearing in public, and deftly yanked it out) and *GQ* in the other; "Genesis, Ruth, Esther, and John—but mostly the Song of Songs." And in response to my look of frank disbelief, she began to recite, in a tone redolent of Pentecostal summer camp, all the while hoisting *GQ* aloft with its bare-torsoed male-model cover spread:

---

1. *GQ* is, of course, *Gentlemen's Quarterly*, while *GLQ* is, presumably, the *Gay and Lesbian Quarterly* (its subtitle is *A Journal of Lesbian and Gay Studies*).

10. THE SONG OF SONGS IN THE HISTORY OF SEXUALITY

"I charge you, O daughters of Jerusalem, if ye find my beloved, that ye tell him, that I am sick of love."

"What is thy beloved more than another beloved, O thou fairest among women? What is thy beloved more than another beloved, that thou dost so charge us?"

"My beloved is white and ruddy, the chiefest among ten thousand. His head is as the most fine gold, his locks are bushy, and black as a raven. His eyes are as the eyes of doves by the rivers of waters, washed with milk, and fitly set. His cheeks are as a bed of spices, as sweet flowers; his lips like lilies, dropping sweet smelling myrrh. His hands are as gold rings set with the beryl; his belly is as bright ivory overlaid with sapphires. His legs are as pillars of marble, set upon sockets of fine gold; his countenance is as Lebanon, excellent as the cedars. His mouth is most sweet; yea, he is altogether lovely. This is my beloved, and this is my friend, O daughters of Jerusalem...."

Beautiful Brides

The arduous task of queering the Song of Songs, a text that is ostensibly an unequivocal celebration of male-female sexual love, was accomplished over many centuries by the fathers and doctors of the church (as well as by Jewish sages of blessed memory, although they were hampered by a modesty and restraint to which their Christian cousins were seldom subject). Night after night in their cells, by flickering candlelight, they que(e)ried the Song of Solomon, strenuously enquiring after its spiritual meaning and confidently setting it forth. And as they did so their austere cells were transformed into lavish theaters. What follows is a series of preliminary portraits of some of the more remarkable performers.

We begin with Origen of Alexandria (ca. 185–253), whose commentary and homilies on the Song of Songs set the stage for so much that would follow. Actually, Origen not only set the stage; he himself took to the stage, amid rapturous applause, in his celebrated role as the "Bride" of the Song, played opposite the "Bridegroom," who is Christ. Here is a short snippet from his performance:

> For there is a certain spiritual embrace, and O that the Bridegroom's more perfect embrace may enfold my Bride! Then I too shall be able to say what is written in this same book: *His left hand is under my head, and His right hand will embrace me* [Song 2:6].... And if He will condescend to make my soul His Bride too and come to her, how fair must she then be to draw Him down from heaven to herself, to cause Him to come down to earth, so that He may visit His beloved one! With what beauty must she be adorned, with what love must she burn that He may say to her the things which He said to the perfect Bride...! (*Homilies on the Song of Songs* 1.2–3; trans. from Origen 1957)

Christendom had to wait almost a thousand years for an artiste able to match Origen's performance. Indeed, Bernard of Clairvaux (1091?–1153) not only matched it; he outdid Origen in effusiveness. Listen to Bernard as he warms up: "[L]et him who is the most handsome of the sons of men, let him kiss me with the kiss of his mouth [Song 1:1].... [E]ven the very beauty of the angels can only leave me wearied. For my Jesus utterly surpasses these in his majesty and splendor. Therefore I ask of him what I ask of neither man nor angel: that he kiss me with the kiss of his mouth" (*Sermons on the Song of Songs* 2.2).[2] Now listen to this declaration of passion: "It is simply that I am in love.... It is desire that drives me on, not reason.... I ask, I crave, I implore: let him kiss me with the kiss of his mouth" (9.2). And for a gender-bending finale:

> While the bride is conversing about the Bridegroom, he ... suddenly appears, yields to her desire by giving her a kiss.... The filling up of her breasts is a proof of this. For so great is the potency of that holy kiss, that no sooner has the bride received it than she conceives and her breasts grow rounded with the fruitfulness of conception, bearing witness, as it were, with this milky abundance. Men with an urge to frequent prayer will have experience of what I say.... [T]here comes an unexpected infusion of grace, our breast expands..., and our interior is filled with an overflowing love; and if somebody should press upon it then, this milk of sweet fecundity would gush forth in streaming richness. (9.7)

But even Bernard would be hard-pressed to hold his hard-won place as Christendom's most extravagant interpreter of the celebrated role of the Bride in the face of the stiff competition that was to follow—Denis the Carthusian (1402?–1471), for example, known, not for nothing, as the Ecstatic Doctor.[3] Divas such as Denis, however, would soon be exposed as hopeless hams by the elegant interpretation of the role enacted by the Mystical Doctor, St. John of the Cross (1542–1591). Here is a choice snippet from his performance, sung with real emotion and a seemly economy of gesture:

> There He gave me His breast;
> There he taught me a sweet and living knowledge;
> And I gave myself to Him,

---

2. For the translation used, see Bernard of Clairvaux 1971–80.

3. Translated and annotated extracts from Denis's commentary are available in Turner 1995, 411–48 ("But how, oh you poor silly little soul..., how can you have the presumption, the boldness, even the least self-assurance to ask a kiss of him, of whom the heavens, the earth, the seas are all in awe...").

10. THE SONG OF SONGS IN THE HISTORY OF SEXUALITY 229

Keeping nothing back;
There I promised to be His bride. (*Spiritual Canticle* 27)[4]

What are we to make of these intensely erotic readings of the Song of Songs? During the past century or more, literal readings of the Song have all but displaced the allegorical readings that proliferated and predominated in preceding centuries.[5] But whereas the enabling assumption of the literal readings is that the Song concerns the mutual attraction between a man and a woman, the enabling assumption of the allegorical readings is that the Song concerns the mutual attraction between two males: between a community or individual, on the one hand, classically conceived as male,[6] and a divine being, on the other hand, also conceived as male.

For classical Jewish and Christian commentators, the Song simply could not be what it seemed to be. That would have been unthinkable. Paradoxically, however, allegorizing it only had the effect of turning it into something yet more unthinkable—not just the torrid expression of a sizzling sexual relationship between a horny young woman and her hunky young man, hidden away among the books of sacred Scripture like a sex manual in a monastery library or a rabbinic house of study, but the expression of an erotic relationship between two *male* parties instead. The allegorical approach to the Song sprang ultimately from disinclination on the part of pious male exegetes to engage in unspiritual fleshing out of its nubile female protagonist,[7] inti-

---

4. For the translation used, see John of the Cross 1964. Essentially, the *Spiritual Canticle* is a free poetic paraphrase of the Song of Songs.

5. Under "allegorical," here and throughout, I am subsuming three different "senses of sacred Scripture" that the medieval mind, in particular, took pains to distinguish, namely, the allegorical, the anagogical and the tropological. My usage of the term "literal," too, is rough and ready by medieval standards; by the thirteenth century the term had become subject to some exquisite refinements.

6. By which I simply mean that whether in Jewish or Christian allegorical exegesis of the Song through the ancient, medieval and early modern periods, the expositor in all but a tiny handful of the extant texts is a male who addresses himself primarily to an audience of male peers, synecdochic stand-ins for Israel or the Church. The first *possible* exception to the rule is the anonymous twelfth-century Christian commentary on the Song known as the *St. Trudperter Hohelied* (St. Trudperter Song of Songs), and the first *certain* exceptions are Mechtilde of Magdeburg's thirteenth-century *Das fliessende Licht der Gottheit* (The Flowing Light of the Godhead), which includes mystical meditation on selected verses from the Song, and Teresa of Avila's sixteenth-century *Conceptos del amor de Dios sobre unas palabras de los Cantares* (Conceptions of Divine Love in Some Words of the Canticles).

7. The poem (if indeed it is *a* poem and not a mini-anthology of love lyrics) contains three voices: a female voice, a male voice and a group voice. Of the three, however,

mate knowledge of whose body or libidinal life is served up in every stich. A staggering profusion of delicious nonsense arose as a result of this disinclination or discomfort. "*The meeting of your thighs....* This refers to the coming together of Jews and Gentiles in the one Church of Christ.... *Your two breasts* are the two Testaments, from which the children begotten in Christ draw milk for their growth"—the litany of examples is endless.[8]

With exquisite irony, however, the austere expositor's attempt to evade the perilous embrace of the Song's female lover through allegory plunges him instead into the arms of another lover—a *male* lover, no less, whom he takes to be God or Christ. ("Each soul living in charity is an individual Bride of Christ," croons Denis the Carthusian, "and so our Lord and Saviour holds her close to him with the arms of love" [*Commentary on the Song of Songs* 42].) With astonishing ease the male expositor is seduced by the Song into whispering Shulamith's[9] white-hot words of passion into the ear of the fantasized male personage in whose muscular arms he has eagerly taken refuge. ("Join with the Bride in saying what she says," urges Origen, "so that you may hear also what she heard" [*Homilies on the Song of Songs* 1.1].) Allegorical exegesis of the Song thereby becomes a sanctioned space—a stage, indeed—for some decidedly queer performances. Finding himself upon this stage, the monk, priest, prelate, or rabbi (for the restraint I earlier ascribed to the latter is only relative, as it happens),[10] however respectable or repressed he might be in "real" life, is possessed by a divine madness. Throwing off his religious garb and all his inhibitions with it, he paints his nails, decks himself out in flamboyant costumes, and camps it up with abandon. "I am the beautiful Bride in sooth," purrs Origen, sashaying across the stage, "and I show not my naked face to any save Thee only, whom I kissed tenderly but now" (*Homilies on the Song of Songs* 1.8).

---

the female's is the most prominent, delivering most of the lines and initiating most of the exchanges, as Phyllis Trible first argued in her now classic "Love's Lyrics Redeemed" (1978c). Trible is only one of many feminist biblical scholars who have been drawn to the Song on that account (see further "Unsafe Sex" below).

8. The two offered here are drawn from Nicholas of Lyra (1270?–1349), *The* Postilla Litteralis *on the Song of Songs* 62–63. For a continuous 382-page catena of ancient and medieval interpretations of the Song, lavishly studded with such gems, see Littledale 1869.

9. Shulamit(h), or the Shulam(m)ite, is the name traditionally given to the female protagonist of the Song (cf. 6:13: "Come back, come back, O Shulammite [*haššûlammît*]...").

10. I engage elsewhere with the rabbinic tradition of Song of Songs interpretation (Moore 2001, 29–39).

ALLEGORY'S DOUBLE CROSS (WHICH TURNS THE CROSS-BEARING CHRISTIAN INTO A CHRISTIAN CROSS-DRESSER)

It is customary to see Origen as the fountainhead of the Christian allegorical exposition of the Song.[11] Through him the Jewish allegorical interpretation of the Song flowed into the church and irrigated its ascetic imagination (Urbach 1971; Kimelman 1980). Intriguingly, the conduit for this stunningly queer body of commentary may himself have been a gender anomaly. For if Origen's reading of the Song was scrupulously spiritual, his reading of Matt 19:12 (Jesus' expression of approval for those "who have made themselves eunuchs for the kingdom of heaven") was scrupulously literal—at least if Eusebius is to be credited. Squirming uncomfortably and crossing his legs tightly, Eusebius offers an elliptical account of Origen's painfully literal reading of this highly enigmatic verse (*Hist. eccl.* 6.8.1–3). But whereas the literal reading of Matthew that Eusebius ascribes to Origen was strikingly at odds with his spiritual reading of the Song in one sense, in another sense it was not. For Origen deals with the textual body of the Song in precisely the same way that he has dealt with his own sexual body, amputating from it anything that might prove an occasion for sin (cf. Matt 18:8: "And if your hand or your foot causes you to sin, cut it off…"). He reenacts on the Song that which he has already enacted on his own flesh. In short, he submits the Song to castration. Of course, one could also argue that Origen, in commenting at such spectacular length upon the Song, was attempting to replace that which, on Eusebius's account, he had excised from his own flesh, and one could thereby read his "twenty thousand lines" as a monumental attempt to substitute the phallus for the penis.[12]

In either case, however, Origen's queer reading of the Song could be said to have proceeded smoothly from the Song's own propensity to blur gender boundaries (cf. Landy 1983, 73–112; Meyers 1986)—to "masculinize" the female body (as in 4:4, for example, "Your neck is like the tower of David, built in courses; on it hang a thousand bucklers, all of them shields of warriors") and to "feminize" the male body (as in the intensely sensual description of it in 5:10–16), and, on occasion, to employ the same images for both bodies (deer and dove, for instance). The gender-blurring imagery of the Song overruns the margins of the page and "contaminates" the commentaries of Origen and his successors, where it proliferates and mutates uncontrollably.

---

11. Although the first Christian known to have allegorized the Song was Hippolytus of Rome, fragments of whose commentary on it (ca. 200?) survive.

12. The phrase "twenty thousand lines" comes from Jerome's prologue to his Latin translation of the *Homilies*.

But Origen's queer reading of the Song could also be said to have proceeded smoothly from the transgressive body that tradition so aptly assigned to him. Of eunuchs in general in the world of late antiquity, and Origen in particular, Peter Brown remarks:

> The eunuch was notorious (and repulsive to many) because he had dared to shift the massive boundary between the sexes.... He had opted out of being male. By losing the sexual "heat" that was held to cause his facial hair to grow, the eunuch was no longer recognizable as a man. He was a human being "exiled from either gender." Deprived of the standard professional credential of a philosopher in late antique circles—a flowing beard—Origen would have appeared in public with a smooth face, like a woman or like a boy frozen into a state of prepubertal innocence. He was a walking lesson in the basic indeterminacy of the body. (1988, 169)

As it happens, however, the thrilling being who is the ultimate object of desire in Origen's commentary on the Song, and whom he terms "the Bridegroom," is "himself" anatomically indeterminate. He is obviously quite a man—utterly masterful, utterly capable of displaying his "husband's power" to the "virginal" soul and initiating her into the "perfect mystery," as Origen delicately puts it (*Commentary on the Song of Songs*, Prologue 4)—yet he is not *all* man. And not only because he is also divine but because he is also a woman.

We receive the first inkling of this when, with a ceremonious flourish, Origen unhooks the straps of Song 1:2, "For Thy breasts are better than wine," and the hidden glory of the Bridegroom flops forth.[13] The Bride is "moved deeply by the beauty of His breasts" (*Commentary on the Song of Songs* 1.2), and, "after she has been found worthy to receive kisses from the Bridegroom's own mouth, and to enjoy his breasts, says to Him: 'Thy breasts are above wine'" (1.4). These superb breasts owe nothing to silicon, moreover; they are packed with something altogether superior: "treasures of wisdom and knowledge are concealed in them." And when the Bride "reflects upon the teaching that flows forth from the Bridegroom's breasts, she is amazed and marvels" (1.2). Moaning softly, s/he wraps her moist lips around the Bridegroom's erect nipples, which leak luscious drops of teaching. "Because He tastes so sweet and so delightful," gurgles Origen, his head buried in the Bridegroom's bosom, milk dripping down his beardless chin, "all other flavours will seem harsh and bitter to [the spiritual man] now; and therefore he will feed on Him

---

13. The Bridegroom owes his hermaphroditic cleavage to the Greek (Septuagint) and Latin (Vulgate) translations of Song 1:2, which read *mastoi sou* and *ubera tua*, respectively ("your breasts"), whereas the Hebrew (Masoretic) text has *dōdêkā* ("your love," or, conceivably, "your lovemaking"; so Bloch and Bloch 1995).

alone" (1.4). All of which is to say that Origen's own gender indeterminacy has communicated itself, somehow, to the Bridegroom.

Who in turn communicated it to the Bridegrooms of so many of the commentaries that succeeded Origen's, in a veritable epidemic of gender undecidability. A stunning example occurs in Aponius's *In Canticum canticorum explanatio* (ca. 680), which, commenting on Song 8:10, "I am a wall, and my breasts like towers," identifies the wall as "the Manhood of Christ," upon which "the towering breasts" are supported (Littledale 1869, 371). The mind boggles, or merely bogs down, as it attempts to bring this surreal spectacle into focus. What sort of body might be up to the challenge of coupling with this hyper-endowed prodigy, we wonder, this monument to gendered excess—and gender indeterminacy? How about this one, which Gregory of Elvira, writing a little earlier, fantasized on the basis of Song 1:2: "Instead of the two breasts of the she-goat of the Law, written on tablets of stone by the finger of God, Christians, like cows, have the four breasts of the Evangelists, full of the sweet milk of wisdom" (*Tractatus de epithalamio* 1.9, in Matter 1990, 88).

How paradoxical to have to reassert in the face of these lush spectacles of sensory overload that the allegorical impulse in Song of Songs interpretation stemmed from the radical repudiation of the flesh. Yet that would appear to have been the case. Allegorical exegesis was the child of ascesis. Celibate Christian expositors employed allegory to unsex the salacious Song and render it sublimely spiritual. For these interpreters, the Song was a ticking time bomb within Scripture itself, an occasion of sin just waiting to happen, which only the ingenuity of the allegorist could successfully defuse. Only the male who was castrated—literally, or at least metaphorically—could approach this text with impunity. The Song of Songs was a book for eunuchs. Or at least a book for monks.

But monks, too, came increasingly to seem like gender anomalies as the Middle Ages wore on. Daniel Boyarin explains: "[S]ince the monk within [medieval] Christian culture has a binary opposite in the knight, the former can be removed from the category of 'real men' within Christianity and stand as an oppositional force to it. Monks, then, effectively form a distinct gender within Christian society, one that is removed from the paternal and sexual order" (1997, 26). All of which leads one to wonder: Was this why medieval monks evinced such immense fascination with the Song of Songs, or rather with its allegorization? Torrid expressions of the soul's ardent desire for spiritual congress with Christ under the voluptuous figure of a bride's ardent desire for sexual congress with her bridegroom proceeded with astonishing ease from the pens of this clerical class. Why? Because these gender contortionists already constituted a third gender in relation to their cultural habitat anyway?

One is further tempted to drape these *spiritual* cross-dressers in the same conceptual garb that Marjorie Garber runs off for *literal* cross-dressers in *Vested Interests*, her encyclopedic cultural history of cross-dressing. "[O]ne of the most consistent and effective functions of the transvestite in culture," she argues, "is to indicate the place of what I call 'category crisis'" (1992, 16). By this she means

> a failure of definitional distinction, a borderline that becomes permeable, that permits of border crossings from one (apparently distinct) category to another.... The binarism male/female ... is itself put into question or under erasure in transvestism, and a transvestite figure, or a transvestite mode, will always function as a...mechanism of displacement from one blurred boundary to another. An analogy here might be the so-called "tagged" gene that shows up in a genetic chain, indicating the presence of some otherwise hidden condition. It is not the gene itself, but its presence, that marks the trouble spot, indicating the likelihood of a crisis somewhere, elsewhere.
>
> In a similar way, I will argue, the apparently spontaneous or unexpected or supplementary presence of a transvestite figure in a text (whether fiction or history, verbal or visual, imagistic or "real") that does not seem, thematically, to be primarily concerned with gender differences or blurred gender indicates a *category crisis elsewhere*, an irresolvable conflict or epistemological crux that destabilizes comfortable binarity, and displaces the resulting discomfort onto a figure that already inhabits, indeed incarnates, the margin. (1992, 16–17, her emphasis)

In the case of the classic medieval commentaries on the Song of Songs, I am tempted to merge Garber's reflections on category crisis with those of Boyarin on the medieval monk as constituting a distinct gender[14] and speculate that the routine apparitional emergence of "transvestite" figures (males in female guise) in these commentaries—texts that are not concerned thematically with gender difference, much less with gender bending—indicates a category crisis in medieval society centered on the anomalously gendered person of the male celibate. In the commentaries—more specifically, in the authorial personae created in the commentaries—the already anomalous figure of the male celibate is torqued up to an exquisite (and cathartic) extreme until it becomes an entity who (surreptitiously) inhabits, indeed incarnates, the margin: a male

---

14. Garber herself in her chapter on "Religious Habits" writes of the perceived femininity of the priest or monk in medieval society—"beardless, wearing a cassock that could be thought to resemble a woman's skirt, devoid of political power, living in quiet obedience, and performing domestic chores" (1992, 218). The chapter carries a telling epigraph from Sydney Smith's 1855 novel, *Lady Holland's Memoir*: "As the French say, there are three sexes—men, women, and clergymen."

10. THE SONG OF SONGS IN THE HISTORY OF SEXUALITY 235

author who, not in the name of fiction but of ultimate truth, internalizes a feminine persona so completely that he speaks fluently in her voice, feels with her emotions, and throbs with her sexuality; a male author who might be said to personify queer gender identity, in that "he" puts powerfully into question the binary category of gender itself.

And yet I have little desire to idealize patristic and medieval commentators on the Song of Songs as exotic exemplars of a third gender or third sex. The contempt for the flesh on the part of male celibates that found expression in the allegorical exposition of the Song was also—or especially—contempt for *female* flesh. Bernard of Clairvaux, the most prolix commentator of all on the Song, requiring eighty-six sermons to get to the end of its second chapter, discovered the path that would eventually lead to these sermons while in full flight from female flesh, according to his intimate friend and biographer William of Saint Thierry. In boyhood, Bernard's eyes, then roaming free, would alight from time to time upon a female form. Bernard's member, rudely aroused from slumber, would crane its neck forward curiously for a glimpse of its own, causing its owner to flee in confusion and dunk the offending organ (himself still appended to it) in an icy pond until it consented to withdraw its head. Thus it was that Bernard resolved to become a monk.[15] And it was from this same frigid pond, proof against the wiles of the temptress and the treacherous head of the serpent, that Bernard would deliver all eighty-six of his exquisite sermons on the Song, its pages dripping with icy water.

Allegorical exposition of the Song replicates the deadly struggle of male celibacy itself. What must be overcome in either instance is the sexual, the sensual, the fleshly, the female. Small wonder that no other book of sacred Scripture received more reverent attention from male ascetics in the ancient and medieval church. The most sensual book in the Bible became the book of professional celibates, past masters of repression and sublimation.[16] The repressed returns, of course, although not with a vengeance so much as a wicked sense of humor: the monk, priest or prelate is deftly transformed into a drag queen as he strives manfully to play the feminine role thrust upon him by the spiritual reading of the Song.[17] And the final ironic twist is the fact that the feminine is what elicits his distrust, if not his outright disgust, ordinar-

---

15. The anecdote is William's, even if the words are not; see William of St. Thierry et al. 1960, 20. William began his biography around 1147 and covered the first forty years of Bernard's life. After William's death, Arnold of Bonnevaux and others took up the tale.

16. Not that *all* commentators on the Song were celibate. Gregory of Nyssa, for one, seems to have been married.

17. Cf. Butler 1990, 137: "The performance of drag plays upon the distinction between the anatomy of the performer and the gender that is being performed."

ily. This is the double-cross of allegory that turns the cross-bearing Christian into the Christian cross-dresser. Through the (r)use of allegory, the exegete eagerly embraces that from which he is actively in flight.

By annexing a mystical—and mystified—femaleness to his own male body, however, the allegorical expositor renders the literal female body redundant. The woman of the Song—and, by extension, woman in general—is symbolically annihilated in the very gesture through which she is appropriated. The symbolic world created by these male celibates in their allegorical elaborations of the Song is as free of the polluting presence of real women as the chapterhouse at Clairvaux, an inner sanctum of homosocial sanctity and the literary setting of Bernard's eighty-six sermons on the Song, delivered to an implied audience of women-free men, the minutiae of whose daily live are so disposed that they are almost never obliged to lay eyes on a flesh-and-blood daughter of Eve. The ecclesiastical tradition of Song of Songs interpretation thus presents us with the paradoxical spectacle of male ascetics endlessly preening themselves in front of a mirror. Allegory enables them to gaze upon the female body in the Song without actually having to see it. In its contours and crevices they only see themselves.

The Commentator Removes His Makeup

Like a man who awakes bleary-eyed and hungover one overcast morning to discover to his immense horror that he is in another man's bed, entwined in its owner's arms, commentary on the Song of Songs began to recoil sharply from allegory in the course of the nineteenth century. Slipping stealthily out of bed and hastily adjusting its clerical collar, it tiptoed out of the room. Like reformed and newly sober men, late nineteenth- and early twentieth-century commentators labored to straighten out the queer reading to which the Song had so long been subjected. The Song was turned instead into a celebration of, indeed a warrant for, heterosexuality. R. F. Littledale bewails the beginnings of this transformation in his 1869 tome on the Song—specifically, "the [emerging] assertion that its design is to teach a higher morality with regard to love and marriage." He objects: "There is not the faintest hint in any writer, Jewish or Christian, before the nineteenth century, that such a lesson is inculcated by the Song of Songs" (1869, xxvii).[18] But the transformation, once underway, proved irreversible. Littledale's German contemporary, Franz Delitzsch, could

---

18. Littledale has overlooked Johann David Michaelis (d. 1791), who, in his notes to Bishop Robert Lowth's *De sacra poesi Hebraeorum praelectiones* (1753), opined that the Song extols conjugal love, "the attachment of two delicate persons who have been long united in the sacred bond," and inquired: "Can we suppose such happiness unworthy of

already announce confidently in his 1875 commentary: "The Song transfigures natural but holy love. Whatever in the sphere of the divinely-ordered marriage relation makes love the happiest, firmest bond uniting two souls together, is presented to us here in living pictures" (1980, 5).[19]

The new homiletics of heteronormativity in Song of Songs interpretation found especially succinct expression in a mid-twentieth-century endorsement of its erotics by the distinguished Old Testament scholar, H. H. Rowley. "The Church has always consecrated the union of man and woman in matrimony, and taught that marriage is a divine ordinance," he wrote, "and it is not unfitting that a book which expressed the spiritual and physical emotions on which matrimony rests should be given a place in the Canon of Scripture" (1952, 234). Roland E. Murphy, who himself has been arguing this very point since at least the middle of the twentieth century, sums it up nicely in his recent commentary on the Song: "While the Song is not designed to elaborate theological doctrine or teach ethics, its unapologetic depiction of rapturous, reciprocal love between a man and a woman does model an important dimension of human existence, an aspect of life that ancient Israel understood to be divinely ordained and sanctioned" (1990, 100).

Of course, it is not only impeccably credentialized biblical scholars such as Rowley and Murphy who have read the Song as championing the sanctity of heterosexuality, thereby slapping a fig leaf on the "carnal" reading and recruiting it for mainstream morality. In the course of a fascinating stretch of the 300-page lead-in to his own massive commentary on the Song, Marvin Pope treats us to a wealth of twentieth-century opinion, mainly Christian but also Jewish, much of it lacking professional polish, which contends that the Song is essentially a celebration of divinely ordained heterosexual love, supremely enshrined in heterosexual marriage (1977, 192–205). Of particular interest are the reasons advanced in a doctoral dissertation that Pope quotes for the superiority of the literal reading over the allegorical reading. The Song should "be used only with extreme care in a mystical sense in hymnody, prayers or sermons. So to use the book is to distort its meaning. Whatever use in worship to which [it] is put, it must be consistent with its content concerning the love between a man and a woman" (Dempsey 1963, 157, quoted in Pope 1977, 197). In effect, for this writer, the allegorical tradition constitutes a threat to a heterosexual reading of the Song. He is able to report with satisfac-

---

being recommended as a pattern to mankind, and of being celebrated as a subject of gratitude to the great Author of happiness?" (quoted in Ginsburg 1857, 87).

19. The interpretation of the Song as a series of ancient Hebrew wedding songs also made its appearance in the late nineteenth century—in J. G. Wetzstein's appendix to Delitzsch's commentary, for example, but particularly in the work of Karl Budde (1894, 1898).

tion, however: "During the last century the traditional allegorical approach to Canticles has been for the most part abandoned because of the discoveries of scholarship, the spread of a more natural view of love and sex, and a realization that in the final analysis Canticles is love poetry" (1963, 158, quoted in Pope 1977, 197). And also because of the rise of heterosexuality?

The "invention" of heterosexuality appears to have coincided approximately with the invention of electricity, photography, automotive engineering, and other indispensable appurtenances of modernity.[20] Is it entirely a matter of chance that the emergence of heterosexuality, with its sharply delineated and strictly policed sexual borders, should happen to coincide with the decline of the allegorical interpretation of the Song of Songs, with its ill-defined and poorly policed sexual borders? "Before" heterosexuality, "normal" men could get up to things with other men that they could not so easily get up to "after" heterosexuality—*intimate* things, erotic or otherwise. Daniel Boyarin notes the scope for forms of male intimacy even within Jewish rabbinic culture, a culture that "has always been heteronormative, even if not heterosexual, that is, homophobic" (1997, 16).

> "Who is a friend?" a midrash asks. "He that one eats with, drinks with, reads with, studies with, sleeps with, and reveals to him all of his secrets—the secrets of Torah and the secrets of the ways of the world." "Sleeps with" does *not* have the euphemistic value that it has in English or German, but the text is certainly reaching for a very intense and passionate level of male-male physical intimacy here. The "way of the world" is a somewhat ambiguous metaphorical term that can refer to several areas of worldly life, including

---

20. As well as with the invention of homosexuality. The terms "homosexual(ity)" and "heterosexual(ity)" both date from 1869. Michel Foucault famously locates the discursive construction of homosexuality in the late nineteenth century and the (then nascent) sciences of psychology and psychiatry. As defined by earlier legal and religious codes, "sodomy was a category of forbidden acts; their perpetrator was nothing more than the juridical subject of them" (Foucault 1978, 42). The homosexual, in contrast, was "a personage, a past, a case history, and a childhood…. Nothing … was unaffected by his sexuality…. It was everywhere present in him: at the root of all his actions…; written immodestly on his face and body because it was the secret that always gave itself away. It was consubstantial with him, less as a habitual sin than as a singular nature…. The sodomite had been a temporary aberration; the homosexual was now a species" (1978, 42–43). David Greenberg excavates the same early sexological terrain as Foucault, but in considerably more detail (1988, 397–433). Jonathan Katz extends Foucault's project in a different direction, highlighting the role of Freud and popularized Freudianism in the transformation of heterosexuality from an obscure late-Victorian sexual pathology (the compulsion to seek sexual pleasure for its own sake rather than as a means of procreation) into the gold standard of twentieth-century normality (1995, 57–82). For a useful companion to Katz, see Richardson 1996.

business, but especially sex. Male intimacy, it seems, for the talmudic culture includes the physical contact of being in bed together while sharing verbally the most intimate of experiences, a pattern not unknown in other cultures.... Thus, while we cannot draw inferences about the sexual practices of rabbinic men from such a passage, we can certainly, it seems to me, argue that it bespeaks a lack of "homosexual panic" such as that necessitated by the modern formation known as "heterosexuality." (1997, 16–17, quoting *Schechter Aboth* 10)

I would argue, just as confidently, that the consummately queer body of allegorical commentary on the Song of Songs, both Jewish and Christian, that we have been pondering in this essay similarly bespeaks, indeed presupposes, a lack of homosexual panic in the cultures in which it was conceived—in which case the pervasiveness of homosexual panic in twentieth-century Western culture would explain the rejection of the allegorical approach to the Song even by male readers innocent or wary of the "discoveries" of critical biblical scholarship (such as the non-Solomonic authorship of the book or its pronounced family resemblance to other ancient Near Eastern love poetry).

Among the critical scholars themselves (who until very recently have all been male),[21] the interpretation of the Song as a celebration of heterosexual love has long been commonplace, as we have seen. One strongly suspects that, as polished products of heterosexuality, these scholars have problems internalizing the central voice of the Song—the feminine voice—that preheterosexual scholars (ancient, medieval, early modern) did not have. In other words, they have trouble throwing themselves wholeheartedly into the role of a vivacious young woman in love. The intrinsic queerness of that role sits too strangely in a culture that has scripted them to be superlatively straight at all times. If they are ordained clergy, indeed (and again, until relatively recently, almost all of them have been), the culture has already cast them in a dizzyingly different role: that of the ultimate custodians of its straightness.

But the final twist in this footnote to the history of sexuality is possibly the trickiest of all.

The New Allegorists

In their attempts to take the literal interpretation of the Song to its logical conclusion, a number of recent commentators have inadvertently fallen back on the allegorical method. Marvin Pope and Michael Goulder have been espe-

---

21. As far as I have been able to discover, Exum 1973 was the first published contribution by a woman to critical scholarship on the Song.

cially notable in this regard. Few modern readings of the Song are as resolutely heterosexual as theirs. In stark contrast to the "old" allegorists, who gave even sexual details of the Song a spiritual reading, these "new" allegorists give a sexual reading even to details that are ostensibly nonsexual.

First, Goulder. Confronted with Song 8:5b, which he translates as "Under the apple-tree I awakened you;/ there your mother writhed with you,/ there she who bore you writhed," Goulder suspects that the phrase "I awakened you" (*'ôrartîka*—the "you" is therefore masculine) "refers to sexual arousal." He further suspects that "Under the apple-tree" is likewise a double entendre,"

> [f]or it could be that the place where she aroused him is an anatomical place as well as a place in a glade; and that it is thought of as an apple tree by virtue of the two fruits hanging down above the "trunk"; that there is a special force to "under," because it is at the under end of this tree that the nerves are concentrated that make for such arousal; and it is "there" that women ... are in turn aroused to ecstasy in the moment of union. (1986, 7–8)

Faced with 6:12, which he renders poetically as "Ere I had thought it, he made me, my life did, my own people's chariot,/ Come from Nadiv," Goulder explains: "When first he saw her, the king compared the princess to his mare in the chariots (*rikebê*) of Pharaoh (1.9): now, she says, he has made her a chariot of her own people—that is, she is still the mare, but he is now the 'charioteer.'" Still unsure as to Goulder's meaning? Let him rein in your wilder imaginings: "The Hebrews had thus already discovered that sexual union could take place in more than one position" (1986, 51).

Neither does Goulder shrink from translating 7:10b, a line he assigns to the "princess," as "To touch my love's erectness, and my lips to kiss his sleepers!" or from paraphrasing the entire verse as follows: "He says, 'Your mouth is like wine' [7:10a] with its kisses: yes, she replies daringly, 'It goes to my beloved to his "uprightness."'" And again: "'Your mouth is intoxicating,' says the king: 'it goes,' replies the princess with a twinkle, 'to my beloved's "uprights," it glides with my lips over his "sleepers"'" (1986, 58–59). What Goulder imagines these "sleepers" to be is never explicitly stated—but then it doesn't need to be, so skillfully does he draw ancient Hebrew sexual slang out of the ether. And the imagined oral ministrations (guaranteed to arouse the "sleepers" from slumber?) are not all one-way traffic. Confronted, finally, by 8:2, which Goulder renders in rhyme as

> I'd take you to my mother's,
> To drink my spiced wine—
> You'd show me how—and taste the sweet

10. THE SONG OF SONGS IN THE HISTORY OF SEXUALITY   241

Of pomegranate mine

he is able to state confidently, "The sexual meaning is not in doubt.... The only question is what sort of sexual activity is envisaged. We may think of straightforward sexual union.... On the other hand, we have to consider the alternative that the 'drinking' is meant literally.... It seems probable then that she is speaking here of oral sex on his side, as a preamble to the full union of 8.3 (celebrated at v. 5b)" (1986, 62). And so on.

What prevents me, however, from hailing Michael Goulder as the new allegorist par excellence of the Song of Songs is the palpable discomfort that his own steamy readings induce in him. He worries audibly and at length that the details of his translations and exegesis reveal the Song to be nothing more "than a piece of high-class pornography" (1986, 79). Like Martin Luther before him, Goulder cannot quite bring himself to contemplate an unmitigated carnal interpretation of the Sublime Song. Consequently, he is driven to argue that the Song contains a hidden theological message—one that, when fully unveiled, turns out to be positively prescient: "Jews and Gentiles are equal in the sight of God. Such theological insights do not receive explicit expression before the Epistle to the Ephesians" (1986, 78). In Goulder's fascinating commentary on the Song of Songs, then, "old" allegorist and "new" allegorist do deadly battle, the old allegorist eventually pinning the new allegorist to the ground—but not before the latter has blurted out everything he has wanted to say.

Pope, in contrast, is prey to no such conflicts. His transformation of the Sublime Song into the Suggestive Song is accomplished entirely without qualms. But he does open up a Pandora's box in the process (out of which a topless Pandora pops on cue—although that is just the beginning). Let us start with Pope's treatment of Song 7:2a (Heb. 7:3a), generally rendered by translators along the following lines: "Your navel is a rounded bowl/ that never lacks mixed wine" (RSV). The owner of the navel is feminine in the Hebrew (*sorēk*). Peering intently into the little cavity, however, Pope begins to doubt that it really is a navel after all. He argues that the Hebrew word traditionally translated as "navel" would be better rendered here as "vulva." "Since the movement of the description of the lady's charms is from the feet upward," he tactfully explains, "the locus of the evermoist receptacle between the thighs and the belly would seem to favor the lower aperture. The liquid, too, would seem to make the navel unlikely since navels are not notable for their capacity to store or dispense moisture" (1977, 617–18).

Convinced that he has caught a glimpse of a vulva, Pope seems to become obsessed by the thought of it. Thus he cannot resist translating Song 7:8c–d (Heb. 7:9c–d) as "Let your breasts be like grape clusters/ The scent of your vulva like apples" instead of the more usual "Let your breasts be like grape clusters/ The scent of your *breath* [*'appēk*] like apples." But Pope had earlier ascribed a still more fragrant perfume to this aromatic vulva. With regard to Song 4:13a, "*šĕlāḥayik* is a pomegranate grove," he suggests that *šĕlāḥayik* denotes a "more intimate portion" of the heroine's anatomy than most translators have been willing to contemplate, and boldly renders the part-verse as "Your groove a pomegranate grove" (1977, 453, 490–91).[22]

The most telling and thought-provoking portion, however, of Pope's new allegorical reading of the Song of Songs, is his partial decoding of 5:2–6. The passage, in Pope's own translation, reads:

> I slept, but my mind was alert.
> Hark, my love knocks.
> Open to me, my sister,
> My darling, my dove, my perfect one!
> For my head is drenched with dew,
> My locks with the night mist.
> I have removed my tunic
> How shall I put it on?
> I have washed my feet
> How shall I soil them?
> My love thrust his "hand" into the hole,
> And my inwards seethed for him.
> I rose to open for my love,
> And my hands dripped myrrh,
> My fingers liquid myrrh,
> On the handles of the bolt.
> I opened to my love,
> But my love had turned and gone.
> My soul sank at his flight.
> I sought, but could not find him.
> I called him, but he did not answer me.

Pope offers the following explanation for his decision to turn "hand" (*yad*) into a naughty word by slipping it into a sexy pair of quotation marks: "Given the attested use of 'hand' as a surrogate for phallus"—earlier he has adduced Isa 57:8–10 and the Qumran Manual of Discipline (1QS 7:13) in this regard, along with certain Ugaritic texts—"there can be no question that, whatever

---

22. H. H. Hirschberg had anticipated Pope in this instance, however, rendering *šĕlāḥayik* less sexily as "your vagina" on the basis of a cognate Arabic word (1961, 379–80).

the context, the statement 'my love thrust his "hand" into the hole' would be suggestive of coital intromission, even without the succeeding line descriptive of the emotional reaction of the female" (1977, 519).

"Whatever the context...." This is an extraordinary claim in *its* context, because disregard for context is meant to be the hallmark, not of the "literal" reading of the Song (of which Pope's *magnum opus* is the most ambitious example ever attempted), but of the "allegorical" reading. The immediate context of this line militates strongly against Pope's reading, as we shall see in a moment. Like the "old" allegorists, however, Pope is not about to let context stand in the way of the *desired* reading. Precisely at this point in Pope's commentary, the distinction between the literal and the allegorical collapses, for by inviting us to read even *one* word in this passage euphemistically, Pope opens a sluice gate. We automatically enclose the "hole" also in quotation marks (even if Pope himself is too delicate to do so), and these mental quotation marks then begin to run rampant all over the passage. In effect, Pope has invited us to turn the entire passage into an allegory of "coital intromission." Let's give it a try.

If Pope is correct in his interpretation of Song 5:4a ("My love thrust his 'hand' into the hole"), surely 5:2c ("Open to me") can mean only one thing: "Open your legs to me"—and, indeed, Pope does not disappoint us in his handling of this part-verse. "The word 'door' is recognized even by the most modest commentators as a figure for a female unusually open and receptive to sexual overtones," he asserts. Moreover, "the request to 'open' in the preceding verse could in certain circumstances have sexual connotations" (1977, 514–15). But now we encounter our first obstacle. The reason given for this impassioned outburst of unbridled lust—"Open your legs!"–seems rather incongruous at first blush: "For my head is drenched with dew,/ My locks with the night mist." But might not the "head" in question be the man's glans, we feel compelled to ask, in which case the drops of "dew" would be the visible proof of his ardor, while the "locks" would, of course, be the luxuriant tangle of his pubic hair (raven black, perhaps, to match his wavy tresses [cf. 5:11])?[23] Admittedly, the "night mist" with which the "locks" are said to be drenched present us with more of a challenge, unschooled as we are in the allegorical method.

Still more obdurate are the lines that follow, spoken this time by the woman: "I have removed my tunic/ How shall I put it on?" What we should expect to hear at this steamy juncture in the proceedings is *not* something along the lines of "I'm stripped and ready for action, and now you want me to

---

23. Actually, the Hebrew term *qĕwûssôtay*, which Pope translates as "my locks," can be rendered more simply as "my hair."

get dressed again?" The latter part of the verse, however, is less enigmatic: "I have washed my feet/ How shall I soil them?" Pope remarks: "In view of the well-known use of 'feet' as a euphemism for genitals, the language is at least suggestive" (1977, 515). He adds: "The language of the lady may represent a bit of coy pretense intended to tease the eager male" (1977, 515). "Coy," however (which my dictionary defines as "Shrinking modestly or coquettishly from familiarity; shy; demure…"), is hardly the adjective that leaps to my mind to describe a statement that might be paraphrased as: "I have washed my pussy, and now you want me to get it messy again?" But now we encounter our biggest problem yet. The next seven lines of the poem seem to be out of sequence. We should expect "I rose to 'open' for my love," followed by "I 'opened' to my love," climaxing in "My love thrust his 'hand' into the 'hole,'" but that is not what we have here, the thrusting of the "hand" into the "hole" mysteriously preceding any "opening" whatsoever on the part of the "hole."

Certain of the remaining details, however, have been ably handled by yet another new allegorist. Undeterred by contextual inconveniences, Lyle Eslinger has snatched the baton from Pope and pushed the hyperheterosexual reading of the passage to unprecedented extremes. First he picks up Pope's interpretation of Song 8:8–9. This passage reads:

> We have a little sister, and she has no breasts.
> What shall we do for our sister, on the day
> when she is spoken for?
> If she is a wall, we will build upon her a
> battlement of silver; but if she is a door,
> we will enclose her with boards of cedar. (RSV)

At issue here is the girl's virginity, Pope suspects. Her family's concern is "to keep her closed until the proper time for opening" (1977, 680). This provides Eslinger with the opening *he* needs, however: "Given this explicit identification of the girl with a door, and the *double entendre* of 5.2–5, in which the door plays a central role, it is possible that the *kappôt hammanʿûl* of 5.5d may mean something besides 'the handles of the bolt' (RSV and Pope)" (1981, 275).

The exegetical footwork that follows resists easy summary, so I shall take the liberty of skipping ahead to Eslinger's conclusion. The seemingly innocent reference to "the handles of the bolt," expertly coaxed open by Eslinger, now parts to reveal a superlatively intimate part of female anatomy. At that moment the Song of Songs seems to shimmer, shift shape, and become—what? A hardcore centerfold spread, which teasingly transmutes into a gynecological illustration from an anatomical textbook (pornography always threatening to teeter over into anatomy, in any case, and vice versa). Any textbook in particular, though? Yes, *Cunningham's Manual of Practical Anatomy*, thirteenth edition, from which Eslinger extracts the following terms that, for him, uncover the secret meaning of the mysterious part-verse that he is probing: "Regarding the specific anatomical identity of the *kappôt hammanᶜûl* it is possible to suggest the vaginal vestibule and bulbs, along with the bulbospongiosus muscle as the locking or barring mechanism (*hammanᶜûl*) and the labia minora and majora as the plural appendages which together form the walls of the vulvic cavity" (1981, 276).

Eslinger's dramatic gesture of uncovering is a singularly electrifying example of that hyperheterosexual reading of the Song of Songs that I have termed the new allegorical reading. Yet it is a mere Hippolytan fragment,[24] casually whipped out en route to a rereading of some verses from Deuteronomy.[25] The "literal" reading of the Song, its reclamation from seventeen centuries of homoerotic exegesis and its transformation into an unmitigated celebration of heterosexual love and lust, is still in its infancy. The carnal interpretation of the Song still awaits its Origen.[26]

---

24. See n. 12 above.

25. Those in which Israel is sternly instructed to lop off the *kappâ* (traditionally translated "hand") of any woman so depraved as to presume to grab the crotch of a man who is beating her husband (Deut 25:11–12). Armed with his reading of Song 5:5, as well as of Gen 32:26, 33, Eslinger argues that *kappâ* here refers to the external female genitalia.

26. Although his advent may well be at hand. I refer to Roland Boer, whose hyper-risqué readings of the Song are beginning to trickle into print (1999b, 2000; cf. 1998). These readings are a major focus of the essay that follows.

11

UNSAFE SEX: FEMINISM, PORNOGRAPHY, AND THE SONG OF SONGS*

Co-authored with Virginia Burrus

During my early years at Drew Theological School, I team-taught "Gender and Sexuality in the Bible and Early Christianity" with my colleague in early church history, Virginia Burrus. The Song of Songs was one of the more pleasant rest stops on the mad dash from Genesis to Augustine that was that overly ambitious course. Thus it was that I discovered that Virginia had many things to say about the Song that I had not thought to think. Out of that collegial dialogue the following collaboration emerged.

It was a propitious period in Song of Songs scholarship. The second feminist essay collection on the Song had recently appeared (Brenner and Fontaine 2000), along with other important and provocative work on sex and gender in the book. Virginia and I resolved to co-write an article that would presuppose "The Song of Songs in the History of Sexuality," but only in order to press beyond it by meticulously teasing out the implications of certain queer construals of the Song (notably that of Roland Boer [1999b, 2000]) for certain feminist construals of the Song (notably the tradition flowing from the pioneering work of Phyllis Trible [1978c]) and vice versa.

The article's original abstract is perhaps worth quoting in full, as it may serve to focus the argument of what is, I suspect, frequently a dense and demanding read:

> How should the Song of Songs be read? As that rarest of biblical texts, one that gives voice to female desire in the context

---

* Originally published in *Biblical Interpretation* 11 (2003): 24–52.

of a sexual relationship characterized by equality and mutuality rather than domination and submission? Or as yet another vehicle for male pornographic fantasy and sexual aggression? Attempting to shift the (dualistic) terms of this burgeoning debate on the Song, this article explicitly situates itself at the intersection of feminist and queer theories, focusing especially on s/m eroticism as a site where these theories forcefully collide and delicately collude, and arguing that feminist and queer politics can ill-afford to exclude each other.

This was a project that I would not have had the capacity—or the courage—to attempt on my own. As with the other co-authored essays in this collection, I am grateful for the reciprocal ventriloquism of collaborative authorship that enabled me to say more than I knew and mean more than I said.

The Joy of Sex

The attempts of ancient and medieval commentators on the Song of Songs to evade the carnal embrace of its female lover through allegorical exposition merely had the effect of plunging them instead into the arms of another lover, a male lover, God or Christ.[1] With astonishing ease, these austere male interpreters were seduced by the Song into whispering Shulamith's white-hot words of passion into the ear of the divine male personage in whose muscular arms they had eagerly taken refuge. Allegorical exegesis of the Song thereby became a sanctioned space, or stage, for some decidedly queer performances.

Eventually, however, commentary on the Song began to recoil from allegory. Late nineteenth- and early twentieth-century exegetes labored manfully to straighten out the queer reading to which the Song had so long been subjected, a task arguably made imperative by the recent invention and rapid dissemination of heterosexuality. Thus it was that the Song was transformed into a celebration of, indeed a warrant for, heterosexual love and marriage. As early as 1875, Franz Delitzsch was able to announce: "The Song transfigures natural but holy love. Whatever in the sphere of the divinely-ordered marriage relation makes love the happiest, firmest bond uniting two souls

---

1. The first two paragraphs of the present essay are a précis of the previous essay, "The Song of Songs in the History of Sexuality."

together, is presented to us here in living pictures" (1980 [1875], 5).[2] Similar assertions proliferated in the decades that followed and echo intermittently down to the present.[3]

But it was not only from within the sanctum of biblical scholarship or the bosom of the church that the conjugal interpretation of the Song sounded forth. It also found unexpected expression in Julia Kristeva's 1983 essay on the lovers of the Song, which nestles snugly in her *Histoires d'amour*, side by side with similar essays on other notable lovers, not least Don Juan and Romeo and Juliet. With regard to the interpretation of the Song, argues Kristeva, "[i]t is probably of prime importance that we are dealing with conjugal love" (1987a [1983], 98). Her conjugal exposition of the Song achieves full expression in "A Wife Speaks," the concluding section of her essay:

> She, the wife, for the first time ever, begins to speak before her king, husband, or God; to submit to him, granted. But as an amorous loved one. It is she who speaks and sets herself up as equal, in her legal, named, unguilty love, to the other's sovereignty. The amorous Shulamite is the first woman to be sovereign before her loved one. Through such hymn to the love of the married couple, Judaism asserts itself as a first liberation of women. By virtue of being subjects: loving and speaking. The Shulamite, by virtue of her lyrical, dancing, theatrical language, and by the adventure that conjugates a submission to legality and the violence of passion, is the prototype of the modern individual. Without being queen, she is sovereign through her love and the discourse that causes it to be. Limpid, intense, divided, quick, upright, suffering, hoping, the wife—a woman—is the first common individual who, on account of her love, becomes the first Subject in the modern sense of the term. (1987a, 99–100)

The popular perception of Kristeva as a doyenne of "French feminist theory" is doubtless partly misleading, given the complexity of her relationship to feminism as ordinarily understood, a complexity spectacularly in evidence in the passage just quoted. For what the sentiments expressed therein seem to amount to—sentiments accentuated more than masked by Kristeva's soaring style and penchant for hyperbole—is a version of "love patriarchalism," lightly secularized: legally subject to her husband, the wife is nonetheless equal to him in love—and that is all the "liberation" she requires. Swimming blithely against the current of two decades of feminist criticism and activism, Kristeva

---

2. Declarations such as Delitzsch's went hand-in-glove with the interpretation of the Song as a series of ancient Hebrew wedding songs, which also made its appearance in the late nineteenth century.

3. See the further quotations assembled on pp. 237–38 above.

here implicitly extols heterosexual marriage as the generative matrix of emancipated female subjectivity.

Kristeva is also defiant, or perhaps merely innocent, of the scholarly consensus that, by the time she writes, has stripped the Song of its traditional matrimonial framework and reconstrued it instead as a paean to unmarried love and lust, with no wedding veil in sight and no apparent intent to procreate. The feminist trajectory in this general swerve in critical discourse on the Song is furthermore characterized by an intense emphasis on the essential equality of its male and female protagonists—an unqualified equality, not hedged in by hierarchy, and hence distinct from the kind celebrated by Kristeva. Alicia Ostriker, indeed, in a footnote to her contribution to the second *Feminist Companion to the Song of Songs*, chastises Kristeva roundly for her "palpable misreadings" of the Song, which seem "dependent not only on Kristeva's view of the lover as 'king, husband, or God,' but on her assumption that an amatory relationship is necessarily a submissive one" (Ostriker 2000, 49 n. 26). For Ostriker, in contrast, "What is extraordinary in the Song is precisely the absence of structural and systemic hierarchy, sovereignty, authority, control, superiority, submission, in the relation of the lovers" (49–50). And again: "the Song is, in effect, the quintessence of the non-patriarchal.... It includes no representation of hierarchy or rule, no relationship of dominance and submission, and (almost) no violence" (43). Ostriker's claims are by no means unique; rather, they echo a refrain that has resounded through decades of feminist commentary on the Song, beginning, it seems, with Phyllis Trible's contention that in the Song "there is no male dominance, no female subordination, and no stereotyping of either sex" (1978c, 161).[4]

What assumptions regarding sex and sexuality undergird this and similar assertions in Trible's "Love's Lyrics Redeemed," her celebrated essay on the Song? Trible's curiously ambiguous stance on the marital status of the lovers of the Song provides a promising point of departure for our reflections. On the one hand, Trible *explicitly* represents the lovers as an unmarried couple: "Never is this woman called a wife, nor is she required to bear children. In fact, to the issues of marriage and procreation the Song does not speak" (1978c, 162). On the other hand, Trible *implicitly* represents the lovers of the Song as being in a relationship that exemplifies marriage as it was meant to be—an effect of her primary strategy of reading the Song against the backdrop of Gen 2–3. "[T]he Song of Songs redeems a love story gone awry," she argues, namely, that of the

---

4. For similar claims, see the catena of quotations assembled in Exum 1998, 227. Exum quotes Athalya Brenner, Marcia Falk, Julia Kristeva, Carol Meyers, and Renita Weems, in addition to Trible. Carey Ellen Walsh might also be added to the list (see Walsh 2000, esp. 4).

second Genesis creation account. In consequence, she repeatedly represents the lovers of the Song as a prelapsarian Adam and Eve:

> Born to mutuality and harmony, a man and a woman live in a garden where nature and history unite to celebrate the one flesh of sexuality. Naked without shame or fear..., this couple treat each other with tenderness and respect. Neither escaping nor exploiting sex, they embrace and enjoy it. Their love is truly bone of bone and flesh of flesh, and this image of God male and female is indeed very good.... Testifying to the goodness of creation, then, eroticism becomes worship in the context of grace. (1978c, 161)

And again:

> In the end she [the woman of the Song] speaks directly and only to her lover, the bone of her bone and the flesh of her flesh. The man of Genesis 2 once left his father and mother to cleave to his woman (v. 24); now the woman of the Song bids her lover to make haste, and in this bidding all others are left behind. The circle of intimacy closes in exclusion when two become one. (1978c, 152)

Similar sentiments continue to echo in feminist commentary. Introducing the first *Feminist Companion to the Song of Songs*, a collection that included "Love's Lyrics Redeemed," Athalya Brenner announces matter-of-factly, "The primary subject matter of the SoS is earthy enough—heterosexual love and its erotic manifestations" (1993, 28). The ensuing decade, which saw the rapid proliferation and dissemination of queer theory, might be thought to have rendered such assertions problematic.[5] Yet even in the second *Feminist Companion to the Song of Songs*, which appeared seven years after the first volume, the Song continues to be read unselfconsciously through the prism of an unproblematized heterosexuality. "I first sat down to read the Song of Songs as a teenager, for a high school English class," Alicia Ostriker recalls, in an essay written specially for the second volume. "I had no trouble understanding it. The unutterably sweet words seemed to come not from outside but from within myself, as if my most intimate truth were projected onto the screen of the page" (2000, 36). Here and in the longer passage from which this quotation is extracted, the Song is construed as a series of erotic love lyrics in

---

5. The huge and heterogeneous body of work associated with the term *queer theory* (influential early examples included Foucault 1978; Butler 1990; Sedgwick 1990; de Lauretis 1991) has tended overwhelmingly to be social constructionist in thrust, arguing that neither heterosexuality nor homosexuality are transhistorical essences but instead are historical formations of relatively recent vintage.

which a man and a woman give spontaneous expression to an innate sexual orientation that encapsulates the essence, indeed the truth, of their inmost identities as gendered subjects—which is simply another way of saying that the Song is here assumed to be a consummate expression of heterosexual love and desire and that heterosexuality itself is correspondingly assumed to be a transhistorical constant rather than a historical construct, a constructedness that Ostriker's essay fails to register: although the adult Ostriker marks her distance from the adolescent Ostriker by noting the "rapt innocence" of the latter's reading of the Song (2000, 36), the mature reading that she proceeds to offer is scarcely less affirming of a timeless and idealized heterosexuality than the adolescent reading. Trible's take on the Song invites a similar critique. Like Ostriker, Trible does not explicitly employ the terms "heterosexual" or "heterosexuality" in her essay; one might well argue nonetheless that what the essay implicitly celebrates is heterosexual love epitomized by marriage—argue, moreover, that Trible tacitly represents the Song as the charter document of heterosexuality itself, by shuffling it with the myth of sexual origins in Gen 2–3 and enabling it to trump and displace the latter.

In the wider domain of feminist theory and criticism, heterosexuality has long been suspected of enshrining an eroticization of gender inequality.[6] In light of such concerns, what are we to make of the efforts, not just of Trible, but of an entire "school" of feminist commentary on the Song, to read it, from within the unproblematized horizon of a transhistorical heterosexuality, as the model expression of an erotics of gender *equality*? What else but an attempted redemption, if not an outright reinvention, of heterosexual sex?[7] Implicit

---

6. So strong is the perceived link between heterosexuality and sexism that much so-called "second wave" feminism has been characterized by a theoretical and political tendency to equate (some version of) lesbianism and feminism. As an early example, consider the "radicallesbians" manifesto, which proclaimed that the essence of being a "woman" is to "get fucked by men" and issued a consequent call to refuse "femininity" as an irretrievably patriarchal construction in favor of a woman-centered sociality and identity (radicallesbians 2004 [1970]). Compare Monique Wittig: "'Woman' has meaning only in heterosexual systems of thought and heterosexual economic systems. Lesbians are not women" (1992, 32). Or consider Adrienne Rich's term "the lesbian continuum," by which she means "to include a range—through each woman's life and throughout history—of woman-identified experience, not simply the fact that a woman has had or consciously desired genital sexual experience with another woman" (1986, 51). The rather more "ascetic" antiporn position of Catharine MacKinnon (1989) stridently equates heterosex with gender oppression, without however envisioning the possibility of a "lesbian" escape.

7. Leo Bersani (1988, 215) discusses and critiques "the redemptive reinvention of sex" that underlies the agenda not only of most feminist (whether "lesbian" or "straight") theorizing about sex but also of much gay male theorizing about sex. As will become clear, we take his challenge seriously.

is a scathing critique of "unredeemed" heterosexual sex, which is to say of eroticized gender inequality—or of sex as ordinarily understood. Here, too, feminist scholarship on the Song reflects broader trends in feminist theory and criticism—for instance, Luce Irigaray's bold (and controversial) attempts, now spanning several decades and many books, at a radical reconception, both theoretical and practical, of "the encounter between woman and man, between women and men" (1996, 11). Yet there are hints of trouble in paradise. Introducing the second *Feminist Companion to the Song of Songs*, Carole Fontaine, in between noting how feminist biblical scholars have "appropriated this book as peculiarly their own" and asserting that "it would be hard to find a feminist scholar who does not share, cross-culturally and cross-every other way, some of our collective delight in reading this book," urges that we "allow ourselves the pleasures of reading as women on a topic that revels in sexuality (*however dismal the literal realities may be*)" (Fontaine 2000, 13, 15, emphasis added). If the phrase "reading as women" evokes an essentialism that is strategically deployed (if often also implicitly deconstructed) in feminist interventions that seek to open up a specifically "feminine" realm of culture or textuality, the parenthetical remark, with its evocation of a constrastingly bleak realm of "literal" sex, hints at the inherent difficulty and consequent fragility of a feminist heteroerotics centered on disciplined opposition to patriarchy and hierarchy. "There is a big secret about sex," queer critic Leo Bersani quips; "most people don't like it" (1988, 197). And, stereotypically, feminists are among those who like it least.

Now, pornography epitomizes the kind of sex that most people, feminist or not, claim to like least of all. The egalitarian erotics attributed to the Song by successive feminist critics has permitted a frankly literal reading of its sexual innuendos, while simultaneously preserving it from charges of being pornographic. Contrast the awkward predicament of a mainstream historical-critical exegete, such as Michael Goulder, who, traversing the Song without the benefit of this guardrail, worries audibly in his 1986 book, *The Song of Fourteen Songs*, that the details of his thoroughly sexual translations and interpretations reveal the Sublime Song to be nothing more "than a piece of high-class pornography" (1986, 79).[8] By the mid-1990s, however, David Clines is able to propose, without any apparent qualms, that pornography is precisely what the Song of Songs amounts to, emboldened as he is by the critical sensibility dubbed "ideological criticism" that by then has crystallized in Anglo-American biblical studies, so that unsightly aspects of a biblical text that hitherto might have occasioned embarrassed apologetics now become occasions for unabashed uncoverings:

---

8. See further pp. 240–41 above.

> I start again here from the assumption that we are dealing with a male text, and I am interested in how that text constructs the woman.... In the Song, the woman is everywhere constructed as the object of male gaze.... To her male spectators, the readers of the poem, of course, she cannot say, "Do not stare at me"; for she has been brought into existence precisely to be stared at, and the veil she would willingly cover herself with is disallowed by the poet's gaze. She has been the victim of male violence and anger (1.6), and she bears the marks of it on her face; and now the poet invites his readers to share his sight of the woman's humiliation. That is the very stuff of pornography. (1995c, 117–19; cf. Polaski 1997)[9]

At first, or even second, glance, Clines's reading of the Song, which, in effect, imputes an *exploitative* erotics to it, might seem to be worlds apart from the readings of Trible and other feminist interpreters who, with equal certainty, attribute an *egalitarian* erotics to it—and, to a degree that should not be simply elided, these readings *are* thoroughly at odds with each other. What they seem to share, however, is an unstated yet palpable set of assumptions about what constitutes "good sex," on the one hand, and "bad sex," on the other. "I have the suspicion," muses Clines, "that a work that came into the world as an erotic, perhaps pornographic, literature for the male taste proves ultimately to be irredeemable in polite society.... In a feminist age too, it will not do, for it cannot shake off all traces of the needs it was created to serve" (1995c, 113–14).

It is perhaps not surprising that "the strongest critique of sexual relations in the Song ... comes from men," as Cheryl Exum has remarked, whereas female commentators—elsewhere quick to denounce pornographic strains in the Hebrew Bible—have been markedly reluctant to pronounce "irredeemable" what "appears to be [the] final refuge" for readers who desire "to have an ancient book"—best of all a biblical book?—"that celebrates woman's equality and whose protagonist is an active, desiring autonomous [female] subject" (2000, 26). Exum cannily advises women not only to be willing to join men in the feminist critique of what may after all turn out to be yet another androcentric and misogynistic biblical text but also to continue to insist on their right to appropriate it positively, even through positive "misreadings" (2000, 35). But that "a feminist age" might actually have uses for the pornographic,

---

9. While Polaski does not explicitly label the Song "pornography," he does follow Clines in thoroughly depicting the woman as a construction of the male gaze. He goes beyond Clines, however, via Foucault, to argue that the woman has fully internalized the male gaze, that she "glories" in it, even (Polaski 1997, 74), and that she thereby becomes the agent of her own subjection: "The Shulammite has become her *own* watchman" (1997, 79, his emphasis).

even positive uses, is a possibility that apparently has not occurred to Exum any more than to Clines.

Indeed, it may well be that aversion to the pornographic reading, along with attraction to the heteronormative reading, is a virtually "irredeemable" feature of the modern interpretive tradition. Whereas the denial of carnality provided the condition for the queerly spiritualized eroticism of premodern readings of the Song, the repression of pornography is inherent to the frank "sexuality" of modern readings of it—feminist or otherwise. This is merely another way of saying that contemporary commentary on the Song is a late extension of the pivotal phenomenon that Michel Foucault locates in the late nineteenth century: a colossal "incitement to discourse" on sex, resulting in a veritable discursive explosion, *but all under the cover of a rhetoric of prohibition.* What emerges is "a censorship of sex" that is at the same time "an apparatus for producing an even greater quantity of discourse about sex" (Foucault 1978, 23). Through a proliferation of discourses, disciplines, technologies, and regimes of knowledge and power (not least among them, psychoanalysis), the modern individual is produced as a sexual subject, possessor of a "truth" about desire that remains nonetheless hidden, buried, in need of discovery, confession, release—or "liberation" (1978, 17–35).[10] Thus, "censorship" and "sexuality" are two sides of the same coin, and movements of "sexual liberation" frequently prove surprisingly continuous with the repressive discourses they claim to supersede—for, one way or another, sexuality has always been "liberating" itself.

"Sexuality," as Foucault understands it, is furthermore at the root of notions of sexual "identity" or "orientation," defined by the fundamental binary of hetero- versus homosexuality.[11] As Jonathan Katz argues, the "invention" of heterosexuality builds upon an earlier marital ideal of "true love" in such a way as to articulate the notion of a "sexual instinct" that is neither reducible to, nor altogether detachable from, the carnal instinct to reproduce, on the one hand, or the spiritual purity of disembodied love, on the other (1995, 40–51). The contradictions entailed in this irretrievably heteronormative notion of "sexuality" become particularly visible at the point of its perpetuation of a complementary, gendered division of sexual labor, in which woman is aligned with spirituality and ethics and man with fleshly desire. In this unstable context, the very existence of female desire is made tenuous, while sexuality itself remains shadowed by moral doubt (1995, 31–32).

---

10. Cf. Carr 2000, 235: "In place of general sexual repression, we have the specific story of the repression of the original erotic meaning of the Song. In place of more general sexual liberation, we have scholarly recovery of the original erotic meaning of the Song."

11. This perspective is developed more fully in Halperin 1990 and Katz 1995.

We are suggesting that feminist interpretation of the Song of Songs has successfully disrupted, but by no means cleanly "liberated" itself from, the modern ideology of heteronormativity, with its distinctive inflection of the ideal of "true love" as "an intense spiritual feeling powerful enough to justify marriage, reproduction, and an otherwise unhallowed sensuality" (1995, 44). Earlier we noted the intense gravitational pull that the ideology of heterosexual marriage exerts in Trible's pioneering feminist reading of the Song, notwithstanding her certainty that the relationship celebrated in the Song is not (yet?) a matrimonial one. In retrospect, Kristeva's take on the Song now seems less exceptional than it did at first glance, merely giving overt expression to the heterosexism that, potentially at least, finds covert expression in celebratory feminist readings of the Song.

But what of pornography? In relation to heterosexuality, pornography can be said to constitute a double sign. On the one hand, it is the sign of what is *excluded* by heterosexuality (epitomized by heteronormativity, with its teleologies of matrimony and/or monogamy). On the other hand, it is the sign for what is just barely *included* in heterosexualty—an "unhallowed sensuality." If pornography is a particular and extreme instance of the incitement to sexual discourse, liberating what is only constituted in the first place by repression,[12] *resistance* to pornographic readings will undeniably remain crucial to feminist strategy. Paradoxically, however, outright *censorship* of the pornographic may also prove problematic for feminist interpretations. This is especially the case for any feminism that seeks not to "reinvent" heterosexuality but rather to subvert or evade it—for example, by retrieving the eroticism of an ancient text, such as the Song of Songs, that predates both (modern) "sexuality" and (an equally modern) "pornography," that is other than heterosexual, yet also not homosexual, thereby eluding the hamfisted clutches of those dualistic categories altogether. Such is the interest motivating the current essay.

Only one contemporary commentator that we know of has seemed willing to disrupt the sexual orthodoxy (which is the orthodoxy of "sexuality" itself) that has dominated feminist scholarship on the Song. To his work we now turn.

The Pleasures of Perversity

Roland Boer's twin essays on the Song of Songs (1999b, 2000) veer between erudite expositions of arcane theory (Lacanian, mainly) and X-rated exegesis.[13]

---

12. Cf. Baudrillard 1987, 22: "Pornography is only the paradoxical limit of the sexual."
13. Also see Boer 1998, which, while it does not deal directly with the Song of Songs, is nevertheless closely aligned thematically with the other two essays.

For a typical blast of Boer's X-egesis (or should that be sexegesis?), consider his paraphrase of Song 2:8–17:

> Beth Rabbim and Leb Bannon make their appearance here. (*I haven't heard of them, but both of them have kinky reputations.*) It begins with a long tongue darting over Beth's very ample breasts, "leaping over the mountains, bounding over the hills" (2:8). As the camera pans out, somewhat shakily, the large pink nose and muzzle of a "gazelle" (2:9) come into view. Beth has her eyes closed and groans, enjoying the rough tongue of the animal. But now a "young stag" (2:9) walks over, sniffs Beth's face and then her cunt. Its huge cock is distended as it gazes at Beth's mons venus, pondering her interwoven pubes: "Look, there he stands behind our wall, gazing in at the windows, looking in at the lattice" (2:9). (*Oh my God, I think, he's not going to fuck her, is he?*) (1999b, 66, his emphasis)

Yes, he is, as it happens, although not as a stag but as a satyr, together with the gazelle, which has now undergone a similar metamorphosis; and the reader is spared no detail of their multipositional *ménage à trois*. Throughout this essay, indeed, scholars of the Song are afforded a rare opportunity to further expand their interdisciplinary expertise by acquainting themselves with the *termini technici* of the pornographic film industry—"the meat shot," "the money shot" ("Do we not also find the money shot in the Song?" [1999b, 60]), "getting wood," "the stunt cock," and so on—an opportunity that, however, will not be relished by all. Accustomed as we are to the vast vat of vanilla pudding that is conventional biblical scholarship, Boer's spicy sexegetical romp will send many of us scrambling for the disciplinary spittoon. Yet Boer's experiment should not be dismissed too quickly. Among other things, it constitutes a productive provocation for close reflection on feminism's relationship to the erotic in general, and the erotics of the Song of Songs in particular—a labor of reflection that Boer himself never really undertakes, however: he is particularly silent on the feminist trajectory of Song of Songs interpretation and the relationship of his own reading to it.

Boer's reading is distinguished not merely by the claim that the Song is pornographic (a position he shares with Clines), nor even solely by the extravagant terms in which he claims it ("the Song … is part of the invention of pornography" [1999b, 56]), but by his positive assessment of the Song *as* a pornographic text. Boer is presumably aware that his proporn reading invites double censorship from at least some feminist biblical scholars, first for denying them scarce biblical resources for a kinder, gentler sexuality, and second for *enjoying* it so much; but he is also aware that pornography—together with sadomasochism and other "perverse" sexual practices—has produced fierce public debates not only *with* but also (and perhaps more significantly) *within* feminism itself. At least since the "sex wars" of the 1980s, antiporn feminists who favor censorship have been knocking heads with sex radicals of various stripes, many also strongly aligned with feminism.[14] Feminism—scarcely a monolith as either a political or an intellectual phenomenon—has thus produced not only some of the toughest critiques of pornography but also some of the toughest critiques of censorship. "One would think," notes Lynda Hart wryly (echoing the sentiments of Gayle Rubin), "that women didn't join the feminist movement in order to have their sexual practices policed by feminists themselves" (1998, 47).

So it is that Boer can legitimately infer a feminist alliance for his own unabashedly pornographic exegetical project by citing feminist philosopher Judith Butler's critique of the position that pornography, like rape, is based on domination, and that all domination-based sexuality is inherently oppressive (Boer 1999b, 54–55; 1998, 152–53). That Butler herself is not only far from the positions of antiporn feminists as diverse as Catharine MacKinnon and Monique Wittig,[15] but is also herself critiqued by feminist proponents of (queer) s/m for having pathologized sadomasochistic practices even while opposing censorship (Hart 1998, 104–5), reminds us how complex, heterogeneous, and unstable are the recent discourses of feminism and sexuality, not least at their points of overlap and interaction. Among the important contributions of Boer's work on the Song is that it brings scholarship on the eroticism of this text for the first time to the perimeter of the contested and messy territory of feminist discourses on sex and sexuality, where purity proves elusive and pleasure is ever mingled with danger. As this is just the territory we wish to explore further, let us stay with Boer's commentary a little longer.

Upon the Song, Boer performs an analysis that is strategically pornographic, indeed hyper-pornographic, the pornographic, for him, being the privileged form of political opposition to censorship (1999b, 55; 1998, 153). Enacted at the edge of excess and beyond, Boer's whimsical X-egetical antics may, in the end, however, deliver not merely a "hyper-" but also a "failed" pornography, as Karmen MacKendrick (1999, 29) describes the Marquis de Sade's extravagant textual acts—and for many of the same honorable reasons.[16] Just as Boer's text shuttles between the numbing expanses of high theory and

---

14. An incisive political-historical account of the relevant debates within feminism is provided by Duggan and Hunter 1995. For a different angle, see Butler 1994.

15. See n. 6 above.

16. Sade, mediated by Lacan, features briefly in Boer's discussion of the relation of pain to sexual perversity in the Song (Boer 2000, 283). A subsequent essay by Boer (which does not, however, deal with the Song) accords Sade a more prominent role. Accompanied by Masoch, Deleuze, Freud, and Lacan, Sade participates in a decidedly queer symposium hosted by Yahweh himself (Boer 2001).

the eye-popping intimacy of the pornographic film loop, so too does Sade's text shuttle between scenes of graphic—well, *sadism*—and rambling, frequently numbing, discourses on philosophy and politics. "The philosophical reflections that intersperse [Sade's text] would make for *very* slow one-handed reading," as MacKendrick drily notes. Sade's text, read as pornography, is "self-subverting" because of the element of interruption, but also because of the element of repetition: "Sade's narrative climaxes are immediately irrelevant (it is only the next that matters)" (1999, 29, her emphasis). Boer's text, too, may be read as effectively disrupting the alternating sequence of frenzied build-up and orgasmic release typical of pornography. Boer's text, like Sade's, is itself an exceedingly slow one-handed read, not only because of the regular intrusion of dense theoretical interludes, but also because the sex comes so often and so fast, endlessly inventive yet relentlessly repetitious, peppered with itemized lists and logical permutations, and all so utterly undercontextualized as to leave even the Divine Marquis, himself possessed of scant patience in matters of contextualization, wholly in the shade. The taxonomic thrust of Boer's exegetical extravagances comes to a minimalistic climax—or rather a vertiginous series of successive mini-climaxes, enacted with machine-gun rapidity—near the conclusion of "The Second Coming":

> Apart from [its] incessant terminology of sex, the whole Song may also be read allegorically as a series of sexual episodes, a poetic porn text: group sex in 1:2–4; a male-female combination with some extras, including shepherds and a bestial phantasy, in 1:5–2:7; animals and humans in 2:8–17; a man with a dildo in 3:1–5; an ode to the phallus and a gay scene in 3:6–11; water sports, especially piss and ejaculate, between two females in 4:1–15; a female-male SM sequence in 4:16–5:9; queer savouring of a grotesque male body in 5:10–16; swinging in 6:1–3; a lesbian sequence in 6:4–12; group female scopophilia in 7:7/6–10/9; and an orgy in 8:1–14. (2000, 296–97)

In Boer's text, "too much happens too often," breeding not contempt so much as sheer exhaustion, as MacKendrick says of Sade's text (1999, 54), even when Boer's text does *not* read like the subject index of a sexological monograph. Boer's most draining sequence, perhaps, is the "Schlong of Schlongs" section of "Night Sprinkle(s)" (1999b, 64–70), an orgiastic XXX-travaganza that fills page after page, working its way tirelessly and systematically through every imaginable sexual act (with a couple of all-but-unimaginable acts tossed in for good measure).

Is this "authorial misstep," as feminist biblical scholar Alice Bach dubs the parallel sequence in Boer's "King Solomon Meets Annie Sprinkle," really "self-serving and icky" (Bach 1998, 303)? True, Boer's eroticism is excessive and nonteleological, and as such inefficient, not to say pointless—but that precisely *is* the point, we might answer Bach on Boer's behalf (although without denying that she, too, has a point). Calculated misstep is the technique by which Boer's text begins to exceed and thereby escape the repressive regime of heteronormative sexuality—of which pornography is a notable, but by no means necessarily subversive, byproduct, we would argue (at that point arguing both with *and* against Boer). In other words, by taking the pornographic reading to the point of "failure," Boer begins to succeed at productive perversity: ceasing merely to react, his commentary begins effectively to resist the Censor and the near-ubiquitous ideological apparatus that is ever at the latter's disposal.

Performing a "strong," even violent, reading of the Song as hyper-erotic literature, Boer tops the biblical text.[17] Like all good tops, he is a persuasive as well as a forceful partner.[18] Like all good bottoms, the Song resists even as it surrenders to his will.[19] The Song of Songs is indeed a perverse text, it seems to us. Its excessive eroticism, like that of Boer's commentary, runs counter to the conventionally pornographic—yet it does so differently. If in Boer's pornographic rescripting of the Song "too much happens too often," in the Song itself, one might say, "nothing ever happens at all, leaving the reader in a constant ... state of suspense"—as MacKendrick describes Leopold von Sacher-Masoch's languid erotic opus *Venus in Furs*. "The point is not merely to avoid climax," she continues; "Masoch's characters ... deliberately arouse their desires and delight in this arousal," but only the better to "enjoy their own frustration" (1999, 54). They are thus "at a significant remove" from the gratification-greedy individuals conjured up by antiporn polemic "who cannot tolerate ... the frustration of being told no" (1999, 61).[20] Looked at from the bottom, indeed, the Song of Songs begins to seem surprisingly akin to Masoch's magnum opus: presenting a slowly shifting, subtly repetitious series of elaborately described scenes that fire anticipation, the Song also curtails conventional narrative momentum and frustrates the readerly desire for narrative consumption, saturating the text instead with the perverse pleasure of prolonged suspense. That the Song goes nowhere, ultimately, has been recognized by numerous commentators, including some as ideologically at odds

---

17. Elsewhere he seems to prefer to play the bottom (see Boer 2001, 80 n. 1).

18. Cf. MacKendrick 1999, 129: "Intensity requires making others want the pain imposed on them, without its ceasing to be painful."

19. For the masochist, pain and restraint "entail an exceptionally forceful enhancement of the always unexpected resistant power of the body, specifically a resistance to the seemingly irresistible disciplinary power of contemporary culture." Conversely, "to (try to) top to no response is to expend one's force into a void" (MacKendrick 1999, 101, 128).

20. See the handsome reprint of Masoch's *Venus in Furs* issued alongside Gilles Deleuze's theoretical essay "Coldness and Cruelty," in Deleuze and Sacher-Masoch 1989.

as Julia Kristeva and Alicia Ostriker. Kristeva observes how the lovers of the Song "do not merge but are in love with the other's absence" (1987a, 89), while Ostriker notes that, "Notwithstanding the efforts of generations of commentators to impose a coherent narrative plot on the Song, it goes nowhere and ends without closure" (2000, 47). Carey Ellen Walsh argues, "The Song's importance as a book is in its voicing of desires unconsummated.... Not having this couple consummate is the point and the power of this book" (2000, 34–35). Ariel Bloch and Chana Bloch, for their part, remark that, "Despite the brothers and watchmen, the Song has none of the dark complication of many familiar love stories. For Romeo and Juliet, love is wedded to loss and death; for Tristan and Isolde, or for Heathcliff and Catherine, love itself is a form of suffering.... But ... the lovers in the Song exhibit few of the usual symptoms. They don't suffer love, they savor it" (1995, 7). Or perhaps they merely savor suffering.

Ceasing to react either with or against pornography, our reading thus sets foot in the slippery territory that MacKendrick dubs the "counterpleasures." These pleasures, which resist rather than oppose, she defines as ones "that queer our notion of pleasure, consisting in or coming through pain, frustration, refusal. They are pleasures of exceptional intensity, refusing to make sense while still demanding a philosophical unfolding.... They are pleasures that refuse the sturdy subjective center, defying one's own survival, promising the death not of the body but, for an impossible moment, of the subject" (1999, 8). What possible spaces might feminism occupy in the death of the subject achieved through complex and subtle practices of perversity? This is a question we must ask and ask again. The answers will necessarily be partial, and partly unsatisfying, for the counterpleasures by their very nature pursue their goals—political as well as erotic—only by indirect routes; their structure is such as to thwart teleology at every turn. They cannot, in other words, simply be a feminist *tool*, but they may be a feminist *ally*. For feminists, there can no replacement for (supersession of) the opposition to patriarchy or (hetero)sexism. But opposition has its limits, its entrapments even. Allied to feminism, the counterpleasures may enable it to resist, not only its own internal orthodoxies (the inevitable by-product of opposition), but also the multiple hierarchies that—diversely—constrain female subjects from without. As performative or ritual practices (overlapping complexly with liturgy and asceticism), the counterpleasures may serve feminist ends by exposing, intensifying, parodying, displacing, and dislodging obdurate relations of power inscribed within gender (but not only gender)—techniques akin to the "consciousness-raising" and cathartic therapies long familiar to feminism, but a feminism here driven to acknowledge more deeply the inevitable and inextricable entanglement of all human relationality in asymmetrical dynamics of power.

The feminist trajectory of Song of Songs interpretation that can be said to stem from Phyllis Trible's "Love's Lyrics Redeemed" represents, in essence, a denial of these dynamics—a denial, that is, of the ubiquity of power relations in human transactions—through a utopian reinvention of sex itself as characterized by absolute equality and mutuality. That the blueprint for such a reinvention should turn up in the Bible, of all places, is a tribute to Trible's exegetical ingenuity. But how might the Song appear were it read as a text of counterpleasure instead?

THE WOUNDS OF LOVE

The Song of Songs *bottoms out* at 5:6–7:

> I opened to my beloved,
> but my beloved had turned and gone.
> My soul failed me when he spoke.
> I sought him, but found him not;
> I called him, but he gave no answer.
> The watchmen found me, as they went about in the city;
> they beat me, they wounded me,
> they took away my mantle,
> those watchmen of the walls.

This sequence reopens and repeats 3:2–4, but whereas the earlier scene ended with a meeting ("scarcely had I passed them [the watchmen], when I found him whom I love"—3:4), the later scene ends with a beating. Nowhere has this beating received more sustained scrutiny than in Fiona Black and Cheryl Exum's "Semiotics in Stained Glass: Edward Burne-Jones's Song of Songs" (1998). The stained glass of the title, which constituted the visual incitement for their reflections, is a window depicting the Song of Songs designed by the British Pre-Raphaelite artist Edward Burne-Jones, which they discovered in the medieval church of Saint Helen in Darley Dale, Derbyshire. Burne-Jones selected twelve scenes from the Song to represent it, one of which is the beating scene: a burly watchman has gripped the woman roughly by the wrist and forced her to the ground (alternatively, he has already flattened her and is now dragging her to her feet); clenched in his other fist is a lantern, which he has thrust into her face—although the lantern is not readily visible to the viewer, as Black and Exum note, so that at first glance his fist rather seems raised to smash her in the face. Black and Exum observe how critical commentators on the Song have long been stumped by this seemingly gratuitous beating; either they pass over it in silence or offer unconvincing explanations for its presence.

Black and Exum do not attempt to conceal their own disquiet at Burne-Jones's representation of the scene, barely ameliorated by the fact that, in their view, the artist has balked at depicting the scene in all its bloody brutality: in the stained-glass panel the woman is not "wounded," nor is she in any immediate danger from her attacker's fists, one of which grips her wrist, as we said, while the other clutches the lantern (Black and Exum 1998, 337–38).[21] Yet their assessment of the window's impact—its punch, if you will—is, in the end, an ambiguously positive one:

> Burne-Jones's window has sent us back to the source text with a heightened sense of the disruptive power of these details for traditional sanguine readings of this text. What would happen to the place of honour held by the biblical Song of Songs if, rather than suppressing these recalcitrant details, we foregrounded them? (1998, 342)

What, indeed? "What Burne-Jones's window has most impressed upon us is the importance of a counterreading of the biblical text," they continue" (1998, 342)—and they carry us to the brink of such a counterreading, although it is perhaps more ours than theirs.

"Song 3.1–5 and 5.2–8 are commonly referred to as dream sequences," they earlier noted, "because they both begin with the woman in her bed at night; but the text never states that she is dreaming and it is quite possible to imagine that she is lying in bed awake, thinking about her lover" (1998, 339 n. 57).[22] She is fantasizing, then, but what is she fantasizing about? "[W]hy would the woman's fantasy about her lover's approach and her response, already aborted when her lover disappears, continue to the point of violence to the dreamer? Is this a woman's fantasy, the kind of dream a woman would have…?" The implied answer is no, one suspects. They continue: "or is it—and the entire biblical Song—a male fantasy representing what a male author might like to think a woman dreams about?" (1998, 339–40). One simi-

---

21. Black returns to the window and its beating scene in a more recent essay (2001), in which she allies a "counter-coherent" strategy of reading to the Kristevan concept of the disordering "abject" in such a way as to foreground the complex textual disturbance effected by the watchmen's beating: if the woman's search disrupts order, so also does the violence of her repression, and the scene remains unsettled and unsettling.

22. Walsh (2000, 113) takes this line of speculation to its logical climax: "This passage, in essence, is a biblical wet dream of a woman. It is also an allusion to autoeroticism, the Bible's sole scene of masturbation, with the woman's hand and fingers involved, dripping with her own wetness, and the man vanishing. This copious moistness and repeated opening is the woman's desire and probable climax. The description of dripping fingers, followed by still silence, is a not-too-cloaked reference to a woman's orgasm."

larly suspects that, for Black and Exum, this is the more likely option. But what sort of man might be disposed to suppose or imagine that a woman dreams or fantasizes about being beaten by men? Black and Exum do not feel a need to be specific. Instead, they conclude with a telling question: "Is our inability to account for this scene a result of our unwillingness to consider what is most disturbing about it?" (1998, 34). What precisely is it that haunts the shadows of Black and Exum's text and, by extension, the margins of their Song of Songs, a text they resolutely refuse to reduce to a light-filled tale of romantic love? "[T]his picture of a man attacking a woman is difficult to negotiate," they remark at one point (1998, 337). Would it be doubly difficult to negotiate— all but impossible, indeed, within the dominant feminist trajectory of Song of Songs interpretation—were the picture to be construed instead, through a blissful act of willful misreading, to be the oblique representation of a specific woman's insistent desire to suffer physical pain at the hands of a man (or another woman)? Would it be any less difficult to negotiate if, through a further act of interpretive violence, impelled by desire, it were somehow transmuted so as to become a still more oblique representation of a specific *man's* desire to suffer physical agony at the hands of a woman (or another man)—or, rather, under her (or his) heel, preferably stiletto and tipped with steel?

Again, Roland Boer rushes in where biblical feminists (sensibly?) fear to tread. In the "Schlong of Schlong's" section of "Night Sprinkle(s)," Boer rewrites the Song as a screenplay for a porn video, as we noted earlier. As it happens, he represents Song 5:2–7 as an s/m scene, helpfully providing the bondage ropes that the text apparently omitted to mention: "'the sentinels found' her, tied her up, 'beat' her and 'wounded' her, leaving her without her 'mantle'" (5:7). "The S/M of fisting ['he thrust his hand into the hole'—5:5] has given way to that of bondage, beating and pain"—all of which elicits a parenthetical question from Boer's narrator: "*Is this coerced domination or the desired and pleasurable dynamic of power? It is hard to tell*" (1999b, 69, his emphasis). Yet the beating is only one of two elements that, in Boer's mind, seemingly, qualify this scene for the X-rated s/m sticker. The denial of the object of desire is, apparently, the other element. Following Sue Lammith's fisting by Frank Incense—"his hand moving back and forth inside her" stimulates "an ecstacy reminiscent of the ultimate orgasm of childbirth"—we read: "The S/M tendency of this scene develops further, for as she 'opened to [her] beloved' he 'turned and was gone,'" eliciting a further parenthetical aside from Boer's narrator: "*OK, I was mentally leafing through my Lacan, finding the place on the insatiability of desire*" (1999b, 69, his emphasis).[23] This second

---

23. Insatiability, compulsive repetition, and nonclosure are themes that Boer develops further in "The Second Coming" (2000).

element—the indefinite withholding of the object of desire—is especially important, it seems to us, for the scene in question, encapsulating a theme that, arguably, permeates the entire Song, and concludes it although without concluding: as we have already noted, the Song goes nowhere, ultimately, and ends without closure. Arguably, too, this theme itself encapsulates the erotic economy of s/m, which is actually a countereconomy: s/m subverts heteronormative lack-based economies of desire, as the point is no longer to "get" what you "lack"—whether it be the phallus, a baby, or even your orgasm—not to "get" anything or anywhere, in fact, but rather to continue to *want*, ever more intensely, ever more insistently, and hence ever more pleasurably.[24]

Boer's (passing) construal of the second watchmen scene in terms of an erotics of denial is, however, not unprecedented—and not because some other postmodernist chanced upon the reading before him. One needs to backtrack a little further than that. At least one notable fourth-century interpreter seems to have actively enjoyed this scene from the bottom. For Gregory of Nyssa, the "sadomasochistic" moment in the text becomes an interpretive key to the Song's larger meaning, unlocking the infinite mysteries of divine eros. Like the smitten woman (or so he imagines), Gregory knows that pain and ecstasy coincide in desire and that the only true goal for a lover is found in love's unending detours and deferrals; thus the most violent frustration of desire—the searching "bride's" stripping, beating, and wounding—is reconceived by him as the source of the soul's deepest pleasure. Gregory not only rejoices in the agony of his own unfulfilled desire; he actively wills that the pain be intensified. "Perhaps these may seem to some to be the words of one who grieves rather than of one who rejoices—'they beat' and 'they wounded' and 'they took away my veil'; but if you consider the meaning of the words carefully, you will see that these are utterances of one who glories greatly in the most beautiful things" (*Hom.* 12.1359).[25] With her veil removed, the soul can at last see clearly, and the beating, in the course of which she is stripped of her obscuring veil, is thus "a good thing," he assures us (going on to compile a list of biblical beatings that might make Sade himself salivate; *Hom.* 12.1361–1362). "The soul that looks up towards God and conceives that good desire for his eternal beauty constantly experiences an ever new yearning for that which lies ahead,

---

24. Cf. MacKendrick 1999, 126: "In the everyday (nonecstatic) economy of investment, expenditure is loss (and desire is lack, founded upon the need to fill what is empty, replace what is lost). This is precisely the economy of productivity, the teleological economy found in the security of the center."

25. Our readings of Gregory's homilies on the Song of Songs are based on the Greek text provided in Dünzl 1994. Where available, we have followed the partial English translation of the homilies found in Musurillo 1961.

and her desire is never given its full satisfaction" (*Hom.* 12.1366), he declares serenely, thereby leaving the yearning woman to wander the dark streets and alleyways *ad infinitum*, confident that the watchmen, like stern guardian angels, will find her and whip her, again and again—and this too is "a good thing." "In this way she is, in a certain sense, wounded and beaten because of the frustration of what she desires." But "the veil of her grief is removed when she learns that the true satisfaction of her desire consists in constantly going on with her quest and never ceasing in her ascent, seeing that every fulfillment of her desire continually generates another desire for the transcendent" (*Hom.* 12.1369–1370).

The erotics of deferral are by no means confined, however, to the second watchmen scene in Gregory's reading of the Song. They feature still more intensely in Song 2, as he interprets it (*Hom.* 4). "Stay me with sweet oils, fill me with apples: for I am wounded by love. His left hand is under my head, and his right hand embraces me," chants the woman (2:5–6). Gregory takes this to mean that the bride has been wounded by the divine groom's dart of desire. "O beautiful wound and sweet beating!" she exclaims. Pricked by the potent arrow and infected with insatiable desire, she herself *becomes* an arrow: the divine archer's right hand draws her near to him, while his left hand directs her head toward the heavenly target (*Hom.* 4.127–129). Making his way to the end of Song 2, Gregory notes that the bride seeks a place of repose "in the cleft of the rock" (*Hom.* 6.178; cf. Song 2:14). This image merges with an earlier one in the same chapter of the bridegroom as an apple tree into whose shade the bride has entered (v. 3), evoking for Gregory Moses' theophanic climax in "the cleft of the rock" (Exod 33:22; cf. 20:21), which in turn facilitates his rescripting of the apple-tree scene as wedding-night lovemaking, replayed and thereby prolonged (on his reading) in the first watchmen scene of Song 3:1–4: "thinking to achieve that more perfect participation in her union with the divine Spouse," she finds herself, "just as Moses [was]," enveloped in the secret inner space of a sacred darkness (*Hom.* 6.181).[26] Subtle gender ambiguities and reversals (the bride as arrow resting in the bridegroom's cleft) are thus overlain by a queer image of Moses penetrating God's cleft, which then renders the original exchange (between bride and bridegroom) queerer still, as Gregory interprets the bride's experience "in the cleft" as a surprise honeymoon encounter with an unexpectedly feminine lover who teasingly leaves her ravenous for yet more heavenly delights. "Far from attaining perfection, she has not even begun to approach it," Gregory asserts (*Hom.* 6.181),

---

26. This is not the only time that Gregory invokes the cleft in the rock of Exod 33:22 to supplement his reading of Moses' entry into the "darkness" of God in Exod 20:21; see his *Life of Moses* 2.230 (discussed in Burrus 2000, 127–28, 130).

in seeming admiration at the divine top's consummate skills. Immortality, for Gregory, is undying desire; and so the desire that suffuses the Song, on his reading of it, can only be the kind that does not admit of satiation. Ultimately, Gregory traces out the dim contours of a *theological* reading of the Song from the bottom, a mode of reading to which we shall return in our final section.

For now, however, we need to come to terms with the fact that even with Gregory's bottom-hugging reinscription of the Song's erotics, we are, admittedly, still within the realm of "a male fantasy representing what a male author might like to think a woman dreams about" (to echo Black and Exum's qualm about the Song itself, specifically its beating scene). But it is a "male" fantasy radically destabilized in its maleness. For Gregory, "Shulamith, c'est moi": her violent dreams or fantasies (if that indeed is what they are) are his own, and he imagines himself not on the giving but on the receiving end of the watchman's stick—even as he *also* imagines that he, however feminized, may subsequently become an arrow directed toward a male lover's "cleft." Not bad for a "church father," perhaps, yet Black and Exum's question, originally addressed to the Song's beating scene, still presses insistently: "Is this a *woman's* fantasy, the kind of dream a *woman* would have?" They mean a "real" woman, presumably.[27] For if, as we have already noted, the implied answer is no, this is surely *not* because Black and Exum are ignorant of the fact that certain women *do* fantasize about being physically overpowered, even about being beaten, but rather because they think it would be better if they didn't. Nevertheless, it is worth asking back: Why shouldn't the text become *less*, not more, disturbing when the beating is represented *as* a fantasy, and a woman's fantasy as that (or even a queerly femme Father's)?

If it may be argued that the feminist policing of women's daydreams seems even more bizarre than the feminist policing of female sexuality more generally, it must also be acknowledged that Black and Exum are in good company in worrying about the insidious psychological effects of graphic images of male domination and female submission. Women who take pleasure in fantasies of erotic violence, whether such women be casual consumers of bodice-ripping romances or serious practitioners of sadomasochistic sex, have consistently concerned and scandalized liberal feminism. Actively enjoying what, some would argue, are internalized renditions of their own abjectness under patriarchy, such women have appeared to be perpetrators of patriarchy as well as its victims. Yet the power of fantasy not only to affect but even to constitute reality should not be underestimated (see Hart 1998, 17–18). By taking female

---

27. Cf. Lynda Hart's critique of Leo Bersani's appropriation of the feminine for purposes of the privileged inscription (or, rather, the privileged "shattering") of a (gay) male subjectivity (Hart 1998, 87–91).

fantasies of erotic violence seriously, we may come less to fear their potential for passively shoring up an oppressive sexual status quo than to acknowledge their capacity to subvert it actively from within. The patriarchal sexual order is, arguably, already disrupted when a woman constructs herself as an actively desiring subject, even if—*perhaps especially if*—what she desires is a good beating. Within the terms of a Freudian psychoanalytic theory suspiciously complicit in the formation of heterosexuality, a girl accomplishes the difficult process of becoming a "woman" in part by sublimating fantasies of violence into fantasies of tender affection, thereby accepting her culturally prescribed role as guardian of the hearth of civilization. Should feminism not, then, have some place for "girls" who refuse to become "real women"—that is, "women" the way men like to imagine them (see Hart 1998, 22–31)? At issue here is the potential, indeed the propensity, of erotic fantasy not merely to resemble but also dissemble, and thereby reassemble, reality, engaging in a transgressive mimicry rather than a compliant mimesis.[28]

Yet the line between the female masochist and the battered woman may continue to blur troublingly—as though it were actually impossible to distinguish in the end between a woman whose rapist claims "she asked for it" and a woman who quite literally asks for it, in the "contractual" context of s/m eroticism. This is not only because within s/m practice itself, "the mantra 'safe, sane, and consensual' is an ideal" none of the terms of which "can be easily accessed" (Hart 1998, 75); more than that, it is because s/m is characterized by a subtle play of resemblance and dissimilarity, a structure of risk, that, for its practitioners, accounts for much of its seductive appeal—and, indeed, lends it much of its subversive potential. As MacKendrick puts it, "both [pain and restraint] entail an exceptionally forceful enhancement of the always unexpected resistant power of the body, specifically a resistance to the seemingly irresistible disciplinary power of contemporary culture" (1999, 101). Or, to put it another way, s/m *marks the difference* between an intricate transaction, on the one hand, in which the power and overpowering of resistance delicately collude, each deriving its pleasure from the other, and a sheerly oppositional imposition of will, on the other hand, that is at once repressive and oppressive (cf. MacKendrick 1999, 129).

Above our entire discussion of the beating scene in the Song, therefore, a crucial question looms: how to distinguish ultimately between the painfilled pleasure of a bottom and the pleasureless pain of a battered woman? *Both readings of the scene are valid and, indeed, for feminists, indispensable,*

---

28. Hart (1998, 86) invokes "mimicry," as articulated (differently) by both feminist theorist Luce Irigaray and postcolonial theorist Homi Bhabha, to describe the "dissonant displacements" of oppressive models effected by s/m eroticism.

we would contend. Here as elsewhere, feminist and queer politics can ill afford to ignore each other. An adequately theorized feminist erotics may require that we both continue to denounce, and dare to celebrate, the beating of the woman in the Song; that we let genders oscillate and eroticisms queer; that we both remain within, and subversively exceed, the normative enclosure of modern "sexuality." Resisting subjectification—not least, sexual subjectification—may well be the act that necessarily underlies all political resistance, above all feminist resistance—as well as all approaches to the "sacred."[29]

Missing God

For some contemporary readers of the Song, as for some ancient readers, the violent assault of the watchmen may be an indispensable fantasy. (For others, it may not.) One cannot exercise power in the absence of resistance, or resistance in the absence of power; and one cannot transgress, or transcend, one's own boundaries alone. "That is why one needs an other: reader, god, top, bottom" (MacKendrick 1999, 156).

We have had much to say about readers in these pages, and not a little about tops and bottoms. But *God*? God has gone missing from readings of the Song since the ascent of "sexuality" and the demise of allegory (the latter two developments being intimately interlinked, as we began this essay by noting). And in the meantime, of course, God has gone missing more generally. This essay might seem an unlikely stage on which to perform the return of the repressed divine. And yet, as we attempt to nudge our own reading of the Song around yet another bend, to turn it further toward counterpleasurable perversity, what could possibly be queerer than … a theological reading? It might be argued, indeed, that the counterpleasures, through violently willing transgression between and *beyond* human subjects, open up upon the "sacred" or even the "divine." "One might say that God is still love, but love has changed," muses MacKendrick (1999, 157). How, then, has *God* changed as a consequence?

"I miss God. I miss the company of someone utterly loyal," confesses the female protagonist of Jeanette Winterson's beguiling novel *Oranges Are Not the Only Fruit*.

---

29. Georges Bataille argues that eroticism has a "sacramental" character, and that its purpose is "to destroy the self-contained character of the participators as they are in their normal lives" (1986, 17). His construal of the "sacred" follows the path of negative theology, and resists the notion of a discrete, personal "God."

> I miss God who was my friend. I don't even know if God exists, but I do know that if God is your emotional role model, very few human relationships will match up to it. I have an idea that one day it might be possible, I thought once it had become possible.... As it is, I can't settle, I want someone who is fierce and will love me until death and know that *love is as strong as death* [Song 8:6], and be on my side for ever and ever. I want someone who will destroy and be destroyed by me. There are many forms of love and affection, some people can spend their whole lives together without knowing each other's names. Naming is a difficult and time-consuming process; it concerns essences, and it means power. But on the wild nights who can call you home? Only the one who knows your name. Romantic love has been diluted into paperback form and has sold thousands and millions of copies. Somewhere it is still in the original, written on tablets of stone. I would cross seas and suffer sunstroke and give away all I have, but not for a man, because they want to be the destroyer and never the destroyed. That is why they are unfit for romantic love. There are exceptions and I hope they are happy. (1985, 170, emphasis added)

The God whom Winterson's protagonist misses seems at first glance to be the very God whom feminists have censured, and censored, in their readings of the Hebrew prophets (Hosea and Ezekiel in particular), precisely because he is said to function as a transcendental role model for wife abusers and other men who find violence against women to be erotically exciting and/or socially justifiable (e.g., Setel 1985; Exum 1996, 101–28; Brenner 1997, 153–74). And, indeed, Winterson's God is not unlike the "pornoprophetic" God; yet he is also not identical to him. For starters, is he really a "he"? Winterson's character has, after all, been compelled to leave her home and church for loving "the wrong sort of people," namely, women (1985, 127). In the passage that we have quoted, too, the divine "friend" whom she misses so intensely subtly transmutes, as the passage unfolds, into one for whom she would cross seas, suffer sunstroke, and gladly relinquish all that she possesses—but who is not, and must not be, male: a divine *girl*friend, then? And one willing—eager, indeed— not only "to destroy" but also "to be destroyed"?

The God whom Winterson so misses might well be the God who has been missing from the Song of Songs as the modern critical tradition has constructed it. Against a scholarly consensus that (to quote Brenner again) affirms, or rather assumes, that "[t]he primary subject matter of the SoS is ... heterosexual love and its erotic manifestations" (1993, 28), the task of queering the Song asserts its urgency. The "literal" tradition of Song of Songs interpretation, which has become synonymous with the critical tradition, was built on the ruins of the allegorical tradition, which is to say that the modern heterosexual construal of the Song—which constantly risks relapsing into a heterosexist construal, as we have been arguing—was predicated on the banishment of God from the Song. How better, then, to counter the heterosexist reading of the Song than by staging a return of the divine repressed? Yet the God who returns to the Song cannot simply be identical to the God who long ago exited the Song, queer though the latter undoubtedly was. The God who returns will need to be queerer still, an infinitely malleable lover, embracing and exceeding all imaginable "positions" (gendered or otherwise), equally at home on the contemporary altars of sadomasochistic ritual as in the prayer closets of ancient and medieval monks.[30] This God, who is now nowhere in the Song, would, once again, be everywhere in the Song, in command and under command by turns.

---

30. Note the call of Marcella Althaus-Reid (2000, 95): "Then indecent theologians must say: 'God, the Faggot; God, the Drag Queen; God, the Lesbian; God, the heterosexual woman who does not accept the constructions of ideal heterosexuality; God, the ambivalent, not easily classified sexuality.'" In chapter subsections entitled "Systematic Theology from the Margins of Sexuality" and "Black Leather: Doing Theology in Corset and Laced Boots," Althaus-Reid considers both pornography and (s/m) fetishism as theological resources (2000, 144–51). Mark Jordan (2002, 163–70) similarly pushes the envelope of theological reflection to include the sadomasochistic.

12
SEX AND THE SINGLE APOSTLE*

This essay's placement in the present volume is dictated by the fact that it looks backwards and forward at once. In common with "Taking It Like a Man," it takes Foucault's work on Greek and Roman sex as its point of departure and launches from there into a textual case study of the construction, enactment, and inherent instability of hegemonic Greco-Roman masculinity, the text in question being the Letter to the Romans. Like the two essays on the Song of Songs, moreover, the present essay derives its principal insights from queer theory (or the critical sensibility for which that term is a cipher). Although focused primarily on Paul's incalculably influential pronouncements on homoeroticism in Rom 1:26–27, the essay ventures a series of arguments about Romans in general. It contends that righteousness in Romans is essentially a masculine trait and sinfulness is essentially a feminine trait, so that the story that Romans tells is a saga of soteriological sex change, the Jesus of Romans being a woman forever in the process of becoming a man—arguments that a more rigorous application of queer theory then proceeds to deconstruct in order to press toward a more nuanced conclusion.

Where the essay looks forward (most immediately, to the next two essays in this collection, both of which engage with colonialism and imperialism) is in the right-hand column of its main section. There I analyze certain of the ideological functions assigned to Rom 1:26–27, and Rom 1:18–32 more broadly, during the height of the British Empire. The analysis attempts to blend queer and postcolonial theory, and that is a combination with

---

*First published in David J. A. Clines and Stephen D. Moore, eds., *Auguries: The Jubilee Volume of the Sheffield Department of Biblical Studies* (JSOT Supplement Series 269; Sheffield: Sheffield Academic Press, 1998), 250–74, under the title "Que(e)rying Paul."

which I continue to experiment (see Moore 2009)—although I might have done far more with it in my book on postcolonialism (Moore 2006), as I now belatedly realize.

Why two columns? Here as elsewhere I use the two-column format to solve a technical problem: the emergence in an essay of a parallel argument that has taken on a life of its own such that it can no longer be confined to the footnotes but begs inclusion in the main text.

If you were able to direct your eyes into secret places, to unfasten the locked doors of sleeping chambers and to open these hidden recesses to the perception of sight, you would behold that being carried on by the unchaste which a chaste countenance could not behold. You would see what it is an indignity even to see…. (Cyprian, *To Donatus* 9 [on Rom 1:26–27])[1]

The gods bless you.
May you sleep then
on some tender
girlfriend's breast.
(Sappho of Lesbos, Fragment 126)[2]

Michel Foucault begins the third volume of his *History of Sexuality*, devoted to discourses of sexuality in the Roman period, with an examination of the *Oneirokritika* (Dream Analysis or Dream Taxonomy) of Artemidoros of Daldis, an itinerant dream analyst of the second century C.E. (Foucault 1986, 1–36). "[A] man's book that is addressed mainly to men" (1986, 28), the *Oneirokritika* is designed as a handbook for other dream analysts, although it is also addressed to the "general reader" who will be able to use it to decipher his own dreams.[3] This general reader, or dreamer, is envisioned as a family man with possessions, quite often with a trade or business, and "apt to have servants or slaves" (1986, 6). But the real value of this text, for Foucault, inheres in the fact that while it is the only one from this period to present anything approximating a systematic exposition of the varieties of sexual acts, "it is not in any sense a treatise on morality, which would be primarily concerned with formulating judgments about those acts and relations" (1986, 9). Instead it discloses

---

1. Translation from Deferrari 1947.
2. Translation from Barnard 1958.
3. More specifically, the first three books of the *Oneirokritika* seem to be addressed to the general public and the last two to Artemidoros's own son.

"schemas of valuation that were generally accepted" (1986, 3). Indeed, John J. Winkler, whose celebrated *The Constraints of Desire: The Anthropology of Sex and Gender in Ancient Greece* accords a no less prominent place to the *Oneirokritika*, goes so far as to claim that the text "represents not just one man's opinion about the sexual protocols of ancient societies"—the opinion of a free, literate man, to be precise—"but an invaluable collection of evidence—a kind of ancient Kinsey report—based on interviews with thousands of clients" (1990, 33; cf. 23ff.).[4]

The relevant chapters of the *Oneirokritika* begin: "The best set of categories for the analysis of intercourse [*synousia*] is, first, intercourse which is according to nature [*kata physin*] and convention [*nomon*] and customary usage [*ethos*], then intercourse against convention [*para nomon*], and third, intercourse against nature [*para physin*]" (1.78).[5] The relevance of the *Oneirokritika* for the interpretation of Rom 1:26–27, Paul's incalculably influential pronouncement on homoeroticism and the primary subject of this essay, thus begins to become apparent. "Their women exchanged natural relations [*tēn physikēn chrēsin*] for unnatural [*eis tēn para physin*]," writes Paul, "and the men likewise gave up natural relations [*tēn physikēn chrēsin*] with women...."[6] "Intercourse which is according to nature and convention" in the *Oneirokritika* turns out to be that in which a man has sex with a social inferior—but not just a *female* inferior (such as his wife, his female slave, "women who mind workshops and stalls," or a prostitute), for sex with a male slave also falls into this category, provided only that the slave assumes the passive role. "To be penetrated [*perainesthai*] by one's house slave is not good," Artemidoros avers (1.78). Why? Not because of the act of anal penetration in itself, nor even the slave's maleness, argues Winkler, "but because a social inferior is represented as a sexual superior" (1990, 37).

The active/passive antithesis is one that Foucault returns to repeatedly in the second and third volumes of *The History of Sexuality*. At one point, for instance, he notes that although the dividing line of gender in antiquity did

---

4. There seems to be widespread agreement on this general point (even allowing for a dash of hyperbole in Winkler's formulation of it); see, e.g., in addition, Pack 1955, 287; Brooten 1996, 176–78.

5. Winkler's translation, here and in what follows. *Oneirokritica* 1.78–80 in translation forms an appendix to his book (1990, 210–16). For a translation of the entire work, see White 1975; for a full-length study of it, see Blum 1936.

6. What makes it all the more relevant is that the appeal to a concept of nature is lacking both in the Levitical (18:22; 20:13) and rabbinic pronouncements on homoeroticism—although Paul's Hellenistic Jewish contemporaries Philo and Pseudo-Phocylides do also have recourse to *physis* in their own statements on homoeroticism (Philo, *Special Laws* 1.325; 2.50; 3.37–39; *Abraham* 135–135; Pseudo-Phocylides, *Sentences* 3, 190–192, 213–214).

run principally between male and female, its route was far more circuitous ultimately. More precisely, the line ran "between what might be called the 'active actors' in the drama of pleasures, and the 'passive actors': on one side, those who were the subject of sexual activity…, and on the other, those who were the object-partners, the supporting players.…" The active actors were men, of course, "but more specifically they were adult free men." And the passive actors included women, of course, "but women made up only one element of a much larger group that was sometimes referred to as a way of designating the object of possible pleasure: 'women, boys, slaves'" (Foucault 1985, 47). David Halperin reduces these principles to a simple formula: "Sexual partners came in two different kinds—not male and female but 'active' and 'passive,' dominant and submissive" (1990, 33). Or as Clement of Alexandria no less pithily put it: "To do [*to dran*] is the mark of the man; to suffer [*to paschein*] is the mark of the woman" (*The Instructor* 3.19.2).

Returning to Artemidoros (1.78–79), we discover that "intercourse against convention [*para nomon*]" involves incest or oral-genital contact (for reasons not entirely clear, almost as great a taboo attached to the latter as to the former in the ancient Mediterranean world).[7] "Intercourse against nature [*para physin*]," finally, turns out to be a ragbag category containing most of the possible (and seemingly impossible) permutations that remain: penetrating oneself anally with one's own penis, fellating oneself (regular masturbation falls into the natural and conventional category), the penetration of a woman by another woman, and sex with a god or goddess, a corpse, or an animal (1.80). "What idea or ideas of nature generate this heterogeneous list of things *para physin*?" muses Winkler (1990, 38).[8] Not reproductive potential, obviously, since both the preceding categories, the natural-conventional and the unconventional, contain sexual acts that are nonreproductive: sodomy is natural and conventional, for example, while fellatio is unconventional, although not unnatural. The underlying rationale seems rather to be "that unnatural acts do not involve any representation of human social hierarchy.… Bestiality is not 'unnatural' in the sense of being what modern psychology calls a

---

7. The reasons are, perhaps, clearest in the case of cunnilingus. The dominant sexual ideology of that world was relentlessly phallocentric, but cunnilingus, "which does not require the intervention of a penis…, offer[ed] no place for the phallus to assert its power" (Williams 1999, 202–203; cf. Parker 1997, 51–52; Richlin 1992, 25–26, 69).

8. Compare the quotation from a "certain Chinese encyclopaedia" with which Foucault's *The Order of Things* opens, a surreal taxonomy that divides animals into such classes as "belonging to the Emperor," "embalmed," "tame," "sucking pigs," "fabulous," "stray dogs," "drawn with a very fine camelhair brush," "that from a long way off look like flies," and so on, all of which leaves Foucault marveling at "the stark impossibility of thinking *that*" (1970, xv, his emphasis).

perversion; rather it is outside the conventional field of social signification. If a man gains advantage over a sheep, so what?" (1990, 38–39). (The sheep herself might not be quite so dismissive, of course.)

The most telling item in the unnatural category, however, and the most significant for our understanding of Rom 1:26–27, is the penetration of a woman by another woman—provided, of course, that verse 26b ("Their women exchanged natural intercourse for unnatural") actually refers to sexual relations between women, as most modern commentators on Romans have supposed,[9] and not to "heterosexual" anal or oral intercourse, say, or even bestiality.[10] What are the grounds for this supposition? In the first place, the *homoiōs* of verse 27 ("and the men *likewise*, giving up natural intercourse with women, were consumed with passion for each other") strongly suggests that the women's unnatural intercourse similarly resulted from *their* being consumed with passion for each other. The correspondence between the unnatural activities of the women, on the one hand, and those of the men, on the other, suggested by *homoiōs*, also militates against the bestial interpretation of verse 26b: whatever the men are up to, it doesn't seem to involve four-legged partners. The bestial interpretation also stumbles on verse 24: "God gave them up ... to the degrading of their bodies *among themselves* [*en autois*]." No barks, bleats, grunts, or neighs intersperse with the human cries of passion that resound through this passage. And as for the women's unnatural intercourse being anal or oral sex with men, explicit castigations of either activity as being contrary to nature are lacking in Greco-Roman sources (even including Jewish sources), whereas sexual relations between women are denounced as unnatural by an impressive array of authors over a long span of time, including Plato, Seneca the Elder, Martial, Ovid, Ptolemy, Dorotheos of Sidon, Manetho, Pseudo-Phocylides, Tertullian, Clement of Alexandria, John Chrysostom—and Artemidoros.[11] Quietly slipping in behind this august company, therefore, I take Rom 1:26b to refer to sexual relations between women. But what precisely is it about such activity that caused the hackles to rise on these ancient authors?

Commenting on Artemidoros's allusion to unnatural intercourse between women, Winkler rightly insists that the expression should not be domesti-

---

9. Though not most ancient commentators, who saw in v. 26b a reference to male-female vaginal sex rendered "unnatural" by reason of the female assuming a "masculine" role (Martin 1995b, 348 n. 40; see further Brooten 1985).

10. Dissident voices include James Miller's (1995), who suggests that "heterosexual" anal or oral sex is envisioned here, and Klaus Haacker's (1994), who suspects that bestiality is the issue.

11. The arguments just presented rely heavily on Brooten's superb treatment of Rom 1:26b (1996, esp. 241–53).

cated by some soft-focus translation such as "lesbian sex," "for that would be to gloss over the very point where ancient Mediterranean sexual significations diverge from our own, hence the point where they are most revealing" (1990, 39). In the Greco-Roman world, sex, by definition—"natural" and "conventional" sex, that is—was male-initiated and utterly centered on the penis and the act of penetration (1990, 43). That the male organ should loom large in Artemidoros's dream book, therefore, given that book's propensity to reflect commonly held sexual attitudes and assumptions, is scarcely surprising.[12] At one point in the *Oneirokritika*, the penis elicits the following eulogy:

> The penis is like a man's parents since it contains the generative code [*spermatikos logos*], but it is also like his children since it is their cause. It is like his wife and girlfriend since it is useful for sex. It is like his brothers and all blood relations since the meaning of the entire household depends on the penis. It signifies strength and the body's manhood, since it actually causes these: for this reason some people call it their "manhood" [*andreia*]. It resembles reason and education since, like reason [*logos*], it is the most generative thing of all.... It is like the respect of being held in honor, since it is called "reverence" and "respect." (1.45)

In short, it can do everything but beg, roll over, and fetch the newspaper. In the sphere where we should most expect it to shine, however—the bedroom—it is rather less versatile. The act of penetration seems to constitute the quintessence of sexual activity for Artemidoros. "No caresses, no complicated combinations, no phantasmagoria," as Foucault remarks (1986, 28). This is in full continuity with the phallocentric conception of the sexual act reflected in a wide range of ancient Greek and Latin texts, its reduction to a penetrative, ejaculatory schema assumed to encompass all sexual activity (1986, 129, 136; Halperin 1990, 30; Walters 1997, 30).

Sexual relations between women can only be articulated in the *Oneirokritika*, therefore, in the significant terms of the system, which is to say, in terms of a penetrator and a penetratee. "Sexual relations between women are here classed as 'unnatural,'" notes Winkler, "because 'nature' assumes that what are significant in sexual activity are (i) men, (ii) penises that penetrate, and (iii) the articulation thereby of relative statuses through relations of dominance" (1990, 39). Women are not intrinsically equipped—not anatomically equipped, that is—to display these "natural" relations of dominance, of social hierarchy, in the sexual act. And they had better not try! "Women had better not ape [*mēde ... mimēsainto*] the conjugal role [*lechos*] of men,"

---

12. On the ubiquity of the phallus in Roman culture in particular, see Kellum 1996; cf. Keuls 1985, esp. 65–97 passim; Williams 1999, 18, 86–95, 172–73.

warns the Hellenistic Jewish author known as Pseudo-Phocylides (*Sentences* 192, my trans.).

The reduction of sexual relations to the act of penetration enables sex to become a simple yet effective instrument for expressing hierarchical relations. Foucault puts it memorably:

> Artemidorus sees the sexual act first and foremost as a game of superiority and inferiority: penetration places the two partners in a relationship of domination and submission. It is victory on one side, defeat on the other; it is a right that is exercised for one of the partners, a necessity that is imposed on the other. It is a status that one asserts, or a condition to which one is subjected. (1986, 30)

Penetration was not all of sex, then as now, needless to say. In the ancient Mediterranean world, however, it does appear to have been that aspect of sexual activity commonly thought to express social relations of honor and shame, aggrandizement and loss, domination and submission (cf. Winkler 1990, 40), or, more generally, movement up or down that treacherously slippery social ladder whose greased rungs marked discrete levels of status and prestige (see further Hallett and Skinner 1997, Part 3).

What's That Peculiar Thing Poking through the Tear in Saint Paul's Epistle to the Romans?

Is this how Paul, too, saw the sexual act? There is, of course, no way to know for certain. We may be tempted to give him the benefit of the doubt. He did choose to remain celibate, after all (1 Cor 7:7–8; 9:5, 15), which, being translated into the Priapean terms in which we have been trading, means that he did not use his penis to affirm his social status. (His phallic use or abuse of authority is another matter, of course, one that has often been addressed in recent years.) Yet the problem that now protrudes so obscenely through the tear that began to appear in Rom 1:26–27 as we perused Artemidoros's pronouncements on sex cannot be sewn up—or zipped up—so easily. So startlingly congruent, indeed, are these verses with the sociosexual script that I have been fleshing out that it seems

Things That Cannot Be Thought without Shame or Horror

Consider the case of a society one of whose constitutive conditions is the systemic subjugation of the feminine. Consider further that the definitive display of this subjugation is, according to the society's elite spokesmen, the act of sexual penetration. In such a society, this act becomes the arbitrary object of a massive symbolic investment—arbitrary, because a penis inserted in a vagina or an anus has no more intrinsic social

to matter very little in the end whether Paul himself was fully cognizant of what he was saying or whether he was merely a dummy on the knee of a ventriloquist culture that spoke through him to audiences that he, or it, could never have imagined—most recently ourselves. In any case, taking a leaf from the *Amplified New Testament*, I now submit the following amplified translation of Rom 1:26b–27:[1]

> Their women exchanged natural relations (of domination versus submission, designed to display social hierarchy, they themselves assuming the inferior position by accepting penile penetration) for unnatural relations (in which no display of domination or submission occurred and consequently no social hierarchy was exhibited, because no penile penetration took place), and the men likewise gave up natural relations with women (the male assuming the dominant position, penetrating the woman and thereby exhibiting and reaffirming his social superiority over her) and were consumed with passion for one another, men committing shameless acts with men (in which one partner would necessarily end up the loser in the zero-sum game of honor versus shame, passively accepting penetration and thus defeat at the hands of the other)....

My argument, in short, is that Rom 1:26–27 is but the tip of a sociosexual iceberg. And that the iceberg, like most, is a chilling one.

Of course, we have barely begun to scratch its surface. Romans 1:18–32, the larger subunit within which our verses occur, is a saga of crime and punishment. The plot paraphrase of this saga, sketched out in what follows, began as significance than a digit inserted in a nostril, say, or a hot dog inserted in a bun. For the society's moral custodians, however, the idea that certain insubordinate females might brazenly usurp the definitive masculine role of sexual penetrator is a deeply disturbing one. But the idea that they might actively choose to bypass penetrative sex altogether, finding nonpenetrative sex preferable, for whatever reason, is literally unthinkable: it falls soundlessly outside the bounds of the system and cannot even be posed as a problem within it.

These general observations, however, are by no means restricted to ancient Mediterranean societies. Even in nineteenth-century Britain—at least as represented by the patriarchs of polite British society—sexual relations could still be conceived only in terms of a penetrator and a penetratee,[1] same-sex relations merely

---

1. "( ) signify additional phases of meaning included in the Greek word, phrase or clause" (Siewert 1958, ix). For the basic translation I am using the RSV.

1. Not that same-sex relations, even between women, are widely conceived in any other terms even today (see Faderman 1981, 31–37; Rich-

12. SEX AND THE SINGLE APOSTLE

a series of jottings in the margins of Bernadette Brooten's *Love between Women: Early Christian Responses to Female Homoeroticism* (1996), an impressive 113 pages of which is devoted to the elucidation of Rom 1:26–27 (with emphasis, as might be expected, on 1:26b)—and that against the panoramic backdrop of the six chapters on "Female Homoeroticism in the Roman World" that, in effect, prepare for it (although their value far exceeds this function)—making it far and away the most exhaustive investigation of these verses ever undertaken. Brooten has left no stone unturned in her meticulous mapping of this tiny, but hotly contested, patch of text, and has begun to describe what has crawled out from underneath them. It seems to me, however, that what has slithered out is even more unsightly than Brooten has realized. Borrowing her pen and sketchpad, therefore, and drawing on the work of other scholars also (notably Stanley Stowers), I shall attempt to press beyond Brooten's analysis in what follows (although without presuming for a moment that she would recognize my sketch as a logical extension of her own).

First of all, why does Paul mention female homoeroticism before male: "Their women exchanged natural relations for unnatural, and the men likewise gave up natural relations with women..."? Does he regard the former as the more heinous aberration of the two (so heinous, in fact, that he is unwilling to go into detail on it, reserving what meager details there are in these verses for the lesser aberration of male homoeroticism)? Brooten finds support for this view in a fourth-century comment by John Chrysostom on this passage to the effect that homoerotic sexual contact is even more shameful for women than for men (Brooten 1996, 240; Chrysostom, *On the Epistle to the Romans*, Homily 4.1). But what ultimately lends plausibility to this interpretation of Rom 1:26–27 is the hegemonic "logic" involving insertions that God or nature never intended. As such, same-sex relations automatically assumed the status of an inferior copy (or, on occasion, Satanic parody) of an authentic (divinely instituted) original. But when the two parties engaged in sexual congress were not only female but British as well, no model whatsoever could be wheeled into the parlor, the church or the courtroom within which they might be conceptually encaged and displayed.

Consider the historical anecdote with which Bernadette Brooten opens her discussion of Rom 1:26–27 in her *Love between Women*: "The place: Edinburgh, Scotland. The time: 1811. Miss Marianne Woods and Miss Jane Pirie, two schoolteachers accused of having had a sexual relationship with each other, deny the charges and sue their accusers for libel" (1996, 189).[2] The charges

---

ardson 1996, esp. 2–9; Wilton 1996).

2. For a full account of the proceedings, Brooten refers us to Faderman 1983

of the Greco-Roman sex/gender system as it is expressed in so many of the other elite, male-authored texts that have come down to us,[2] a logic I began to unpack in the preceding section (and one with which Brooten is intimately familiar, although she omits to apply it to the question of why Paul indicts female homoeroticism first, or why he declines to gloss its "shamefulness," reserving the more lurid details for male homoeroticism, and causing Brooten to conclude that, "as for many other writers throughout history, female homoeroticism is unspeakable for Paul" [1996, 240]). Female homoeroticism constituted more of a threat to the logic or symbolic economy of Greco-Roman sex and gender than either anal intercourse or fellatio between males (the twin specters implicitly summoned up on the flickering screen of Rom 1:27). It even constituted more of a threat than bestiality or necrophilia. A person of either sex who copulated with an animal at least preserved his or her gender identity intact, either "mounting" the animal or "being mounted" by it, as his or her anatomical equipment dictated (cf. Brooten 1996, 252). A man who penetrated a corpse likewise retained the essential mark of his masculine identity.

A woman who had sex with another woman, however—which, being translated into the dominant sexological categories of ancient Mediterranean culture, could only mean a woman who penetrated or mounted another woman, using her in the manner of a man and thereby constructing a counterfeit, indeed monstrous, masculinity for herself—becoming a monster, in fact[3]—threatrest principally on the testimony of a sixteen-year-old schoolgirl, Jane Cumming. In the course of the trial, however, doubts are raised that sexual relations between women are even possible. This elicits a "memorandum" from the Senior Counsel for the defense (the schoolteachers' accusers), which begins as follows: "Because the Lord Ordinary in hearing had expressed doubt of the existence of the vice in question, the defendant begs leave to provide proofs of the Authorities with regard to the practice of tribadism" (quoted in Faderman 1983, 211). The evidence produced is principally antiquarian in character. It includes Lucian of Samosata's *Dialogues of the Courtesans* 5.1–4 (quoted at length) and a list of references to relevant passages in other Greco-Roman authors:

(itself a book-length version of Faderman 1981, 147–54). On consulting Faderman, one is referred in turn to Anon. 1975, in which the transcripts of the trial are collected. Yet another account of the trial can be found in Roughead 1931.

---

2. The term "elite" must be applied with caution to Paul, although it does seem to stick nonetheless (see Martin 1995a, 51–52).

3. Ovid, for example, characterizes female homoeroticism as *prodigiosa*, "monstrous" (*Metamorphoses* 9.727), as does Martial (*Epigrams* 1.90.8). John Chryso-

ened by her hubris to shatter the very mold that shaped Greco-Roman gender identity in the first place. Such a woman—if that indeed is what "she" was—pissed in the sacred waters of gender itself and sent ripples of alarm through the minds and texts of elite Greco-Roman males, the letter to the Romans included. For the purity of gender was no mere abstraction for such males; rather they perceived it as having social consequences of the most concrete and immediate kind. Brooten is incisive on this point: "Female-female and male-male sexual relations in the Roman world and in Rom 1:26-27 are both parallel and not parallel to one another. They both exemplify homoeroticism, but they differ socially, since, within this gender hierarchy, a man loses status in adopting a passive role, while a woman theoretically gains status by giving up a passive role" (1996, 266). In principle the thought of a woman *gaining* status was more worrying for elite males than the thought of a man *losing* status. Why? Because

Juvenal, Ovid, Martial, Phaedrus. It also includes Rom 1:26b.

And the verdict? No less august a body than the House of Lords itself decides in 1819 in favor of Woods and Pirie, unable to accept that two British Christian women above the lower classes could be capable of the heinous act attributed to them—if, indeed, British women of any class could be deemed capable of it. Lord Justice Clerk Hope: "There is not a prostitute so blasted as these women are described by Miss Cumming." Lord Gillies: "No such case was ever known in Scotland, or in Britain.... I do believe that the crime here alleged has no existence" (quoted in Faderman 1981, 149). Whence, then, the accusation? Where is the fire from which this noxious smoke has arisen? Lord Meadowbank notes with undisguised disdain that the principal witness, Miss Cumming, is "wanting in the advantages of legitimacy and a European complexion" (quoted in Faderman 1983, 153). The daughter of a deceased Scottish

---

stom later dubs it *allokoton lyssan*, "monstrous insanity" (*On the Epistle to the Romans* 4.1). And monsters give rise to nightmares, such as Seneca the Younger's vision of a Dildo Monster who, not content with penetrating other females, penetrates males as well (*Moral Epistles* 95.20), or Martial's yet more horrific vision of a Clitoris Monster, one Philaenis, "*tribas* of the very *tribades*," who buggers boys and screws eleven girls each day, "quite fierce with the erection of a husband" (*Epigrams* 7.67.1–3). Even the strap-on dildo (Greek *olisbos*; Latin *iuvamen* [?]), which the ancients deemed an indispensable accessory of the woman-loving woman (e.g., Aristophanes, *Lysistrata* 109–10; Seneca the Elder, *Controversiae* 1.2.23; Lucian of Samosata, *Dialogues of the Courtesans* 5.4 §292; b. 'Aboda Zara 44a), is itself a freakish implement in Pseudo-Lucian's *Erōtes* 28, which speaks of "mysterious monstrosities empty of [male] seed [*asporon terastion ainigma*]." Tamsin Wilton notes how even today female homoeroticism is frequently perceived as "an alien monstrosity prowling around outside the fold of gender conformity" (1996, 126).

as a culture that pivoted on the concept of "limited good," there was only so much status (read "honor") to go around. Loss of honor on the part of one male in this zero-sum economy entailed automatic increase of honor for another male. But increase of honor on the part of a *female*—itself an anomalous notion, since the Roman concept of honor encapsulated the essence of *masculine* virtue—could only result in loss of honor for *all* males. Female homoeroticism was therefore a crime against *man*.

But, of course, it was also a crime against God. This brings us to the question, not simply of why Paul places *female* homoeroticism at the head of his list of "dishonorable passions" (*pathē atimia*), but of why he separates *all* homoeroticism out for special mention instead of merely including it in the vice list that follows (1:29–31)? Because homoerotic relations epitomize—indeed, mimic in miniature—human rebellion against God and refusal of the honor due to him ("they did not honor [*ouch ... edoxasan*] God as God"—Rom 1:21), the thorny problem with which Paul is wrestling in this difficult stretch of Romans.

This brings us in turn to the relationship of homoeroticism to idolatry in our passage. Romans 1:18–23 sternly indicts those who, in choosing empty idols over the one true God ("they exchanged the glory of the immortal God for images"), rebelled against his authority and refused to submit to his power. Romans 1:24–27 proceeds to imply that the punishment fit the crime: "Therefore [*dio*] God gave them up in the lusts of their hearts to impurity, to the degrading of their bodies among themselves, because they exchanged the truth about God for a lie and worshiped and served the creature rather than the creator...." Their refusal of the divinely ordained relations of superordination and subordination between creature and creator is mirrored in their refusal of the divinely ordained relations of super-

gentleman and an Indian woman, she had spent the first eight years of her life in India. Meadowback suggests that the girl's imagination has been set ablaze by her lewd and lascivious Indian nurses: "It is an historical fact and matter of notoriety that the language of the Hindoo female domestics turns chiefly on the commerce of the sexes" (quoted in Faderman 1983, 153).[3] Lord Boyle sums up the situation: "[H]owever well known the crime here charged may be among Eastern nations, this is the first instance on record, of such an accusation having ever been made in this country" (quoted in Faderman 1981, 150).

The lords' confident pronouncements on the sexual proclivities of Asian women should come as no surprise. Since the Renaissance at least, Asia, Africa and the Americas had been what

---

3. "I detect something inscrutable and disturbing about this child of India," Meadowbank later declares (quoted in Faderman 1983, 189).

ordination and subordination between male and female. A startling homology therefore emerges in which God is to the human being as the active, erect, penetrating male is to the passive, open, penetrated female.

But the homology implicit in this passage is much more intricate than that. Romans 1:22–23 states: "Claiming to be wise, they became fools; and they exchanged the glory of the immortal God for images resembling a mortal human being or birds or four-footed animals or reptiles." In common with many other commentators, Brooten observes: "Paul draws upon motifs of Jewish antipagan polemic. Both the Wisdom of Solomon … and Philo of Alexandria … explicitly polemicize against Egyptian animal worship"—although animals also played a role in Greek and Roman religion, as Brooten reminds us; for example, the snakes that were an essential part of the Roman *lararium*, that chapel within a Roman house dedicated to its tutelary deities (1996, 231–32). Philo obligingly spells out the rationale for his own scornful denunciation of animal worship: "The Egyptians have promoted to divine honours irrational animals.... [T]hey render worship to them, they the civilized to the uncivilized and untamed, the reasonable to the irrational, … the rulers and masters to the naturally subservient and slavish" (*On the Contemplative Life* 8–9, LCL trans.).

We are now in a position to unfurl the implicit rationale of Rom 1:18–27 in turn. Because the human beings whom Paul is indicting refused to honor the divinely ordained hierarchy whereby the lesser submits to the greater—a refusal emblematized by their worship of animals, creatures that by nature are inferior to humans and designed to serve them—God punished them by consigning them to shameful practices that sabotaged another divinely ordained hierarchy, that of male over female. In other words, humans refused to honor the divinely instituted hierar-

Anne McClintock has termed "a porno-tropics for the European imagination—a fantastic magic lantern of the mind onto which Europe projected its forbidden sexual desires and fears" (1995, 22). In consequence, non-European peoples were regularly imagined by Europeans to be especially susceptible to homoerotic temptations. "Harem stories, in particular, fanned fantasies of lesbianism," as Ania Loomba notes.

> In his account of early seventeenth-century Turkey, for example, George Sandys contemplates what happens when women are cloistered with each other, engaged in long hours of massaging and pampering their bodies: "Much unnaturall and filthie lust is said to be committed daily in the remote closets of these darksome [bathhouses]: yea, women with women; a thing incredible, if former times had not given thereunto

chy that should have regulated divine-human relations (God over "man"). This refusal or rebellion found emblematic expression in, or was epitomized by, these sinful humans' reversal of a *second* divinely instituted hierarchy, that which should have regulated human-animal relations ("man" over animal). And God punished these rebels by permitting them to overturn a *third* divinely instituted hierarchy, that which should have regulated male-female relations (man over woman), thereby rubbing their noses in their sin (cf. 2:6).[4] The full homology inherent in Rom 1:18–27 can now be set out in full:

> FEMALE is to MALE
> as
> ANIMAL is to HUMAN
> and as
> HUMAN is to GOD.

In the symbolic world of Rom 1:18–32, therefore, "natural" sex is to "true" worship as "unnatural" sex is to idolatry[5]—which is to say that the submissiveness that the female should display in relation to the male (the *sine qua non* of "natural" sex) finds its ultimate warrant in the submissiveness that the human being should display in relation to God. The absolute inequality that is intrinsic to the act of divine worship—such worship being, in effect, the celebration of such both detection, and punishment." (1998, 155, quoting Sandys 1615, 69)[4]

But what act precisely was it that the House of Lords in 1819 deemed a British woman incapable of? What act would it have been unthinkable to attribute to such a person? What act constituted such a vicious symbolic assault on the institution of gender itself that it could not be granted even a notional existence in British society, but could only be conceived as something external, alien and monstrous, something that the uncivilized, dark-skinned women of the Orient indulged in, something altogether Other? Why, the sexual penetration of one woman by another,

---

4. The author of the Wisdom of Solomon also attributes a tit-for-tat mentality to God: "In return for their [the Gentiles'] foolish and wicked thoughts, which led them astray to worship irrational serpents and worthless animals, you sent upon them a multitude of irrational creatures to punish them, that they might learn that one is punished by the very things by which one sins" (11:15–16, NRSV; cf. 12:23, 27; *Testament of Gad* 5:1).

5. And so the punishment (being "given up" by God to unnatural sex) perfectly fits the crime (idolatry). I shall return to this below.

4. The European orientalization of female homoeroticism finds an interesting parallel in the tendency in ancient Latin literature to dissociate the *tribas* (or woman-penetrating woman) from Rome both geographically and temporally by Hellenizing her and retrojecting her into the past (see Hallett 1997, 266).

inequality—is tacitly adduced in Rom 1:18–32 to sanction inequality between male and female, an inequality whose ritual expression is the "natural" sex act, the act of penile penetration. Sex in this symbolic economy is nothing other—*can* be nothing other—than eroticized inequality.[6] And this inequality is immeasurably productive, masculine and feminine subjects themselves being manufactured through the eroticization of dominance and submission. To elaborate, were Paul in Romans willing or able to reflect explicitly on the theory of gender that undergirds his discourse, he might well appeal to Gen 3:16 in support of it. "Male and female he created them" (Hebrew *zākār ûnĕqēbâ bārā' 'ōtām*; Greek *arsen kai thēlu epoiēsen autous*)—so the first Genesis creation account describes the institution of anatomical sex (1:27). But the second creation account describes the institution of gender: "Your desire shall be for your husband/man, and he shall lord it over you" (3:16; Hebrew *wĕ'el-'îšēk tĕšûqātēk wĕhû' yimšāl-bāk*; Greek *kai pros ton andra sou hē apostrophē sou, kai autos sou kyrieusei*), which, being further translated, means nothing other than "*masculine* and *feminine* he created them." The intricate interpenetration of desire, domination, and submission (at once creative Trinity and sadomasochistic *ménage à trois*), succinctly suggested in this immensely influential verse, is precisely what brings gender to birth, for the author of Romans no less than for the author(s) of Genesis.

Thus far I have been attempting to exhume the imbedded cultural assumptions about homoerotic behavior that underlie Rom 1:26–27, to

of course. What finally clinched the verdict in favor of the two Scottish schoolteachers was the fact that the primary witness, Jane Cumming, had never claimed to have seen an artificial phallus being employed in the alleged sexual relationship.[5]

---

5. Although she did claim to have heard a sound "like putting one's finger into the neck of a wet bottle" (quoted in Faderman 1983, 147), a remark that elicits a bizarre game of Twenty Questions:

"Was it anything like the drawing of a cork?" John Clerk says.

"No."

"Was it like a person clapping or patting another on the cheek or shoulders?"

"No."

"Miss Cumming," Lord Robertson asks, "was it perhaps like a person dabbing their hands in water?"

"It was not quite like that, but more like it I think than rubbing or clapping."

"Miss Cumming," Lord Robertson asks again, "have you ever

---

6. Carol Smart notes: "It has been a main element of much feminist writing that heterosexuality is about the eroticisation of power difference" (1996, 168). Sheila Jeffreys, in particular, has made this theme her own (e.g., 1990, 1996), and the term "eroticized inequality" is hers.

explain why such behavior should not only be an affront to Paul's god, but should actually epitomize sinful humanity's disordered relationship with him. Implicit in any conception of "wrong" relationship, however, is a corresponding conception of "right" relationship. If homoeroticism can be said to epitomize a *wrong* relationship with Paul's deity, what would be logically entailed in a *right* relationship with him? Were we to press Paul's implicit characterization of homoeroticism to its logical conclusion, what would come into view? It is time to turn over this particular stone and see what adheres to its underside.

A right relation of creature to creator is implicitly modeled in our passage by a right relation of female to male, specifically a right sexual relation. What, therefore, are we to conclude? That a right relation to God would mean being properly underneath him,[7] breathless under his massive bulk, legs spread wide? And are we also to conclude that women who engage in homoerotic activity are "confused people, who do not do what they really want" (cf. Brooten 1996, 199), because they do not *know* what they really want? What do they really want, anyway? The answer commonly comes to succinct expression in that quintessential site of masculine discourse, the male locker room. What women who love women want, what they need, to straighten them out and cure them of their condition, is *a good fucking*.

In Rom 1:18–32, "confused" people everywhere are epitomized by women-loving women. And God's "wrath" against such people (1:18) is

---

7. Elsewhere in Romans we find *hē hypandros gynē* (7:2), the only New Testament occurrence of this telling expression. Elizabeth Castelli notes how contemporary translations of it, such "a married woman" (e.g., RSV, NAB, NRSV), conceal "the hierarchical formulation of the Greek…, literally, 'the woman who is under a man'" (1994, 283). As it happens, the term is also used by Artemidoros (*Oneirokritika* 1.78).

But in that case no sexual act could have occurred. The legal principle was classic in its stark simplicity: *No dildo, no dyke*.

In pronouncing upon Rom 1:26b, therefore, the schoolteacher's barrister, John Clerk, argued that if it indeed referred to sexual relations between women, a prosthetic phallus must needs be envisioned:

> [T]he defendant's counsel … alleged that this crime was mentioned in the New Testament. And if they were right it is the only one of all their authorities entitled to the slightest regard. The New Testament passage which the defendant's counsel refers to is in the first chapter of the

---

heard a dairy maid making up butter? Was it anything like a dairy maid patting butter?" (quoted in Faderman 1983, 163)

And so on. Faced with the unimaginably "unnatural," language slides backwards down an analogical slope.

12. SEX AND THE SINGLE APOSTLE

the direct result of their unreasonable refusal of his stiff solution to their plight, of their declining to assume the passive position in relation to him, spreading their legs or bending over as abject acknowledgment of his absolute authority and infinite superiority. Paul's god thus turns out to be an oversized (and over-endowed?) Roman male in the classic patriarchal mold, with a permanent erection and not enough orifices in which to insert it. Intriguingly, this Priapean personage is the exact antithesis of the celibate Paul's own public persona, suggesting how little conscious control Paul has exercised over the creation of his god. What should we conclude? That Paul is once again a dummy in the lap of a ventriloquist and masculinist culture whose voice resounds through his letters (and whose permanently erect member he is blithely unaware of, despite his being perched upon it)? Or that Paul, on the contrary, is no dummy, the fact that he has surreptitiously created a Jewish-Christian Priapus suggesting instead that he has unconsciously allowed his sexuality to shape his theology?

Now, the tale that Paul tells about his Priapus is not one of unending frustration. In the fullness of time, this ithyphallic personage did have the perfect orifice offered to him, and in a spirit of perfect submission. For Paul's anguished outlining of humanity's *plight*—universal sin ("Since all have sinned and fall short of the glory of God...")—is but the prelude to his triumphant unveiling of God's *solution*—Jesus Christ ("...they are now justified by his grace as a gift, through the redemption that is in Christ Jesus"—Rom 3:24). This universal sin is epitomized, or, better, synecdochically figured (the part standing in for the whole), by homoerotic sexual relations, especially between women, as we have seen. But why is *Jesus* the solution? Because Jesus submitted himself absolutely to God (cf. Phil 2:5–8;

Romans: "For this cause God gave them up into vile affections; for even their women did change the natural use into that which is against nature." It is very evident that even supposing this passage had referred to some infamous congress between two women, the proper inference would be that it was by the use of an instrument. (Quoted in Faderman 1983, 220)

The spectacle of a phallus-wielding woman, however, coupled with the accompanying spectacle, almost as inducive of gender vertigo, of "men" who mistake their anuses for vaginas, was too much for most eighteenth- and nineteenth-century clerical commentators on Rom 1:26–27, prompting near-apoplectic outbursts of indignation. Exemplary in this regard is John Brown's *The Self-Interpreting Bible*, a mammoth, worm-eaten tome that sat in a corner of the conference room in the

Rom 5:19), uniquely exemplifying the obedience to, and reverence for, God's authority that God demands of every human being. Stripped naked and spread out on the cross, run through with sundry phallic objects, Jesus in his relationship to God perfectly models the submissiveness that should also characterize the God-fearing female's proper relationship to the male. This is the sexual substratum of Paul's soteriology.

And it comes to vivid visual expression in the various artistic depictions of a female Christ on the cross that have appeared in recent decades, beginning in 1975, apparently, with Edwina Sandys's controversial *Christa*, a bronze sculpture first displayed in the Episcopal Cathedral of St. John the Divine in New York. A similar sculpture by James M. Murphy exhibited at Union Theological Seminary nine years later, this time in clay and entitled *Christine on the Cross*, carried the inversion of the traditional image to its logical conclusion. Murphy turned the familiar cross on its head—literally: the woman's legs are spreadeagled and her feet nailed to the dropped crossbar, while her arms are pulled above her head and her hands nailed together to the vertical bar. But what does it all mean? The artist's own interpretation of the sculpture is that it is a graphic embodiment and denunciation of systemic misogyny.[8] Does the trail of blood we have been tracking through the early chapters of Romans lead inexorably, then, through the doors of St. James's Chapel at Union Theological Seminary to form a spreading pool at the base of this unsettling sculpture of a cruelly tortured woman symbolically spreadeagled upon a cruciform bed of pain? Not exactly, because

Department of Biblical Studies at the University of Sheffield, my whilom employer, and glowered down at my colleagues and me while we engaged in our ungodly deliberations. First published in 1778 and highly regarded in its day, *The Self-Interpreting Bible* paraphrases Rom 1:24–27 as follows:

> To punish their thus setting up false objects of worship, and representing Him in so unjust, false, and shameless a manner, and regarding and worshipping the basest of creatures more than Himself, God, their infinitely glorious and blessed Creator, Preserver, and Governor, in His righteous judgement, withdrew His abused light and restraints, left them to themselves, and gave them up to their own vicious inclinations, which hurried them, both men and women, into such shocking, lustful, disgraceful, and

---

8. So Crawford 1983, 26, quoted in Ford 1996, 292. Ford provides details of six artistic representations of crucified female Christs, five sculptures and one painting, issuing from Africa, Australia, Canada, Latin America, and the United States (1996, 291–92).

12. SEX AND THE SINGLE APOSTLE

the closer we come to the writhing figure whose own cross thrusts up through the bloodstained pages of the crucifixated letter to the Romans—a dim figure silhouetted against the sun—the less certain we become about whether we are looking at a woman or a man. For the Pauline Jesus' spectacular act of submission—his consummate "feminine" performance—is simultaneously and paradoxically a demonstration of his masculinity, as we are about to see.

Mastery—of others, but most especially of oneself—was the supreme index of masculinity in the Greco-Roman intellectual milieu of the mid-first century C.E., and had been for quite some time.[9] Against this towering backcloth, it is hard to resist reading the Pauline Jesus' submission unto death as a bravura display of self-mastery, and hence a spectacular performance of masculinity. Yet one is hard pressed to discover any Pauline scholars who have set foot on this stage.

Stanley Stowers comes closest in his *Rereading of Romans*, making a compelling case for construing this letter as, in part, yet another Greco-Roman discourse on self-mastery. "The theme of self-mastery would have loomed very large for ancient readers of Romans," argues Stowers—and it still loomed large for patristic interpreters of the letter, as he later observes—

> but it is scarcely noticed by modern readers.... [T]he concept of self-mastery has none of the powerfully loaded social and cultural meaning for us that it did for people in Paul's day. Even apparent similarities between self-mastery and the modern concept of self-discipline mislead because the ancient and modern conceptions of the person and society differ so greatly. The rhetoric of Romans pushes the theme of self-mastery, or the lack of it, into the foreground in three ways.

unnatural abuse of their bodies as cannot be thought of or mentioned without shame or horror.

Brown's use of the term "Governor" for God, while commonplace, at least in traditional ecclesiastical English, is interesting. What does Brown imagine? That the heathen, in the absence of the "light and restraints" imposed by their (civilizing?) "Governor," simply slid back into their native moral degeneracy? The logic that undergirds this fiery reading of Rom 1:24–27 is, one suspects, a colonialist logic.

Brown himself does not use the term "heathen" in his paraphrase of the passage, but many other eighteenth- and nineteenth-century commentators do.[6] Consider what befalls our passage when the wicked of Rom 1:18–32 are said not to

---

9. See 177, 179–80, 184–85 above.

6. It is not that Brown had no use for the term. The other great work he bequeathed to posterity, *A Dictionary of the Holy Bible*, contains an illuminating article on "Gentiles, Heathen," as we shall see.

> First, Romans tells the story of sin and salvation, problem and solution, punishment and reward at its most basic level as a story of the loss and recovery of self-control. Second, the letter represents the readers as characters in this basic story that concerns self-mastery. Third, Romans relates this story of loss to the story of God's righteous action through Jesus Christ so that Christ becomes an enabler of the restored and disciplined self. (1994, 42)

And hence an enabler, and himself a paragon, of masculinity, so that the salvation proffered to the reader of Romans amounts to—what? The attainment of true manhood, this being necessary in order to enter into fellowship with Paul's (hypermasculine) god?

Stowers himself does not draw this conclusion. Gender is a peripheral concern in "Readers in Romans and the Meaning of Self-Mastery," the (masterful) chapter of *A Rereading of Romans* in which Stowers substantiates the argument summarized in the above quotation. Yet it is but a short step from Stowers's position to the conclusion that Romans is implicitly about masculinity. Consider a further passage from his chapter, one of the few to deal directly with gender: "Gender hierarchy lies close to the heart of the discourse on self-mastery. Life is war, and masculinity has to be achieved and constantly fought for. Men are always in danger of succumbing to softness, described as forms of femaleness or servility.... To achieve self-mastery means to win the war; to let the passions and desires go unsubdued means defeat, a destruction of hard-won manliness" (1994, 45). All of this we have already seen. But Stowers now makes the crucial link with Rom 1:26–27: "The centrality of this gender defeat explains why leaving assigned gender roles for same sex love serves as the illustration in 1:26–27 of the extent to which Gentiles have succumbed to passions and desires" (1994, 45–46). This be "Gentiles" or "pagans" but "heathen," as, for instance, in William Sanday and Arthur Headlam's late-nineteenth century commentary on Romans, which contains a notable excursus on 1:18–32 entitled "St. Paul's Description of the Condition of the Heathen World" (1895, 49–52). When a contemporary British New Testament scholar uses the term "pagan," he or she almost always does so with reference to certain products of Greco-Roman culture and in order to distinguish them from other products of that culture termed "Jewish" or "Christian." But when an eighteenth- or nineteenth-century British New Testament scholar used the term "heathen," an eighteenth- or nineteenth-century reality was automatically conjured up in addition to an ancient one. The article on "Gentiles, Heathen" from the nineteenth-century revised edition of John Brown's 1768 *Dictionary of the Holy Bible* provides an instructive illustration of the ease with which the heathen of old and the contemporary heathen

would seem to mean that homoerotic relations, specifically between males this time, are, for Paul, emblematic of the loss of masculinity that loss of mastery over the passions always and inevitably entails. And this in turn means that Paul's discourse on *sin* in Romans—Romans, remarkably, containing forty-eight of the sixty-four occurrences of the term "sin" (*hamartia*) in the Pauline letters, even including the disputed letters (so Dunn 1998, 111), and sin, for Paul, being, above all, that which masters and enslaves (Rom 6:16–23)—is simultaneously a discourse on *masculinity*. Which in its turn means that Paul's Jesus, as the one who uniquely overcame sin, is implicitly held up as the supreme exemplar of masculinity for Jew and Gentile alike—a hypostatized Masculinity, if you will, to which all human beings can now aspire, whether or not they have been blessed with male genitalia. (For one of the more striking features of masculinity in Greco-Roman antiquity was its relative independence from anatomy: females, too, could be paragons of masculinity.)[10] Or to translate back into Stowers's terms:

> The letter establishes the audience's relation to the theme of self-mastery also by making Christ an enabler of the mastery over self that the readers are already depicted as having by virtue of their new lives. The arguments in chapters 5–8 aim to change the readers' understanding of how they have attained mastery over their passions and desires: not through the law but through their identification with Jesus Christ. According to 6:1–7:6, Jesus' death is somehow a cause of

could be conflated. Of the heathen of old we are told:

> For many ages before Christ, these nations were destitute of the true religion, and gave themselves up to the grossest ignorance, or most absurd idolatry, superstition, and horrid crimes. Their most learned men, with all their boasted pretensions to wisdom, were, as well as others, absurd in the main, and complied with, or promoted the absurd customs they found among their countrymen. They were strangers to the covenants of promise—without God and without hope in the world—living in subjection to Satan, and in the most horrid, and often most unnatural lusts, Rom. i.22, 25. (1851, 461)

And of the eighteenth- and nineteenth-century heathen we are told: "As the nations were of old

---

10. See 191–95 above. This topos has acquired a new lease of life in contemporary gender theory, as, for example, in Judith Halberstam's *Female Masculinity* (1998). Eve Sedgwick remarks: "[L]ike men, I as a woman am also a producer of masculinities and a performer of them" (1995, 13).

the encoded readers' "death to sin," which means that the readers can now be free from enslavement to their passions and desires. Chapter 8 combines this motif of liberation from passions through the Spirit with the themes of freedom from condemnation and a filial relationship with God leading to future reward. (1994, 44–45)

What this edifying paragraph conceals, however—indeed, what Stowers's entire chapter conceals, although only barely: it crouches in the corners—is a rather less edifying reality. *Righteousness in Romans is essentially a masculine trait*; it is, in fact, the very mark of masculinity. What then is *un*righteousness, sin, with its cunning accomplice, "the flesh"? What else but loss of self-mastery, lack of masculinity—in a word, femininity. *Sinfulness, therefore, is essentially a feminine trait in Romans.* Commentators on Romans have occasionally glimpsed this, but failed to acknowledge what they were seeing. James Dunn, for example, states: "And in [Rom] 7:14 Paul's 'I' laments that he is 'fleshly, sold under sin,' like a defeated captive in war, sold into slavery" (1998, 112). Like a feminized male, in other words. But that sinfulness should be found to be a feminine state in Paul's thought is scarcely surprising; it is merely the gendered logic of Greco-Roman moral philosophy in Jewish-Christian guise.[11]

destitute of the knowledge and worship of the true God, the word Heathen or Gentile sometimes denotes such as are without the church, are ignorant, atheistical, idolatrous"—and so on down to the concluding encapsulation of the heathen as "all Antichristian nations, whether Papists or not" (1851, 461).

"Heathen," however, was a pregnant term, even a strategic term, not only in British ecclesiastical discourse of the period but also in British imperial discourse (to the extent that the two could be disentangled). Reflecting upon nineteenth-century India, for example, R. S. Sugirtharajah remarks: "As a way of legitimizing European intervention, colonizers were actively involved in producing images which reinscribed the cultural and religious differences between imperialists and imperialized natives. One such image was of the 'Other' as the heathen—the antithesis of all civilized and Christian values" (1998a, 46). The term "heathen" in a nineteenth- or early twentieth-century Brit-

---

11. As with Philo, for instance (who is more up-front than Paul about his contempt for the feminine): "For progress [toward virtue] is indeed nothing else than the giving up of the female gender by changing into the male, since the female gender is material, passive, corporeal, and sense-perceptible, while the male is active, rational, incorporeal, and more akin to mind and thought" (*Questions and Answers on Exodus* 1.8, LCL trans.; cf. *Questions and Answers on Genesis* 2.12, 49; *The Worse Attacks the Better* 28; *On the Embassy to Gaius* 319).

Romans implicitly presents Jesus' submission to God as a model for the submission that should characterize the female's proper relationship to the male, as we have seen. Yet Jesus is not allowed to become mired in femininity, to sink into a softness, a flabbiness, from which he might not be able to extricate himself, in which he might lose his own hardness, his own manliness. For his spectacular act of submission is simultaneously a demonstration of self-mastery. The redemption of femininity is accomplished through its transmutation into masculinity, and this transmutation is effected through self-mastery. The passage from sin to righteousness that Romans proclaims, therefore, is not only *christological* through and through: it is also *gendered* through and through. And the story that Romans tells is a saga of soteriological sex change. For the Jesus of Romans is a woman forever in the process of becoming a man. And that is what queer theory has to teach us about Pauline theology.

But it is not only Paul's Christ who now looks considerably queerer than when we started out. For what is true of his Christ is also true of Paul himself. Paul reinvented Jesus of Nazareth, but in so doing Paul also reinvented himself. Paul modeled himself on the Jesus whom he had modeled, mimicked the Jesus whom he had made. "Mimic me, as I mimic Christ [*mimētai mou ginesthe*,

ish commentary on Rom 1:18–32, therefore—the period when the British Empire had succeeded in hauling its bloated bulk up to the dizzying pinnacle from which it was soon to plunge—readily conjured up the stereotypical spectacle of the "unsaved" dark-skinned mass of polytheistic humanity, in need of Christ, and in need of civilizing, and hence in need of colonizing.

The amalgamation of the academic, the ecclesiastical and the imperial is accentuated in the Sanday-Headlam commentary cited earlier (altogether a more polished product than Brown's bilious tracts) by the fact that at least one of its authors happened to be a pillar of the university that was the intellectual jewel in the crown of the British Empire; and that both authors happened to be officers, not just of the academy, but also of the church that had succeeded spectacularly in making Englishness a global religion.[7] The

---

But what of Gal 3:28: "There is no longer Jew or Greek, there is no longer slave or free, there is no longer male and female [*arsen kai thēlu*], for all of you are one in Christ Jesus"? An adequate unpacking of this verse, or rather of its immense cultural baggage, would require at least as much effort as Rom 1:26–27, the sort of effort Daniel Boyarin puts into it (1994, 180–200). But my suspicion in light of our discussion of Romans is that what Gal 3:28 implicitly proclaims is the replacement of two sexes with one gender—masculinity in the theological trappings of "righteousness," which every believer, regardless of anatomical equipment, is required to put on.

---

7. In Ireland, for instance, the violent suppres-

kathōs kagō Christou]," he urged his Corinthian flock (1 Cor 11:1; cf. 4:16; 1 Thess 1:6; 2 Thess 3:7, 9). But this self-engendering performance was also a performance of gender: Paul permitted his Jesus to enter him. "I have been crucified with Christ," he groans in Galatians, "and it is no longer I who live, but it is Christ who lives in me [*en emoi*]. And the live I now live in the flesh I live by faith in the Son of God, who loved me and gave himself for me" (Gal 2:19–20; cf. Rom 6:3–6). In this male-male love affair, Jesus is the penetrator, Paul the penetratee. Jesus is active and initiatory (cf. Gal 1:12), Paul is passive and receptive. In refashioning Jesus of Nazareth, therefore, in constructing this Christ-in-a-closet (the closet lovingly crafted with tools borrowed from the Carpenter himself?), Paul refashions himself, becoming—what? He becomes a man whose identity inheres in his utter submission to another man. As such, he becomes a "man," or a (wo)man, or an unman.[12] The dominant male who has placed Paul in this passive role is, of course, no longer Jesus of Nazareth, the lowborn Galilean peasant (Paul's appetite for humiliation and rough trade—for a rough tradesman?—does have its limits, apparently), but instead the Christ of fate: the ravishing being whom Paul was fated to be with—and be under—from all

Right Revd. William Sanday was the Lady Margaret Professor of Divinity and Canon of Christ Church at Oxford University, while the Right Revd. Arthur C. Headlam was a Fellow of All Souls College at the same institution. Reading Sanday and Headlam on "St. Paul's Description of the Condition of the Heathen World," it is hard to avoid the suspicion that their outraged hero is storming not just through the streets of Corinth but also through the streets of Calcutta, fulminating against all heathenish practices, present no less than past, so fully do they seem to share his intense revulsion "at the vices which he

---

12. The term "unman" is borrowed from Jonathan Walters (1991, 31; 1997, 41). See further Skinner 1997, 18, quoting Ellen Oliensis: "[A]ny asymmetrical relation between two Roman men is conceivably also a sexual relation"; also Skinner 1993, 120: "In the Greco-Roman world … power was openly eroticized—so openly and so thoroughly as to undermine biological gender identity." Walters, too, writes of a Roman "concept of manliness which is irreducibly bound up with the holding of power over others, and which is radically incompatible with being the object of power to another," to the extent that Juvenal (*Satire* 2.143ff.) can imply that a gladiator is even less of a man than a sexually penetrated male (1998, 152).

---

sion of Roman Catholicism went hand-in-glove with the violent suppression of the Irish language ("Gaelic" as it is commonly called, although not by the Irish themselves), the eradication of superstition and the imposition of true religion being conjoined with the eradication of a barbaric tongue and the imposition of civilized speech. On language as a colonial instrument, see Fanon 1967, 17–40; Thiong'o 1986, 4–33. Specifically on the Irish context, see Kiberd 1995, esp. 9–17, 133–54.

eternity (Rom 8:29-30). This heavenly man (cf. 1 Cor 15:48-49) derives his own identity in turn, however, from his utter submission to a still more dominant male—the most dominant male of all (the one whose testosterone-bloated bulk casts a menacing shadow over the women-loving-women of Rom 1:26b)—which is to say (yet again) that Paul's Christ is not all man either, and not only because he is divine, but also because he is supine: "When all things are subjected to him, then the Son himself will also be subjected to him who puts all things under him [*ho huios hypotagēsetai tō hypotaxanti autō ta panta*]..." (1 Cor 15:28). And it is Paul's own abjectly submissive role within this all-male threesome as "slave of Christ" (*Christou doulos*—Gal 1:10; cf. Rom 6:16-23) that, more than anything else, now defines his radically reconfigured identity as a Christian. Small wonder that Paul has no need of a woman (1 Cor 7:7-8; 9:5, 15). Why should he need one when, in terms of the phallobsessive gender logic of his culture (and ours?), he quite simply is one? Other logics are, however, possible. More than that, they are necessary.

How else might we counter Paul's reading of homoeroticism in Rom 1:26-27? Taking my lead once again from Bernadette Brooten, I shall concentrate on homoerotic relations between women. "The Greek term for 'intercourse,' *chrēsis*, literally means 'use,'" as she notes. "Greek authors from the classical period through late antiquity use both the noun *chrēsis* and the verb *chraomai* ('to use') in a sexual sense. A man 'uses' or 'makes use of' a woman or a boy" (1996, 245).[13] He uses found prevailing among the heathen," "given over especially to sins of the flesh" as they were (and are?). Such gods as their "lawless fancies" invented "left them free to follow their own unbridled passions. And the Majesty on High angered at their willful disloyalty, did not interfere to check their downward career" (1895, 49-50). That the Majesty on High might not be an altogether separate, or separable, entity from the Majesty in Buckingham Palace is suggested by even a casual perusal of another instructive Sanday and Headlam excursus, this time on Rom 13:1-7 ("Let every person be subject to the governing authorities..."), and entitled "The Church and the Civil Power" (1895, 369-73). But let us return to the sins of the flesh, to wallow in them one last time.

In the nineteenth century no less than the first, the moral degeneracy of the benighted heathen could be conveniently encapsulated in the most shocking spectacle of all: that of their women sacrilegiously

---

13. The Greek of Rom 1:27, *homoiōs te kai hoi arsenes aphentes tēn physikēn chrēsin tēs thēleias...*, was rendered literally by the King James translators as "likewise also the men, leaving the natural use of the woman...." Most modern translators blanch at this rendering, however, opting for a soft-focus translation instead; KJV's great-

them for sexual pleasure, sexual release. But he also uses them to display his social status, as we saw, to demonstrate his "superiority" in relation to their "inferiority." Now let us turn yet again to Rom 1:26b, "Their woman exchanged natural use/intercourse [*metēllaxan tēn physikēn chrēsin*] for unnatural." "'Their women' exchanged the culturally accepted form of men 'using' them for another form of sexual contact," is Brooten's etic paraphrase of this assertion (1996, 245). She continues:

> As the subject of an active verb, "their women" acted as agents in changing their form of sexual contact. The active verb (*metēllaxan* ["exchanged"]) with a feminine subject (*hai thēleiai* ["the women"]) is striking. The specific terms for sexual intercourse are usually active when they refer to men and passive when they refer to women. Thus, a man penetrates (*perainei*) a woman, while a woman is penetrated (*perainetai*) by a man.... The case is the same for marriage: a man marries (*gamizei*) a woman, while a woman is married (*gamizetai*) by a man....
>
> "To exchange" is, of course, not a verb that means "to have sexual intercourse" or "to marry." Nevertheless, in the context of the widespread cultural view of women as sexually passive, for women actively to "exchange natural intercourse for unnatural" stands out. (1996, 245–46)

Brooten would seem to be suggesting that the practices here condemned by Paul—female homoerotic practices—can be counterread as active resistance to phallic, patriarchal power, Paul himself inadvertently providing us with the

grandchild NRSV, for example, has: "in the same way also the men, giving up natural intercourse with women...."

thrusting their hands into the sacred flame to seize the one organ that nature never intended them to have and to penetrate each other with it in the manner of men (not caring that the organ they usurp has been torn from the groins of real men, who now lie bleeding all about). When it comes to Rom 1:26, Sanday and Headlam do not disappoint. "God gave them up to the vilest passions," they write. "Women behaved like monsters who had forgotten their sex" (1895, 40). This reading, however, is offered as part of the paraphrastic translation with which their treatment of each section of Romans begins. The verse-by-verse commentary proper on Rom 1:18–32 that follows passes over 1:26 in perfect silence.[8] Compare the memorable scene in E. M. Forster's *Maurice* in which the issue of same-sex love is similarly consigned to the closet by

---

8. And over 1:27 likewise, except for a brief comment on the participle *apolambanontes*, "receiving back/receiving one's due" (1895, 46).

12. SEX AND THE SINGLE APOSTLE

cue through his assignation of active agency to these outlaw women.

Where might we go from here? We could take the tiny opening proffered by the active verb and prise it apart as far as it will go. One way to do so would be to employ Foucault as a lever, but also as a foil. The heroes of the second and third volumes of his *History of Sexuality* are Greek and Roman individuals for whom the sex act was a "technology of the self," part of a voluntary regime of improvised "ethical" practices, which together comprised an "art of existence" (*technē tou biou*) in the service, not just of self-transformation, but of self-invention. Notoriously, however, all these individuals happen to be male, for Foucault, who flatly states:

> [T]his ethics was not addressed to women.... It was an ethics for men: an ethics thought, written, and taught by men, and addressed to men—to free men obviously. A male ethics, consequently, in which women figured only as objects or, at most, as partners that one had best train, educate and watch over when one had them under one's power, but stay away from when they were under the power of someone else. (1985, 22)[14]

---

14. This is one of several such disclaimers that punctuate *The Use of Pleasure* and *The Care of the Self*. They have not prevented feminist critics from hauling Foucault over the coals (e.g., Richlin 1991; 1998; Hunt 1992; MacKinnon 1992; McNay, 1992, esp. 75ff.; Greene 1996; duBois 1998; Foxhall 1998)—nor should they, since he proceeds to idealize this androcentric ethic anyway. A more emphatic disclaimer was issued by Foucault in an interview: "The Greek ethics were linked to a purely virile society with slaves, in which women were underdogs whose pleasure had no importance, whose sexual life had to be oriented toward, determined by, their status as wives.... All that is quite disgusting!" (1984, 344, 346). But not disgusting enough, apparently.

an Oxbridge don. David Halperin's *One Hundred Years of Homosexuality* opens with a rerun of the scene:

> "Omit: a reference to the unspeakable vice of the Greeks." With those words, uttered in "a flat toneless voice," the Dean of a Cambridge college in the seventh chapter of E. M. Forster's self-suppressed novel, *Maurice* (originally composed in 1913–14 and first released for publication upon the novelist's death in 1970), interrupts a student who has been dutifully translating aloud from the text of an unnamed classical Greek author. (1990, 1)

Why this particular vice should have required such a vigilant labor of denial and repression, especially among elite males, for whom gender, sexuality and social status were inextricably intertwined, should by now be apparent.

But what the active verb in Rom 1:26b conjures up, albeit in spectral form, is a spectacle undreamed of even (or especially?) by Foucault, that of Greco-Roman *women* actively engaged in "technologies of the self," in radical self-(re)invention, exchanging the culturally prescribed passive role in sexual relations for something else—something altogether unspecified but meriting the (promising) adjective "unnatural" nonetheless (which, in the context, readily admits the etic synonym "countercultural")—and thereby acceding to sexual agency.[15]

That such a reading should manage to spring up in the arid wasteland of Rom 1:18–32 is rather remarkable. But is the climate not too harsh for it? Sadly it is. Watch what happens.

Even the fragile autonomy that the active verb *metēllaxan* confers upon these gender renegades is ultimately illusory, according to our passage. For these shockingly unfeminine females are still being shafted by a male. The active verb "exchanged" is overshadowed in our text by a much bigger active verb, whose subject is God, and is forced to submit to it: "Therefore God gave them up [*paredōken*] in the lusts of their heart to impurity, to the degrading of their bodies among themselves.... God gave them up [*paredōken*] to degrading passions. Their women exchanged their natural sexual use for unnatural"—all of which can now be paraphrased as follows. Even as these aberrant women lie entwined in each other's arms, they are being impaled on God's irresistible purpose, being quietly punished by him—so quietly, so surreptitiously, in fact, that they are entirely unaware of it and slumber on in

So who, then, are these women-become-monsters who slither sensuously out of the darker recesses of Sanday's and Headlam's imaginations, causing them to shudder briefly and lapse into troubled silence? They are the selfsame monsters that other prominent representatives of the British ruling class declared to be dark-skinned, Oriental and altogether un-British in the trial of the two female schoolteachers earlier in the same century, in an attempt to cleanse the land of their loathsome spectral presence and drive them back into the amoral cesspool out of which they crawled. In short, they are *heathen* monsters. These nineteenth-century heathen, whose moral turpitude is, like their first-century counterparts, epitomized by their women-loving women, are practically begging for the locker-room "cure,"[9] so sorely are they in need of Christ,

---

15. Amy Richlin has recently attempted a similar counterreading of Pliny the Elder's *Natural History* that presents the dimly glimpsed women therein as subjects engaged in active self-fashioning (see Richlin 1997b, along with her parallel effort in 1998, 152–62).

9. See p. 288 above on the cure. Note, too, that the century that witnessed the birth of modern men's team sports and "muscular Christianity"

a stupor, as though drugged. Even though they imperil, by their monstrous behavior, hierarchical gender binarism, and hence the very foundations of the cosmos itself, threatening to bring the entire natural and cultural order crashing down in ruins, gender is silently reasserting itself even as they sleep. Their activity is being transmuted into passivity, pliancy, penetrability. The Impenetrable Penetrator (that condition being the quintessence of Roman manhood) remains fully in charge, and his superiority and their inferiority is being properly displayed on behalf of all males everywhere—which, for Paul and the hegemonic hypermasculinity for which he is here the mouthpiece, is all that matters ultimately.

of civilizing, of colonizing. In a word, they are in need of *invasion*, the imperialistic equivalent of "a good fucking"—in this case, one administered in the missionary position. And that is precisely what they get.

It is high time, however, to explore this locker room more thoroughly. What if some of its lockers actually turned out to be closets?

---

also witnessed the birth of the locker room.

The Locker Room

Paul need not have the last word. The trick will be to reason according to rules not laid down by him or his culture. My queering of Paul and his Christ has, up to now, played into Paul's hands. I was merely waltzing with him to his own whistled tune, and whether he happened to be wearing the evening gown or the tuxedo made little difference in the end. In characterizing the submissive Christ or the submissive Paul, the "penetrated" Christ or the "penetrated" Paul, as "feminine" or "feminized" I was reading into Paul's pregnant silences and attempting to complete his unfinished sentences for him. But my calculations were based on the Greco-Roman gender equations: active = masculine, passive = feminine. I was factoring Jesus and Paul into these equations and duly jotting down the results. These equations are hardly axiomatic, however, to put it mildly. Numerous feminist scholars have critiqued them and the concepts of appropriate gender behavior enshrined in them. What might queer theory (or the critical sensibility for which that term is shorthand) contribute to such critiques?

We might begin by asking what logic dictates that a submissive male be characterized as "feminine" or "feminized" in the first place. To so characterize the submissive male is to code the erotic exchange in terms that are ineluctably "hetero." It is to supply the "missing" female in the exchange by dressing one of the partners in conceptual drag and declaring him to be the woman. But the bottom line is that there *are* no females in the inner sanctum of Paul's theology. There are only males acting upon other males: God, Jesus, Paul. Now, this male sanctum is a locker room, as it happens. And most of the action takes place in the showers. "The Lord is enveloped in clouds," declares the Psalmist (97:2). Here the clouds are of steam. And the symbolic action dimly glimpsed through them is inflexibly hierarchical. Jesus submits himself obediently to God's excruciating demands. Paul submits himself to Jesus in turn, opens himself utterly to Jesus, is entered and possessed by Jesus. And throughout this steamy scene there is not a single female face in sight, not to mention a female orifice. Richard Rambuss rightly cautions in his *Closet Devotions* "that we avoid peremptorily re-encoding every representation of the penetrable male body as feminized *because* penetrated. Are male bodies without their own orifices?" he asks rhetorically (1998, 38, his emphasis).[13]

The defensive clenching of male orifices is the most characteristic gesture of Greco-Roman discourses on sex. Within the constrictive bounds of these discourses, a "man" is, by definition, an impenetrable penetrator, as we have seen, a body whose exits must never be used as entrances. To translate into contemporary queer idiom, the Greco-Roman man can only ever be a "top" and must never be a "bottom." He is an assless cock, a bottomless top, a top who does not have a bottom of his own (cf. Simpson 1994, 135ff.). Greco-Roman discourses on sex conjure up a sex/gender system in which every sexual act *must* involve a masculine and a feminine partner—to the extent that when an anatomically female partner is lacking, an anatomically male partner must be conscripted to play the woman. Within the terms of this system, therefore, sex can only ever be a masculine-feminine activity: sex can only ever be heterosex. Greco-Roman discourses on sex thus enshrine a hyperheteronormativity—and centuries "before" heterosexuality.

But there is more. Within the cramped confines of this phallofixated system, sexual acts even between persons of the same sex automatically become displaced expressions of gender hierarchy. Sex becomes a mechanism for producing and maintaining gender hierarchy—one with an inbuilt safety

---

13. Rambuss continues: "Accounts that fashion a paradoxically 'female' or a 'bisexual' Jesus often do so at the cost of too quickly effacing the primary maleness of his body and its operations, as well as, perhaps more importantly, the possibilities a male Christ affords for a homoeroticized devotional expression" (1998, 38). His remarks are directed to recent interpreters of the devotional verse of the English metaphysical poets (John Donne, George Herbert, Thomas Traherne, and especially Richard Crashaw).

valve to ensure that the mechanism cannot be used for any other purpose. For whether the sexual partners happen to be a man and a woman, or a man and a "woman" (in the case of two males), or a "man" and a woman (in the case of two females), the superiority of the man and the inferiority of the woman is symbolically affirmed—endlessly reaffirmed—in and through the act of penetration. This symbolic reiteration of gender hegemony was the quintessence of sex for Greek and Roman male elites,[14] rendering the concept of nonpenetrative "lesbian" sex literally unthinkable (the phallus is the switch that activates the mechanism; without it no sex is possible). Greco-Roman heteronormativity thus turns homosex—even homosex between women—into an expression of misogyny.

In this essay I have been arguing that Paul, too, inhabited this conceptual enclosure (which more and more has come to resemble a factory floor), and that his "theological system" (to the extent that he can be said to have had *one*), traditionally thought to be encapsulated in his letter to the Romans, has not only been *infected* by this sex/gender system but partly *produced* by it.

Any changes introduced into the sex/gender system, therefore, would have immediate repercussions for the theological system. What sorts of changes? First and most obviously, perhaps, the abandonment of fixed sexual roles of domination and submission, conceptually correlated with the performance of masculinity and femininity respectively, for fluid sexual roles of "domination" and "submission," neither being automatically correlated with either gender. This would be a relatively minor adjustment. It would loosen the symbolic screws of a cast-iron concept of gender hierarchy, although without actually dismantling it.

Yet a reversal even on this modest scale would have massive repercussions for Pauline theology, given Paul's passionate conviction (classically expressed in Rom 1:18–32, as we have seen) that proper relations between human beings, even—or especially—sexual relations, necessarily mirror proper relations between human beings and God. Any expansion of the domain of the permissible in human sexual relations would, therefore, result in a corresponding transformation of human-divine relations. What transformed relations might we then envision between the three central characters in Paul's epochal passion play—between God and Jesus, Jesus and Paul, God and Paul? What else but those in which Paul would not only open himself utterly to Jesus, but Jesus, reciprocally, would open himself utterly to Paul. More significantly still,

---

14. And probably not just male elites. Craig Williams notes that the sexual preconceptions and prejudices evident in Roman graffiti seem to mirror those of the elite literary sources, notwithstanding the fact "that these graffiti were written by and for a broader cross-section of society than the literary texts" (1999, 257).

God would open himself to each of them in turn. The Bottomless Top, the conceptual pivot of Paul's entire theosexual system, would become a top with a bottom. God would get a bottom of his own.

And what might God not be ready for then? Sexual activity that would offer only the most precarious of toeholds to hierarchy, or none at all, and thus would constitute a divine warrant for radically egalitarian forms of social behavior? Nonphallic sexual activity, even? The trick would be to take that which is farthest outside the camp in Romans, that which is most anathemized—sex between women, as we have seen—and usher it into the center, into the tabernacle itself, thereby causing the models of divine-human relations, male-female relations, and even human-animal relations currently displayed in Romans to reform themselves radically in relation to it. This essay is offered as a prolegomenon to such a project.

Further Reading on Queer Studies

Burrus, Virginia. 2004. *The Sex Lives of Saints: An Erotics of Ancient Hagiography*. Divinations: Rereading Late Ancient Religion. Philadelphia: University of Pennsylvania Press. Queer, s/m and postcolonial theories weave through Burrus's close readings of the earliest Christian hagiographies.

Butler, Judith. 2004. *Undoing Gender*. London: Routledge. Butler's *Gender Trouble* (1990) is widely regarded as the quintessential specimen text of queer theory. *Undoing Gender* covers much of the same ground but in a more accessible, circumspect, and thoroughgoing fashion.

Foucault, Michel. 1978. *The History of Sexuality*, vol. 1: *An Introduction*. (French orig. 1976.) Translated by Robert Hurley. New York: Random House. Probably Foucault's most influential book. Argues that sexuality is a discursive construct, and locates its invention particularly in the late nineteenth century. Foucault's brand of constructionism has been extremely important for queer theory.

Goss, Robert E., and Mona West, eds. 2000. *Take Back the Word: A Queer Reading of the Bible*. Cleveland: Pilgrim. Twenty-one essays, most focused on a specific biblical text, and all intent on claiming the Bible for LGBT persons and communities.

Guest, Deryn. 2005. *When Deborah Met Jael: Lesbian Biblical Hermeneutics*. London: SCM. Meticulously outlines a lesbian biblical hermeneutic rooted in the lived experience of lesbians and LGBT folk generally.

Guest, Deryn, Robert E. Goss, Mona West, and Thomas Bohache, eds. 2006. *The Queer Bible Commentary*. London: SCM. A team of thirty-one scholars provides commentary on every book of the Bible. The volume's methodological range is described as spanning "feminist, queer, deconstructionist, postcolonial and utopian theories, the social sciences, and historical critical discourses" (xiii).

Halperin, David. 2002. *How to Do the History of Homosexuality*. Chicago: University of Chicago Press. Primarily a study of ancient Greek and Roman sex that further intensifies the already pronounced Foucauldianism of Halperin's *One Hundred*

Years of Homosexuality (1990). His extended critique of Bernadette Brooten's *Love between Women* (1996) is of particular interest to students of early Christian sex.

Loughlin, Gerard, ed. 2007. *Queer Theology: Rethinking the Western Body*. Oxford: Blackwell. Twenty-one essays divided into six parts: "Queer Lives"; "Queer Church"; "Queer Origins"; "Queer/ing Tradition"; "Queer/ing Modernity"; and "Queer Orthodoxy."

Martin, Dale B. 2006. *Sex and the Single Savior: Gender and Sexuality in Biblical Interpretation*. Louisville: Westminster John Knox. Seeks to counter biblical interpreters who attempt, through appeal to what the New Testament texts "actually" say about sex and marriage, to disguise their homophobia as responsible exegesis.

Moore, Stephen D. 2001. *God's Beauty Parlor: And Other Queer Spaces in and around the Bible*. Contraversions: Jews and Other Differences. Stanford, Calif.: Stanford University Press. An introduction to queer theory along with queer readings of the Song of Songs, Romans, Revelation, and the "beautiful" Jesus of popular imagination.

———. 2009. "Metonymies of Empire: Sexual Humiliation and Gender Masquerade in the Book of Revelation." Pages 71–97 in *Postcolonial Interventions: Essays in Honor of R. S. Sugirtharajah*. Edited by Tat-siong Benny Liew. The Bible in the Modern World 23. Sheffield: Sheffield Phoenix. Reads Revelation's Whore and Lamb with Judith Butler.

Sedgwick, Eve Kosofsky, ed. 1997. *Novel Gazing: Queer Readings in Fiction*. Durham, N.C.: Duke University Press. Seventeen essays attempt to turn queer theory into critical practice.

Stone, Ken. 2005. *Practicing Safer Texts: Food, Sex and Bible in Queer Perspective*. Queering Theology. New York: T&T Clark. Analyzes a series of Hebrew Bible texts in which both food and sex appear, on the assumption that food and sex are each useful for thinking the other.

Stone, Ken, ed. 2001. *Queer Commentary and the Hebrew Bible*. JSOTSup 334. Sheffield: Sheffield Academic Press. Seven exegetical essays, several of them highly audacious, on Hebrew Bible texts and themes, followed by three response essays.

Stone, Ken, and Holly Toensing, eds. Forthcoming. *Bible Trouble: Queer Readings at the Boundaries of Biblical Scholarship*. Semeia Studies. Atlanta: Society of Biblical Literature.

POSTCOLONIALITY

13

QUESTIONS OF BIBLICAL AMBIVALENCE AND AUTHORITY UNDER A TREE OUTSIDE DELHI; OR, THE POSTCOLONIAL AND THE POSTMODERN*

This essay took its first faltering steps as a paper that I wrote in 2000 for the inaugural session of the SBL New Testament Studies and Postcolonial Studies Consultation. My brief for the session was to address the relationship of postcolonialism and poststructuralism. I decided to toss postmodernism into the mix: Why balk at a colossal challenge when one is already faced with an enormous one? The result is a rather dense essay, perhaps the densest in this entire collection, which is certainly nothing to cheer about. My current preoccupation with postcolonial theory (broadly speaking, the poststructuralist analysis of colonialism, imperialism, and their ever more complex afterlives: neocolonialism, late capitalism, globalization...) is not a purely intellectual one. It, too, is deeply rooted in my biography, as the essay at one point attempts to explain. As a white male, nonetheless (and Ireland's sun-starved climate does produce some of the whitest males on the planet—ironically, given that country's dismally downtrodden history), I needed some initial encouragement to engage with the (post)colonial, and that encouragement came from Fernando Segovia. For that I will always be in his debt.

Effectively, this essay is a companion to the one with which this collection opens. But whereas my treatment of postmodernism and poststructuralism in the earlier essay is triangulated with aesthetic modernism (the literary and artistic avant-garde), my

---

*First published in Stephen D. Moore and Fernando F. Segovia, eds., *Postcolonial Biblical Criticism: Interdisciplinary Intersections* (The Bible and Postcolonialism 8; New York: T&T Clark, 2005), 79–96.

treatment of postmodernism and poststructuralism in the present essay is triangulated with colonialism, postcolonialism and neocolonialism (that other legacy of modernity). Postmodernism loses its virtue in its transition between the two essays (also see the headnote to "The 'Post-' Age Stamp"); and the (Christian) Bible, too, assumes a more sinister aspect, now "bearing both the standard of the cross and the standard of empire," as Homi Bhabha, postcolonial theorist par excellence and protagonist of the tale the present essay tells, memorably puts it (1994e, 92). The essay's title is a homage to Bhabha's 1985 article, "Signs Taken for Wonders: Questions of Ambivalence and Authority under a Tree Outside Delhi, May 1817" (Bhabha 1994g), technically the first example of postcolonial biblical criticism, albeit *avant la lettre* and arising as far outside the field of biblical studies as can reasonably be imagined.

Prefatory "Post-"script

Driven by the subaltern history of the margins of modernity—rather than by the failures of logocentrism—I have tried, in some small measure, to revise the known, to rename the postmodern from the position of the postcolonial. (Bhabha 1994f, 175)

Postcolonialism and postmodernism: one would be hard pressed by now to intone two more overdetermined, and overinflated, critical terms.[1] Is the "post" in postcolonialism the same as the "post" in postmodernism,[2] so that

---

1. The term "postcolonialism," for instance, "designates too many things, all at once," as Aijaz Ahmad complains. "It is said to refer, first, to conditions that are said to prevail in the former colonies, such as India. But the same term is also made to refer to a *global* condition of the relations between the West and the Rest...—so that 'postcoloniality' becomes a 'post' not only of colonialism but also of an indeterminate larger thing. At the same time, the term 'postcolonial' also comes to us as the name of a *discourse* about the condition of 'postcoloniality,'" and a discourse that presumes a "prior consent to theoretical postmodernity," what is more. "Between postcoloniality as it exists in a former colony like India, and postcoloniality as the condition of discourse practised by such critics as Homi Bhabha," he concludes sardonically, "there would appear to be a very considerable gap" (Ahmad 1996, 283, his emphasis). Robert Young proposes jettisoning the term "postcolonialism" altogether and replacing it with "tricontinentalism" (2001, 57).

2. A question especially associated with Kwame Anthony Appiah (1991), although his voice is but one in a cacophonous chorus that has addressed this perplexing relationship—

the two terms are merely alternative names for the same phenomenon? At first glance, perhaps, it might appear that a case could be made for this position, particularly if "postmodernism," or, better for our purposes, "postmodernity," is understood as that which has replaced or displaced "modernity" (to resort for the moment to a rather crude chrono-logic), the latter being understood in turn as the combined and cumulative product of the European Reformation, scientific revolution, and Enlightenment—together with the corollary colonization of the non-European world. Colonial exploitation, not least the slave trade, has often been said to have enabled the economies of early (and not so early) modern Europe in the material realm; while in the psychic realm, the non-European world, conceived as quinessentially "superstitious" and "primitive," served conveniently as the constitutive Other for Europe's dominant image of itself as quintessentially "rational" and "civilized" (cf. Moore-Gilbert 1997, 123). But if modernity is to be regarded as in no small part an effect of European colonialism, might not postmodernity and postcolonialism be regarded in consequence, not only as natural allies, but even as virtual synonyms?

To argue thus, however, would be to indulge in an overbenign reduction of the concept of postmodernity, or, to revert to the more common term, postmodernism.[3] As the latter term is now frequently used, it names much more than an antihegemonic reaction to or repudiation of the world-annexing impulses of European modernity. In its more bloated forms, indeed, postmodernism is a code word for the cultural logic of late capitalism (see Jameson 1991), whose signal features include mass culture, mass media, multinational corporations and information technology—although, seen from the "underside," as it were, this same set of features appear as the dissolution of traditional societies, asymmetrical systems of economic exchange, crippling national debt, limited access to technology, and so on.

Postmodernism, thus distended, however, is, if anything, a synonym not for *post*colonialism so much as for *neo*colonialism. The latter term, which is less evocative, perhaps, of a state "beyond" colonialism than of the West's continued domination of the Rest (see Nkrumah 1965; Young 2001, 44–56), better names the socioeconomic and sociopolitical constraints within which the majority of the world's population conducts its daily affairs. I am reminded of a now misplaced magazine article that tells of a certain Afri-

---

and arrived at a range of incommensurate conclusions. See, in addition, Tiffin 1988; Adam and Tiffin 1989; Mukherjee 1991; Ashcroft, Griffiths and Tiffin 1995, Part 4 ("Postmodernism and Postcolonialism"); Bhabha 1994f; 1996; Moore-Gilbert 1997, 121–30; Xie 1997; Quayson 2000; cf. Chioni Moore 2005.

3. Not that these two terms are invariably synonymous either; see pp. 13–14 above.

can village's recent attempts to honor the parousia of the CEO of Microsoft Corporation, a visitation preceded by a gift to the village of a state-of-the-art PC. Bill Gates arrived with his entourage to discover that the computer had been hooked up to the sole electrical outlet in the village, thereby becoming a shrine to the *deus absconditus* of neocolonialism and a poignant symbol of the village's simultaneous inclusion in and exclusion from the benefits of global capitalism—or of "postmodernism," in the distended sense. Far from being a synonym for "postcolonialism," indeed, "postmodernism," as neocolonialism, might instead be the primary phenomenon presently in need of postcolonial critique.

And yet there can be no clean subject-object separation of postcolonialism and postmodernism either, if for no other reason than that a third term regularly mediates between them in such a way as to muddy any clear distinction between them. That term is "poststructuralism."[4] In the minds of most who ponder such matters, poststructuralism (epitomized by, although by no means confined to, Derridean deconstruction) is quintessential academic postmodernism—postmodernism *as* academic discourse. And postcolonial theory—the most visible manifestation of contemporary postcolonial studies, itself epitomized by the names of Edward Said, Gayatri Chakravorty Spivak, and Homi Bhabha is—for the most part, poststructuralist through and through. Said's *Orientalism* (1978a), for instance, commonly regarded as the charter document of postcolonial theory, makes strategic use of the analytic categories of Michel Foucault (but also those of Antonio Gramsci) to excavate the West's multi-discursive construction of the "Orient." The book analyzes the emergent academic disciplines, political discourses, literary representations and elaborate cultural stereotypes by which the East, and especially the Middle East, became the West's constitutive other, particularly during the incremental expansion and consolidation of Europe's colonial empires in the eighteenth and nineteenth centuries. The book then proceeds to track Orientalism's labyrinthine ideological legacy down to the mid-twentieth century and beyond.[5] Said's dealings with Foucault, however, never entirely uncritical, were subsequently marked with increasing caution; "[Foucault's] Eurocentrism was almost total," he remarked at one point (2000, 196).[6] Spivak's embrace of poststructuralist thought, primarily that of Jacques Derrida, has been more consistent. She has remained remarkably "loyal" to deconstruction

---

4. For a definition of which, see pp. 1–2 n. 1 above.
5. Said 1986 and 1997 reconsider and further refine the concept of Orientalism.
6. Similarly in *Culture and Imperialism*, Said's most sustained example of postcolonial literary and cultural criticism, he takes Foucault to task for his "theoretical oversight" of "the imperial experience" (1993, 41; cf. 26–27).

13. QUESTIONS OF BIBLICAL AMBIVALENCE AND AUTHORITY   313

through the decades, never renouncing it no matter how unfashionable it has become (see esp. Spivak 1999, 423ff.). At the same time, she has never been content simply to mimic or replicate the signal Derridean moves (cf. Spivak 2005). Rather, her work has been instrumental in realigning, redirecting and reinventing deconstruction by transforming it into cultural criticism, or—to borrow a term from the subtitle of her earliest essay collection—"cultural politics" (Spivak 1988b). Bhabha's relationship to Derrida has also been marked by a complex mix of dependence and independence, as we shall see. All in all, however, Bhabha has been more eclectic than Spivak in his borrowings from poststructuralism. He is also significantly indebted to Jacques Lacan, and, to a lesser degree, to Foucault, Roland Barthes, Julia Kristeva, and even Louis Althusser (to add a "structuralist" name to the familiar "poststructuralist" litany), as well as to Mikhail Bakhtin.[7]

Postcolonial theory (or colonial discourse analysis, to restore its original name to it) has comfortably assumed its appointed place (all *too* comfortably, some would argue—more on this below) within the Anglo-American academy alongside New Historicism, "third-wave" feminism, queer theory, cultural studies, and other theory-savvy critical movements that all, to a greater or lesser degree, bring critical sensibilities forged in the crucible of an often generic poststructuralism to bear upon assorted "material" domains (history, not least the colonial variety; gender; sex and sexuality; popular culture), frequently in explicit reaction to the first, neo-formalist, putatively apolitical phase of French poststructuralism's appropriation in the Anglophone academy. Said's *Orientalism*, in particular, can be regarded as a crucial catalyst in the politicization, not just of Anglo-American poststructuralism, but of the Anglo-American literary academy more generally,[8] a transformation that began in earnest in the early 1980s and has been unrelenting ever since.

---

7. Excellent (if exacting) individual chapters on Said, Spivak, and Bhabha can be found in Young 1990; Childs and Williams 1997; Moore-Gilbert 1997. Shorter introductions to all three can be found in Hawley 2001. Moore-Gilbert has had a second shot at Spivak and Bhabha (Moore-Gilbert 2000), while Young has returned to Said (Young 2001, 383–94). Full-length books have also appeared on Said (e.g., Ashcroft 2001; Hussein 2002; Marrouchi 2004), Spivak (Morton 2002; 2007; Sanders 2006), and Bhabha (Huddart 2006). Said has been an interlocutor for a handful of biblical scholars; see esp. Whitelam 1996; Sugirtharajah 1998a; Friesen 2001; Frilingos 2004; Ahn 2006. Biblical-scholarly engagements with Bhabha have been more numerous; see, e.g., Liew 1999; Brett 2000; Runions 2002; Samuel 2002; 2007; Thurman 2003; Han 2005; Ahn 2006. For a rare biblical-scholarly engagement with Spivak, see Donaldson 2005.

8. Also worth noting in this regard is Said's once influential article, "The Problem of Textuality: Two Exemplary Positions" (1978b), which pitted a rhetorically politicized Foucault against a depoliticized Derrida.

Not surprisingly, perhaps, the spectacle of poststructuralism's systematic politicization, especially within the U.S. academy, has itself elicited political critique, none more scathing, perhaps, than that of Aijaz Ahmad (1992), whose primary target happens to be postcolonial theory, the bull's-eye on the target being Edward Said. According to Ahmad (and the summary of his extended arguments that follows is a partial and rather freely paraphrastic one), postcolonial theory replicates troublingly within the Western academy the international division of labor characteristic of global capitalism, whereby raw materials generated in the Third World (in this case, the archival products of colonialism: administrative records, missionary tracts, traces of indigenous voices, and so on) are exported to the First World, where they are turned into refined or luxury products by a privileged intelligentsia (themselves thoroughly insulated from the harsh material realities of Third World existence) for consumption by a metropolitan elite of fellow-scholars and graduate students, which in fact constitutes their primary audience, all direct engagement with the extraacademic world, least of all the working class or underclass, even within the U.S. itself, being foreclosed almost as a matter of course.

Symptomatic of the complicity of postcolonial theory with late capitalist ideology, presumably (to echo Ahmad further, but also to extrapolate from him), would be the fact that some of the wealthiest Western universities, ornate pillars of the social and political establishment, reserve some of their most coveted and most lucrative positions for "politicized" theorist-critics, not least leading postcolonial theorist-critics: Spivak holds a prestigious chair at Columbia, as did Said until his recent death, while Bhabha holds a no less prestigious one at Harvard (having ascended there in incremental stages by way of the University of Sussex and the University of Chicago, his stock, like that of Spivak, formerly of the University of Pittsburgh, inexorably rising with that of postcolonial studies). Such allegations, while crude, can have a deep impact nonetheless. A few semesters ago, to recite a personal example, an Argentinian student in one of my courses read aloud, and in shocked tones, an excerpt from Ahmad's blistering broadside at the outset of a class discussion of postcolonial theory, after which many members of the class seemed to find it all but impossible to take the topic seriously.

Rajeswari Sunder Rajan (1997) has attempted to respond on behalf of the accused (although the accusations he is countering are not those of Ahmad per se so much as the related ones of Arif Dirlik [1994]). "The operation of global capitalism as cause," notes Rajan, "is so pervasive that it is only too easy to establish that intellectuals in particular (and of every persuasion) are coopted within its system" (1997, 597). He goes on to suggest that what would be of significantly more interest would be "the identification of criticism or critics who could be considered exempt from the embrace of capitalism's reward

13. QUESTIONS OF BIBLICAL AMBIVALENCE AND AUTHORITY

system" (1997, 597). Rajan doesn't altogether succeed, however, in deflecting Dirlik's (or Ahmad's) accusations; for there are rewards and rewards, and the rewards attaching to an endowed chair at Harvard or Columbia are one thing, while those attaching to, say, a position at an inner-city community college are another altogether (to remain for now within the U.S., although the remuneration for such a position, even at entry level, would far exceed, even in real terms, that for a senior position at, say, the University of Havana, to cull but one example from a great many possible ones). But the argument now threatens to undercut itself, for faculty at community colleges and other institutions at the base of the U.S. pyramid of higher learning typically lack the institutional motivation and support to engage in research and publication, so that the only First World postcolonial intellectuals whose theoretical positions would, in accordance with the implicit canons advanced by Ahmad and Dirlik, be fully "authenticated" by their institutional locations would be those whose voices would be altogether absent from published academic debate—unlike those of Ahmad and Dirlik themselves.

What *is* highly instructive, nonetheless (and both Ahmad and Dirlik serve to remind us forcibly of it), is how the U.S. can brazenly lavish its most exalted academic honors upon the very intellectual class that tends to be most critical both of its domestic arrangements and international operations, seemingly in the sure and certain knowledge that the pronouncements of such intellectuals, once they exit the academic sphere, will plummet silently into a bottomless well of public indifference (unlike those of the Dixie Chicks, say, whose moderate interrogation of Operation Iraqi Freedom raised a storm of public reaction).[9] "I always counsel people against the decision to go into the

---

9. The successful Texas country group's lead singer Natalie Maines announced in a concert in London in March 2003 that she was "ashamed the president of the United States is from Texas" (referring, of course, to George W. Bush), after which country stations across the U.S., in response to calls from irate listeners, began to pull the Dixie Chicks' songs from their playlists. Postcolonial theory, for its part, did succeed the same year in making at least one splash in the extraacademic sphere in a hearing on Capitol Hill that bizarrely turned into a seminar on postcolonial theory. As Gaurav Desai and Supriya Nair (2005, 7) tell it, "On June 10, 2003 ... a U.S. Congressional Subcommittee on Select Education met to discuss 'International Programs in Higher Education and Questions of Bias.' Ostensibly a routine evaluation conducted before the reauthorization of the next cycle of funding of Title VI in the Higher Education Act, the proceedings were marked by the testimony of Stanley Kurtz, a research fellow at the Hoover Institution and contributing editor of the *National Review Online*. Kurtz ... alleged that area studies programs funded by Title VI monies were fundamentally anti-American in orientation and critical of American foreign policy. This was, he asserted, in no small part a result of the dominance of postcolonial scholarship in the academy. 'The ruling intellectual paradigm in academic area studies,' Kurtz testified, 'is called "post-colonial theory." Post-colonial theory was founded by

academy because they hope to be effective beyond it," literary theorist Stanley Fish announced at a much-publicized symposium on the future of "theory" staged at the University of Chicago in April 2003 (Eakin 2003, D9).[10] For Aijaz Ahmad, as we noted earlier, Edward Said epitomizes theory's scandalous shortcomings. Yet it is precisely Said who might be said to constitute the outstanding contemporary exception to Fish's cynical rule: until his premature death in 2003 from leukemia, Said was a leading U.S. academic intellectual whose outspoken (and theory-honed) views on Israeli-Palestinian relations in particular, expressed in numerous newspaper and magazine articles and radio and television interviews, and anchored in years of active service on the Palestinian National Council, made him a familiar and formidable name to an indeterminate but surely sizeable international public, many or most of whom had never heard of postcolonial studies.

And what of Homi Bhabha—interestingly enough, the only one of the more than two dozen academic luminaries assembled around the table at the Chicago symposium on theory's alleged bankruptcy to venture a defense of theory's political efficacy (see Eakin 2003, D9; Bhabha 2004)? What I myself have encountered repeatedly in recent years, as have several of my immediate colleagues in neighboring theological disciplines, is that a striking number of students coming into our classes, international students in particular, with intense commitments to social justice, vernacular hermeneutics, liberative praxis, and activist politics, feel themselves personally addressed by Homi Bhabha and discover in critical categories such as colonial ambivalence, mimicry, and hybridity analytic tools that enable them to reconceptualize their own relationships to their frequently complex sociocultural locations in ways that they experience as transforming and even empowering—as do I myself.

In the cultural crucible in which I spent my own formative years, that of postcolonial, hyper-Catholic, southern Ireland of the 1950s and 1960s, the

---

Edward Said. Said is famous for equating professors who support American foreign policy with the 19th-century European intellectuals who propped up racist colonial empires. The core premise of post-colonial theory is that it is immoral for a scholar to put his knowledge of foreign languages and cultures at the service of American power.'" The ensuing debate included a statement from Congressman Timothy Ryan: "I think that the fact that our federal money is going to teach ... post-colonial theory, I think [sic], speaks volumes about what kind of country we live in and what we stand for, that that would even be an option" (1995, 9). Desai and Nair conclude: "[This] rather muddled formulation rests on the by now numbingly familiar apotheosis of democratic debate in this country but perhaps more complacently depends on the arguable irrelevance of critiques to state dominance. And yet the gnat must have some sting to warrant even momentary congressional energy" (1995, 9–10).

10. For the published proceedings of the symposium, see Mitchell 2004.

Bible was an English book—*the* English book, indeed—so much so that when in due course I went in search of a college degree program in biblical studies, the only avenues open to me in the Irish republic were the degrees offered at the University of Dublin, Trinity College, that enduring monument to British colonial rule in Ireland, founded by Elizabeth I in 1592 to educate the sons of the Protestant Anglo-Irish aristocracy, and effectively closed to Catholics until the 1960s. My training in biblical studies at Trinity was simultaneously an induction in postcolonial studies, although I was insufficiently aware of it at the time. In any case (although I would not want to make too much of it), it is my own (necessarily eroded) identity as a member of that most unlikely of postcolonial peoples—a nation of white west-Europeans whose formative history includes some 800 years of colonial intervention (and not as agent, but as object)[11]—that equips me now with a keen appetite for pondering the complexities that characterize the often tortuous exchanges between colonizer and colonized during colonial occupation and after official decolonization (and not just in Ireland, of course), relations of domination and submission, coercion and co-option, attraction and revulsion (the very relations that most preoccupy Bhabha, as we shall see, and are the objects of his most incisive analyses)—and with tracing the Bible's ever-shifting place in this intricate web of exchanges.

Bhabha's Bible

> And the holiest of books—the Bible—bearing both the standard of the cross and the standard of empire finds itself strangely dismembered. (Bhabha 1994e, 92)

To begin again, but differently: postcolonial studies, poststructuralism, biblical interpretation—at least one notable interfacing of these three reading practices has already occurred, and occurred not in a corner but in a text that, arguably, ranks alongside Said's *Orientalism* as, simultaneously, the most celebrated and most contested product of contemporary postcolonial studies. I speak of Bhabha's 1994 essay collection, *The Location of Culture*, and specifically of "Signs Taken for Wonders: Questions of Ambivalence and Authority under a Tree Outside Delhi, May 1817," which was originally published in

---

11. In applying the adjective "colonial" in blanket fashion to this entire 800-year span, I am putting a simple spin on a complex issue. For an elaborately nuanced discussion of the ways in which the labels "colonial" and "postcolonial" may or may not be applied to different phases of Irish history, see Howe 2000, 7–20. Further primers on Ireland and postcoloniality include Lloyd 1993; Kiberd 1995; Carroll and King 2003.

318   THE BIBLE IN THEORY

1985, is the sixth of the book's eleven essays, and as such is a centerpiece of sorts. Not unlike other essays of eighties vintage engaged in heady fusions of poststructuralism and historiography—New Historicist essays in particular—this one too opens with a historical anecdote.[12]

The date: May 1817. The place: a grove of trees "just outside Delhi" (Bhabha 1994g, 102). An Indian catechist, Anund Messeh, has just arrived at the scene, having journeyed hurriedly and excitedly from his mission in Meerut, apparently in response to a report that a throng of some five hundred souls, men, women and children, are seated in the shade of the trees and engaged in scriptural reading and debate. The following exchange, attributed to Anund and an elderly member of the assembly by the *Missionary Register* of January 1818, whence Bhabha exhumed it, ensues:

> "Pray who are all these people? and whence come they?" "We are poor and lowly, and we read and love this book."—"What is that book?"—"The book of God!"—"Let me look at it, if you please." Anund, on opening the book, perceived it to be the Gospel of our Lord, translated into the Hindoostanee Tongue, many copies of which seemed to be in the possession of the party: some were PRINTED, others WRITTEN by themselves from the printed ones. Anund pointed to the name of Jesus, and asked, "Who is that?"—"That is God! He gave us this book."—"Where did you obtain it?"—"An Angel from heaven gave it us, at Hurdwar fair."—"An Angel?"—"Yes, to us he was God's Angel: but he was a man, a learned Pundit." (Doubtless these translated Gospels must have been the books distributed, five or six years ago, at Hurdwar by the missionary.)… "These books," said Anund, "teach the religion of the European Sahibs. It is THEIR book; and they printed it in our language, for our use." (Bhabha 1994g, 102–3)

In the space of some half-dozen sentences, the supplier of this divine book undergoes a rapid series of renamings that cascade in a dizzying descent. First, God himself is said to have provided the book out his bounty, then his Angel, then a mere mortal, albeit a "learned Pundit" and missionary, and finally the "European Sahibs." The transcendent Word has again become flesh—first

---

12. The anecdote frequently played a strategic role in New Historicism, infecting the teleological metanarratives of traditional historiography with elements of the contingent and the unassimilable (see further pp. 101–6 above). I would hesitate to ascribe an elaborate theory of the anecdote to "Signs Taken for Wonders" (even within New Historicism, such theory only rarely came to full expression; see esp. Fineman 1989; cf. Gallagher and Greenblatt 2000, 20–74 passim), but Bhabha does attempt to blow some sizeable holes in the metanarrative fabric of nineteenth-century colonial discourse by means of his own anecdote, as we shall see.

13. QUESTIONS OF BIBLICAL AMBIVALENCE AND AUTHORITY   319

brown flesh and then white flesh. Shimmering undecidably at the juncture of two incommensurate cultures, it belongs to both and neither at once.

The anecdote's intense attraction for Bhabha is hardly surprising. Bhabha's intellectual idiom is a generic poststructuralism, as we noted earlier, Derridean primarily, though Lacan also looms large on the Bhabhan mindscape, as does Foucault on occasion, and assorted other Parisian *penseurs*. Sizeable swathes of Bhabha's text approximate the near illegible density of early Derrida. Without the Derridean decoder ring, indeed, Bhabha simply cannot be deciphered. And many of the early Derridean mana-words—not least *writing, inscription, doubling, repetition, the book, the text*—are also Bhabhan obessions, not to say fetishes (fetishism itself being another Bhabhan obsession)—hence the allure of this anecdote for Bhabha, which he reads as an epiphanic scene insistently repeated, "played out in the wild and wordless wastes of colonial India, Africa, the Caribbean," namely, "the sudden, fortuitous discovery of the English book" (1994g, 102)—in this case the quintessential English book, the one that is at once the book of mission and the book of empire. What fascinates Bhabha is the way in which this found book, redolent with originary meaning and authority, universal and immutable, is inevitably and inexorably dislocated and evacuated, hallowed and hollowed at one and the same time, as it is subjected to linguistic and cultural reformulation and deformation—to reiteration, repetition, reinscription, doubling, dissemination, and displacement (to recite a deconstructive litany that is as familiar to the reader of Bhabha as to the reader of Derrida).

Bhabha is not without his own conceptual and terminological apparatus, however, drawn largely from Freud via Lacan—although, in hyper-eclectic fashion, also from a range of other theorist-critics as diverse as Fanon and Bakhtin—and given a highly distinctive inflection: *ambivalence, mimicry,* and *hybridity* are merely some of its better known categories (the Bhabhan mana-words, indeed). Nor does he hesitate to declare his distance from Derrida on occasion, most notably seven pages into the essay under discussion, when he announces his "departure from Derrida's objectives in 'The Double Session,'" the Derridean text he has been milking, and a strategic redirection of attention from "the vicissitudes of interpretation" in the act of reading "to the question of the effects of power" in the colonial arena (Bhabha 1994g, 108; cf. Derrida 1981b). In the event, Bhabha doesn't stray very far from Derrida; we are immediately told that the announced "departure" will actually constitute a "return" to some underdeveloped themes in Derrida's essay. The question I wish to ponder here, however—hardly a novel question, I realize, although one that, so far as I am aware, has not yet been the subject of protracted reflection in the context of biblical studies—is whether or to what extent strategies of reading whittled in the laps of some of the master texts of the European philosophical tradition—for that is what Derrida's texts have by now become—or in the laps of some of the master texts of the European psychoanalytic tradition, in the case of Lacan, are adequate to the task of analyzing European colonialism and its effects, including the mobilization and counter-mobilization of biblical texts in colonial arenas.

What Bhabha's deployment of poststructuralist, largely Derridean, thought does enable, arguably, is a more adequate appreciation of the *complexity* of the cultural space occupied by the Bible in British India. While Bhabha readily acknowledges that Said's *Orientalism* was seminal for his own project (Bhabha 1994d, ix), he just as readily takes Said to task for his (largely implicit) characterization of colonial discourse, epitomized by Orientalist discourse, as self-confident and self-consistent, monolithic and monologic, animated by a single unifying intention (the will to power), as well as for his corollary assumption that colonization itself is characterized by a one-sided possession of power on the part of the colonizer.[13] Aided and abetted by Freud, as refracted through Lacan, but also through Fanon, Bhabha calls each of these assumptions acutely into question.[14] For Bhabha, colonial discourse is characterized above all by *ambivalence*, which is to say simultaneous attraction and repulsion, as distinct from pure unequivocal opposition. Consequently, colonial discourse is riddled with contradictions and incoherences, traversed by anxieties and insecurities, and hollowed out by originary lack and internal heterogeneity. For Bhabha, moreover, the locus of colonial power, far from being unambiguously on the side of the colonizer, inheres instead in a shifting, unstable, potentially subversive, "in-between" or "third" space between colonizer and colonized, which is characterized by *mimicry*, on the one hand, in which the colonized heeds the colonizer's peremptory injunction to imitation, but in a manner that constantly threatens to teeter over into parody or mockery; and by *hybridity*, on the other hand, another insidious product of the colonial encounter that further threatens to fracture the colonizer's identity and authority by exposing the colonizer's culture as always already infected by impurity and alterity.[15]

---

13. In *Culture and Imperialism* (1993), Said himself set out to complicate his earlier characterization of the colonizer-colonized relationship, as he explained in an interview (2002, 4–5).

14. Bhabha's relationship to Fanon is itself somewhat complex, however, because he also takes Fanon to task (specifically, the Fanon of *The Wretched of the Earth* [1961]) for his "Manichaean" locating of power too asymmetrically on the side of the colonizer (Bhabha 1994c, esp. 61–63).

15. See esp. Bhabha 1994a, 129–38, for ambivalence; 1994e for ambivalence and mimicry; 1994g, 111–22, for hybridity; and 1990 and 1994b, 37–39, for the "Third Space."

13. QUESTIONS OF BIBLICAL AMBIVALENCE AND AUTHORITY 321

What Bhabha doesn't address, directly at least, is what all of this might mean for the colonizer's book—which is, of course, to say the "European" book par excellence, the Bible—but it requires but little reflection to see that it means the book's *deconstruction*. (Could Bhabha's essential Derrideanism lead us to expect anything else?) If Said's conception of colonial discourse and colonial power admits, in principle at least, of a Bible that can function more or less straightforwardly as an effective instrument of the colonizer's will to subjugate the colonized, Bhabha's conception of colonial discourse and colonial power conjures up a rather different Bible, a far more mercurial Bible, which, as it permeates the cultural space of the colonized, effortlessly adapts to its contours, is rewritten in the process of being reread, and thereby subverts the colonizer's claims on its behalf of univocity and universality.

In the face of the subtle hermeneutical spectacle with which Bhabha implicitly presents us, however, all sorts of uncomfortable questions arise, many of which have already been posed in one form or another by Bhabha's critics.[16] Several touch on ostensibly universalizing moves in Bhabha's own text, most notably his exportation, lock, stock, and barrel, to the colonies of European psychoanalytic theory in the Freudian-Lacanian mode (e.g., Young 1990, 144; Moore-Gilbert 1997, 140–51).[17] This colonial export business is merely one aspect of a problem that is much larger than Bhabha, however, that of the blanket application of "First World" theory more generally to "Third World" cultures. (In biblical studies, the analogue has been a kind of methodological imperialism in which only methods and theories manufactured in Europe or North America have been deemed adequate to the task of exegesis—and not only by the manufacturers themselves, resulting in an incessant stream of students from Africa, Latin America, and especially Asia to study in European and North American universities and seminaries.) Yet in the case of Bhabha, what is most problematic, perhaps, is not his *use* of psychoanalytic theory per se but his failure to acknowledge its cultural specificity. In this regard, he has been compared unfavorably to Fanon, who also makes use of Freudian and even Lacanian categories (e.g., Fanon 1967, 161 n. 25), but never uncritically or unselfconsciously.

Still more problematic in Bhabha's writings is the thorny issue of *agency* (see, e.g., Parry 2004, 13–36, 55–74 passim)—although the limitations of his work in this regard are paradoxically bound up with its moments of greatest insight. Bhabha's basic approach to colonialism and its aftermath, it might be said, provides an exemplary, if incomplete, analytic model. To state it (all

---

16. Huddart 2005, 149–69, usefully surveys a wide range of critical reactions to Bhabha's work

17. For the attempt of the accused to respond to the charge, see Bhabha 2002, 29–32.

too) simply, critical approaches that concentrate exclusively on the "outward" appurtenances of colonialism and its counter-effects, such as military interventions, administrative infrastructures, nationalist movements, civil disobedience, or armed insurrections—not to deny for a moment the importance of analyzing such fundamental phenomena—cannot account adequately for the immensely complex relations of collusion and resistance, desire and disavowal, dependence and independence that can characterize the exchanges between colonizer and colonized during colonial occupation *and* after official decolonization. Isolating and unraveling these often tortuous relations, tensions, and affiliations accounts for Bhabha's most impressive achievements, and his indispensable tools to this end have been those forged in the fires of poststructuralist thought.[18] As he himself has put it:

> My growing conviction has been that the encounters and negotiations of differential meanings and values within "colonial" textuality, its governmental discourses and cultural practices, have enacted, *avant la lettre*, many of the problematics of signification and judgment that have become current in contemporary theory—aporia, ambivalence, indeterminacy, the question of discursive closure, the threat to agency, the status of intentionality, the challenge to "totalizing" concepts, to name but a few. (1992, 439)[19]

---

18. *European* poststructuralist thought (to resurrect the earlier issue)? Yes, on the face of it, although Robert Young, for one, has made a spirited case against seeing poststructuralism as simply or straightforwardly European, Euro-American, or Western. He argues: "In fact, the 'high European theory' of structuralism and poststructuralism is of broadly non-European origin: structuralism was developed by the Prague school as an anti-western strategy, directed against the hierarchical cultural and racial assumptions of imperialist European thought. Many of those who developed the theoretical positions known collectively as poststructuralism came from Algeria and the Maghreb. Though structuralism and poststructuralism were taken up and developed in Europe, both were indeed alien, and fundamentally anti-western in strategy" (2001, 67–68). Young's chapter on Derrida, in particular, subtitled "Derrida in Algeria" (2001, 411–26), pushes this line of argument to the limit—and possibly over.

19. Elsewhere, in an interview, Bhabha recalls that while working as a graduate student on the novels of V. S. Naipaul he was reminded of the fact that "in literature at least, no colonized subject had the illusion of speaking from a place of plenitude or fullness. The colonial subject was a kind of split subject and 'knew' it both phenomenologically and historically. Whereas I was being taught that such splitting of the subject was the general condition of the psyche (Lacan) … there was a much more specific or 'local' historical and affective apprehension of this which was part of the personhood of the postcolonial subject. The 'decentering of the self' was the very condition of agency and imagination in these colonial or postcolonial conditions, and it becomes more than a theoretical axiom; it becomes a protean, everyday practice, a way of living with oneself and other" (2002, 21).

13. QUESTIONS OF BIBLICAL AMBIVALENCE AND AUTHORITY 323

Bhabha's psychoanalytic and poststructuralist version of postcolonial criticism is most in its element, one might say, when applied to "normal" colonial relations, as opposed to overtly coercive colonial relations when the use of armed force is paramount. That is when Bhabhan concepts such as mimicry and hybridity come into their own. Both implicitly and explicitly, Bhabha ascribes considerable subversive potential to such phenomena. Yet where is this subversion, this sabotage, this resistance to colonial domination actually occurring? In the consciousness of the individual colonized subject? Or in his or her subconscious? Or unconscious? Or is its real locus instead in the tide of discourse that ebbs and flows between colonizer and colonized, causing the colonizer's identity and authority to be surreptitiously eroded in and through his discursive impositions on the colonized? Is the colonizer, then, the ultimate agent of his own discursive undoing? Characteristically, Bhabha never tackles such questions head on.[20]

"Signs Taken for Wonders," however, is one essay in which Bhabha is more than usually emphatic that the colonized are engaged in active subversion of the colonizer's discourse, in this case the colonizer's Scripture. Ostensibly, the encounter of the catechist Anund Messeh with the throng of five hundred outside Delhi in May 1817 is enacted amid *ruins*. As Bhabha reports, a letter from a representative of the Indian Church Missionary Society sent to London that same month expressed the desire that the Indian "heathens," suitably catechized, themselves "be made the instruments of pulling down their own religion, and of erecting in its ruins the standards of the Cross" (1994g, 106). Bhabha's countervailing desire, understandably enough, is that of interpreting these ruins, or runes, differently, by reading *with* the natives assembled under the tree outside Delhi, and *against* the narrator of the *Missionary Register* anecdote, for whom these natives, seemingly, are a gormless, guileless, and generally ignorant lot.

To take up the anecdote where we earlier left off: "'These [Gospel] books,' said Anund, 'teach the religion of the European Sahibs. It is THEIR book; and they printed it in our language, for our use.' 'Ah! no,' replied [his interlocutor], 'that cannot be, for they eat flesh'" (Bhabha 1994g, 103). Bhabha remarks (and here I am both paraphrasing and amplifying his comment) that this "canny" observation effectively challenges the assumption that the authority of the "English book" is universal and self-evident by underscoring the cultural specificity and relativity of its provenance. Bhabha's exegesis of this canny rejoinder, and of the natives' subsequent declaration that they are willing to be baptized, but "will never take the Sacrament [of the Eucha-

---

20. Even in the essay in *The Location of Culture* entitled "The Postcolonial and the Postmodern," whose subtitle is "The Question of Agency" (1994f).

rist] ... because the Europeans eat cow's flesh, and this will never do for us" (1994g, 104)—statements he characterizes as "insurgent interrogations in the interstices" of colonial authority (1994g, 105)—occupies a further five pages of dense meditation.

What is being accomplished under the tree outside Delhi, however, at least on Bhabha's reading, is nothing less than the hybridization of the "English book." The colonizers' missionary strategy of distributing Hindi Bibles to the native populace, Bible's calculated to function as timebombs that will eventually decimate the native's indigenous religious culture from within, has exploded in the colonizers' faces. "After our experience of the native interrogation," claims Bhabha, "it is difficult to agree entirely with Fanon that the psychic choice is to 'turn white or disappear.' There is the more ambivalent, third choice: camouflage, mimicry, black skins/white masks," he adds, reading Fanon against Fanon, and quoting Lacan: "It is not a question of harmonizing with the background but, against a mottled background, of being mottled—exactly like the technique of camouflage practised in human warfare" (Bhabha 1994g, 120–21, quoting Lacan 1978, 99). And it is as a "masque of mimicry" that Bhabha ultimately construes the anecdote of the encounter under the tree outside Delhi, a moment of "civil disobiedience" enacted openly under the eye of colonial power by means of the subtle strategy that he terms "sly civility" (1994g, 121; cf. 1994h).

And it is surely in "civil" colonial encounters such as this one—and most of all in "textual" encounters—that Bhabhan theory is at its most persuasive, if it is ever to be persuasive at all. For if it is to be objected—as indeed it has been (e.g., Moore-Gilbert 1997, 134–35)—that, in the larger scheme of things, any amount of colonial ambivalence, mimicry, or hybridity did not, in the end, effectively hamper British administration and exploitation of India, it is no less evident that the colonizers at least failed to impose their religious ideology uniformly upon the Indian populace.

In the end, however, Bhabha does not seem to know quite what to do with the Bible. "And what is the significance of the Bible?" "Signs Taken for Wonders" eventually inquires, only to answer lazily, "Who knows?" (1994g, 121), a shrug of the shoulders all the more surprising for the fact that the essay has already implicitly provided an answer. The significance of the Bible in the Indian colonial situation, it has suggested, was that it was an especially fraught site of simultaneous compliance and resistance (the Indian Bible thus turns out, not altogether unexpectedly, to be a Bhabhan Bible). That it could, and did, function as a colonialist instrument of coercion and co-option hardly needs belaboring.

But the extent to which it could simultaneously function as an instrument of native resistance in that situation is further suggested by a final excerpt from the *Missionary Register* of May 1817, which Bhabha quotes, although without comment, thereby ending his essay. The author of this excerpt is yet another missionary to the Indians (this one British, unlike Anund Messeh), who can hardly contain his frustration:

> Still [every Indian] would gladly receive a Bible. And why? That he may store it up as a curiosity; sell it for a few pice; or use it for waste paper.... [A]n indiscriminate distribution of the scriptures, to everyone who may say he wants a Bible, can be little less than a waste of time, a waste of money and a waste of expectation. For while the public are hearing of so many Bibles distributed, they expect to hear soon of a corresponding number of conversions. (1994g, 122)

In the colonial context, the practice of eagerly acquiring the European Book of books only to barter it without first having read it, or especially to employ it as waste paper,[21] might well be construed as the epitome of a *materialist* reading of the colonial Bible, a singularly sly and canny affirmation of the ineluctable materiality of this Sign of signs, and hence its cultural specificity and relativity. Simultaneously and consequently, however, these casual yet highly charged gestures might also be construed as the epitome of a *resistant* reading of the colonial Bible, one that resists precisely by refusing to read. More precisely still even, these gestures might be said to resist by resolutely remaining at the level of the material signifier, the papery substance itself—miraculously thin, almost transparent, yet wholly tangible nonetheless—refusing its translation, its sublation, into a transcendental, transcontextual, transcultural signified. Arguably, such a mode of reading would also be an entirely apt, if altogether paradoxical, model for a biblical critical practice that would aspire to be "postcolonial" and "poststructuralist" at once—or to put it another way (a still more simplistic way), "political" and "postmodern" at once. And such a critical practice might, among other things, entail gingerly picking up the tangled thread that Homi Bhabha so abruptly drops at the end of "Signs Taken for Wonders" and patiently picking at it until some of the denser knots that bind the biblical texts to diverse colonial contexts—knots themselves constituted by elaborate acts of reading—begin to unravel.

---

21. Or worse? South African liberation theologian Itumeleng Mosala, on a visit to Drew Theological School in February 2000, began his public lecture with an eyebrow-raising anecdote of two opponents of apartheid held in a single, bleak prison cell, one bereft of toilet tissue and every other creature comfort, but thoughtfully furnished with twin Bibles; of the difficult decision facing each prisoner in consequence; and of the symbolic stakes in each course of action.

14
"The Romans Will Come and Destroy Our Holy Place and Our Nation": Representing Empire in John*

This essay is one of three freestanding exegetical chapters in my book *Empire and Apocalypse*; the other two treat Mark and Revelation. On the face of it, the present essay would seem to be the one least influenced by postcolonial theory. The Revelation chapter sets forth the influential analytic categories of Homi Bhabha (colonial ambivalence, mimicry, and hybridity) and proceeds to apply them to Revelation, while the Mark chapter also explicitly adduces Bhabha and reads the Gospel as an elaborate instance of colonial ambivalence. In the present essay, however, I am experimenting with a more oblique approach to theoretical exegesis. The footnotes teem with references to mainstream Johannine scholarship. But while this work serves to refine the reading (providing an "indispensable guardrail," as Derrida might say [1976, 158]), it is not what drives it or fuels its engine. The excruciatingly close style of reading that characterizes the latter sections of the essay (enough to cause even its author's eyes to glaze over occasionally), a style obsessively attentive to ambiguities and inconsistencies, logical tensions and unintentional effects, owes everything to ingrained habits of analysis that are best described as deconstructive (even if Derrida never features in the footnotes). Or so I would like to imagine, anyway.

What I am about, then, in this essay is not so much applying the postcolonial theory of Homi Bhabha or Gayatri Spivak

---

* First published in Stephen D. Moore, *Empire and Apocalypse: Postcolonialism and the New Testament* (The Bible in the Modern World 12; Sheffield,: Sheffield Phoenix, 2006), 45–74.

to John's representations of empire as replicating Bhabha's and Spivak's signal strategy: that of deploying a deconstructive sensibility to tease out the tortuous complexities and contradictions of life under colonialism and imperialism. Alternatively, I'm merely doing bad historical criticism—a possibly I don't entirely discount, actually, having almost unlimited faith as I do in historical criticism's alchemical ability to take whatever is poured into it from outside (in this case, postcolonial theory of the deconstructive variety) and transform it into a disguised version of itself. But that is the subject of another essay, or several (Moore and Sherwood 2010a, 2010b, 2010c).

Prologue: Of Christs and Conquistadores

The true light that enlightens everyone was coming into the world. (John 1:9)

We penetrated deeper and deeper into the heart of darkness.... We were wanderers on prehistoric earth, on an earth that wore the aspect of an unknown planet. We could have fancied ourselves the first men taking possession of an accursed inheritance, to be subdued at the cost of profound anguish and of excessive toil. (Conrad 1902, 43)

Here, sailing toward an alien land in uncharted waters, and yet it was as if he were coming home. (Falconer 2002, 9)

The Fourth Gospel numbers among its distant descendants the diverse travel narratives of modern European colonialism. For the Johannine Jesus, too, is an envoy from a distant realm who claims the world through which he is journeying and all its inhabitants for the supreme power whom he purports to represent. This is the sensibility that Musa Dube incisively brings to the Fourth Gospel (1998, esp. 122–24; cf. Dube and Staley 2002a, 1, 9). For Dube, the Johannine Jesus is a precursor of the "earth-swallowing" Mr. Kurtz, a Conradian traveler journeying into *The Heart of Darkness* that is the unredeemed Johannine cosmos: "The light shines in the darkness, and the darkness has not overcome it" (John 1:5).[1]

---

1. Dube quotes Conrad on Kurtz: "I saw him open his mouth wide ... as though he had wanted to swallow ... all the earth" (Conrad 1902, 74, in Dube 1998, 122).

14. THE ROMANS WILL COME AND DESTROY OUR HOLY PLACE

A further illuminating intertext for the Fourth Gospel, it seems to me, is a rather more recent novel, Colin Falconer's *Feathered Serpent* (2002), a vivid and wrenching narrative of the Spanish conquest of Mexico. The eponymous Feathered Serpent is the Aztec deity Quetzalcóatl. But in the fertile hermeneutic imagination of the novel's compelling female protagonist, Ce Malinali Tenepal—better known to posterity as La Malinche[2]—Feathered Serpent is also Hernán Cortés. More precisely, the arrival of the conquistador in her land is interpreted by Malinali as the long-awaited advent of Feathered Serpent. The physical aspect of Quetzalcóatl had been imprinted in her mind since childhood: almost human, he is tall, bearded, and fair-skinned, the most beautiful of the gods (Falconer 2002, 23). When she is confronted with the unfathomable Other, then, in the persons of the ragtag Spanish landing party, the appearance of their leader trumpets forth his identity:

> Out there on the river is the great canoe they speak of, flying a banner with the red cross of Feathered Serpent.[3] There can be no doubt. The day has finally come.
> "Look," I whisper to Rain Flower.
> "I see it, Little Mother."
> "I told you! It has happened!"
> But still I cannot see *him*. I know he is not the god with the corn silk hair and turquoise eyes or the fire-haired one ... not any of these other bearded, pink-faced creatures, many of them with faces pitted like lava stone, others with...
> *There!*
> For a moment it is hard to breathe. He is just as I have imagined him, as I saw him on the pyramid at Cholula, as he has been depicted a thousand times on statues and carvings and reliefs in temple walls: a dark beard, black hair falling to his shoulders, his face framed by his helmet, which is itself decorated with a quetzal-green plume.[4] The gray eyes watch me intently, as if he, too, has experienced this same moment of recognition.
> And now he approaches. (2002, 35)

---

2. La Malinche makes her first appearance in the historical record in Bernal Díaz del Castillo's 1568 eyewitness account of the Spanish conquest, *Historia verdadera de la conquista de la Nueva España*. Díaz, however, as a loyal son of Spain, does not brand her a traitor to her people. That infamous characterization of her comes of age in Félix Varela's 1826 novel *Jicoténcal* and the nineteenth century Mexican independence movement. See further Cypess 1991; Alarcón 1997; Harris 2004. For an earlier attempt to bring La Malinche into dialogue with a biblical text, see Maldonado 1995.

3. The cross happens to be a symbol of fertility in her culture (*Feathered Serpent*, p. 36).

4. Another of Quetzalcóatl's symbols, as is later made explicit (Falconer 2002, 60).

I, for my part, meanwhile, find myself no less predisposed to identify this mesmerizing stranger with yet another divine being. Although he is not Quetzalcóatl, this other god's totem is also the serpent: "And as Moses lifted up the serpent [*ton ophin*] in the wilderness, so must the Son of Man be lifted up, that whoever believes in him may have eternal life" (John 3:14–15; cf. 12:32–34). Of course, the Fourth Gospel declines to describe the physical appearance of its protagonist. But the blank silhouette thereby outlined afforded imperial Christianity the opportunity to imprint its own idealized features onto the conquering hero of the Johannine travel narrative. Appropriately enough, therefore, Falconer's Cortés in his physical aspect is a virtual twin of the Christ endlessly produced and reproduced by the early modern European imagination:

> Montecuhzoma took an agave thorn from the shrine and stabbed at his own flesh, repeatedly, until the blood ran down his arms. "Did you see this stranger who claimed to be Quetzalcóatl?"
> "Yes, my lord. His skin was white, like chalk, and he had a dark beard and a straight nose." (2002, 60)[5]

Like the denizens of Jerusalem who agonize over Jesus' identity (John 7:25–27, 31), the Mexica debate the identity of the incomprehensible stranger. "The ancient prophecies are fulfilled!" Malinali assures them; "Feathered Serpent has returned!" "Is he truly a god?" one of them dubiously inquires, to which Malinali replies, in effect, that his divinity is written all over his face: "Look at his white face, his black beard. Do you not recognize him?" (2002, 50). Within the densely ironic weave of the narrative, Malinali has become the unwitting mouthpiece for the conquistadors' own self-representation as emissaries of Christ, conformed to his image and likeness. Like the Samaritan woman of John 4:1–42, Malinali is the female personification of her people—more accurately, the personification of her people as susceptible to seduction and eventual domination by the unfathomable stranger: "Many Samaritans from that city believed in him because of the woman's testimony.... So when the Samaritans came to him, they asked him to stay with them..." (4:39–40; cf. Dube 2002, 57, 69, 71).[6]

---

5. These features are coupled with dark hair falling to his shoulders, as we saw earlier.

6. Further on this recurrent trope whereby the seduction of a native woman by a foreign conqueror becomes "a micro-colonization pregnant with allegorical implications," see Harris 2004, 244 (from which this pithy quote comes), also Hulme 1985 and Donaldson 2002. As Harris notes, in the chronicles of the conquest of the Americas, the trope can be traced all the way back to Columbus's diary (2004, 244).

Cortés/Christ represents himself to the Mexica as harbinger of "the good news of the one true religion" (Falconer 2002, 51). More ambitiously, he explains that he has been "sent by his most Catholic majesty, Charles V, king of Spain … to show … the way to true religion" (50), impelling Malinali to muse: "I wonder who this great god might be that Feathered Serpent serves in this way. He must surely be referring to Olintecle, the Father of All Gods" (51). Her identification of Cortés's Lord as his heavenly Father later finds elegant expression in her explanation to a fellow native that "The bearded god speaks Castilian, the language spoken in heaven" (82). The immeasurable superiority of the "Cloud Lands" (70) from whence Cortés/Christ has journeyed ("My kingdom is not of this world"—John 18:36) confers upon him absolute authority over the patently inferior lands that he has condescended to visit. Shocked at the stranger's stunning arrogance, a representative of the local elite protests to Malinali, "He has only just arrived in our lands," to which she serenely responds, "They are his lands, so he may do as he wishes" (51).

In the far distance, meanwhile, the uncertain outline of the swordless (cf. John 18:10–11) but world-conquering Johannine Jesus shimmers softly in the harsh Samaritan sun (cf. 4:6), and his hypnotic voice, only faintly distorted, carries over the centuries and the seas to his sword-wielding, world-conquering followers poised on the shores of yet another Samaria: "I tell you, lift up your eyes, and see how the fields are already white for harvest.… For here the saying holds true, 'One sows and another reaps.' I sent you to reap that for which you did not labor; others have labored, and you have entered into their labor" (4:35–38).

Of course, there are other voices also in the Fourth Gospel; there are even other incarnations of its protagonist. But are there also other paths out of Samaria that lead elsewhere than to Mexico by way of Rome? How best to characterize the political ideology of this Gospel?

"I Find This Man to Be Politically Innocuous"

John is at once the most—and the least—political of the canonical Gospels. It is the *most* political, because both popular support for, and official opposition to, Jesus' mission in this Gospel are each accorded a rationale that is more explicitly political than in the Synoptic Gospels.[7] Consider John 6:15, on the one hand, in which the people are poised to "take [Jesus] by force to make him king" (cf. 12:12), and 11:48, on the other hand, in which the religious authori-

---

7. Recognition of which fact began in earnest, apparently, with Schlier 1956 [1941]; cf. 1968, esp. 224–25. Notable among more recent readings of John as a deeply political text are Rensberger 1988 and Cassidy 1992.

ties anxiously articulate the potentially catastrophic political consequences of this popular fervor: "If we let him go on like this, every one will believe in him, and the Romans will come and destroy our holy place and our nation." Consider, too, the unique prominence given to the theme of Jesus' kingship in the Johannine passion narrative. Apart from a single reference to him as "Son of God" (19:7), "King of the Jews" is the only title used of Jesus throughout that narrative. The term *basileus* ("king," "emperor") occurs no fewer than eleven times, and the term *basileia* ("kingdom," "kingship," "empire") an additional three, in the relatively terse exchanges between Pilate and Jesus and Pilate and Jesus' accusers—which is to say that John represents the charges brought against Jesus as *political* charges with a consistency and single-mindedness that is altogether absent from the Synoptic tradition. Yet John is also the *least* political of the canonical Gospels, it might equally be argued, because the same passion narrative seems to place Jesus' kingship front and center only in order to depoliticize it.

Throughout the Roman trial and crucifixion narrative in John, Jesus is—yet is not—"King of the Jews." His kingship is an object of incessant ambivalence in the narrative (18:33–40; 19:14–15, 19–22), and also of mockery and mimicry (19:2–5).[8] And yet, like any other trial, John's Roman trial disallows an ambivalent verdict. The reader encoded and embedded in the text, constructed and called into being through engagement with the text, is expected to take sides. Far from being granted a godlike position above, behind, or beyond the text, the reader is summoned to adopt one or other of the roles scripted in advance by the text and, indeed, dramatized within it.[9] And Johannine commentators have tended traditionally and overwhelmingly to assume Pilate's role, improvising on his lines, and siding with him over against "the Jews" on the issue of Jesus' kingship. Raymond Brown speaks for most when he writes of the latter stages of the trial, "Pilate now understands that Jesus claims no political kingship, for he has found Jesus innocent" (1970, 885). The implicit tone is one of approval: Pilate is correct in his estimate. And the meaning of "innocent" here would appear to be "politically unthreatening."[10]

If Jesus' royal claim, however, is not to be construed as a threat to Roman hegemony—imperial, colonial, political, military, or cultural—the embarrass-

---

8. Alternatively, or simultaneously, depending on how we read, it is Jewish nationalism that is the object of such treatment in the passion narrative. See Rensberger 1984, 402ff., which is paralleled in Rensberger 1988, 94ff.

9. Further on this deconstructive trope, see pp. 85–86 above.

10. Other scholars are more explicit and emphatic than Brown in this regard. Hans Kvalbein, for instance, states that John 18:28—19:19 "shows a Jesus who is no political challenge to the Roman Empire," and has no intention "of undermining the Roman authorities" (2003, 227–28). Kvalbein is echoing Martin Hengel (1991).

ing question arises: Of what use is it then? To anyone but the Romans, that it. If the Roman prefect's "I find no crime in him [*egō oudemian hueriskō en autō aitian*]" (18:38) is to be construed—approvingly and unequivocally—as meaning that the Jewish Messiah's brand of kingship is not, in the end, a threat to the Roman emperor's brand, then pro-Roman apologetics would here seem to be extending themselves to the limit and paving the royal road to the fourth century and an unproblematic fusion of Christianity and Rome.

In an irony not foreseen by this consummately ironic Evangelist, the only characters in the drama proposing a more satisfactory interpretation of Jesus' kingship—one singularly at odds with Jesus' own interpretation, that of Pilate, and that of most Johannine commentators—are "the Jews." "The Jews" expound a Christology that runs counter to Pilate's—and Jesus' own—apolitical Christology. "The Jews" expound a Christology whose long-delayed fruit, it might even be said, is less fourth-century Constantinian Christianity than late twentieth-century liberation theology, prompting the following paraphrase of the dialogue:

> Pilate: "Your accusations notwithstanding, I find this man to be politically innocuous."
> "The Jews": "Nothing could be further from the truth. He imperils the imperial status quo. He is actually more of an affront to the emperor, and hence a more serious threat to you, even than that militant insurgent Barabbas."

In that they were wrong, however, if history is to be the judge.

Hurrying to the Praetorium

More even than in Mark, the face of Rome in John is the blurred face of the Prefect of Judea, Pontius Pilate. This is not only because, unlike Mark, and Matthew and Luke following him, no centurion hovers at the foot of the cross in John as an ancillary personification in the passion narrative of Roman imperial authority. It is also because the figure of Pilate looms considerably larger in the Fourth Gospel in general than in the Synoptics, and for two reasons. First, the Johannine Pilate is simply accorded more lines than his Synoptic counterparts, and memorable lines at that. The relative complexity of the Johannine Pilate as a character owes much to such enigmatic utterances as "Am I a Jew?" (18:35); "What is truth?" (18:38); "Behold the man!" (19:5); and "What I have written I have written" (19:22).[11] Second, the Judean religious

---

11. For literary studies of the characterization of John's Pilate, see, for example, Culpepper 1983, 142–43, and esp. Conway 1999, 154–63.

leadership is accorded a far more effaced role in the Johannine trial narrative than in the Synoptic trial narratives, which has the effect of casting the Roman leadership, almost wholly embodied in the person of Pilate, in still sharper relief—*almost* wholly, because there is, apparently, one further Roman of rank in John's passion narrative.[12]

On a literal reading of John 18:3, 12—one matter-of-factly embraced by quite a number of scholars (e.g., Barrett 1978, 518, 524; Rensberger 1984, 399–400; 1988, 90; Brown 1994, 1:248–51; O'Day 1995, 801–2; cf. Schnackenburg 1982, 3:222–23)—a cohort (*speira*) of Roman troops under the command of a tribune (*chiliarchos*) is present at Jesus' arrest. The term *speira* ordinarily designates six hundred soldiers. John thus floods the garden with Roman troops, by implication, cramming them in shoulder-to-shoulder and cheek-to-jowl, so that they overwhelmingly outnumber the other named component of the arresting party, "the attendants [*hypēretai*] of the chief priests and the Pharisees" (18:3; cf. 18:12). From the outset, then, and to a degree entirely unmatched by its Synoptic counterparts, the Johannine passion narrative represents its towering protagonist as engaged in a toe-to-toe contest with Roman imperial might—and with Rome hitting the canvas hard early in the first round: "When he said to them *Egō eimi*, they drew back and fell to the ground" (18:6).

It is not that the Jewish leadership plays no role whatsoever in this championship bout, but only that its role is strictly secondary. The Johannine narrator seems to want to march us briskly through Jesus' interrogations by Annas and Caiaphas in order to get us as expeditiously as possible to the interrogation by Pilate. In place of the energetic, crisis-inducing questioning of Jesus attributed to the high priest in Mark and Matthew, culminating in the high priest's dramatic rending of his robe and impassioned condemnation of the accused (Mark 14:53–65; Matt 26:57–68; cf. Luke 22:66–71), we find in John only the bland summary statement, "The high priest [here referring to Annas, apparently] then questioned Jesus about his disciples and his teaching" (18:19). The interrogation does, to be sure, evoke a spirited response from the Johannine Jesus (18:20–21), but nothing nearly as momentous as the Markan Jesus' "I am [the Christ, the Son of the Blessed One]" (14:62), his first and final public spilling of his "messianic secret."

---

12. The only other such Roman in the entire Fourth Gospel if we resist the temptation to conflate the *basilikos* ("courtier," "royal official") of John 4:46, 49 with the *hekatonrarchos* ("centurion") of Matt. 8:5, 8, 13, and Luke 7:2, 6, in line with a commentarial tradition that, while by no means unanimous, has had a long history; for an early instance of it, see Bernard 1928, 1:167.

14. THE ROMANS WILL COME AND DESTROY OUR HOLY PLACE

Following his questioning by Annas, Jesus is passed on to Caiaphas. Presumably we are to imagine that Jesus is interrogated by Caiaphas as well, but the text does not say so explicitly, much less indicate the content of the questioning. Jesus is "sent … bound to the house of Caiaphas the high priest" (18:24), only to be "led … from the house of Caiaphas to the praetorium" and the Roman prefect (18:28). So heavily foregrounded in the Johannine passion narrative, then, is Jesus' confrontation with Rome, personified by the Prefect of Judea, as to relegate the confrontation with the local Judean elite to the periphery and all but evacuate it of content—a curiously anticlimactic twist to this climactic phase of the plot, given the plot-propelling antagonism that has characterized the protagonist's relations with "the Jews" in so many of the scenes leading up to his arrest.

Viewed differently, however, this anticlimax is not altogether devoid of narrative logic. All of the outraged or incredulous questions or accusations put to Jesus by "the Jews" that the narrator can devise have already been "reported" in the body of the narrative, and responded to either by Jesus or the narrator, and hence do not need repeating at its climax—questions or charges such as:

- "It has taken us forty-six years to build this temple, and will you raise it up in three days?" (2:20)
- "Is not this Jesus, the son of Joseph, whose father and mother we know? How does he now say, 'I have come down from heaven'?" (6:42)
- "How can this man give us his flesh to eat?" (6:52)
- "Who are you?" (8:25)
- "Are we not right in saying that you are a Samaritan and have a demon?" (8:48; cf. 7:20)
- "Are you greater than our father Abraham…? And the prophets…? Who do you claim to be?" (8:53)
- "You are not yet fifty years old, and have you seen Abraham?" (8:57)
- "Are we also blind?" (9:40)
- "If you are the Christ, tell us plainly." (10:24)
- "We stone you for no good work but for blasphemy; because you, being a man, make yourself God." (10:33)

This onslaught of questions and accusations distributed throughout the narrative has the effect of simultaneously preempting and delocalizing Jesus' official trial and conferring the character of a displaced trial on the narrative at large. Martin Kähler famously dubbed Mark's Gospel "a passion narrative with an extended introduction" (1964 [1896], 80 n. 11). But the trial and hence the passion of Jesus looms still larger in John's Gospel. The Johannine plot (such as it is) unfolds in an outsized courtroom, with "the world," epitomized in this instance by "the Jews," as plaintiff, Jesus as defendant, and God as judge.[13] By the time we arrive at the official trial before the local Judean leadership, therefore, there is exceedingly little left to say—as Jesus himself reminds his interrogators: "I have spoken openly to the world; I have always taught in synagogues and in the temple, where all Jews come together; I have said nothing secretly. Why do you ask me?" (18:20–21). There is considerably more to say to the Roman leadership, in contrast, an entirely fresh dialogue partner for the dialogue-loving protagonist.[14] And whereas the principal topic of Jesus' dialogues with "the Jews" was his relationship to the God of Israel, the principal topic of his dialogue with the Roman prefect will be his relationship to that other, more proximate, god, the Roman emperor.[15]

Pilate Picks Up the Lash

The face of Rome in the Fourth Gospel is the face of Pontius Pilate, as we already remarked, which is also to say that when Rome finally assumes a speaking role in this Gospel (beyond the three words accorded to it in 18:5, 7, that is) it is in the person of the prefect of Judea. But it is not in his ordinary capacity as chief administrator and head bureaucrat that Pilate makes his entrance in John so much as in his extraordinary capacity as chief inquisitor and head torturer: Pilate's questioning of the accused is punctuated by Pilate's scourging of the accused.

Now, we are probably not to suppose that the Roman prefect applies the scourge to the peasant upstart with his own hands—or are we? In the Markan

---

13. The widespread recognition that a trial motif permeates the Fourth Gospel (see, e.g., 3:19; 5:22, 30; 8:16, 26; 9:39; 16:8–11) owes much to Blank 1964. For a more recent study of the motif, see Lincoln 2000.

14. Contrast Jesus' silence before Pilate in Mark, broken only by the taciturn "You have said so [*su legeis*]" (15:2).

15. Granted, the emperor in question, Tiberius, was not deified at his demise because the Senate refused to vote him the honor. His provincial subjects, however, knew better. As Robert L. Mowery notes: "Tiberius ... is identified as *theou Sebastou huios* ['son of the divine Augustus'] by various inscriptions and coins, and he is called *theou huios* ['Son of God'] by inscriptions located in such widely-scattered regions as Egypt, Achaia, Asia, Cilicia, and even the northern shore of the Black Sea. Tiberius is called a god by various Greek inscriptions and coins, and he is hailed as both 'god' and 'son of god Sebastos' by a few Greek sources. Early Christians who heard about these imperial honors may not have known that Tiberius was never officially declared a *divus* by the Roman Senate" (2002, 102).

account of the Roman trial we read that "having flogged Jesus, [Pilate] handed him over to be crucified" (*kai paredōken ton Iēsoun phragellōsas hina staurōthē*—15:15), while Matthew parrots Mark, only reshuffling Mark's syntax (*ton de Iēsoun phragellōsas paredōken hina staurōthē*—27:26).[16] More decisively even than the Markan formulation, however, the Johannine formulation seems to thrust the lash into the prefect's hand: "Then Pilate took Jesus and scourged him" (*Tote oun elaben ho Pilatos ton Isoun kai emastigōsen*—19:1). Why not simply take the statement at face value altogether, and understand it to be claiming that Pilate himself, quite literally, scourged Jesus?[17] Or would this be an overly literal interpretation of the Greek construction? After all, recourse to the eminently flexible and resourceful aorist tense was koine Greek's standard way of saying that X had Y flogged, or scourged, or crucified, or subjected to any other action entailing indirect agency, as example after example indicates.[18] But the ambiguity inherent in the Greek construction, taken in and of itself, does leave open the possibility Pilate himself is the direct agent of the scourging.

Of course, a possibility is not always a plausibility, for it is never merely a matter of grammar. And so it will be objected that the spectacle of Pilate himself scourging the accused would have been beneath his dignity as a Roman official. But perhaps the Johannine author is not unduly concerned with the dignity of Roman officials, or even with verisimilitude (and it is with the twists of his narrative rather than the turns of the history that putatively underlies it that I myself am concerned with here). Is the image of the prefect personally laying into the peasant troublemaker with a flagrum or flagellum intrinsically less verisimilar than the image of a full Roman cohort being dispatched to arrest this unarmed peasant—and falling prostrate before him in the process (18:3–6)—or of the prefect responding with fear to the peasant's claims to

---

16. The Lukan passion narrative, meanwhile, discreetly omits any description of the scourging, even though Jesus (18:33) and Pilate (23:16) have predicted it. Two different verbs are used, *mastigoō*, "scourge," in 18:33 (also the verb that John uses, as we shall see), and *paideuō*, "chastise," in 23:16, both in contrast to Mark and Matthew's *phragelloō*, "flog."

17. Note how the agency ascribed to Pilate in 19:1 parallels that ascribed to his soldiers in 19:2: "Then Pilate took Jesus and scourged him. And the soldiers plaited a crown of thorns, and put it on his head, and arrayed him in a purple robe...."

18. See Plutarch, *Caesar* 29.2, for instance: "Marcellus, while he was consul, beat with rods [*ekisto rabdois*] a senator of Novum Comum who had come to Rome..." (LCL trans.). Or Josephus, *Jewish War* 2.14.9: "they also arrested and brought before [Gessius] Florus [Prefect of Judea] many of the peaceful citizens, whom he first scourged and then crucified [*hous mastixin proaikisamenos anestaurōsen*]..." (LCL trans., modified). Similar examples could be multiplied from accounts of flagellation and crucifixion alone in the relevant Greek literature.

divine sonship (19:8)? So far as I have been able to ascertain, nevertheless, even the most encyclopedic Johannine commentaries, for all their exhaustive industry, fail to register Pilate's direct agency in the scourging as even an easily dismissible interpretation.

In the end, however, whether or not the prefect administers the scourging in person is a moot, if not uninteresting, point given the Johannine wording of the event: "Then Pilate took Jesus and scourged him." The agency of the underlings who, in accordance with the traditional assumption, actually administer the flogging is entirely erased in this formulation: they are every bit as much instruments in the hands of the prefect as are the scourges gripped in their own hands—and are made so by this standard grammatical construction that unsettlingly deconstructs the distinction between direct and indirect agency. Language itself, then, thrusts the lash into the prefect's hand. Moreover, as we are about to see, it represents Rome as always already wielding the whip.

The successive episodes of the Roman trial narrative unfold in accordance with an inflexible numerical logic, familiar to readers of the Fourth Gospel, reaching a climax with the first drawing of the victim's blood. For as has often been remarked, John structures the Roman trial in seven chiastic episodes (a number with which he is, of course, much taken), and it is in the middle episode of the chiasm that the scourging occurs[19]—which is to say, on the topmost level of the narrative pedestal. Imperial Rome, in the person of Pontius Pilate, confronts Jesus atop that pedestal, flagrum in hand (symbolically at least, if not actually), the inquisitor now become torturer.

Commentators regularly note the apparent oddity of the Johannine placement of the scourging—not immediately preceding the crucifixion, as in Mark and Matthew, but in the middle of the Roman trial. Brown, in common

---

19. Brown (1994, 1:758), building on certain prior proposals, plausibly suggests the following chiastic structure for the Roman trial narrative:

1. *Outside* (18:28–32)	=	7. *Outside* (19:12–16a)
Jews demand death		Jews obtain death
2. *Inside* (18:33–38a)	=	6. *Inside* (19:9–11)
Pilate and Jesus on kingship		Pilate and Jesus on power
3. *Outside* (18:38b-40)	=	5. *Outside* (19:4–8)
Pilate finds no guilt; choice of Barabbas		Pilate finds no guilt; "Behold the man"
	4. *Inside* (19:1–3)	
	Soldiers scourge Jesus	

Scene 4, however, would be better titled "Pilate scourges Jesus," following John's own formulation of the event—and rendering unnecessary Brown's caveat: "Pilate appears as a major actor in every episode of [the Roman trial narrative] except...the middle episode containing the scourging and mockery of Jesus" (1994, 1:758; cf. 1:827).

14. THE ROMANS WILL COME AND DESTROY OUR HOLY PLACE 339

with many, distinguishes three functions for Roman floggings: a punishment for lesser crimes (and probably what Pilate has in mind in Luke 23:16); "a chastisement bordering on inquisitional torture to extract information from the prisoner or get him to confess"; or a prelude to crucifixion intended both to increase the condemned's suffering and shorten his sojourn on the cross (1994, 1:851–52). But Brown is unable to fit the Johannine scourging into this tripartite schema: "Harder to classify is the scourging of Jesus in John 19:1; Pilate's motive seems to be to make Jesus look wretched so that 'the Jews' will be satisfied and accept his release" (1994, 1:852). Brown's (implicit) disqualification of the second option, that the Johannine Jesus' scourging is "a chastisement bordering on inquisitional torture," typifies that of the commentarial tradition generally, as does his inability to account satisfactorily for the placement of the scourging in the middle rather than at the end of the Roman trial.

This tendency in the tradition provides Jennifer Glancy (2005) with her cue to argue compellingly that the Johannine scourging is best construed as an instance of Roman judicial torture.[20] A stark definition proffered in the *Digest of Justinian* (and quoted in Glancy 2005, 118) encapsulates the Roman stance on judicial torture: "By torture we mean the infliction of anguish and agony on the body to elicit the truth" (48.10.15.41; cf. 48.19.28.2). Sources attesting to this practice are numerous, ranging from Acts 22:24, the only unequivocal instance of judicial torture in the New Testament, in which a Roman tribune orders Paul "to be examined with scourges [*mastixin anetazesthai auton*] that he might fully know what crime [the mob] were clamoring he had committed,"[21] to a letter of Pliny, governor of Bithynia, to the emperor Trajan, which includes the statement: "I deemed it that much more necessary to extract the real truth, by means of torture [*per tormenta*], from two female slaves, who were styled deacons."[22]

To read the Johannine scourging as judicial torture, however, is not to sieve all the mystery out of it. For the account of the torture is extraordinarily condensed. The problem is not so much the lack of graphic detail on the manner in which the accused is scourged[23] as the lack of questions directed to him to motivate and accompany the ordeal. In much the same

---

20. A suggestion formerly made in passing by C. H. Dodd (1963, 102–3) and independently by Edward Peters (1985, 27), as Glancy acknowledges. Keener 2003, 2:1120 n. 463 lists further scholars who have ventured the suggestion, although Glancy develops it much more fully.
21. My translation.
22. Pliny the Younger, *Letters* 10.96, my translation.
23. In contrast to other contemporary accounts of scourging; see further 150–51 above.

way in which the Jewish trial in John is evacuated of content in its telling, as we have seen, most of the charges and questions that should have constituted it having already been disseminated through the preceding narrative, so too are the questions that should punctuate the scourging dissociated from it and displaced around it:

- "Are you the King of the Jews?" (18:33)
- "So you are a king?" (18:37)
- "Where are you from?" (19:9)
- "Do you refuse to speak to me? Do you not know that I have power to release you, and power to crucify you?" (19:10).

Torture, it goes without saying, is not the preserve of empire. Yet, as history has persistently taught us (most recently at Abu Ghraib and Guantánamo Bay), empire and torture tend to be inextricably intertwined. The Roman Empire, as is commonly argued, had as its fundamental enabling condition the institution of slavery (e.g., Bradley 1994, 31–81; Thompson 2003, 1–34). But what in turn was the fundamental condition of slavery? Not to have one's own physical person at one's disposal would seem to be the obvious answer. And the permanent possibility, not to say outright probability, of rape, flogging, or other forms of physical abuse or torture—including judicial torture—can be said to have epitomized the slave's lack of autonomy over his or her body. Put another way, if the slave ensured the efficient operation of the empire, the permanent possibility of physical punishment, epitomized by torture, was what ensured the efficient operation of the slave. And what was true of the slave was also true, albeit to a lesser degree, of noncitizens generally, not least in backwater territories of the empire such as the province of Judea. The relationship between empire and torture, therefore, while ordinarily oblique, was nonetheless symbiotic, even fundamental and central, in the Roman imperial order.

And it is that relationship that comes to veiled but succinct expression in the Johannine Roman trial narrative. So far as I can discover, nobody has yet managed to explain satisfactorily in relation to Johannine theology—or ideology, for that matter—why 19:1–3, Jesus' brutal torture within the Roman praetorium by scourging, crowning with thorns, blows to the body and/or face and psychological abuse should be the central term in the seven-term chiasm that structures the Roman trial narrative, and hence the term that is singled out for special emphasis.[24] What I would suggest, however, is that this emphasis makes excellent sense when set in relation to Roman imperial ideol-

---

24. On the significance of chiastic central terms, see, e.g., Welch 1981, 10; Breck 1994, 330–50, esp. 335.

ogy—or, rather, the implicit Johannine critique of such ideology. The central term in the chiasm, namely, torture, is none other than the central mechanism designed to keep every Roman subject—slave, peasant, every other noncitizen, and, in certain cases, even citizens themselves—firmly in their respective, and respectful, places in relation to Roman imperial authority, and never more so than when torture is the prelude to death. Whether or not the Fourth Evangelist may plausibly be said to have intended it,[25] therefore, his placement of the torture scene as the foregrounded feature of the chiasm that structures his account of Roman judicial procedure admits—indeed invites—interpretation as a singularly scathing indictment of the Roman imperial order in general and of Roman justice in particular.

Johannine Atonement: Propitiating Caesar

In the Fourth Gospel, in stark contrast, say, to the book of Revelation, the Roman Empire is never represented as the *object* of divine punishment, whether realized or merely anticipated. Rome is only ever the *agent* of punishment in John. More even than in Mark, moreover, it is the Judean elite in John—the Judean comprador class, so to speak, and the primary referent, apparently, of the Johannine epithet "the Jews" (*hoi Ioudaioi*)[26]—who are the object of unrelenting, scathing criticism, both explicit and implicit, while their Roman overlords (ostensibly, at least) are let off the hook. In Mark, arguably, the actions of the Judean elite vis-à-vis the misunderstood protagonist are implicitly represented as precipitating the annihilation of Jerusalem and its temple (e.g., Telford 1980; Mack 1988). The corresponding situation in John, however, is considerably more ambiguous and oblique.

Consider John 11:47–52 in particular:

> So the chief priests and the Pharisees assembled the council [*synedrion*] and said, "What are we to do, because this man is performing many signs? If we let him go on like this, everyone will believe in him, and the Romans

---

25. What the Evangelist probably intended was to highlight the soldiers' ironic acclamation of Jesus as "King of the Jews" (19:2–3), as Conway insightfully suggests (1999, 158 n. 267). But the mock coronation occurs in the context of Jesus' torture—is itself, indeed, an intrinsic feature of the torture that permeates and unifies this scene. Narratively, then, the torture is the more basic element whose chiastic centering needs explaining, and should not be swept too swiftly under the christological rug.

26. "The term is mostly, although … not always, used for the authorities headquartered in Jerusalem" (Keener 2003, 1:221), a position particularly associated with Urban von Wahlde (1981–82; 1983). For further discussion of this complex issue, see Motyer 1997, 54–56; Reinhartz 2001, 72–75.

will come and destroy our holy place[27] and our nation" [*kai eleusontai hoi Rōmanoi kai arousin hēmōn ton topon kai to ethnos*]. But one of them, Caiaphas, being high priest that year, said to them, "You know absolutely nothing, nor do you understand that it more expedient for you that one man die for the people than that the entire nation perish." Now he did not say this of his own accord, but being high priest that year he prophesied that Jesus was about to die for the nation, and not for the nation only, but to gather into one the scattered children of God. (11:47–52, my trans.)

This unique passage assigns political motivation to the indigenous Judean leadership with a degree of explicitness that is entirely lacking in the Synoptic tradition. In the Synoptics (or so it has commonly been argued), Jesus' symbolic action in the temple is the event that, above all else, consolidates the Judean elite's opposition to him and precipitates his arrest (cf. Mark 11:18; 14:57–58; Matt 26:59–61; Luke 19:45–47; Acts 6:12–14). The temple incident cannot, of course, assume this catalytic role in the Fourth Gospel, occurring as it does at the outset of Jesus' public activity (2:13–22). On the face of it, too, John would seem to have passed up on the other major incident that might have provided a neat logical segue into the Judean elite's expressed concern about a calamitous Roman backlash—namely, the festival crowd's explicit and enthusiastic acclamation of the Galilean upstart as "King of Israel" upon his entry into Jerusalem.[28] Instead, what would appear to be a more politically neutral event—the raising of Lazarus from the dead—is assigned the role of bringing the Judean leadership's anxieties about a Roman military intervention to a head.

On closer examination, however, it appears that their fears are not misplaced. On the contrary, their analysis of the situation is commendably shrewd. For while the raising of Lazarus might at first glance seem an altogether unlikely pretext for concerns about a Roman retaliation, certain details in the ensuing narrative (esp. 12:9–11, 17–19) make the rationale plain. "Everyone" is starting to "believe in him," and what they are believing, apparently, and not just believing but openly proclaiming, is that he is the long-awaited King of Israel (12:12–13; cf. 1:49; 6:15), certainly a provocation, if not an open invitation, to the Romans to "come and destroy" the nation and the temple that, more than any other public symbol, epitomizes the nation's identity. "Everyone," then, is starting to believe that Jesus is what he does—

---

27. With the majority, I take *hēmōn … ton topon* (literally, "our place") to refer to the Jerusalem temple rather than the city of Jerusalem (cf. John 4:20; Acts 6:13–14; 7:7).

28. The other event in the narrative that has the effect of causing the crowds to acclaim Jesus king is yet another one of the "many signs" "this man is performing" (11:47), namely, the multiplication of the loaves and fish (6:1–15).

and does not—claim to be, namely, the King of Israel. If they "let him go on like this," "everyone will believe" that he is the divinely appointed deliverer destined to wrest the nation back from the Romans, and the Romans will indeed clamp down with frightful force. But even if the indigenous Judean elite succeed in stopping Jesus by engineering a shameful execution for him, patently incompatible with claimed messianic status, "the Romans will come" anyway. The Romans will still come and destroy the temple and the nation—but not as divinely orchestrated punishment for Israel's perceived rejection of its Messiah, as in Mark. It is supersessionism, not theodicy, that is the primary theological engine wheeled out by John to make sense of the temple's destruction—or so it seems at first. As we are about to discover, the latter engine is secretly housed within the former.

For John, the Jerusalem temple must be destroyed because it is destined to be replaced by that other temple that is Jesus' body (2:19–22; cf. 4:20–21). Jesus himself will be the new temple and thus the new gathering place for "the scattered children of God." But he will also be the sacrificial lamb (1:29, 36) who by "[dying] for the nation" will render the new temple cult efficacious. The grip of Johannine irony on the unwitting Judean elite is thus a veritable stranglehold in the passage we are considering. If they permit the popular acclaim of the Galilean peasant as Messianic King of Israel to continue unchecked, the Romans will descend with irresistible force to annihilate their holy place and even their nation. But if they intervene decisively to squelch that popular acclaim by engineering the Galilean's execution—the Romans will *still* descend with irresistible force, etc., as the Gospel's postwar audience is only too well aware. Either way, responsibility for the temple's obliteration is laid squarely (and unfairly) at the feet of "the Jews," epitomized by the Judean elite. "Destroy this temple...," Jesus challenges "the Jews" in 2:19. "He was speaking of the temple of his body [*tou naou tou sōmatos autou*]," the narrator is quick to add (2:21). But within the starkly simplifying universe of Johannine supersessionism, the injunction "Destroy this temple...," addressed to "the Jews," applies to the literal temple as much as to the spiritual temple and implicitly identifies "the Jews" as the real agents of that destruction. It is they, not the Romans, who bear ultimate responsibility for it.

Johannine irony runs riot, then, around the theme of the temple. Consequently, the high priest's "prophecy" in 11:47–52 is anything but straightforward; it is in fact riddled with peculiarities. The ostensible logic of the utterance is plain enough. The Galilean upstart must be consigned to destruction by the Romans so that the "nation" (*to ethnos*)[29] may be spared

---

29. Which term I take to refer primarily to the Judean temple-state.

destruction by the Romans. The narrator's labeling of the utterance as prophecy (*eprophēteusen hoti emellen Iēsous apothnēskein...*—11:51) is designed to announce its truth. But the "nation," epitomized by its sacred city and "holy place," *was* eventually destroyed by the Romans, notwithstanding the consignment of Jesus to the Romans by the local Judean leadership. Therefore the prophecy misses its mark.

Of course, to construe the prophecy thus is to give it a literal reading, whereas the implied author apparently intends it to be taken spiritually: "he prophesied that Jesus was about to die for the nation, and not for the nation only, but to gather into one the scattered [*dieskorpismena*] children of God" (11:51–52). But the antecedent narrative has piled up too much literal freight to admit of instant transformation by a cursory wave of the spiritualizing wand: the chief priests' and Pharisees' warning, "the Romans will come and destroy our nation," followed by the high priest's counsel, "it more expedient for you that one man die for the people than that the entire nation perish," reinforced by the narrator's own "he prophesied that Jesus was about to die for the nation," leaves only the afterthought-like clause "and not for the nation only but to gather into one the scattered children of God" to suggest that the high priest might have been saying more than he knew—and to suggest it insufficiently, since the image of dispersal so readily summons up as its primary or literal referent the Jewish Diaspora, Israel without borders, and only secondarily summons up Jewish and/or Gentile Christianity.[30]

This is not to imply, however, that Caiaphas's statement is utterly devoid of theological resonance. Jesus must be punished, must be executed, must be sacrificed so that the populace at large may be spared. The substitutionary logic anticipates the doctrine of atonement.[31] Jesus must die a substitutionary death, according to the high priest. But to propitiate what or whom? *Rome* is Caiaphas's implicit answer, or, if the "what" be personified as a "whom," *Caesar*. Substitution, propitiation, atonement is here elaborated in a register that is ineluctably physical, not metaphysical. Moreover, this statement is actually the most explicit, and as such the primary, interpretation in the Fourth Gospel of Jesus' death as substitution. The mechanism of substitution, propitiation, atonement that comes to explicit expression in this passage is the same mechanism that implicitly drives John 1:29, "Behold the Lamb of God

---

30. As Keener notes (2003, 2:857 n. 204), many commentators hold that Gentile Christians only are in view here, while others argue that both Jewish and Gentile Christians are envisioned.

31. See pp. 156ff. above.

who takes away the sin of the world!" (cf. 1:36), as well as the more subtle allusions to the substitutionary nature of Jesus' death in 19:14, 29, 36.[32]

Yet even if the basic mechanism is the same, it may be objected that the entity being placated is different in each instance: God on the one hand, Caesar on the other. What the high priest's prophecy reveals, however (so that he does after all say more than he knows), is a complicating factor within the relatively undeveloped Johannine version of the doctrine of atonement that ordinarily goes unremarked. It is only by appeasing Caesar that God can be appeased; or to put it another way, the propitiation of Caesar is the necessary precondition for the propitiation of God in the Fourth Gospel—which is simply to say in turn that the torture and execution of the Son of God are performed in the symbolic presence of the Roman emperor in the first instance, as even a cursory reading of the Johannine passion narrative reveals (see especially 19:12, 15).

But the degree of emphasis put on Caesar's placation throughout the trial narrative (in which the only real question at issue is whether or not Jesus is to be considered a threat to Caesar's authority) is such as to thrust the corresponding theme of God's placation exclusively into the realm of subtle allusion—or, to switch to a different discursive register, into the realm of the repressed. Crushed under the ponderous weight accorded to the theme of being in a right relationship to the Roman emperor versus not being in a right relationship to him, the theme of divine propitiation only finds expression through oblique means throughout the Roman trial and execution narrative. Essentially this dynamic is the familiar psychoanalytic one. Unconscious truth—here equivalent to Johannine theological truth—can only come to displaced expression in the seams and secret pockets of conscious discourse and action—here the arrest, trial, torture and execution of the protagonist. And the role of the unconscious material in this narrative is, as we might expect, subversive in relation to the conscious or manifest material. In the Johannine passion narrative, the implicit, concealed or unconscious material subverts the explicit, ostensive or conscious material by suggesting that the propitiation of Caesar is only the *apparent* issue in Jesus' trial, torture, and execution. The "real" issue is the propitiation of that other deity, the Jewish one—a theme that carries us even deeper into psychoanalytic territory, since the God-Jesus relationship in the Fourth Gospel is obsessively framed as a Father-Son relationship.[33]

---

32. For a recent discussion of Jesus' substitutionary death in John, see Waetjen 2005, 284–85.

33. But that will have to await another essay.

Implicit, too, in this conscious-unconscious dynamic is the subversion of one empire by another empire—so that Pilate's concern on behalf of Caesar is not, after all, misplaced. In the cracks and fissures of the Roman imperial order, the Fourth Gospel tells us, the empire of God takes root. To be sure, God's empire (*hē basileia tou theou*) is far less an explicit theme in the Fourth Gospel than in the Synoptic Gospels; but that does not mean that it is any less present or potent. For, ultimately, the Johannine resistance to Roman colonization might be said to be an alternative program of colonization more ambitious even than the Roman one: the annexation of the world by nonmilitary means.

The conquest, however, begins at home. For it is in this Gospel, more than any other, that Jesus is routinely represented as usurping and absorbing Jewish identity markers and sacred spaces (cf. Reinhartz 2002, 182). Jesus' incessant march up and down the Holy Land in the Fourth Gospel is, in effect, a reconquest of the Holy Land (etymologically, after all, Jesus is Joshua). The Roman expulsion of the Jewish populace from its sacred city, following the Bar Kokhba revolt (132–135 C.E.), combined with the Roman renaming of the city as Aelia Capitolina, all anticipated by Rome's earlier destruction of city and temple (70 C.E.), might be said to be the material counterpart of the systematic spiritual dispossession of Judaism enacted in the Fourth Gospel. When Christianity eventually *becomes* Rome in the fourth century, the circle of dispossession is completed, both spiritually and materially. Before long, Rome and Jerusalem have become the twin spiritual centers of imperial Christianity, while the displaced Jews, branded with the mark of Cain, continue to wander the earth homeless.

The Romans Will Come ... on the Clouds of Heaven

The Son of Man will come (*erchomai*) in clouds, says Mark (13:26; 14:62; cf. 8:38). The Romans will come (*erchomai*), says John (11:48). How are these two comings related? The defining characteristic of both ancient Jewish and early Christian apocalyptic eschatology, arguably, is the concept of an imminent, public, unambiguous and climactic divine irruption on the stage of human history. The Fourth Gospel, however, in contrast to the Synoptic Gospels, famously lacks an explicit parousia scenario, the central element of the Christian apocalyptic drama.[34] But this absence has profound implications for the presence of Rome in the Fourth Gospel. In the absence of a dramatized parousia, Rome can be said to assume apocalyptic agency in this Gospel, lend-

---

34. At the most, John 5:28–29, together with 6:39–40, 44, 54 and 12:48, might be read as implicit anticipations of an undramatized parousia. For discussion of the issue, see, e.g., Ridderbos 1997, 199; Brown and Moloney 2003, 241.

ing uncanny veracity to the climactic confession of "the Jews" in the Roman trial scene, "We have no king/emperor but Caesar [*ouk echomen basileia ei mē Kaisara*]" (19:15). It is Caesar rather than God—or, rather, Caesar *as* God—whose potential (and potentially catastrophic) intervention assumes apocalyptic proportions in the Fourth Gospel: "the Romans will come and destroy both our holy place and our nation" (11:48).

The Johannine Jesus himself is in denial of this uncomfortable fact, as is the implied author, his ventriloquist. "You would have no power over me unless it had been given you from above," Jesus tells Pilate, gesturing heavenward; "therefore the one who handed me over to you is guilty of a greater sin" (19:11). This assertion falls prey, however, to its own inherent ambiguity: the prefect would also have no power over the accused if it had not been bestowed on him by the emperor. And the statement is further fractured by a second instability: its first clause implicitly ascribes to the divine Judge responsibility for the death-torture of his Son, while the second clause explicitly—and awkwardly—attempts to displace that responsibility onto others (Judas or the Judean religious leadership, depending on how one reads).[35] The result is a curiously weak assertion.

Thomas's celebrated acclamation of the risen Jesus similarly accords covert homage to the Roman emperor. Luminous artistic depictions of the risen Lord, from the ancient Church all the way down to the closing moments of Mel Gibson's *The Passion of the Christ*, have no basis in the Fourth Gospel, which ascribes only three traits to his resurrected body: it can be mistaken for that of a person on the lower rungs of the social ladder, a slave or common laborer ("Supposing him to be the gardener [*ho kēpouros*]…"—20:14–15; cf. 21:4); incongruent with the first trait, it can also pass through locked doors (20:19, 26); and entirely congruent with the first trait, it bears the scars of brutal physical maltreatment ("Unless I … place my finger in the mark of the nails and place my hand in his side…"—20:25; cf. 20:20, 27).

Of this eternally scarred body, Jennifer Glancy has remarked: "Thomas's exclamation, 'My Lord and my God!,' ascribes authority and sovereignty not to the one who imposes the mark but to the marked man" (2005, 134). I both agree and disagree with this statement. John has cunningly, and catachrestically,[36] adopted and adapted an acclamation employed in Roman

---

35. Early Brown attempts to grapple with the "difficult logic" of the second clause (1970, 879, his expression), but most subsequent commentators—including later Brown (1994, 1:842)—gloss over it.

36. Associated with Gayatri Spivak, the term *catachresis* denotes the process whereby the colonized strategically appropriate and redeploy specific elements of colonial or imperial culture or ideology (see further Moore 2006, 37–38, 105–106).

imperial court ceremonial, reapplying it to the risen Jesus.[37] The acclamation thus glistens with freshly applied meaning, but the original meaning still seeps through the palimpsest. Thomas's exclamation pays awed homage to the ambiguous figure standing before him whose divine nature has enabled him to transcend the ritual degradation of his body. But it simultaneously pays homage to the absent, yet present, figure of the Roman emperor whose own divine authority, reaching effortlessly across the Mediterranean, has caused his peasant subject's body to be inscribed eternally, and hence indelibly, with the marks of a slave.[38] Once again the Johannine text concedes inadvertently through subtle ambiguities in its narrative argumentation that Caesar's immeasurable bulk, center and anchor of the world out of which the text emerges, cannot simply be wafted away with a casual wave of the theological wand. In its furtive acknowledgement of this fundamental, unyielding reality, Johannine theology shows itself to be surreptitiously intermeshed with Roman imperial ideology, specifically that of the imperial cult. The imperial cult overtly celebrates what the Fourth Gospel covertly concedes, namely, the irreducible fact of Caesar's omnipotence—all of which brings us back to the lack of apocalyptic eschatology in the Fourth Gospel and the manner in which Rome automatically rushes in to fill the theological vacuum engendered by that lack. For it is not only nature that abhors a vacuum, seemingly; the supernatural abhors it as well.

In the Fourth Gospel, no end to Caesar's reign is prophesied or threatened, whether explicitly as in Revelation or implicitly as in the Synoptic apocalypses. Unlike those other texts, the Fourth Gospel does not depict the Roman Empire as destined to be destroyed or replaced by the new Christian empire from without, commencing with the public manifestation of the glorified Son of Man to friend and foe alike ("Behold, he is coming with the clouds, and every eye will see him…"—Rev 1:7). Instead, by implication, the Fourth Gospel depicts the Roman Empire as destined to be transformed by Christianity from within. This assertion depends on a certain assumption, namely, that Rome can reasonably be construed as a major, if unspecified, component of "the world" (*ho kosmos*) to which John incessantly refers. But if "the world"

---

37. As argued in particular by Cassidy (1992, 13–16, 55), with reference to the *dominus et deus noster* ("our Lord and God") title applied to Domitian. The title was certainly applied to the emperor by sycophants such as Martial (*Epigrams* 5.8; 7.34; 8.2; 9.66; 10.72), but it is unlikely that Domitian applied it to himself, contrary to what Seutonius claims (*Domitian* 15.2; cf. Jones 1992, 108–109). The title "savior of the world" (*ho sōtēr tou kosmou*) in John 4:42 similarly evokes Roman imperial propaganda (Koester 1990; Cassidy 1992, 34–35). Dube memorably remarks on this verse: "The Johannine Jesus now emerges fully clothed in the emperor's titles" (2002, 66).

38. Roman crucifixion being, above all, "the slave's punishment" (see pp. 162–63 above).

does not contain Rome—is not, indeed, permeated by Roman power, and for all intents and purposes coextensive with it—then what weight, freight or purchase could the term possibly have in John's own world?[39] If "the world" is primarily the Roman world, however,[40] then the negative depiction of "the world" in the Fourth Gospel—as plunged in darkness (8:12; 9:5; cf. 12:35; 1:5), given over to evil works (7:7), ignorant of the only true God (17:25; cf. 14:17; 17:3), ruled by Satan (12:31; 14:30; 16:11), hostile to Jesus and those who believe in him (7:7; 15:18–25; 17:14; cf. 16:20)—functions as a veiled or implicit denunciation of the Roman Empire.

At the same time, however, "the world" is also explicitly represented in the Fourth Gospel as the object of God's extravagant love (3:16), Jesus' salvific self-sacrifice (1:29; 3:17; 12:47) and the disciples' future witness and mission (14:31; 16:8; 17:21, 23; cf. 4:35–42), issuing, incrementally but inexorably, in the annexation and transformation of "the world"—its "unworlding," if you will. "And I, when I am lifted up from the earth," the Gospel's paradoxical protagonist declares, anticipating his imperial enthronement on the cross, "will draw everyone to myself [*pantas helkusō pros hemauton*]" (12:32)—given enough time, that is. But no other Gospel writer (not even Luke) allows Jesus' followers quite as much time to unworld "the world," to appropriate and colonize it,[41] because no other Jesus is in less of a hurry to return.

What Revelation gets stunningly wrong, therefore, John gets uncannily right. What Revelation is entirely incapable of imagining or foreseeing is that Rome will eventually become Christianity and Christianity will eventually become Rome. But that is precisely what the Fourth Gospel seems to intuit, against all the odds. In tacitly allowing Rome to survive and thrive into the indefinite future, the Fourth Gospel shows itself to be the charter document of Constantinian Christianity not just in terms of its Christology, which is how it is normally seen, but also in terms of its political theology.

Yet again, however, this theology is neither stable nor self-consistent. For it is also the product of a narrative that contains, embedded within in, the most trenchant critique of Roman imperialism of any of the canonical Gos-

---

39. I thus find Adele Reinhartz's otherwise excellent analysis of John's relations to Rome too tentative on this point. She writes: "More elusive is the question of whether the 'world' as used in this Gospel includes a reference to the Roman empire" (2002, 179).

40. The Jewish, and, most importantly, Judean world being the major subset of that Roman world in the narrative world of this Gospel (see, e.g., 7:3–4; 12:19; 18:20).

41. As such, this unworlding is also a "worlding"—Spivak's term (e.g., 1990b, 1, 129; 1999, 211–13) for the process whereby a colonizing agent assimilates a subject people and territory to his own worldview through systemic acts of epistemic violence: renaming, remapping, etc. The all-encompassing Johannine conceptual vocabulary likewise performs a worlding of non-Johannine reality—or "the world," to give it its Johannine appellation.

pels, not only in its implicit inclusion of Rome in a "world" denounced in utterly uncompromising terms, but also in its placement of its protagonist's judicial torture as the central term in the chiastic structure of its Roman trial narrative, as discussed earlier, and the searing critique of the fundamental operations of the *imperium Romanum* that that placement entails. Simultaneously and contradictorily, meanwhile, John's rejection of a death-sentence verdict for Rome—a sentence that would ordinarily be carried out through the parousia scenario integral both to the Synoptic tradition and ancient Christian apocalyptic more generally—makes it the Gospel of the imperial status quo. The assessment with which this chapter began will thus serve also to end it: John is at once the most—and the least—political of the canonical Gospels.

Further Reading in Postcolonial Studies

Ashcroft, Bill, Gareth Griffiths, and Helen Tiffin. 2001. *Post-colonial Studies: The Key Concepts*. 2nd ed. London: Routledge. An A-Z mini-encyclopedia of postcolonial studies composed of more than one hundred short essays.

Carter, Warren. 2008. *John and Empire: Initial Explorations*. New York: T&T Clark. The most exhaustive treatment yet of any biblical text in its relations to empire. Reads the Fourth Gospel as a complex work of "imperial negotiation."

Desai, Guarav, and Supriya Nair, eds. 2005. *Postcolonialisms: An Anthology of Cultural Theory and Criticism*. New Brunswick, N.J.: Rutgers University Press. Thirty-seven selections divided into the following parts: "Ideologies of Imperialism"; "The Critique of Colonial Discourse"; "The Politics of Language and Literary Studies"; "Nationalisms and Nativisms"; "Hybrid Identities"; "Gender and Sexualities"; "Reading the Subaltern"; "Comparative (Post)colonialisms"; and "Globalization and Postcoloniality."

Dube, Musa W. 2000. *Postcolonial Feminist Interpretation of the Bible*. St. Louis: Chalice. Postcolonial feminist reading of the conquest narrative in Joshua and the Canaanite woman pericope in Matthew, including interpretations of the latter episode developed by nonacademic African women.

Dube, Musa W., and Jeffrey L. Staley, eds. 2002. *John and Postcolonialism: Travel, Space and Power*. Bible and Postcolonialism 7. New York: T&T Clark. Includes essays on such issues as ethnicity, decolonization, colonial evangelism, gender, nation, hybridity, and border-crossing as they impinge on John and its relations to empire.

Horsley, Richard A., ed. 2008. *In the Shadow of Empire: Reclaiming the Bible as a History of Faithful Resistance*. Nine well-known scholars read selected biblical texts as anti-imperial resistance literature. The empires range from Assyria to Rome, and the scholars are Norman Gottwald, Walter Brueggemann, Jon Berquist, John Dominic Crossan, Neil Elliott, Warren Carter, Brigitte Kahl, Greg Carey, and Horsley himself.

Loomba, Ania, Suvir Kaul, Matti Bunzl, Antoinette Burton, and Jed Esty, eds. 2005. *Postcolonial Studies and Beyond*. Durham, N.C.: Duke University Press. An interdisciplinary cast of contributors reflect on the past, present, and possible future(s) of postcolonial studies.

Marchal, Joseph A. 2008. *The Politics of Heaven: Women, Gender, and Empire in the Study of Paul*. Paul in Critical Contexts. Minneapolis: Fortress. Philippians is the principal focus of this theory-savvy study, which refuses to separate feminist and postcolonial analysis.

Moore, Stephen D. 2006. *Empire and Apocalypse: Postcolonialism and the New Testament*. Bible in the Modern World 12. Sheffield: Sheffield Phoenix. Includes exegetical chapters on Mark, John, and Revelation.

Moore, Stephen D., and Fernando F. Segovia, eds. 2005. *Postcolonial Biblical Criticism: Interdisciplinary Intersections*. Bible and Postcolonialism 8. New York: T&T Clark. Roland Boer, Laura Donaldson, David Jobling, Tat-siong Benny Liew, and the editors variously relate postcolonial studies and postcolonial biblical criticism to feminism, racial/ethnic studies, poststructuralism, and Marxism.

Moore, Stephen D., and Mayra Rivera, eds. 2010. *Planetary Loves: Spivak, Postcoloniality, and Theology*. Transdisciplinary Theological Colloquia. New York: Fordham University Press. Includes essays by eleven theologians and three biblical scholars, as well as an extended public conversation with Gayatri Chakravorty Spivak.

Moore-Gilbert, Bart. 1997. *Postcolonial Theory: Contexts, Practices, Politics*. London: Verso. Still the best introduction to postcolonial theory, although in need of updating. Includes lengthy chapters on Edward Said, Gayatri Spivak, and Homi Bhabha.

Segovia, Fernando F., and R. S. Sugirtharajah, eds. 2007. *A Postcolonial Commentary on the New Testament Writings*. Bible and Postcolonialism 13. New York: T&T Clark. In this landmark volume, an international team of twenty-one contributors provides postcolonial commentary on all the books of the New Testament.

Sugirtharajah, R. S. 2002. *Postcolonial Criticism and Biblical Interpretation*. Oxford: Oxford University Press. Possibly the best textbook introduction to postcolonial biblical criticism.

———, ed. 2005. *The Postcolonial Biblical Reader*. Oxford: Blackwell. An anthology of twenty essays, spanning both Testaments, and divided into four parts: "Theoretical Practices"; "Empires Old and New"; "Empire and Exegesis"; and "Postcolonial Concerns."

Thatcher, Tom. 2009. *Greater Than Caesar: Christology and Empire in the Fourth Gospel*. Minneapolis: Fortress. Presents a detailed exegetical argument for the position that John's Christology is, first and foremost, John's response to Rome.

Young, Robert J. C. 2003. *Postcolonialism: A Very Short Introduction*. Oxford: Oxford University Press. In effect, a very short version of Young's magisterial *Postcolonialism: An Historical Introduction* (2001) designed for readers looking for preliminary orientation.

POSTTHEORY

15
A Modest Manifesto for New Testament Literary Criticism: How to Interface with a Literary Studies Field That Is Postliterary, Posttheoretical, and Postmethodological*

There is a tale I have been spinning for more than two decades now, a tale of two disciplines. It tells how New Testament scholars have adopted and adapted—often to the point of outright reinvention—various methods and movements in literary studies (the tale always being complicated by the fact that I myself have been engaged all the while in that very same enterprise). In the particular installment of the saga that is the present essay, the principal players are several of the usual suspects: poststructuralism, postcolonial studies, queer theory, and masculinity studies. This time around, however, cultural studies takes center stage. In the essay I echo the argument frequently made that cultural studies is the critical phenomenon least amenable to, and least assimilable to, literary studies as traditionally conceived and practiced, principally because it is postliterary in thrust. But I also argue that similarly in biblical studies, although for somewhat different reasons, cultural studies constitutes the most serious (and, I would add, salutary) threat to the inherited identity of the discipline that we have yet encountered, an identity more than two centuries in the making and hence formidably resistant to dismantling and recrafting.

This argument, however, inheres within a larger one. The essay also contends that literary studies (even apart from cultural studies) is an enterprise more at odds with biblical studies than is generally realized by biblical scholars, even those most interested in, and most influenced by, literary criticism. I argue that all

---
*First published in *Biblical Interpretation* 15 (2007): 1–25.

of the major recent developments in literary studies are essentially postmethodological in their manner of reading and general way of proceeding. As such they constitute a trenchant yet timely challenge to biblical scholars, and above all to biblical literary critics, to come clean and confess, own up to their professional preoccupation with methodology—a preoccupation frequently amounting to an obsession—understand what underlies it, and finally press beyond it.

Of course, I myself need to confront that challenge as much as anyone else working in the interdiscipline of biblical and literary studies. As will be patently obvious to readers of these essays, my own obsession with methodology has been, and continues to be, considerable. In urging that we biblical scholars finally shake off our methodone addiction, therefore, I am attempting to talk myself out of a topic on which to write (although admittedly with little fear of ever fully succeeding).

We asked the candidate what her dream course would be, and she said she would like to teach a course in "theory and—and, um—" (there was a long silence) "theory and *non*theory." Our chair asked, "*non*theory, what's that?" And she said, "well, nontheory—like, *you* know, poems, stories, plays." And he said, "Oh yes, what we used to call literature." (Gilbert 2001, 252)

In the old days, rock music was a distraction from your studies; now it may well be what you are studying. (Eagleton 2003, 3)

Twenty years ago, it was still possible to pack all of the existing books on postmodernism, across all disciplines, into a good-sized, but by no means outsized, footnote. And less than twenty years ago, it was still possible to pack most of the self-avowed postmodernists in biblical studies into a minivan. Where the minivan was headed on that occasion I no longer remember. But I do recall one of its occupants advising the driver to be alert lest a gang of historical critics crammed into a bigger, meaner vehicle run us off the road, thereby ridding biblical studies of the scourge of postmodernism at a stroke. Those were heady days, giddy with self-aggrandizement, several of us being so naïve as to believe that historical criticism's stranglehold on the discipline would gradually and inexorably lessen as the acknowledged pillars and official gatekeepers, comfortably sprawled in prestigious chairs in all the leading research universities, would retire or depart for the great senior common room in the sky and be replaced with—well, postmodernists, of course, and other committed iconoclasts. How poorly we understood the rigid rules of dynastic succession that ensure the stability of our discipline through the generations.

It seems to me, indeed, that historical criticism's hegemony in the international field of biblical studies has not diminished significantly during the past two decades—although substantiating that opinion would require another essay. This is not to imply, however, that New Testament literary criticism—my principal focus here—has been cryogenically frozen during this period. For one thing, the "time-warp factor" (cf. Moore 1989, 178), long so pronounced in such criticism, has noticeably decreased. By this I mean in particular that deconstruction and other varieties of poststructuralism, extending to New Historicism, were not taken up in New Testament studies until long after their first flowering, and even their eventual decline, in literary studies, whereas most of the major developments of the 1990s in literary studies, in contrast—cultural studies, postcolonial studies, queer theory, masculinity studies, and autobiographical criticism—had all been taken up in New Testament studies even before that decade had come to an end.[1] Contemporary New Testament literary critics tend, on the whole, to be more attuned to real-time literary studies than their time-traveling predecessors (and I include my own early professional persona in the latter category).

Theory and Posttheory

By the mid-1980s, poststructuralism had become the dominant discourse in U.S. literary studies—a rather sad and curious fate for a congeries of critical positions that, collectively, made so much of the marginal and the peripheral and relentlessly subjected dominant discourses to principled interrogation.[2] Eugene Goodheart, long a critic of poststructuralism, nuances its ascent in the 1970s and 1980s:

> What I am describing did not occur everywhere in the academy. I suspect that many institutions of higher learning in the country have not experienced an academic transformation, and that there are still places where the older traditions of teaching prevail.... But the transformation did take place in the leading institutions which have a disproportionate influence not only on the academic, but also on the cultural life generally. (1999, 20–21)[3]

---

1. I detail these appropriations below.
2. For an extended definition of poststructuralism, see pp. 162–63 above.
3. In biblical studies, meanwhile, corresponding transformation of the field has not extended to the leading institutions. Even in North America, biblical scholars with serious interests in literary criticism, literary theory, critical theory, cultural theory, or other

The institutionalization of poststructuralism within the Modern Language Association, meanwhile, the principal professional association within the field(s) of literary studies, received vivid symbolic expression in 1986 with the election of arch-deconstructionist J. Hillis Miller to its presidency. For quite some time, in short, poststructuralism has occupied a role in U.S. literary studies not unlike that of historical criticism in biblical studies as the sine qua non for initiation into the discipline.

The wholesale "poststructuralization" (if I may be permitted that barbarism) of literary studies does much to explain its limited impact on New Testament studies. For the varieties of literary criticism that have been most widely embraced in the latter field are those that assimilate most smoothly with traditional historical criticism, most especially redaction criticism. Narrative criticism, for all its undeniable novelty twenty years ago, seems in retrospect to have been a singularly painless extension of redaction criticism. What yokes narrative criticism to redaction criticism is a shared preoccupation (ordinarily unstated in the case of narrative criticism) with uncovering the Evangelist's original intentions. The intricate narrative designs that the narrative critic is typically intent on unearthing are precisely those that the Evangelist putatively implanted in the first place. Reader-response criticism, too, at least in the formalist version of it that caught on in New Testament studies (only one of several possible versions, however), implicitly harnesses itself to the quest for authorial intentions to the extent that its characteristic preoccupation is with tracking the "implied reader" through the narrative, a reader who is on a tight leash held by the author and who jumps obediently through all the readerly hoops that the author has ingeniously manufactured. Deconstruction, in contrast, in common with other varieties of poststructuralist criticism, characteristically reads against the grain of authorial intentionality, and hence by extension against the definitive recovery project of redaction criticism. Deconstruction sticks in the craw of redaction criticism and resists easy incorporation into its maw.

And it is not only redaction criticism that finds deconstruction difficult to swallow. Theological exposition and historical reconstruction remain the primary preoccupations of mainstream New Testament scholarship more generally. By theological exposition I mean the meticulous elucidation of the theological themes, perspectives and agendas of both the narrative and epistolary literature of the New Testament. Deconstruction, meanwhile, subjects the theological, or more properly the "metaphysical" in all its philosophical and theological guises, to stringent interrogation. Yet this blanket statement requires immediate qualification; for apophatic or negative theology,

---

related domains tend to be isolated voices—when not absent altogether—in the principal PhD-granting institutions.

at least, has proved immensely alluring to Derrida and other deconstructors (e.g., Derrida 1992a, 1992b).[4] Indeed, even if deconstruction has failed to make significant inroads in New Testament studies,[5] New Testament theology and deconstruction are not necessarily incommensurable discourses; for deconstruction can illuminate many corners—and not a few supposedly open spaces—of New Testament theology that traditional scholarship has left opaque, precisely because there is much in the New Testament narratives and letters that resists assimilation to the theological categories employed by New Testament scholars.[6]

With regard to historical reconstruction, that other definitive project of mainstream New Testament scholarship, there is the complication that various poststructuralisms, not least deconstruction, have problematized inherited conceptions of history and historiography. Poststructuralism has commonly been seen in New Testament studies, indeed, as singularly ahistorical in thrust—not an altogether unreasonable deduction, admittedly. By and large, poststructuralism in New Testament studies did surf the wave of reaction to historical criticism that had been building since the 1970s. Historiography and poststructuralism achieved at least one notable fusion, meanwhile, in U.S. literary studies. But New Historicism—for it is that to which I refer, and I shall return to it again—has itself made relatively little headway in biblical studies, and what inroads have been made have been mainly in the field of Hebrew Bible.[7]

Thus far I have been writing as though deconstruction still ruled the roost in U.S. literary studies, but, of course, it does not. Even the hold of the more generic poststructuralism that succeeded deconstruction, infiltrating almost every corner of the field in the 1980s and 1990s, seems of late to be loosening. "High theory," epitomized by poststructuralist theory, is currently in a state of perceived decline, although what has taken or will take its place is still veiled from view. Introducing *After Theory*, Terry Eagleton cautions:

---

4. Classically associated with such figures as Pseudo-Dionysius and Meister Eckhart, negative theology is a self-subverting discourse that strategically enacts its own inadequacy to the task of enclosing the divine in human thought or language.

5. Although not for want of trying; see, e.g., Phillips 1990b; Jobling and Moore 1992; Moore 1992, 1994; Seeley 1994; The Bible and Culture Collective 1995; Aichele 1996; Counet 2000; Price 2000; Sherwood 2004b; Jennings 2005; Smith 2005; Nutu 2007; and Wilson 2007 (to list only monographs and edited collections).

6. I have argued this case in detail with regard to Mark and Luke-Acts in Moore 1992.

7. Further on New Historicism, see ch. 5 above, together with the bibliography on pp. 122–24.

> Those to whom the title of this book suggests that "theory" is now over, and that we can all relievedly return to an age of pre-theoretical innocence, are in for a disappointment. There can be no going back to an age when it was enough to pronounce Keats delectable or Milton a doughty spirit. It is not as though the whole project was a ghastly mistake on which some merciful soul has now blown the whistle, so that we can all return to whatever it was we were doing before Ferdinand de Saussure heaved over the horizon. (2003, 1–2)[8]

Reports of theory's recent or imminent demise, even assuming they are not exaggerated, are not good news, it seems to me, for biblical critics with pronounced interests in literary studies. For theory has long functioned as a kind of lingua franca in our particular region of the humanities. The absorption of "theory" back into "reading" and the corresponding decentering of theory and theoreticians in favor of a renewed foregrounding of literature and literary authors may be cheering news indeed for theory-weary literary critics, but hardly for biblical literary critics restlessly searching for ever-new angles on the same old texts. For the lightning bolt of inspiration is, on the whole, more likely to strike the biblical critic browsing works with such titles as *Deconstructions: A User's Guide* (Royle 2000), or *Queer Studies: An Interdisciplinary Reader* (Corber and Valocchi 2003), or *Postcolonialisms: An Anthology of Cultural Theory and Criticism* (Desai and Nair 2005) than browsing works with such titles as *The Art of Shakespeare's Sonnets* (Vendler 1999), or *Jane Austen's Letters* (Austen 1995), or *T. S. Eliot: His Mind and Personality* (Hoskot 1979).

Poststructuralism and the Political

Hand in hand with the "poststructuralization" of literary studies during the past twenty-five years or so has gone a "politicization" of literary studies. The latter began in no small part, indeed, as a reaction against the former, a backlash against the perceived apoliticism of American deconstruction, in particular, of the late 1970s and early 1980s.[9] This political reaction, however, while frequently setting poststructuralism aside altogether, has more often tended to harness it instead for the analysis of a steadily expanding set of social realia: gender and sexuality; race and ethnicity; colonialism, postcolonialism, and neocolonialism; popular culture; and social class (this last, however, being

---

8. Further on theory's alleged decline, see ch. 16 below.
9. Two influential expressions of this backlash were Said 1978b, which took Derridean deconstruction to task for its abstraction and neglect of the political, and Lentricchia 1980, a trenchant critique of deconstructive "formalism."

the least-attended topic on the list). Poststructuralism and the political have forged potent fusions in critical phenomena ranging from cultural studies, New Historicism and gender studies to postcolonial and queer studies—which is to say in virtually every high-profile "movement" in literary studies since the heyday of "Yale deconstruction" in the late 1970s and early 1980s. The "politicization" of U.S. literary studies has been even more widespread than its "poststructuralization." This "politicization" preceded poststructuralism in the U.S. academy in the forms of Marxist and especially feminist criticisms, and even at present shows no signs of abating. More than poststructuralism, it remains the "untranscendable horizon" in contemporary literary studies to the extent that it seems at present all but impossible to imagine what might possibly succeed it as the dominant intellectual ethos of the discipline.

Biblical studies, too, of course, although certainly in a less concerted fashion than literary studies, has increasingly veered into the "political" in recent decades. I would venture to say, however, that literary studies has provided little direct impetus for this swerve in biblical studies. Notable political developments in literary studies, such as New Historicism, postcolonial studies and queer studies, have only been taken up in biblical studies in the past decade or less, and remain on the fringes of the field. Feminist biblical criticism and other liberationist trajectories in hermeneutics and exegesis have more effectively catalyzed the political turn in biblical studies. Emblematic of that turn was Elisabeth Schüssler Fiorenza's landmark presidential address to the Society of Biblical Literature in 1987, subsequently published as "The Ethics of Biblical Interpretation" (Schüssler Fiorenza 1988). Schüssler Fiorenza's accession to the presidency of the SBL, coupled with her challenging address, signaled at least a temporary movement to the center of the discipline of what had formerly been peripheral. Poststructuralism, however—emblematic, as I have argued, of extrabiblical literary studies in this period—remained in the margins, Schüssler Fiorenza's distrust of malestream historical criticism being coupled with a distrust of postmodernism in general and poststructuralism in particular.[10] In general, whereas a self-consciously political stance has frequently, even regularly, gone hand in hand with poststructuralism in literary

---

10. Schüssler Fiorenza's SBL presidency thus signified something quite different from J. Hillis Miller's MLA presidency of the previous year, the latter being widely billed as signaling the "triumph of theory" (read: poststructuralism) in literary studies—not least because the title of his presidential address contained that very expression (see Miller 1987). For detailed discussion of Schüssler Fiorenza's stance on postmodernism, see The Bible and Culture Collective 1995, 260–67.

studies in recent decades, their conjunction in biblical studies has been far more the exception than the rule.[11]

Literary Studies after Literature

By the mid-1990s, postcolonial studies, cultural studies, and queer theory had emerged as the most fashionable trends in U.S. literary studies, with masculinity studies hot on their heels. It is in the nature of fashions quickly to become unfashionable, but ten years on these developments still seem to dominate the scene, and nothing comparably visible has yet reared its head in the field.[12] It appears that there are more substantial reasons than sheer trendiness, then, for the vast critical literature that each of these areas has spawned. Each of them also constitutes a considerable resource for New Testament studies, it seems to me, and each has barely begun to be engaged by New Testament scholars.

Queer theory, for instance, has the capacity to shift the increasingly tired debates on biblical texts that apparently deal with homosexuality into a radically different register—precisely by problematizing the concept of "homosexuality" itself. As is now well known, the inaugural volume of Foucault's *History of Sexuality* (1978), effectively the charter document of queer theory, argues that "homosexuality," far from being the name of a phenomenon that has remained more or less stable through history, is instead a discursive product of relatively recent vintage.[13] By this logic, whatever Paul is attacking in those lethal two verses of Romans, say, that have destroyed an incalculable number of lives, cannot be equated with what is customarily labeled "homosexuality" in contemporary Western societies.[14] Queer theory thus provides the professional New Testament scholar—and, more crucially, the local pastor—with resources for reading a particularly combustible handful of biblical texts differently.

---

11. Fusions of feminism and deconstruction constitute one set of exceptions (e.g., Graham 1991; Phillips 1994; Rutledge 1996; Sherwood 1996; and ch. 4 above). Certain of David Jobling's essays engage in broader mergings of deconstruction and the political (e.g., 1990, 1992). Foucauldian readings constitute yet another set of exceptions (e.g., Castelli 1991a, 1991b; Polaski 1999; and chs. 3 and 7 above).

12. With the arguable exception of ecocriticism (see, e.g., Glotfelty and Fromm 1996; Rosendale 2002; Garrard 2004; Buell 2005; Gersdorf and Mayer 2006), which I plan to engage in a separate study.

13. On queer theory/queer studies, including queer reading of biblical texts, see the bibliography on pp. 304–5 above.

14. See further ch. 12 above.

15. A MODEST MANIFESTO

To limit queer biblical commentary, however, to the tiny handful of biblical texts that explicitly touch on homoeroticism would be to miss a major contribution of queer theory as it has been deployed in literary studies. For heterosexuality has been queer theory's object of investigation as much as homosexuality (e.g., Katz 1995; Richardson 1996; Boyarin 1997; Warner 1999; Thomas 2000; Ingraham 2005).[15] Queer theory has dealt deconstructively with sexuality in general, and by extension with gender in general, but most especially, perhaps, with masculinity, disclosing the queerness with which masculinity as construction and performance is inflected and infected in Western and other cultures. Masculinity has, meanwhile, also become an explicit object of investigation in New Testament studies.[16] To date, however, this burgeoning body of work has made little direct use of queer theory.[17] Instead it has drawn mainly and increasingly on a specific corpus of work in the field of classics dealing with the protocols, codes, and conventions of masculinity in ancient Mediterranean culture—and not incidentally, in the process, showing ancient masculinities to be a foreign country in relation to modern masculinities.[18] This body of work in classics may, however, be regarded as sibling to queer theory in literary studies, to the extent that Foucault's *History of Sexuality* has constituted the most significant generative matrix for each of the two areas.[19] There is, as such, a potential compatibility between queer theory in literary studies, on the one hand, and much recent work on sex and gender in the field of classics, on the other, that has yet to be exploited by most of the New Testament critics currently analyzing the gender performances of assorted males in the New Testament, principally Jesus and Paul.

---

15. Pride of place on any such list, however, belongs to a work that preceded "queer theory" proper—Adrienne Rich's 1980 manifesto, "Compulsory Heterosexuality and Lesbian Existence" (reprinted in Rich 1986).

16. See, e.g., Glancy 1994; Eilberg-Schwartz 1994, 223–37; Parsons 1995; Moore 1996, 102–38; 2001, 90–199 passsim; Clines 1998; Smith 1999; Kahl 2000; D'Angelo 2002; Moore and Anderson 2003; Frilingos 2004, 64–115; Conway 2008.

17. For partial exceptions, see Pippin 1999, 117–25, and Moore 2001, 113–23, 163–72 (= 295–304 above).

18. Most of the essays in Moore and Anderson 2003 fall into this category, for example, as does Conway 2008, the first complete monograph on New Testament masculinities. For a comprehensive introduction to the study of masculinity in the ancient Mediterranean world, see Williams 1999.

19. The second and third volumes of the *History of Sexuality* (Foucault 1985; 1986) deal with Greek and Roman antiquity respectively, and devote much attention to masculinity. See further 274–79 passim above.

The influence of postcolonial studies on literary studies during the past fifteen years has been even more extensive than that of queer theory.[20] What of the influence of postcolonial studies on New Testament studies? While limited, it has been surprisingly complex.[21] Only consider the ways in which postcolonial studies has been taken up within the Society of Biblical Literature. The now disbanded program unit The Bible in Africa, Asia, the Caribbean and Latin America (henceforth, BAACLA) served as the first forum for postcolonial studies within the society. At the 1998 annual meeting, BAACLA featured a panel discussion of *The Postcolonial Bible* (Sugirtharajah 1998b), while the 1999 meeting included a BAACLA session on "Postcolonial Studies and New Testament Studies." My initial point is a simple one. Throughout its admittedly short history, postcolonial biblical criticism has, more often than not, been less another spillover from literary studies than a distinctive inflection of liberation hermeneutics, most especially contextual hermeneutics.[22] This is not to suggest, however, that postcolonial biblical criticism of this stripe is a seamlessly smooth outgrowth of liberation hermeneutics. On the contrary, its most prolific exemplar, R. S. Sugirtharajah, has mounted an energetic internal critique of the liberationist tradition from a postcolonial perspective (2001, 203–75; 2002, 103–23). Not for the first time has a theory or methodology with its disciplinary locus in literary studies morphed into something distinctively different when adopted and adapted by biblical critics: consider the analogous transformation of structural narratology into narrative criticism, or that of ideology critique (classically, Marxist-driven) into ideological criticism (normally, not Marxist-driven).

The customizing of postcolonial studies by New Testament critics becomes yet more apparent when we consider the still small but steady stream of books with the word "empire" in their titles that has trickled forth in recent years: *Paul and Empire* (Horsley 1997), *Matthew and Empire* (Carter 2001), *Unveiling Empire: Reading Revelation Then and Now* (Howard-Brook and Gwyther 1999), *Jesus and Empire* (Horsley 2002), *The Bible and Empire* (Sugirtharajah 2005a)…—to which cluster may be added by reason of a shared preoccupation with the theme of empire still other recent works, such as *Liberating Paul*

---

20. For a brief introduction to postcolonial studies, see Moore 2006, 3–23, together with ch. 13 above. Detailed introductions include Ashcroft, Griffiths, and Tiffin 2001; Young 2001; Desai and Nair 2005.

21. And the literature has been quite extensive; see, e.g., Donaldson 1996; Sugirtharajah 1998a; 1998b; 1999a; 2001; 2002; 2003; 2005a; Liew 1999; Dube 2000; Segovia 2000; Dube and Staley 2002b; Kim 2004; Moore and Segovia 2005; Moore 2006; Segovia and Sugirtharajah 2007.

22. Also variously termed vernacular hermeneutics, cultural exegesis, cultural interpretation, intercultural interpretation and cultural studies.

(Elliott 1994), *Paul and Politics* (Horsley 2000), *Paul and the Roman Imperial Order* (Horsley 2004), *Hearing the Whole Story: The Politics of Plot in Mark's Gospel* (Horsley 2001), and *The Gospel of Matthew in Its Roman Imperial Context* (Riches and Sim 2005), to name but the main examples. Can this work usefully be labeled "postcolonial biblical criticism"? I'm not sure that it can. It is certainly no coincidence that it emerges at a time when postcolonial studies has been widely disseminated throughout the humanities. But exceedingly seldom does the "X and Empire" work draw on extrabiblical postcolonial studies. "Empire studies" would be a more apt term for it. And it is probably safe to predict that it stands a far better chance of making significant inroads in mainstream New Testament studies than any brand of postcolonial biblical criticism that requires navigation through the frequently dense discourse of postcolonial theory. Not the least reason why literary studies has had a merely superficial impact on biblical studies, all told, is that literary studies is a field that embraces difficulty of one sort—the sort monumentalized in disciplinary landmarks such as Jacques Derrida's *Of Grammatology* or Homi Bhabha's *The Location of Culture*—whereas biblical studies is a field that embraces difficulty of another sort—the sort enshrined in the Documentary Hypothesis or the Synoptic Problem.

Let us turn, finally, to cultural studies, the fourth critical phenomenon that overran U.S. literary studies in the 1990s—not that it originated in the 1990s or even the 1980s: by the time it caught on in the U.S. literary academy it already had a thirty-year history in tow.[23] American cultural studies has frequently been castigated for jettisoning the Marxist underpinnings of its formative British phase.[24] Even domesticated and defanged, however, cultural studies may still turn out to have been the most momentous shift of all in U.S. literary studies. For however radical other brands of criticism may appear to be, "literature," however conceived or reconceived, remains their object of analysis. Deconstructionists read Shelley, Proust, and Joyce; postcolonial critics read Conrad, Kipling, and Chinua Achebe; queer theorists read E. M. Forster and Jean Genet; while New Historicists read Shakespeare and, well, Shakespeare. But practitioners of cultural studies read *Cosmopolitan*, *Maxim*, and *Martha Stewart Living*; commercials, infomercials, infotainment, and CNN; hip-hop culture, highbrow culture, and fast-food culture; Wall Street and Wal-Mart; plastic surgery and plastic garden gnomes; and so on in

---

23. A history that, according to the standard recital, began in Britain in the 1950s. For a potted version of that history, see Moore 1998a, esp. 3–13. For the unabridged version, see Turner 2003. Broader introductions to cultural studies include Grossberg, Nelson, and Treichler 1992; Storey 1996, 2003; During 1999, 2005; Abbas and Erni 2004; Leistyna 2004.

24. See Moore 1998a, 17–18, for a catena of quotations from the castigators.

an endlessly proliferating list.[25] What has tended to fill traditionally minded literature professors with dismay or disgust in recent years has been less the spectacle of the best and brightest graduate students pressing the classics of the various literary canons through a Frenchified theoretical shredder than the spectacle of such students now laboring earnestly to decode the semiotics of *American Idol* or the Victoria's Secret catalogue or the lyrics of hip-hop or thrash metal. To certain of the more apocalyptic minds among these anxious or appalled traditionalists, indeed, it is not entirely unimaginable that the academic study of the literary canons will gradually become an esoteric discipline, comparable to the study of, say, Old or Middle English in current academic culture. At the very least, literature's place at the center of "literary studies" can no longer be comfortably assumed.[26]

What of cultural studies' relationship to biblical studies? As with postcolonial studies, only more so, cultural studies has assumed a form within biblical studies for which one would be hard pressed to find a precise analogue within literary studies. Fundamental in this regard has been Fernando Segovia's influential framing of the landmark collection *Reading from This Place* (Segovia and Tolbert 1995a, 1995b), and other work of this stripe, as "cultural studies."[27] Cultural studies in this mode is a brand of biblical criticism in which the critic explicitly foregrounds his or her sociocultural location—or "face and voice," as Segovia more pithily puts it (1995b, 12)—in the act of interpretation. This device is especially identifiable with a rising tide of distinctive biblical scholarship recently issuing from the Two-Thirds World and from minority scholars in North America.[28] The sociocultural context out of which the critic explicitly writes is rarely itself the object of analysis in such work, but rather is made the instrument for illuminating the biblical text.

---

25. This is a rather partial presentation of cultural studies, admittedly (as is Eagleton's similar encapsulation of it [2003, 2–5]). It is another academic discipline, when all is said and done (notwithstanding its recurrent efforts to be otherwise), which means that much of it occurs not in Technicolor but in muted shades of gray. My point, however, is that any of the topics listed above—along with innumerable others of the same ilk—would be eminently *viable* objects of analysis for contemporary cultural studies.

26. An early testament to this crisis was the "forum" of thirty-two letters on the strained relations between literary studies and cultural studies published in the March 1997 issue of *PMLA*, the MLA's flagship journal.

27. For the framing, see Segovia 1995a, 1–32, and especially Segovia 1995b, 1–17. His framing is all the more interesting for the fact that the volumes' contributors do not themselves label their work "cultural studies." Segovia 2000 further develops his conception of cultural studies.

28. See, e.g., Mosala 1989; Felder 1991; Sugirtharajah 1991, 1999b; Smith-Christopher 1995; Wimbush 2000; Dube 2001; Liew and Yee 2002; Patte 2004.

In literary studies meanwhile, as intimated earlier, the term "cultural studies" most readily evokes the academic analysis of contemporary popular culture—principally, although by no means exclusively, Western popular culture. How might this version of cultural studies translate into biblical studies? As critical examination of the Bible as cultural icon, presumably, most especially as an icon of contemporary culture, and popular culture in particular. Cultural studies in this mode might turn its analytic attention to any one of a dizzying array of objects, ranging from *The Passion of the Christ* and its impassioned reception to the controversies swirling around U.S. monuments to the Ten Commandments; from the Bible's multiple identities within the teeming abyss of the Internet ("My name is Legion, for we are many") to its less conflicted identity within the Bush White House; and from its overt deployment in the intraecclesial homosexuality wars to its more occluded employment in nonreligious cinema and popular music. Significant studies of the Bible as cultural icon have, of course, already appeared, most notably studies of the Bible in both classical and contemporary art and of the Bible in film.[29] Certain of these studies label themselves explicitly as exercises in cultural studies, while others do not. But are any of them to be regarded as "literary criticism"? Not in any readily recognizable sense, but it is perhaps now the fate of literary criticism within biblical studies to wander ever further from its origins, as is already the case with literary criticism within literary studies.

Beyond Method

The four recent developments in literary studies that we have been considering—postcolonial studies, cultural studies, queer studies, and masculinity studies—share a common, underremarked feature. That feature is also present in autobiographical criticism, which, while not as visible in contemporary literary studies as the other four developments, has nevertheless yielded a sig-

---

29. See, e.g., Bal 1991; Exum 1996, 1999; Bach 1996; Aichele 2000; Aichele and Walsh 2002; Walsh 2003; Runions 2003; Corley and Webb 2004; Plate 2004. Cultural studies experiments that range more broadly include Phy 1985; Exum and Moore 1998; and esp. Moore 1998b; Boer 1999a. Between them, the latter two volumes include explorations of such topics as Mrs. Thatcher's Bible; representations of the Bible in the supermarket tabloid *Weekly World News*; biblical allusions in (non-Christian) rock music; and readings of biblical texts with such pop-cultural intertexts as pornography; the MacDonald's culinary experience; and the brilliant, burnout career of Guns n' Roses frontman Axl Rose. Similarly omnivorous in scope is Black 2006. For a full-length study of the Bible in/and contemporary popular music, see Dowsett 1998. The SBL has had a Bible and Cultural Studies program unit since 1996, although cultural-studies papers at SBL have by no means been limited to that forum.

nificant body of work in biblical studies.[30] (One thing that any such list of recent trends occludes, however, is the continuing central influence of feminist studies, which so frequently informs, or even shapes, activity in these newer areas, although it also frequently exists in some tension with them.) None of these newer areas—and this is the common feature—offer much in the way of a "methodology," at least as we understand that term in biblical studies.

The high-profile developments in U.S. literary studies of the 1970s and 1980s—deconstruction, reader-response criticism, New Historicism—were different. Deconstruction was nothing if not a methodology, despite the ritual protests of its acolytes that it was anything but. At its best, deconstruction was a highly pliable strategy of reading. But it was also an eminently *repeatable* strategy of reading—which I take to be as good a rough-and-ready definition of "method" as any. Deconstruction shuttled constantly between rigidity and flexibility. At its worst, it was a reading-by-numbers procedure whose precise outcome was a foregone conclusion. In the hands of its more adept practitioners, however, it was capable of surprising even the jaded critic. Reader-response criticism, for its part, offered a range of distinctive methodologies to the critical consumer in the guise of assorted "reader" costumes to try on—Stanley Fish's Surprised Reader and Wolfgang Iser's Implied Reader being the most striking, perhaps, and the costumes that New Testament literary critics were most eager to wear (see further Moore 1989, 71–107). New Historicism, in apparent contrast, was *almost* what deconstruction claimed to be—not a method. And yet even New Historicism yielded certain readily identifiable and, yes, repeatable strategies of reading, as we shall see.

It seems to me that postcolonial studies, cultural studies, queer studies, masculinity studies and autobiographical criticism are in a somewhat different boat, methodologically speaking. British cultural studies did develop certain distinctive methodological procedures during the 1970s and early 1980s (as outlined in Moore 1998a, 7–8). By the time cultural studies began to take the U.S. academy by storm in the late 1980s and early 1990s, however, it had all but uncoupled itself from methodology as such. What is distinctive (and controversial) about U.S. cultural studies is its preferred objects of analysis, as noted earlier, not its analytical procedures.[31] What of postcolonial studies? Despite the colossal critical literature that this field has spawned, it has yielded

---

30. See pp. 171–72 above.

31. A lack (if that indeed is what it is) that Schwoch, White, and Gaonkar 2005 attempts to redress. The thing to be noted for our purposes, however, is that the volume emerges out of a general perception that the question of method in cultural studies is a puzzling and vexing one.

remarkably little in the way of readily identifiable methodologies or even general strategies of reading. What does immediately leap to mind are the immensely influential concepts set forth (in thoroughly unsystematic fashion) by Homi Bhabha in certain of the early essays collected in *The Location of Culture* (1994d)—colonial ambivalence, mimicry, and hybridity.[32] These three interrelated concepts do provide a productive reading grid that can readily, if not unproblematically, be superimposed on texts emerging from empire, including biblical texts.[33] Gayatri Spivak's no less influential oeuvre, however, offers exceedingly slim pickings for the method-hungry biblical critic,[34] as, indeed, does Edward Said's, the latter arguably only yielding the overly general strategy of "contrapuntal reading" (Said 1993, esp. 51, 66–67).[35]

Queer studies and masculinity studies, too, along with autobiographical criticism, offer extremely little in the way of iterable methodological procedures. They seem to offer nothing comparable even to Derrida's early (and endlessly cited) description of deconstruction as an operation conducted in two successive phases, "reversal" and "reinscription";[36] or of Aram Veeser's encapsulation of New Historicism (at least as practiced by its preeminent exponent, Stephen Greenblatt) as an analytic strategy that typically moves through five successive "moments": anecdote, outrage, resistance, containment, and autobiography.[37] Queer studies and masculinity studies do effect a radical reconceptualization of sex, sexuality and/or gender that draws the critic's eye inexorably to certain features of a text and even predetermines the broad contours of a reading. But each of these developments, along with postcolonial studies and cultural studies, seems to me to have more in common methodologically with feminist studies, say, than with deconstruction, reader-response criticism or New Historicism. In literary studies, as in biblical studies, feminist critics have not been associated with any one methodology. Feminist scholarship has been a radically eclectic enterprise, methodologically speaking. What feminist scholars do share in common, it seems to me, is a critical sensibility, an encompassing angle of vision that, in a more

---

32. See further pp. 319–20 above.
33. See, e.g., Runions 2002; Thurman 2003; Moore 2006, 97–121. For general reflection on Bhabha and the Bible, see pp. 317–25 above.
34. Although one can do a surprising amount with a few scraps; see especially Donaldson 2005.
35. New Testament scholars who have engaged with Said include Friesen 2001 and Frilingos 2004, both of whom devote space to Said in their respective introductions. Tellingly, however, Said disappears from view once these scholars turn to the task of exegeting Revelation.
36. On which see p. 91 above.
37. On which see pp. 101ff. above.

fundamental fashion than a methodological framework, brings previously unperceived or disavowed data into focus (cf. Fonow and Cook 1991). And it seems to me, too, that postcolonial studies, cultural studies, queer studies, and masculinity studies operate similarly. Autobiographical criticism, for its part, also diverges from traditional methodology, the critic's personal history forming the explicit reading frame into which the text is placed and in relation to which it assumes fresh meaning.

This postmethodological swerve in literary studies (effected unselfconsciously, so far as I can tell, with no manifestos to herald it) offers an instructive contrast to our established modes of reading in biblical studies. For methodology has long been the sine qua non of biblical studies as an academic discipline. Methodology is what is meant to keep our discourse on the Bible from being subjective, personal, private, pietistic, pastoral, devotional or homiletical. Methodology, in short, is what maintains the partition between sermon and scholarship. The homily has long been the constitutive other of biblical criticism, and methodology the enabling condition of such criticism—"methodology" throughout being a cipher for "objectivity," "neutrality," "disinterestedness," and the other related and foundational values of biblical studies as an academic discipline, values that are rarely trumpeted nowadays, at least in Anglophone biblical scholarship (evidence of the impact of postmodernism on the field), but that continue to hold sway, seemingly, over most practitioners of the discipline anyway, at least to the extent that they resist seeing their own scholarship as advocacy for the interests of their class or any other, that being the perceived preserve of other scholars who wear their political agenda on their sleeve (evidence of the lack of impact of postmodernism on the field).[38]

But our quarantining of the biblical critical from the homiletical has not occurred without cost. Most obviously, our obsession with method has made for a mountainous excess of dull and dreary books, essays, and articles: here, first, in numbing dry detail is my method; now watch and be amazed while I apply it woodenly to this unsuspecting biblical text. Can we move beyond methodology in biblical studies without writing sermons pure and simple? That, I would suggest, is an important, perhaps even a central, challenge for those of us in biblical studies interested in engaging in authentic interdisciplinary dialogue with contemporary literary studies.

---

38. In her response to the SBL paper on which this essay is based, Mary Ann Tolbert noted that homiletics, too, is a field much preoccupied with method. It seems to me, however, that methodology plays a substantially different role in homiletics than in traditional biblical scholarship. Its function in homiletics is hardly that of facilitating a disinterested stance on the part of the interpreter in relation to the biblical text.

Yet it is not as though I am advocating a move into terra incognita. At least one flourishing variety of biblical criticism, discussed in brief above, itself seems to be flirting with the sermon, and largely independently of any influence from literary studies. I refer to contextual hermeneutics, vernacular hermeneutics, cultural exegesis, cultural interpretation, intercultural interpretation, cultural studies…—all terms used interchangeably for the same critical sensibility, as we saw. What contextual hermeneutics has in common with the sermon is a shared central concern to bring an ancient text into meaningful and explicit dialogue with a contemporary context. A decade or so ago, I confessed to a certain discomfort with contextual hermeneutics' blurring of the professional and the personal, along with its concomitant blurring of the critical and the homiletical.[39] But now I find myself wanting to dwell a while in this discomfort, to take its measure and plumb its depths, recognizing it to be nothing other than the sensitized underbelly of the system of exclusions that constitutes my professional identity as a biblical scholar.

Contextual hermeneutics, while seldom, if ever, claiming or admitting as much, seems to press significantly "beyond method," and while that is by no means its most important feature, it is probably its least discussed. Within the realm of contextual hermeneutics, biblical scholarship as a disciplinary practice threatens to crumble and come apart, it seems to me, even more than it does within the realm of deconstructive biblical criticism. And it comes apart precisely in order to be reformed as something other than what biblical scholarship originally was, which is to say—among other things, and somewhat reductively no doubt—a white European ideology.

I see contextual hermeneutics, then—or cultural studies, if you prefer the Segovian moniker—as occupying approximately the same position within contemporary biblical studies as cultural studies—the "other" cultural studies, that is to say, the extrabiblical kind—occupies within contemporary literary studies. Each in its own way is the critical development that most threatens the inherited identity of its respective discipline. And I can imagine no more forward-looking project for biblical literary criticism—a literary criticism, however, in which the appellative privileging of the "literary" would itself be thrown into question—than to attempt to combine these two types of cultural studies, the biblical studies type and the literary studies type. Such a project would entail dislodging the written biblical text from its traditionally privileged place at the center of biblical studies (for whether in the postliterate West or in the pre- and postliterate developing world, the *written* biblical

---

39. See p. 136 above.

text is seldom the primary "text" anyway)[40] and simultaneously pushing into a postmethodological space—which, I hasten to add, is altogether different from a premethodological space. Isn't it time that we exited the methodone clinic once and for all?

---

40. Within the U.S., look no further than the *Passion of the Christ* phenomenon. And even when the object of biblical obsession is still a text, it is not necessarily the biblical text; the staggering sales of the *Left Behind* series have not put the lie to the truism that in mainline Protestant U.S. churches Revelation is among the least read biblical books, since it is not Revelation itself that is being read. On the oral Bible in the Two-Thirds World, see, most recently, Draper 2004.

16
AFTER "AFTER THEORY," AND OTHER APOCALYPTIC CONCEITS IN LITERARY AND BIBLICAL STUDIES*

Co-authored with Yvonne Sherwood

As this volume has shown, the history of poststructuralism both inside and outside the field of biblical studies has been a complicated one. Within the field of literary studies, poststructuralism has been the object of repeated reinvention—deconstruction, New Historicism, postcolonial theory, queer theory...—and each new version has, sooner or later and to a greater or lesser degree, been appropriated for biblical exegesis. Most recently, a poststructuralist version of ecocriticism centered on human-animal relations and catalyzed especially by Derrida's "The Animal That Therefore I Am" (2002b; cf. Derrida 2003, 2008, 2009) has emerged in literary studies and begun to mushroom.

Side by side, however, with this entrepreneurial success story of poststructuralism's successive career changes is a competing tale of poststructuralism's final demise. And it is the latter drama that is the central focus of this final essay, which originated as a conference paper that Yvonne Sherwood and I co-wrote in 2007 for a joint AAR/SBL session on the "after theory" and "post-poststructuralism" debate in literary studies and its complex ramifications for biblical and theological studies. As the previous essay noted in brief, "high theory," epitomized by poststructuralism, is currently in a perceived state of decline in many sectors of the literary studies field. Given that theory has long been the

---

* This essay is a revised and expanded version of a paper prepared for a joint session of the Bible, Theology, and Postmodernity Group and the Reading, Theory and the Bible Section at the Joint Annual Meeting of the American Academy of Religion and the Society of Biblical Literature Annual Meeting in San Diego, 2007.

lingua franca of literary studies, its alleged demise raises fundamental questions about the future of that discipline as well as its present and recent past.

In this essay, Yvonne and I shuttle back and forth between literary studies and biblical studies and reflect on the roles that theory has played in each field, where it presently finds itself, and where it may yet be headed. Ultimately, we find the rumors of theory's recent demise less interesting than evidence of its recent transformation. Something novel has emerged between theory and the Bible, we argue, and it has emerged outside the field of biblical studies. While biblical scholars have been engaging theory to vamp up an uncomfortably old-fashioned discipline, theorists in unprecedented numbers have been engaging the uncomfortable relic that is the Bible and have begun using old-fashioned words besides, many of them "biblical" words. Paradoxically, however, rather than being less of a challenge to traditional biblical scholarship than previous modes of theorizing, this "turn to religion" in theory is actually more of a challenge, we would argue, and hence even more of a provocation to reexamine our ingrained disciplinary habits and inclinations.

Our route to these conclusions is through the detour of defamiliarization. Taking the long road to the rear entrance of the biblical studies fortress—the road that passes through literary studies—we attempt at every turn to expose the acute *strangeness* of biblical literary criticism and of critical biblical scholarship in general. Yvonne began her academic life in English Literature, so that strangeness has never been lost on her. I've had to work harder to see it, and working with her has helped me to bring it into sharper relief. For her gift of comfortable alienation I am profoundly grateful.

After Theory, or, Revolt in the Cafeteria

Poststructuralism has long epitomized "high theory" in literary studies—or "Theory," as we shall term it for convenience. Poststructuralism's relationship to Theory has generally been synecdochic, the part standing in for the whole. It is no accident that Theory's most visible early outing as a term was in Jonathan Culler's *On Deconstruction*, a book that arguably did more than any other to popularize deconstruction, itself a further synecdoche for poststructuralism, in Anglo-American literary studies. As the book opens we find Culler ruminating how "works of literary theory are [now] closely and vitally related to other writings within a domain as yet unnamed but often called 'theory' for short. This domain is not 'literary theory,'" continues Culler, "since many of its most interesting works do not explicitly address literature.... [T]he most convenient designation is simply the name 'theory'" (1982, 8). Much more recently, Culler has defined Theory as an umbrella term for "discourses that come to exercise influence outside their apparent disciplinary realm because they offer new and persuasive characterizations of problems or phenomena of general interest: language, consciousness, meaning, nature and culture, the functioning of the psyche, the relations of individual experience to larger structures, and so on" (2007, 4).

Over the past three decades, the term *Theory*, at once vague and specific, has stood in for a paradoxically expansive yet selective body of work: Russian formalism, French structuralism, semiotics, poststructuralism, deconstruction, Lacanian and post-Lacanian psychoanalytic theory, assorted Marxisms and neo-Marxisms, reader-response criticism and *Rezeptionsästhetik*, "French feminist theory," "third-wave" feminist theory, gender studies, queer theory, New Historicism, cultural materialism, cultural studies, postcolonial studies, and (academic) postmodernism *tout court*, along with carefully selected slices of what is known (often polemically) as "continental philosophy." Theory's national origins are thus seen to lie quite specifically in a transatlantic alliance between France and the United States with walk-on parts for a few Russians, Germans, and Italians and a brief detour through Birmingham (England, not Alabama) for cultural studies. Theory's A-list has included such assorted luminaries as Jacques Derrida, Michel Foucault, Jacques Lacan, Roland Barthes, Julia Kristeva, Louis Althusser, Gilles Deleuze, Luce Irigaray, Paul de Man, Edward Said, Fredric Jameson, Gayatri Spivak, Judith Butler, Homi Bhabha, Slavoj Žižek, and Donna Haraway, to name but a few representative figures. Theory does not include figures like Jung or Weber; it may not even include figures like Adorno or Habermas.[1] And although its corpus is corpulent and expansive, Theory is hardly a single body. In its short life it has seen as many sectarian schisms as post-Reformation Christianity. Proponents of cultural materialism, say, are as prone to parody New Historicists or postcolonial critics to parody postcolonial theorists as evangelical Christians are to parody Roman Catholics—or other evangelical Christians. Not surprisingly, therefore, attacks on Theory have been equally conflicted, with Theory serving as a repository for mutually exclusive accusations. Charged with being at once too high (arcane, scholastic, esoteric) and too low (vulgar, materialist, pop-

---

1. For the filleted version of Theory and what it excludes, see Anderson 2006, 1.

cultural), Theory has become a target for both "right" and "left," at once too "politically correct" and too apolitical, remote, and disengaged.

Thus far we have been writing as though Theory still ruled the roost in literary studies, but its hold has slackened noticeably in recent years. "High theory," epitomized by poststructuralist theory, is currently in a state of perceived decline. In the field of literary studies, book titles such as *After Theory* (Docherty 1996; Eagleton 2003), *Reading after Theory* (Cunningham 2002), and *What's Left of Theory?* (Butler, Guillory, and Thomas 2000b)[2] suggest that Theory is currently croaking its last gasp—although, of course, it's also possible that the authors of such books are standing over Theory with a pillow, intent on bringing on the very death they are describing. Even for the authors of these would-be obituaries, however, what has taken or will take Theory's place is still veiled from view, awaiting apocalypse. Introducing *After Theory*, eponymous exemplar of the "after Theory" phenomenon and arguably its most influential product, Terry Eagleton cautions that those who suppose that "Theory" is now slipping into the past, "so that we can all relievedly return to an age of pre-theoretical innocence, are in for a disappointment" (2003, 1).[3] The very debate engendered by Eagleton and others, however, centered on death notices or their disproval, conspires to creates a sense of Theory as, at the very least, an "obtrusive ghost" in literary studies (Rabaté 2002, 10).

Reports of Theory's recent or imminent demise, in any case, even assuming they are not exaggerated,[4] are hardly electrifying news for biblical scholars. Theory can hardly be said to have risen to sufficiently Luciferian height in biblical studies to undergo any meaningful fall. Rather than being cast from the celestial heights, it would have to be thrown from a basement window. Theory-weary book titles are hardly a fixture of contemporary biblical studies. We do not find biblical scholars reflexively reaching for the particular eschatological trope of Theory's decline and fall to limn an as yet dimly glimpsed future designed, as all such futures are, to polemically reorient the present. The first reason for this is the obvious one: any call for an

---

2. See also Derrida et al. 2004, a book whose engagement with the "after theory" debate is more oblique. For the proceedings of a particularly public and influential moratorium on Theory conducted in Chicago in April 2003 by a distinguished group of Theorists, see Mitchell 2004. With the announced demise of Theory in general, questions are now being asked as to whether specific types of Theory, some until recently deemed hale and hearty, are also at death's door; see, e.g., Agnani et al. 2007 (titled "The End of Postcolonial Theory?").

3. Further still on theory's rise and alleged decline, see Bové 1992; Eddins 1995; Harris 1996; Perloff 2007; and esp. Patai and Corral 2005b.

4. A number of critics (e.g., McQuillan et al. 1999; Davis 2003) argue that such reports *are* exaggerated and that Theory will continue to play a crucial role in the humanities.

apocalypse of Theory from within biblical studies would sound absurd. Apocalypses are not minor fires started by pyromaniacs but last-ditch emergency measures reserved for overbearing worlds that need imagining otherwise. To get a decent apocalyptic fire going, you need something momentous and massive (the Roman Empire, say, would do nicely; the American Empire would do just as well) to send up in flames.

Academics are as adept as any other constituency at imagining themselves as members of a beleaguered minority. Self-reflective articles written from an acknowledged perspective of privilege and majority are ever in short supply. That being said, visions of victimhood can only go so far. The image of traditionally minded biblical scholars marooned in a small rowing boat or huddling on a small island on a globe that has been thoroughly colonized by Theory would sound paranoid and absurd. "Theory's Empire" in biblical studies is approximately the size of Tobago or the Falkland Islands. This is the underwhelming reality that John J. Collins is up against in his recent *The Bible after Babel*, a rare biblical studies contribution to the "After Theory" genre. But even Collins is compelled to admit a few pages into his book: "It is not the case that the postmodernists have captured the field. Far from it" (2005, 3).[5]

Far from it, indeed. Through our (admittedly jaundiced) eyes, Theory, while certainly alive and sometimes even kicking in biblical studies, seems all too often to be used as garnish, a soupçon of Zeitgeist spice, on modes of critical practice that remain fundamentally unaffected by it; or it tends to circulate among a few overworked usual suspects and a few fervent new recruits who preach to the converted in the Theory-ghettos of the Society of Biblical Literature Annual Meeting. Literary critic Valentine Cunningham misreads the menu, claiming that Theory has "spread … slickly" and "glibly" like a "gumbo" into such unlikely fields as geography, law, music, and even theology—by which he apparently means biblical studies, as the sole item of evidence trotted out for the Theorization of theology is the existence of *The Postmodern Bible* (Cunningham 2005, 32; cf. The Bible and Culture Collective 1995). Cunningham has mistaken the gumbo for the main course when it is merely a side dish at most.

Litcrit asylum seekers from "Theory's Empire" like Cunningham do, however, enable us better to gauge the jaw-dropping gulf that has gradually opened up between their field and ours around the issue of Theory. We look on agog while Daphne Patai and Will Corral, industrious compilers of the 725-page *Anthology of Dissent* from *Theory's Empire*, lament that job

---

5. Similar in tone is Barr 2005. The faint apocalypticism of the book's subtitle (*Biblical Studies at the End of a Millennium*) is amplified in certain of its chapters, particularly the one entitled "Postmodernism" (141–62).

applicants nowadays, "ostensibly in literature," seem unable to do anything but trot out increasingly tired truisms about the "construction of national identity," "globalization," "epistemic violence," "border crossings," "transgressive sexuality," and the like (2005a, 11). We are bemused by Jonathan Culler's take on Theory as the "discursive space within which literary and cultural studies now occur, even if we manage to forget it, as we forget the air we breathe" (2007, 3). We marvel as Terry Eagleton bemoans the "quietly spoken middle-class students" who "huddle diligently in libraries" and work on vampirism and eye-gouging, cyberfeminism and incest, pubic hair, the literature of latex, and (most disturbing of all, no doubt) the TV sitcom *Friends* (2003, 2–6).

Parodic license notwithstanding, the institutionalization of Theory within the Modern Language Association is routinely assumed even—or especially—by those most hostile to Theory. So institutionalized, indeed, has Theory become, according to Patai and Corral, that it is no longer *haute cuisine* but cafeteria fare: "more and more students these days approach theory as a tedious obligation, no longer as an exciting subject they wish to explore. In other words, theory in the classroom is, today, often little more than a routine practice, as predictable and dull as cafeteria food" (2005a, 13). "Oh no, not the gouged eyeballs again!" the hapless EngLit student might well exclaim. Once upon a time, the best and brightest of the Ivy League's literature students, among them Theorists-to-be of the stature of Gayatri Spivak and Barbara Johnson, sat at the feet of Paul de Man, doyen-to-be of American deconstruction, absorbing his darkly luminous classroom pronouncements and puzzling over their meaning afterwards in the corridors. These days, Ivy League students are far more prone to ironize the fashionability and revolutionary caché of Theory, if the testimony of a Yale undergraduate writing recently in *The New York Times Magazine* is to be credited:

> Lit theory is supposed to be the class where you sit at the back of the room with every other jaded sophomore wearing skinny jeans, thick-framed glasses, an ironic T-shirt and oversize retro headphones, just waiting for the lecture to be over so you can light up a Turkish Gold and walk to lunch while listening to Wilco. That's pretty much the way I spent the course, too, through structuralism, formalism, gender theory and postcolonialism. (Handler 2007, 36)

For his generation, as he goes on to explain, the revolutionary aura of Theory is precisely what makes it seem so passé. Theory can now only be an ironic gesture at best, the equivalent of retro headphones: "We are a generation for whom even revolution seems trite, and therefore as fair a target for bland imitation as anything else" (2007, 43). Theory thus becomes little more than an intellectual fashion accessory that seems quaintly, if earnestly, out-of-date. Geriatric names such as Jacques Lacan might be replaced by younger names such as Slavoj Žižek, but the product line is looking increasingly tired nonetheless.

Contrast biblical studies, in which Theory is at less risk, at least for now, of going the way of the tie-dye T-shirt, love beads, and the lava lamp. Our aim in this essay, however, is not to launch yet another ad campaign to sell Theory to biblical scholars or sell them on it. The time for that, at least, might well be past. Our intent, rather, is diagnostic and analytic. We want to look at what has happened, what has failed to happen, and what might yet happen in biblical studies under the heading of "Theory" and reflect on what these various "whats" reveal about the very different disciplinary spaces occupied by biblical studies and literary studies. Contending that Theory's most important contribution is the self-reflexive and metacritical moves it makes possible, our reflection on Theory's reception in biblical studies is intended to defamiliarize the peculiarities of our own disciplinary space.

Theory before Theory

Biblical studies is such a radically different discipline from literary studies that neither Theory, nor what critics are against when they declare themselves against Theory, quite translate. So different are these two disciplinary domains, in fact, that were we biblical scholars to take up the campaign against Theory in the terms in which it has been voiced in literary studies, we would, as will gradually become apparent, be arguing against ourselves.

When Theory "officially" arrived on the scene in literary studies, it met itself at the door to the extent that it entered a discipline that had already taken a theoretical turn. The New Criticism that had been dominant mode of Anglo-American literary criticism from the late 1930s onward shuttled between "practical" criticism and metacritical reflection—Theory *avant la lettre*—the latter activity steadily assuming ever-greater autonomy. By the early 1940s, Theory had begun to step out of the shadows. The word is boldly emblazoned in the title of René Wellek and Austin Warren's 1942 landmark *Theory of Literature*. William K. Wimsatt's *The Verbal Icon* from 1954, another New Critical classic, is no less theoretical in orientation. By turning New Criticism into New Theory, Yale literature professors such as Wellek, Wimsatt, and Cleanth Brooks (whose *Well Wrought Urn* from 1947 also veers into Theory) were unwittingly setting the stage for the Francophile theorists of the next generation, "some of whom were their own students" (Dickstein 1995, 62).

When Theory "officially" arrived on the scene in literary studies, then—and it did so most flashily at the conference that Johns Hopkins University hosted in 1966 to welcome French structuralism to America[6]—it entered a discipline that was already well-accustomed to working between literature and philosophy (in the broad, nonanalytic sense), or, if you prefer, to thinking quasi-philosophically and proto-Theoretically in the ample space afforded by literature. The discipline was already replete with "abstract" reflection—enough, for example, to fill 683 pages of David Lodge's 1972 anthology, *Twentieth Century Criticism*, with only a handful of those pages issuing from the French *maîtres à penser* in the person of Roland Barthes. "Traditional" literary critics such as William Empson, Lionel Trilling, and Frank Kermode had been busy for decades writing on such abstract topics as ambiguity, sincerity and authenticity, time, mortality, and endings. The reading of literature for many such critics was intimately intertwined with the task of reflecting on the human condition, albeit in an often elitist Arnoldian way (that was crying out for "Theoretical" demystification). It was also bound to an at once spiritualized and secularized, large and modest, sense of "soul." As theology retracted from a putative universal to a specialized preserve of the tribe called Christians, and Anglo-American philosophy became more doggedly "analytic," literature, largely a nineteenth-century invention, came to serve as a vital refuge for "vagrant values" such as the deviant, the erotic, the visionary, the sublime, the ineffable, and the transcendent (cf. Eagleton 2003, 99)—albeit a mode of transcendence that often had a very uncomfortable, even antithetical, relationship to God(s).

What passed for normal critical practice in literary studies was, therefore, fundamentally different from its counterpart in biblical studies. The investigation of the chronological relationship between manuscripts and quartos, the quest for the identity of the "dark lady" and Shakespeare's relationship to her, the refining of textual editions, and other para-historical-critical preoccupations were but a part of critical practice. Lectures and papers about literature were frequently self-consciously performative and evangelistic. The task was to produce a piece of writing that would seduce the reader or hearer into reading or rereading Wallace Stevens or *The Yellow Wallpaper*. The labor of criticism often entailed conspicuous wordsmithery and frequently took the form of stitching different works together by means of a marginal-seeming metaphorical or thematic thread. "Strong" and idiosyncratic readings were applauded, as was overt authorship. The critic stood forth as critic-writer rather than self-effacing commentator hiding bashfully behind the literary

---

6. In the persons of Barthes, Lacan, and Derrida (then a much lesser luminary than the other two), among others. The conference proceedings were published in Macksey and Donato 1970. 1966 also witnessed a thematic double issue of *Yale French Studies* (36/37) entitled *Structuralism*, which included articles by Lacan, Lévi-Strauss, and Todorov.

text. A lecture or paper might take as its task a reflection on the paradoxical representation of truth and lying in fiction, but dealing as it did in fiction, it would have been peculiar to think of its function as a definitive exposition of the work's "truth." For literary specialists such a view would have been ripe for mockery—as it was in David Lodge's now aging but still apposite caricature of literary academia in his novel *Changing Places*. Lodge's character Morris Zapp dreams of completing a series of commentaries on the novels of Jane Austen, "one novel at a time, saying absolutely everything that could possibly be said about them ... so that when each commentary was written there would be simply *nothing further to say* about the novel in question"—the object, however, not being that of "enhanc[ing] others' enjoyment and understanding of Jane Austen" but of "put[ting] a definitive stop to the production of any further garbage on the subject" (Lodge 1975, 34, his emphasis).

It is hardly surprising that Theory found a natural habitat in such an environment. Nor is it surprising that the particular species of Theory that took root was not structuralism, with its compulsion to explain and exhaust, but deconstruction. In its early American manifestation, deconstruction was characterized by an untiring insistence on literature's sublime capacity always to exceed anything that the critic might think to say about it, and as such was more of a New New Critical phenomenon than was generally realized at the time. This has become ever more clear in hindsight. Typical is Rita Felski's recent observation:

> Participants in the so-called theory revolution of the last few decades often extolled the iconoclasm of their intellectual interventions, yet in practice these theories rarely if ever spawned entirely new ways of reading, but modified and fine-tuned techniques of interpretation that had been developed over decades, in some cases over centuries.
>
> We may be reminded, at this point, of the frequently made observation that deconstruction's success in the United States derived from its ability to latch on to, while burnishing with new glamour and prestige, techniques of close reading popularised during the heyday of New Criticism. (2008, 110–11)[7]

Theory glided in as, in some ways at least, a smooth extension of normal critical practice in literary studies insofar as it coupled consideration of audaciously large questions with intricate engagement with the minutiae of the words on the page.

---

7. Recognition of the New New Critical character of "Yale deconstruction," in particular, is as old as Yale deconstruction itself; see esp. Lentricchia 1980, 282–317 (a scathing chapter on Paul de Man).

Theory's progress, however, was uneven. It moved in with lava-like swiftness in some contexts but with glacial slowness in others. The incursions of Theory into literature departments were often gradual and belated. Outside of the charmed circle of elite departments in which the leading Theorists themselves tended to cluster, many departments were only beginning tentatively to dip their toes in Theory by the late 1980s, students being exposed to it in small (inoculating?) doses in the form of what Julian Wolfreys has termed the "Theory tourism" of the lone and detached Theory course (1999, 1–11 passim). Paul de Man's insistence that Theory has always been accompanied by a resistance to Theory (1986, 3–20) is entirely apposite.[8] To that resistance and what aroused it we now turn.

The Inhumanity of Theory

With the arrival of Theory in literary studies as a source of regeneration and redefinition came the equally vital stimulus of Theory as that over against which to define or situate oneself. As both welcome guest and unwelcome intruder, Theory provoked myriad performances of disciplinary redefinition or reconsolidation. But here again, just where we might expect close conjunction with biblical studies and the raising of voices essentially interchangeable with those of James Barr, say, in *History and Ideology in the Old Testament* (2005, esp. 141–78) or John Collins in *The Bible after Babel* (2005), the differences are striking and instructive. The campaign against Theory in literary studies has been spearheaded by figures such as Harold Bloom, whose own early work (esp. Bloom 1975) extolled such unhistorical-critical-sounding activities as "strong misreading" and "poetic misprision"; Christopher Ricks, who writes on Bob Dylan as well as Victorian poetry (Ricks 2004) and so slums it in "low" or popular culture (albeit to redeem Dylan for poetry); and Valentine Cunningham, whose *In the Reading Gaol* (1993) is a virtuoso performance of criticism-as-literature, with headings such as "Textual Stuff," "Handkerchief Othello," "Give Me an Aposiopestic Break," and "The Wor(l)d of Mrs Woolf."

Insofar as they have made common cause, campaigns against Theory have tended to unite around a soteriological, protectionist impulse: a desire to save the Author (a long-endangered species) and, by extension, the human as that which, in an ambiguously secularized world, is the source of the spiritual and the repository of meaning, all the more precious for being smaller than a god. Terry Eagleton's *After Theory* relies heavily for its rhetorical armature on this trope of the reassertion and protection of the human. Working with a suspiciously pruned version of Theory (cf. Anderson 2006, 1), Eagleton sets Theory

---

8. Admittedly, this is a simplified take on de Man's complex argument.

up (in both senses) as that which excludes, by definition, all the truly important human stuff such as love, religion, suffering, ethics, birth, and death. Revealingly, a large proportion of the metaphors he employs come down to differences between the human and the animal, giving his book a curiously Aesopian flavor. We are urged to retrieve the human from the clutches of Theory, red in tooth and claw, by working our way through a menagerie of parables about the parochial stoat, the tiger in the bathroom, the unusually literate zebra, and good and bad toads (Eagleton 2003, 55, 106, 110, 157).

To acquire a clearer sense, however, of why Theory is currently demonized in certain sectors of literary studies, one needs to turn from Eagleton to other, more traditionally minded representatives of the profession. And who better to speak for the traditionalist position than the late René Wellek, principal author of the aforementioned New Critical classic *Theory of Literature* and one of the most respected literary critics of his generation. "Destroying Literary Studies" is at once the title of a 1983 article by Wellek and his answer to the question of what the more recent brand of Theory is up to:

> The day-to-day task of criticism is the sifting of the enormous production of books, and even the ranking and grading of writers. That we teach Shakespeare, Dante, or Goethe rather than the newest best-seller or any of the romances, Westerns, crime, and detective novels, science fiction, and pornography on the racks of the nearest drug store is an act of evaluation. We exercise choice the minute we take up a classical text whose value is certified by generations of readers, in deciding what features we shall pay attention to, what we shall emphasize, appreciate, and admire, or ignore and deprecate. It is now unfashionable to speak of a love of literature, of enjoyment of and admiration for a poem, a play, or a novel. But such feelings surely must have been the original stimulus to anyone engaged in the study of literature. Otherwise he might as well have studied accounting or engineering. Love, admiration, is, I agree, only the first step. Then we ask why we love and admire or detest. We reflect, analyse, and interpret; and out of this understanding grow evaluation and judgment, which need not be articulated expressly. Evaluation leads to the definition of the canon, of the classics, of the tradition. In the realm of literature the question of quality is inescapable. If this is "elitism", so be it. (2005 [1983], 47–48)

Wellek's jeremiad ends, somewhat poignantly, with the hope that "this new 'absurdist' wave ... has already crashed on the shore" (2005, 51). He would live another twenty-two years, long enough to see droves of graduate students turn their back on the literature stacks of the university libraries altogether to head for "the racks of the nearest drug store" instead for material on which to write their doctoral dissertations.

Lost love is a leitmotif wending its way through Daphne Patai and Will Corral's voluminous anti-Theory anthology (2005b). "This is what drew many of us to literature and criticism in college," one of the contributors, Morris Dickstein, reminisces. "The study of literature demanded a sheer love of language and storytelling for their own sake, yes, but the great writers also had something to say; the cognitive mysteries and affective intensities of the work of art lay before the young would-be critic like a land of dreams" (2005, 61). That the Great Authors have been displaced by the Great Theorists is what many of the contributors find hardest to swallow. "[T]he critics seem less interested in considering what literary works have to say to us than in applying a particular theory to them," John Ellis complains (2005, 92). "And so these new professionals spiral away from anything resembling what one stubbornly continues to describe as the study of literature," adds Frank Kermode (2005, 614). Harold Fromm goes further:

> [T]he use of literature as a weapon to fight this war against capitalism and patriarchy is all to often a violation of the creative skills and large consciousness behind the novels and poems that gives us so much psychological nourishment.... Works of literary genius emerge from the same human soil as everything else, and nothing is finally sacred, but reductive readings produce crabbed and crippled forms of aesthetic response, constricting rather than expanding consciousness. (2005, 455)

This elegaic lament for the tradition that extolled Great Books, Literary Masterpieces, and Authorial Genius that runs like a refrain through *Theory's Empire* would be unimaginable in Eagleton's *After Theory*. It dovetails neatly, nonetheless, with Eagleton's charge that Theory threatens the human. Patai and Corral summarize the sentiments of their contributors thus: "critics are called upon to transmit the abiding worth of literature to the coming generations. If this does not happen, our essayists fear, the humane and life-enhancing properties of literary works will be lost to us as literary studies, and literature itself, are disfigured in the distorting mirrors of the fun house of theoretical posturing" (2005b, 587). Two of these essayists inquire how the avowed goal of so much Theory, which they take to be that of human emancipation, can actually be achieved by Theory, since so much of it is so unabashedly antihumanist (Freadman and Miller 2005, 78–79).

The critique of Theory as antihuman(e)/antihumanist, which is intimately bound up with the "demise of literature" critique, is also closely tied to the third main plank of the anti-Theory platform, the identity-politics critique. "Summoning philosophical allies from Paris," Todd Gitlin protests, "the partisans of difference as a supreme principle tack together a ramshackle unity based not so much on a universalist premise or ideal as on a common enemy—the

Straight White Male who, trying to obscure his power and interests, disguises himself as the human in 'humanism.' With the identity groupings, humanism is dead, a dirty word…" (2005, 404). All of which (to give editors Patai and Corral the last word) brings us back once again to literature:

> [I]dentity politics has for decades been on a collision course with the serious study of literature. Perhaps the most expressive, and most familiar, emblem of this clash is the label "Dead White Males" with which the entire Western canon (always excluding, of course, the still fashionable French *maîtres à penser*) is now routinely dismissed. The obverse of this blanket rejection is the "standpoint epistemology" that privileges, say, the writings of "women of color." The greater the claim for past oppression and marginalization, the greater the presumed validity of a group's contributions today. (2005b, 397)

By defending the human(e) against Theory, Eagleton contributes to the general thrust of anti-Theory protests—at least insofar as he can: rhapsodic elegies at the graveside of the Western literary canon or bitter denunciations of minoritarian discourse are hardly within bounds for any self-respecting literary Marxist.

Theory is regularly caricatured in anti-Theory polemic as a depersonalizing force that would dissolve the human into mere textuality or reduce literary criticism to the lowest common denominators of race-gender-class sloganeering. It is often accused of missing the meaning of literary works: not in the sense of the one true meaning, a concept that has seldom mattered in literary criticism anyway, but the kind of meaning that Theory tends to dissolve in unsavory ideological subtexts. *Jane Eyre*, for example, must be defended against the kind of reading that would reduce it to an epiphenomenal effect of nineteenth-century imperialism, racism, and classism or dissipate its transcendental human value in the grubby economics of the slave trade.[9]

Large sectors of the anti-Theory camp, then, are devoted to the protection of the Author, but not in the same way that biblical scholars have sought to protect the Author. What is to be defended is not the Author as ultimate author-ity (sovereign creator of originally intended meanings, which have been unknowingly scattered and lost by precritical readers and must now, as in some gnostic myth of return, be recovered and reconstructed by critical scholars), but the Author's humanity, individuality, idiosyncrasy, creativ-

---

9. The sort of thing that Gayatri Spivak is alleged to do in her highly influential reading of *Jane Eyre* (Spivak 1985). The article (which has been reprinted in at least a dozen anthologies) begins: "It should not be possible to read nineteenth-century British literature without remembering that imperialism, understood as Britain's social mission, was a crucial part of the cultural representation of England to the English" (1985, 243).

ity, and genius—all now threatened with consignment to the prison house of language and the impersonality of semiotic systems. The self-appointed bodyguards of the Author in *Theory's Empire* love to conscript paragons of authorship such as Virginia Woolf or Margaret Atwood to the cause, seizing on authorly ripostes such as "To read on a system ... is very apt to kill what it suits us to consider the more humane passion for pure and disinterested reading" (Woolf) and "I think I am a writer, not a sort of *tabula rasa* for the Zeitgeist or a non-existent generator of 'texts'" (Atwood).[10] The living, beating heart of authorial sensibility and creativity needs defending from poststructuralist Theories of language that would dissolve all formerly autonomous agents, not least Authors, in an acid-bath of textuality, intertextuality, semioticity, and undecidability.

Since the Author was still reflexively clutching her literary creation as she sank into the acid-bath, it, too, needed rescuing. One of the most common rallying-cries against Theory has been its alleged propensity to reduce literature to a "text"—a term that smacked, and still smacks, for many of the uglification of academic prose, quasi-scientism, and the reduction of something that had once felt like a site of communion between author and reader to an object to be analyzed and dissected. Literature needed to be protected from Theoretical über-systems that were "cold-blooded" (to employ Eagleton's term [2003, 79]), mechanical, reductive, and doctrinaire. Often these objections emanated not just from the professorial rearguard but from students who wanted to be left alone to read without Theory intruding between them and the novel, play, or poem like a lumpish, unwelcome visitor. Nothing could be less attractive to such students than, say, the geometrical rigidity of the semiotic square. The scene of intimate, unmediated reading that they imagined was Romantic, but also reminiscent of the Reformation Protestant communing with the Word direct.[11]

Yet the campaign against Theory in literary studies, acrimonious as it has been, has produced almost no campaign buttons or stump speeches in biblical studies. Why? Because it doesn't translate, because there is no need for it, and because polemic against the "cold-blooded" and system- and minutiae-obsessed would have us thrusting accusing fingers in our own faces. It is hard to imagine biblical scholars uniting around a critique of the cold-blooded, since we don't really think of ourselves as "warm-blooded." Being warm-

---

10. Woolf's comment appears as an epigram to Cunningham 2005, while Atwood's comment is cited in Patai and Corral 2005a, 9, as "emblematic of the reaction to theory of most creative writers, whose status many theorists have been eager to usurp."

11. We are, of course, talking about the Reformation ideal. In practice, unmediated communion proved deeply problematic.

blooded is not something we think of as a primary criterion for membership in our discipline. The aberrations the anti-Theorists ascribe to Theory would, in biblical studies, merely describe business as usual.

For example, whereas the objectification and deconstruction of "the text" felt to many like a transgression in literary studies, it somehow seems less jarring in biblical studies. The biblical text has, in effect, long been seen as an "always already" deconstructed object. This is most evident in "textual criticism" (so appropriately named): its operative assumption is the ineluctable *difference* between the imperfect object present to our senses (the current edition of the *Biblia Hebraica Stuttgartensia* or the *Novum Testamentum Graece*) and the text in the putatively perfect state that the critic painstakingly seeks to reconstruct (the biblical autographs). For textual criticism, that driest and dustiest of biblical disciplines and, one might imagine, furthest removed from the exotic excesses of Theory, the text is a para-poststructuralist object. Incurably infected with self-division, it is "at least dual" (Culler 2007, 100). It is, in fact, myriad. The original, ideal, immaterial text always floats serenely free and beyond the reach of the object-text—the text-in-fragments, that is, violently marked and marred by the history of its material transmission. Although certain of the premises of textual criticism are on a head-on collision course with Theory (not least around the dream of accessing origin and intention), "textuality," that Theoretical concept par excellence,[12] has certain uncanny affinities with textual criticism. Sizeable swathes of Roland Barthes's "The Death of the Author," for instance, that once-celebrated manifesto for textuality, might well have been written with the bottomless waste paper basket of the biblical manuscript tradition in mind: "We know now that a text is not a line of words releasing a single 'theological' meaning (the 'message' of the Author-God), but of a multidimensional space in which a variety of writings, none of them original, blend and clash. The text is a tissue of quotations" (1977a [1968], 146). Or consider this equally well-known sentence from Derrida: "a text … is henceforth no longer a finished corpus of writing, some content enclosed in a book or its margins, but a differential network, a fabric of traces referring endlessly to something other than itself, to other differential traces…" (1979a, 84).[13] Small wonder, then, if the concept of textuality should feel faintly familiar, at least, to biblical critics.[14] One of the first lessons that every initiate into

---

12. See further 5 n. 2 above.

13. For a more somber take on textuality, much of which also fits our topic, however, see Jameson 1987. De Man 1986, 21–26, is also relevant.

14. Even if they feel simultaneously compelled to disavow it. See our discussion of the fate of intertextuality in biblical studies below.

our guild learns, after all, is that the biblical text is never simply given: it is, yet it also is not, and can never fully be.

Then there is our obsession with textual minutiae. We have long made our home in the kind of textual details that a traditionally minded literary critic would likely deem incidental or secondary, peripheral or tangential: the etymologies of the personal names in the Mari tablets; the probable geographical location of the land of Nod; the botanical identity of Jonah's *qiqayon* plant; fragmentary funerary texts from Ugarit; shopping lists from Oxyrhynchus; Western noninterpolations in Luke; *hapax legomena* in the Pastoral Epistles; the significance of locusts in the diet followed at Qumran—the list is infinitely long and ever more bizarre. In literary studies, meanwhile, preoccupation with the ostensibly incidental or tangential has, ironically enough, been associated not with the traditionalists in the discipline but rather with some of its least traditional—and hyper-Theoretical—practitioners, such as deconstructionists and New Historicists. The tangential obsession comes to classic expression in another oft-cited statement by Derrida: "I do not 'concentrate', in my reading ... either exclusively or primarily on those points that appear to be the most 'important', 'central', 'crucial'. Rather, I deconcentrate, and it is the secondary, eccentric, lateral, marginal, parasitic, borderline cases which are 'important' to me and are a source of many things, such as pleasure, but also insight into the general functioning of a textual system" (1988d, 44). As biblical scholars, however, we do not need Derrida's paternal blessing in order to dig happily with our buckets and spades in the ample margins of the biblical text. As Tim Beal has observed, biblical commentary and Theory share a certain "pointlessness," since both are diffused across a dizzying range of details and tangents and deconcentrate on the particular (1999, xi). Digging in the margins has been both our business and our pleasure for centuries.

In a final twist of irony, the turn to Theory for at least some of us in biblical studies actually had much to do with an attempted "humanization" of our discipline. Our first attraction to Theory arose at least in part from a desire to talk about "larger human themes" in our work (even if we never used that language, even to ourselves)—themes such as bodies and embodiment, pain and pleasure, sex and death—but also more alien themes such as ecstasy and mysticism. We were drawn to overtly arational, parareligious, poststructuralist meditations and to deconstructive flirtations with negative theology—the tantalizingly impossible quest for transcendence in the determinedly low-ceilinged space of Theory. In an interesting twist, it felt like blasphemy in biblical studies—a field that for all its theological veneer tends to aspire to "rational" and scientific modes of argumentation—to venture into the poetic and mystical regions of these religious texts.

Theory and Methodolatry

It is not mysticism, however, so much as methodology that accounts for Theory's modest attractions for biblical scholars. Literary critics have been predisposed to resist the straitjacket of system and method, as we shall see, but biblical scholars have been predisposed to embrace it. Theory, insofar as it has been assimilated at all in biblical studies, has been assimilated mainly as system and method. Theory has fueled the biblical-scholarly susceptibility to methodolatry and methodone addiction.[15] Method is our madness. Out of the ample range of options that Theory offered biblical scholars in the 1970s and 1980s, nothing was more warmly received than structuralism, semiotics, semiotic squares, actantial models, and other sharp-cornered narratological devices. The first three biblical studies journals founded as forums for methodologies other than the historical critical— *Linguistica Biblica* in 1970, *Semeia* in 1974, and *Sémiotique et Bible* in 1975—were founded either principally or exclusively as forums for biblical structuralism and its closest kin: semiotics, narratology, generative poetics, sociolinguistics, and the like.

All in all, structuralism's impact on biblical studies has far exceeded its impact on literary studies, just as poststructuralism's impact on literary studies has far exceeded its impact on biblical studies. Structuralism had no sooner arrived from France than American literary critics began to tinker with it, loosen its screws, file its sharp edges, and transform it into something they soon began to call "poststructuralism"—a term that, as Derrida would wryly remark, was unknown in France until its "return" from the United States (1988c, 2). The attraction of poststructuralism, epitomized by deconstruction, was precisely that it was *not* structuralism, which is to say that it eschewed the structuralist project of turning literary criticism into a science by constructing ultimate explanatory models or methods that would lift the lid off literature once and for all and expose the hidden mechanisms that made it tick. Deconstruction, in contrast, was content to become "the straight-man or foil of a literary language that everywhere outwit[ted] its powers of conceptual command" (Machin and Norris 1987, 18). One of the most insistent tropes of deconstruction (as witnessed by the work of Paul de Man, J. Hillis Miller, Barbara Johnson and Shoshan Felman, and occasionally that of Derrida) was the notion that the critic, while appearing to comprehend the literary text from a position securely outside or above it, is in fact being encircled and contained by the text, enveloped within its folds, unwittingly acting out an interpretative role that the text has scripted, even dramatized, in advance. In retrospect it is hardly surprising that it was poststructuralism, not structuralism, that took

---

15. Further on this addiction, see pp. 370–72 above.

root and flourished in ground that had been prepared for decades by the New Critics, who themselves knew well how to genuflect before literature. And nowhere was the unstructuralist character of poststructuralism more evident than in the assertion that early on became a mantra of American deconstruction: "Deconstruction is not a method."[16]

But deconstruction could not *not* be a method in biblical studies. Rita Felski has commented incisively on the compulsive tendency of academic disciplines to re-create elements incorporated from other disciplines in their own image and likeness:

> While literary critics, for example, are often expected to position themselves in terms of gender, race, or sexuality, scant attention is paid to disciplinary location, surely the most salient influence on how we write and read. Only when we venture abroad are we forced into a realization of the sheer contingency and strangeness of our mother tongue. Literature scholars recruited to serve on interdisciplinary hiring committees soon discover how puzzling their working assumptions can seem to scholars in other fields. These methodological differences are modified but far from dissipated by the spread of interdisciplinary work. Victorianists may pride themselves on stretching the boundaries of their field by writing on drains or Darwin, yet to outsiders their arguments, interpretations, and use of evidence unequivocally proclaim their English department training. Disciplines, in other words, are defined less by subject matter than by method. (2008, 112)

We would want to add, however, that some disciplines are more deeply defined by method than others. Specifically, we would contend that method does not mean as much for literary critics as for biblical critics. What defines the biblical studies discipline is less that it *possesses* method than that it is *obsessed with* method and as such *possessed by* method.

As such, biblical scholarship turns everything it touches into method, even concepts as methodologically unpromising as intertextuality. The term was coined by Julia Kristeva, as is well-known, at the heady height of Parisian (post)structuralism (Kristeva 1980d [1969]), and exuberantly glossed by Roland Barthes, for whom the text, as intertext, was

> woven entirely with citations, references, echoes, cultural languages … antecedent or contemporary, which cut across it through and through in a vast stereophony. The intertextual in which every text is held, it itself being the text-between of another text, is not to be confused with some origin

---

16. Due in no small part to Derrida's own insistence: "Deconstruction is not a method and cannot be transformed into one" (1988c, 3).

of the text: to try to find the "sources", the "influences" of a work, is to fall in with the myth of filiation; the citations which go to make up a text are anonymous, untraceable, and yet already read: they are quotations without inverted commas. (1977b [1971], 160)

What happens when such a radical term enters the biblical-scholarly lexicon, as it began to do decades ago? Does it result in the unraveling of biblical scholarship as we know it, fixated as it is on sources, influences, and "the myth of filiation"? Not in the least. What happens for the most part instead is business as usual, the ongoing preoccupation with pentateuchal source-paternity, inter-Isaianic *ménages à trois*, Synoptic *ménages à trois*, and all the other intensely intersubjective authorial exchanges[17] that elicit quiet excitement in the average biblical scholar—so much so that the editor of the wonderfully titled *Intertextuality in Ugarit and Israel* is emboldened to begin his introduction with the blasé announcement, "To the Bible scholar, intertextuality is nothing new" (de Moor, 1998, ix),[18] while the author of an intertextual analysis of Matthew and Paul can just as casually remark, "It has been argued that *the method of intertextuality*, which has been used so profitably in New Testament scholarship, can be employed with equal benefit in a study of Matthew's Gospel and the Pauline epistles" (Sim 2009, 418, emphasis added).[19] Faced with the domesticating capacity of such a discipline, what chance did deconstruction ever have of making a difference in it, much less a *différance*?

Indeed, the reception—or not—of deconstruction in biblical studies reveals much about the nature of the discipline. Ill-equipped to preconceive of it as anything but another method, biblical scholars immediately turned deconstruction into "deconstructionism," according it a place in the already long assembly line of critical "-isms" that lie at the center of the biblical studies enterprise: textual criticism, source criticism, tradition criticism, form criticism, redaction criticism, composition criticism, genre criticism, rhetorical criticism, feminist criticism, canonical criticism, social-scientific criticism, structuralism, narrative criticism, reader-response criticism, ideological criti-

---

17. Contrast Kristeva 1980d, 69: "the notion of intertextuality replaces the notion of intersubjectivity...."

18. De Moor continues: "The way in which Jewish works of the Second Temple period and the New Testament used the Old Testament forced exegetes to address the issue of intertextuality long before this postmodern shibboleth was coined" (1998, ix).

19. Hays 1989 was one of the earliest consolidators of the method, as Sim acknowledges (2009, 403). Certain of the essays collected in Fewell 1992 represented a different trajectory, one less concerned with authorial intentionality than with what exceeds and subverts it; but that has not been the version of intertextuality that has caught on in biblical studies.

cism, womanist criticism, autobiographical criticism, deconstructionism....
This particular "-ism" was assigned a series of spectacularly reductive definitions, along the lines of "Deconstructionism denies that texts have any single correct meaning or can have any single correct interpretation,"[20] which made it sound less like another useful addition to the biblical scholar's interpretive toolkit than a reason for early retirement. At the same time, the *word* "deconstruction(ism)," evoking difficult procedures and complex methodological machinery, began to pop up regularly in our academic prose. The notion of advanced critical machinery for highly trained operators appealed to our biblical scholarly sensibilities. Curiosity was seldom sufficiently piqued, however, to impel one to plunge directly into the machine's manuals—Derrida's *Of Grammatology*, say, or de Man's *Allegories of Reading*—and attempt to extract the methods presumably at their core.

Unhistorical Criticism

In a move that was at once inevitable and unfortunate, Theory as it entered biblical studies was stamped quite specifically as *literary* Theory, campaigning for freedom from *history's* empire. The original wagon train setting off into the sunset of Theory was packed with self-proclaimed dissidents, discontents, refugees, and asylum seekers from the totalitarian state of historical criticism, campaigning for the right to do something, anything, else—and the overdetermined heading of (literary) Theory came to stand for that anything, and everything, else. The advent of Theory in biblical studies was caught up in the dichotomy of the literary and the historical, or in much-loved terms that smacked reassuringly of scientific specialization, the "synchronic" and the "diachronic." The dichotomization of Theory and historiography was inevitable given historical criticism's monopoly of the field, but it also served to ensure from the outset that Theory's impact on the field would be minimal. To invite the accusation or even the suspicion that one's work was "ahistorical" was to put oneself beyond the pale of "serious" biblical scholarship and beyond the kinds of questions that the guild was predisposed to recognize as the ones that really mattered. That is why tirades against Theory have been few and far between in biblical studies—Theory has had too little impact, all told, to merit much attention—while the confrontation between historical "mini-

---

20. To distill the essence of such definitions, Colin Davis remarks of them in the literary studies context: "Why bother to read Derrida when you could rely on grotesque caricatures of his thought to rebut him?" (2003, 2–3). For recent examples in biblical studies, see Carvalho 2006, 422; Powell 2009, 58–59.

malism" and "maximalism" is frequently the occasion for sell-out duels and pistols at dawn.

Ironically, however, even as the wagon train of Theorists was trundling out of historical-critical territory in biblical studies, literary Theorists were busy rediscovering history, or claiming that they had been misunderstood as asserting an ahistorical formalism. In reaction to the perceived formalism of "Yale deconstruction," Theory in literary studies began to take a sharp historiographical turn, resulting in such field-reorienting phenomena as colonial discourse analysis (later to be relabelled postcolonial theory) and New Historicism.[21] New "historicisms" replaced old "formalisms," and "formalism" became something of a term of abuse in literary circles.[22] Had biblical literary criticism in its first youthful flush of attraction to Theory been more attuned to and more taken with these poststructuralist experiments in historiography, what difference, if any, might it have made for Theory's reception and dissemination in biblical studies? We can only speculate.

Yet it is not as though the fixation with history characteristic of biblical scholarship had no effect whatsoever on biblical literary critics, even those ostensibly in flight from historical criticism. For the importation of Theory into biblical studies soon led to an almost obsessive concern with the author, tethered as he was to history, and his troubled relationship with the reader. Reader-oriented Theory, in particular, quickly morphed into a debate about the power of the historical author, abetted by his intratextual henchman the implied author, relative to that of the reader in their perpetual tug-of-war over the text's meaning, a tussle in which the reader could only ever be on the losing side, given the biblical scholar's fixation on authorial intentions. No works of reader-response criticism were more warmly received by biblical scholars than Wolfgang Iser's *The Implied Reader* (1974) and *The Act of Reading* (1978), notwithstanding the fact that they were repeatedly panned by secular literary critics for seeming to offer the reader a bill of rights and independence

---

21. Edward Said's *Orientalism* (1978a) came to be seen retrospectively as the charter document of colonial discourse analysis (and then of postcolonial theory), while Stephen Greenblatt's *Renaissance Self-Fashioning* (1980) came to be seen as the seminal text of New Historicism (although Greenblatt did not coin the term until 1982).

22. More recently, the very concept of formalism has been problematized, certain critics arguing that it was in fact, and of necessity, always covertly attached to histories, contexts, authors, and referents. See, e.g, Butler, Guillory, and Thomas 2000a, viii–x; Culler 2007, 9–12, 99–116, esp. 101–3. Butler et al. argue that deconstruction's reply to New Criticism insisted that "There is always that which calls the form into question, and that is not simply another formal element, but a resistant remainder that sets limits to formalism itself" (2000a, ix), while Culler argues that "the text itself" was always a "complicated positivity," even for the New Critics (2007, 102).

from the author with one hand while surreptitiously tearing it up with the other.[23] To this day, meanwhile, no major works of reader-response criticism have received less attention from biblical reader-response critics than David Bleich's *Subjective Criticism* (1978), Norman Holland's *5 Readers Reading* (1975), and other work similarly focused on the unpredictable meanderings of "real" readers as opposed to the lockstep goose-stepping of "ideal" readers.[24] Real readers did not fit well into the machinery of method. We were much more comfortable with readerly cyborgs—ideal readers, intended readers, model readers, inscribed readers, encoded readers, implied readers, informed readers, competent readers, narratees, readers-in-the-text—who had been preprogramed by historical authors to read in rigidly predetermined ways.

Civil Servants of the Biblical Text

A further curious feature of the reception of Theory in biblical studies has been a tendency to defer indefinitely intimate engagement between the Bible and Theory by engaging instead in extensive, earnest, metacritical surveys of the pros and cons of, say, "deconstructionism." Long, chaste courtships seem to be yet another aspect of our ecclesiastical legacy as biblical scholars. It has been our self-revealing habit, as it has not been the habit of secular literary critics, to survey Theories and methodologies from the perspective of *acceptability*: How far is this an acceptable or appropriate Theory or method? Instead of declaring themselves against Theory because it curbs readerly freedom and idiosyncrasy, as Theory's discontents in literary studies are prone to do, surveyors of Theory in biblical studies tend to appeal implicitly to models of sin and consider it a self-evidently damning charge if the practitioners of a certain Theory can be said to be "going too far." A good kind of engagement with Theory—a level-headed survey that would combine a proper appreciation for utility with a salutary caution against going too far (not least on the first date)—is contrasted with a bad kind of engagement with Theory, too much in the thrall of, say, cultish gurus such as Derrida or Foucault. There is something of an institutional anxiety about writing on biblical texts in a strong and audacious way that might identify one as an afficionado and practitioner of raw, unprocessed Theory. Theory in mediated and very dilute form becomes the icon of Good Theory, stopping well short of what is assumed (often without reading) to be Theory's wilder, more extravagant, more excessive side.

---

23. For a catena of quotations from literary critics who take Iser to task for granting his reader freedom in theory only to withdraw it in practice, see Moore 1989, 102.

24. For more recent attempts to complicate overly generic and idealized "reader constructs," see the essays collected in Flynn and Schweickart 2004.

Best of all, in some circles at least, is avoiding incriminating association altogether with the faddish gurus of Theory—and much headache-inducing reading in a field not one's own—by acquiring one's Theory second-hand, with the brand names removed. Thrift-store Theory, if you will. As an extreme example of this exercise, consider Philippe Guillaume's recent *Journal of Biblical Literature* article, "Dismantling the Deconstruction of Job" (2008). The Theory enthusiast, dully trawling the table of contents of this particular issue of *JBL*, with little expectation of electrification ("Let's see, 'Who Led the Scapegoat in Leviticus 16:21?'..."), would likely come awake on encountering Guillaume's title—a knowing allusion, he or she might well imagine, to Derrida's instructive equation of deconstruction with dismantling (e.g., Derrida 1988c, 3). If he or she were old enough, or had read obsessively enough in the annals of early American deconstruction, he or she might even be put immediately in mind of the thrust-and-parry of those heady early days of High Theory—sallies such as J. Hillis Miller's "Deconstructing the Deconstructors" (1975), much admired in its time.[25] Our imagined reader might shake his or her greying head in bemusement at the thought that these second-order deconstructive shenanigans had taken thirty-odd years to migrate into the staid pages of *JBL*.

What bitter disappointment would await our reader, then, once his or her fumbling fingers had found the article. For not only does Guillaume's study not reference any extrabiblical deconstructor, living or dead; it does not even reference any intrabiblical attempts to harness extrabiblical deconstruction for the interpretation of Job, such as David Clines's moderately well-known essay "Deconstructing the Book of Job" (1990). Instead, Guillaume's article is a response to André LaCocque's "The Deconstruction of Job's Fundamentalism" (2007), an earlier *JBL* article that itself does not reference any extrabiblical deconstruction—although it does reference Clines's essay, albeit in passing (2007, 92 n. 33, 93 n. 34), so that it is left to Guillaume to effect the absolute watering-down of LaCocque's already watery brew. All of which serves, at least, to explain the conditions under which article titles with the word "Deconstruction" in them can appear in the table of contents of mainstream biblical studies journals such as *JBL*. They can appear only if the word has ceased to mean anything substantive and is so cut off from anything outside the internal world of biblical scholarly debate that it is all but lifeless from lack

---

25. Joseph Riddel, the deconstructor who was the particular target of Miller's thrusts, came back with a riposte, "A Miller's Tale" (Riddel 1975), which vertiginously attempted to deconstruct Miller's deconstruction of Riddel's deconstruction of the poetry of William Carlos Williams.

of oxygen. In short, they can appear only if the word has become yet another name for biblical historical criticism.

The largely cautious and chaste reception of Theory in biblical studies also seems to betray a fear of writing that stands in stark contrast to secular literary criticism. Literary critics can regularly be found engaging the performative and risky power of words, almost as if they are wilfully confusing the job description of the critic with that of the writer. Critics of James Joyce slip quite comfortably into pun to craft a critical discourse on Joycean writing that itself slides from "syntax" to "sintalks" and shuttles between the "trivial" and the "quadrivial," while T. S. Eliot scholars have recourse to critical poetry in order to write meaningfully about phrases such as "the intolerable shirt of flame."[26] Nor is this simply an effect of contagion generated by modernist literature. Hoary staples of the literature curriculum, like *Hamlet*, often find themselves written about in works with headings such as "Erasures, Poison and Nothing," "At the Centre: Wordplay," or "Silence, Soliloquy, Court Speech, Noise"[27]—the kind of thing that happens to Jeremiah, Jonah, or John only rarely, in studies that seem, by definition, far further from the center of the discipline than they would be in literary studies. As noted earlier, even self-declared anti-Theorists such as Valentine Cunningham are capable of writing with a stylistic élan that makes most biblical-scholarly prose seem colorless by comparison; while reading "Theoretical" essays such as Kristeva's "Stabat Mater" (1987b), Cixous's "Bathsheba or the Interior Bible" (1998), or certain of Derrida's numerous forays into the Bible plunges us altogether into a mode of writing that seems entirely alien to biblical criticism.[28] What seems so foreign (French as opposed to Anglo-German?) is the slippage into a poetic-philosophical language that "make[s] writing and hearing ... pair up and dance" (Cixous 2004, vii).

That we don't go in for this kind of thing (much) in biblical studies is clearly not attributable to the kinds of texts we have in front of us. The biblical God and his many amanuenses manipulate words as cavalierly and startlingly as a Joyce or Derrida. Our set texts include the wild writing of the prophets, texts that muddy the line between oral performance and literary act and so are particularly prone to exploit false etymologies, puns, and the physical shape of words (see Sherwood 2001). Then there is the gaudy proto-surrealism of Daniel and Revelation. Even the language of the Gospels is not the colorless,

---

26. As exemplified, say, by the following books, plucked almost at random from the library shelves: Milesi 2003; Riquelme 1991.

27. All three taken from Calderwood 1983.

28. For Derrida's distinctive mode of Bible study, see, e.g., Sherwood 2004b; Twomey 2005.

abstract, propositional language of a modern theological treatise; rather, the language is consistently concrete, graphic, and pictographic. Standard biblical-scholarly style, meanwhile, works untiringly to strip these vivid, visceral texts of their residual hieroglyphic brilliance.[29]

Our writerly reticence and reserve stems not from the texts on which we write but rather from a fear of breaking with the unwritten regulations that determine our professional style as biblical scholars. For credibility and authority rely, more than we might care to admit, on style. Critics such as Steven Shapin and Barbara Shapiro have argued compellingly (Shapin 1994; Shapiro 1994) that truth is in part a social category and that establishing one's credentials to represent truth, and hence one's credibility, requires conforming to certain distinct social markers, not least stylistic markers and other markers of self-expression. That our herd behaviour as biblical scholars includes seasonal clustering in various *societies*—The Society of Biblical Literature, The Society for Old Testament Study, The Studiorum Novi Testamenti Societas…—is not accidental. An academic discipline is a collegial body, a social unit, and "fact" is a social as much as an empirical category, established by means of appropriate "epistemological decorum" (cf. Shapin 1994, 193–242 passim). This is the case even, or perhaps especially, with the sciences and those branches of the humanities that aspire to scientific (unmediated) knowledge.

In biblical studies, epistemological decorum is construed rather differently than in literary studies. In biblical studies, the model of the good reader is the commentator. This self-effacing reader does not write but, as his name implies, merely comments. He is a civil servant of the biblical text. He is a patient laborer in the textual field. He is not a shyster, a quack, or even a salesman. He doesn't need to be. The simple fact that you're already reading, or even consulting, his 800-page commentary on Jeremiah or Hebrews tells him that you're already sold on the Bible, lock, stock, and barrel, whether for reasons of profession or piety or professional piety. For his part, he's so deep into the text as to be all but invisible most of the time. For hundreds of pages at a time, there's little or nothing in his own text to indicate that it was written by a living, breathing human being. Relative to the larger-than-life text that he serves, in any case, the circumstances of his own bookish life are inconsequential. He lives vicariously through the text and willingly under its thrall. This we have on the authority of no less eminent a commentator than Walter Brueggemann:

> This text does not require "interpretation" or "application" so that it can be brought near our experience and circumstance. Rather, the text is so power-

---

29. See further pp. 42–51 above.

ful and compelling, so passionate and uncompromising in its anguish and hope, that it requires we submit our experience to it and thereby reenter our experience on new terms, namely the terms of the text. The text does not need to be *applied* to our situation. Rather, our situation needs to be *submitted* to the text for a fresh discernment. It is our situation, not the text, that requires a new interpretation. In every generation, this text subverts all our old readings of reality and forces us to a new, dangerous, obedient reading. (1998, 18, his emphasis)

Ultimately, of course, Brueggemann is channeling the Protestant Reformers here, not least Luther himself who declared: "This queen [Scripture] must rule, and everyone must obey and be subject to her" (Luther 1963, 57). The biblical commentator, then, is a humble and obedient servant of Her Majesty, the Queen. As the quintessentially diffident and retiring nonauthorial author, he is the direct descendent of the Reformation authors, who have a squirmingly uncomfortable love-hate relationship with the presumed arrogance and Pelagianism of overt authorship and who often present themselves as smashing the idols of suffocatingly opulent (Catholic) writing in order to establish something that is, in Luther's phrase, "*rain und pur*."[30]

It is not, of course, the case that biblical critics are congenitally more humble than literary critics, or less intent on making a name for themselves and a tower with its top in the heavens; it is rather that one makes that name through almost opposite social-writerly rules. Decorum and modesty are high indicators of solidity and respectability, and hence of truth, in biblical studies, as is a posture of obedience to the biblical text and to the inherited traditions of critical biblical scholarship—which is why it is always a good badge of disciplinary membership to accuse a fellow biblical scholar of "going too far," thus marking oneself as one who goes only as far as is proper or necessary and never so far as to appear excessive or unseemly. Such moderation and decorum guarantee good team players who are content to churn out works of scholarship that add but minor variations to already "established" interpretations—the sort of work of which the biblical commentary is emblematic—and thereby move the lumbering disciplinary beast along, step by slow step, through a process of incremental tweaking, poking, prodding, and massaging.

This model of reading, along with its results, is likely to strike our (no less stereotypical and admittedly idealized) literary critic as rather dreary, for in literary studies the inherited social-stylistic model is of the strong, if not flamboyant, authorial signature. In literary studies, credibility is not jeopar-

---

30. On "*rain und pur*" ("clear and pure") as an anthem of German Protestant aesthetics, see Matheson 2000, 7.

dized by writing that is self-consciously writing, nor is there an imperative to tie every observation down with the tether of substantiation, suspending footnote after ponderous footnote from the page of the article or monograph[31] until the band of "main" text has grown so dangerously thin that it can barely support the weight of erudition appended to it. And whereas the author of a commentary or monograph on a biblical text can safely assume that the reader is already a committed consumer of this text, embedded as it is in an altogether unvarying and entirely inflexible canon, the author of a literary-critical book or essay operates in an environment in which canonical boundaries are essentially fluid and periodically subject to fluctuation. The latter critic, unable to assume that the reader is already invested in the text, must devise ever new hooks to grab his or her interest and is inclined to see critical writing more as an exercise in rhetoric: writing as seduction.

The Return of the Big, Flabby, Old-Fashioned Words

In the first encounters between Bible and Theory, Theory tended to be regarded as secular, sexy, demystifying stuff that a few adventurous or despairing biblical scholars could import from elsewhere in order to sex up a discipline that seemed hopelessly behind the times. The appeal to, and of, Theory reflected a certain cultural-academic cringe about working in Bible that was in itself symptomatic of the strange cultural place that the Bible had come to occupy in the order of knowledge that we term "the modern." After all, biblical studies was a discipline whose eponymous object, the Bible, epitomized for the secular Western mindset, more than any other single cultural emblem, the irrational, the delusional, the medieval, the morally questionable, and so much else of that ilk. As such, it also signified that which was remote, archaic, and—precisely—behind the times: the time before the modern, the other than the modern. Biblical scholarship itself ceaselessly fed and fattened this conception of the Bible by analyzing it primarily as an ancient document, through modes and methods of analysis that worked hard to be credibly modern, but made the Bible the product of a world alien and antithetical to the modern world. Incessant critical labor and the objectivity of scientific methodology set biblical scholarship apart from devotional Bible study (or so we thought)— marking our emphatic distance from the kind of thing that colleagues in other disciplines tended to imagine that we were up to, when they did not imagine outright that we were testifying, praying in tongues, and issuing altar calls in the classroom.

---

31. Like certain of the footnotes in the present tome. Old habits die hard.

In the first wave of their reception in biblical studies, Theory and/as postmodernity served to scratch our itch to belong fully in the university (while also intensifying that itch, as scratching is prone to do). Theory as a cipher for postmodernity became a means not only of pushing biblical studies more firmly into the "present" but also of propelling it into the "future." What got sidelined in this scramble for critical respectability was the question of how and why the Bible had been constructed as, necessarily, behind (and other to) the modern times. Theory came to stand for a "literary" that was "anything but history," but without the important question being asked of why the Bible had become so firmly bound up with history in the first place. Theory became a way of restoring narrativity, the readerly, the writerly, the body, ideology, the ethical, the lyrical, the mystical, the para-rational, and the present to a history-obsessed discipline, without raising the question of how and why the scholar's Bible had become a site from which these things had to be excluded.

Something new is now emerging, however, between Theory and the Bible that enables us to tackle precisely these kinds of questions. These are questions that have relevance well beyond the boundaries of the tightly demarcated disciplinary fiefdom known as biblical studies. Not surprisingly, therefore, those posing the questions are, almost without exception, not professional biblical scholars. While biblical scholars have long been engaging Theory to vamp up a fundamentally old-fashioned and thoroughly untrendy profession, Theorists have long been engaging the old uncomfortable relic that is the Bible and, more recently, have begun using old-fashioned words besides. For starters, even a partial list of the leading French intellectuals who, since the 1960s, have written on or around the Bible—and, at times, written, and Theorized, through it—reads like a *Who's Who in High Theory*: Roland Barthes, Hélène Cixous, Gilles Deleuze, Jacques Derrida, Luce Irigaray, Julia Kristeva, Jacques Lacan,[32] Emmanuel Levinas, Jean-Luc Nancy, Michel Serres....[33] Derrida was the most prolific of these occasional and unorthodox biblical commentators. By his death in 2004 he had written on, or with, such biblical scenes and themes as the creation and fall, the tower of Babel, Abraham's hospitality to the angels, the "sacrifice" of Isaac, the burial of Sarah, the wandering in the desert, "shibboleth," the tactile Synoptics and the relatively touch-phobic Fourth Gospel, Jesus' healings of the blind, the Last Supper, doubting Thomas, the conversion of Saul/Paul, and the Apocalypse of John.

Beginning in the 1990s, however, Theory, Bible, and religion began to try out some new steps. Derrida led the dance, as much as anybody, and at an age

---

32. "Writing" through his amanuensis Jacques-Alain Miller.

33. Many of these writings are summarized in The Bible and Culture Collective 1995 and/or anthologized in Jobling, Pippin, and Schleifer 2001.

when he might have been content to sit it out. During the last decade or so of his life, Derrida's previously muted interest in religion, including biblical religion, intensified and took several new turns (see esp. Derrida 1995, 2002a; Derrida and Vattimo 1998). Meanwhile, other prominent European intellectuals, notably Alain Badiou, Giorgio Agamben, and Slavoj Žižek were busily Theorizing with, of all things, the theology of Saint Paul, following in the footsteps of Jacob Taubes (Badiou 2003; Agamben 2005; Žižek 2003; cf. Taubes 2004).[34] What Derrida, the Paul-infatuated philosophers, and sundry other participants in this unlikeliest "return to religion" were up to—all differently, however—can best be understood by contrasting it with what Theory-besotted biblical scholars were up to during the same period. While these biblical scholars were busy applying Theory understood—as it also tended to be in 1980s literature departments—as an extension of a very modern practice of demystification or secularization,[35] certain Theorists were busy interrogating the idea of secularization itself, deliberately begging the question by insistently returning us to "religion." While Theory was being plundered in biblical studies for vogueish neologisms and modish post-isms, Theory outside of biblical studies was turning away from neologisms toward big, bad, old-fashioned words such as universalism, democracy, ethics, humanism, religion, faith, belief, Christianity, the theopolitical, the messianic, Paul, truth, justice, forgiveness, friendship, the kingdom, the neighbor, hospitality, and even, for God's sake, evil.[36]

---

34. Taubes's book emerged from a series of lectures delivered in 1987. Another notable "Theoretical" encounter with Paul occurs in Lyotard and Gruber 1999, esp. 13–28; and see now in addition Caputo and Alcoff 2009; Harink 2010. Jean-Luc Nancy, for his part, snubs Paul to philosophize instead with "The Epistle of Saint James" (Nancy 2008).

35. The present authors would unhesitatingly number themselves among these biblical scholars. Sherwood would classify her early work (esp. Sherwood 1996) as an exercise in demystification or secularization. Fresh from an English Literature department, she regarded the conjunction of Bible and Theory as something akin to the coupling of a prophet and a prostitute: religious object meets "secular" Theory in an impious, and rather exciting, clash. While exposing the deconstructive fragility of violent hierarchies within the Bible, however, she left foundational disciplinary and modern hierarchies—not least between the modern subject and the religious object—firmly intact. Moore, meanwhile, was staging parallel secularizing demystifications (or demystifying secularizations) of the biblical God and biblical God-talk (e.g., Moore 1996), but again in ways that necessitated a tidy separation between the modern (and even the postmodern) subject and the religious object.

36. See, e.g., Derrida 1997a, 1997b, 2001, 2005; Derrida and Dufourmantelle 2000. See also the books on Paul listed above and, in addition, the special issue of *differences* devoted to universalism (7:1, 1995; its contents include Balibar 1995; Schor 1995; Scott 1995); Laclau 1995; de Vries 1999; Butler and Žižek 2000; Garber, Hanssen and Walklowitz

The "return to the Bible" entailed in this larger "return to religion," so called, does not promise or threaten a renaissance or revival of the Bible in any sense that confessional communities would readily recognize, nor does it simply reenact the conviction that we must all somehow engage with the Bible as towering cultural artifact because we cannot get around it or get over it. Rather, in the wake of Theory (in both senses of the phrase), the Bible is coming to be seen as a key site where foundational, but unsustainable, "modern" separations were made—and decompose. What might this mean for biblical scholarship per se? By engaging anew with the formative history of our discipline, we can investigate and interrogate the process whereby critical discourse on the Bible became a means for the consolidation of certain antitheses fundamental to modernity, such as religion and reason, history and myth, theology and philosophy, the cultural and the universal, modern subject and ancient object.

Jonathan Sheehan's *The Enlightenment Bible* (2004) offers one example of such study. It is not yet another history of modern biblical scholarship—that is, an inward-turned aetiological saga of the evolutionary process by which *homo biblicus academicus*, taking his first unsteady steps in early modern Europe, began to walk upright, to jog, and then to run, eventually arriving at the present, to be cheered and applauded by all his biblical-scholarly descendants. Rather, it is an investigation of the broader cultural negotiations that took place in the sixteenth through the nineteenth centuries around the Bible as symptomatic cultural space. A still more incisive example of such study—because more informed, and formed, by Theory—is Ward Blanton's *Displacing Christian Origins*, which argues that we need a "radical engagement" with our own "disciplinary history" if Theory is ever going to generate anything more than a series of "sideshow[s] at the SBL" (2007, 17). In a canny demonstration of what the relationship between Bible and Theory might become—or of one shape, at any rate, that it might take—Blanton uses nineteenth- and twentieth-century debates about Christian origins to talk about such issues as the "enabling break" between the secular subject and the religious object, philosophy's allergy to positive religion (including the separation of philosophy and the Bible), and how biblical criticism came to obsess about the "danger" of narcissistically projecting oneself into the text, this being the very "possibility for the continuation of the guild" (2007, 52–53). In Blanton's book, seminal biblical critics such as Strauss, Schweitzer, and Deissman engage with seminal

---

2000; Badiou 2001; Žižek 2001a, 2001b; Weed and Rooney 2003; Scott 2004; and *The Dark God*, a special issue of the hyper-Theoretical psychoanalytic journal *UMBR(a)* (1, 2005), whose editorial is entitled "The Object of Religion," and whose back jacket issues the challenge, "I defy all of you: I can prove to you that you believe in God's existence."

modern philosophers such as Hegel, Nietzsche, and Heidegger in a dialogue moderated by such postmodern Theorists as Derrida, Žižek, and Agamben. This strong encounter between Bible and Theory contrasts starkly with the weak use of Theory in certain forms of biblical literary criticism that surreptitiously revert back to truisms that biblical criticism has always thrived on, as we saw, such as the contamination of the historical object by the contemporary subject, who is never quite objective enough.

As work such as that of Agamben, Badiou, Derrida, Nancy, and Žižek outside the field of biblical studies, work such as that of Blanton within it, and work such as that of John Caputo on its margins suggests (see esp. Caputo 2006),[37] the Bible, like religion, is now being used a resource for philosophers to think beyond the limits of empiricism, ontology, and metaphysics. The "return to the Bible" in Theory and philosophy—or philosophical Theory—is, however, a move that constitutes a philosophical scandal, since it seeks to include within philosophy that which, by philosophy's own self-definition, must necessarily be excluded from philosophy. The Bible has become a resource for unsettling settled identities and shaking up the way we think about established concepts. Badiou, for example, uses the Pauline corpus to produce alternative ways of conceptualizing such foundational notions as universalism and the subject and to critique "identitarian fanaticism" that, he argues, promotes capitalism's globalizing project (2003, 5–7). "Saint Paul" thereby becomes (and not just for Badiou, as we have seen) an exceedingly unlikely but extremely productive site where contemporary Theoretical questions—in this case, the limits of identity and the potential of the universal—are hashed out.

What such studies further suggest is that we are on the cusp of more significant and more searching engagements between Bible and Theory than before—engagements that promise more than further neologisms, "post"-isms, and the Next Big Thing or the Latest (Grotesquely Adjectivized) Big Name ("Toward a Žižekian Reading of Zephaniah," "Acts in Agambenian Perspective," etc.). These new encounters have the potential to push the conjunction of Bible and Theory beyond rote readings of the biblical texts in which everything that may be said or thought has already been determined in advance by our disciplinary DNA. One dimension of this new engagement with Theory would take its lead from recent reactivations of the Bible in Theory and engage with what philosophers, in particular, have been doing with the Bible, while resisting the temptation simply to repeat the protective mantra that they are not reading Paul, say, as they should (read: as we would). This reflex gesture reinforces the proprietary wall that biblical specialists have

---

37. Caputo is a philosopher of religion and his principal interlocutors in this book are Derrida, Paul, and Jesus.

always erected around the Bible, ensuring in advance that any engagement with Theory will remain strictly superficial and ultimately inconsequential.

A second dimension of this intensified encounter with Theory would be a revisiting of our own disciplinary origins—not for the purpose, however, of performing yet another aetiological recital of the epic emergence and ascent of our scholarly tribe, designed to explain and legitimize the styles of biblical scholarship that most of us still practice. Rather, our purpose would be to unpick the locks of the disciplinary mechanism itself and expose its inner operations, to probe the discomfort zones that mark the edges of acceptable and normative practice in our guild, to examine the system of exclusions that constitute our professional identities as biblical scholars, and to reflect on how this system relates to that order of knowledge we call "modern." Whereas what might be called the first wave of engagement between Bible and Theory promised new postmodern gadgets to affix to the same old disciplinary machine, what might be called the second wave does not. This second wave would thus have little to contribute to reflections on "the future of biblical studies" or "biblical scholarship in the twenty-first century"—critical genres that tend overwhelmingly to think in terms of the discipline's survival and self-sustenance through variety and innovation and that typically translate into advocacy for those new methods that seem to sit most solidly and securely upon the foundations established by the older methods. Instead, this second wave would offer metacritical analyses of our disciplinary pasts that would radically dismantle the default categories in which we operate as biblical scholars. This, admittedly, is hardly a comfortable prospect. But it is precisely in this self-risking mode that the engagement between Bible and Theory promises intellectual relevance beyond our own self-replicating enclave.

Further Reading on the "After Theory" Debate

McQuillan, Martin, Graeme MacDonald, Robin Purves, and Stephen Thomson, eds. 1999. *Post-theory: New Directions in Criticism*. Edinburgh: Edinburgh University Press. An exceptionally smart set of essays on theory's uncertain place in contemporary literary studies and the humanities generally.

Butler, Judith, John Guillory, and Kendall Thomas, eds. 2000. *What's Left of Theory? New Work on the Politics of Literary Theory*. London: Routledge. Among the questions this volume engages are the following: "[M]ust 'theory' be left behind in order for left literary analysis to emerge? Has the study of literature passed beyond its encounter with theory?" (x).

Collins, John J. 2005. *The Bible after Babel: Historical Criticism in a Postmodern Age*. Grand Rapids: Eerdmans. A rare biblical studies example of a critical subgenre common in literary studies. A traditionally minded scholar takes stock of assorted seismic upheavals in his field, not least those stemming from theory.

Davis, Colin. 2004. *After Poststructuralism: Reading, Stories and Theory*. London: Routledge. Reflects on the "theory wars," assessing the principal arguments for and against theory and arguing that theory is far from dead and will continue to play a significant role in the humanities.

Eagleton, Terry. 2003. *After Theory*. New York: Basic Books. The most widely read obituary on theory. Argues theory's inhumane inability to come to terms with many of the human themes that matter most, such as love, evil, death, morality, religion, and revolution.

Mitchell, W. J. T., ed. 2004. The Future of Criticism: A *Critical Inquiry* Symposium. *Critical Inquiry* 30:324–483. The proceedings of a public dialogue conducted at the University of Chicago by a distinguished group of theorist-critics convened to address propositions such as that "the great era of theory is now behind us" and "theory ... has backed off from its earlier sociopolitical engagements and its sense of revolutionary possibility."

Moore, Stephen D., and Yvonne Sherwood. 2010a. Biblical Studies "after" Theory: Onwards Towards the Past. Part One: After "after Theory," and Other Apocalyptic Conceits. *Biblical Interpretation* 18.1:1–27.

———. 2010b. Biblical Studies "after" Theory: Onwards Towards the Past. Part Two: The Secret Vices of the Biblical God. *Biblical Interpretation* 18.2:87–113.

———. 2010c. Biblical Studies "after" Theory: Onwards Towards the Past. Part Three: Theory in the First and Second Waves. *Biblical Interpretation* 18.3:191–225. Parts 1 and 3 represent a much-expanded version of the concluding essay of the present volume, while part 2 loops back to examine the invention of the biblical scholar in the eighteenth century and thereby illuminate the field's current relations to theory.

Patai, Daphne, and Will H. Corral, eds. 2005. *Theory's Empire: An Anthology of Dissent*. New York: Columbia University Press. The forty-seven essays assembled in this 725-page anthology span three decades. All of them are critical of theory *tout court*, or of different styles of theory, ranging from early American deconstruction to postcolonial and queer theory.

Rabaté, Jean-Michel. 2002. *The Future of Theory*. Blackwell Manifestos. Oxford: Blackwell. A broad-ranging apologia for theory that considers its alleged demise and argues its abiding relevance.

Works Cited

Abbas, Ackbar, and John Nguyet Erni, eds. 2004. *Internationalizing Cultural Studies: An Anthology*. Oxford: Blackwell.
Abel, Elizabeth, ed. 1982. *Writing and Sexual Difference*. Chicago: University of Chicago Press.
Abraham, Nicolas, and Maria Torok. 1986. *The Wolf Man's Magic Word: A Cryptonymy*. Translated by Nicholas Rand. Minneapolis: University of Minnesota Press.
Adam, A. K. M. 1995. *What Is Postmodern Biblical Criticism?* GBS. Minneapolis: Fortress.
———, ed. 2000. *Handbook of Postmodern Biblical Interpretation*. St. Louis: Chalice.
———, ed. 2001. *Postmodern Interpretations of the Bible—A Reader*. St. Louis: Chalice.
———. 2006. *Faithful Interpretation: Reading the Bible in a Postmodern World*. Minneapolis: Fortress.
Adam, Ian, and Helen Tiffin, eds. 1989. *Past the Last Post: Theorizing Post-Colonialism and Post-modernism*. Hemel Hampstead, U.K.: Harvester Wheatsheaf.
Agamben, Giorgio. 2005. *The Time That Remains: A Commentary on the Letter to the Romans*. Translated by Patricia Dailey. Meridian: Crossing Aesthetics. Stanford, Calif.: Stanford University Press.
Agnani, Sunil, et al. 2007. The End of Postcolonial Theory? A Roundtable with Sunil Agnani, Fernando Coronil, Gaurav Desai, Mamadou Diouf, Simon Gikandi, Susie Tharu, and Jennifer Wenzel. *PMLA* 122:633–51.
Ahmad, Aijaz. 1992. *In Theory: Classes, Nations, Literatures*. London: Verso.
———. 1996. The Politics of Literary Postcoloniality. Pages 276–93 in *Postcolonial Theory: A Reader*. Edited by Padmini Mongia. London: Arnold.
Ahn, Yong-Sung. 2006. *The Reign of God and Rome in Luke's Passion Narrative: An East Asian Global Perspective*. BibInt 80. Leiden: Brill.
Aichele, George. 1996. *Jesus Framed*. Biblical Limits. London: Routledge.
———, ed. 2000. *Culture, Entertainment and the Bible*. JSOTSup 309. Sheffield: Sheffield Academic Press.
Aichele, George, and Richard Walsh, eds. 2002. *Screening Scripture: Intertextual Connections between Scripture and Film*. Harrisburg, Pa.: Trinity Press International.
Alarcón, Norma. 1997. Traddutora, Traditora: A Paradigmatic Figure of Chicana Feminism. Pages 278–97 in *Dangerous Liaisons: Gender, Nation and Postcolonial Perspectives*. Edited by Anne McClintock, Aamir Mufti, and Ella Shohat. Minneapolis: University of Minnesota Press.

Althaus-Reid, Marcella. 2000. *Indecent Theology: Theological Perversions in Sex, Gender, and Politics*. London: Routlege.
Anderson, Amanda. 2006. *The Way We Argue Now: A Study in the Cultures of Theory*. Princeton: Princeton University Press.
Anderson, Gary A. 1987. *Sacrifices and Offerings in Ancient Israel: Studies in Their Social and Political Importance*. HSM 41. Atlanta: Scholars Press.
———. 1992. Sacrifice and Sacrificial Offerings (Old Testament). *ABD* 5:870–86.
Anderson, Hugh. 1985. 4 Maccabees. Pages 531–64 in vol. 1 of *The Old Testament Pseudepigrapha*. Edited by James H. Charlesworth. New York: Doubleday.
———. 1992. Fourth Maccabees. *ABD* 4:452–54.
Anderson, Janice Capel, and Stephen D. Moore. 2003. Matthew and Masculinity. Pages 134–48 in Moore and Anderson 2003.
Anderson, Janice Capel, and Jeffrey L. Staley, eds. 1995. *Taking It Personally: Autobiographical Biblical Criticism*. *Semeia* 72. Atlanta: Scholars Press.
Anonymous. 1975. *Miss Marianne Woods and Miss Jane Pirie against Dame Helen Cumming Gordon*. (Trial transcript.) New York: Arno.
Anselm of Canterbury. 1966. *Saint Anselm: Basic Writings.* Proslogium; Monologium; Gaunilon's *On Behalf of the Fool*; Cur Deus Homo. Edited and translated by S. N. Deane. 2nd ed. LaSalle, Ill.: Open Court.
Appiah, Kwame Anthony. 1991. Is the Post- in Postmodernism the Post- in Postcolonialism? *Critical Inquiry* 17:336–57.
Ashcroft, Bill. 2001. *Edward Said*. Routledge Critical Thinkers. London: Routledge.
Ashcroft, Bill, Gareth Griffiths, and Helen Tiffin, eds. 1995. *The Post-colonial Studies Reader*. London: Routledge.
———. 2001. *Key Concepts in Post-colonial Studies*. 2nd ed. London: Routledge.
Ashley, Kathleen, Leigh Gilmore and Gerald Peters, eds. 1994. *Autobiography and Postmodernism*. Amherst: University of Massachusetts Press.
Aspegren, Kerstin. 1990. *The Male Woman: A Feminine Ideal in the Early Church*. Edited by René Kieffer. Stockholm: Almqvist & Wiksell.
Attridge, Derek. 1988. Unpacking the Portmanteau, or Who's Afraid of *Finnegans Wake*? Pages 140–55 in Culler 1988b.
Aune, David C. 1994. Mastery of the Passions: Philo, 4 Maccabees and Earliest Christianity. Pages 125–58 in *Hellenization Revisited: Shaping a Christian Response within the Greco-Roman World*. Edited by Wendy E. Helleman. Lanham, Md.: University Press of America.
Austen, Jane. 1995. *Jane Austen's Letters*. Edited by Deirdre Le Faye. Oxford: Oxford University Press.
Bach, Alice. 1998. On the Road Between Birmingham and Jerusalem. *Semeia* 82:297–305.
———, ed. 1996. *Biblical Glamour and Hollywood Glitz*. *Semeia* 74. Atlanta: Scholars Press.
Badiou, Alain. 2001. *Ethics: An Essay on the Understanding of Evil*. Translated by Peter Hallward. London: Verso.
———. 2003. *Saint Paul: The Foundation of Universalism*. Translated by Ray Brassier. Cultural Memory in the Present. Stanford, Calif.: Stanford University Press.

Baer, Richard A., Jr. 1970. *Philo's Use of the Categories of Male and Female.* ALGHJ 3. Leiden: Brill.
Bailey, Randall C., Tat-siong Benny Liew, and Fernando F. Segovia, eds. 2009. *They Were All Together in One Place? Toward Minority Biblical Criticism.* Semeia Studies 57. Atlanta: Society of Biblical Literature.
Bal, Mieke. 1987. *Lethal Love: Feminist Literary Readings of Biblical Love Stories.* Indiana Studies in Biblical Literature. Bloomington: Indiana University Press.
———. 1991. *Reading "Rembrandt": Beyond the Word-Image Opposition.* Cambridge: Cambridge University Press.
Balibar, Etienne. 1995. Ambiguous Universality. *differences* 7: 48–74.
Banfield, Ann. 1982. *Unspeakable Sentences: Narration and Representation in the Language of Fiction.* London: Routledge & Kegan Paul.
Barclay, John M. G. 1996. *Jews in the Mediterranean Diaspora: From Alexander to Trajan (323 B.C.E.-117 C.E).* Edinburgh: T&T Clark.
Barnard, Mary, trans. 1958. *Sappho: A New Translation.* Berkeley and Los Angeles: University of California Press.
Barr, James. 2005. *History and Ideology in the Old Testament: Biblical Studies at the End of a Millennium.* 2nd ed. Oxford: Oxford University Press.
Barrett, C. K. 1978. *The Gospel according to St. John.* 2nd ed. Philadelphia: Westminster.
———. 1982a. *Essays on John.* Philadelphia: Westminster.
———. 1982b. Paradox and Dualism. Pages 215–21 in Barrett 1982a.
———. 1982c. Symbolism. Pages 65–79 in Barrett 1982a.
Barth, Karl. 1933. *The Epistle to the Romans.* Translated by Edwyn C. Hoskyns. Oxford: Oxford University Press.
———. 1956–61. *The Doctrine of Reconcilation.* Vol. 4 of *Church Dogmatics.* 3 pts. Edited by Geoffrey W. Bromiley and Thomas F. Torrance. Translated by Geoffrey W. Bromiley. Edinburgh: T&T Clark.
———. 1960. *Anselm: Fides Quaerens Intellectum.* Translated by Ian W. Robertson. London: SCM.
Barthes, Roland. 1954. *Michelet par lui-même.* Paris: Éditions du Seuil.
———. 1971. Réponses. *Tel Quel* 47:89–107.
———. 1975. *The Pleasure of the Text.* Translated by Richard Miller. New York: Hill & Wang.
———. 1976. *Sade/Fourier/Loyola.* Translated by Richard Miller. New York: Hill & Wang.
———. 1977a. The Death of the Author [French orig. 1968]. Pages 142–48 in idem, *Image, Music, Text.* Translated by Stephen Heath. New York: Hill & Wang.
———. 1977b. From Work to Text [French orig. 1968]. Pages 155–64 in *Image, Music, Text.* Translated by Stephen Heath. New York: Hill & Wang.
———. 1977c. *Roland Barthes by Roland Barthes.* Translated by Richard Howard. New York: Noonday.
———. 1978. *A Lover's Discourse: Fragments.* Translated by Richard Howard. New York: Hill & Wang.
———. 1980. *La Chambre claire: Note sur la photographie.* Paris: Gallimard & Seuil.

———. 1981. *Le Grain de la voix: Entretiens 1962-1980*. Paris: Éditions du Seuil.
———. 1988. Introduction to the Structural Analysis of Narratives [French orig. 1966]. Pages 95–135 in idem, *The Semiotic Challenge*. Translated by Richard Howard. New York: Hill & Wang.
Bataille, Georges. 1986. *Erotism: Death and Sensuality*. Translated by Mary Dalwood. San Francisco: City Lights. [French orig. 1957]
Baudrillard, Jean. 1987. *Forget Foucault*. Translated by Nicole Dufresne. New York: Semiotext(e). [French orig. 1977]
Beal, Timothy K. 1999. *Esther*. In Tod Linafelt and Timothy K. Beal, *Ruth and Esther*. Berit Olam: Studies in Hebrew Narrative and Poetry. Collegeville, Minn.: Liturgical Press.
Beasley-Murray, George R. 1987. *John*. WBC 36. Waco, Tex.: Word.
Begley, Adam. 1994. The I's Have It: Duke's "*Moi*" Critics Expose Themselves. *Lingua Franca* 4:54–59.
Benstock, Shari, ed. 1988. *The Private Self: Theory and Practice of Women's Autobiographical Writing*. Chapel Hill: University of North Carolina Press
Bernard, John Henry. 1928. *A Critical and Exegetical Commentary on the Gospel according to St. John*. 2 vols. Edited by A. H. McNeile. ICC. Edinburgh: T&T Clark.
Bernard of Clairvaux. 1971–80. *On the Song of Songs I–IV*. Vols. 2–5 of *The Works of Bernard of Clairvaux*. Edited by M. Basil Pennington. Translated by Kilian Walsh and Irene Edmonds. Kalamazoo, Mich.: Cistercian Publications.
Bersani, Leo. 1988. Is the Rectum a Grave? Pages 197–222 in *AIDS: Cultural Analysis, Cultural Activism*. Edited by Douglas Crimp. Cambridge: MIT Press.
Bhabha, Homi K. 1990. The Third Space: Interview with Homi K. Bhabha. Pages 207–21 in *Identity: Community, Culture, Difference*. Edited by Jonathan Rutherford. London: Lawrence & Wishart.
———. 1992. Postcolonial Criticism. Pages 437–65 in *Redrawing the Boundaries: The Transformation of English and American Literary Studies*. Edited by Stephen Greenblatt and Giles Gunn. New York: Modern Language Association of America.
———. 1994a. Articulating the Archaic. Pages 123–38 in Bhabha 1994d.
———. 1994b. The Commitment to Theory. Pages 19–39 in Bhabha 1994d.
———. 1994c. Interrogating Identity: Frantz Fanon and the Postcolonial Prerogative. Pages 40–65 in Bhabha 1994d.
———. 1994d. *The Location of Culture*. London: Routledge.
———. 1994e. Of Mimicry and Man: The Ambivalence of Colonial Discourse. Pages 85–92 in Bhabha 1994d.
———. 1994f. The Postcolonial and the Postmodern: The Question of Agency. Pages 171–97 in Bhabha 1994d.
———. 1994g. Signs Taken for Wonders: Questions of Ambivalence and Authority under a Tree outside Delhi, May 1817. Pages 102–22 in Bhabha 1994d.
———. 1994h. Sly Civility. Pages 93–101 in Bhabha 1994d.
———. 1996. Postmodernism/Postcolonialism. Pages 307–22 in *Critical Terms for Art History*. Edited by Robert S. Nelson and Richard Shiff. Chicago: University of Chicago Press.

———. 2002. Speaking of Postcoloniality, in the Continuous Present: A Conversation [with John Comaroff]. Pages 15–46 in Goldberg and Quayson 2002.
———. 2004. Statement for the *Critical Inquiry* Symposium. *Critical Inquiry* 30:342–49.
Biale, David. 1982. The God with Breasts: El Shaddai in the Bible. *HR* 21:240–56.
Bible and Culture Collective. 1995. *The Postmodern Bible*. New Haven: Yale University Press.
Bickerman, Elias J. 1976. The Date of Fourth Maccabees [Orig. 1945]. Pages 275–81 in vol. 1 of idem, *Studies in Jewish and Christian History*. AGJU 9. Leiden: Brill.
Bilde, Per. 1988. *Flavius Josephus between Jerusalem and Rome: His Life, His Works, and Their Importance*. JSPSup 2. Sheffield: JSOT Press.
Black, Fiona C. 2001. Nocturnal Egression: Exploring Some Margins of the Song of Songs. Pages 93–104 in Adam 2001.
———, ed. 2006. *The Recycled Bible: Autobiography, Culture, and the Space Between*. SemeiaSt 51. Atlanta: Society of Biblical Literature.
Black, Fiona C., and J. Cheryl Exum. 1998. Semiotics in Stained Glass: Edward Burne-Jones's Song of Songs. Pages 315–42 in Exum and Moore 1998.
Blank, Josef. 1964. *Krisis: Untersuchungen zur johanneischen Christologie und Eschatologie*. Freiburg: Lambertus.
Blanton, Ward. 2007. *Displacing Christian Origins: Philosophy, Secularity and the New Testament*. Chicago: University of Chicago Press.
Bledstein, Adrien Janis. 1993. Are Women Cursed in Genesis 3.16? Pages 142–45 in *A Feminist Companion to Genesis*. Edited by Athalya Brenner. FCB 2. Sheffield: JSOT Press.
Bleich, David. 1978. *Subjective Criticism*. Baltimore: Johns Hopkins University Press.
Blinzler, Josef. 1959. *The Trial of Jesus: The Jewish and Roman Proceedings against Jesus Christ Described and Assessed from the Oldest Accounts*. Translated by Isabel McHugh and Florence McHugh. Westminster, Md.: Newman.
Bloch, Ariel, and Chana Bloch. 1995. *The Song of Songs: A New Translation with an Introduction and Commentary*. New York: Random House.
Bloom, Harold. 1975. *A Map of Misreading*. Oxford: Oxford University Press.
Blum, Claes. 1936. *Studies in the Dream-Book of Artemidoros*. Uppsala: Almqvist & Wiksell.
Boer, Roland. 1998. King Solomon Meets Annie Sprinkle. *Semeia* 82:151–82.
———. 1999a. *Knockin' on Heaven's Door: The Bible and Popular Culture*. Biblical Limits. London: Routledge.
———. 1999b. Night Sprinkle(s): Pornography and the Song of Songs. Pages 53–70 in Boer 1999a.
———. 2000. The Second Coming: Repetition and Insatiable Desire in the Song of Songs. *BibInt* 8:276–301.
———. 2001. Yahweh as Top: A Lost Targum. Pages 75–105 in *Queer Commentary and the Hebrew Bible*. Edited by Ken Stone. JSOTSup 334. Sheffield: Sheffield Academic Press.
Boers, Hendrikus. 1988. *Neither on This Mountain Nor in Jerusalem: A Study of John 4*. SBLMS 35. Atlanta: Scholars Press.
Boff, Leonardo. 1987. *Passion of Christ, Passion of the World: The Facts, Their Inter-

pretation, and Their Meaning Yesterday and Today. Translated by Robert R. Barr. Maryknoll, N.Y.: Orbis.

Bolin, Anne. 1992. Vandalized Vanity: Feminine Physiques Betrayed and Portrayed. Pages 79–99 in *Tattoo, Torture, Mutilation, and Adornment: The Denaturalization of the Body in Culture and Text*. Edited by Frances E. Mascia-Lees and Patricia Sharpe. SUNY Series on the Body in Culture, History, and Religion. Albany: State University of New York Press.

Booth, Wayne C. 1983. *The Rhetoric of Fiction*. 2nd ed. Chicago: University of Chicago Press.

Børresen, Kari Elisabeth, ed. 1995. *The Image of God: Gender Models in Judaeo-Christian Tradition*. Minneapolis: Fortress.

Bové, Paul. 1992. *In the Wake of Theory*. Middletown, Conn.: Wesleyan University Press.

Boyarin, Daniel. 1990. The Eye in the Torah: Ocular Desire in Midrashic Hermeneutics. *Critical Inquiry* 16:532–50.

———. 1993. *Carnal Israel: Reading Sex in Talmudic Culture*. The New Historicism: Studies in Cultural Poetics 25. Berkeley and Los Angeles: University of California Press.

———. 1994. *A Radical Jew: Paul and the Politics of Identity*. Contraversions: Critical Studies in Jewish Literature, Culture, and Society 1. Berkeley and Los Angeles: University of California Press.

———. 1995. Are There Any Jews in "The History of Sexuality"? *Journal of the History of Sexuality* 5:333–55.

———. 1997. *Unheroic Conduct: The Rise of Heterosexuality and the Invention of the Jewish Man*. Berkeley and Los Angeles: University of California Press.

Bradley, Keith. 1994. *Slavery and Society at Rome*. Cambridge: Cambridge University Press.

Brainum, Jerry. 1994. Spank That Baby Fat! *Flex* July: 211.

Branderburger, Egon. 1984. *Markus 13 und die Apokalyptik*. FRLANT 134. Göttingen: Vandenhoeck & Ruprecht.

Breck, John. 1994. *The Shape of Biblical Language: Chiasmus in the Scriptures and Beyond*. Crestwood, N.Y.: St. Vladimir's Seminary Press.

Breitenstein, Urs. 1978. *Beobachtungen zu Sprache, Stil und Gedankengut des Vierten Makkabäerbuchs*. Basel: Schwabe.

Brenner, Athalya. 1993. On Feminist Criticism of the Song of Songs. Pages 28–37 in *A Feminist Companion to the Song of Songs*. Edited by Athalya Brenner. FCB 1. Sheffield: Sheffield Academic Press.

———. 1997. *The Intercourse of Knowledge: On Gendering Desire and "Sexuality" in the Hebrew Bible*. BibInt 26. Leiden: Brill.

Brenner, Athalya, and Carole R. Fontaine, eds. 2000. *The Song of Songs*. FCB 2/6. Sheffield: Sheffield Academic Press.

Brett, Mark G. 2000. *Genesis: Procreation and the Politics of Identity*. London: Routledge.

Brodski, Bella, and Celeste Schenck, eds. 1984. *Life/Lines: Theorizing Women's Autobiography*. Ithaca, N.Y.: Cornell University Press.

Bronner, Leila Leah. 1983–84. Gynomorphic Imagery in Exilic Isaiah (40–66). *Dor le Dor* 12:71–83.

———. 1994. *From Eve to Esther: Rabbinic Reconstructions of Biblical Women*. Louisville: Westminster John Knox.

Brooks, Cleanth. 1947. *The Well Wrought Urn: Studies in the Structure of Poetry*. New York: Harcourt Brace.

Brooten, Bernadette, J. 1985. Patristic Interpretations of Romans 1:26. Pages 287–91 in *Historica-Theologica-Gnostica-Biblica*. Vol. 1 of *Studia Patristica XVIII: Papers of the Ninth International Patristics Conference, Oxford 1983*. Edited by Elizabeth A. Livingstone. Kalamazoo, Mich.: Cistercian Publications.

———. 1996. *Love between Women: Early Christian Responses to Female Homoeroticism*. Sexuality, History, and Society. Chicago: University of Chicago Press.

Brown, Joanne Carlson, and Rebecca Parker. 1989. For God So Loved the World? Pages 1–30 in *Christianity, Patriarchy, and Abuse: A Feminist Critique*. Edited by Joanne Carlson Brown and Carole R. Bohn. New York: Pilgrim.

Brown, John. 1778. *The Self-Interpreting Bible, Containing the Sacred Text of the Old and New Testaments*. 2 vols. Bungay: Brightly & Child. [1813 reprint]

———. 1851. *A Dictionary of the Holy Bible, Corrected and Improved according to the Advanced State of Information at the Present Day, by the Rev. James Smith, A.M.* London: Blackie & Son. [Orig. 1768]

Brown, Norman O. 1966. *Love's Body*. Berkeley and Los Angeles: University of California Press.

Brown, Peter. 1980. *The Book of Kells*. London: Thames & Hudson.

Brown, Peter Robert Lamont. 1988. *The Body and Society: Men, Women, and Sexual Renunciation in Early Christianity*. New York: Columbia University Press.

Brown, Raymond E. 1966. *The Gospel according to John I–XII*. AB 29. Garden City, N.Y.: Doubleday.

———. 1970. *The Gospel according to John XIII–XXI*. AB 29A. Garden City, N.Y.: Doubleday.

———. 1977. *The Birth of the Messiah: A Commentary on the Infancy Narratives in Matthew and Luke*. New York: Doubleday.

———. 1994. *The Death of the Messiah: From Gethsamane to the Grave. A Commentary on the Passion Narratives in the Four Gospels*. 2 vols. ABRL. New York: Doubleday.

Brown, Raymond E., and Francis J. Moloney. 2003. *An Introduction to the Gospel of John*. New York: Doubleday.

Brownstein, Rachel M. 1996. Interrupted Reading: Personal Criticism in the Present Time. Pages 29–39 in Veeser 1996b.

Brueggemann, Walter. 1998. *A Commentary on Jeremiah: Exile and Homecoming*. Grand Rapids: Eerdmans.

Budde, Karl. 1894. Was ist das Hohelied? *Preussische Jahrbücher* 78:92–117.

———. 1898. Das Hohelied erklärt. Pages 9–48 in Karl Budde, Alfred Bertholet, and D. G. Wildeboer, *Die fünf Megillot*. Kurzer Hand-Commentar zum Alten Testament 6. Tübingen: Mohr Siebeck.

Buell, Lawrence. 2005. *The Future of Environmental Criticism: Environmental Crisis and Literary Imagination*. Blackwell Manifestos. Oxford: Blackwell.

Bultmann, Rudolf. 1952–55. *The Theology of the New Testament*. Translated by Kendrick Grobel. 2 vols. New York: Charles Scribner's Sons.

———. 1960. The Task of Theology in the Present Situation. Pages 158–65 in *Existence and Faith: Shorter Writings of Rudolf Bultmann*. Edited and translated by Schubert M. Ogden. New York: Living Age.

———. 1961. New Testament and Mythology. Pages 1–44 in *Kerygma and Myth: A Theological Debate*. Edited by Hans Werner Bartsch. Translated by G. R. Beasley-Murray et al. Philadelphia: Westminster.

———. 1971. *The Gospel of John*. Translated by G. R. Beasley-Murray, R. W. N. Hoare, and J. K. Riches. Philadelphia: Westminster.

Burnett, Fred W. 1990. Postmodern Biblical Exegesis: The Eve of Historical Criticism. *Semeia* 51:51–80.

Burrus, Virginia. 2000. *"Begotten, Not Made": Conceiving Manhood in Late Antiquity*. Figurae: Reading Medieval Culture. Stanford, Calif.: Stanford University Press.

Butler, Judith. 1990. *Gender Trouble: Feminism and the Subversion of Identity*. London: Routledge.

———. 1994. Against Proper Objects. *differences* 6:1–26.

Butler, Judith, John Guillory, and Kendall Thomas. 2000a. Preface. Pages viii–xii in Butler, Guillory, and Thomas 2000b.

Butler, Judith, John Guillory, and Kendall Thomas, eds. 2000b. *What's Left of Theory? New Work on the Politics of Literary Theory*. London: Routledge.

Butler, Judith, and Slavoj Žižek, eds. 2000. *Contingency, Hegemony, Universality: Contemporary Dialogues on the Left*. London: Verso.

Calderwood, James L. 1983. *To Be and Not to Be: Negation and Metadrama in Hamlet*. New York: Columbia University Press.

Calvet, Louis-Jean. 1995. *Roland Barthes: A Biography*. Translated by Sarah Wykes. Bloomington: Indiana University Press.

Campbell, Douglas A. 1992. *The Rhetoric of Righteousness in Romans 3.21–26*. JSNTSup 65. Sheffield: Sheffield Academic Press.

Caputo, John D. 2006. *The Weakness of God: A Theology of the Event*. Indiana Series in the Philosophy of Religion. Bloomington: Indiana University Press.

Caputo, John D., and Linda Martin Alcoff, eds. 2009. *St. Paul among the Philosophers*. Indiana Series in the Philosophy of Religion. Bloomington: Indiana University Press.

Carr, David. 2000. Gender and the Shaping of Desire in the Song of Songs. *JBL* 119:233–48.

Carroll, Clare, and Patricia King, eds. 2003. *Ireland and Postcolonial Theory*. Notre Dame, Ind.: University of Notre Dame Press.

Carter, Warren. 2001. *Matthew and Empire: Initial Explorations*. Harrisburg, Pa.: Trinity Press International.

Carvalho, Corrine L. 2006. *Encountering Ancient Voices: A Guide to Reading the Old Testament*. Winona, Minn.: Saint Mary's Press.

Cassidy, Richard J. 1992. *John's Gospel in a New Perspective: Christology and the Realities of Roman Power*. Maryknoll, N.Y.: Orbis.

Castelli, Elizabeth A. 1991a. *Imitating Paul: A Discourse of Power.* Literary Currents in Biblical Interpretation. Louisville: Westminster John Knox.
———. 1991b. Interpretations of Power in 1 Corinthians. *Semeia* 54:197–222.
———. 1991c. "I Will Make Mary Male": Pieties of the Body and Gender Transformation of Christian Women in Late Antiquity. Pages 29–49 in *Body Guards: The Cultural Politics of Gender Ambiguity.* Edited by Julia Epstein and Kristina Straub. London: Routledge.
———. 1994. Romans. Pages 272–300 in Schüssler Fiorenza 1994.
Chance, John K. 1994. The Anthropology of Honor and Shame: Culture, Values, and Practice. *Semeia* 68:139–52.
Chatman, Seymour. 1978. *Story and Discourse: Narrative Structure in Fiction and Film.* Ithaca, N.Y.: Cornell University Press.
Childs, Brevard S. 1974. *The Book of Exodus.* OTL. Philadelphia: Westminster.
Childs, Peter, and Patrick Williams. 1997. *An Introduction to Post-colonial Theory.* London: Prentice Hall/Harvester Wheatsheaf.
Chioni Moore, David. 2005. Is the Post- in Postcolonial the Post- in Post-Soviet? Toward a Global Postcolonial Critique. Pages 514–38 in Desai and Nair 2005.
Christensen, Duane L. 1991. *Deuteronomy 1–11.* WBC 6A. Dallas: Word.
Cixous, Hélène. 1972. *The Exile of James Joyce or the Art of Replacement.* Translated by Sally A. J. Purcell. New York: David Lewis.
———. 1980a. The Laugh of the Medusa. Translated by Keith Cohen and Paula Cohen. Pages 245–64 in Mark and de Courtivron 1980.
———. 1980b. Sorties. Translated by Ann Liddle. Pages 90–98 in Marks and de Courtivron 1980.
———. 1998. Bathsheba or the Interior Bible. Pages 3–19 in idem, *Stigmata: Escaping Texts.* London: Routledge.
———. 2004. *Portrait of Jacques Derrida as a Young Jewish Saint.* New York: Columbia University Press.
Clément, Catherine. 1983. *The Lives and Legends of Jacques Lacan.* Translated by Arthur Goldhammer. New York: Columbia University Press.
Clines, David J. A. 1990. Deconstructing the Book of Job. Pages 65–80 in *The Bible as Rhetoric: Studies in Biblical Persuasion and Credibility.* Edited by Martin Warner. Warwick Studies in Philosophy and Literature. London: Routledge.
———. 1995a. David the Man: The Construction of Masculinity in the Hebrew Bible. Pages 212–43 in Clines 1995b.
———. 1995b. *Interested Parties: The Ideology of Writers and Readers of the Hebrew Bible.* JSOTSup 205; Gender, Culture, Theory 1. Sheffield: Sheffield Academic Press.
———. 1995c. Why Is There a Song of Songs and What Does It Do to You If You Read It? Pages 94–121 in Clines 1995b.
———. 1998. Ecce Vir, or, Gendering the Son of Man. Pages 352–75 in Exum and Moore 1998.
Cohen, Martin S. 1983. *The Shi'ur Qomah: Liturgy and Theurgy in Pre-Kabbalistic Jewish Mysticism.* Lanham, Md.: University Press of America.
———. 1985. *The Shi'ur Qomah: Texts and Recensions.* Tübingen: Mohr Siebeck.

Cohn, Dorrit. 1978. *Transparent Minds: Narrative Modes for Presenting Consciousness in Fiction.* Princeton: Princeton University Press.

Collins, John J. 1981. *Daniel, First Maccabees, Second Maccabees with an Excursus on the Apocalyptic Genre.* Old Testament Message 16. Wilmington, Del.: Michael Glazier.

———. 1993. *Daniel: A Commentary on the Book of Daniel.* Hermeneia. Minneapolis: Fortress.

———. 2005. *The Bible after Babel: Historical Criticism in a Postmodern Age.* Grand Rapids: Eerdmans.

Conrad, Joseph. 1902. *Heart of Darkness and Selections from The Congo Diary.* New York: The Modern Library. [1999 reprint]

Conway, Colleen M. 1999. *Men and Women in the Fourth Gospel: Gender and Johannine Characterization.* SBLDS 167. Atlanta: Scholars Press.

———. 2008. *Behold the Man: Jesus and Greco-Roman Masculinity.* Oxford: Oxford University Press.

Corber, Robert J., and Stephen Valocchi, eds. 2003. *Queer Studies: An Interdisciplinary Reader.* Oxford: Blackwell.

Corley, Kathleen E., and Robert L. Webb, eds. 2004. *Jesus and Mel Gibson's* Passion of the Christ*: The Film, the Gospels and the Claims of History.* New York: Continuum.

Cornwell, Andrea, and Nancy Lindisfarne, eds. 1994. *Dislocating Masculinity: Comparative Ethnographies.* Male Orders. London: Routledge.

Cosgrove, Charles H. 1984. The Divine *Dei* in Luke-Acts: Investigations into the Lukan Understanding of God's Providence. *NovT* 26:168–90.

Counet, Patrick Chatelion. 2000. *John, a Postmodern Gospel: Introduction to Deconstructive Exegesis Applied to the Fourth Gospel.* BibInt 44. Leiden: Brill.

Coward, Harold, and Toby Foshay, eds. 1992. *Derrida and Negative Theology.* Albany, N.Y.: State University of New York Press.

Cranfield, C. B. 1975–79. *A Critical and Exegetical Commentary on the Epistle to the Romans.* 2 vols. ICC. Edinburgh: T&T Clark.

Crawford, Bobbie. 1983. A Female Crucifix. *Daughters of Sarah* 14:26.

Crossan, John Dominic. 1973. *In Parables: The Challenge of the Historical Jesus.* New York: Harper & Row.

———. 1975. *The Dark Interval: Toward a Theology of Story.* Niles, Ill.: Argus Communications.

———. 1976. *Raid on the Articulate: Comic Eschatology in Jesus and Borges.* New York: Harper & Row.

———. 1979. *Finding Is the First Act: Trove Folktales and Jesus' Treasure Parable.* SemeiaSt 9. Missoula, Mont.: Scholars Press.

———. 1980. *Cliffs of Fall: Paradox and Polyvalence in the Parables of Jesus.* New York: Seabury.

———. 1982. Difference and Divinity. *Semeia* 23:29–40.

———. 1983. *In Fragments: The Aphorisms of Jesus.* San Francisco: Harper & Row.

———. 1985. *Four Other Gospels: Shadows on the Contours of Canon.* New York: Winston.

———. 1988. *The Cross That Spoke: The Origins of the Passion Narrative*. San Francisco: Harper & Row.
———. 1991. *The Historical Jesus: The Life of a Mediterranean Jewish Peasant*. San Francisco: HarperSanFrancisco.
———. 1994a. *The Essential Jesus: Original Sayings and Earliest Images*. San Francisco: HarperSanFrancisco.
———. 1994b. *Jesus: A Revolutionary Biography*. San Francisco: HarperSanFrancisco.
———. 1995. *Who Killed Jesus? Exploring the Roots of Anti-Semitism in the Gospel Story of the Death of Jesus*. San Francisco: HarperSanFrancisco.
Culler, Jonathan. 1982. *On Deconstruction: Theory and Criticism after Structuralism*. Ithaca, N.Y.: Cornell University Press.
———. 1988a. The Call of the Phoneme. Pages 1–16 in Culler 1988b.
———, ed. 1988b. *On Puns: The Foundation of Letters*. Oxford: Blackwell.
———. 2007. *The Literary in Theory*. Cultural Memory in the Present. Stanford, Calif.: Stanford University Press.
Cullmann, Oscar. 1959. *The Christology of the New Testament*. Translated by S. C. Guthrie and C. A. M. Hall. Philadelphia: Westminster.
Culpepper, R. Alan. 1983. *Anatomy of the Fourth Gospel: A Study in Literary Design*. Foundations and Facets. Philadelphia: Fortress.
Cunningham, D. J. 1968. *Cunningham's Manual of Practical Anatomy*. 13th ed. 3 vols. Revised by G. J. Romanes. Oxford: Oxford University Press.
Cunningham, Valentine. 1993. *In the Reading Gaol: Postmodernity, Texts and History*. Oxford: Blackwell.
———. 2002. *Reading after Theory*. Blackwell Manifestos. Oxford: Blackwell.
———. 2005. Theory, What Theory? Pages 24–41 in Patai and Corral 2005b.
Cypess, Sandra Messinger. 1991. *La Malinche in Mexican Literature: From History to Myth*. Austin: University of Texas Press.
D'Angelo, Mary Rose. 2002. The ANHP Question in Luke-Acts: Imperial Masculinity and the Deployment of Women in the Early Second Century. Pages 44–72 in *A Feminist Companion to Luke*. Edited by Amy-Jill Levine. FCNTECW 3. Sheffield: Sheffield Academic Press.
Darling Young, Robin. 1991. The "Woman with the Soul of Abraham": Traditions About the Mother of the Maccabean Martyrs. Pages 67–82 in *"Women Like This": New Perspectives on Jewish Women in the Greco-Roman World*. Edited by Amy-Jill Levine. SBLEJL 1. Atlanta: Scholars Press.
Davidson, Cathy N. 1993. *Thirty-Six Views of Mt. Fuji: On Finding Myself in Japan*. New York: Dutton.
Davidson, Robert. 1973. *Genesis 1–11*. CBC. Cambridge: Cambridge University Press.
Davis, Colin. 2003. *After Poststructuralism: Reading, Stories and Theory*. London: Routledge.
Davis, Robert Con, ed. 1983. *Lacan and Narration: The Psychoanalytic Difference in Narrative Theory*. Baltimore: John Hopkins University Press.
Deferrari, R. J., ed. and trans. 1947. *Fathers of the Church: A New Translation*. 86 vols. Washington, D.C.: Catholic University of America Press.

Deissmann, Adolf. 1900. Das vierte Makkabäerbuch. Pages 149–76 in vol. 2 of *Die Apokryphen und Pseudepigraphen des Alten Testaments*. Edited by Emil Kautzsch. Tübingen: Mohr Siebeck.

De Lauretis, Teresa, ed. 1991. *Queer Theory: Lesbian and Gay Sexualities. differences* 3:2 [thematic issue].

Deleuze, Gilles. 1988. *Foucault*. Edited and translated by Sean Hand. Minneapolis: University of Minnesota Press.

Deleuze, Gilles, and Leopold von Sacher-Masoch. 1989. *Masochism: Coldness and Cruelty/Venus in Furs*. New York: Zone.

Delitzsch, Franz. 1980. *Proverbs, Ecclesiastes, Song of Solomon*. Translated by M. G. Easton. Grand Rapids: Eerdmans. [German orig. 1875]

De Man, Paul. 1971. *Blindness and Insight: Essays in the Contemporary Rhetoric of Reading*. Minneapolis: University of Minnesota Press.

———. 1979. *Allegories of Reading: Figural Language in Rousseau, Nietzsche, Rilke, and Proust*. New Haven: Yale University Press.

———. 1986. *The Resistance to Theory*. Theory and History of Literature 33. Minneapolis: University of Minnesota Press.

De Moor, Johannes Cornelis. 1998. Introduction. Pages ix–xi in *Intertextuality in Ugarit and Israel: Papers Read at the Tenth Joint Meeting of The Society for Old Testament Study and Het Oudtestamentisch Werkgezelschap in Nederland & België, Held at Oxford, 1997*. Edited by Johannes Cornelis de Moor. Leiden: Brill.

Dempsey, Robert Brinkerhoff. 1963. The Interpretation and Use of the Song of Songs. PhD dissertation. Boston University School of Theology.

Derrida, Jacques. 1976. *Of Grammatology*. Translated by Gayatri Chakravorty Spivak. Baltimore: Johns Hopkins University Press.

———. 1978a. *Edmund Husserl's* Origin of Geometry: *An Introduction*. Translated by John P. Leavey Jr. Stony Brook, N.Y.: Nicholas Hays.

———. 1978b. *Writing and Difference*. Translated by Alan Bass. Chicago: University of Chicago Press.

———. 1979a. Living On: Border Lines. Translated by James Hulbert. Pages 75–176 in Harold Bloom et al., *Deconstruction and Criticism*. New York: Continuum.

———. 1979b. *Spurs: Nietzsche's Styles/Éperons: Les Styles de Nietzsche*. Translated by Barbara Harlow. Chicago: University of Chicago Press.

———. 1981a. *Dissemination*. Translated by Barbara Johnson. Chicago: University of Chicago Press.

———. 1981b. The Double Session. Pages 173–286 in Derrida 1981a.

———. 1981c. *Positions*. Translated by Alan Bass. Chicago: University of Chicago Press.

———. 1982. *Margins of Philosophy*. Translated by Alan Bass. Chicago: University of Chicago Press.

———. 1984a. *Signéponge/Signsponge*. Translated by Richard Rand. New York: Columbia University Press.

———. 1984b. Two Words for Joyce. Translated by Geoff Bennington. Pages 145–59 in *Post-Structuralist Joyce*. Edited by Derek Attridge and Daniel Ferrer. Cambridge: Cambridge University Press.

———. 1985a. *The Ear of the Other: Otobiography, Transference, Translation*. Edited by Christie McDonald. Translated by Avital Ronell and Peggy Kamuf. Lincoln: University of Nebraska Press.
———. 1985b. Interview: Choreographies. Pages 163–85 in Derrida 1985a.
———. 1986a . Fors: The Anglish Words of Nicolas Abraham and Maria Torok. Translated by Barbara Johnson. Pages xi–xlviii in Abraham and Torok 1986.
———. 1986b. *Glas*. Translated by John P. Leavey Jr. and Richard Rand. Lincoln: University of Nebraska Press.
———. 1986c. Proverb: "He That Would Pun...." Pages 17–21 in *Glassary*. Edited by John P. Leavey Jr. Lincoln: University of Nebraska Press.
———. 1986d. Shibboleth. Translated by Joshua Wilner. Pages 307–47 in *Midrash and Literature*. Edited by Geoffrey H. Hartman and Sanford Budick. New Haven: Yale University Press.
———. 1986e. Des Tours de Babel. Translated by Joseph F. Graham. Pages 165–207 in *Difference in Translation*. Edited by Joseph F. Graham. Ithaca, N.Y.: Cornell University Press.
———. 1987a. *The Post Card: From Socrates to Freud and Beyond*. Translated by Alan Bass. Chicago: University of Chicago Press.
———. 1987b. *Psyché: Inventions de l'autre*. Paris: Galilée.
———. 1987c. *The Truth in Painting*. Translated by Geoff Bennington and Ian McLeod. Chicago: University of Chicago Press.
———. 1987d. *Ulysse gramophone: Deux mots pour Joyce*. Paris: Galilée.
———. 1987e. Women in the Beehive: A Seminar with Jacques Derrida. Pages 189–203 in *Men in Feminism*. Edited by Alice Jardine and Paul Smith. New York: Methuen.
———. 1988a. Hear Say Yes in Joyce. Translated by Tina Kendall and Shari Benstock. Pages 27–75 in *James Joyce: The Augmented Ninth. Proceedings of the Ninth International James Joyce Symposium*. Edited by Bernard Benstock. Syracuse, N.Y.: Syracuse University Press.
———. 1988b. An Interview with Derrida (from *La nouvel observateur*). Translated by David Allison et al. Pages 71–82 in Wood and Bernasconi 1988.
———. 1988c. Letter to a Japanese Friend. Translated by David Wood and Andrew Benjamin. Pages 1–5 in Wood and Bernasconi 1988.
———. 1988d. *Limited Inc*. Edited by Gerald Graff. Translated by Samuel Weber and Jeffrey Mehlman. Evanston, Ill.: Northwestern University Press.
———. 1988e. Telepathy. Translated by Nicholas Royle. *Oxford Literary Review* 10:3–41.
———. 1992a. How to Avoid Speaking: Denials. Translated by Ken Frieden. Pages 73–142 in Coward and Foshay 1992.
———. 1992b. Post-Scriptum: Aporias, Ways and Voices. Translated by John P. Leavey Jr. Pages 283–323 in Coward and Foshay 1992.
———. 1993. Circumfession: Fifty-Nine Periods and Periphrases. Translated by Geoffrey Bennington. Pages 3–315 in Geoffrey Bennington and Jacques Derrida, *Jacques Derrida*. Chicago: University of Chicago Press.
———. 1995. *The Gift of Death*. Translated by David Wills. Chicago: University of Chicago Press.

———. 1997a. *Deconstruction in a Nutshell: A Conversation with Jacques Derrida.* Edited by John D. Caputo. New York: Fordham University Press.
———. 1997b. *Politics of Friendship.* Translated by George Collins. London: Verso.
———. 2001. *On Cosmopolitanism and Forgiveness.* Translated by Mark Dooley and Michael Hughes. London: Routledge.
———. 2002a. *Acts of Religion.* Edited by Gil Anidjar. Translated by Samuel Weber et al. London: Routledge.
———. 2002b. The Animal That Therefore I Am (More to Follow). Translated by David Wills. *Critical Inquiry* 28:369–418.
———. 2003. And Say the Animal Responded? Translated by David Wills. Pages 121–46 in *Zoontologies: The Question of the Animal.* Edited by Cary Wolfe. Minneapolis: University of Minnesota Press.
———. 2005. *Rogues: Two Essays on Reason.* Translated by Pascale-Anne Brault and Michael Naas. Stanford, Calif.: Stanford University Press.
———. 2008. *The Animal That Therefore I Am.* Edited by Marie-Louise Mallet. Translated by David Wills. New York: Fordham University Press.
———. 2009. *The Beast and the Sovereign.* Vol. 1. Translated by Geoffrey Bennington. Seminars of Jacques Derrida. Chicago: University of Chicago Press.
Derrida, Jacques, and Anne Dufourmantelle. 2000. *Of Hospitality: Anne Dufourmantelle Invites Jacques Derrida to Respond.* Translated by Rachel Bowlby. Cultural Memory in the Present. Stanford, Calif.: Stanford University Press.
Derrida, Jacques, Frank Kermode, Toril Moi, and Christopher Norris. 2004. *life.after.theory.* New York: Continuum.
Derrida, Jacques, and Gianni Vattimo, eds. 1998. *Religion.* Translated by David Webb et al. Stanford, Calif.: Stanford University Press.
Desai, Gaurav, and Supriya Nair, eds. 2005. *Postcolonialisms: An Anthology of Cultural Theory and Criticism.* New Brunswick, N.J.: Rutgers University Press.
DeSilva, David A. 1995a. *Despising Shame: Honor Discourse and Community Maintenance in the Epistle to the Hebrews.* SBLDS 152. Atlanta: Scholars Press.
———. 1995b. The Noble Contest: Honor, Shame, and the Rhetorical Strategy of 4 Maccabees. *JSP* 13:31–57.
De Vries, Hent. 1999. *Philosophy and the Turn to Religion.* Baltimore: Johns Hopkins University Press.
Dickstein, Morris. 2005. The Rise and Fall of "Practical" Criticism: From I. A. Richards to Barthes and Derrida. Pages 60–77 in Patai and Corral 2005b.
Dillon, Richard J. 1978. *From Eye-Witnesses to Ministers of the Word: Tradition and Composition in Luke 24.* AnBib 82. Rome: Pontifical Biblical Institute.
Dirlik, Arif. 1994. The Postcolonial Aura: Third World Criticism in an Age of Global Capitalism. *Critical Inquiry* 20:328–56.
Docherty, Thomas. 1996. *After Theory.* Edinburgh: Edinburgh University Press.
Dodd, C. H. 1932. *The Epistle of Paul to the Romans.* Moffatt New Testament Commentary. London: Hodder & Stoughton.
———. 1963. *Historical Tradition in the Fourth Gospel.* Cambridge: Cambridge University Press.

———. 1968. *The Interpretation of the Fourth Gospel*. Cambridge: Cambridge University Press.
Donaldson, Laura E., ed. 1996. *Postcolonialism and Scriptural Reading*. Semeia 75. Atlanta: Scholars Press.
———. 2002. The Breasts of Columbus: A Political Anatomy of Postcolonialism and Feminist Religious Discourse. Pages 41–61 in *Postcolonialism, Feminism and Religious Discourse*. Edited by Laura E. Donaldson and Kwok Pui-lan. London: Routledge.
———. 2005. Gospel Hauntings: The Postcolonial Demons of New Testament Criticism. Pages 97–114 in Moore and Segovia 2005.
Dover, K. J. 1989. *Greek Homosexuality, Updated and with a New Postscript*. Cambridge: Harvard University Press. [Orig. 1978]
Dowsett, Andrew C. 1998. Theology in the Discography: The Bible and Popular Music. PhD dissertation. University of Sheffield.
Draper, Jonathan A., ed. 2004. *Orality, Literacy, and Colonialism in Southern Africa*. SemeiaSt 46. Atlanta: Society of Biblical Literature.
Dreyfus, Hubert L., and Paul Rabinow. 1983. *Michel Foucault: Beyond Structuralism and Hermeneutics*. 2nd ed. Chicago: University of Chicago Press.
Dube, Musa W. 1998. Savior of the World, but Not of This World: A Postcolonial Reading of Spatial Construction in John. Pages 118–35 in Sugirtharajah 1998b.
———. 2000. *Postcolonial Feminist Interpretation of the Bible*. St. Louis: Chalice.
———, ed. 2001. *Other Ways of Reading: African Women and the Bible*. GPBS. Atlanta: Society of Biblical Literature.
———. 2002. Reading for Decolonization (John 4.1–42). Pages 51–75 in Dube and Staley 2002b.
Dube, Musa W., and Jeffrey L. Staley. 2002a. Descending from and Ascending into Heaven: A Postcolonial Analysis of Travel, Space and Power in John. Pages 1–10 in Dube and Staley 2002b.
———, eds. 2002b. *John and Postcolonialism: Travel, Space and Power*. The Bible and Postcolonialism 7. New York: Continuum.
DuBois, Page. 1991. *Torture and Truth*. London: Routledge.
———. 1998. The Subject in Antiquity after Foucault. Pages 85–103 in Larmour, Miller and Platter 1998.
Duggan, Lisa, and Nan D. Hunter. 1995. *Sex Wars: Sexual Dissent and Political Culture*. London: Routledge.
Duke, Paul D. 1985. *Irony in the Fourth Gospel*. Atlanta: John Knox.
Dunn, James D. G. 1988. *Romans 1–8*. WBC 38A. Dallas: Word.
———. 1998. *The Theology of Paul the Apostle*. Edinburgh: T&T Clark.
Dünzl, Franz, ed. and trans. 1994. *Gregor von Nyssa, In Canticum Canticorum homiliae. Homilien zum Hohenlied*. 3 vols. Freiburg: Herder.
Dupont-Sommer, André. 1939. *Le Quatrième Livre des Machabées: Introduction, traduction et notes*. Paris: Librairie Ancienne Honoré Champion.
Duras, Marguerite. 1980. Smothered Creativity. Translated by Virginia Hules. Pages 111–13 in Mark and de Courtivron 1980.
During, Simon, ed. 1999. *The Cultural Studies Reader*. 2nd ed. London: Routledge.

———. 2005. *Cultural Studies: A Critical Introduction*. London: Routledge.
Dutton, Kenneth R. 1995. *The Perfectible Body: The Western Ideal of Male Physical Development*. New York: Continuum.
Eagleton, Terry. 2003. *After Theory*. New York: Basic.
Eakin, Emily. 2003. The Latest Theory Is That Theory Doesn't Matter. *The New York Times*, 19 April, D9.
Eakin, Paul John. 1985. *Fictions in Autobiography: Studies in the Art of Self-Invention*. Princeton: Princeton University Press
Eco, Umberto. 1989. *The Middle Ages of James Joyce: The Aesthetics of Chaosmos*. Translated by Ellen Esrock. London: Hutchinson Radius.
Eddins, Dwight, ed. 1995. *The Emperor Redressed: Critiquing Critical Theory*. Tuscaloosa: University of Alabama Press.
Edwards, W. D., W. J. Gabel, and F. E. Hosmer. 1986. On the Physical Death of Jesus Christ. *Journal of the American Medical Association* 255:1455–63.
Ehrman, B. D., and M. A. Plunkett. 1983. The Angel and the Agony: The Textual Problem of Luke 22:43–44. *CBQ* 45:401–16.
Eichrodt, Walther. 1961. *Theology of the Old Testament*. Translated by J. A. Baker. OTL. Philadelphia: Westminster.
Eilberg-Schwartz, Howard. 1990. *The Savage in Judaism: An Anthropology of Israelite Religion and Ancient Judaism*. Bloomington: Indiana University Press.
———. 1992a. The Problem of the Body for the People of the Book. Pages 17–46 in Eilberg-Schwartz 1992b.
———, ed. 1992b. *People of the Body: Jews and Judaism from an Embodied Perspective*. SUNY Series on the Body in Culture, History, and Religion. Albany: State University of New York Press.
———. 1994. *God's Phallus and Other Problems for Men and Monotheism*. Boston: Beacon.
Elliott, Neil. 1994. *Liberating Paul: The Justice of God and the Politics of the Apostle*. Maryknoll, N.Y.: Orbis.
Elliott, Scott. 2009. "The Son of Man Goes as It Is Written of Him": The Figuration of Jesus in the Gospel of Mark. PhD dissertation. Drew University Theological School.
Ellis, John. 2005. Is Theory to Blame? Pages 92–108 in Patai and Corral 2005b.
Ellmann, Richard. 1982. *James Joyce*. 2nd ed. Oxford: Oxford University Press.
Ernst, Josef. 1977. *Das Evangelium nach Lukas*. Regensburger Neues Testament. Regensburg: Pustet.
Erskine, Andrew. 1990. *The Hellenistic Stoa: Political Thought and Action*. Ithaca, N.Y.: Cornell University Press.
Esler, Philip F. 1987. *Community and Gospel in Luke-Acts: The Social and Political Motivations of Lucan Theology*. New York: Cambridge University Press.
Eslinger, Lyle. 1981. The Case of the Immodest Lady Wrestler in Deuteronomy XXV 11–12. *VT* 31:269–81.
———. 1987. The Wooing of the Woman at the Well: Jesus, the Reader and Reader-Response Criticism. *Literature and Theology* 1:167–83.

Exum, J. Cheryl. 1973. A Literary and Structural Analysis of the Song of Songs. *ZAW* 85:47–79.

———. 1996. *Plotted, Shot, and Painted: Cultural Representations of Biblical Women.* JSOTSup 215; Gender, Culture, Theory 3. Sheffield: Sheffield Academic Press.

———. 1998. Developing Strategies of Feminist Criticism/ Developing Strategies for Commentating the Song of Songs. Pages 206–49 in *Auguries: The Jubilee Volume of the Sheffield Department of Biblical Studies.* Edited by David J. A. Clines and Stephen D. Moore. JSOTSup 269. Sheffield: Sheffield Academic Press.

———, ed. 1999. *Beyond the Biblical Horizon: The Bible and the Arts.* Leiden: Brill.

———. 2000. Ten Things Every Feminist Should Know about the Song of Songs. Pages 24–35 in Brenner and Fontaine 2000.

Exum, J. Cheryl, and Stephen D. Moore, eds. 1998. *Biblical Studies/Cultural Studies: The Third Sheffield Colloquium.* JSOTSup 266; Gender, Culture, Theory 7. Sheffield: Sheffield Academic Press.

Faderman, Lillian. 1981. *Surpassing the Love of Men: Romantic Friendship and Love between Women from the Renaissance to the Present.* New York: William Morrow.

———. 1983. *Scotch Verdict: Miss Pirie and Miss Woods v. Dame Cumming Gordon.* New York: William Morrow.

Falconer, Colin. 2002. *Feathered Serpent: A Novel of the Mexican Conquest.* New York: Three Rivers.

Fanon, Frantz. 1967. *Black Skin, White Masks.* Translated by Charles Lam Markmann. New York: Grove. [French orig. 1952]

———. 1968. *The Wretched of the Earth.* Translated by Constance Farrington. New York: Grove. [French orig. 1961]

Farmer, William R. 1994. *The Gospel of Jesus: The Pastoral Relevance of the Synoptic Problem.* Louisville: Westminster John Knox.

Fee, Gordon D. 1994. *God's Empowering Presence: The Holy Spirit in the Letters of Paul.* Peabody, Mass.: Hendrickson.

Felder, Cain Hope, ed. 1991. *Stony the Road We Trod: African American Biblical Interpretation.* Minneapolis: Fortress.

Felman, Shoshana. 1982. Turning the Screw of Interpretation. Pages 94–207 in *Literature and Psychoanalysis. The Question of Reading: Otherwise.* Edited by Shoshana Felman. Baltimore: Johns Hopkins University Press.

———. 1987. *Jacques Lacan and the Adventure of Insight: Psychoanalysis in Contemporary Culture.* Cambridge: Harvard University Press.

Felski, Rita. 2008. From Literary Theory to Critical Method. *Profession* 2008:108–16.

Fewell, Danna Nolan, ed. 1992. *Reading between Texts: The Bible and Intertextuality.* Literary Currents in Biblical Interpretation. Louisville: Westminster John Knox.

Fishbane, Michael. 1994. Arm of the Lord: Biblical Myth, Rabbinic Midrash, and the Mystery of History. Pages 271–92 in *Language, Theology and the Bible: Essays in Honor of James Barr.* Edited by Samuel E. Balentine and John Barton. Oxford: Clarendon.

Fitzmyer, Joseph A. 1981. *The Gospel According to Luke I–IX.* AB 28. Garden City, N.Y.: Doubleday.

———. 1985. *The Gospel according to Luke X–XXIV.* AB 28A. Garden City, N.Y.: Doubleday.
———. 1993. *Romans: A New Translation with Introduction and Commentary.* AB 33. New York: Doubleday.
Flynn, Elizabeth A., and Patrocinio P. Schweickart, eds. 2004. *Reading Sites: Social Difference and Reader Response.* New York: Modern Language Association of America.
Folkenflik, Robert, ed. 1993. *The Culture of Autobiography: Constructions of Self-Representation.* Stanford, Calif.: Stanford University Press.
Fonow, Mary Margaret, and Judith A. Cook, eds. 1991. *Beyond Methodology: Feminist Scholarship as Lived Research.* Bloomington: University of Indiana Press.
Fontaine, Carole R. 2000. Preface. Pages 13–16 in Brenner and Fontaine 2000.
Ford, Joan Massingbaerde. 1996. The Crucifixion of Women in Antiquity. *Journal of Higher Criticism* 3:290–309.
Foster, Hal, ed. 1983. *The Anti-Aesthetic: Essays on Postmodern Culture.* Port Townsend, Wash.: Bay Press.
Foster, William, ed. 1943. *The Voyage of Sir Henry Middleton to the Moluccas, 1604–1606.* Hakluyt Society Series 2/88. London: Haklyut Society.
Foucault, Michel. 1962. *Maladie mentale et personalité.* 2nd ed. Paris: Universitaires de France.
———. 1965. *Madness and Civilization: A History of Insanity in the Age of Reason.* Translated by Richard Howard. New York: Pantheon. [Abridged trans. of *Histoire de la folie à l'âge classique.* Paris: Plon, 1961]
———. 1970. *The Order of Things: An Archaeology of the Human Sciences.* New York: Vintage.
———. 1973. *The Birth of the Clinic: An Archaeology of Medical Perception.* Translated by Alan Sheridan. New York: Pantheon.
———, ed. 1975. *I, Pierre Rivière, Having Slaughtered My Mother, My Sister, and My Brother...: A Case of Parricide in the 19th Century.* Translated by Frank Jellinek. New York: Pantheon.
———. 1977a. *Discipline and Punish: The Birth of the Prison.* Translated by Alan Sheridan. New York: Vintage.
———. 1977b. Nietzsche, Genealogy, History. Pages 139–64 in *Language, Counter-Memory, Practice: Selected Essays and Interviews.* Edited by Donald F. Bouchard. Translated by Donald F. Bouchard and Sherry Simon. Ithaca, N.Y.: Cornell University Press.
———. 1978. *An Introduction.* Vol. 1 of *The History of Sexuality.* Translated by Robert Hurley. New York: Pantheon.
———. 1979. What Is an Author? Translated by Josué V. Harari. Pages 141–60 in *Textual Strategies: Perspectives in Post-structuralist Criticism.* Edited by Josué V. Harari. Ithaca, N.Y.: Cornell University Press.
———. 1980a. Body/Power. Pages 55–62 in Foucault 1980c.
———. 1980b. The Eye of Power. Pages 146–65 in Foucault 1980c.
———. 1980c. *Power/Knowledge: Selected Interviews and Other Writings, 1972–1977.* Edited by Colin Gordon. Translated by Colin Gordon et al. New York: Pantheon.

———. 1980d. Prison Talk. Pages 37–54 in Foucault 1980c.
———. 1980e. Questions on Geography. Pages 63–77 in Foucault 1980c.
———. 1983. The Subject and Power. Pages 208–26 in Dreyfus and Rabinow 1983.
———. 1984. On the Genealogy of Ethics: An Overview of Work in Progress. Pages 340–72 in *The Foucault Reader*. Edited by Paul Rabinow. New York: Pantheon.
———. 1985. *The Use of Pleasure*. Vol. 2 of *The History of Sexuality*. Translated by Robert Hurley. New York: Pantheon.
———. 1986. *The Care of the Self*. Vol. 3 of *The History of Sexuality*. Translated by Robert Hurley. New York: Pantheon.
———. 1988a. Behind the Fable. Translated by Pierre A. Walker. *Critical Texts* 5:1–5.
———. 1988b. On Power. Pages 96–109 in Foucault 1988d.
———. 1988c. Politics and Reason. Pages 57–85 in Foucault 1988d.
———. 1988d. *Politics, Philosophy, Culture: Interviews and Other Writings, 1977–1984*. Edited by Lawrence D. Kritzman. Translated by Alan Sheridan et al. London: Routledge.
———. 1988e. Technologies of the Self. Pages 16–49 in *Technologies of the Self: A Seminar with Michel Foucault*. Edited by Luther H. Martin, Huck Gutman, and Patrick H. Hutton. Amherst: University of Massachusetts Press.
———. 1989a. Clarifications on the Question of Power. Pages 179–92 in Foucault 1989c.
———. 1989b. The Discourse of History. Pages 11–34 in Foucault 1989c.
———. 1989c. *Foucault Live (Interviews, 1966–84)*. Edited by Sylvere Lotringer. Translated by John Johnson. New York: Semiotext(e).
———. 1991. Governmentality. Pages 87–104 in *The Foucault Effect: Studies in Governmentality*. Edited by Graham Burchell, Colin Gordon, and Peter Miller. Chicago: University of Chicago Press.
Fowler, Robert M. 1989. Postmodern Biblical Criticism. *Forum* 5:3–30.
Foxhall, Lin. 1998. Pandora Unbound: A Feminist Critique of Foucault's *History of Sexuality*. Pages 122–37 in Larmour, Miller, and Platter 1998.
Freadman, Richard, and Seumas Miller. 2005. The Power and Limits of Literary Theory. Pages 78–91 in Patai and Corral 2005b.
Freedman, Diane P. 1996. Autobiographical Literary Criticism as the New Belletrism: Personal Experience. Pages 3–16 in Veeser 1996b.
Freedman, Diane P., Olivia Frey, and Frances Murphy Zauhar, eds. 1993. *The Intimate Critique: Autobiographical Literary Criticism*. Durham, N.C.: Duke University Press.
Freedman, Harry, and Maurice Simon, eds. 1939. *Deuteronomy and Lamentations*. Vol. 7 of *Midrash Rabbah*. Translated by J. Rabbinowitz and A. Cohen. London: Soncino.
Freud, Sigmund. 1900. *The Interpretation of Dreams*. Vols. 4 and 5 of Freud 1953–74.
———. 1901. *The Psychopathology of Everyday Life*. Vol. 6 of Freud 1953–74.
———. 1905a. *Jokes and Their Relation to the Unconscious*. Vol. 8 of Freud 1953–74.
———. 1905b. *Three Essays on the Theory of Sexuality*. Pages 125–245 in vol. 7 of Freud 1953–74.
———. 1913. *Totem and Taboo*. Vol. 13 of Freud 1953–74.

———. 1915. Instincts and Their Vicissitudes. Pages 109–40 in *On the History of the Psycho-Analytic Movement, Papers on Metapsychology, and Other Works*. Vol. 14 of Freud 1953–74.

———. 1953–74. *The Standard Edition of the Complete Psychological Works*. Edited and translated by James Strachey. London: Hogarth.

Freudenthal, Jakob. 1869. *Die Flavius Josephus beigelegte Schrift über die Herrschaft der Vernunft [IV Makkabäerbuch], eine Predigt aus dem ersten nachchristlichen Jahrhundert*. Breslau: Schletter.

Friesen, Steven J. 2001. *Imperial Cults and the Apocalypse of John: Reading Revelation in the Ruins*. Oxford: Oxford University Press.

Frilingos, Christopher A. 2004. *Spectacles of Empire: Monsters, Martyrs, and the Book of Revelation*. Divinations: Rereading Late Ancient Religion. Philadelphia: University of Pennsylvania Press.

Fromm, Harold. 2005. Oppositional Opposition. Pages 454–57 in Patai and Corral 2005b.

Fussel, Samuel Wilson. 1991. *Muscle: Confessions of an Unlikely Bodybuilder*. New York: Avon.

———. 1994. Bodybuilder Americanus. Pages 43–60 in *The Male Body: Features, Destinies, Exposures*. Edited by Laurence Goldstein. Ann Arbor: University of Michigan Press.

Gagnon, Madeleine. 1980. Body I. Pages 179–80 in Mark and de Courtivron 1980.

Gaines, Charles, and George Butler. 1974. *Pumping Iron: The Art and Sport of Bodybuilding*. New York: Simon & Schuster.

Gallagher, Catherine, and Stephen Greenblatt. 2000. *Practicing New Historicism*. Chicago: University of Chicago Press.

Gallop, Jane. 1982. *The Daughter's Seduction: Feminism and Psychoanalysis*. Ithaca, N.Y.: Cornell University Press.

———. 1985. *Reading Lacan*. Ithaca, N.Y.: Cornell University Press.

———. 1988. *Thinking through the Body*. New York: Columbia University Press.

Garber, Marjorie. 1992. *Vested Interests: Cross-Dressing and Cultural Anxiety*. London: Routledge.

Garber, Marjorie, Beatrice Hanssen, and Rebecca L .Walklowitz, eds. 2000. *The Turn to Ethics*. London: Routledge.

Garrard, Greg. 2004. *Ecocriticism*. New Critical Idiom. London: Routledge.

Garrett, Susan R. 1989. *The Demise of the Devil: Magic and the Demonic in Luke's Writings*. Minneapolis: Fortress.

———. 1991. "Lest the Light in You Be Darkness": Luke 11:33–36 and the Question of Commitment. *JBL* 110:93–105.

Gasparro, Giulia Sfameni. 1995. Image of God and Sexual Differentiation in the Tradition of *Enkrateia*. Pages 134–69 in Børresen 1995.

Gates, Henry Louis, Jr. , ed. 1986. *"Race," Writing and Difference*. Chicago: University of Chicago Press.

———. 1994. *Colored People: A Memoir*. New York: Knopf.

Georgi, Dieter. 1985. Rudolf Bultmann's *Theology of the New Testament* Revisited.

Pages 75–87 in *Bultmann, Retrospect and Prospect: The Centenary Symposium at Wellesley*. Edited by Edward C. Hobbs. HTS 35. Philadelphia: Fortress.

Gersdorf, Catrin, and Sylvia Mayer, eds. 2006. *Nature in Literary and Cultural Studies: Transatlantic Conversations on Ecocriticism*. Nature, Culture and Literature 3. Amsterdam: Rodopi.

Gilbert, Sandra. 2001. New Uses for Old Boys: An Interview with Sandra Gilbert. Pages 244–54 in *Professions: Conversations on the Future of Literary and Cultural Studies*. Edited by Donald E. Hall. Urbana: University of Illinois Press.

Gilmore, David D. 1990. *Manhood in the Making: Cultural Concepts of Masculinity*. New Haven: Yale University Press.

Gilmore, Leigh. 1994. *Autobiographics: A Feminist Theory of Women's Self-Representation*. Ithaca, N.Y.: Cornell University Press.

Ginsburg, Christian D. 1857. *The Song of Songs: Translated from the Original Hebrew, with a Commentary, Historical and Critical*. London: Longman, Green.

Ginzberg, Louis. 1909–59. *The Legends of the Jews*. 7 vols. Translated by Henrietta Szold et al. Philadelphia: The Jewish Publication Society of America.

Gitlin, Todd. 2005. The Cant of Identity. Pages 400–410 in Patai and Corral 2005b.

Glancy, Jennifer A. 1994. Unveiling Masculinity: The Construction of Gender in Mark 6:17–29. *BibInt* 2:34–50.

———. 2005. Torture: Flesh, Truth, and the Fourth Gospel. *BibInt* 13:107–36.

Gleason, Maud W. 1995. *Making Men: Sophists and Self-Presentation in Ancient Rome*. Princeton: Princeton University Press.

Glotfelty, Cheryll, and Harold Fromm, eds. 1996. *The Ecocriticism Reader: Landmarks in Literary Ecology*. Athens, Ga.: University of Georgia Press.

Goldberg, David Theo, and Ato Quayson, eds. 2002. *Relocating Postcolonialism*. Oxford: Blackwell.

Goldhill, Simon. 1995. *Foucault's Virginity: Ancient Erotic Fiction and the History of Sexuality*. Cambridge: Cambridge University Press.

Goldstein, Jonathan A. 1983. *II Maccabees*. AB 41A. Garden City, N.Y.: Doubleday.

González, Justo L. 1995. Reading from My Bicultural Place: Acts 6:1–7. Pages 139–47 in Segovia and Tolbert 1995a.

Goodheart, Eugene. 1999. *Does Literary Studies Have a Future?* Madison: University of Wisconsin Press.

Gottstein, Alon Goshen. 1994. The Body as Image of God in Rabbinic Literature. *HTR* 87:171–95.

Goulder, Michael D. 1986. *The Song of Fourteen Songs*. JSOTSup 36. Sheffield: JSOT Press.

Goux, Jean-Joseph. 1990. *Symbolic Economies: After Marx and Freud*. Translated by Jennifer Curtiss Gage. Ithaca, N.Y.: Cornell University Press.

Graham, Susan Lochrie. 1991. Silent Voices: Women in the Gospel of Mark. *Semeia* 54:119–36.

Gray, Bennison. 1975. *The Phenomenon of Literature*. The Hague: Mouton.

Greenberg, David F. 1988. *The Construction of Homosexuality*. Chicago: University of Chicago Press.

Greenblatt, Stephen. 1980. *Renaissance Self-Fashioning: From More to Shakespeare*. Chicago: University of Chicago Press.

———. 1988. *Shakespearean Negotiations: The Circulation of Social Energy in Renaissance England*. The New Historicism: Studies in Cultural Poetics 4. Berkeley and Los Angeles: University of California Press.

———. 1990. *Learning to Curse: Essays in Early Modern Culture*. London: Routledge.

———. 1991. *Marvelous Possessions: The Wonder of the New World*. Chicago: University of Chicago Press.

———. 1996. Laos Is Open. Pages 221–34 in Veeser 1996b.

Greene, Ellen. 1996. Sappho, Foucault, and Women's Erotics. *Arethusa* 29:1–14.

Grossberg, Lawrence, Cary Nelson, and Paula Treichler, eds. 1992. *Cultural Studies*. London: Routledge.

Grosz, Elizabeth. 1990. *Jacques Lacan: A Feminist Introduction*. London: Routledge.

Gruber, Mayer I. 1992. The Motherhood of God in Second Isaiah. Pages 3–15 in idem, *The Motherhood of God and Other Studies*. South Florida Studies in the History of Judaism 57. Atlanta: Scholars Press.

Grundmann, Walter. 1961. *Das Evangelium nach Lukas*. THKNT 3. Berlin: Evangelische Verlagsanstalt.

Guest, Deryn, Robert E. Goss, Mona West, and Thomas Bohache, eds. 2006. *The Queer Bible Commentary*. London: SCM.

Guillaume, Philippe. 2008. Dismantling the Deconstruction of Job. *JBL* 127:491–99.

Gunn, Janet Varner. 1982. *Autobiography: Toward a Poetics of Experience*. Philadelphia: University of Pennsylvania Press

Gutman, Isaiah. 1949. The Story of the Mother and Her Seven Sons in the *Agadah* and in II and IV Maccabees [Hebrew]. Pages 25–37 in *Commentationes Iudaico-Hellenisticae in memoriam Iohannis Lewy*. Edited by Moshe Schwabe and Isaiah Gutman. Jerusalem: Magnes.

Haacker, Klaus. 1994. Exegetische Gesichtspunkte zum Thema Homosexualität. *TBei* 25:173–80.

Habermas, Jürgen. 1983. Modernity—an Incomplete Project. Pages 3–15 in Foster 1983.

Hadas, Moses. 1953. *The Third and Fourth Books of Maccabees*. New York: Harper & Row.

Haenchen, Ernst. 1984. *John 1: A Commentary on the Gospel of John Chapters 1–6*. Translated by Robert W. Funk with Ulrich Busse. Hermeneia. Philadelphia: Fortress.

Halberstam, Judith. 1998. *Female Masculinity*. Durham, N.C.: Duke University Press.

Hall, Edith. 1989. *Inventing the Barbarian: Greek Self-Definition through Tragedy*. Oxford: Clarendon.

Hallett, Judith P. 1997. Female Homoeroticism and the Denial of Roman Reality. Pages 255–73 in Hallett and Skinner 1997.

Hallett, Judith P., and Marilyn B. Skinner, eds. 1997. *Roman Sexualities*. Princeton: Princeton University Press.

Halperin, David M. 1990. *One Hundred Years of Homosexuality: And Other Essays on Greek Love*. London: Routledge.

———. 1995. *Saint Foucault: Towards a Gay Hagiography*. Oxford: Oxford University Press.
Halperin, David M., John J. Winkler and Froma I. Zeitlin, eds. 1990. *Before Sexuality: The Construction of Erotic Experience in the Ancient Greek World*. Princeton: Princeton University Press.
Hamburger, Käte. 1973. *The Logic of Literature*. Translated by Marilynn Rose. Bloomington: Indiana University Press.
Hamilton, Paul. 1996. *Historicism*. New Critical Idiom. London: Routledge.
Hamm, Dennis. 1986. Sight to the Blind: Vision as Metaphor in Luke. *Bib* 67:457–77.
Han, Jin Hee. 2005. Homi Bhabha and the Mixed Blessing of Hybridity in Biblical Hermeneutics. *The Bible and Critical Theory* 1:4. Online: http://publications.epress.monash.edu/loi/bc.
Handler, Nicholas. 2007. The Posteverything Generation. *The New York Times Magazine*, 30 September, 36, 43.
Hanson, Paul D. 1979. *The Dawn of Apocalyptic: The Historical and Sociological Roots of Jewish Apocalyptic Eschatology*. 2nd ed. Philadelphia: Fortress.
Harink, Douglas, ed. 2010. *Paul, Philosophy, and the Theopolitical Vision: Critical Engagements with Agamben, Badiou, Žižek and Others*. Theopolitical Visions 7. Eugene, Ore.: Cascade.
Harris, Amanda Nolacea. 2004. Imperial and Postcolonial Desires: *Sonata de Estío* and the Malinche Paradigm. *Discourse* 26:235–57.
Harris, Wendell V. 1996. *Beyond Poststructuralism: The Speculations of Theory and the Experience of Reading*. University Park: Pennsylvania State University Press.
Hart, Lynda. 1998. *Between the Body and the Flesh: Performing Sadomasochism*. Between Men—Between Women: Lesbian and Gay Studies. New York: Columbia University Press.
Hartman, Geoffrey. 1989. The State of the Art of Criticism. Pages 86–101 in *The Future of Literary Theory*. Edited by Ralph Cohen. London: Routledge.
Hassan, Ihab. 1987. *The Postmodern Turn: Essays in Postmodern Theory and Culture*. Columbus: Ohio State University Press.
Hawley, John C., ed. 2001. *Encyclopedia of Postcolonial Studies*. Westport, Conn.: Greenwood.
Hays, Richard B. 1989. *Echoes of Scripture in the Letters of Paul*. New Haven: Yale University Press.
Heidegger, Martin. 1971. *The Question Concerning Technology and Other Essays*. Translated by William Lovitt. New York: Harper & Row.
Hengel, Martin. 1977. *Crucifixion in the Ancient World and the Folly of the Message of the Cross*. Translated by John Bowden. Philadelphia: Fortress.
———. 1989. *The Zealots: Investigations into the Jewish Freedom Movement in the Period from Herod I until 70 A.D.* Translated by David Smith. Edinburgh: T&T Clark.
———. 1991. Reich Christi, Reich Gottes und Weltreich im Johannesevangelium. Pages 163–84 in *Königsherrschaft Gottes und himmlischer Kult in Judentum, Urchristentum und in der hellenistischen Welt*. Edited by Martin Hengel and Anna Maria Schwemer. Tübingen: Mohr Siebeck.

Henten, J. W. van. 1986. Datierung und Herkunft des Vierten Makkabäerbuches. Pages 137–45 in *Tradition and Reinterpretation in Jewish and Early Christian Literature: Essays in Honor of Jürgen C. H. Lebram*. Edited by J. W. van Henten et al. Leiden: Brill.

Herion, Gary A. 1992. Wrath of God (Old Testament). *ABD* 6:989–96.

Heschel, Abraham J. 1962. *The Prophets*. Philadelphia: Jewish Publication Society of America.

Hirschberg, Harris Hans. 1961. Some Additional Arabic Etymologies in Old Testament Lexicography. *VT* 11:373–85.

Hogan, Patrick Colm, and Lalita Pandit, eds. 1990. *Criticism and Lacan: Essays and Dialogue in Language, Structure, and the Unconscious*. Athens: University of Georgia Press.

Holland, Norman N. 1975. *5 Readers Reading*. New Haven: Yale University Press.

Honer, Anne. 1985. Beschreibung einer Lebens-Welt: Zur Empirie des Bodybuilding. *Zeitschrift für Soziologie* 14:131–39.

Hooke, S. H. 1962–63. The Spirit Was Not Yet. *NTS* 9:372–80.

Hooker, Morna D. 1991. *The Gospel according to Saint Mark*. Black's New Testament Commentary. Peabody, Mass.: Hendrickson.

Horsley, Richard A. 1987. *Jesus and the Spiral of Violence: Popular Jewish Resistance in Roman Palestine*. San Francisco: Harper & Row.

———, ed. 1997. *Paul and Empire: Religion and Power in Roman Imperial Society*. Harrisburg, Pa.: Trinity Press International.

———, ed. 2000. *Paul and Politics: Ekklesia, Israel, Imperium, Interpretation*. Harrisburg, Pa.: Trinity Press International.

———. 2001. *Hearing the Whole Story: The Politics of Plot in Mark's Gospel*. Louisville: Westminster John Knox.

———. 2002. *Jesus and Empire: The Kingdom of God and the New World Disorder*. Minneapolis: Fortress.

———. 2004. *Paul and the Roman Imperial Order*. Harrisburg, Pa.: Trinity Press International.

Horsley, Richard A., and John S. Hanson. 1985. *Bandits, Prophets, and Messiahs: Popular Movements in the Time of Jesus*. New Voices in Biblical Studies. Minneapolis: Winston.

Hoskot, S. S. 1979. *T. S. Eliot: His Mind and Personality*. Philadelphia: Richard West.

Hoskyns, Edwyn C. 1947. *The Fourth Gospel*. Edited by Francis N. Davey. 2nd ed. London: Faber & Faber.

Howard-Brook, Wes, and Anthony Gwyther. 1999. *Unveiling Empire: Reading Revelation Then and Now*. Maryknoll, N.Y.: Orbis.

Howe, Stephen. 2000. *Ireland and Empire: Colonial Legacies in Irish History and Culture*. Oxford: Oxford University Press.

Huddart, David. 2006. *Homi K. Bhabha*. Routledge Critical Thinkers. London: Routledge.

Hull, John M. 1974. *Hellenistic Magic and the Synoptic Tradition*. London: SCM.

Hulme, Peter. 1985. Polytropic Man: Tropes of Sexuality and Mobility in Early Colonial Discourse. Pages 17–32 in *Europe and Its Others*. Edited by Francis Barker et al. Colchester: University of Essex Press.

Hunt, Lynn. 1992. Foucault's Subject in *The History of Sexuality*. Pages 78–93 in Stanton 1992.

Hussein, Abdirahman A. 2002. *Edward Said: Criticism and Society*. London: Verso.

Hutcheon, Linda. 1988. *A Poetics of Postmodernism: History, Theory, Fiction*. London: Routledge.

Huyssen, Andreas. 1986. *After the Great Divide: Modernism, Mass Culture, Postmodernism*. Bloomington: Indiana University Press.

Idel, Moshe. 1988. *Kabbalah: New Perspectives*. New Haven: Yale University Press.

Ingraham, Chrys, ed. 2005. *Thinking Straight: The Power, the Promise, and the Paradox of Heterosexuality*. London: Routledge.

Irigaray, Luce. 1985a. *Speculum of the Other Woman*. Translated by Gillian C. Gill. Ithaca, N.Y.: Cornell University Press.

———. 1985b. *This Sex Which Is Not One*. Translated by Catherine Porter. Ithaca, N.Y.: Cornell University Press.

———. 1989. Equal to Whom? Translated by Robert L. Mazzola. *differences* 1:59–76.

———. 1996. *I Love to You: Sketch of a Possible Felicity in History*. Translated by Alison Martin. London: Routledge.

Iser, Wolfgang. 1974. *The Implied Reader: Patterns of Communication in Prose Fiction from Bunyan to Beckett*. Baltimore: Johns Hopkins University Press.

———. 1978. *The Act of Reading: A Theory of Aesthetic Response*. Baltimore: Johns Hopkins University Press.

Jacob, Benno. 1974. *The First Book of the Bible: Genesis*. Edited and translated by Ernest I. Jacob and Walter Jacob. New York: Ktav.

Jameson, Fredric. 1987. The Ideology of the Text. Pages 17–71 in idem, *Situations of Theory*. Vol. 1 of *The Ideologies of Theory: Essays, 1971–1986*. Theory and History of Literature 49. Minneapolis: University of Minnesota Press.

———. 1991. *Postmodernism, or, the Cultural Logic of Late Capitalism*. Durham, N.C.: Duke University Press.

Janowitz, Naomi. 1992. God's Body: Theological and Ritual Roles of *Shi'ur Komah*. Pages 183–202 in Eilberg-Schwartz 1992b.

Jay, Martin. 1986. In the Empire of the Gaze: Foucault and the Denigration of Vision in Twentieth-Century French Thought. Pages 175–204 in *Foucault: A Critical Reader*. Edited by David Couzens Hoy. Oxford: Blackwell.

Jeffreys, Sheila. 1990. *Anticlimax: A Feminist Perspective on the Sexual Revolution*. London: Women's Press.

———. 1994. *The Lesbian Heresy: A Feminist Perspective on the Lesbian Sexual Revolution*. London: Women's Press.

———. 1996. Heterosexuality and the Desire for Gender. Pages 75–90 in Richardson 1996.

Jennings, Theodore W., Jr. 2005. *Reading Derrida/Thinking Paul: On Justice*. Cultural Memory in the Present. Stanford, Calif.: Stanford University Press.

Jobling, David. 1990. Writing the Wrongs of the World: The Deconstruction of the Biblical Text in the Context of Liberation Theologies. *Semeia* 51:81–118.

———. 1992. Deconstruction and the Political Analysis of Biblical Texts: A Jamesonian Reading of Psalm 72. *Semeia* 59:95–127.
Jobling, David, Tina Pippin, and Ronald Schleifer, eds. 2001. *The Postmodern Bible Reader*. Oxford: Blackwell.
John of the Cross. 1964. *The Collected Works of St. John of the Cross*. Translated by Kieran Kavanaugh and Otilio Rodriguez. New York: Doubleday.
Johnson, Barbara. 1980. *The Critical Difference: Essays in the Contemporary Rhetoric of Reading*. Baltimore: Johns Hopkins University Press.
———. 1987. *A World of Difference*. Baltimore: Johns Hopkins University Press.
Jones, Ann Rosalind. 1985. Writing the Body: Toward an Understanding of *L'Écriture féminine*. Pages 361–78 in *The New Feminist Criticism: Essays on Women, Literature, and Theory*. Edited by Elaine Showalter. New York: Pantheon.
Jones, Brian W. 1992. *The Emperor Domitian*. London: Routledge.
Jones, Gareth. 1991. *Bultmann: Towards a Critical Theology*. Cambridge: Polity.
Jordan, Mark D. 2002. *The Ethics of Sex*. New Dimensions to Religious Ethics. Oxford: Blackwell.
Joyce, James. 1939. *Finnegans Wake*. London: Faber & Faber.
Kahl, Brigitte. 2000. No Longer Male: Masculinity Struggles behind Galatians 3:28? *JSNT* 79:37–49.
Kähler, Martin. 1964. *The So-Called Historical Jesus and the Historic, Biblical Christ*. Edited and translated by Carl E. Braaten. Philadelphia: Fortress. [German orig. 1896]
Kaplan, Alice. 1993. *French Lessons: A Memoir*. Chicago: University of Chicago Press.
Käsemann, Ernst. 1980. *Commentary on Romans*. Edited and translated by G. W. Bromiley. Grand Rapids: Eerdmans.
Katz, Jonathan Ned. 1995. *The Invention of Heterosexuality*. New York: Dutton.
Keener, Craig S. 2003. *The Gospel of John: A Commentary*. 2 vols. Peabody, Mass.: Hendrickson.
Kelber, Werner H. 1990. In the Beginning Were the Words: The Apotheosis and Narrative Displacement of the Logos. *JAAR* 58:69–98.
Kellum, Barbara. 1996. The Phallus as Signifier: The Forum of Augustus and Rituals of Masculinity. Pages 170–83 in *Sexuality in Ancient Art: Near East, Egypt, Greece, and Italy*. Edited by Natalie Boymel Kampen. Cambridge Studies in New Art History and Criticism. Cambridge: Cambridge University Press.
Kermode, Frank. 2005. Changing Epochs. Pages 605–620 in Patai and Corral 2005b.
Keuls, Eva C. 1985. *The Reign of the Phallus: Sexual Politics in Ancient Athens*. Berkeley and Los Angeles: University of California Press.
Kiberd, Declan. 1995. *Inventing Ireland*. London: Jonathan Cape.
Kim, Jean K. 2004. *Woman and Nation: An Intercontextual Reading of the Gospel of John*. BibInt 69. Leiden: Brill.
Kimelman, Reuven. Rabbi Yohanan and Origen on the Song of Songs. *HTR* 73:567–95.
Klauck, Hans-Joachim. 1989. *4 Makkabäerbuch*. Jüdische Schriften aus hellenistisch-römischer Zeit 3.6. Gütersloh: Gerd Mohn.
———. 1990. Brotherly Love in Plutarch and in 4 Maccabees. Pages 144–56 in *Greeks,*

Romans, and Christians: Essays in Honor of Abraham J. Malherbe. Edited by David L. Balch, Everett Ferguson, and Wayne A. Meeks. Minneapolis: Fortress.

Klein, Alan M. 1993. *Little Big Men: Bodybuilding Subculture and Gender Construction.* SUNY Series on Sport, Culture, and Social Relations. Albany: State University of New York Press.

Koester, Craig R. 1990. "The Savior of the World" (John 4:42). *JBL* 109:665–80.

Kofman, Sarah. 1973. Un philosophe "unheimlich." Pages 107–204 in Lucette Finas et al., *Écarts: Quatres essais à propos de Jacques Derrida.* Paris: Fayard.

Kosta, Barbara. 1994. *Recasting Autobiography: Women's Counterfictions in Contemporary German Literature and Film.* Ithaca, N.Y.: Cornell University Press.

Kraemer, Ross S. 1994. The Other as Woman: An Aspect of Polemic among Pagans, Jews, and Christians in the Greco-Roman World. Pages 121–44 in *The Other in Jewish Thought and History: Constructions of Jewish Cultural Identity.* Edited by Laurence J. Silberstein and Robert L. Cohn. New York: New York University Press.

Krauss, Rosalind. 1980. Poststructuralism and the "Paraliterary." *October* 13:36–40.

Kressel, G. M. 1994. An Anthropologist's Response to the Use of Social Science Models in Biblical Studies. *Semeia* 68:153–61.

Kristeva, Julia. 1974. *La Révolution du langage poétique: l'avant-garde à la fin du XIXe siècle, Lautréamont et Mallarmé.* Paris: Éditions du Seuil.

———. 1980a. Oscillation between Power and Denial. Pages 165–67 in Mark and de Courtivron 1980.

———. 1980b. Postmodernism? Pages 136–41 in *Romanticism, Modernism, Postmodernism.* Edited by Harry R. Garvin. Lewisburg, Pa.: Bucknell University Press.

———. 1980c. Woman Can Never Be Defined. Pages 137–41 in Mark and de Courtivron 1980.

———. 1980d. Word, Dialogue, and Novel. Pages 64–91 in idem, *Desire in Language: A Semiotic Approach to Literature and Art.* Translated by Leon S. Roudiez. New York: Columbia University Press.

———. 1982. *Powers of Horror: An Essay on Abjection.* Translated by Leon S. Roudiez. New York: Columbia University Press.

———. 1987a. A Holy Madness: She and He. Pages 83–100 in Kristeva 1987c.

———. 1987b. Stabat Mater. Pages 234–64 in Kristeva 1987c.

———. 1987c. *Tales of Love.* Translated by Leon S. Roudiez. New York: Columbia University Press.

———. 1989. Holbein's Dead Christ. Pages 238–69 in vol. 1 of *Fragments for a History of the Human Body.* Edited by Michel Feher with Ramona Naddoff and Nadia Tazi. New York: Zone.

Kvalbein, Hans. 2003. The Kingdom of God and the Kingship of Christ in the Fourth Gospel. Pages 215–32 in *Neotestamentica et Philonica: Studies in Honor of Peder Borgen.* Edited by David E. Aune, Torrey Seland, and Jarl Henning Ulrichsen. Leiden: Brill.

Lacan, Jacques. 1970. Of Structure as an Inmixing of an Otherness Prerequisite to Any Subject Whatever. Pages 186–200 in Macksey and Donato.

———. 1977a. *Écrits: A Selection.* Translated by Alan Sheridan. New York: Norton.

———. 1977b. Preface. Pages vii–xv in Lemaire 1977.

———. 1978. *The Four Fundamental Concepts of Psycho-Analysis*. Translated by Alan Sheridan. New York: Norton.

———. 1981. *Le Séminaire, livre III: Les psychoses*. Edited by Jacques-Alain Miller. Paris: Éditions du Seuil.

———. 1982a. Desire and the Interpretation of Desire in *Hamlet*. Translated by James Hulbert. Pages 11–52 in *Literature and Psychoanalysis. The Question of Reading: Otherwise*. Edited by Shoshana Felman. Baltimore: Johns Hopkins University Press.

———. 1982b. *Feminine Sexuality: Jacques Lacan and the* école freudienne. Edited by Juliet Mitchell and Jacqueline Rose. Translated by Jacqueline Rose. New York: Norton.

———. 1988a. *The Seminar of Jacques Lacan. Book I: Freud's Papers on Technique, 1953–1954*. Edited by Jacques-Alain Miller. Translated by John Forrester. New York: Norton.

———. 1988b. Seminar on "The Purloined Letter." Translated by Jeffrey Mehlman. Pages 28–54 in *The Purloined Poe: Lacan, Derrida, and Psychoanalytic Reading*. Edited by John P. Muller and William J. Richardson. Baltimore: Johns Hopkins University Press.

———. 1990. Introduction to the Names-of-the-Father Seminar. Translated by Jeffrey Mehlman. Pages 81–95 in Jacques Lacan, *Television/A Challenge to the Psychoanalytic Establishment*. Edited by Joan Copjec. Translated by Denis Hollier et al. New York: Norton.

Laclau, Ernesto. 1995. Universalism, Particularism and the Question of Identity. Pages 93–108 in *The Identity in Question*. Edited by John Rajchman. London: Routledge.

LaCocque, André. 2007. The Deconstruction of Job's Fundamentalism. *JBL* 126:83–97.

Landy, Francis. 1983. *Paradoxes of Paradise: Identity and Difference in the Song of Songs*. Bible and Literature. Sheffield: Almond.

Lang, Candace. 1996. Autocritique. Pages 40–54 in Veeser 1996b.

Larmour, David H. J., Paul Allen Miller, and Charles Platter, eds. *Rethinking Sexuality: Foucault and Classical Antiquity*. Princeton: Princeton University Press.

Leclercq, Henri. 1907–53. Flagellation (Supplice de la). Pages 1638–43 in vol. 5 of *Dictionnaire d'archéologie chrétienne et de liturgie*. Edited by Fernand Cabrol and Henri Leclercq. Paris: Letouzey et Ané.

Leistyna, Pepi, ed. 2004. *Cultural Studies: From Theory to Action*. Oxford: Blackwell.

Lejeune, Philippe. 1989. *On Autobiography*. Edited by Paul John Eakin. Translated by Katherine Leary. Minneapolis: University of Minnesota Press

Lemaire, Anika. 1977. *Jacques Lacan*. Translated by David Macey. New York: Routledge & Kegan Paul.

Lentricchia, Frank. 1980. *After the New Criticism*. Chicago: University of Chicago Press.

———. 1989. Foucault's Legacy: A New Historicism? Pages 231–42 in Veeser 1989.

———. 1994. *The Edge of Night*. New York: Random House.

Léon-Dufour, Xavier. 1986. *Life and Death in the New Testament*. Translated by Terrence Prendergast. San Francisco: Harper & Row.

Levine, Amy-Jill. 1995. "Hemmed in on Every Side": Jews and Women in the Book of Susanna. Pages 175–90 in Segovia and Tolbert 1995a.
Liew, Tat-siong Benny. 1999. *Politics of Parousia: Reading Mark Inter(con)textually*. BibInt 42. Leiden: Brill.
Liew, Tat-siong Benny, and Gale A. Yee, eds. 2002. *The Bible in Asian America*. Semeia 90/91. Atlanta: Scholars Press.
Lightfoot, R. H. 1956. *St. John's Gospel*. Edited by C. F. Evans. Oxford: Oxford University Press.
Lincoln, Andrew T. 2000. *Truth on Trial: The Lawsuit Motif in the Fourth Gospel*. Peabody, Mass.: Hendrickson.
Lindars, Barnabas. 1972. *The Gospel of John*. NCBC. London: Marshall, Morgan & Scott.
Lindner, Helgo. 1972. *Die Geschichtsauffassung des Flavius Josephus im Bellum Judaicum: Gleichzeitig ein Beitrag zur Quellenfrage*. AGJU 12. Leiden: Brill.
Lingis, Alphonso. 1994. *Foreign Bodies*. London: Routledge.
Lionnet, Françoise. 1989. *Autobiographical Voices: Race, Gender, Self-Portraiture*. Ithaca, N.Y.: Cornell University Press.
Littledale, Richard Frederick. 1869. *A Commentary on the Song of Songs from Ancient and Mediaeval Sources*. London: Joseph Masters & Son.
Litz, A. Walton. 1961. *The Art of James Joyce: Method and Design in* Ulysses *and* Finnegans Wake. Oxford: Oxford University Press.
Lloyd, David. 1993. *Anomalous States: Irish Writing and the Postcolonial Moment*. Durham, N.C.: Duke University Press.
Lodge, David, ed. 1972. *Twentieth Century Literary Criticism*. London: Longman.
———. 1975. *Changing Places: A Tale of Two Campuses*. London: Secker & Warburg.
Lohfink, Gerhard. 1971. *Die Himmelfahrt Jesu: Untersuchungen zu den Himmelfahrtsund Erhöhungstexten bei Lukas*. Munich: Kösel-Verlag.
Loomba, Ania. 1998. *Colonialism/Postcolonialism*. New Critical Idiom. London: Routledge.
Lührmann, Dieter. 1987. *Das Markusevangelium*. HNT 3. Tübingen: Mohr Siebeck.
Lust, Johan, Erik Eynikel, and Katrin Hauspie, comps. 1992. *A Greek-English Lexicon of the Septuagint*. Vol. 1. Stuttgart: Deutsche Bibelgesellschaft.
Luther, Martin. 1963. *Lectures on Galatians, 1–4*. Vol. 26 of *Luther's Works*. Translated by Jaroslav Pelikan. St. Louis: Concordia. [German orig. 1535]
Lutz, Cora E. 1947. Musonius Rufus, "The Roman Socrates." *Yale Classical Studies* 10:3–147.
Lyotard, Jean-François. 1984. *The Postmodern Condition: A Report on Knowledge*. Translated by Geoff Bennington and Brian Massumi. Minneapolis: University of Minnesota Press.
Lyotard, Jean-François, and Eberhard Gruber. 1999. *The Hyphen: Between Judaism and Christianity*. Translated by Pascale-Anne Brault and Michael Naas. Philosophy and Literary Theory. Amherst, N.Y.: Humanity.
MacCannell, Juliet Flower. 1986. *Figuring Lacan: Criticism and the Cultural Unconscious*. Lincoln: University of Nebraska Press.
Machin, Richard, and Christopher Norris. 1987. Introduction. Pages 1–10 in *Post-*

structuralist Readings in English Poetry. Edited by Richard Machin and Christopher Norris. Cambridge: Cambridge University Press.

Mack, Burton L. 1988. *A Myth of Innocence: Mark and Christian Origins*. Philadelphia: Fortress.

MacKendrick, Karmen. 1999. *Counterpleasures*. SUNY Series in Postmodern Culture. New York: State University of New York Press.

MacKinnon, Catharine. 1989. *Toward a Feminist Theory of the State*. Cambridge: Harvard University Press.

———. 1992. Does Sexuality Have a History? Pages 117–36 in Stanton 1992.

Macksey, Richard, and Eugenio Donato, eds. 1970. *The Structuralist Controversy: The Languages of Criticism and the Sciences of Man*. Baltimore: Johns Hopkins University Press.

Malbon, Elizabeth Struthers. 1983. Fallible Followers: Women and Men in the Gospel of Mark. *Semeia* 28:29–48.

Maldonado, Robert D. 1995. Reading Malinche Reading Ruth: Toward a Hermeneutic of Betrayal. *Semeia* 72:91–110.

Malina, Bruce J., and Jerome H. Neyrey. 1991. Honor and Shame in Luke-Acts: Pivotal Values of the Mediterrainean World. Pages 25–66 in *The Social World of Luke-Acts: Models for Interpretation*. Edited by Jerome H. Neyrey. Peabody, Mass.: Hendrickson.

Malmede, Hans H. 1986. *Die Lichtsymbolik im Neuen Testament*. Wiesbaden: Harrassowitz.

Marcus, Laura. 1994. *Auto/Biographical Discourses: Theory, Criticism, Practice*. New York: St. Martin's.

Marks, Elaine, and Isabelle de Courtivron, eds. 1980. *New French Feminisms: An Anthology*. New York: Schocken.

Marrouchi, Mustapha. 2004. *Edward Said at the Limits*. Albany: State University of New York Press.

Marshall, I. Howard. 1978. *The Gospel of Luke: A Commentary on the Greek Text*. NIGTC. Grand Rapids: Eerdmans.

Martin, Dale B. 1990. *Slavery as Salvation: The Metaphor of Slavery in Pauline Christianity*. New Haven: Yale University Press.

———. 1995a. *The Corinthian Body*. New Haven: Yale University Press.

———. 1995b. Heterosexism and the Interpretation of Romans 1:18–32. *BibInt* 3:332–55.

Matarazzo, Mike. 1993. Pile It On! Thank God for the Offseason. *Flex* December: 21–24.

Matheson, Peter. 2000. *The Imaginative World of the Reformation*. Edinburgh: T&T Clark.

Matter, E. Ann. 1990. *The Voice of My Beloved: The Song of Songs in Western Medieval Christianity*. Philadelphia: University of Pennsylvania Press.

Mattila, Sharon Lea. 1996. Wisdom, Sense Perception, Nature, and Philo's Gender Gradient. *HTR* 89:103–29.

McClintock, Anne. 1995. *Imperial Leather: Race, Gender and Sexuality in the Colonial Contest*. London: Routledge.

McIntyre, John. 1992. *The Shape of Soteriology: Studies in the Doctrine of the Death of Christ*. Edinburgh: T&T Clark.

McKnight, Edgar V. 1988. *Postmodern Use of the Bible: The Emergence of Reader-Oriented Criticism*. Nashville: Abingdon.

McLaughlin, Thomas. 1990. Figurative Language. Pages 80–90 in *Critical Terms for Literary Study*. Edited by Frank Lentricchia and Thomas McLaughlin. Chicago: University of Chicago Press.

McNay, Lois. 1992. *Foucault and Feminism*. Boston: Northeastern University Press.

McQuillan, Martin, Graeme MacDonald, Robin Purves and Stephen Thomson. 1999. The Joy of Theory. Pages ix–xx in *Post-theory: New Directions in Criticism*. Edited by Martin McQuillan et al. Edinburgh: Edinburgh University Press.

Meyer, Marvin W. 1985. Making Mary Male: The Categories of "Male" and "Female" in the Gospel of Thomas. *NTS* 31:554–70.

Meyers, Carol. 1986. Gender Imagery in the Song of Songs. *Hebrew Annual Review* 10:209–23.

———. 1988. *Discovering Eve: Ancient Israelite Women in Context*. Oxford: Oxford University Press.

Milesi, Laurent, ed. 2003. *James Joyce and the Difference of Language*. Cambridge: Cambridge University Press.

Milgrom, Jacob. 1991. *Leviticus 1–16: A New Translation with Introduction and Commentary*. AB 3. New York: Doubleday.

Miller, D. A. 1992. *Bringing Out Roland Barthes*. Berkeley and Los Angeles: University of California Press.

Miller, James. 1993. *The Passion of Michel Foucault*. New York: Simon & Schuster.

Miller, James E. 1995. The Practices of Romans 1:26: Homosexual or Heterosexual? *NovT* 37:1–11.

Miller, J. Hillis. 1975. Deconstructing the Deconstructors. *Diacritics* 5:24–31.

———. 1987. The Triumph of Theory, the Resistance to Reading, and the Question of the Material Base. *PMLA* 102:281–291.

Miller, Nancy K. 1991. *Getting Personal: Feminist Occasions and Other Autobiographical Acts*. London: Routledge

Miller, Patricia Cox. 1992. The Devil's Gateway: An Eros of Difference in the Dreams of Perpetua. *Dreaming* 2:45–63.

Miller, Robert J., ed. 1995. *The Complete Gospels: Annotated Scholars Version*. San Francisco: HarperSanFrancisco.

Mitchell, W. J. T., ed. 2004. The Future of Criticism: A *Critical Inquiry* Symposium. *Critical Inquiry* 30:324–483.

Moberly, R W. L. 1983. *At the Mountain of God: Story and Theology in Exodus 32–34*. JSOTSup. 22. Sheffield: JSOT Press.

Moi, Toril. 1985. *Sexual/Textual Politics: Feminist Literary Theory*. New York: Methuen.

Montrose, Louis A. 1989. Professing the Renaissance: The Poetics and Politics of Culture. Pages 15–36 in Veeser 1989.

———. 1996. *The Purpose of Playing: Shakespeare and the Cultural Politics of the Elizabethan Theatre*. Chicago: University of Chicago Press.

Moo, Douglas. 1991. *Romans 1–8*. Wycliffe Exegetical Commentary. Chicago: Moody Press.

Moore, Stephen D. 1989. *Literary Criticism and the Gospels: The Theoretical Challenge*. New Haven: Yale University Press.

———. 1992. *Mark and Luke in Poststructuralist Perspectives: Jesus Begins to Write*. New Haven: Yale University Press.

———. 1994. *Poststructuralism and the New Testament: Derrida and Foucault at the Foot of the Cross*. Minneapolis: Fortress.

———. 1996. *God's Gym: Divine Male Bodies of the Bible*. London: Routledge.

———, ed. 1997. *The New Historicism*. *BibInt* 5:4 [thematic issue].

———. 1998a. Between Birmingham and Jerusalem: Biblical Studies and Culture Studies. Pages 1–32 in Moore 1998b.

———, ed. 1998b. *In Search of the Present: The Bible through Cultural Studies*. Semeia 82. Atlanta: Scholars Press.

———. 2001. *God's Beauty Parlor: And Other Queer Spaces in and around the Bible*. Contraversions: Jews and Other Differences. Stanford, Calif.: Stanford University Press.

———. 2006. *Empire and Apocalypse: Postcolonialism and the New Testament*. The Bible in the Modern World 12. Sheffield: Sheffield Phoenix.

———. 2007. Revelation. Pages 436–54 in *A Postcolonial Commentary on the New Testament Writings*. Edited by Fernando F. Segovia and R. S. Sugirtharajah. The Bible and Postcolonialism 13. New York: T&T Clark.

———. 2008. Afterword: Things Not Written in This Book. Pages 253–58 in *Anatomies of Narrative Criticism: The Past, Present, and Futures of the Fourth Gospel as Literature*. Edited by Tom Thatcher and Stephen D. Moore. SBLRBS 55. Atlanta: Society of Biblical Literature.

———. 2009. Metonymies of Empire: Sexual Humiliation and Gender Masquerade in the Book of Revelation. Pages 71–97 in *Postcolonial Interventions: Essays in Honor of R. S. Sugirtharajah*. Edited by Tat-siong Benny Liew. Sheffield: Sheffield Phoenix.

Moore, Stephen D., and Catherine Keller. 2005. Derridapocalypse. Pages 189–207 in *Derrida and Religion: Other Testaments*. Edited by Yvonne Sherwood and Kevin Hart. Chicago: University of Chicago Press.

Moore, Stephen D., and Yvonne Sherwood. 2010a. Biblical Studies "after" Theory: Onwards Towards the Past. Part One: After "After Theory," and Other Apocalyptic Conceits. *BibInt* 18:1–27.

———. 2010b. Biblical Studies "after" Theory: Onwards Towards the Past. Part Two: The Secret Vices of the Biblical God. *BibInt* 18:87–113.

———. 2010c. Biblical Studies "after" Theory: Onwards Towards the Past. Part Three: Theory in the First and Second Waves. *BibInt* 18.1:191–225.

Moore, Stephen D., and Janice Capel Anderson, eds. 2003. *New Testament Masculinities*. SemeiaSt 45. Atlanta: Society of Biblical Literature.

———. 2008. *Mark and Method: New Approaches in Biblical Studies*. 2nd ed. Minneapolis: Fortress.

Moore, Stephen D., and David Jobling, eds. 1991. *Poststructuralism as Exegesis. Semeia* 54. Atlanta: Scholars Press.
Moore, Stephen D., and Mayra Rivera, eds. 2010. *Planetary Loves: Spivak, Postcoloniality, and Theology.* Transdisciplinary Theological Colloquia. New York: Fordham University Press.
Moore, Stephen D., and Fernando F. Segovia, eds. 2005. *Postcolonial Biblical Criticism: Interdisciplinary Intersections.* The Bible and Postcolonialism 6. New York: T&T Clark International.
Moore-Gilbert, Bart. 1997. *Postcolonial Theory: Contexts, Practices, Politics.* London: Verso.
———. 2000. Spivak and Bhabha. Pages 451–66 in Schwarz and Ray 2000.
Moriarty, Michael. 1991. *Roland Barthes.* Stanford, Calif.: Stanford University Press.
Morton, Stephen. 2002. *Gayatri Chakravorty Spivak.* Routledge Critical Thinkers. London: Routledge.
———. 2007. *Gayatri Spivak: Ethics, Subalternity and the Critique of Postcolonial Reason.* Key Contemporary Thinkers. Cambridge: Polity.
Mosala, Itumeleng J. 1989. *Biblical Hermeneutics and Black Theology in South Africa.* Grand Rapids: Eerdmans.
Motyer, Stephen. 1997. *Your Father the Devil? A New Approach to John and "the Jews."* Carlisle: Paternoster.
Mowery, Robert L. 2002. Son of God in Roman Imperial Titles and Matthew. *Bib* 83:100–110.
Moxnes, Halvor. 1996. Honor and Shame. Pages 19–40 in *The Social Sciences and New Testament Interpretation.* Edited by Richard Rohrbaugh. Peabody, Mass.: Hendrickson.
Muecke, D. C. 1969. *The Compass of Irony.* London: Methuen.
Mukherjee, Aron P. 1991. Whose Post-colonialism and Whose Postmodernism? *World Literature Writers in English* 30:1–9.
Mulvey, Laura. 1975. Visual Pleasure and Narrative Cinema. *Screen* 16:6–18.
Murnaghan, Sheila. 1988. How a Woman Can Be More Like a Man: The Dialogue between Ischomachus and His Wife in Xenophon's *Oeconomicus*. *Helios* 15:9–22.
Murphy, Roland E. 1990. *The Song of Songs: A Commentary on the Book of Canticles or the Song of Songs.* Hermeneia. Minneapolis: Fortress.
Musurillo, Herbert, ed. and trans. 1961. *From Glory to Glory: Texts from Gregory of Nyssa's Mystical Writings.* New York: Charles Scribner's Sons.
Nancy, Jean-Luc. 2008. *Dis-Closure: The Deconstruction of Christianity.* Translated by Bettina Bergo et al. Perspectives in Continental Philosophy. New York: Fordham University Press.
Neusner, Jacob. 1985. *Genesis Rabbah: The Judaic Commentary to the Book of Genesis. A New American Translation.* 3 vols. BJS. Atlanta: Scholars Press.
Newman, Charles. 1985. *The Post-modern Aura: The Act of Fiction in an Age of Inflation.* Evanston, Ill.: Northwestern University Press.
Newsom, Carol A., and Sharon H. Ringe, eds. 1992. *The Women's Bible Commentary.* Louisville: Westminster John Knox.

Newton, Judith Louder. 1990. Historicisms New and Old: "Charles Dickens" Meets Marxism, Feminism, and West Coast Foucault. *Feminist Studies* 16:449–70.

Niditch, Susan. 1992. Genesis. Pages 10–25 in Newsom and Ringe 1992.

Nkrumah, Kwame. 1965. *Neo-Colonialism: The Last Stage of Imperialism*. London: Heinemann.

Nolland, John. 1989. *Luke 1–9:20*. WBC 35a. Dallas: Word.

North, Helen F. 1966. *Sophrosyne: Self-Knowledge and Self-Restraint in Greek Literature*. Cornell Studies in Classical Philology 35. Ithaca, N.Y.: Cornell University Press.

Nötscher, Friedrich. 1969. *"Das Angesicht Gottes schauen" nach biblischer und babylonischer Auffassung*. Darmstadt: Wissenschaftliche Buchgesellschaft.

Nuttall, Geoffrey F. 1978. *The Moment of Recognition: Luke as Story-Teller*. London: University of London/Athlone Press.

Nutu, Ela. 2007. *Incarnate Word, Inscribed Flesh: John's Prologue and the Postmodern*. The Bible in the Modern World 6. Sheffield: Sheffield Phoenix.

Nygren, Anders. 1949. *Commentary on Romans*. Translated by Carl C. Rasmussen. Philadelphia: Muhlenberg.

O'Day, Gail R. 1986. *Revelation in the Fourth Gospel: Narrative Mode and Theological Claim*. Philadelphia: Fortress.

———. 1992. John. Pages 381–93 in Newsom and Ringe 1992.

———. 1995. The Gospel of John: Introduction, Commentary, and Reflections. Pages 491–865 in *Luke; John*. Vol. 9 of *The New Interpreter's Bible*. Edited by Leander E. Keck. Nashville: Abingdon.

Okure, Teresa. 1988. *The Johnnnine Approach to Mission: A Contextual Study of John 4:1–42*. WUNT 2. Tübingen: Mohr Siebeck.

Olney, James. 1972. *Metaphors of Self: Meaning in Autobiography*. Princeton: Princeton University Press.

———, ed. 1980. *Autobiography: Essays Theoretical and Critical*. Princeton: Princeton University Press.

Olsson, Birger. 1974. *Structure and Meaning in the Fourth Gospel: A Text-Linguistic Analysis of John 2:1–11 and 4:1–42*. ConBNT 6. Lund: Gleerup.

Ong, Walter J. 1981. *The Presence of the Word: Some Prolegomena for Cultural and Religious History*. Minneapolis: University of Minnesota Press.

Oppenheim, A. Leo. 1977. *Ancient Mesopotamia: Portrait of a Dead Civilization*. 2nd ed. Chicago: University of Chicago Press.

Origen. 1957. *The Song of Songs: Commenary and Homilies*. Translated by R. P. Lawson. Ancient Christian Writers: The Works of the Fathers in Translation 26. London: Longmans, Green.

Ostriker, Alicia. 2000. A Holy of Holies: The Song of Songs as Countertext. Pages 36–54 in Brenner and Fontaine 2000.

Owens, Craig. 1983. The Discourse of Others: Feminists and Postmodernism. Pages 57–82 in Foster 1983.

Pack, Roger. 1955. Artemidoros and His Waking World. *Transactions and Proceedings of the American Philological Association* 86:280–90.

Paglia, Camille. 1992. Alice in Muscle Land. Pages 79–82 in idem, *Sex, Art, and American Culture: Essays.* New York: Vintage.
Pardes, Ilana. 1992. *Countertraditions in the Bible: A Feminist Approach.* Cambridge: Harvard University Press.
Parker, Holt N. 1997. The Teratogenic Grid. Pages 47–65 in Hallett and Skinner 1997.
Parry, Benita. 2004. *Postcolonial Studies: A Materialist Critique.* London: Routledge.
Parsons, Mikeal C. 1995. Hand in Hand: Autobiographical Reflections on Luke 15. *Semeia* 72:125–52.
Patai, Daphne, and Will H. Corral. 2005a. Introduction. Pages 1–18 in Patai and Corral 2005b.
———, eds. 2005b. *Theory's Empire: An Anthology of Dissent.* New York: Columbia University Press.
Patte, Daniel. 1995a. Acknowledging the Contextual Character of Male, European-American Critical Exegeses: An Androcritical Perspective. Pages 35–55 in Segovia and Tolbert 1995a.
———. 1995b. *Ethics of Biblical Interpretation: A Reevaluation.* Louisville: Westminster John Knox.
———, et al., eds. 2004. *Global Bible Commentary.* Nashville: Abingdon.
Paul, Diana Y. 1979. *Women in Buddhism: Images of the Feminine in the Mahāyāna Tradition.* Berkeley, Calif.: Asian Humanities.
Perloff, Marjorie. 2007. Presidential Address 2006: It Must Change. *PMLA* 122:652–62.
Perreault, Jeanne. 1995. *Writing Selves: Contemporary Feminist Autobiography.* Minneapolis: University of Minnesota Press.
Personal Narratives Group, eds. 1989. *Interpreting Women's Lives: Feminist Theory and Personal Narratives.* Bloomington: Indiana University Press.
Pesch, Rudolf. 1986. *Die Apostelgeschichte.* 2 vols. EKKNT 5. Zurich: Benziger; Neukirchen-Vluyn: Neukirchener.
Peters, Edward. 1985. *Torture.* Oxford: Blackwell.
Pfitzner, Victor C. 1967. *Paul and the Agon Motif: Traditional Athletic Imagery in the Pauline Literature.* NovTSup 16. Leiden: Brill.
Phillips, Gary A. 1988. The Authority of Exegesis and the Responsibility of the Critic: The Ethics and Ethos of Criticism. Paper presented at the AAR/SBL Annual Meeting, Chicago.
———. 1989. Biblical Exegesis in the Postmodern Age: Hearing Different Voices and Rethinking Critical Practice. Paper presented at the Westar Institute Spring Meeting, Sonoma, Calif.
———. 1990a. Exegesis as Critical Praxis: Reclaiming History and Text from a Postmodern Perspective. *Semeia* 51:7–50.
———, ed. 1990b. *Poststructural Criticism and the Bible: Text/History/Discourse.* Semeia 51. Atlanta: Scholars Press.
———. 1994. The Ethics of Reading Deconstructively, or Speaking Face-to-Face: The Samaritan Woman Meets Derrida at the Well. Pages 283–325 in *The New Literary Criticism of the New Testament.* Edited by Elizabeth Struthers Malbon and Edgar McKnight. Sheffield: Sheffield Academic Press.

Phy, Allene Stuart, ed. 1985. *The Bible and Popular Culture in America*. The Bible in American Culture 2. Philadelphia: Fortress; Chico, Calif.: Scholars Press.

Pippin, Tina. 1999. *Apocalyptic Bodies: The Biblical End of the World in Text and Image*. Biblical Limits. London: Routledge.

Plate, S. Brent, ed. 2004. *Re-viewing the Passion: Mel Gibson's Film and Its Critics*. New York: Palgrave Macmillan.

Plevnik, Joseph. 1993. Honor/Shame. Pages 95–103 in *Biblical Social Values and Their Meanings: A Handbook*. Edited by John J. Pilch and Bruce J. Malina. Peabody, Mass.: Hendrickson.

Plummer, Alfred. 1922. *A Critical and Exegetical Commentary on the Gospel according to St. Luke*. 5th ed. ICC. New York: Scribner.

Plunkett, Regina St. G. 1988. The Samaritan Woman: Partner in Revelation. Paper presented at the New England Regional Meeting of the Society of Biblical Literature, Boston.

Polaski, Donald. 1997. What Will Ye See in the Shulamite? Women, Power, and Panopticism in the Song of Songs. *BibInt* 5:64–81.

Polaski, Sandra Hack. 1999. *Paul and the Discourse of Power*. The Biblical Seminar 62; Gender, Culture, Theory 8. Sheffield: Sheffield Academic Press.

Pomeroy, Sarah B. 1994. *Xenophon*, Oeconomicus: *A Social and Historical Commentary with a New English Translation*. Oxford: Clarendon.

Pope, Marvin H. 1977. *Song of Songs: A New Translation with Introduction and Commentary*. AB 7C. Garden City, N.Y.: Doubleday.

Porsch, Felix. 1974. *Pneuma und Wort: Ein exegetischer Beitrag zur Pneumatologie des Johannesevangeliums*. Frankfurter theologische Studien 16. Frankfurt: Knecht.

Powell, Mark Allan. 2009. Literary Approaches and the Gospel of Matthew. Pages 44–82 in *Methods for Matthew*. Edited by Mark Allan Powell. Methods in Biblical Interpretation. Cambridge: Cambridge University Press.

Price, Robert M. 2000. *Deconstructing Jesus*. Amherst, N.Y.: Prometheus.

Quayson, Ato. 2000. Postcolonialism and Postmodernism. Pages 87–111 in Schwarz and Ray 2000.

Rabaté, Jean-Michel. 2002. *The Future of Theory*. Oxford: Blackwell.

Rad, Gerhard von. 1972. *Genesis: A Commentary*. Translated by John H. Marks. OTL. Philadelphia: Westminster.

radicallesbians. 2004. The Woman-Identified Woman [Orig. 1970]. Pages 239–41 in *Feminist Theory: A Reader*. Edited by Wendy Kolmar and Frances Bartkowski. 2nd ed. Mountain View, Calif.: Mayfield.

Radl, Walter. 1975. *Paulus und Jesus im lukanischen Doppelwerk: Untersuchungen zu Parallelmotiven im Lukasevangelium und in der Apostelgeschichte*. Bern: Herbert Lang; Frankfurt: Peter Lang.

Ragland-Sullivan, Ellie. 1986. *Jacques Lacan and the Philosophy of Psychoanalysis*. Urbana: University of Illinois Press.

Rajak, Tessa. 1983. *Josephus: The Historian and His Society*. London: Duckworth.

Rajan, Rajeswari Sunder. 1997. The Third World Academic in Other Places; or, the Postcolonial Intellectual Revisited. *Critical Inquiry* 23:596–616.

Rajchman, John. 1988. Foucault's Art of Seeing. *October* 44:89–117.

Rambuss, Richard. 1998. *Closet Devotions*. Durham, N.C.: Duke University Press.
Redditt, Paul L. 1983. The Concept of *Nomos* in Fourth Maccabees. *CBQ* 45:249-70.
Reindl, Joseph. 1970. *Das Angesicht Gottes im sprachgebrauch des Alten Testaments*. Leipzig: St. Benno-Verlag.
Reinhartz, Adele. 2001. *Befriending the Beloved Disciple: A Jewish Reading of the Gospel of John*. New York: Continuum.
———. 2002. The Colonizer as Colonized: Intertextual Dialogue between the Gospel of John and Canadian Identity. Pages 170-92 in Dube and Staley 2002b.
Reiss, Timothy. 1982. *The Discourse of Modernism*. Ithaca, N.Y.: Cornell University Press.
Renehan, Robert. 1972. The Greek Philosophical Background of Fourth Maccabees. *Rheinisches Museum für Philologie* 115:232-38.
Rengstorf, Karl Heinrich. 1971. Sēmeion, Sēmainō, Sēmeioō, Asēmos, Episēmos, Eusēmos, Sussēmon. Pages 200-269 in vol. 7 of *Theological Dictionary of the New Testament*. Edited by Gerhard Friedrich. Translated by Geoffrey W. Bromiley. Grand Rapids: Eerdmans.
Rensberger, David. 1984. The Politics of John: The Trial of Jesus in the Fourth Gospel. *JBL* 103:395-411.
———. 1988. *Johannine Faith and Liberating Community*. Philadelphia: Westminster.
Rich, Adrienne. 1986. Compulsory Heterosexuality and Lesbian Existence [Orig. 1980]. Pages 23-75 in idem, *Blood, Bread, and Poetry: Selected Prose 1979-1985*. New York: Norton.
Richardson, Diane, ed. 1996. *Theorising Heterosexuality: Telling It Straight*. London: Taylor & Francis.
Riches, John, and David C. Sim, eds. 2005. *The Gospel of Matthew in Its Roman Imperial Context*. New York: T&T Clark.
Richlin, Amy. 1991. Zeus and Metis: Foucault, Feminism, Classics. *Helios* 18:160-80.
———. 1992. *The Garden of Priapus: Sexuality and Aggression in Roman Humor*. 2nd ed. London: Routledge.
———. 1993. Not before Homosexuality: The Materiality of the *Cinaedus* and the Roman Law against Love between Men. *Journal of the History of Sexuality* 3:523-73.
———. 1997a. Gender and Rhetoric: Producing Manhood in the Schools. Pages 90-110 in *Roman Eloquence: Rhetoric in Society and Literature*. Edited by William J. Dominik. London: Routledge.
———. 1997b. Pliny's Brassiere. Pages 197-220 in Hallett and Skinner 1997.
———. 1998. Foucault's *History of Sexuality*: A Useful Theory for Women? Pages 138-70 in Larmour, Miller, and Platter 1998.
Ricks, Christopher. 2004. *Dylan's Visions of Sin*. New York: Ecco.
Riddel, Joseph. 1975. A Miller's Tale. *Diacritics* 5:56-65.
Ridderbos, Herman N. 1997. *The Gospel according to John: A Theological Commentary*. Translated by John Vriend. Grand Rapids: Eerdmans.
Riquelme, John Paul. 1991. *Harmony of Dissonances: T. S. Eliot, Romanticism, and Imagination*. Baltimore: Johns Hopkins University Press.
Robinson, James M., ed. 1988. *The Nag Hammadi Library in English*. San Francisco: HarperSanFrancisco.

Robinson, John A. T. 1952. *The Body: A Study in Pauline Theology*. Studies in Pauline Theology 5. London: SCM.

Rose, Jacqueline. 1982. Introduction. Pages 27–57 in Lacan 1982b.

———. 1986. *Sexuality in the Field of Vision*. London: Verso.

Rosendale, Steven, ed. 2002. *The Greening of Literary Scholarship: Literature, Theory, and the Environment*. Iowa City: University of Iowa Press.

Ross, Marlon B. 1990. Contingent Predilections: The Newest Historicisms and the Question of Method. *The Centennial Review* 34:485–538.

Roudinesco, Elisabeth. 1990. *Jacques Lacan & Co.: A History of Psychoanalysis in France, 1925–1985*. Translated by Jeffrey Mehlman. Chicago: University of Chicago Press.

Roughead, William. 1931. *Bad Companions*. New York: Duffield & Green.

Rowley, H. H. 1952. The Interpretation of the Song of Songs. Pages 189–234 in idem, *The Servant of the Lord and Other Essays*. London: Lutterworth.

Royle, Nicholas. 1995. *After Derrida*. Manchester: Manchester University Press.

———, ed. 2000. *Deconstructions: A User's Guide*. New York: Palgrave Macmillan.

Runions, Erin. 2002. *Changing Subjects: Gender, Nation and Future in Micah*. Playing the Texts 7. Sheffield: Sheffield Academic Press.

———. 2003. *How Hysterical: Identification and Resistance in the Bible and Film*. New York: Palgrave Macmillan.

Rutledge, David. 1996. *Reading Marginally: Feminism, Deconstruction, and the Bible*. BibInt 21. Leiden: Brill.

Sáez, Ñacuñán. 1992. Torture: A Discourse on Practice. Pages 126–44 in *Tattoo, Torture, Mutilation, and Adornment: The Denaturalization of the Body in Culture and Text*. Edited by Frances E. Mascia-Lees and Patricia Sharpe. SUNY Series on the Body in Culture, History, and Religion. Albany: State University of New York Press.

Said, Edward W. 1978a. *Orientalism*. New York: Vintage.

———. 1978b. The Problem of Textuality: Two Exemplary Positions. *Critical Inquiry* 4:673–714. Reprinted in revised form in Said 1983, 178–225.

———. 1983. *The World, the Text, and the Critic*. Cambridge: Harvard University Press.

———. 1986. Orientalism Reconsidered. Pages 210–29 in *Literature, Politics and Theory*. Edited by Francis Barker et al. London: Methuen.

———. 1993. *Culture and Imperialism*. New York: Vintage.

———. 1997. Orientalism and Beyond. Pages 34–73 in *Postcolonial Criticism*. Edited by Bart Moore-Gilbert, Gareth Stanton, and Willy Maley. London: Longman.

———. 2000. Michel Foucault, 1927–1984. Pages 187–97 in idem, *Reflections on Exile and Other Essays*. Cambridge: Harvard University Press.

———. 2002. In Conversation with Neeladri Bhattacharya, Suvir Kaul, and Ania Loomba. Pages 1–14 in Goldberg and Quayson 2002.

Samuel, Simon. 2002. The Beginning of Mark: A Colonial/Postcolonial Conundrum. *BibInt* 10:405–19.

———. 2007. *A Postcolonial Reading of Mark's Story of Jesus*. Library of New Testament Studies 340. New York: T&T Clark.

Sanday, William, and Arthur C. Headlam. 1895. *A Critical and Exegetical Commentary on the Epistle to the Romans*. ICC. Edinburgh: T&T Clark.

Sanders, E. P. 1985. *Jesus and Judaism*. Philadelphia: Fortress.

———. 1993. *The Historical Figure of Jesus*. New York: Penguin.

Sanders, Mark. 2006. *Gayatri Chakravorty Spivak: Live Theory*. New York: Continuum.

Sandmel, Samuel. 1971. *Philo's Place in Judaism: A Study of Conceptions of Abraham in Jewish Literature*. New York: Ktav.

———. 1978. *Judaism and Christian Beginnings*. Oxford: Oxford University Press.

Sandys, George. 1615. *A Relation of a Journey Begun An. Dom. 1610: Fovre bookes. Containing a description of the Turkish Empire, of Aegypt, of the Holy Land, of the remote parts of Italy, and ilands adioyning*. London: Allot.

Sarna, Nahum M. 1989. *Genesis/Berēšit: The Traditional Hebrew Text with the New JPS Translation*. The JPS Torah Commentary. Philadelphia: Jewish Publication Society.

Sarracoll, M. John. 1903–5. *The Voyage Set Out by the Right Honourable the Earle of Cumberland, in the Yere 1586. Written by M. John Sarracoll Marchant in the Same Voyage*. Edited by Richard Hakluyt. Vol. 11 of *The Principal Navigations, Voyages, Traffiques & Discoveries of the English Nation*. Glasgow: James MacLehose & Sons.

Sarup, Madan. 1993. *An Introductory Guide to Post-structuralism and Postmodernism*. 2nd ed. Athens: University of Georgia Press.

Satlow, Michael L. 1994. "They Abused Him Like a Woman": Homoeroticism, Gender Blurring, and the Rabbis in Late Antiquity. *Journal of the History of Sexuality* 5:1–25.

———. 1995. *Tasting the Dish: Rabbinic Rhetorics of Sexuality*. BJS 303. Atlanta: Scholars Press.

———. 1996. "Try to Be a Man": The Rabbinic Construction of Masculinity. *HTR* 89:19–40.

———. 1997. Jewish Constructions of Nakedness in Late Antiquity. *JBL* 116:429–54.

Scarry, Elaine. 1985. *The Body in Pain: The Making and Unmaking of the World*. Oxford: Oxford University Press.

Schäfer, Peter. 1988a. *Hekhalot-Studien*. Tübingen: Mohr Siebeck.

———. 1988b. *Shi'ur Qoma*: Rezensionen und Urtext. Pages 75–83 in Schäfer 1988a.

———. 1988c. Zum Problem der redaktionellen Identität der Hekhalot Rabbati. Pages 63–74 in Schäfer 1988a.

Schlier, Heinrich. 1956. Jesus und Pilatus nach dem Johannesevangelium [Orig. 1941]. Pages 56–74 in idem, *Die Zeit der Kirche: Exegetische Aufsätze und Vorträge*. 4th ed. Freiburg: Herder.

———. 1968. The State according to the New Testament. Pages 215–38 in idem, *The Relevance of the New Testament*. Translated by W. J. O'Hara. Freiburg: Herder & Herder.

Schnackenburg, Rudolf. 1968. *The Gospel according to St. John*. Vol. 1. Translated by Kevin Smyth and Cecily Hastings. Herder's Theological Commentary on the New Testament. New York: Herder & Herder.

———. 1982. *The Gospel according to St. John*. Vol. 3. Translated by David Smith and G. A. Kon. Herder's Theological Commentary on the New Testament. New York: Herder & Herder.
Schneiderman, Stuart. 1983. *Jacques Lacan: The Death of an Intellectual Hero*. Cambridge: Harvard University Press.
Schneiders, Sandra M. 1991. *The Revelatory Text: Interpreting the New Testament as Sacred Scripture*. San Francisco: HarperCollins.
Scholem, Gershom. 1965. *Jewish Gnosticism, Merkabah Mysticism, and Talmudic Tradition*. 2nd ed. New York: Jewish Theological Seminary of America.
———. 1971. *Major Trends in Jewish Mysticism*. 3rd ed. New York: Schocken.
———. 1987. *Origins of the Kabbalah*. Edited by R. J. Zwi Werblowsky. Translated by Allan Arkush. Philadelphia: Jewish Publication Society; Princeton: Princeton University Press.
Schor, Noami. 1995. French Feminism Is a Universalism. *differences* 7:15–47.
Schubert, Paul. 1954. The Structure and Significance of Luke 24. Pages 165–86 in *Neutestamentliche Studien für Rudolf Bultmann, zu seinem siebzigsten Geburtstag*. Edited by Walther Eltester. Berlin: Topelmann.
Schürmann, Heinz. 1969. *Das Lukasevangelium. I. Teil: Kommentar zu 1.1–9.50*. HTKNT 3.1. Freiburg: Herder.
Schüssler Fiorenza, Elisabeth. 1983. *In Memory of Her: A Feminist Theological Reconstruction of Christian Origins*. New York: Crossroad.
———. 1984. *Bread Not Stone: The Challenge of Feminist Biblical Interpretation*. Boston: Beacon.
———. 1988. The Ethics of Biblical Interpretation: Decentering Biblical Scholarship. *JBL* 107:3–17.
———, ed. 1994. *A Feminist Commentary*. Vol. 2 of *Searching the Scriptures*. New York: Crossroad.
Schuster, Nancy. 1981. Changing the Female Body: Wise Women and the Bodhisattva Career in Some *Maharatnakutasutras*. *Journal of the International Association of Buddhist Studies* 4:24–69.
Schwan, Alexander. 1976. *Geschichtstheologie Konstitution und Destruktion der Politik: Friedrich Gogarten und Rudolf Bultmann*. Berlin: de Gruyter.
Schwartz, Regina M. 1992. Nations and Nationalism: Adultery in the House of David. *Critical Inquiry* 19:131–50.
Schwarz, Henry, and Sangeeta Ray, eds. 2000. *A Companion to Postcolonial Studies*. Blackwell Companions in Cultural Studies. Oxford: Blackwell.
Schweitzer, Albert. 1968. *The Quest of the Historical Jesus: A Critical Study of Its Progress from Reimarus to Wrede*. Translated by W. Montgomery. New York: Macmillan. [German orig. 1906]
Schwoch, James, Mimi White, and Dilip Gaonkar, eds. 2005. *The Question of Method in Cultural Studies*. Oxford: Blackwell.
Scott, Joan W. 1995. Universalism and the History of Feminism. *differences* 7:1–14.
———. 2004. French Universalism in the Nineties. *differences* 15:32–53.
Sedgwick, Eve Kosofsky. 1990. *Epistemology of the Closet*. Berkeley and Los Angeles: University of California Press.

———. 1993. *Tendencies*. Durham, N.C.: Duke University Press.
———. 1995. Gosh, Boy George, You Must Be Awfully Secure in Your Masculinity! Pages 11–20 in *Constructing Masculinity*. Edited by Maurice Berger, Brian Wallis, and Simon Watson. London: Routledge.
Seeley, David. 1990. *The Noble Death: Graeco-Roman Martyrology and Paul's Concept of Salvation*. JSNTSup 28. Sheffield: Sheffield Academic Press.
———. 1994. *Deconstructing the New Testament*. BibInt 5. Leiden: Brill.
Segovia, Fernando F. 1995a. "And They Began to Speak in Other Tongues": Competing Modes of Discourse in Contemporary Biblical Criticism. Pages 1–32 in Segovia and Tolbert 1995a.
———. 1995b. Cultural Studies and Contemporary Biblical Criticism: Ideological Criticism as Mode of Discourse. Pages 1–17 in Segovia and Tolbert 1995b.
———. 1995c. Toward a Hermeneutics of the Diaspora: A Hermeneutics of Otherness and Engagement. Pages 57–73 in Segovia and Tolbert 1995a.
———. 2000. *Decolonizing Biblical Studies: A View from the Margins*. Maryknoll, N.Y.: Orbis.
Segovia, Fernando F., and Mary Ann Tolbert, eds. 1995a. *Social Location and Biblical Interpretation in the United States*. Vol. 1 of *Reading from This Place*. Minneapolis: Fortress.
———. 1995b. *Social Location and Biblical Interpretation in Global Perspective*. Vol. 2 of *Reading from This Place*. Minneapolis: Fortress.
Segovia, Fernando F., and R. S. Sugirtharajah, eds. 2007. *A Postcolonial Commentary on the New Testament Writings*. The Bible and Postcolonialism 13. New York: T&T Clark.
Setel, T. Drorah. 1985. Prophets and Pornography: Female Sexual Imagery in Hosea. Pages 86–95 in *Feminist Interpretation of the Bible*. Edited by Letty M. Russell. Philadelphia: Westminster.
Shapin, Steven. 1994. *A Social History of Truth: Civility and Science in Seventeenth-Century England*. Chicago: University of Chicago Press.
Shapiro, Barbara. 1994. The Concept "Fact": Legal Origins and Cultural Diffusion. *Albion* 26: 227–52.
Shaw, Brent D. 1996. Body/Power/Identity: Passions of the Martyrs. *JECS* 4:269–312.
Sheehan, Jonathan. 2004. *The Enlightenment Bible: Translation, Scholarship, Culture*. Princeton: Princeton University Press.
Sherwood, Yvonne. 1996. *The Prostitute and the Prophet: Hosea's Marriage in Literary-Theoretical Perspective*. Sheffield: Sheffield Academic Press. Repr. as *The Prostitute and the Prophet: Reading Hosea in the Late Twentieth Century*. New York: T&T Clark International, 2004.
———. 2001. Of Fruit and Corpses and Wordplay Visions: Picturing Amos 8.1–3. *JSOT* 92:5–27.
———. 2004a. Introduction: Derrida's Bible. Pages 1–20 in Sherwood 2004b.
———, ed. 2004b. *Derrida's Bible (Reading a Page of Scripture with a Little Help from Derrida)*. New York: Palgrave Macmillan.
Siewert, Francis E., ed. 1958. *Amplified New Testament*. Grand Rapids: Zondervan.

Sim, David C. 2009. Matthew and the Pauline Corpus: A Preliminary Intertextual Study. *JSNT* 31:401–22.
Simms, George Otto. 1988. *Exploring the Book of Kells*. Dublin: O'Brien.
Simpson, David. 1996. Speaking Personally: The Culture of Autobiographical Criticism. Pages 82–94 in Veeser 1996b.
Simpson, Mark. 1994. *Male Impersonators: Men Performing Masculinity*. London: Routledge.
Skinner, Marilyn B. 1993. *Ego Mulier*: The Construction of Male Sexuality in Catullus. *Helios* 20:107–30.
———. 1996. Zeus and Leda: The Sexuality Wars in Contemporary Classical Scholarship. *Thamyris* 3:103–23.
———. 1997. Introduction: *Quod multo fit aliter in Graecia*. Pages 1–25 in Hallett and Skinner 1997.
Sly, Dorothy. 1990. *Philo's Perception of Women*. BJS 209. Atlanta: Scholars Press.
Smart, Carol. 1996. Collusion, Collaboration and Confession: On Moving beyond the Heterosexuality Debate. Pages 161–77 in Richardson 1996.
Smith, Abraham. 1999. "Full of Spirit and Wisdom": Luke's Portrait of Stephen (Acts 6:1–8:1a) as a Man of Self-Mastery. Pages 97–114 in *Asceticism and the New Testament*. Edited by Leif E. Vaage and Vincent L. Wimbush. London: Routledge.
Smith, James A. 2005. *Marks of an Apostle: Deconstruction, Philippians, and Problematizing Pauline Theology*. SemeiaSt 53. Atlanta: Society of Biblical Literature.
Smith, Robert. 1995. *Derrida and Autobiography*. Cambridge: Cambridge University Press.
Smith, Sidonie. 1987. *The Poetics of Women's Autobiography: Marginality and the Fictions of Self-Representation*. Bloomington: Indiana University Press.
Smith, Sidonie, and Julia Watson, eds. 1992. *De/Colonizing the Subject: The Politics of Gender in Women's Autobiography*. Minneapolis: University of Minnesota Press.
Smith-Christopher, Daniel, ed. 1995. *Text and Experience: Towards a Cultural Exegesis of the Bible*. The Biblical Seminar 35. Sheffield: Sheffield Academic Press.
Sontag, Susan. 1973. *On Photography*. New York: Penguin.
South, James T. 1992. *Disciplinary Practices in Pauline Texts*. Lewiston, N.Y.: Mellen.
Spanos, William V. 1987. *Repetitions: The Postmodern Occasion in Literature and Culture*. Baton Rouge: Louisiana State University Press.
Spengemann, William. 1980. *The Forms of Autobiography: Episodes in the History of a Literary Genre*. New Haven: Yale University Press.
Spivak, Gayatri Chakravorty. 1985. Three Women's Texts and a Critique of Imperialism. *Critical Inquiry* 12: 243–61.
———. 1988a. Can the Subaltern Speak? Pages 271–313 in *Marxism and the Interpretation of Culture*. Edited by Cary Nelson and Larry Grossberg. Urbana: University of Illinois Press.
———. 1988b. *In Other Worlds: Essays in Cultural Politics*. London: Routledge. [Orig. 1987]
———. 1990a. The New Historicism, Political Commitment and the Postmodern Critic [with Harold Veeser]. Pages 152–68 in Spivak 1990b.

———. 1990b. *The Post-colonial Critic: Interviews, Strategies, Dialogues*. Edited by Sarah Harasym. London: Routledge.

———. 1999. *A Critique of Postcolonial Reason: Toward a History of the Vanishing Present*. Cambridge: Harvard University Press.

———. 2005. Touched by Deconstruction. *Grey Room* 1:95–104.

Stanton, Domna, ed. 1992. *Discourses of Sexuality: From Aristotle to AIDS*. Ann Arbor: University of Michigan Press.

Stanton, Elizabeth Cady. 1895–98. *The Woman's Bible*. 2 vols. New York: European Publishing Company.

Staley, Jeffrey Lloyd. 1988. *The Print's First Kiss: A Rhetorical Investigation of the Implied Reader in the Fourth Gospel*. SBLDS 82. Atlanta: Scholars Press.

———. 1995. *Reading with a Passion: Rhetoric, Autobiography, and the American West in the Gospel John*. New York: Continuum.

Stanley, Liz. 1992. *The Auto/Biographical I: The Theory and Practice of Feminist Auto/Biography*. New York: St. Martin's.

Stern, David. 1991. *Parables in Midrash: Narrative and Exegesis in Rabbinic Literature*. Cambridge: Harvard University Press.

Sternberg, Meir. 1978. *Expositional Modes and Temporal Ordering in Fiction*. Baltimore: Johns Hopkins University Press.

Storey, John, ed. 1996. *What Is Cultural Studies? A Reader*. London: Arnold.

———. 2003. *Cultural Studies and the Study of Popular Culture*. 2nd ed. Athens: University of Georgia Press.

Stout, Jeffrey. 1987. A Lexicon of Postmodern Philosophy. *RSR* 13:18–22.

Stowers, Stanley K. 1988. 4 Maccabees. Pages 922–34 in *Harper's Bible Commentary*. Edited by James L. Mays. San Francisco: Harper & Row.

———. 1994. *A Rereading of Romans: Justice, Jews, and Gentiles*. New Haven: Yale University Press.

Sturrock, John. 1979. Roland Barthes. Pages 52–80 in *Structuralism and Since: From Lévi-Strauss to Derrida*. Edited by John Sturrock. Oxford: Oxford University Press.

Sugirtharajah, R. S., ed. 1991. *Voices from the Margin: Interpreting the Bible in the Third World*. Maryknoll, N.Y.: Orbis.

———. 1998a. *Asian Biblical Hermeneutics and Postcolonialism: Contesting the Interpretations*. Maryknoll, N.Y.: Orbis.

———, ed. 1998b. *The Postcolonial Bible*. The Bible and Postcolonialism 1. Sheffield: Sheffield Academic Press.

———, ed. 1999a. *Postcolonial Perspectives on the New Testament and Its Interpretation*. *JSNT* 73 [thematic issue].

———, ed. 1999b. *Vernacular Hermeneutics*. The Bible and Postcolonialism 2. Sheffield: Sheffield Academic Press.

———. 2001. *The Bible and the Third World: Precolonial, Colonial and Postcolonial Encounters*. Cambridge: Cambridge University Press.

———. 2002. *Postcolonial Criticism and Biblical Interpretation*. Oxford: Oxford University Press.

———. 2003. *Postcolonial Reconfigurations: An Alternative Way of Reading the Bible and Doing Theology*. St. Louis: Chalice.

———. 2005a. *The Bible and Empire: Postcolonial Explorations*. Cambridge: Cambridge University Press.

———, ed. 2005b. *The Postcolonial Biblical Reader*. Oxford: Blackwell.

———, ed. 2008. *Still at the Margins: Biblical Scholarship Fifteen Years after* Voices from the Margin. New York: T&T Clark.

Sullivan, Sir Edward. 1920. *The Book of Kells*. London: The Studio.

Tasker, Yvonne. 1993. *Spectacular Bodies: Gender, Genre and the Action Cinema*. London: Routledge.

Taubes, Jacob. 2004. *The Political Theology of Paul*. Translated by Dana Hollander. Cultural Memory in the Present. Stanford, Calif.: Stanford University Press.

Taylor, Mark C. 1984. *Erring: A Postmodern A/theology*. Chicago: University of Chicago Press.

———. 1987. *Altarity*. Chicago: University of Chicago Press.

Telford, William R. 1980. *The Barren Temple and the Withered Tree*. JSNTSup 1. Sheffield: JSOT Press.

Thiong'o, Ngugi wa. 1986. *Decolonising the Mind: The Politics of Language in African Literature*. London: James Curry.

Thomas, Calvin, ed. 2000. *Straight with a Twist: Queer Theory and the Subject of Heterosexuality*. Urbana: University of Illinois Press.

Thompson, F. H. 2003. *The Archaeology of Greek and Roman Slavery*. London: Duckworth.

Thurman, Eric. 2003. Looking for a Few Good Men: Mark and Masculinity. Pages 137–62 in Moore and Anderson 2003.

Tiffin, Helen. 1988. Post-colonialism, Post-modernism and the Rehabilitation of Postcolonial History. *Journal of Commonwealth Literature* 23:169–81.

Tilley, Maureen A. 1994. The Passion of Perpetua and Felicity. Pages 829–58 in Schüssler Fiorenza 1994.

Tindall, William. 1959. *A Reader's Guide to James Joyce*. London: Thames & Hudson.

Todorov, Tzvetan. 1981. *Introduction to Poetics*. Translated by Richard Howard. Minneapolis: University of Minnesota Press.

Tolbert, Mary Ann. 1989. *Sowing the Gospel: Mark's World in Literary-Historical Perspective*. Minneapolis: Fortress.

Tompkins, Jane P., ed. 1980. *Reader-Response Criticism: From Formalism to Post-Structuralism*. Baltimore: Johns Hopkins University Press.

———. 1993. Me and My Shadow. Pages 23–40 in Freedman, Frey, and Zauhar 1993.

———. 1996a. Let's Get Lost. Pages 268–81 in Veeser 1996b.

———. 1996b. *A Life in School: What the Teacher Learned*. New York: Perseus.

Torgovnick, Marianna de Marco. 1994. *Crossing Ocean Parkway: Readings by an Italian American Daughter*. Chicago: University of Chicago Press.

Townshend, R. B. 1913. The Fourth Book of Maccabees. Pages 653–85 in vol. 2 of *Apocrypha and Pseudepigrapha of the Old Testament*. Edited by R. H. Charles. Oxford: Clarendon.

Trible, Phyllis. 1976. God, Nature of, in the OT. Pages 368–69 in the supplementary volume of *The Interpreter's Dictionary of the Bible*. Edited by Keith Crim et al. Nashville: Abingdon.

———. 1978a. *God and the Rhetoric of Sexuality*. OBT. Philadelphia: Fortress.

———. 1978b. A Love Story Gone Awry. Pages 72–143 in Trible 1978a.

———. 1978c. Love's Lyrics Redeemed. Pages 144–65 in Trible 1978a.

———. 1984. *Texts of Terror*. OBT 13. Philadelphia: Fortress.

Turner, Denys. 1995. *Eros and Allegory: Medieval Exegesis of the Song of Songs*. Cistercian Studies 156. Kalamazoo, Mich.: Cistercian Publications.

Turner, Graeme. 2003. *British Cultural Studies: An Introduction*. 3rd ed. London: Routledge.

Twomey, Jay. 2005. Reading Derrida's New Testament: A Critical Appraisal. *BibInt* 13:374–403.

Tyler, Stephen A. 1987. *The Unspeakable: Discourse, Dialogue, and Rhetoric in the Postmodern World*. Madison: University of Wisconsin Press.

Ulmer, Gregory L. 1983. The Object of Post-criticism. Pages 83–110 in Foster 1983.

———. 1985. *Applied Grammatology: Post(e)-Pedagogy from Jacques Derrida to Joseph Beuys*. Baltimore: Johns Hopkins University Press.

———. 1988. The Puncept in Grammatology. Pages 164–89 in Culler 1988b.

Urbach, Ephraim E. 1971. The Homiletical Interpretation of the Sages and the Expositions of Origen on Canticles, and the Jewish-Christian Disputation. *Scripta Hierosolymitana* 22:248–75.

———. 1975. *The Sages: Their Concepts and Beliefs*. 2 vols. Translated by Israel Abrahams. Jerusalem: Magnes.

Vawter, Bruce. 1977. *On Genesis: A New Reading*. New York: Doubleday.

Veeser, H. Aram, ed. 1989. *The New Historicism*. London: Routledge.

———. 1991. Re-Membering a Deformed Past: (New) New Historicism. *The Journal of the Midwest Modern Language Association* 24:3–13.

———. 1994. The New Historicism. Pages 1–33 in *The New Historicism Reader*. Edited by H. Aram Veeser. London: Routledge.

———. 1996a. Introduction: The Case for Confessional Critics. Pages ix–xxvii in Veeser 1996b.

———. 1996b. *Confessions of the Critics*. London: Routledge.

Vendler, Helen. 1999. *The Art of Shakespeare's Sonnets*. Cambridge: Belknap.

Via, E. Jane. 1987. Women in the Gospel of Luke. Pages 38–55 in *Women in the World's Religions: Past and Present*. Edited by Ursula King. New York: Paragon House.

Vogt, Kari. 1995. "Becoming Male": A Gnostic and Early Christian Metaphor. Pages 170–86 in Børresen 1995.

Waetjen, Herman C. 2005. *The Gospel of the Beloved Disciple: A Work in Two Editions*. New York: T&T Clark.

Wahlde, Urban C. von. 1981–82. The Johannine "Jews": A Critical Survey. *NTS* 28:33–60.

———. 1983. The Gospel of John and the Presentation of Jews and Judaism. Pages 67–84 in *Within Context: Essay on Jews and Judaism in the New Testament*. Edited by David P. Efroymson et al. Collegeville, Minn.: Liturgical Press.

Walsh, Carey Ellen. 2000. *Exquisite Desire: Religion, the Erotic, and the Song of Songs.* Minneapolis: Fortress.

Walsh, Richard. 2003. *Reading the Gospels in the Dark: Portrayals of Jesus in Film.* Harrisburg, Pa.: Trinity Press International.

Walters, Jonathan. 1991. "No More Than a Boy": The Shifting Construction of Masculinity from Ancient Greece to the Middle Ages. *Gender & History* 5:20–33.

———. 1997. Invading the Roman Body: Manliness and Impenetrability in Roman Thought. Pages 29–43 in Hallett and Skinner 1997.

———. 1998. Juvenal, *Satire 2*: Putting Male Sexual Deviants on Show. Pages 148–54 in *Thinking Men: Masculinity and Self-Representation in the Classical Tradition.* Edited by Lin Foxhall and John Salmon. Leicester-Nottingham Studies in Ancient Society 7. London: Routledge.

Walters, Margaret. 1978. *The Nude Male: A New Perspective.* New York: Paddington.

Wansink, Craig S. 1996. *Chained in Christ: The Experience and Rhetoric of Paul's Imprisonments.* JSNTSup 130. Sheffield: Sheffield Academic Press.

Warner, Michael. 1999. *The Trouble with Normal: Sex, Politics and the Ethics of Queer Life.* New York: Free.

Warner, William. 1992. Spectacular Action: Rambo and the Popular Pleasures of Pain. Pages 672–88 in Grossberg, Nelson, and Treichler 1992.

Warrior, Robert Allen. 1989. Canaanites, Cowboys, and Indians: Deliverance, Conquest, and Liberation Theology Today. *Christianity and Crisis* 29:261–265.

Washington, Harold C. 1997. Violence and the Construction of Gender in the Hebrew Bible: A New Historicist Approach. *BibInt* 5:324–63.

Watson, Julia, and Sidonie Smith. 1992. Introduction: De/Colonization and the Politics of Discourse in Women's Autobiographical Practices. Pages xiii–xxxi in Smith and Watson 1992.

Weed, Elizabeth, and Ellen Rooney, eds. 2003. *Humanism. differences* 14:1 [thematic issue].

Weider, Joe, with Bill Reynolds. 1983. *The Weider System of Bodybuilding.* Chicago: Contemporary.

Weinfeld, Moshe. 1972. *Deuteronomy and the Deuteronomic School.* Oxford: Clarendon.

———. 1991. *Deuteronomy 1–11.* AB 5. New York: Doubleday.

Weissler, Chava. 1992. *Mizvot* Built into the Body: *Tkhines* for *Niddah*, Pregnancy, and Childbirth. Pages 101–16 in Eilberg-Schwartz 1992b.

Welch, John W. 1981. *Chiasmus in Antiquity: Structures, Analysis, Exegesis.* Hildesheim: Gerstenberg.

Wellek, René. 2005. Destroying Literary Studies [Orig. 1983]. Pages 41–51 in Patai and Corral 2005b.

Wellek, René, and Austin Warren. 1942. *Theory of Literature.* New York: Harcourt Brace.

Wenham, Gordon J. 1987. *Genesis 1–15.* WBC 1. Dallas: Word.

Westermann, Claus. 1984. *Genesis 1–11.* Translated by J. J. Scullion. Continental Commentaries. Minneapolis: Augsburg.

White, Hayden. 1979. Michel Foucault. Pages 81–115 in *Structuralism and Since: From Lévi-Strauss to Derrida*. Edited by John Sturrock. Oxford: Oxford University Press.
White, Robert J., ed. and trans. 1975. *The Interpretation of Dreams*: Oneirocritica *by Artemidoros*. Park Ridge, N.J.: Noyes.
Whitelam, Keith. 1996. *The Invention of Ancient Israel: The Silencing of Palestinian History*. London: Routledge.
William of St. Thierry et al. 1960. *Bernard of Clairvaux: The Story of His Life as Recorded in the* Vita Prima Bernardi *by Certain of His Contemporaries, William of St. Thierry, Arnold of Bonnevaux, Geoffrey and Philip of Clairvaux, and Odo of Deuil*. Translated by Geoffrey Webb and Adrian Walker. London: Mowbray.
Williams, Craig A. 1999. *Roman Homosexuality: Ideologies of Masculinity in Classical Antiquity*. Oxford: Oxford University Press.
Williams, Patricia J. 1991. *The Alchemy of Race and Rights: Diary of a Law Professor*. Cambridge: Harvard University Press.
Wills, Lawrence M. 1990. *The Jew in the Court of the Foreign King: Ancient Jewish Court Legends*. Harvard Dissertations in Religion 26. Minneapolis: Fortress.
Wilson, Andrew P. 2007. *Transfigured: A Derridean Reading of the Markan Transfiguration*. New York: T&T Clark.
Wilton, Tamsin. 1996. Which One's the Man? The Heterosexualization of Lesbian Sex. Pages 125–42 in Richardson 1996.
Wimbush, Vincent L., ed. 2000. *African Americans and the Bible: Sacred Texts and Social Textures*. New York: Continuum.
Wimsatt, William K., Jr. 1954. *The Verbal Icon: Studies in the Meaning of Poetry*. Lexington: University of Kentucky Press.
Winkler, John J. 1990. *The Constraints of Desire: The Anthropology of Sex and Gender in Ancient Greece*. The New Ancient World. London: Routledge.
Winterson, Jeanette. 1985. *Oranges Are Not the Only Fruit*. New York: The Atlantic Monthly Press.
Wittig, Monique. 1992. *The Straight Mind and Other Essays*. Boston: Beacon.
Wolfreys, Julian. 1999. Introduction: Border Crossings, or Close Encounters of the Textual Kind. Pages 1–11 in *Literary Theories: A Reader's Guide*. Edited by Julian Wolfreys. New York: New York University Press.
Wolfson, Elliot R. 1992. Images of the Divine Feet: Some Observations on the Divine Body in Judaism. Pages 143–82 in Eilberg-Schwartz 1992b.
Wood, David, and Robert Bernasconi, eds. 1988. *Derrida and Différance*. Evanston, Ill.: Northwestern University Press.
Wyschogrod, Edith, David Crownfield, and Carl A. Raschke, eds. 1989. *Lacan and Theological Discourse*. Albany: State University of New York Press.
Xie, Ming. 1997. The Postmodern as the Postcolonial: Recognizing Chinese Modernity. *Ariel* 28:11–32.
Young, Robert J. C. 1990. *White Mythologies: Writing History and the West*. London: Routledge.
———. 2001. *Postcolonialism: An Historical Introduction*. Oxford: Blackwell.

Young, Steve. 1994. Being a Man: The Pursuit of Manliness in *The Shepherd of Hermas*. *JECS* 2:237–55.

Zahn, Theodor. 1921. *Das Evangelium des Johannes ausgelegt*. 6th ed. Leipzig: Deichert.

Žižek, Slavoj. 2001a. *The Fragile Absolute: Or, Why Is the Christian Legacy Worth Fighting For?* London: Verso.

———. 2001b. *On Belief*. Thinking in Action. London: Routledge.

———. 2003. *The Puppet and the Dwarf: The Perverse Core of Christianity*. Short Circuits. Cambridge: MIT Press.

Index of Modern Authors

Abbas, Ackbar 365 n. 23
Abel, Elizabeth 30–31
Abraham, Nicolas 56 n. 5
Adam, A. K. M. 9 n. 1, 23
Adam, Ian 311 n. 2
Adams, Rachel 221
Agamben, Giorgio 401, 403
Agnani, Sunil 376
Ahmad, Aijaz 310 n. 1, 314–16
Ahn, Yong-Sung 313 n. 7
Aichele, George 3, 23, 122, 359, 367 n. 29
Alarcón, Norma 329 n. 2
Alcoff, Linda Martin 401 n. 34
Althaus-Reid, Marcella 271 n. 30
Anderson, Amanda 375 n. 1, 382
Anderson, Gary A. 214 n. 33
Anderson, Hugh 177–78 n. 4, 190 n. 36
Anderson, Janice Capel 6, 127, 171, 175, 222, 363 n. 16, 363 n. 18
Appiah, Kwame Anthony 310 n. 2
Ashcroft, Bill 311 n. 2, 313 n. 7, 350, 364 n. 20
Ashley, Kathleen 139
Aspegren, Kerstin 194 n. 44, 194 n. 46, 195
Attridge, Derek 46
Aune, David C. 178
Austen, Jane 360, 381

Bach, Alice 259–60, 367 n. 29
Badiou, Alain 401, 402 n. 36, 403
Baer, Richard A., Jr. 194 n. 44
Bailey, Randall C. 128
Bal, Mieke 211 n. 30, 367 n. 29

Balibar, Etienne 401 n. 36
Banfield, Ann 69
Barclay, John M. G. 178 n. 4
Barnard, Mary 274 n. 2
Barr, James 377 n. 5, 382
Barrett, C. K. 84 nn. 3–4, 86, 89 n. 14, 92, 93, 334
Barth, Karl 157–59
Barthes, Roland 2 n. 1, 3, 5 n. 2, 12–13, 19, 51, 74 n. 35, 122, 142–44, 313, 375, 380, 387, 390, 400
Bataille, Georges 12, 22, 65 n. 21, 269 n. 29
Baudrillard, Jean 256 n. 12
Beal, Timothy K. 122, 388
Beasley-Murray, George R. 85 n. 6, 86, 88
Begley, Adam 127, 139, 145
Belsey, Catherine 122
Benstock, Shari 139
Bernard, John Henry 334 n. 12
Bersani, Leo 252 n. 7, 253, 267 n. 27
Bhabha, Homi K. 2 n. 1, 268 n. 28, 310–14, 316–25, 327–28, 351, 365, 369, 375
Biale, David 212 n. 32
Bible and Culture Collective 9, 23, 359 n. 5, 361 n. 10, 377, 400 n. 33
Bickerman, Elias J. 177–78 n. 4
Bilde, Per 104
Black, Fiona C. 171, 262–64, 267, 367 n. 29
Blank, Josef 336 n. 13
Blanton, Ward 402–3
Bledstein, Adrien Janis 220 n. 44

Bleich, David 394
Blinzler, Josef 150
Bloch, Ariel 232 n. 13, 261
Bloch, Chana 232 n. 13, 261
Bloom, Harold 382
Blum, Claes 275 n. 5
Boer, Roland 245 n. 26, 247, 256–60, 264–65, 351, 367 n. 29
Boers, Hendrikus 96 n. 24
Boff, Leonardo 155
Bohache, Thomas 255, 304
Bolin, Anne 203 n. 2
Booth, Wayne C. 73
Bové, Paul 376 n. 3
Boyarin, Daniel 176 n. 2, 205 n. 7, 209 n. 22, 211 n. 30, 221, 233–34, 238, 295 n. 11, 363
Bradley, Keith 340
Brainum, Jerry 216
Branderburger, Egon 113 n. n
Breck, John 340 n. 24
Breitenstein, Urs 178 n. 6, 186 n. 24, 196 n. 48
Brenner, Athalya 247, 250 n. 4, 251, 270
Brett, Mark G. 313 n. 7
Bronner, Leila Leah 209 n. 22, 221
Brooks, Cleanth 379
Brooten, Bernadette, J. 275 n. 4, 277 n. 9, 281–83, 285, 288, 297–98, 305
Brown, Joanne Carlson 155
Brown, John 289, 291–92, 295
Brown, Norman O. 72
Brown, Peter 50 n. 16
Brown, Peter Robert Lamont 232
Brown, Raymond E. 56 n. 2, 58 n. 6, 61 n. 13, 83, 85 n. 6, 86, 90, 92, 96, 149 n. 2, 152 n. 6, 332, 334, 338–39, 346 n. 34, 347 n. 35
Brownstein, Rachel M. 129, 132, 139
Brueggemann, Walter 350, 397–98
Budde, Karl 237 n. 19
Buell, Lawrence 362 n. 12
Bultmann, Rudolf 14, 86, 92, 159–61
Bunzl, Matti 351
Burnett, Fred W. 9 n. 1

Burrus, Virginia 6, 247, 266 n. 26, 304
Burton, Antoinette 351
Butler, George 214 n. 33
Butler, Judith 2 n. 1, 225, 235 n. 17, 251 n. 5, 258, 304, 305, 375, 376, 393 n. 22, 401 n. 36, 404

Cahoone, Lawrence E. 23
Calderwood, James L. 396 n. 27
Calvet, Louis-Jean 143–44
Campbell, Douglas A. 178 n. 4
Caputo, John D. 16 n. 4, 122, 401 n. 34, 403
Carr, David 255 n. 10
Carroll, Clare 317 n. 11
Carroll, Robert 123, 222
Carter, Warren 350, 364
Carvalho, Corrine L. 392 n. 20
Cassidy, Richard J. 331 n. 7, 348 n. 37
Castelli, Elizabeth A. 75 n. 36, 162, 164 n. 17, 167, 194 nn. 45–46, 288 n. 7, 362 n. 11
Chance, John K. 189 n. 33
Chatman, Seymour 67, 73
Childs, Brevard S. 212
Childs, Peter 313 n. 7
Chioni Moore, David 311 n. 2
Christensen, Duane L. 204 n. 3
Cixous, Hélène 18–22, 49 n. 15, 122, 396, 400
Clément, Catherine 59 n. 9
Clines, David J. A. 23, 177 n. 2, 221, 253–55, 257, 273 n., 363 n. 16, 395
Cohen, Martin S. 207–8, 217 n. 38
Cohn, Dorrit 74
Collins, John J. 23, 183, 197 n. 51, 377, 382, 404
Conrad, Joseph 328, 365
Conway, Colleen M. 122, 222, 333 n. 11, 341 n. 25, 363 n. 16
Cook, Judith A. 370
Corber, Robert J. 360
Corley, Kathleen E. 367 n. 29
Cornwell, Andrea 177 n. 2

INDEX OF MODERN AUTHORS

Corral, Will H.   376 n. 3, 377–78, 384–85, 386 n. 10, 405
Cosgrove, Charles H.   63 n. 18
Counet, Patrick Chatelion   359 n. 5
Cranfield, C. B.   158 n. 12
Crawford, Bobbie   290 n. 8
Crossan, John Dominic   93 n. 20, 100–101, 106 n. h, 107–9, 111, 114–15, 117–20, 122 n. 7, 350
Culler, Jonathan   1, 38, 374–75, 378, 387, 393 n. 22
Culpepper, R. Alan   74 n. 33, 83 n. 2, 333 n. 11
Cunningham, D. J.   245
Cunningham, Valentine   376–77, 382, 386 n. 10, 396
Cypess, Sandra Messinger   329 n. 2

D'Angelo, Mary Rose   363 n. 16
Darling Young, Robin   177 n. 3, 182 n. 15, 186 n. 27, 193, 196–97
Davidson, Cathy N.   138
Davidson, Robert   205
Davies, Philip R.   171
Davis, Colin   376 n. 4, 392 n. 20, 405
Davis, Robert Con   59 n. 9
De Courtivron, Isabelle   20
Deferrari, R. J.   274 . 1
Deissmann, Adolf   193 n. 40, 196 n. 48, 402
De Lauretis, Teresa   251 n. 5
Deleuze, Gilles   65 n. 21, 258 n. 16, 260 n. 20, 375, 400
Delitzsch, Franz   236–37, 248–49
De Man, Paul   2 n. 1, 56, 86 n. 7, 95 n. 21, 375, 378, 381 n. 7, 382, 389
De Moor, Johannes Cornelis   391
Dempsey, Robert B.   237–38
Derrida, Jacques   2 n. 1, 3, 6, 11–16, 18–19, 27–38, 40–42, 47–50, 53, 56 n. 3, 58, 62, 65 n. 21, 77 n. 39, 79, 81–82, 84, 86 n. 7, 87, 91–92, 122–24, 143 n. 8, 146, 175, 312–13, 319–20, 322 n. 18, 327, 359, 365, 369, 373, 375, 376 n. 2, 380 n. 6, 387–89, 390 n. 16, 392 n. 20, 394–96, 400–401, 403
Desai, Gaurav   315–16 n. 9, 350, 360, 364 n. 20
DeSilva, David A.   189 nn. 33–34
De Vries, Hent   401 n. 36
Dickstein, Morris   379, 384
Dirlik, Arif   314–15
Docherty, Thomas   376
Dodd, C. H.   85 n. 6, 86 n. 8, 92, 158, 339 n. 20
Donaldson, Laura E.   313 n. 7, 330 n. 6, 351, 364
Donato, Eugenio   380 n. 6
Dover, K. J.   176 n. 2, 190
Dowsett, Andrew C.   367 n. 29
Draper, Jonathan A.   372 n. 40
Dreyfus, Hubert L.   157
Dube, Musa W.   328, 330, 348 n. 37, 350, 364 n. 21, 366 n. 28
DuBois, Page   150, 154, 299 n. 14
Dufourmantelle, Anne   401 n. 36
Duggan, Lisa   258 n. 14
Duke, Paul D.   82, 83 n. 2, 85
Dunn, James D. G.   158 n. 12, 163, 293, 294
Dünzl, Franz   265 n. 25
Dupont-Sommer, André   178 nn. 4 and 6, 192 n. 40, 196
Duras, Marguerite   23
During, Simon   365 n. 23
Dutton, Kenneth R.   202 n. 1, 220 n. 42

Eagleton, Terry   356, 359, 366 n. 25, 376, 378, 380, 382–85, 405
Eakin, Emily   316
Eakin, Paul John   139
Eco, Umberto   43
Eddins, Dwight   376 n. 3
Edwards, W. D.   92
Ehrman, Bart D.   76 n. 37
Eichrodt, Walther   213
Eilberg-Schwartz, Howard   177 n. 2, 206, 212 n. 31, 222, 363 n. 16
Elliott, Neil   350, 365

458   THE BIBLE IN THEORY

Elliott, Scott   54
Ellis, John   384
Ellmann, Richard   44, 49, 50 nn. 16–17
Erni, John Nguyet   365 n. 23
Ernst, Josef   63
Erskine, Andrew   188 n. 30, 189 n. 35
Esler, Philip F.   60
Eslinger, Lyle   85 n. 6, 244–45
Esty, Jed   351
Exum, J. Cheryl.   221, 239 n. 21, 250 n. 4, 255, 262–64, 267, 270, 367 n. 29
Eynikel, Erik   192 n. 39

Faderman, Lillian   280 n. 1, 281 n. 2, 283–84, 287–88 n. 5
Falconer, Colin   328–31
Fanon, Frantz   221, 296 n. 7, 319–21, 324
Farmer, William R.   130
Fee, Gordon D.   167 n. 19
Felder, Cain Hope   366 n. 28
Felman, Shoshana   22, 53, 59 n. 9, 85, 389
Felski, Rita   381, 390
Fewell, Danna Nolan   391 n. 19
Fishbane, Michael   218 n. 40
Fitzmyer, Joseph A.   58 n. 6, 64 n. 19, 69, 163 n. 15
Flynn, Elizabeth A.   394 n. 24
Folkenflik, Robert   139
Fonow, Mary Margaret   370
Fontaine, Carol R.   247, 253
Ford, Joan Massingbaerde   290 n. 8
Foster, William   102
Foucault, Michel   2 n. 1, 3, 12, 23, 53–54, 65–67, 69–71, 73, 74 n. 33, 75–76, 99, 121 n. 4, 122, 123, 137, 142, 145 n. 12, 146, 153–54, 156–57, 160–62, 167–70, 175–76, 180 n. 10, 184–85, 188, 225–26, 238, 251 n. 5, 254 n. 9, 255, 273–76, 278–79, 299–300, 304, 312–13, 319, 363, 375, 394
Fowler, Robert M.   9 n. 1, 10–11, 13–14, 16
Foxhall, Lin   299 n. 14

Freadman, Richard   384
Freedman, Diane P.   128, 133, 139, 171, 172
Freedman, Harry   193 n. 41, 197 n. 52
Freud, Sigmund   2 n. 1, 12, 18, 42, 45–47, 56, 59, 64–65, 83 n. 1, 129, 148, 170, 221, 238 n. 20, 258 n. 16, 268, 319–21
Freudenthal, Jakob   192 n. 40, 195, 196 n. 48
Frey, Olivia   128, 171
Friesen, Steven J.   313 n. 7, 369 n. 35
Frilingos, Christopher A. 313 n. 7, 363 n. 16, 369 n. 35
Fromm, Harold   362 n. 12, 384
Fussel, Samuel Wilson   202 n. 1, 213–16, 219–20

Gabel, W. J.   92
Gagnon, Madeleine   18
Gaines, Charles   214 n. 33
Gallagher, Catherine   123, 318 n. 12
Gallop, Jane   22, 30–31, 53, 59 n. 9, 63 n. 17
Gaonkar, Dilip   368 n. 31
Garber, Marjorie   234, 401 n. 36
Gardiner, Judith Kegan   222
Griffiths, Gareth   311 n. 2, 350, 364 n. 20
Garrard, Greg   362 n. 12
Garrett, Susan R.   69, 75
Gasparro, Giulia Sfameni   185 n. 22
Gates, Henry Louis, Jr.   2 n. 1, 133
Georgi, Dieter   160 n. 13
Gersdorf, Catrin   362 n. 11
Gilbert, Sandra   356
Gilmore, David D.   189 n. 33
Gilmore, Leigh   139
Ginsburg, Christian D.   237 n. 18
Ginzberg, Louis.   209, 211 n. 30
Gitlin, Todd   384
Glancy, Jennifer A.   177 n. 2, 339, 347, 363 n. 16
Gleason, Maud W.   190, 195
Glotfelty, Cheryll   362 n. 12
Goldhill, Simon   176 n. 2

Goldstein, Jonathan A.   179, 196 n. 49
González, Justo L.   136
Goodheart, Eugene   357
Goss, Robert E.   225, 304
Gottstein, Alon Goshen   205 n. 7
Goulder, Michael D.   239–41, 253
Goux, Jean-Joseph   56–57
Graham, Susan Lochrie   6, 99–100, 123, 362 n. 11
Gray, Bennison   68 n. 24, 69
Greenberg, David F.   206 n. 9, 238 n. 20
Greenblatt, Stephen   100–102, 106, 109–11, 113 n. o, 115–116, 117 n. u, 119–20, 121 n. 3, 123, 162, 318 n. 12, 369, 393 n. 21
Greene, Ellen   299 n. 14
Greene, Graham   106
Grossberg, Lawrence   365 n. 23
Grosz, Elizabeth   63 n. 17
Gruber, Eberhard   401 n. 34
Gruber, Mayer I.   221
Guest, Deryn   225, 304
Guillaume, Philippe   395
Guillory, John   376, 393 n. 22, 404
Gunn, Janet Varner   139
Gutman, Isaiah   178 n. 6
Gwyther, Anthony   364

Haacker, Klaus   277 n. 10
Habermas, Jürgen   13, 375
Hadas, Moses   177–78 n. 4, 178 n. 6, 190, 192 n. 38, 192–93 nn. 40–41, 196
Haenchen, Ernst   86
Halberstam, Judith   293 n. 10
Hallett, Judith P.   171, 279, 286 n. 4
Halperin, David M.   176 n. 2, 220 n. 43, 255 n. 11, 276, 278, 299, 304
Hamburger, Käte   68–69, 74 n. 33
Hamilton, Paul   107
Hamm, Dennis   55 n. 1, 65 n. 22
Han, Jin Hee   313 n. 7
Handler, Nicholas   378
Hanson, John S.   109
Hanson, Paul D.   216
Hanssen, Beatrice   401 n. 36

Harink, Douglas   401 n. 34
Harris, Amanda Nolacea   329 n. 2, 330 n. 6
Harris, Wendell V.   376 n. 3
Hart, Lynda   258, 267–68
Hartman, Geoffrey   43 n. 12
Hassan, Ihab   10
Hauspie, Katrin   192 n. 39
Hawley, John C.   313 n. 7
Hays, Richard B.   391 n. 19
Headlam, Arthur C.   292, 295–98, 300
Heidegger, Martin   12, 16 n. 4, 54–55, 62, 65 n. 21, 403
Heller, Joseph   106
Hengel, Martin   122 n. 8, 151–52, 155, 332 n. 10
Hens-Piazza, Gina   123
Herion, Gary A.   216
Heschel, Abraham J.   216 n. 35
Hirschberg, Harris Hans   242 n. 22
Hogan, Patrick Colm   59 n. 9
Holland, Norman N.   394
Honer, Anne   202 n. 1
Hooke, S. H.   91 n. 16
Hooker, Morna D.   113 n. n
Horsley, Richard A.   109, 350, 364–65
Hoskot, S. S.   360
Hoskyns, E. C.   85 n. 6, 92
Hosmer, F. E.   92
Howard-Brook, Wes   364
Howe, Stephen   317 n. 11
Huddart, David   313 n. 7
Hull, John M.   321 n. 16
Hulme, Peter   330 n. 6
Hunt, Lynn   299 n. 14
Hunter, Nan D.   258 n. 14
Hussein, Abdirahman A.   313 n. 7
Hutcheon, Linda   11, 22
Huyssen, Andreas   12, 14, 17

Idel, Moshe   208
Ingraham, Chrys   363
Irigaray, Luce   18–19, 21, 23, 63 n. 17, 65, 72, 122, 253, 268 n. 28, 375, 400
Iser, Wolfgang   13, 368, 393–94

Jacob, Benno 205
Jameson, Fredric 10, 20 n. 7, 23, 311, 375, 387 n. 13
Janowitz, Naomi 208 n. 16
Jay, Martin 65 n. 21
Jeffrey L. Staley 85 n. 6, 95 n. 22, 127, 137, 140–42, 145–46, 171, 172, 328, 350, 364 n. 21
Jeffreys, Sheila 287 n. 6
Jennings, Theodore W., Jr. 123, 359 n. 5
Jobling, David 3, 24, 123, 351, 359 n. 5, 362 n. 11, 400 n. 33
Johnson, Barbara 53, 84, 86 n. 7, 378, 389
Jones, Ann Rosalind 22
Jones, Brian W. 348 n. 37
Jones, Gareth 160 n. 13
Jordan, Mark D. 271 n. 30
Joyce, James 12, 19, 20 n. 7, 28, 36–37, 42, 44–47, 49–50, 54, 365, 396

Kahl, Brigitte 350, 363 n. 16
Kähler, Martin 335–36
Kaplan, Alice 138
Käsemann, Ernst 158 n. 12
Katz, Jonathan Ned 238 n. 20, 255, 363
Kaul, Suvir 351
Keener, Craig S. 339 n. 20, 341 n. 26, 344 n. 30
Kelber, Werner H. 89 n. 12, 90, 95
Keller, Catherine 123
Kellum, Barbara 278 n. 12
Kermode, Frank 380, 384
Keuls, Eva C. 278 n. 12
Kiberd, Declan 296 n. 7, 317 n. 11
Kim, Jean K. 364 n. 21
Kimelman, Reuven 231
King, Patricia 317 n. 11
Kitzberger, Ingrid Rosa 172
Klauck, Hans-Joachim 177 n. 4, 192 n. 37, 198 n. 54
Klein, Alan M. 202 n. 1, 203, 215, 217–18
Koester, Craig R. 348 n. 37
Kofman, Sarah 58

Kosta, Barbara 139
Kraemer, Ross S. 195 n. 47
Krauss, Rosalind 12
Kressel, G. M. 189 n. 33
Kristeva, Julia 2 n. 1, 5, 12, 18–22, 49 n. 15, 78 n. 40, 122, 249–50, 256, 261, 263 n. 21, 313, 375, 390, 391 n. 17, 396, 400
Krondorfer, Björn 222
Kuefler, Mathew 222
Kvalbein, Hans 332 n. 10

Lacan, Jacques 2 n. 1, 5, 12, 18, 21, 32, 36, 42, 45–46, 48, 49 n. 15, 53, 57–65, 74 n. 34, 83 n. 1, 87, 94, 96, 122, 142, 146, 256, 258 n. 16, 264, 313, 319–21, 322 n. 19, 324, 375, 379, 380 n. 6, 400
Laclau, Ernesto 401 n. 36
LaCocque, André 395
Landy, Francis 231
Lang, Candace 132
Leclercq, Henri 150
Leistyna, Pepi 365 n. 23
Lejeune, Philippe 139
Lemaire, Anika 59 n. 8
Lentricchia, Frank 107, 131, 133, 138, 360 n. 9, 381 n. 7
Léon-Dufour, Xavier 161
Levine, Amy-Jill 6, 136
Liew, Tat-siong Benny 128, 305, 313 n. 7, 351, 364 n. 21, 366 n. 28
Lightfoot, R. H. 89, 90 n. 15
Lincoln, Andrew T. 336 n. 13
Lindars, Barnabas 86
Lindisfarne, Nancy 177 n. 2
Lindner, Helgo 104
Lingis, Alphonso 202 n. 1, 220 n. 42
Lionnet, Françoise 140
Littledale, Richard Frederick 230 n. 8, 233, 236
Litz, A. Walton 45
Lloyd, David 317 n. 11
Lodge, David 380, 381
Loomba, Ania 285, 351

INDEX OF MODERN AUTHORS

Loughlin, Gerard 305
Lührmann, Dieter 113 n. n
Lust, Johan 192 n. 39
Luther, Martin 241, 398
Lutz, Cora E. 198 n. 55
Lyotard, Jean-François 17, 20 n. 7, 24, 401 n. 34

MacCannell, Juliet Flower 59 n. 9
MacDonald, Graeme 404
Machin, Richard 389
Mack, Burton L. 341
MacKendrick, Karmen 258–61, 265 n. 24, 268–69
MacKinnon, Catharine 252 n. 6, 258, 299 n. 14
Macksey, Richard 380 n. 6
Malbon, Elizabeth Struthers 34 n. 4
Maldonado, Robert D. 329 n. 2
Malina, Bruce J. 189 n. 33
Malmede, Hans H. 62 n. 16
Marchal, Joseph A. 351
Marcus, Laura 139
Marks, Elaine 20
Marrouchi, Mustapha 313 n. 7
Marshall, I. Howard 63
Martin, Dale B. 163, 177 n. 2, 277 n. 9, 282 n. 2, 305
Matarazzo, Mike 214–15
Matheson, Peter 398 n. 30
Mattila, Sharon Lea 194 n. 44
Mayer, Sylvia 362 n. 12
McClintock, Anne 285
McIntyre, John 156
McKnight, Edgar V. 10, 13–14
McLaughlin, Thomas 92 n. 19
McNay, Lois 299 n. 14
McQuillan, Martin 376 n. 4, 404
Meyer, Marvin W. 194 n. 45
Meyers, Carol 220 n. 44, 231, 250 n. 4
Milesi, Laurent 396 n. 26
Milgrom, Jacob 213
Miller, D. A. 220 n. 43
Miller, J. Hillis 86 n. 7, 358, 361 n. 10, 389, 395

Miller, Jacques-Alain 400 n. 32
Miller, James 170
Miller, James E. 277 n. 10
Miller, Nancy K. 128–33, 136, 139, 145, 172
Miller, Patricia Cox 194 n. 46
Miller, Robert J. 151
Miller, Seumas 384
Miscall, Peter 23
Mitchell, W. J. T. 316 n. 10, 376 n. 2, 405
Moberly, R W. L. 212 n. 31
Moi, Toril 22, 65
Moloney, Francis J. 346
Montrose, Louis A. 99, 119–20
Moo, Douglas 157–58
Moore-Gilbert, Bart 311, 313 n. 7, 321, 324, 351
Moriarty, Michael 144
Morton, Stephen 313 n. 7
Mosala, Itumeleng J. 325 n. 21, 366 n. 28
Motyer, Stephen 341 n. 26
Mowery, Robert L. 336 n. 15
Moxnes, Halvor 189 n. 33
Muecke, D. C. 83 n. 2
Mukherjee, Aron P. 311 n. 2
Mulvey, Laura 65
Murnaghan, Sheila 194 n. 43
Murphy, Roland E. 237
Musurillo, Herbert 265 n. 25

Nair, Supriya 315–16 n. 9, 350, 360, 364 n. 20
Nancy, Jean-Luc 400, 401 n. 34, 403
Nelson, Cary 365 n. 23
Neusner, Jacob 210 n. 25
Newman, Charles 13, 16
Newton, Judith Louder 107
Neyrey, Jerome H. 189 n. 33
Niditch, Susan 211
Nkrumah, Kwame 311
Nolland, John 60 n. 11, 61 n. 13
Norris, Christopher 389
North, Helen F. 184
Nötscher, Friedrich 210 n. 27
Nuttall, Geoffrey F. 55 n. 1

Nutu, Ela 359 n. 5
Nygren, Anders 158

O'Day, Gail R. 82, 84, 85 n. 5, 86–87
Okure, Teresa 82, 87 n. 9, 94
Olney, James 129 n. 2, 139
Olsson, Birger 85 n. 6
Ong, Walter J. 10, 64
Oppenheim, A. Leo 219
Ostriker, Alicia 250–52, 261
Owens, Craig 17, 65

Pack, Roger 275 n. 4
Paglia, Camille 202 n. 1
Pandit, Lalita 59 n. 9
Pardes, Ilana 211 n. 30
Parker, Holt N. 276 n. 7
Parker, Rebecca 155–56
Parry, Benita 321
Parsons, Mikeal C. 177 n. 2, 363
Patai, Daphne 376 n. 3, 377–78, 384–85, 386 n. 10, 405
Patte, Daniel 134–35, 137
Paul, Diana Y. 193 n. 42
Perloff, Marjorie 376 n. 3
Perreault, Jeanne 139
Personal Narratives Group 139
Peters, Edward 339 n. 20
Pfitzner, Victor C. 185–86
Phillips, Gary A. 3, 9, 11, 134, 135 n. 7, 359 n. 5, 362 n. 11
Phy, Allene Stuart 367 n. 29
Pippin, Tina 24, 363 n. 17, 400 n. 33
Plate, S. Brent 367 n. 29
Plevnik, Joseph 189 n. 33
Plummer, Alfred 56 n. 2
Plunkett, M. A. 76 n. 37
Plunkett, Regina St. G. 84, 86–87
Polaski, Donald 254, 362 n. 11
Polaski, Sandra Hack 123
Pomeroy, Sarah B. 180 n. 10, 194
Pope, Marvin H. 237–39, 241–44
Porsch, Felix 96
Powell, Mark Allan 392 n. 20
Price, Robert M. 359 n. 5

Purves, Robin 404

Quayson, Ato 311 n. 2

Rabaté, Jean-Michel 376, 405
Rabinow, Paul 157
Rad, Gerhard von 205
radicallesbians 252 n. 6
Ragland-Sullivan, Ellie 63 n. 17
Rajak, Tessa 104
Rajan, Rajeswari Sunder 314–15
Rajchman, John 65 n. 21
Rambuss, Richard 302
Raschke, Carl A. 16 n. 4
Redditt, Paul L. 178–79 n. 7
Reindl, Joseph 210 n. 27
Reinhartz, Adele 341 n. 26, 346, 349 n. 39
Reiss, Timothy 13
Renehan, Robert 178 n. 6, 180
Rengstorf, Karl Heinrich 56
Rensberger, David 331 n. 7, 332 n. 8, 334
Rich, Adrienne 252 n. 6, 363 n. 15
Richardson, Diane 238 n. 20, 363
Riches, John 365
Richlin, Amy 276 n. 7, 299–300 nn. 14–15
Ricks, Christopher 382
Riddel, Joseph 395 n. 25
Ridderbos, Herman N. 346 n. 34
Riquelme, John Paul 396 n. 26
Rivera, Mayra 351
Robinson, James M. 194 n. 45
Robinson, John A. T. 165
Rooney, Ellen 402 n. 36
Rose, Jacqueline 55, 65
Rosendale, Steven 362 n. 12
Ross, Marlon B. 112 n. m
Roudinesco, Elisabeth 59 n. 9, 62–63
Roughead, William 282 n. 2
Rowley, H. H. 237
Royle, Nicholas 360
Runions, Erin 313 n. 7, 367 n. 29, 369 n. 33

INDEX OF MODERN AUTHORS

Rutledge, David 123, 362 n. 11

Sacher-Masoch, Leopold von 260
Sáez, Ñacuñán 154
Said, Edward W. 312–14, 316, 320, 351, 360 n. 9, 369, 375, 393 n. 21
Samuel, Simon 313 n. 7
Sanday, William 292, 295–98, 300
Sanders, E. P. 107
Sanders, Mark 313 n. 7
Sandmel, Samuel 186–87 n. 28, 193
Sandys, George 285–86
Sarna, Nahum M. 205
Sarracoll, M. John 106, 113 n. o
Sarup, Madan 157, 160
Satlow, Michael L. 176 n. 2, 181 n. 12
Savran, David 121
Scarry, Elaine 162
Schäfer, Peter 207 n. 11
Schleifer, Ronald 24, 400 n. 33
Schlier, Heinrich 331 n. 7
Schnackenburg, Rudolf 83, 85 n. 6, 90, 94, 334
Schneiderman, Stuart 59 n. 9
Schneiders, Sandra M. 84, 86–87
Scholem, Gershom 207–9
Schor, Noami 401 n. 36
Schürmann, Heinz 63
Schüssler Fiorenza, Elisabeth 20, 34 n. 4, 361
Schuster, Nancy 193
Schwan, Alexander 160 n. 13
Schwartz, Regina M. 137
Schweickart, Patrocinio P. 394 n. 24
Schweitzer, Albert 100, 402
Schwoch, James 368 n. 31
Scott, Edmund 102
Scott, Joan W. 401 n. 36, 402 n. 36
Sedgwick, Eve Kosofsky 138, 220 n. 43, 225, 251 n. 5, 293 n. 10, 305
Seeley, David 123, 163–65
Seesengood, Robert Paul 172
Segovia, Fernando F. 128, 133, 135, 309, 351, 364 n. 21, 366, 371
Setel, T. Drorah 270

Shapin, Steven 397
Shapiro, Barbara 397
Shaw, Brent D. 177 n. 3, 181 n. 13, 183 n. 18
Sheehan, Jonathan 402
Sherwood, Yvonne 4, 6, 123, 124, 225, 359 n. 5, 362 n. 11, 373–74, 396, 401 n. 35, 405
Siewert, Francis E. 280 n.1
Sim, David C. 365, 391
Simms, George Otto 44–45
Simon, Maurice 193 n. 41, 197 n. 52
Simpson, David 145 n. 12
Simpson, Mark 202 n. 1, 219–20, 302
Skinner, Marilyn B. 176 n. 2, 188 n. 32, 279, 296 n. 12
Sly, Dorothy 195
Smart, Carol 287 n. 6
Smith-Christopher, Daniel 366 n. 28
Smith, Abraham 363 n. 16
Smith, James A. 124, 359
Smith, Robert 143 n. 8
Smith, Sidonie 139–40
Sontag, Susan 68, 74–75, 77
South, James T. 166 n. 18
Spanos, William V. 70 n. 28
Spengemann, William 139
Spivak, Gayatri Chakravorty 2 n. 1, 17, 22, 88 n. 10, 312–14, 327–28, 347 n. 36, 349 n. 41, 351, 369, 375, 378, 385 n. 9
Staley, Jeffrey Lloyd 85 n. 6, 95 n. 22, 127, 137, 140–42, 145, 146 n. 13, 171, 172, 328, 350, 364 n. 21
Stanley, Liz 139
Stanton, Elizabeth Cady 211
Stern, David 205 n. 7
Sternberg, Meir 72
Stone, Ken 305
Storey, John 365 n. 23
Stout, Jeffrey 16
Stowers, Stanley K. 177 n. 2, 178 n. 6, 181 n. 12, 186 n. 26, 191 n. 37, 196 n. 48, 197 n. 54, 281, 291–94
Sturrock, John 143

Sugirtharajah, R. S.   294, 305, 313 n. 7, 351, 364, 366 n. 28
Sullivan, Sir Edward   44

Tasker, Yvonne   202 n. 1
Taubes, Jacob   401
Taylor, Mark C.   14–16, 59 n. 9
Telford, William R.   341
Thatcher, Tom   351
Thiong'o, Ngugi wa   296 n. 7
Thomas, Calvin   363
Thomas, Kendall   376, 393 n. 22, 404
Thompson, F. H.   340
Thomson, Stephen   404
Thurman, Eric   313 n. 7, 369 n. 33
Tiffin, Helen   311 n. 2, 350, 364 n. 20
Tilley, Maureen A.   194 n. 46
Tindall, William   44
Todorov, Tzvetan   74, 380 n. 6
Tolbert, Mary Ann   34, 133, 366, 370 n. 38
Tompkins, Jane P.   128, 130–32, 134, 137–39, 145–46
Torgovnick, Marianna de Marco   138
Torok, Maria   56
Townshend, R. B.   196 n. 48
Treichler, Paula   365 n. 23
Trible, Phyllis   21, 211 n. 30, 212 n. 32, 221, 230 n. 7, 247, 250–52, 254, 256, 262
Turner, Denys   228 n. 3
Turner, Graeme   365 n. 23
Twomey, Jay   124, 396 n. 28
Tyler, Stephen A.   10

Ulmer, Gregory L.   12, 42, 47–48
Urbach, Ephraim E.   205 n. 7, 209 n. 20, 211 n. 30, 231

Valocchi, Stephen   360
Van Henten, J. W.   178 n. 4, 188 n. 29
Van Nortwick, Thomas   171
Vattimo, Gianni   401
Vawter, Bruce   205
Veeser, H. Aram   101, 106–7, 110–11, 112 n. m, 119, 121 n. 1, 123, 124, 128–29, 133, 138, 172, 369
Vendler, Helen   360
Via, E. Jane   72 n. 30
Vogt, Kari   194 n. 46

Waetjen, Herman C.   345 n. 32
Wahlde, Urban C. von   341 n. 26
Walkowitz, Rebecca L.   401 n. 36
Walsh, Carey Ellen   250 n. 4, 261, 263 n. 22
Walsh, Richard   23, 367 n. 29
Walters, Jonathan   188–89, 278, 296 n. 12
Walters, Margaret   220 n. 42
Wansink, Craig S.   181 n. 14
Warner, Michael   363
Warner, William   202 n. 1
Warren, Austin   379
Warrior, Robert Allen   137
Washington, Harold C.   123, 177 n. 2
Watson, Francis   147
Watson, Julia   139–40
Webb, Robert L.   367 n. 29
Weed, Elizabeth   402 n. 36
Weider, Joe   212
Weinfeld, Moshe   204 n. 3, 205 n. 6
Weissler, Chava   209 n. 22
Welch, John W.   340 n. 24
Wellek, René   379, 383
Wenham, Gordon J.   205
West, Mona   225, 304
Westermann, Claus   205 n. 4
White, Hayden   154
White, Mimi   368 n. 31
White, Robert J.   275 n. 5
Whitelam, Keith   313 n. 7
Williams, Craig A.   222, 276 n. 7, 278 n. 12, 303 n. 14, 363 n. 18
Williams, Patricia J.   130 n. 3
Williams, Patrick   313 n. 7
Williams, William Carlos   395 n. 25
Wills, Lawrence M.   183
Wilson, Andrew P.   124, 359 n. 5
Wilton, Tamsin   281 n. 1, 283 n. 3

Wimbush, Vincent L. 366 n. 28
Wimsatt, William K., Jr. 379
Winkler, John J. 176, 188, 190, 195, 275–79
Winterson, Jeanette 269–70
Wittig, Monique 252 n. 6, 258
Wolfreys, Julian 382
Wolfson, Elliot R. 206 n. 9
Wyschogrod, Edith 59 n. 9

Xie, Ming 311 n. 2

Yee, Gale A. 366 n. 28
Young, Robert J. C. 310 n. 1, 311, 313 n. 7, 321, 322 n. 18, 351, 364
Young, Steve 182 n. 16, 185 n. 22

Zahn, Theodor 85
Zauhar, Frances Murphy 128, 171
Zeitlin, Froma I. 176 n. 2
Žižek, Slavoj 375, 379, 401, 402 n. 36, 403

www.ingramcontent.com/pod-product-compliance
Lightning Source LLC
Chambersburg PA
CBHW021350290426
44108CB00010B/177